UNDER TEN MILLION?
ANYTHING'S POSSIBLE!

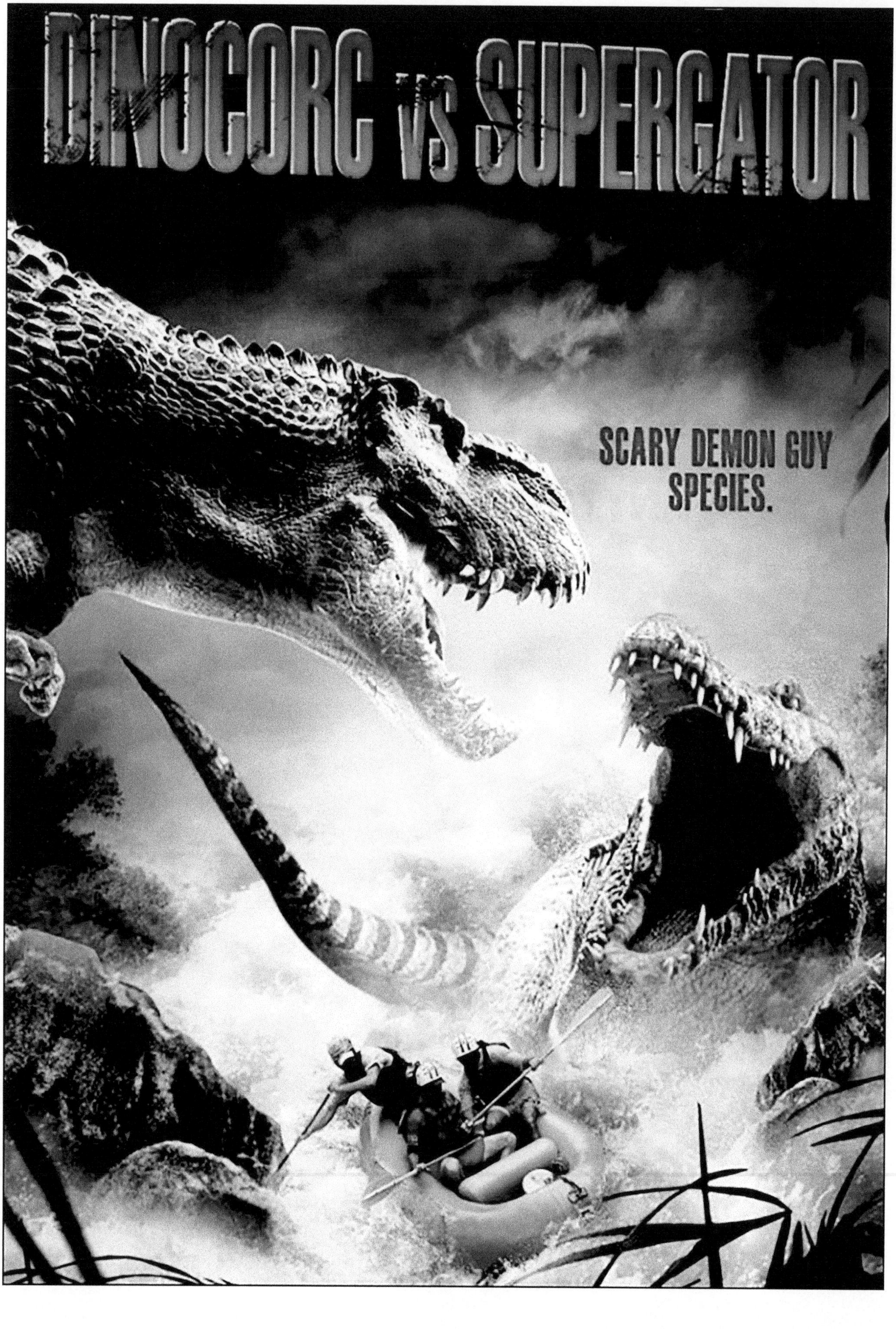
DINOCORC vs SUPERGATOR
SCARY DEMON GUY
SPECIES.

UNDER TEN MILLION? ANYTHING'S POSSIBLE!

Indie Horror, Fantasy, and Sci-Fi Movies
The Very Good, the Very Bad and
the Very, Very Ugly!

BY BARRY ATKINSON

MIDNIGHT MARQUEE PRESS, INC.
BALTIMORE, MARYLAND, USA

Books by Barry Atkinson

Atomic Age Cinema

Heroes Never Die: The Italian Peplum Phenomenon

Indie Horrors

Six-Gun Law
The Westerns of Randolph Scott, Audie Murphy, Joel McCrea and George Montgomery

Six-Gun Law 2
The Westerns of Rory Calhoun, Rod Cameron, Sterling Hayden and Richard Widmark

Six-Gun Law 3
Westerns of the 1950s: The Classic Years

You Are Old Enough Son!

You're Not Old Enough Son

Casebound Color ISBN 978-1-64430-136-4
Paperback Color ISBN 978-1-64430-133-3
Paperback B&W ISBN 978-1-64430-137-1
Library of Congress Catalog Card Number 2023944179
Manufactured in the United States of America
First Printing August 2023

Dedication

To Betty, our little Cretan princess.
We'll be together again one day.

My thanks to David Rimawi of The Asylum
for information on *Monster Island*

TABLE OF CONTENTS

Due west, a distance of 3,450 miles separates my home town in North Cornwall from Gary and Sue Svehla's Baltimore residence, most of it the Atlantic Ocean. Gary and I have never met (a real shame) but "chat" all the time via the internet. *If* we had met face-to-face, I reckon the conversation surrounding the concept of this book would have gone something like this:

Barry: "Gary. What about the manuscript for *Son of Indie Horrors!*, my follow-up to *Indie Horrors!* Anything happening on that front? As you recall, I wrote it on and off between 2010 and 2016 and it's been on the back burner ever since, although I fully appreciate you've put my other projects out on the market in the interim period."

Gary, smiling: "Well, Sue and I *have* been thinking about it. We appreciate all your hard work in putting the book together and we *are* committed to publishing it but does the material appeal to our target audience, the Baby-Boomers? Our readers on the whole prefer the genre

INDIE HORRORS!
The Not-To-Be Missed, The Acceptable, and The Forgettable
Barry Atkinson

from the 1930s through to the 1980s. They are of an age where they buy books on the subject, whereas the modern generation don't; in the main, they get all *their* information free from the internet and various online blogs and sites; nothing is paid for. Naturally, *Son of Indie Horrors!* will be all about modern movies, most of them post-2000."

B: "And, as I read somewhere on the internet recently, going to the cinema "isn't a laugh like it used to be." Well, whoever said that hit the nail on the head! Regrettably, I have to agree with you on the generational indifference towards books, a worrying trend if ever there was one. The other month, a 15-year-old student on television, clutching her obligatory mobile tablet, blithely announced, "I can't see the reason for books." It both horrified and saddened me. Books have been a major part of my life since I was around six years old and still are. I always have a "read" on the go from one month to the next. But personally, I think we ought to give this independent and low-budget stuff a chance. After all, no one else appears to be writing about them. I honestly think we should give them an airing before they disappear entirely off the radar. And many already have. A huge amount of films I reviewed for *Son of Indie Horrors!* never seem to get a showing nowadays."

G: "Okay, I mostly agree with you on that point. A thought. Could we somehow tie in these independent modern movies to their counterparts of old, so that what you've done will appeal to both the Boomers and maybe find a target audience among newer fans who might *then* be tempted to have a look at what went on all those years ago. You can also point out the transition from going out to the movies to home video in all its ramifications and evolutions, because these indie features are straight-to-DVD or TV, with one or two exceptions. Some low-budget features *are* released and some do make money."

B: "Well, I suppose that briefly, the main evolution of the low-budget movie is that nowadays, a great many are issued direct to DVD and/or television, or screened at FrightFests, whereas in the old days, they went the rounds for years as extremely profitable double bills; and double bills as we once knew them died out in English cinemas at the end of the 1960s. I always thought after completing work on *Indie Horrors!* that some of the better Asylum features would have made credible double bills years ago; *The Beast of Bray Road* and *Frankenstein Reborn*, for instance. What a great double "X" presentation that would have made—*and* they would have drawn in the punters [customers]. In

fact, a lot of Asylum's product would be a treat today as double bills—*Mega Shark vs. Kolossus* and *Bigfoot* are just two off the top of my head. Same with New Horizons' *Dinocroc vs. Supergator* paired with Cinetels' *Ogre* which are both in this volume; a terrific monster double attraction, worthy of anything I caught in a cinema 55 years ago. And sorry to ramble on but to ram home the point: My wife's grandson, Tom, visited us a while back and sat through seven [British] X-rated golden oldies during one whole day: *20 Million Miles to Earth*, *It! The Terror from Beyond Space*, *The Land Unknown*, *Indestructible Man*, *The Black Scorpion*, *Invasion of the Body Snatchers* and *The Monster that Challenged the World*. As a 22-year-old, he just couldn't get his head around the fact that I had caught the double bill of *Invasion of the Body Snatchers* and *Indestructible Man* three times in a cinema, all on Sunday screenings; he had real difficulty in visualizing the entire experience, but was deeply jealous all the same!"

G: "What today's horror-mad youngsters are missing!"

B: I know; such a great cinematic period for us Boomers. (Pause). But getting back to the subject in hand: What about this as the route to proceed down? To the original manuscript of *Son of Indie Horrors!* which I'll tinker with, I add, say, around 80 more releases issued between 2010 and 2019 which have taken my fancy and that way, I can emphasize some of the later low-budget features which I personally reckon owe a great deal to the genre *as it was*. By low-budget, I mean anything up to $10,000,000 as opposed to the $200,000,000 or more splashed out on all the current blockbusters. Let's face it, in today's terms, 10 million bucks ain't all that large; hell, I read Daniel Craig's total paycheck for his last Bond movie, including bonus and profit-sharing, was a staggering $60 million. And take Disney's *Avengers: Infinity War* and *Avengers: Endgame*; the pair come in on a colossal combined 680 million dollar budget. That puts the whole thing into perspective."

G: "Incredible, isn't it. And I'll add to that—did you know that HBO spent 25 million on the *first* episode of *Westworld*, the TV series, and the entire series came in at $100 million?"

B: "I didn't realise that. Amazing, particularly when you think that RynoRyder's entertaining found footage quickie *Evidence* was produced for a paltry $12,000. I've seen a lot of indies and lower-budget movies recently and many are not all that bad. In fact, some are bloody (excuse the English expression) good! There's evidence to suggest a mini-horror renaissance is going on out there and whether today's kids buy books or not, it would be nice to get some of this new fodder down in print. Let's give them a chance; embrace them for what they're trying to achieve."

G: "Which is?"

B: "To keep the low-budget horror ball rolling."

G: "Mmm. I suppose the book could work by revamping the whole *Son of Indie Horrors!* idea. But going back on what we were saying, times have drastically changed. When we were kids, we collected models of monsters, film posters, baseball cards and wrote articles in scrappy little journals. Those were nostalgic times for the pair of us, and our reader base. It just doesn't happen like that nowadays. The younger generation don't seem to be as attached to memorabilia relating to the cinema, or memorabilia per se, as we once were. They certainly aren't collectors or hoarders of anything. And as for black-and-white films … forget it! I taught high school English and occasionally had to screen a black-and-white movie to a class. It was as though I was pulling their teeth out!"

them into watching a select few and appreciate that worthwhile cinematic horror/fantasy/sci-fi *does* exist outside of the mega-bucks level, regardless of its post-2000 pedigree. So, to recap: Parts one and two of the new book will be a revised version of *Son of Indie Horrors!*; part three will take the form of an additional 80 plus features. Now, while I'm here, what about an American beer; also, what delights have you got planned for showing in your home cinema tonight? I didn't come all this way *not* to miss out on a Gary Svehla film show!"

Film Ratings used throughout the book

Classic indie/low-budget	*****
As good as the Big Boys	****
Cheaply entertaining	***
Not bad	**
Why did they bother?	*

B: "Yep. Too much technological distraction is the problem; and all of it in color. Of course, in the 1950s, we had nothing but the cinema to amuse us, and most of what we saw was in black-and-white. And before you say it, television in this country during that decade was total crap. I used to collect critical reviews from newspapers and magazines, draw film posters, compile check-lists and even attempted to animate clay models using a home cine camera. And what about the absolute thrill you got when you bought one of those 200-foot 8mm strips of celluloid in its little box showing snippets from *Tarantula* and *The Thing from Another World*, or *First Men in the Moon* in color. That sheer excitement factor is missing from today's moviegoers' mindsets. Tell me, how can anyone derive fun from streaming movies and watching them on a smartphone? I couldn't. It's like a Ray Harryhausen dinosaur compared to a CGI dinosaur. On one hand, you have a solid model you can touch and handle; on the other, nothing, just a mass of pixels. Streaming equates to nothing tangible there, nothing to touch or look at; no celluloid, no DVD, not even the dreaded VHS tape. But things are changing a bit; after all, vinyl is making a comeback, DVD sales are still up so all may not be lost as regards literature on film, be it indie or otherwise."

G: "Correct. You're slowly convincing me, Barry! So somehow your remit is to promote the virtues of the indie/low-budget format and make the result appealing to us oldies *and* the younger set. It should hopefully then be more marketable for everyone involved and, in the long run, it could well convert a few youngsters to the classics that we cherish so much and never get tired of watching."

B: "A tall order but I'll rise to it; I'll give it a go with a mind to get fans out there interested in the merits of the pictures contained within these pages, hopefully to tempt

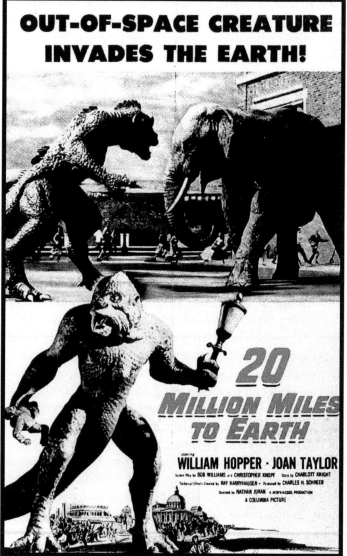

The oldies live on! The Ymir on the rampage in *20 Million Miles to Earth*.

In 2012, Midnight Marquee Press published *Indie Horrors!* in which I reviewed 235 movies (mostly straight-to-DVD/TV/tape fodder) produced under the banner of "independent film production," the majority of which I had seen on numerous foreign channels while living on the Greek island of Crete. The indie horror/fantasy/sci-fi scene has waned slightly since peaking around 2016/2017 (most noticeably Asylum's efforts), the accent now firmly on "mockbusters" or disaster movies to the extent that everything else (horror and sci-fi) has been shunted into the sidelines. By indie, I refer to those films made by Asylum (The Global Asylum), Full Moon, Cinetel Films, Castel Films Romania, Nu Image and a host of other names unfamiliar to the average fan. Low-budget features can be produced by the big boys; some hit the jackpot, others fall by the wayside, but at least they're being made. These days, with up to (and over) $200 million being splashed out on the likes of *Kong: Skull Island*, *Jurassic World: Fallen Kingdom*,

Transformers: The Last Knight, *Pacific Rim*, *Godzilla: King of the Monsters* and all those superhero escapades, 10 million can feel like small change, so it's that figure that I've kept to as the ceiling to the movies contained within this volume; the majority of films described in the following pages fall far, far short of that figure.

Do not compare these indie/low-budget features to the similar-themed big-budget blockbusters that appear on the major circuits, or ridicule and turn your nose up at them. I put this in bold to emphasize the issue. There's absolutely no point. Independent film companies exist in a totally different kind of cinematic universe, quite happy to appeal to its niche audience, providing them (via DVD, TV, streaming, film conventions, FrightFests or a *very* limited and selected cinema release) with a never-ending supply of cut-price goodies and bypassing the masses, most of who are completely unaware of their existence. Cameron's *Avatar*? Yeah, great movie. Jim Wynorski's *Shockwave*? Who? What? *Battle Los Angeles*? Loved it. *Battle of Los Angeles*? Eh? Thought there was only *Battle Los Angeles*. *The 7 Adventures of Sinbad*? Sorry-surely you mean *The 7th Voyage of Sinbad*. *Mega Piranha*? Well, I've heard of *Piranha* but *Mega Piranha*? *Jurassic City*? Are you referring to *Jurassic World*? For those of us weary of the pretentious, who have become blasé to the over-hyped and indifferent to the bloated, are put off by the constant trumpeting surrounding the latest innovations in the field of special effects (and some turn out to be not all *that* special), or have tired of the parade of self-gratulatory A-listers, products like *Hydra, Ice Twisters, Evil Angel, Lake Mungo, Dark Circles, May, The Dinosaur Project, Dr. Moreau's House of Pain, Howl, Ogre, Bigfoot, Autumn, Reptisaurus, Dark Angel: The Ascent, Age of Dinosaurs, Flight 7500, The Reef, Alien Dawn, The Blackout* and *2-Headed Shark Attack* are like a breath of fresh cinematic air—and where else would you come across such a batty sextet of movies such as

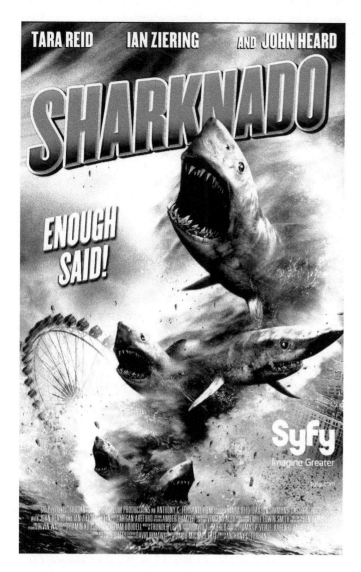

er, slasher/splatter, torture-porn, psychological drama, medical horror, other worlds, ghosts, mad doctors, the supernatural, asylums, haunted houses, dinosaurs, mutated insects, lost/found footage, weather formations, giant reptiles and mega sharks—you name it, it's probably been covered by an indie outfit somewhere; there's something to cater for everyone's tastes, a tasty diet of enriching, altogether more *divergent*, fodder which otherwise would never have been made or seen the light of day. After all, would *any* of the big motion picture companies take the financial risk of tackling something as unconventional as *The Human Centipede (First Sequence)* and its two disgusting sequels? I think not. And as for *Nude Nuns with Big Guns* …!

So the first two parts of this book represent a slightly edited/revamped version of *Son of Indie Horrors!* (*Indie Horrors!* included 20 of Asylums's earliest and classiest pictures: *The Beast of Bray Road, Frankenstein Reborn, I Am Omega, The War of the Worlds* and *Jolly Roger: Massacre at Cutter's Cove* among them; a further 91 are listed here). Bear all the above points in mind when settling down to an indie horror/fantasy movie—you might enjoy what's on offer just that little bit more.

those Asylum has presented to us fans in the shape of their *Sharknado* franchise, except in the realms of indie fantasy cinema? These features hark back in many ways to the innocence, zeal and creativeness displayed in the fantasy output of the '50s and '60s, the genre's golden decades; they are, in fact, the B movies of the modern-day generation, if you like. Example—Asylum's *AE: Apocalypse Earth* can be seen as nothing less than a lively remake of Allied Artists' *World Without End*; 57 years separate the two movies, but what you have is pretty much two very similar productions, making you wonder whether director Thunder Levin took Edward Bernds' sci-fi classic as his template. And that goes for the posters, or DVD covers; richly detailed artwork of the '50s/'60s variety, enticing you to buy despite the dubious contents—but then, isn't that the aim of *all* advertising posters? For example, *Jurassic Attack, Jurassic Hunters* and *Jurassic Shark*'s DVD covers are fantastic "come and get me" pieces of movie advertising—what lies within *might* be a different matter altogether (and in the case of *Jurassic Shark*, it *is* a different matter altogether!)

Disaster, end-of-world, outer space, aliens, vampires, werewolves, zombies, teen horror, Frankenstein, serial kill-

UNDER TEN MILLION? ANYTHING'S POSSIBLE!

The Asylum

Asylum (The Asylum/The Global Asylum) is the leading player among the host of independent film companies at present in operation. Founded in 1997 by David Michael Latt, David Rimawi and Sherri Strain, the company's remit was to produce horror, fantasy and science fiction fodder for the video, DVD and television market on a low-budget basis, setting a ceiling at $1,000,000 (this figure rose to $3,000,000 for the latter entrants in the *Sharknado* series); one or two have been given a limited cinema release, mainly the *Mega Shark* movies. Over 200 features later (this figure includes many titles that do not come under the fantasy/horror/sci-fi banner), much-maligned Asylum shows no sign of slowing up, good news for some, bad news for others. Many buffs detest what critics term their "mockbusters," movies that are flagrantly based on the big money-spinners of the day to lure customers to their product, but with a subtle change in title. In 2008, 20th Century Fox threatened to issue a lawsuit when *The Day the Earth Stopped* was released, a blatant rip-off of *The Day the Earth Stood Still* (legal proceedings were later dropped); Universal-International also went ape when Asylum's *American Battleship* appeared on the shelves at the selfsame time their heavily promoted $209,000,000 *Battleship* was being launched in 2012; the title was swiftly changed to *American Warships* to avoid court reprisals. Deep down, you can't help admiring Asylum's sheer audacity in repeatedly trying to pull off this kind of stunt, but they're not the only copyists doing it; others are just that bit more discreet, particularly when it boils down to naming the picture. In recent years, the company's extensive roster has tended to move away from the gruesome horrors of *Frankenstein Reborn*, *Intermedio*, *Legion of the Dead* and *The Beast of Bray Road*, concentrating more on a stream of disaster mini-epics and alien movies, its retinue of directors, producers, actors, scriptwriters, cinematographers, effects technicians and composers each dabbling in what the other has done on a previous setup; unfortunately, output from 2016 onwards shows a gradual decline in quality and freshness, despite fantastic artwork displayed on the DVD covers; it's becoming increasingly difficult to give these features a top review, however much effort has gone into a specific production. Asylum movies can veer from the truly brilliant to the downright abysmal. On their day, they can come up with the goods big time; an off-day will have you reaching for fast forward on the remote, or the "off" button—you pays your money and you takes your choice. Productions, in the main, are super-glossy and colorful, no denying it, a predominance of busty, well-honed females filling all-male roles to grab the attention of punters; despite comments to the contrary, the low-budget CGI effects can occasionally be absolutely staggering in execution—and most movies come under the 90-minute mark, never outstaying their welcome. Over the years, it has become standard practice to savage *everything* turned out by the company, disregarding any inherent merits a particular movie may have, burying every film made under a blanket of ridiculously inappropriate criticism. Basically, this is grossly unfair, a form of negative cinematic snobbery—Asylum and its multi-tasking crew are not the purveyors of trash/bad taste they're made out to be; they are, and remain, the quintessential independent filmmaking outfit, bringing a touch of levity to an industry so often wrapped up in its own self-grandiloquence. The message is clear: If you don't like the brand, stay away from the product. Let's give credit where credit is due and not simply hate these movies for the sake of it. Whatever you may think about Asylum as a whole and its oddball methods to gain an audience, or how you regard their team of technicians as serious craftsman, you simply cannot ignore the fact that they exist as filmmakers. To do so would be to miss out on some really great indie fare!

Abraham Lincoln vs. Zombies
Asylum 2012; 96 minutes; Director: Richard Schenkman ****
As a 10-year-old child, Abraham Lincoln had to kill his zombified mother; now President of the USA., he not only has the Confederacy to deal with but a fresh outbreak of the undead during the American Civil War.

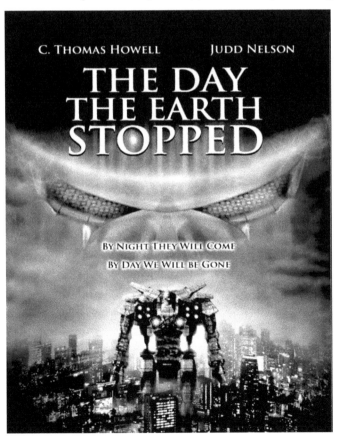

C. THOMAS HOWELL   JUDD NELSON

THE DAY THE EARTH STOPPED

BY NIGHT THEY WILL COME
BY DAY WE WILL BE GONE

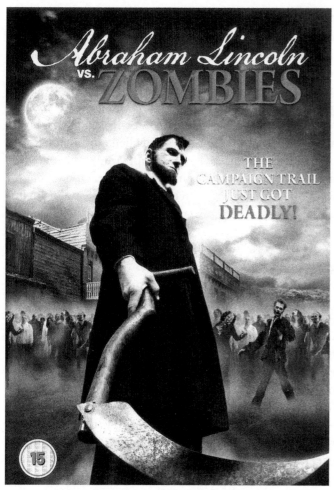

clashes with the undead hordes (Oberst wields a handy scythe, adept at kicking zombie ass), McGraw is the sacrificial lamb, igniting a hidden cache of gunpowder and blowing himself and the zombies, who have been lured into the fort, sky-high. But Norman has had infected blood splashed over her face; 18 months later, she's chained to a cell wall where, on a visit, the President shoots the rabid woman in the head, but not before incurring a fatal scratch. Knowing the outcome, Abraham Lincoln attends that fateful play at Washington's Ford's Theater with his wife on 14 April 1865, aware that an assassin's bullet will not only end his life but hopefully put a stop to a further zombie epidemic led by himself. Tim Gill's bright cinematography, composer Chris Ridenhour's use of old Civil War leitmotifs and Oberst chewing the scenery ensures that *Abraham Lincoln vs. Zombies* is one hoot of a standout zombie flick, placing the flaky-faced ones, for once, a refreshingly unusual change of environment. A wicked slice of Asylum "living dead" entertainment.

AE: Apocalypse Earth

Asylum 2013; 87 minutes; Director: Thunder Levin *****

Earth is under bombardment from alien spacecraft, forcing selected humans to head off into space in the USS *Albert Einstein* in search of a new planet to populate; they eventually find more than they bargained for when they

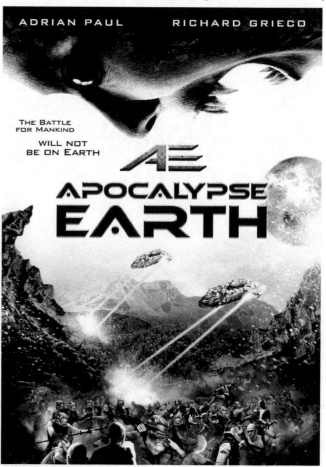

In 2012, two movies were released featuring Abe Lincoln combating the legends of old—Asylum's $150,000 zombie opus and 20th Century Fox's $69,000,000 *Abraham Lincoln Vampire Hunter*. In its own way, Abe versus the zombies is as enjoyably hokey as Abe versus the vampires, despite the vast difference in budgetary costs. Richard Schenkman's at times artful direction and pithy script, combined with Bill Oberst, Jr.'s highly watchable Lincoln, plus tons of zombie incident shot around Georgia's Fort Pulaski Civil War Monument (scene of a strategic battle in 1862), makes for exciting viewing, historical events such as the Gettysburg address craftily manipulated to fit in with the zombie scenario, including an oh-so-smart payoff. Oberst, against government advice, heads a mission comprising a dozen secret servicemen to rebel-held Fort Pulaski to discover why Operation Big Shanty failed, only to find the place crawling with zombies, Confederate General Stonewall Jackson (Don McGraw) a virtual prisoner in his own fortification. McGraw doesn't believe in zombies; as far as he's concerned, they're sick Southerners unfairly treated by the Unionists, but Oberst is determined to bring the affliction under control. Among the fort's mixed retinue is young Theodore Roosevelt (Canon Kuipers), Oberst's old flame-turned-prostitute Mary (Baby Norman) and would-be assassin John Wilkinson (Jason Vail). After numerous

crash-land on a distant Earth-like world. Filmed in the bright green Costa Rican jungles at a cost of $1,000,000, Thunder Levin's sci-fi adventure races through its paces, kicking off on an Earth blasted by rockets and laser beams, to scenes in deep space, and hence to a new world harboring all kinds of menaces: Giant bugs, craft that let loose thunderbolts and a race of murderous invisible people known as The Chameleons. Taking in genre tropes from *Predator*, *World Without End*, *Planet of the Apes*, *The Time Machine* and even *Alien* (Gray Hawkes plays TIM, an android), sit back, grab a drink and take in the action as rugged ex-commando Adrian Paul, Captain Richard Grieco and assorted crash survivors battle huge insects, encounter the remnants of a previous expedition, meet huntress Bali Rodriguez, member of a friendly race, her naturally camouflaged skin matching the jungle surroundings, and tackle a gigantic lizard guarding a spaceship. Paul and Rodriguez fall in lust, romping in a pool, but the pretty little savage is an outcast; only by defeating their invisible enemies will she be welcomed back into her pale-skinned tribe. *AE: Apocalypse Earth* has a certain amount of heart not normally associated with indie sci-fi, Paul wanting to return to Earth to reunite with his family, regardless of the state the planet might be in, others, including besotted Rodriguez, are against the idea. After Paul and company have blown up a few Chameleons, Grieco discovers a ship in working order that blasts off for their home planet, quantum physics coming into the equation—will it be the Earth of now, or in untold years' time? The answer is 325,000 years in the future; the planet they reached when escaping the alien holocaust *was* Earth, the ring around the planet debris from the shattered moon ("We can't go home, Frank. We're already here!"). With feelings too deep for words, Paul, Rodriguez, Grieco and crew troop down the craft's gantry to set up house in this new Garden of Eden, alighting on top of Mount Rushmore, rampant vegetation covering the stone faces of America's former presidents. Solid performances all round, picturesque scenery, decent CGI effects and an intelligent script, combined with nonstop incident packed into an 87-minute running time, elevate *AE: Apocalypse Earth* into the higher echelons of the company's product. This is an Asylum flick elevated to an almost semi-classic level.

Age of Dinosaurs

Asylum 2013; 88 minutes; Director: Joseph J. Lawson *****

Dinosaurs created by cryogenics outfit Geneti-Sharp run riot during a convention, terrorizing the streets of Los Angeles.

Let's get things into perspective. It is pointless comparing *Age of Dinosaurs* to the *Jurassic Park* franchise, as many have done. Universal's *Jurassic World* (2015) had a budget of $150,000,000 and ran for over two hours; Asylum, who

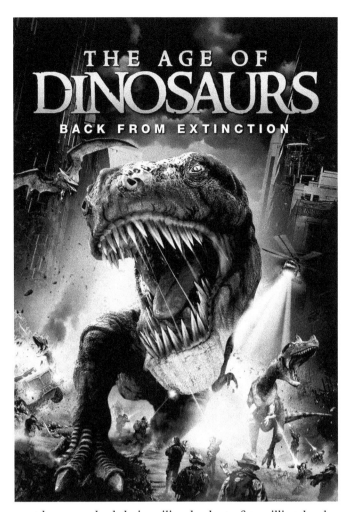

must have reached their ceiling budget of a million bucks, achieves wonders in just under 90 minutes; here, they've pulled it off. The CGI effects are splendid, and you get to see a great deal of the monsters. Agreed, the script is crass in places, but that was a comment leveled at Steven Spielberg's *Jurassic Park* when it first came out in 1993. From an entertainment point of view, it's far more preferable to the overblown "let's have a cliffhanger every five minutes" mentality behind the ponderous *The Lost World: Jurassic Park* (1997) and almost as good as the underrated *Jurassic Park 3* (2001). Moreover, the film comes with a British "15" rating (*JP*'s ratings were aimed at a family audience), meaning the gore count is a lot higher. So sit back and prepare for a roller coaster ride as dinosaurs created by Ronny Cox's company break loose at a convention to sell them worldwide as a form of prehistoric novelty. Veteran Treat Williams plays the hero, a grizzled firefighter having to keep tabs on his text-obsessed teenage daughter (Jillian Rose Reed), giant carnivores and wheeling Pteranodons taking on the LAPD. Joshua Michael Allen and Jose Rosete, the men behind the project, are gobbled up, Cox sacrifices himself to save Williams and Reed, and a few amusing lines ("We wouldn't want them fellas running around the city, now would we? My four grandchildren live out there," states Cox nervously as the growling monsters bat-ter at their glass cages) complement Lawson's deft hand on the camera (he was responsible for the visual effects on over 90 productions, mostly indie, including this one). From the tense opening scene of a scaly monster springing into deadly life in an operating theater to Williams grappling a Pteranodon, perched on Los Angeles' Hollywood sign, Asylum's lively dino-fest, shot in vivid color, doesn't let up for a single second and comes highly recommended, proving that the company's output underwent a renaissance of sorts from 2012 onwards, especially in the special effects department. A five-star dinosaurs-on-the-loose guilty pleasure!

Age of Ice
Asylum 2014; 85 minutes; Director: Emile Edwin Smith *

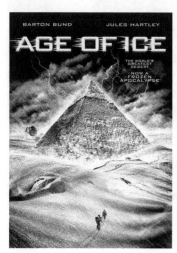

When the Arabian tectonic plate shifts due to an undersea cataclysm, Egypt is engulfed in snow and ice, leading to small pockets of the population heading for a warmer sanctuary.

"It was so cool," beams young Joe Cipriano at the conclusion to this disaster of a disaster movie. For him, maybe, but not for the audience. Once in a while, Asylum gets it all so horribly wrong—*Age of Ice* is a clunker of the first order, disappointingly so when indie aficionados know that the company is perfectly capable of reaching the heights elsewhere. Who, for instance, can honestly swallow people sliding down the frozen 450-foot face of Giza's main pyramid, then simply walking away without a speck of snow on their clothing, let alone any broken bones. How many times must we have to listen to Jordanian Owais Ahmed whining, "I must get in touch with my father," in between him mooning over Barton Bund's simpering daughter, Bailey Spry. "Please tell us we're not screwed," yells wife Jules Hartley to Bund, who grumbles incessantly, "We have to do this together. There is still hope. We have to go on." The trek across icy Egypt seems far longer than Scott's trip to the Antarctic at times, Bund, his family and various hangers-on chancing upon a cavern of waterfalls cascading into warm water. Diving in, they emerge into sunlight and a beach full of paramedics (very handy!), Bund, tears welling up in his eyes, hugging his wife and kids and blurting out, "Just glad our family made it." Granted, scenes of destruction at the start (Cairo in ruins; aircraft colliding on the runway) are executed in Asylum's normal efficient manner, and the frozen dam sequence comes off well, but, overall, this is small return

in a badly acted, poorly scripted entrant in the "Earth is threatened by ice" subgenre (backed by a Middle Eastern musical dirge) that, from a scientific perspective, makes very little sense. An off-day for producer David Michael Latt and his team.

Age of Tomorrow aka Alien Extinction
Asylum 2014; 90 minutes; Director: James Kondelik *****

A colossal meteorite nears Earth, creating an "End of Days" scenario, but when a team of commandos is sent to plant bombs on the rock's surface, they encounter a hostile alien species looking to conquer the planet.

There's a lot going on in James Kondelik's invigorating sci-fi actioner, basically composed of two storylines: Dad Lane Townsend trying to prevent daughter Taylor Coliee from being teleported to the aliens' world via a green beam emitted from a ball-like droid; and Anthony Marks' team of five grunts landing by shuttle and discovering that a huge ship lies within the meteorite that can send its occupants to that green/blue forested alien planet dominated by its ornate spired city. Within the city resides the Queen, a gooey monstrosity hatching eggs, ruler of a dying race that has its eyes (in her case, multiple eyes) on Earth, her assistants a form of other-worldly thug, every captured human contained in glass prisons. Special effects rule the roost as Earth is bombarded by thousands of

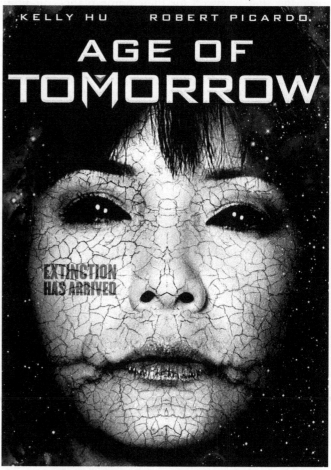

globes whose job is to teleport the entire human population to their planet as slaves, while Marks, physicist Kelly Hu and their squad battle the aliens both in the city and on board their vessel. No happy endings on offer here—an atomic warhead plus hundreds of missiles ordered up by General Robert Picardo destroys the meteorite, only for dozens of other meteorite ships to take its place, surrounding a doomed Earth; Marks and his team are all killed; and Coliee is teleported to the alien city in front of distraught Townsend ("This is our world!") who follows her with more militia, armed with an axe; as the creatures close in on him and battered Coliee in a forest glade and shown a hologram of Earth under siege, he yells defiantly "It's not over—not yet!" However, judging by this pretty powerful fade-out, it *is* all over!

Airplane vs. Volcano
Asylum 2014; 91 minutes;
Directors: James and Jon Kondelik * or *****

A massive underwater explosion off the Hawaiian coast creates a ring of volcanos, trapping a commercial airliner within its deadly center.

Unbelievable! Nonsense! Cornball crap! Bonkers! Cheesy! Cliché-ridden! Trash! Yes, these online comments apply to the Kondelik Brothers' airborne disaster hoot, a movie that gives 1980's *Airplane!* a good run for its money in the "absolute stupidity" stakes. Hunk Dean Cain takes to the controls of Flight 7389 when both pilots are killed by lumps of molten rock and the autopilot has malfunctioned, stewardess Tamara Goodwin sighing over Cain's masculinity in the face of a barrage of volcanic fumes, showers of cinders, heat waves, flowing lava and fireballs, enough to knock any aircraft out of the flaming crimson skies—but not this one! Amid the panicking passengers, young Zachary Haven pukes into a sick bag while Mom Natalie Burtney goes all sloppy over caring cop Lawrence Hilton-Jacobs, who winds up stabbed to death by crazy Anthony Marks, doing a lousy impersonation of a terrified gun-waving terrorist. At Hawaii's military base, cold-eyed Colonel Mike Jerome Putnam barks out orders by rote, junior grunt Morgan West given the go-ahead to instruct fighter command to bomb the volcanic vents; volcanologist Robin Givens hovers in the background, rolling her eyes in mock horror, forever shouting "You need me!" The final 15 minutes will have you laughing out loud into your much-needed beer as Marks ends up in a dinghy on the sea, which erupts beneath him ("Oh my … you are a big bitch!") and the fighters are incinerated by fireballs ("They're getting killed out there!"), but *not* that airliner, one jet managing to hover above the plane (How is it still up there? It's been losing fuel since reel two!); commandos abseil in through the roof and everybody (those still alive, that is) is hauled out one-by-one, dragged up into

the jet by rope, somehow surviving the raging, red-hot inferno around them. Cain, fatally injured, is the sacrificial lamb, steering the aircraft packed with 200 pounds of explosives into volcano number one ("Enough to blow this bastard back to where it came from!"), the resulting detonation extinguishing all seismic activity (Putnam has also perished in the flames). Yes, folks, it's high-fives times back at base, grinning West promoted to sergeant ("Helluva job, soldier!") and Givens sobbing in relief. A fantastically crazy Asylum guilty pleasure for those in the right frame of mind, *not* to be taken seriously—agreed, it's bad and mad, but it's also rather brilliant in a lunatic kind of fashion!

Alien Convergence
Asylum 2017; 87 minutes; Director: Rob Pallatina **

Three meteors smash into power plants in California, releasing giant winged monsters named the Larga that embark on a reign of terror.

And it's up to Caroline Ivari and her crew of disabled service personnel, plus wheelchair-bound dad Stephen Brown, to save the planet by piloting the "Neuro Jet," a revolutionary new plane that responds to thought control. You have to wait 21 minutes for the first alien to appear, a huge winged monstrosity emerging from a crater breathing lethal green vapor that brings down jet fighters and incinerates air bases. Then Ivari and her team get to work, figur-

ing that the creatures, who have arrived from Mars, hate the cold; therefore, impregnating them with liquid nitrogen is the key to their downfall. Investigating a blood-stained cave, Ivari and her colleagues observe a batch of eggs hatching, the slimy offspring merging into one organism that buries itself in the tunnel floor—but that's the end of that particular plot thread. Ivari dons a special helmet that allows her to see the aliens in "real time" and not in fast-motion, and the invaders are destroyed at Tucson after an aerial battle. There's very little in the way of alien invasion effects in this lackluster production, Ivari acting her obligatory "Asylum babe saves the world" part with a minimum of conviction; the aliens are pretty fearsome, all things considered, the one highlight in a mediocre sci-fi outing from the company.

Alien Origin
Asylum 2012; 88 minutes; Director: Mark Atkins **

A military expedition deep in the jungles of Belize has a close encounter of the third kind, resulting in their unexplained disappearance.

It's not the worst lost footage movie ever made—that accolade goes to Asylum's *Monster* (2007). But it comes pretty close. Attractive Belize jungle location work, shot in flashy color around Mayan ruins and caves, disguises the naked truth; apart from an alien skull, a one-second glimpse of its face at the end and the inside of an alien ship, the action, cobbled together from various video sources, consists of nothing more than a group of grunts plus "adventure journalist" Chelsea Vincent running for their lives from an unseen (to us) "something" from another world while searching for two missing archaeologists. In an epilogue filched from Ridley Scott's *Prometheus* (2012),

we are led to believe that primitive hominids were the result of a union between apes and aliens, a "70% match" which, seeing the state the world is in today, won't come as a surprise to a lot of people. Some moderately uneasy moments (flashing lights in the sky; weird scratch marks on trees; creepy cave sequences; strange howling noises)

do little to compensate for the fact that what the public is paying for never fully reveals itself; a well-constructed but ultimately disappointing alien suspenser very short on requisite thrills.

Alien Predator: Hunting Season
Asylum 2018; 87 minutes; Director: Jared Cohn **

In the National Park of Patuca, Honduras, a black ops team disobeys orders to find out the reason behind the disappearance of Unit 2 squad, who were on a mission to investigate an alien spaceship that had crashed into a government building.

Released to cash in on 20th Century Fox's $88,000,000 *The Predator*, Jared Cohn's much leaner effort has chief grunt Xavi Israel, science officer Dutch Hofstetter and seven pumped-up marines spending the first 21 minutes scrambling up and down dusty smoke-filled slopes as they near the building where the alien vessel has buried itself. Coming under attack from energy bolts and bombs resembling black marbles, and to the cry of, "Let's kill all these sons-of-bitches," the squad makes it to the building, enters a tunnel, reaches the interior, discovers "green energy signatures" and commences battle with alien soldiers who detest bright light (the sets are left over from 2016's *Independents' Day*). The dialogue for the most part is garbled, the camerawork wobbly, the action lethargic and Israel gets

his talkative head incinerated by a laser gun. Hofstetter is left all on his own at the end, communicating with a friendly alien and realizing they only wanted to repair their craft and head on back into the Milky Way; war with humans *wasn't* on their agenda. A helicopter comes to pick up Hofstetter as the aliens blast off into the skies. What a pity that the film couldn't capitalize on its splendid opening shot of the alien ship crash-landing on Earth instead of dragging its boot-heels for almost the entire running length; and the acting, overall, leaves a lot to be desired.

Alien Siege
Asylum 2018; 85 minutes; Director: Rob Pallatina **

The USA. is under attack from aliens that want to retrieve a doomsday-type device which has the capability of destroying the universe.

Shades of *Independence Day* as a huge mother ship hovers over Washington, the Capitol Dome is reduced to rubble and alien fighters destroy jet fighters. After a reasonable start, it's back to basics, President Terry Woodberry,

Colonel Arielle Hader, kids Brandon Johnston and Betsy McKinley and adults Matthew Pohlcamp and Christina Licciardi on the run from the invaders who wear gray metallic suits and are seen in blurred focus; their "Achilles Heel" is the neck region where a well-placed bullet can finish them off. Apparently, a refugee alien engineer visited Earth six years back and warned that if the device (carried around in a metal case) was activated, it would release a beacon to "bring them here. They want it back." If you can tear your eyes away from Johnston and McKinley's sets of gleaming, perfectly aligned teeth (is this a toothpaste ad?) and accept the fact that whizz kid Johnston saves the planet by hacking into the White House computer, the final 10 minutes offers a modicum of excitement, a ferocious tentacled monster appearing in the glowing portal of the mother ship, Johnston and Pohlcamp beaming aboard,

dumping the case and its ticking time bomb and beaming back. The vessel implodes, crashing to earth; time for a deeply embarrassing group hug. More alien action and less time spent on umpteen shots of blonde babe McKinley scampering along dusty roads in her hot pants would have elevated this film into something just a bit more acceptable to "alien invasion" buffs.

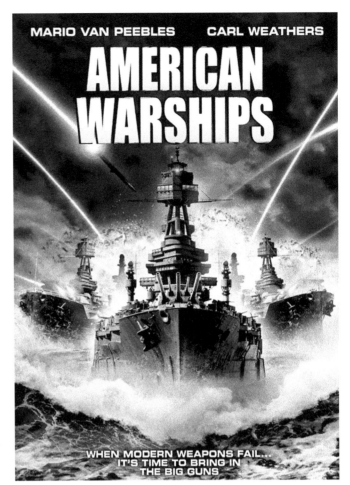

American Warships

Asylum 2012; 89 minutes; Director: Thunder Levin ***

An alien stealth ship opens fire on the American fleet in the Pacific, leading to a possible Third World War when the US president blames the North Koreans and the Chinese for the destruction.

And it's up to Captain Mario Van Peebles, commanding USS *Iowa*, to prove to the Pentagon that an alien race is behind it all, not the Chinese or the Koreans. Coming in at $1,000,000, *American Warships* isn't that far removed from Universal's *Battleships* blockbuster in gung-ho entertainment value, a colorful shoot-'em-up taking place on the high seas that any video games-hooked kid can relate to. Due to be mothballed as a museum piece, warship *Iowa* confronts the alien force, her six big guns eventually brought into play when all else fails to rid the ocean of the craft that employs a cloaking device: Stealth bombers and fighter planes come to grief, as does a team of Navy SEALS who board the main vessel, to be confronted by the insect-like other-worldly crew ("Koreans my ass. That's a damned Martian!"). Museum chick Nikki McCauley helps man the guns, General Carl Weathers sooths the secretary of state's ruffled feathers while Lieutenant Johanna Watts looks more like Van Peeble's daughter than his intended bride-to-be. At the end, after alien ship number one has been blasted to bits, we get to see one of the creatures on board the *Iowa*; shot dead, it evaporates in a pool of blue blood. And did the visitors send a distress signal before being wiped out? That's the burning question as, a year later, Van Peebles and Watts join the queues lining up to see *Iowa*, moored in San Pedro's dock.

The Amityville Haunting

Asylum 2011; 86 minutes; Director: Geoff Meed **

A family moves into the infamous DeFeo residence

where, in 1974, Ronald DeFeo, Jr. murdered his entire family and encounters horrific supernatural disturbances.

When will all this *Paranormal Entity/Activity* found footage stuff ever end, particularly when in most cases, it's not a case of what you don't see but what you *never* get to see. And why do families go and live in houses with such ghastly reputations? "Oh my god, this is so creepy!" shouts a teen at the start, one of five who break into the DeFeo house and pay with their lives. Then Jason Williams and his family move in; within the space of a couple of days, the estate agent and a removal man are both dead from the hands of unseen forces, yet *still* they stay put. "I wanna go somewhere else," moans hysterical wife Amy Van Horne, documented by camcorder-mad son Devin Clark, elder daughter Nadine Crocker glued to her cellphone while younger daughter Gracie Largent talks to an invisible (but not to her) boy. All is not well here! Eighty minutes of found footage/night vision shots later, the family has been wiped out, their deaths shown on the coroner's reports. Fair enough, there are a few spooky moments when ghostly happenings hot up towards the end, DeFeo's malevolent entity manifesting itself as Williams loses his faculties ("Mum. He's fucking crazy!" yells Crocker), but it's all been done before—we know by now where it ultimately leads to so no surprises in store in yet one more entry in the found camcorder footage/haunted house subgenre that, unfortunately, shows no signs of improvement or of letting up.

Android Cop

Asylum 2014; 90 minutes; Director: Mark Atkins *******

The future of law enforcement is here, a part-android police officer teaming up with a Robocop to rid Los Angeles of drug barons operating in a radiation poisoned wasteland known as the Forbidden Zone.

Taking place in 2037, Asylum's reboot of *RoboCop* (1987) features argumentative partners Michael Jai White and Randy Wayne, hot on the trail of Mayor Charles S. Dutton's missing daughter, Larissa Vereza, or her android double: In the future, some people are connected to the circuitry of a robotic doppelgänger and Vereza's has wandered into the Forbidden Zone, which corrupt Dutton is controlling for his own profit, delivering contaminated food parcels to the area and clearing it of citizens with the ultimate aim of grabbing all that real estate for himself— or so we are led to believe in a convoluted screenplay that makes little sense to those not conversant in the laws of

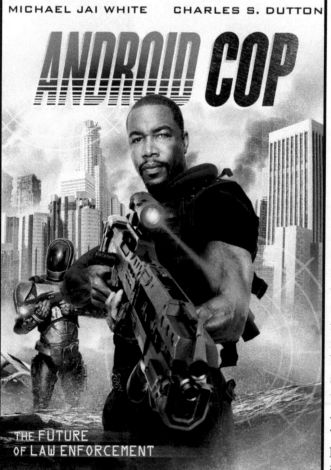

robotics. White doesn't realize he's part human/part machine until the end ("I am a human droid."), going out on the road with monosyllabic, armor-clad Wayne after Vereza has been rescued, the bad cops and drug dealers have been eliminated and guilt-ridden Dutton has put a gun to his head, refusing to pull the plug on his injured daughter. Notwithstanding the plot faults, *Android Cop* is fast-moving, shoot-'em-up fodder put across with flair and an eye for the bleak, futuristic setting; video games-mad kids will love it.

Apocalypse Pompeii

Asylum 2014; 87 minutes; Director: Ben Demaree *******

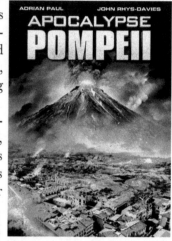

An ex-commando battles the authorities in Naples in his request for a helicopter to rescue his wife and daughter from Pompeii, under threat from erupting Mount Vesuvius.

Cashing in on Tristar's $80,000,000 *Pompeii*, Asylum's disaster effort is presented in the company's usual glossy format (director Ben Demaree handled the pristine photography), shot around Pompeii's actual ruins and in Bulgaria. The plot is far from original, cropping up time and time again in this type of fare: Dad/ex-special forces tough guy Adrian Paul and his team of grunts commandeer a helicopter from a Naples airfield and make for Pompeii where wife Jhey Castles, daughter/amateur volcanologist Georgina Beedle plus various cast members are at the mercy of Vesuvius in full flow, tremors, fireballs, sulfuric gas clouds, a tidal wave of boiling rocks, heat surges, ash and molten lava mirroring the cataclysmic events of 79 AD. Paul eventually rendezvous with the group at Pompeii's grand museum after the ancient city has been partly destroyed and is promptly forgiven by Commander John Rhys-Davies for pinching a 'copter from right under his nose. The effects are serviceable in the normal Asylum manner, the whole shebang made with a certain degree of flourish, a pleasant-enough time-waster which is attractive to look at. Best line in the picture? "This is more fun than taking Kabul from the Taliban!"

Asteroid vs. Earth
Asylum 2014; 91 minutes;
Director: Christopher Douglas-Olen Ray **

A 200-mile-wide asteroid approaches Earth: Scientists calculate that the only way to prevent it from wiping out mankind is to shift the planet off its axis, thus avoiding impact.

And if Earth *was* shifted off its axis, what of the fatal consequences that would follow? Probably even worse than if that gigantic ball of rock had hit us. Never mind, hyperactive computer nerd/genius Charles Byun and geophysicist Tia Carrere hit upon the idea of dropping a nuclear device into the South Pacific's Yap Trench, thereby jolting the planet out of the asteroid's path. Jason Brooks is Carrere's companion/love interest, their submarine heading towards the trench with its cargo of bombs; above surface, General Robert Davi argues with the Russian authorities who want to blast the asteroid out of the heavens which could lead to further worldwide calamities. Strangely, Asylum cut down on the special effects in this one, concentrating a little too much on personal drama and histrionics inside the submarine, which failed to work—we want to see cities destroyed by fire and brimstone, not Carrere overacting like crazy as the sub is split in two, one part surfacing, the other plummeting into the trench (unfortunately, Carrere is in the safe half). The plan comes to nothing, so a team of marines is sent to Saipan Island where Wade F. Wilson sacrifices himself for the sake of humanity, falling backwards into an erupting volcano holding two atomic missiles. One almighty explosion later, Earth trembles in her boots and shifts position, allowing the asteroid to float past into deep space, Brooks planting a smacker on Carrere's grinning face. One tidal wave and a chunk of meteorite hitting China does not a good disaster movie make; among Asylum's extensive repertoire of disaster action flicks, *Asteroid vs. Earth* is one of the more ordinary of the species.

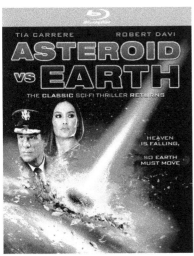

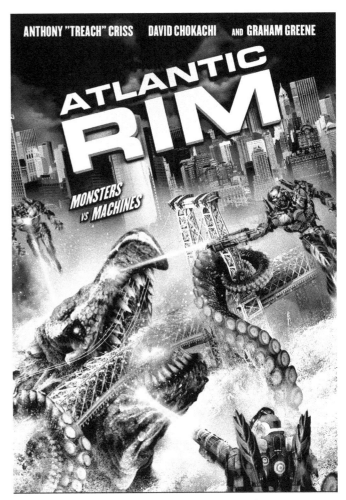

Atlantic Rim aka From the Sea
Asylum 2013; 85 minutes; Director: Jared Cohn ***

Three gigantic super-advanced robots are put into active service when America is threated by a species of aquatic monster.

Hot on the $190,000,000 heels of Guillermo del Toro's 131-minute *Pacific Rim* comes Asylum's cut-price 85-minute version, and just as enjoyable in a cheap kinda way. In the Gulf of Mexico, a deep sea oil rig is scuttled, together with a mini-sub. Descending to 700 fathoms, Green, Red and Blue Bots are employed to find out what went wrong. Attacked by a huge sea monster, the Bots surface, swiftly followed by another gigantic beast; after a tussle in which buildings are wrecked and civilians killed, the creature is destroyed by Red Bot whose commander, David Chokachi, is jailed for negligence. Admiral Graham Greene is informed that the creatures are over one hundred million years old and eggs have been discovered. One hatches, the monster, demolishing a destroyer, heading for New York—Chokachi is busted out of his cell by buddies Anthony 'Treach' Criss and Jackie Moore (she's carrying on with the pair of them), the three are integrated via headsets into their respective Bot's circuitry system ("If the suit gets hurt, the pilot gets hurt.") and off they fly to the Big Apple, a titanic struggle ensuing, including the destruction (yet again!) of the much-abused Statue of Liberty. Chokachi eventually saves the city from being nuked by bad guy Steven Marlow and deposits the monster outside of Earth's atmosphere, in outer space; crash-landing on his return, he picks himself up, dusts himself down and walks off with Moore who still harbors feelings for Criss. A witty script, helter-skelter direction, an amusing turn by Greene as the monosyllabic, stone-faced Admiral, together with acceptable special effects, ensure that Asylum's monster/*Transformers*-style adventure is top entertainment on a Saturday night in.

Atlantic Rim: Resurrection
Asylum 2018; 86 minutes; Director: Jared Cohn ***

Thought wiped out, another alien monster from the ocean depths lurches towards Los Angeles; three out-of-action Bots are called into service to combat the menace.

Brazenly cashing in on Steven S. DeKnight's $150,000,000 *Pacific Rim: Uprising*, Jared Cohn's second stab at the franchise has Michael Marcel, Lindsay Elston and Samm Wiechec clambering into their mighty AI-neural Bots controlled by "spinal cord stimulators" and going head-to-head with a massive crustacean causing havoc in Los Angeles, Steven Richard Harris overseeing the action from an underground bunker. When Marcel is killed in a skirmish, his machine brought down fighting the creature, Elston and Wiechec dispatch the monstrosity, thousands of mini-monsters, a cross between scorpion and spider, exploding from its belly and swarming down the streets; biological warfare is the order of the day, a specimen taken back to the laboratory for analysis. General Terry Woodberry of the Giant Killer Organization gives the order that, "I want anything with more than two legs killed on sight," as two more clawed behemoths emerge from the seas, the babies crawling all over their bodies. Harris and Xavi Israel command the two working Bots and battle the acid-spewing monsters in downtown LA; the giants are eventually destroyed by missiles, the infants demobilized. Injured Harris is comforted by feisty chick medic Jenna Ens while Paul Logan is reunited with hysterical wife Liz

The creatures emerge from the ocean in *Atlantic Rim: Resurrection.*

Fenning and daughter Teagan Sirset; the two women have been on the run throughout the movie, providing viewers with a series of woefully acted vignettes. As the company's monster fests go, the effects, particularly in the second half, are sufficient-enough, not million-dollar standard, perhaps, but pretty close to it, making for an enjoyable romp of the Asylum (if no one else's) variety.

Attila
Asylum 2013; 85 minutes; Director: Emmanuel Itier **

A group of marines discovers the corpse of Attila the Hun in a secret cave and takes it to a military base; Attila comes alive, bent on retrieving the three sections of the sacred staff of Moses which has the power to raise the dead.

If you're going to revive a legendary barbarian from times gone by, why not one of the best? Despite its premise, *Attila* is pretty ordinary stuff, most of the action taking place in sunlit woods where soldier Chris Conrad, military cutie Mikayla S. Campbell and assorted commandos, plus a rival faction, fire round after round at the muscleman with the face of a charcoaled pizza (Cheick Kongo) to no effect, just a shower of sparks bouncing off his well-honed torso. The hooded warrior even survives a rocket launcher! Deep within the classified area of a military fallout shelter, General M. Steven Felty, suffering from cancer, needs Moses' staff to both cure him and reactivate the bodies of young soldiers cut down in their prime (Project Genesis), to be used in an eventual war. The staff's three segments are joined together, Felty drinks blood from the golden skull on top of the staff but goes up in flames, along with a revived corpse—this isn't Attila they've been dealing with, but his son! The real skull-faced Attila materializes out of Felty's remains, fights his errant offspring and the whole base explodes, killing the pair, or does it? A blackened, bloody fist is last seen emerging from the ground, cue perhaps for a sequel which, on this showing, won't, like Attila the Hun, materialize.

Avengers Grimm
Asylum 2015; 81 minutes; Director: Jeremy M. Inman ****

Wicked Rumpelstiltskin kills the king and uses the magic mirror to enter the human world, aiming to rule with an army of thralls; Snow White, Red Riding Hood, Sleeping Beauty, Cinderella and Rapunzel follow through the portal, determined to put an end to his reign of terror.

UNDER TEN MILLION? ANYTHING'S POSSIBLE!

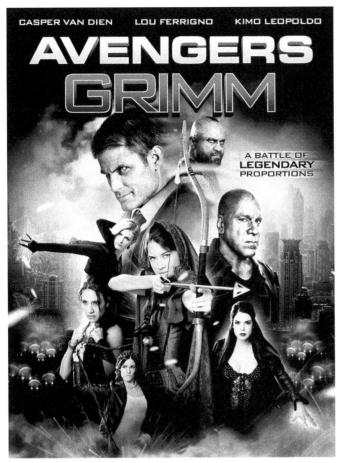

CASPER VAN DIEN   LOU FERRIGNO   KIMO LEOPOLDO

AVENGERS GRIMM

A BATTLE OF LEGENDARY PROPORTIONS

Some are of the opinion that Casper Van Dien has never made a decent movie since 1997's *Starship Troopers*, the actor content to lend his talents to the world of indie cinema. But here, he puts in a spirited performance, playing arch villain Rumpelstiltskin who creates an army of black-eyed thralls out of Los Angeles' citizens and police force, desiring to rule the roost. Elizabeth Peterson (Red Riding Hood) has her own agenda, to kill Kimo Leopoldo (The Wolf), while Lauren Parkinson (Snow White), Milynn Sarley (Cinderella), Mara Fairclough (Sleeping Beauty) and Rileah Vanderbilt (Rapunzel) attempt to eliminate Van Dien and journey back through the portal, a fragment of which the devilish one holds. And let's not forget Lou *The Incredible Hulk* Ferrigno as Iron John, initially against the girls but eventually siding with them after Van Dien has turned his skin to metal. "I'm gonna kill me a princess" growls a member of a S.W.A.T team, no match for these kick-boxing chicks from another dimension, all looking as though they've just stepped out of a New York beauty salon—a bevy of fairy tale Charlie's Angels. Walt Dis-

ney this isn't! You either go along with this kind of low-brow fantasy or you don't. For Asylum fanatics (yes, they do exist!), *Avengers Grimm* (based on Disney's $250,000,000 *Avengers: Age of Ultron* in which Ferrigno spoke the part of Hulk) is fast-moving, tongue-in-cheek fun; imaginative sets in the beginning, corny but enjoyable acting and a bulldozing star turn from Ferrigno, looking a lot younger than his 64 years. It doesn't end happily ever after, either: Ferrigno perishes under tons of falling masonry, Peterson plunges a sword into Leopoldo while Parkinson dies at the hands of Van Dien who disintegrates on trying to transport back through the portal, the portion of mirror smashed, the princesses asking "We're trapped here? We'll keep looking for a way home." One piece of good news—LA's citizens return to normal. On an icy slab in the morgue, Parkinson opens her eyes …

Avengers Grimm: Time Wars
Asylum 2018; 88 minutes; Director: Maximilian Elfeldt **

Snow White, Red Riding Hood, Sleeping Beauty and Alice reunite to defeat a witch from Atlantis who, aided by Rumpelstiltskin, plans to marry Prince Charles Charming III and rule the world.

Avengers Grimm was okay scatterbrained fairy tale fantasy: The follow-up falls flat, nowhere near as inventive, without doubt lacking Casper Van Dien's outlandish turn as arch villain Rumpelstiltskin; here, Eric Feltes plays him as a lank-haired wimp, at the mercy of Katherine Maya's leather-clad, busty Magda, fresh from Atlantis. By coercing Michael Marcel (Prince Charming) to place his power ring on her finger in marriage, she can rule the land but first, she has to get rid of those bitchy thorns in her side, Lauren Parkinson (Snow White), Elizabeth Eileen (Red Riding Hood) and Mara Fairclough (Sleeping Beauty),

"LAYS DOWN THE GAUNTLET.
A MARVEL OF FANTASY ACTION"

"ALL OF YOUR FAIRY TALE FAVORITES"

helped (and hindered) by Christina Licciardi (Alice, aka Looking Glass) and her dopey assistant, Randall Yarborough (Hatter). Plenty of time traveling through the gateway formed by the magic broken mirror glass means that one is never quite sure whether we are supposed to be in the present, the past or the future; the three heroines are pursued through a forest by Maya's robotic mermen, Parkinson stumbles across the graves of her protective seven dwarfs, a medieval castle appears in the mix and back in Los Angeles, Parkinson yells at Maya, "Get your silly ass away from my man!" before tying the knot with Marcel on a sunny Californian beach. As punishment for his ineptness, Feltes is carted off to Atlantis ("I hate the ocean!") by Maya and her black-masked minions, Licciardi telling the newlyweds to, "report to Looking Glass on your return" as she has fresh assignments in store. Disney's $320,000,000 *Avengers: Infinity War* had nothing to worry about in the competition stakes with this lukewarm riposte.

Battle of Los Angeles
Asylum 2011; 90 minutes; Director: Mark Atkins ****

A giant alien spacecraft homes in on Los Angeles, threatening to destroy the city if one of its race, imprisoned by the military in 1942, isn't released to them.

Anything that Columbia can do on a budget of $100,000,000, Asylum can do just as well on a fraction of that sum. Rush-released to cash in on *Battle: Los Angeles*, you just have to applaud the company for its sheer nerve in producing a carbon copy of a major motion picture and somehow getting away with it. The CGI effects at the start are as awesome as Asylum are ever going to achieve—midway through, the plot (if one exists) of Columbia's expensive sci-fi shoot-'em-up is all but forgotten and the film decides to ape *Independence Day*, throwing in a dash of *War of the Worlds* en route. The movie has its faults: The gung-ho script (spat out through gritted teeth by grizzled Tim Abell) will have you squirming in embarrassment; Theresa June Tao's tough army babe is dreadfully forced to the point

of irritation; Nia Peeples' sword-swinging macho-woman act is laughable; and Kel Mitchell's Will Smith impersonation more or less misses the target. Yet it's no good simply lambasting Asylum and all that the company stands for, or nit-picking over their rip-off productions. What they set out to do is often as good as the real thing, and here, *Battle of Los Angeles* succeeds, in spades. There is very little to choose between the direct-to-DVD feature and the big box-office blockbuster; neither could be classed as highbrow entertainment anyway. My money, in this instance, is on Asylum's offering.

Bermuda Tentacles
Asylum/M.O.B. 2014; 89 minutes; Director: Nick Lyon **

Commandos attempt to retrieve the President of America, trapped in a pod over 2,000 feet deep in the Bermuda Triangle, and come up against massive tentacles that are not of this earth.

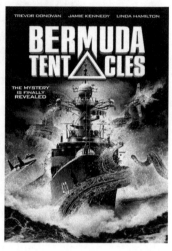

Jettisoned from Air Force One when the plane is hit by lightning, John Savage in his pod sinks to the ocean floor; 2,000 feet above, Admiral Linda Hamilton instructs "risk taker" Captain Trevor Donovan, pert Mya Harrison, the brains behind submersible *Prometheus*, and a team of grunts to plunge into the depths and retrieve Savage. Then Hamilton's fleet is attacked by giant spiny tentacles with mouths ("Do they seem hostile?" she asks biologist Jamie Kennedy. "I dunno," he replies. "They're worms. But they do seem angry."), so Brad Pitt look-alike Donovan has these creatures to contend with, as well as searching for Savage. What he discovers, apart from Savage, is a vast cavern filled with planes and old ships, a nautical graveyard of sorts, the actual insides of a colossal extraterrestrial spacecraft that controls the tentacles; its magnetic force is responsible for all those mysterious disappearances that have occurred over the Bermuda Triangle. *Bermuda Tentacles*, despite good effects work, is oddly lethargic and uninspired, with a tired performance from Hamilton and a scenario containing whiffs of James Cameron's *The Abyss*; the gargantuan alien vessel, emerging at the climax and firing a death ray, looks great though, destroyed by Donovan who then undergoes several minutes of clapping and whooping, embarrassing in the extreme. We know he's a hero, but this is ridiculous. At least he gets to hug pretty Harrison—no wonder director Lyon spends a considerable amount of camera time zooming in on her pretty elfin features. The girl's a cutie!

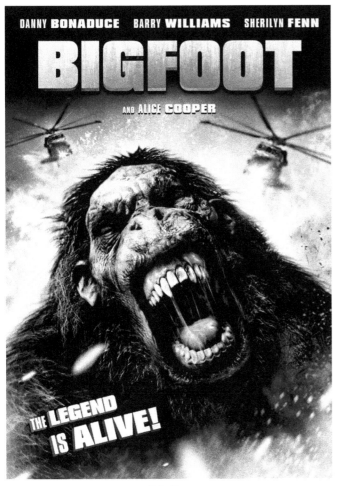

DANNY **BONADUCE** BARRY **WILLIAMS** SHERILYN **FENN**

BIGFOOT

AND **ALICE COOPER**

THE LEGEND IS **ALIVE!**

ing off their heads, swatting them like flies, chasing after cars, tossing vehicles and boats into the air, surviving machine guns and a shell blast, bringing down helicopters, smashing buildings and then retreating to his mountain cave dwelling high up on a cliff à la King Kong. After the monster has stormed through Rapid City, the wrap-up takes place on Mount Rushmore, Bigfoot (badly singed), Bonaduce, Williams and the head of Abraham Lincoln destroyed in a barrage of missiles, statues to the two warring buddies erected in memory of their bravery. It's fairly self-deprecatory in places ("If we respect Bigfoot, he'll respect us."), funny in others (a woman inspecting Bigfoot's footprint is squashed into it by the monster), moves like wildfire and features better-than-average performances from the two leads plus Sherilyn Fenn (cop), Howard Hesseman (mayor) and director Davison as the elderly sheriff. If you get into the spirit of the thing, this is a great big dollop of monster fun from start to finish—yes, *Bigfoot*, on this showing, reigns supreme among the crop of independent creature-features.

Blood Lake: Attack of the Killer Lampreys
Asylum 2014; 87 minutes; Director: James Cullen Bressack **

In a Michigan lake, the lamprey population explodes, threatening nearby rivers, the Mississippi Delta and the local population.

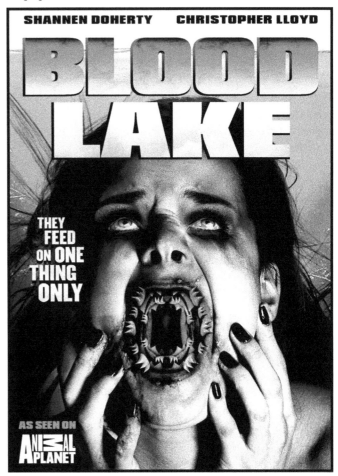

SHANNEN **DOHERTY**   CHRISTOPHER **LLOYD**

BLOOD LAKE

THEY FEED ON ONE THING ONLY

AS SEEN ON
ANIMAL PLANET

Bigfoot
Asylum 2012; 89 minutes; Director: Bruce Davison *****

Deadwood's 1st Annual '80s Flashback Festival receives two visitors—rock legend Alice Cooper and creature of legend Bigfoot.

To all those detractors who aren't enamored with the people over at Asylum and what they are all about, why bother to watch stuff like *Bigfoot* and then tear it to pieces online? Take the movie for what it is, 89 minutes of absolute monster delight, featuring a fabulous 50-foot-high romping, stomping, roaring, head-chewing hairy beast that proceeds to eliminate almost every single cast member by the end credits, plus Abraham Lincoln's face on Mount Rushmore. Agreed, Bigfoot varies in height in some scenes (so did a few of Ray Harryhausen's creations in his films) but he's allowed plenty of screen time; this is an indie CGI beauty to be proud of and relish! In a scenario free from the usual bevy of Asylum brainless bimbos, ex-music buddies Danny Bonaduce and Barry Williams clash over conservation issues and who, years ago, slept with whose mother; Bonaduce wants to slay Bigfoot for the $5,000 bounty; Williams wishes to place the creature (if he can snare it) in a nature reserve. In reel two, glam rocker Alice Cooper, minutes into his act, is kicked to oblivion as the aggrieved shaggy monster embarks on a reign of bedlam, reducing the festival to chaos, stamping on his victims, bit-

"Looks like an anus with teeth!" Correct, and when Mayor Christopher Lloyd sits on the toilet, only for one of the squirmy fanged horrors to, well, go where the sun don't shine, you may want to laugh, cry or switch off in disgust. Asylum's giant eel feature is mundane fodder despite bright photography, fast-paced direction and oodles of gore as thousands of aggressive lampreys embark on a rampage after finishing off the fish population, wriggling in and out of bodily orifices and turning the landscape blood red. Wildlife Services officer Jason Brooks has unsupportive wife Shannen Doherty to contend with (why is it that at the first sign of trouble, these women cold-shoulder their men?) plus sulky teen daughter Ciana Hanna, whose hormones are running riot, just like the slithery menaces in the lake that are getting into the drainage system. Meanwhile, son Koosha Yar keeps wandering off (as kids do in these movies), leading to all and sundry trying to save the boy from being gnawed to death when he's holed up in a house. Lloyd is the baddie, wanting to place tourist revenue before public safety, and on the hour, the scenario is just about played out, going through the motions; Yar is rescued, the lampreys electrocuted en masse in a power plant, although at the end, a large specimen emerges from a pipe, biting a worker on the leg. For his valiant efforts, Brooks receives a group hug, putting a smile on Doherty's frozen features for the first and only time in the picture. Standard creature thrills from Asylum, neither particularly good nor all that bad.

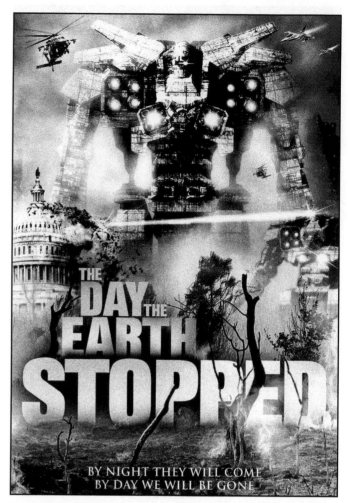

The Day the Earth Stopped
Asylum 2008; 89 minutes; Director: C. Thomas Howell ***

Thousands of giant robots from outer space hover over the world's capital cities, and two alien emissaries also appear with an ultimatum to Earth's leaders: Prove your humanity or we will destroy you.

No, it's not in the same league as 1951's *The Day the Earth Stood Still* (although it gives the 2008 remake a run for its money), but taken in context (this is Asylum, after all, not 20th Century Fox who threatened legal action but subsequently withdrew their impending lawsuit), *The Day the Earth Stopped* is fast-moving, entertaining sci-fi with more-than-reasonable effects. Director C. Thomas Howell plays the hero who latches onto space maiden Sinead Mc-Cafferty (a dead ringer for Angelina Jolie) and attempts, with her help, to convince the hard-nosed (and very stereotypical) grunts that Earth could be destroyed if Man doesn't put a stop to his warlike ways. By coming to the aid of a woman who expires during a traumatic childbirth and restoring her to life, the alien pair ultimately satisfy themselves that humanity and compassion *do* exist on our planet; their mission completed, McCafferty and Bug Hall beam aboard one of the towering robots and shoot off into space with all the others. Perhaps there's one car chase too

many and the dialogue is slightly dumb, but the effects depicting the giants looming over skyscrapers and warding off fighter planes are convincing enough, and McCafferty makes pleasing eye candy. It's the message that counts here; all in all, a pretty decent effort from indie cinema's prime rip-off merchant.

Dragonquest
Asylum 2009; 88 minutes; Director: Mark Atkins **

A young serf is given the daunting task of saving a kingdom from evil forces and a fiery dragon on a rampage.

A below-average *Dungeons and Dragons* slice of hokum from Asylum that drags its heels, even over a running time of 88 minutes. Daniel Bonjour has been told that he is "The Keeper," charged with defeating a warlock appearing from the East. With his magic pendant and grizzled Jason Connery in tow, he sets off on his quest, bumping into kick-boxing warrior Jennifer Dorogi and

UNDER TEN MILLION? ANYTHING'S POSSIBLE!

having a few half-hearted adventures along the way before confronting the warlock and, naturally, reducing him to dust with a beam of light after they engage in combat on the edge of a volcano. There's an enormous serpent residing in a murky green bog, guarding the "Stones of Virtue" (whatever they might be) and a curious scene in a cave when a giant leprous spider emerges, scuttles past Bonjour and promptly disappears. What was that all about? The dire CGI dragon is a mess, one of this company's worst creations, and the obvious attempt at creating a *Lord of the Rings* feel to the proceedings is laughably presented. For non-demanding kids only.

11/11/11

Asylum 2011; 87 minutes; Director: Keith Allan ****

Mum, Dad and son move into a house that was the scene of a bloody massacre, the 10-year-old boy, due to have his 11th birthday on Friday November 11, earmarked by locals as the new Satan.

Keith Allan's creepy mix of *Rosemary's Baby* and *The Omen* begins with that massacre at a dinner party; after finishing the dreadful deed, both gunmen blow their brains out. One year later, Professor John Briddell, pregnant wife Erin Coker and son Hayden Byerly (11 at the time of filming, naturally!) move into the house and, from the start, all does not bode well. Why are there six lines scratched on the wall that bleed blood? Why do various neighbors suddenly suffer violent deaths? What happened to Briddell's predecessor, also a college professor? Why does the doctor and evil nurse Kari Nissena insist on Coker being sedated? Why does nosy old Madonna Magee keep pestering the reserved lad in an effort to "save him"? On Friday November 11 at 11:11 p.m., it has been ordained that a new Satan will rise and take command after the ensuing Armageddon ("Satan is the one and only God."), and young Byerly *is* that new Satan, his goth babysitter (Aurelia Scheppers) teaching him foul manners behind his parents' backs. There's a fair amount of diabolical suspense and tension built up in Asylum's devil-worship flick—on a bigger budget, you get the impression it could have made

the national circuits as an A picture, rated (in England) "18." The *Exorcist*-type finale has all hell (literally!) breaking loose: Interfering Magee gets a machete in the neck and on the hour of 11:11, Byerly morphs into a levitating ghoul. Briddell dispatches two of the six servants of Satan who burst into the room, then kills his son to prevent him from becoming the new Dark Lord; Coker lies dead in the bath, tiny hands glimpsed moving beneath her dress as Briddell is arrested for murder. Another Satan in the making, perhaps …

Empire of the Sharks

Asylum 2017; 89 minutes; Director: Mark Atkins ***

In the future, 98% of the planet's surface is covered in water; an evil warlord rules the roost, controlling thousands of sharks through electronic devices.

Produced back-to-back in South Africa with the inferior *Planet of the Sharks*, Atkins' sub-*Waterworld* feature has Orlando Bloom look-alike Jack Armstrong and black babe Thandi Sebe attempting to rescue a party of captives on grizzled war-

lord John Savage's floating island domain. Everyone is dressed Middle Eastern-style in this fast-moving frolic, Jonathan Pienaar (a dead ringer for Iggy Pop) chewing the scenery as Savage's unhinged sidekick, demanding supplies of fresh water in exchange for the hostages. Blonde Ashley de Lange possesses an ancient amulet that can control sharks, the girl earmarked as a future shark caller; she's also Armstrong's intended. Plenty of gory shark action, including one giant mutated specimen fitted with sensors, and colorful incident abound as Savage and his musclebound tribe (straight out of an Italian peplum movie) try to lay their hands on a vital piece of de-salinization machinery; in the end, the warlord's electric power wilts before Lange's inbuilt power and he's torn to shreds by the predators. Lange is last seen practicing her shark calling skills in an Asylum shark feature that, by their standards, is enjoyable escapism if you engage your brain in neutral and ignore the fact that (a) Armstrong enters the hatch of his submersible in daylight, even though it's below the waves, and (b) breakers are seen in background shots, crashing down into shallow water; most scenes take place (supposedly) in the middle of the ocean.

End of the World
Asylum 2018; 88 minutes; Director: Maximilian Elfeldt **

Colossal solar flares, extreme radiation and coronal mass ejections create apocalyptic weather conditions on Earth.

Putting all their eggs in one basket, Asylum's effects department came up with a barrage of collapsing skyscrapers and office blocks, streets splitting wide open, molten lava flowing through the sidewalks, hurricanes, bolts of lightning, a tsunami, earthquakes, floods, huge black clouds and an active volcano rising above the LA skyline, a collection, if you like, of all those disaster scenes from all those other Asylum disaster movies. Thankfully allowing a crater to swallow four puerile teens at the outset, we had Mom (Jhey Castles) and games nerd son Evan James Henderson dodging every kind of obstacle known to man in their hunt for Dad (Joseph Michael Harris) and daughter Jacqueline Scislowski, while military grunt Sallieu Sesay (who once fancied Castles, and still does) is busy organizing a "mass evac." Everyone is trying to reach a system of caves high up in the hills that contain old military bunkers which, they reason, will protect them from the catastrophes taking place. It's a typical Asylum "can the family reunite in the face of overwhelming odds" vehicle, reasonably directed by Maximilian Elfeldt, the effects achieved with a modicum of expertise. Where it all falls down is in two areas: Harris and Scislowski, after heading for safety in the hills, then return to the ravaged city (and danger) to find a telephone line so that they can contact Castles and Hender-

son; and would teenage computer games geek Henderson *honestly* be able to fly an army helicopter over Los Angeles and then, by chance, locate his father and sister on a rooftop as magma threatens to envelop the building, rescuing them on a rope ladder? Even Castles comments, "It's not a video game," Harris adding, "How did you do that?" How indeed! The film ends in a schmaltzy family hug backed by heavenly choral music, the solar flares subsiding, the planet returning to normal, leaving you with one thought: In Asylum movies (and elsewhere), Los Angeles gets blitzed more times by natural disasters than Tokyo ever did under Godzilla's mighty feet.

Evil Nanny
Asylum 2016; 90 minutes; Director: Jared Cohn ***

A family hires a babysitter for their two children but rue the day they ever took her on when the girl turns out to be a psychotic arsonist bent on claiming their new home as her own.

It's all been done before, of course, most noticeably in John Schlesinger's *Pacific Heights* (Fox, 1990) where Michael Keaton played the tenant from hell who couldn't be budged. Here, Lindsay Elston, after being kicked out of the St. Mary's Home for Wayward Girls (and setting fire

UNDER TEN MILLION? ANYTHING'S POSSIBLE!

to the school sign as she leaves), adopts an alias and takes up a position with Nicole Sterling and Matthew Pohlkamp, looking after their two kids. At first, Elston appears the perfect article, bonding with young Cooper Fontaine and the baby; then she turns into a complete menace, inviting her drug-dealing boyfriend (Stephen Barrington) in her room for sex, throwing rowdy parties, accusing Pohlcamp of molesting her and using every legal loophole in the book to gain possession of the property. For a latter-day Asylum psycho flick, *Evil Nanny* works fine on a basic level, mainly due to Elston's spiky performance as the conniving bitch creating havoc in Sterling's well-ordered household and Jared Cohn's taut direction. However, the climax is a bit hard to swallow, Sterling cuddling the deranged girl in the garden treehouse as the cops, finally aware of who Elston really is, move in, telling her "It's gonna be okay" and that her mother really loved her; would she really have shown such sympathy and repentance after what the mentally unstable babysitter had put her and her family through?

Exorcism: The Possession of Gail Bowers
Asylum 2006; 91 minutes; Director: Leigh Scott ****

In a town somewhere in Florida, a teenage girl is possessed by a demonic entity.

Asylum's answer to both *The Exorcist* and *The Entity* is a smashing little horror tale, staged with a fair amount of verve by Leigh Scott, one of the company's more dynam-

ic directors. The plot is paper-thin, but it's in the telling that counts. Couple Noel Thurman and Griff Furst take on Erica Roby after her parents die. Following a session on an Ouija board with neighbor Rebekah Kochan, Roby is possessed by an invisible "something" and sees shadowy figures on her TV. As her condition worsens (she forces Kochan to kill herself; stigmata break out on her hands; her growling language becomes obscene), Furst calls in a doctor friend (Richard Schick) to diagnose the problem but he proves to be completely useless. Finally, blind priest Thomas Downey is summoned; he performs an exorcism to purge the girl's body of the diabolical being by quoting the Rite of Abraham in the frenetic climax. Minimal effects are an advantage here (no vomiting green slime or Linda Blair-type makeover) and so is the murky, claustrophobic photography. Apart from one glaring error—Kochan dies but nobody appears to notice her absence. Asylum's chilly and occasionally erotic delight is a darned sight more interesting than a host of other demonic possession movies and that includes bigger-budgeted efforts like 2005's tepid *The Exorcism of Emily Rose.*

500 MPH Storm
Asylum 2013; 86 minutes; Director: Daniel T. Lusko *

In the Gulf of Mexico, the Apollo Energy Control Center, harnessing Earth's natural resources via a huge laser beam in an attempt to control weather conditions, malfunctions; as a result, massive storms are created that rock America's Eastern Seaboard.

The U. S. of A. is once more battered by hurricanes, twisters, cyclones and tsunamis courtesy of the Asylum special effects department. The opening is fine, filmed at Albuquerque's International Balloon Festival where, high up, meteorologist Casper Van Dien, wife Sarah Lieving and teenage son Bryan Head note turbulence and darkening skies, descending out of harm's way. Then we are subjected to a barrage of storm-driven effects and a barrage of nonsense from Van Dien's family, especially his brat of a son who blames his father for the appalling conditions. "I wanna go home," he wails as Van Dien drives his 4x4 here, there and everywhere at the speed of light in an effort to escape the clutches of that fearsome "Hypercane," followed by, "You gotta drive faster" from Lieving, screwing up her fine features in mock horror. "Faster," "Go Go Go," and "C'mon!" they yell in unison, our floppy-haired hero depositing the pair at a mountain lodge, rescuing them from a forest fire (in slo-mo), then continually ending up at a disused factory with a bunch of badly acting grunts, obviously the focal point, of what remains unclear. It's noisy, messy and disjointed, with a ludicrous climax, our trio on the roof of that wrecked building, sat-phones in hands, directing coordinates to the control center in order to neutralize the eye of the storm. It works, for around five seconds: The giant beam goes haywire, Van Dien and family board a helicopter discovered standing in the middle of nowhere, the center is knocked out by a missile, Head shouts "Awesome," and the final shot is of the threesome gazing out at a city in smoking ruins. To be honest, *500 MPH Storm* is a chore to sit through, almost an Asylum turkey of storm-like proportions; only Lieving, wasted on this occasion, emerges with any real credibility.

Flight World War II

Asylum 2015; 85 minutes; Director: Emile Edwin Smith **

On a journey to London, Flight 42 encounters an electrical storm and passes through a black hole, finding herself over war-torn France in June 1940.

Given a bit more care and attention (and a bigger budget), Asylum's take on Don Taylor's 1980 *The Final Countdown* could have been a worthy addition to time travel movies of a different kind; instead, amateur dramatics from the cast and questionable World War II facts contribute to a production that fails to live up to its DVD blurb's promise of, "The great-est battle that never happened." Faran Tahir plays the 747's chief pilot, Matias Ponce his buddy, realizing that something is seriously wrong when his plane, emerging from day into night after passing through a huge storm, detects nothing on the radar screen, multiple explosions on the ground below and German Junkers on attack alert. Contacting an English corporal, Robbie Kay, Tahir is forced to believe that they have traveled back in time, even if his shrieking, sobbing, tossed-around, hysterical passengers don't. Two history professors do their best to explain that what everyone is experiencing is an "alternate history," hence the presence of ME262 jets in 1940 and talk of Dunkirk being "a slaughter," while a bearded old gent at the rear scribbles furiously in his diary. The obligatory psycho (Adam Blake) does his best to upset the already upset passengers, stewardess Aqueela Zoll looks pretty and the twist ending has Tahir jettisoning the plane's radar system into the welcoming arms of Kay, a system that apparently helped the allies save Europe from Nazi occupation despite the sterling efforts of Winston Churchill and the boys of the RAF. To ram home the point, once Flight 42 is back in the present and landed at Berlin, the bearded veteran is none other than the English corporal, now 70 years older, who has just put the finishing touches to his book entitled *The Radar System That Saved Europe*. It's ever-so-slightly dull, lacking the essential spectacular effects, making Asylum's other aircraft-in-peril flick, *Airplane vs. Volcano*, seem like a classic in comparison.

40 Days and Nights

Asylum 2012; 82 minutes; Director: Peter Geiger **

A tectonic shift within the Earth's crust causes the sea level to rise worldwide, resulting in a flood of Biblical proportions, an "extinct level event."

In the opening scene, a massive wave sweeps across the Sahara Desert; 78-odd minutes later, a 21st-century Noah's Ark cruises on a calm sea, the crew gazing at the setting sun. What happens in between is straight out of Asylum disaster cliché land: Ark designer Alex Carter secreting himself on board a navy destroyer to steal a device that will modify the ark's ballast units; wife Monica Keena and Christianna Carmine in a 'copter, searching for bee DNA in a flooded canyon; and people racing across country to hitch a ride on the 50,000 people-capacity vessel, cyclones and tsunamis thundering in their rear. Marvel at Denver's skyscrapers under deluge, the Florida Keys road bridge swept away, crass dialogue (Keena, after retrieving only a small portion of DNA from a wrecked train: "No samples means no survival."), the ark resembling a floating cereal giveaway with sails (the turbines pack

up) and Keena's wobbling bottom lip, plus her nipples poking through her soggy vest. The movie ends abruptly on the 79th minute, followed by three minutes of credits, as if all concerned had had enough. At least it's short and blessed with a certain catastrophic panache, in spite of occasional shoddy process work and lame performances from all concerned.

Geo-Disaster
Asylum/SyFy 2017; 87 minutes;
Director: Thunder Levin **

A cloud of dark matter plows through Earth, causing a series of cataclysmic events culminating in a gigantic tidal wave.

In Los Angeles, stepmom Natalie Pelletier has two sullen teenagers on her hands—Maggie Rose Hudson and Isabella Bazler. Meanwhile, up in the San Bernardino Forest area, Pelletier's husband, Matthew Pohlkamp, is trying his damnedest to bond with whiny son Erich Riegelmann ("Come on. Lighten up."). All around them, in Asylum's answer to Warner Bros.' $120,000,000 *Geostorm* released the same month, apocalyptic events are occurring; volcanic eruptions, earthquakes, bad weather, lightning bolts, heavy seas, massive cracks in the crust and collapsing infrastructure. Will husband and new wife

get it together before that mega-tsunami hits? Before you reach for the remote's "off" button, try to ignore Hudson and Riegelmann's "why doesn't anyone understand me" sulky features (difficult, I know), take in some of the better efforts of Asylum's effects department and ponder these all-important questions: Why is that observatory in Puerto Rico only manned by shouty-shouty scientist Tammy Klein ("What is it? It's accelerating towards us! We can't stop it!") and two nerdish assistants?; why is it that when Pohlkamp and Riegelmann's tent plummets into a crevasse for several minutes, they emerge unscathed on a small bank?; what prevents Pohlkamp from pushing his son over the edge when, "You're just a stereotype for a midlife crisis" is flung in his face?; and what stops Pelletier from using her fists when eye-rolling Hudson moans to her, "I wish Dad never married you. Don't you get it? I need a mom." When Bazler suggests taking a vacation "when it's all over," Hudson retorts: "Dork! Look around. Disney World's toast!" The family is eventually reunited in the hills overlooking LA following volcanic explosions, electrical storms, molten lava flowing down the backroads, streaks of lightning encircling the globe, earth tremors, a mammoth vortex sucking in the

atmosphere and the expected tidal wave that sweeps over the city. The boiling magma in the two craters formed by the dark matter hardens and seals the openings, everything returning to normality, including Hudson, who cuddles Pelletier, and Riegelmann, who mutters, "Love you, Dad." In fact the movie ends on a group hug one year later, Pohlkamp stating, in reply to Pelletier's "Where do we go from here?," "It doesn't matter, as long as we're a family." Did someone, somewhere, ask for the vomit bucket?

Ghosthunters
Asylum 2016; 90 minutes; Director: Pearry Reginald Teo ***

When one of their number's wife and daughter are brutally slain by a serial killer, a team of paranormal investigators venture into the victims' house in order to free their tortured spirits.

Released on July 5, 2016 to cash in on Columbia's $144,000,000 *Ghostbusters* which came out a week later, Asylum's effort (18-rated in Britain) harks back to their earlier, bloodier output and isn't all that bad. Getting under way with the savage demise of London Grace (Phyllis Spielman) and daughter Anna Harr at the hands of a masked maniac, the action switches to Stephen Manley, David O'Donnell, Liz Fenning, Crystal Web and rookie reporter Francesca Santoro converging on the house of death. In the attic is a machine that can capture the ec-

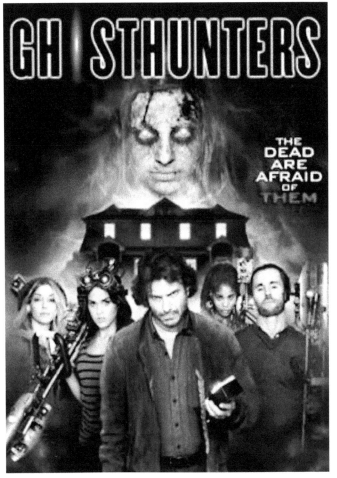

toplasm of ghosts; in this way, Manley can free the spirits of Grace and Harr from the accursed building, bringing them much-needed peace. Using the polarizer, a couple of entities end up in vials as red sticky liquid, the team subjected to supernatural disturbances, especially Santoro who reckons she can see the masked murderer, known as the Night Stalker, through the goggles on her headset; Web is dispatched by a floating knife (although nobody appears to notice). Writer/director Pearry Reginald Teo throws in a plethora of violent images (body parts on hooks) and piles on the sudden shocks with all the subtlety of being hit over the head with a hammer, but it's lively-enough fare for the undiscriminating, Manley disclosed as the killer—and the house is his. He wanted to be part of history, the experimental machine, Unit 7-31, used by Japanese scientists in WWII on prisoners of war to monitor how much stress the human body could take before dying and amplify paranormal activity. Manley, now crazed, stabs O'Donnell to death but is distracted by Grace's raging phantom; the two vials break on the floor, releasing vengeful spirits that attack Manley and kill him, but not before Fenning receives a bullet in the face. Santoro, the only one left, staggers bloody and battered from the place as the cops arrive.

The Giant Killer aka Jack the Giant Killer
Asylum 2013; 87 minutes; Director: Mark Atkins ***

A colossal beanstalk carries Jack off to the Realm of the Clouds where he meets his missing father and an evil queen who plans to return to Earth with an army of giant beasts in retribution for being marooned in her kingdom.

The Asylum team set up camp in the United Kingdom, filming around Manchester, Liverpool and the Welsh countryside in director/writer/photographer Mark Atkins' updated take on the old Jack and the Beanstalk fable, featuring a British cast and excellent special effects interspersed with spells of acting lunacy. On his 18th birthday, Jamie Atkins (Jack) is given a handful of beans; two are planted, a gigantic beanstalk reaches into the heavens and the lad is whisked skywards, meeting his father Harry Dyer who hasn't aged one bit, plus Jane March, a wicked seductress. Dyer's floating castle is a gem direct from the pages of the Jules Verne school of mechanics, as is March's ornate, industrial-styled mountain retreat. The dark-haired vixen plans to conquer the world with her army of gigantic horned six-eyed monsters ("I wish to return to punish all those responsible.") and descends to Earth, taking on the British army, or all 20 of them. It's at this point that the film plummets into absurdity, despite those magnificent roaring, stomping creatures—Welsh actor Steve McTigue's comic book General and his inept squad is straight out of a *Carry On* picture, utterly ludicrous in this fantasy setup, while Agent Ben Cross looks uncomfortable, probably regretting he ever took part in the enterprise. The picture's third section unfor-

tunately drags, Atkins taking on monster number one in a metal *Transformers*-type suit before slaying the thing via a lightning bolt and engaging in lip action with Vicki Glover. Chris Ridenhour and Andrew Morgan Smith's score isn't too bad for an Asylum effort, the set design is imaginative and there's a wealth of incident, but the director's insistence on caricaturizing the British army to such an absurd, cliché-ridden extent simply falls flat on its face—UK viewers will *not* be amused! These amateurish scenes sabotage what could have been one of the company's more rewarding and unusual fantasies.

Halloween Night
Asylum 2006; 85 minutes; Director: Mark Atkins ***

Locked away in an asylum for 10 years after witnessing the rape and murder of his mother for which he was wrongly convicted, a horribly scarred lunatic nursing one almighty grudge escapes and proceeds to slaughter a houseful of teenagers (all in fancy dress) on Halloween night.

Asylum's *Halloween* rip-off is a medley of every other slasher movie made over the past 20 years but is effectively put across. Scot Nery is the boogeyman bent on a mission of revenge, his face resembling a hamburger someone has trodden on, returning to his old house to uncover clues as to who exactly was behind those murders. Turns out it was his father who killed his mother and committed suicide,

sealing the room and setting fire to it. Derek Osedach and Rebekah Kochan play two teens who *nearly* make it to the final reel after everyone else has been chopped up with an axe by the madman; Osedach is mistaken for Nery and accidentally shot by Kochan. Throw in a couple of explicit nude lesbian sex romps (there's a lot of nudity in this movie), a welter of gut-churning butchery (orchestrated with finesse by director Atkins) and the mandatory trick ending and you have an Asylum teenage grue-fest that pretty much hits the horror nail on the head in standard fashion, even though it's far from original in concept.

The Haunting of Whaley House
Asylum 2012; 89 minutes; Director: Jose Prendes ✱✱✱✱

After nightfall, five teenagers and two amateur ghost-busters decide to investigate "America's most haunted house," the infamous Whaley residence in San Diego, with disastrous results.

Asylum's ghost-based movies are better than most (*The Haunting of Winchester House* was brilliant) and Jose Prendes' widescreen offering continues the trend, despite foul-mouthed dialogue ("This house is as haunted as fuck.") and a woeful performance by big black guy Howard Mc-Nair playing Keith, America's most inept investigator of the paranormal. With Camille Saint-Saëns' "Danse Macabre" used over the title credits to set the right mood, tour guide Stephanie Greco takes her four skeptical buddies on

a private nightmare trip through one gloomy room after another, McNair and Graham Denman testing for supernatural presences which are heard on tape and shown briefly (at first) in the background. Then the gray, decaying apparitions of the Whaley family get violent ("You belong to us," they croak): They feed off death, so one by one, Greco's friends are put to the slaughter in a welter of gruesome demises, possessed punk Arielle Brachfeld changing into a Marilyn Manson-type ghoul (vivid make-up) before shooting herself in the chest, just as, in actuality (the film is partly based on fact), Violet Whaley died in 1885. McNair himself has his head squashed after pursuing the spirit of a giggling, malignant little girl, two investigating cops never make it out alive and Greco is the last to perish, falling backwards into a bottomless pit after a repellant creature, the Whaley's pet, has menaced her. The ending has Greco trapped forever in the spooky house, a restless phantom screaming, "I'm alive! I'm alive!" after elderly guide Lynn Lowry has closed the doors on the murder scene. At one point, sexy Mindy Robinson (as Candy Galore!) exposes her well-proportioned breasts in the garden, then promptly disappears from the plot—nice, but rather superfluous to requirements! Produced on a budget of $150,000, *The Haunting of Whaley House* looks cheap in the early stages but bursts into life on the hour, a nifty haunted house flick that gives many similar big-budget offerings from the major studios a real run for their money.

The Haunting of Winchester House
Asylum 2009; 86 minutes; Director: Mark Atkins *****

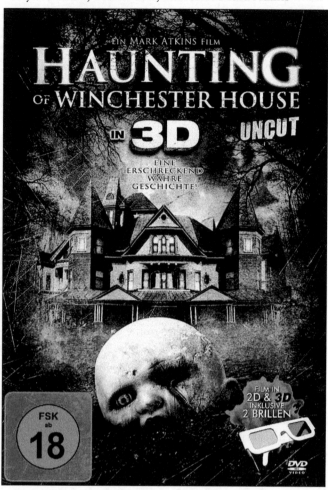

A couple and their young daughter take up caretaker duties in a remote woodland mansion and are immediately tormented by the ghoulish specters of the house's long-dead residents.

And I do mean immediate—no hanging around for things to happen in this unsettling Asylum "things that go bump in the night" chiller as Michael Holmes, Lira Kellerman and daughter Patty Roberts see a haggard old crone, apparitions with disfigured faces, a young girl in white (who died in 1860) and a freakish-looking baby. Atkins effectively cranks up a real sense of dread by having his characters back into all manner of nasties or placing his ghouls in dark, out-of-focus background shots, and underneath it all there is more than one tale unfolding. Are the restless dead tuberculosis or gunshot victims? A family tragedy, maybe? What is the significance behind the small girl's repeated appearances? Is that hollow-eyed, deaf-mute phantom trying to convey something of importance to the terrified couple? What lies in that large ornate box in the dusty attic? Paranormal investigator Tomas Boykin, gifted with second-sight, arrives to put a stop to the manifestations, unsuccessfully as it turns out, and the shock/twist *Others*-type ending (which discloses all of the various plot strands) will take even the most seasoned viewer completely by surprise (spoiler alert: the entire family died in a car crash on their way to the mansion at the start!). The dingy color photography actually works in the film's favor, boosting the clammy, cobwebby atmosphere, as does the whispering, disquieting soundtrack, contributing to a superior supernatural thriller from Asylum. With a well-known star at the helm and a touch more polish, this would have made a respectable cinema release.

Hillside Cannibals
Asylum 2006; 83 minutes; Director: Leigh Scott ***

A couple is terrorized by inbred cannibals, the descendants of the notorious Scottish butcher Sawney Bean, who inhabit caves in the Mojave Desert.

Eighty-three minutes of splatter gore sums up Leigh Scott's garishly photographed answer to Alexandre Aja's *The Hills Have Eyes*, both productions released in March 2006. There's little in the way of plot: Five youngsters head out for the hills; three are butchered by the cannibals, Tom Nagel left chained to a wall and abused while girlfriend Heather Conforto tries to seek help. She rescues Nagel, he's recaptured, fingers scissored off and torso ripped in two; she then enlists the aid of Chriss Anglin who's on the vengeance trail because of his missing daughters ("I'm gonna kill those fucking monsters, every last one of them.") and he's slaughtered, the cave dwellers' "new chief" wearing the ragged facial skin of the dead ex-leader ("Ah'm the new Sawnee Bean!"). Corrupt Sheriff Louis Graham, in with the sect, finally delivers Con-

forto to them after she's nearly been raped and stunned her attacker with a rock, her still corpse looking on as a cannibal couple indulge in graphic sex. Filmed in vivid red colors in Odessa Canyon, Yermo, California, Scott discards all semblance of cinematic finesse in favor of blood, guts, prosthetic scar tissue make-up and copulation of the disgusting variety, the mumbled, caveman-type speech last heard in Hammer's *One Million Years B.C.*, but in its own gruesome, grimy fashion, *Hillside Cannibals* delivers the stomach-churning goods; after all, as is the case with the zombie subgenre, there is only so much you can do with a bunch of flesh-munching disfigured retards.

Ice Sharks
Asylum/SyFy 2016; 85 minutes; Director: Emile Edwin Smith **

The crew of Arctic research station Oasis comes under attack from the "Greenies," an aggressive species of Greenland shark, that leaves them marooned on an ice floe.

In the first few minutes, an Inuit hunter and his dog team are gobbled up by a shark that lurches onto the ice. At the Oasis facility, two scientists are eaten (one on a snowmobile) and shark fins circle the station, acting like saws, cutting into the pack ice which collapses, sending the structure plummeting 90 feet down onto the ocean floor, trapping Edward DeRuiter, Jenna Parker, Kaiwi Lyman and Clarissa

Thibeaux. The four then have to decide on a method of transmitting help to the outside world, and how to cope with the big predators prowling the frigid sea in their vicinity. Don't expect any kind of artistic finesse in this substandard Asylum "sharks on the loose" outing: There's very little blood and guts on the menu (surprising when you consider all the company's other gore-spattered shark features), the CGI effects look wobbly and performances range from passable (DeRuiter) to not-so-good (Lyman, who resembles a surfer dude; in fact, the actor's an ex-surfer!). "Oh my God. Here we go!" yells Thibeaux when Oasis sinks beneath the waves, an indication of how trite the dialogue is, followed by "Don't panic!" from DeRuiter as they realize that there is only one day's air supply left, dead batteries and no radio signal; and how many times must we suffer someone yelling "Copy that!" into a mike. Failing a helicopter attempt to hoist them out of the sea (the chopper crashes, the movie's one effective scene), Oasis (or what remains of it), supported by balloon-like salvage bags, is eventually hauled from the depths by *Icebreaker I*'s winch (just a winch?), complete with a giant shark that's trying to take chunks out of Parker for breakfast; the creature is blasted back into the sea, DeRuiter and Parker go off to play house while Thibeaux mourns the loss of Lyman. A disappointingly tame shark offering from Asylum (shot in Utah), more suitable for the kiddies than those brought up on the 15-rated *Sharknado*/multiple-headed shark flicks which are a lot livelier and far more gruesome in tone.

Independents' Day

Asylum 2016; 91 minutes; Director: Laura Beth Love ****

Massive alien ships hover over the world's major cities, the Orions issuing an ultimatum: Capitulate to our demands, otherwise the entire human race will be wiped out.

Released two weeks before Fox's $175,000,000 *Independence Day: Resurgence*, Laura Beth Love's $500,000 production boasts (for its budget) striking special effects (and plenty of them) plus, to cap it off, an equally striking giant alien. The action is brisk, Madame President Fay Gauthier and her team, plus the rest of the world, given 120 hours to evacuate the planet and board transport ships that will ferry them to the one-kilometer wide Hives (the mother ships) where they will be put down on another world; all those left behind will be exterminated. However, computer whizz kid Brian Tyler Cohen has established that the aliens haven't originated from Orion, their talk of colonizing Earthlings on another planet a fabrication; humans are either jettisoned into space in their thousands before docking at the Hives or they're stored for their much-needed blood. Militia strongman Jes Selane and his First Earth mob are busy upsetting the aliens by blasting away at their craft, even though the devious Orions have shown "good intent" by curing Gauthier's son (Matthew Riley) of his crippled legs. One dead visitor is taken to a lab and dissected, producing a tube of "chemical alien odor," Gauthier hitting on a plan to introduce a virus to mess up the alien computer and meet with the commander on one of the Hives, there to release a contagion that will infect and destroy them. Boarding a transport vessel, Gauthier, Johnny Rey Diaz, Jude B. Lanston and William Castrogiovanni are flown to the Hive armed with a case of lethal vials; Gauthier confronts the big alien boss (a splendid creation), shaking hands (or hand shaking claw) on a deal ("I am the leader of this colony. Your family will not be harmed. You will live on this ship.") and craftily releasing the pathogen.

The Orion dies in agony, as do its crew, the four humans making it back to Earth just as the worldwide Hives explode, along with their transport craft and assorted fighting machines. A feast of jets/humans versus aliens skirmishes ("Take that, space trash!"), highly imaginative shots of the mother ship looming over Washington and that monstrous Orion commander mean that Asylum's space invasion opera scores high marks—and it's far less pretentious than a lot of mega-bucks releases of a similar ilk out there.

Invasion of the Pod People
aka Invasion: The Beginning
Asylum 2007; 85 minutes; Director: Justin L. Jones **

Following a meteorite shower over California, strange tubular plants produce replicas that take over the bodies of their human counterparts.

Yet another slant on *Invasion of the Body Snatchers* with one notable exception: In the Don Siegel classic (and other versions), the replicates were devoid of all feeling; in Asylum's cock-eyed variant, the female aliens turn into rampant lesbians! Sexploitation merchant Russ Meyer could well have produced this movie in the 1960s—a cornucopia of lithe naked female flesh combined with a distinctly amateurish method of filmmaking, a sort of soft-porn alien feature. First off, that appalling soundtrack. It sounds as though Jones made the film in an echo chamber; did they carry out sound checks before shooting? The plot? A model agency is looking for fresh talent. Raven-haired Erica Roby gets roped into trying to lure porn actress Lorraine Smith over to her agency. Smith, though, is the first to be "taken over" by the plant. Next is Roby's foxy boss, Jessica Bork, who then drags Roby off for some group lesbian sex. No happy ending here, either: Danae Nelson, Roby's best friend, corners her in a car at the end, herself one of the pod people. The few male leads in the cast don't offer anything of note—this is one for the boys who like to be titillated. What appears to be slimy red and yellow sheets of polythene constitutes the only bit of effects on show, but at least the movie's more entertaining than 2007's dire Nicole Kidman version, *The Invasion*.

John Carter of Mars aka Princess of Mars
Asylum 2009; 93 minutes; Director: Mark Atkins ****

A marine badly wounded during a terrorist gunfight is teleported to Mars 216, fourth planet in the Alpha Cen-

tauri system, where he becomes embroiled in a conflict between two alien races.

Retitled *John Carter of Mars* to tie in (and cash in) with Disney's $250,000,000 *John Carter* (2012), Mark Atkins' gloriously photographed sci-fi actioner (Atkins' duties included cinematographer) is a delight to sit through: Imaginative other-worldly landscapes (California's Bronson Canyon was the location, filmed using filters), a *Predator*-type species called the Tharks, giant flesh-eating insects, two-legged alien camels, lofty citadels and ex-porn star Traci Lords playing Princess Dejah Thoris. The plot revolves around ownership of a massive pumping station situated in the desert that controls atmospheric conditions; Lords is chief guardian, the Tharks view it with suspicion and bad guy/opium crime boss Chacko Vadaketh has followed Antonio Sabato, Jr. to the planet, wishing to become top dog by taking over the site. Action man Sabato, captured by Thark Matt Lusky, wins the tribes' respect after defeating an army of huge spiders, earns the nickname "Grasshopper" when he uses the planet's low gravitational field to leap vast distances, helps Lusky overthrow Thark tyrant Mitchell Gordon, rescues Lords from her disabled spacecraft, earning her undying love, and goes head-to-head with old foe Vadaketh at the atmosphere control center, the villain carried off by a man-size flying bug. Job done and hostilities at least having quietened down, Saba-

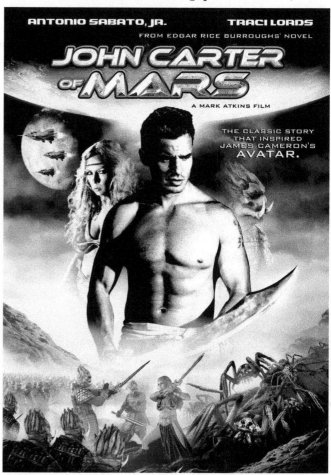

UNDER TEN MILLION? ANYTHING'S POSSIBLE!

to teleports back to Earth where he resumes active duty, vowing to return to Lords' welcoming embrace ("I shall return to the Red Planet and the Princess of Mars."). Atkins focuses a great deal on Sabato's manly physique in a series of arty full-frame shots, the color is exceptional (particularly in the interiors) and the whole entertaining package looks A class. A minor gem from Asylum (note the opening aerial shot, zooming over mountain ranges, a favored credit background display in many Asylum productions.)

Journey to the Center of the Earth
aka Journey to Middle Earth
Asylum 2008; 87 minutes;
Directors: David Jones and Scott Wheeler *

An all-female combat team is accidentally teleported to a cavern 600 kilometers below the Earth's surface, prompting the military to rescue them via a boring machine called the *Deep Digger 1*.

The end credits of this abysmal Asylum fantasy flick state "Based on the novel by Jules Verne." Not in a million years! No doubt made to cash in on the 2008 Brendan Fraser vehicle, David Jones and Scott Wheeler's version of Verne's famous yarn plumbs new depths (literally!) in acting, script, direction and set design, showing a marked drop in standards in a few of Asylum's products from this productive period. Seven vest-wearing, gun-toting macho babes find themselves trapped inside a vast cavern miles underground and it's up to macho Greg Evigan and Dedee Pfeiffer (Michelle Pfeiffer's sister) to come to their rescue in the *DD1*. Menaced by a Tyrannosaurus and a few giant spiders (one bigger than the others), the girls (now reduced to four) eventually get beamed to the surface after the *DD1* has emerged from a volcano, scorched and wrecked. You can run out of adjectives in describing just how irritatingly dreadful this movie is: Pfeiffer's constant Cameron Diaz-type mugging; Evigan's lumpy performance; deplorable CGI effects; a terrible script ("Oh my God, we're all gonna die!" "Screw off." "What do dinosaurs taste like? Chicken?"); the females all behaving like a bunch of spoilt brats who have lost their mobiles; and the *DD1* spewed out of

a grassy, sunlit hillock with no lava visible—you could go on and on. Totally lacking in any Victorian atmosphere and nonsensical to the nth degree, adaptations of classic fantasy fiction novels don't come any crummier than this picture. It's an absolute stinker!

King Arthur and the Knights of the Round Table
Asylum 2017; 88 minutes; Director: Jared Cohn ****

Modern-day descendants of King Arthur and his legendary Knights are visited in Thailand by evil Morgana and Mordred, intent on laying their hands on Excalibur, whatever the cost.

Asylum-bashers have had a field day in lambasting this updating of the Camelot legend (and a rip-off of Guy Ritchie's $175,000,000 *King Arthur: Legend of the Sword*), but within the realms (no pun intended) of Asylum, Jared Cohn's fantasy feature is imaginative, fast-paced fare presented with stacks of glossy dash. Commencing in medieval England, Arthur encasing Morgana ("I am the real Lady of the Lake!") and nephew Mordred in a mighty lump of rock which is jettisoned like a meteor into space, we flash forward 1,500 years to present-day Bangkok (where shooting took place on a $300,000 budget). Marine/Kung Fu expert Eoin O'Brien (Pen, or Pendragon) and girlfriend Kelly B. Jones are joined in their dojo by Alexander Winters, Elidh MacQueen, Jon Nutt and Svitlana Zavialova when vengeful Morgana (Sara Malakul Lane) and Mordred (Russell Geoffrey Banks) arrive on Earth complete with alien powers ("I will get it [Excalibur] back and make the world pay. I am the ultimate sorceress of Camelot."). Lane enlists the aid of a squad of zombies (she administers a potion to her victims' bodies) in her hunt for the sword; but where is it? Excalibur was melted down to make the Holy Grail goblet: O'Brien ("She's come back to kill the Knights of the Round Table. Us!") plunges his arm into a vat of liquid gold after the goblet has been tossed in and pulls out the holy relic, sinking the weapon into Lane's torso during a climactic battle, Banks switching to the side of good. In flashes of jagged lightning, Lane grows to a height of 100 feet, crashing up through the temple walls, and the movie suddenly changes tack (and all the better for it), entering the domain of the Japanese kaiju genre as the giant robotic Morgana snarls and stomps through the streets, demolishing buildings and breathing fire, police and military blazing away ("She's feeding off the magic of the sword."). O'Brien scales her left leg, pulls out the embedded Excalibur and Morgana, groaning and gargling, expires (like Talos in Columbia's *Jason and the Argonauts*), toppling on Banks who's pleased to die ("If I go to Hell, that means I do have a soul."), but not before O'Brien has dubbed him Sir Mordred with Excalibur. As the Knights of the New Camelot recite the laws of chivalry, Cohn's camera pans away from Morgana's huge fallen body lying amid smoking rubble, one of the company's finest of all fade-outs. To give credit where credit's due, Scotty Mullen's script steers just short of triteness, Josh Maas provides bright, sharp photography, Mikel Shane Prather's score isn't intrusive and effects supervisor Joseph J. Lawson pulls out all the stops, especially in that captivating final 10 minutes. Top acting honors has to go to Banks, camping it up by playing Mordred as a gay Goth, talking in an effeminate tone to match his black eyeliner, a real hoot. Yes, indie fans, this is one occasion where Asylum has got it just right!

The Land That Time Forgot aka Dinosaur Island
Asylum 2009; 90 minutes; Director: C. Thomas Howell **

A boat with assorted crew becomes lost in a storm, travels through a portal in the Bermuda Triangle, and ends up on an uncharted island populated by dinosaurs and a group of Germans stranded since the last war.

The spirit of Edgar Rice Burroughs most definitely *doesn't* live on in Asylum's revamp of the Amicus 1974

fantasy vehicle which, at the time, set new standards in tacky monster effects. But what Amicus' juvenile prehistoric romp *did* possess was a sense of wonder and awe, however cardboard the overall look was. Asylum's version clearly lacks both wonder and awe. The island is bereft of the necessary (and essential) prehistoric dioramas, the two squawking female leads (Lindsey McKeon and Anya

Benton) are sexy but can't act, and it's left to the likes of Timothy Bottoms and the director himself to carry the day. Howell's direction, it has to be said, isn't all that bad, and the CGI Tyrannosaurus is more realistically animated than usual. The plot races through the motions: Crew land on island, meet up with T-Rex, a Pterodactyl and rubber tentacles in a lake, discover a bunch of Germans plus their submarine, create fuel from oil deposits, relaunch the sub and inadvertently leave Howell and wife Benton behind to their fate. It's hardly compulsive viewing, even for youngsters, and once again, the company is guilty of uneven sound balance in some sequences; a poor man's *Lost World* by any stretch of the imagination. Surely copyists Asylum could have at least *tried* to retain the essence of the author's novel instead of ignoring it.

Martian Land
Asylum 2015; 86 minutes; Director: Scott Wheeler *

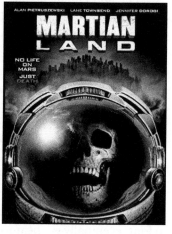

The domed Martian colony of New York is hit by a volcanic sandstorm, and it's down to a group of scientists to stop the colossal whirlwind in its tracks before it destroys MLA— Mars Los Angeles.

Lesbian teen saves mankind on Mars from total wipeout. Yes, that just about describes the plot of *Martian Land*, a plummeting in Asylum's fairly high standards that sums up the company's erratic output to a tee; great product one minute, lousy product the next. Set on a wobbly CGI Mars, Ariana Afsar and doe-eyed girlfriend Chloe Farnworth, marooned in a battered MNY, make for the tunnel connecting the city to MLA while on the windswept Martian surface, her father, Lane Townsend (straight from saving Earth, plagued by similar catastrophes: Yellowstone Park has erupted!) and mum Jennifer Dorogi's new husband, Alan Pietruszewski, swoop around in a dilapidated shuttle, planning to plant EMF Emitters (whatever they are) on relay stations to stabilize the mass. In the meantime, at MLA base, Dorogi, Director of Scientific Research, is at loggerheads with bullish female commander Dionne Neish over who should be running the show, hinting at another one-sided lesbian relationship. "How do we kill it?" yells Neish for the umpteenth time in a voice straight from London's East End, the audience left perplexed as to how and why Afsar is viewed as the Red Planet's savior amid all the shouting and amateur dramatics. On the hour, you will have had enough, but stick with it if only to see Pietruszewski sacrifice himself in order that Townsend and Dorogi are reunited (for the sake of their daughter!), to see Afsar and Farnworth in a girly clinch, to see everyone in tears at the end when the sandstorm, named Zeus, is deflated and to question Neish's acting abilities. One or two half-decent effects are sandwiched between the human non-drama but, all in all, the movie is a bore from start to finish. Asylum, on their day, are capable of much better things than this.

Mega Piranha

Asylum 2010; 92 minutes; Director: Eric Forsberg ****

Genetically engineered to enormous size and strength, a shoal of giant piranha fish escapes from the Venezuelan jungles and heads towards Florida's packed beaches.

In the footsteps (or should that be fins and tentacles?) of *Mega Shark vs. Giant Octopus* comes another slice of outlandish monster nonsense from Asylum featuring one-time '80s pop princess Tiffany, overacting like crazy as a professor not only trying to combat the huge finned terrors but lusting after hunky (but very wooden) Paul Logan. This would have packed them in as a 1960s feature in UK cinemas (with an "X" certificate?); pay no attention to the acting, dumb script or Forsberg's annoying swish-zoom-swoop direction, no doubt aimed at heightening and bringing a sense of urgency to the proceedings. Instead, watch in amazement (and amusement) as the enormous carnivorous piranhas launch their repeated attacks on the Venezuelan and Florida coastlines, leaping out of the water, devouring newsreaders ("Florida is being attacked by giant fish!" screams a woman into her microphone before being gobbled up), smashing into buildings and even chomping up a helicopter midair! At the end of it all, Tiffany tosses her red locks, rolls her eyes and, mouth agape, runs into the steroid-filled arms of Logan as the sun sets, as queasy a moment as the ef-

Mega Piranha goes for a chopper in *Mega Piranha*

fect Forsberg's hyperactive directorial style will have on your stomach. Presented with absolute over-the-top gusto, *Mega Piranha* is one great big hoot from beginning to end, a guilty pleasure that will leave a smile on your face.

Mega Python vs. Gatoroid

Asylum 2011; 91 minutes; Director: Mary Lambert ****

Animal activists release captured pythons into the Florida Everglades; to counteract the menace, alligators fed on dead chickens pumped full of body-building steroids are introduced into the waters. The snakes gobble up the 'gator eggs and in no time at all, colossal pythons are grappling with gigantic alligators, Miami's population at risk of becoming reptile food.

It's difficult to know what's the most enjoyable—seeing the mighty reptiles in combat and feasting on humans or watching bosomy Tiffany (the Ranger) and rake-thin Debbie Gibson (the activist) engaged in a prolonged catfight, the producers capitalizing on the duo's rivalry in the 1980s when both singers were vying for places in the pop charts. Forget the plot and concentrate on the effects which are splendid (for Asylum): Gigantic alligators rip hick hunters from limb to limb in a welter of gore and body parts while 100-foot snakes swallow their prey whole, including ex-Monkees star Micky Dolenz, making a brief guest appearance. Scientist A.

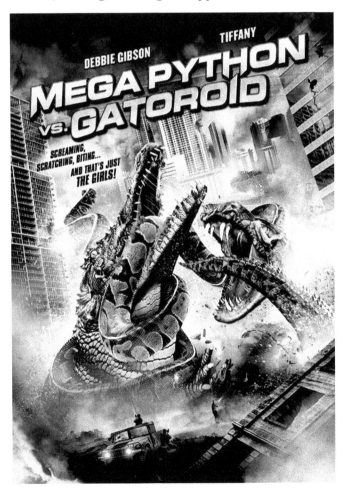

Martinez is the only cast survivor, zooming around in a helicopter after an army of the creatures has descended on Miami, wolfing down trains and dragging an air balloon out of the skies (sporting an Asylum logo!). The two women, having buried their differences, lure the behemoths into a quarry with quantities of pheromone and blast them to bits; Tiffany is eaten alive, Gibson torn in half. A year later, Martinez announces that the Everglades have been restored and are now safe, but in this kind of movie, one never knows! A fun-packed monster romp shot on *Dukes of Hazzard* lines, great entertainment for a Saturday night in.

Mega Shark vs. Crocosaurus
Asylum 2010; 88 minutes;
Director: Christopher Douglas-Olen Ray ***

A 150-foot-long crocodile emerges from a diamond mine in the Republic of Congo, is captured by an adventurer but breaks free from captivity aboard a ship; it then engages in a struggle to the death with a colossal shark known as Megalodon that develops a taste for the giant reptile's eggs.

Jungle explorer Gary Stretch, scientist Jaleel White and special agent Sarah Lieving play the trio trying to save the Californian coastline and Hawaii from being decimated by the two gargantuan beasts of the title, plus

the offspring of the Crocosaurus which are hatching out of 10-foot-high eggs. Asylum's hammy monster-fest ("The official sequel to *Mega Shark vs. Giant Octopus*" proclaim the ads) is enjoyable *only* if you can ignore the following: Variable CGI work, ranging from sufficient to woeful; White babbling on about his "hydrosonic spheres" that look as though they were knocked together from pieces of junk in five minutes; Lieving's expressionless, drone-like performance; the Panama Canal bombed to ruins; the usual parade of stone-faced military chiefs grunting inane one-liners; the crass dialogue: "Launch a full attack. Then shred 'em to bits."; "Listen, you fake-assed pirate."; "They just took out Panama!"; "We're gonna nuke those bastards right out of the water!"; "Sir! The creatures are toast."; the Megalodon somersaulting over battleships; and White's spheres setting off an underwater volcano that destroys the titans and the croc's babies as they converge on Hawaii. The pace is so frantic that you haven't got time to dissect the countless scientific absurdities or wonder how Stretch and company manage to flit from one location to the next in the blink of an eye *or* how a shark, however huge, can swallow a nuclear submarine whole and become a nuclear shark, or … but then I digress. For mindless monster thrills shot in pristine color and deafened by Chris Ridenhour's booming score, *Mega Shark vs. Crocosaurus* will satisfy all grade Z monster lovers everywhere!

Mega Shark vs. Kolossus
Asylum 2015; 89 minutes;
Director: Christopher Douglas-Olen Ray ****

The giant shark Megalodon is still at large off the Brazilian coast and has to do battle with Kolossus, a mighty Russian Cold War robot fueled by an atomic energy source known as Red Mercury.

The fourth entry in Asylum's *Mega Shark* franchise is shot in rapid-paced video style, boasting variable effects (Kolossus comes off much better than Megalodon), bright color and a nonsensical script. SEE! Rio's Christ the Redeemer statue blown sky-high; SEE! A bevy of busty, leather-clad babes, the Unicorn squadron, attempting to defeat mega shark; SEE! Kolossus, a "walking bomb, the doomsday machine," romp all over the countryside, firing death rays from its fingertips; SEE! Megalodon knock ships out of the water and planes out of the sky, gobble up boats and sink an aircraft carrier; SEE! Kolossus hurl Megalodon into space, the shark destroying a satellite station (yes, really!); SEE! The two titans wrestling underwater; and see flirty Doctor Illeana Douglas, feisty action girl Amy Rider, scaredy cat sidekick Edward DeRuiter, deranged scientist Brody Hutzler ("I want to rule the land *and* the sea.") and sour-faced Commanders Tara Price and Ernest "Nuke it!" Thomas zoom from one clumsily edited location (Brazil, Gibraltar, Florida, the Ukraine, the Black Sea) to another in a matter of minutes. Pondering on the film's one great line, "Business

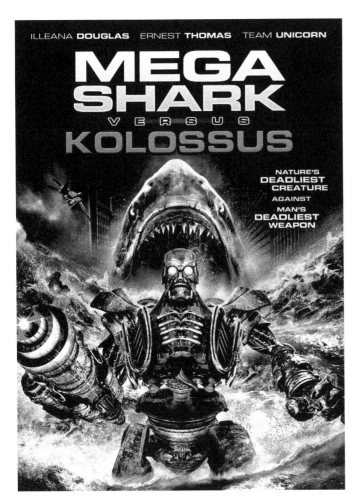

date really soon."), Nero corrupts and mecha shark becomes an amphibious liability, trundling through Sydney's streets on caterpillar tracks, jaws agape, posing a greater menace than the monster cruising around the harbor (yes, the city's famed opera house comes in for a battering as well). Agreed, it's absurd at times (how can Langan flit from New Zealand to Sydney in a matter of seconds?), the final line spoken by Judge, "So long Nero, and thank you," summing up the whole scatty enterprise as mega shark swallows a portion of the disabled mecha shark containing a bomb and is blown into chunks of red meat suitable for Sydney's restaurants; Nelson ends up on a computer memory stick. Well, if this kind of thing worked in 1974's *Godzilla vs. Mecha Godzilla*, it can work here, can't it?

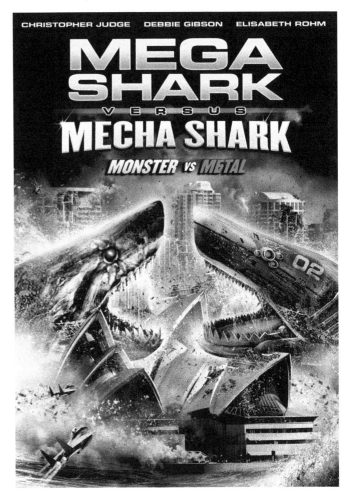

first. Sex and violence later," you might need a stiff drink afterwards to make sure you didn't dream it all up. Great fun!

Mega Shark vs. Mecha Shark
Asylum 2014; 85 minutes; Director: Emile Edwin Smith ****

To combat the threat posed to Sydney by a rampaging giant Megalodon, a colossal mechanical shark is constructed, but when the onboard computer malfunctions, the contraption runs riot in the streets.

The third in the *Mega Shark* series sees Asylum's usual slick production values transforming Los Angeles into Sydney, Australia *and* Egypt's Port Alexandria, seen at the start when mega shark's tail fin flips a tugboat into the pyramids at Giza. To put a stop to the giant predator's activities in the Pacific, Elisabeth Röhm pilots a titanium coated mechanical version fitted with warheads, run by talking computer Nero. Husband Christopher Judge (he has his own mini-metal shark sub) acts as her watchdog, having to fend off impatient Admiral Matt Lagan who has doubts about the submarine's ability to destroy Megalodon. After several battleships, an aircraft carrier and an oil rig have been capsized, mega shark having gone head-to-head with its metal adversary (the two are evenly matched), Sydney is evacuated, ex-pop starlet Debbie Gibson informs the naval authorities that the giant shark is on the lookout for a mate ("We have a 200-foot horny shark on our hands. Find this guy a

Megafault
Asylum 2009; 90 minutes; Director: David Michael Latt ***

In West Virginia, a series of mining detonations sets off a gigantic earthquake that, if unchecked, will travel westwards and split America in half. And it's down to sexy seismologist Brittany Murphy to save the day, with a little help from Eriq LaSalle, the guy who started it all in the first place.

"Disaster/the world is going to end" movies come and go and, really, *Megafault* is no better or worse than the

hundreds that were churned out in the 1970s, the decade for such fare. Asylum's effort boasts pristine color photography and, on a budget of just over a million dollars, some impressive effects: Massive bottomless cracks appearing in the surrounding countryside, spreading like some deadly fungus; buildings collapsing and bursting into flames; an avalanche; and enough explosions to appease all pyromaniacs. Asylum regular Bruce Davison flits in and out of the action as head of a geophysics team while Murphy, scientist one minute, giggly little schoolgirl the next, gets reunited with her husband and daughter (twice) when they become isolated by one calamity after another. LaSalle is the sacrificial lamb, swallowed up as the mighty gap is finally halted in its tracks by a satellite called the Tectonic Weapon, originally designed to create earthquakes on enemy territory. The final shot sees a new Grand Canyon caused by the fault, filmed from space. You may scoff, you may laugh, but consider this—were 1965's *Crack in the World* or 1974's *Earthquake* of higher quality, or more enjoyable, than *Megafault*? Perhaps not!

Megalodon
Asylum 2018; 88 minutes; Director: James Thomas *

A Russian submarine in the South Pacific drills into an undersea cavern, releasing a gigantic prehistoric shark.

The Ruskies are on a spying mission, tapping into security cables on the ocean floor; when the huge released predator wrecks their sub, the three survivors are picked up in a mini-sub by Caroline Harris and her crew and are promptly swallowed by the beast ("So how do we get out of a shark's stomach?"). On board USS military ship *Shaw*,

Admiral Michael Madsen uses electrified bait to retrieve the vessel from the shark's maw, at which point we stray into Russians versus Americans territory at the expense of the Megalodon who doesn't put in an appearance until the final reel. Ego Mikitas stalks Madsen and stone-faced grunt Dominic Pace below decks with a machine gun, meets his end, the crew depart in boats and

cigar-chomping Madsen decides, like all captains before him, to go down with his ship, blowing the USS *Shaw* sky-high and the monster with it. A weak, one-dimensional entry in the "giant shark" series of indie films; the monster is barely seen, Madsen acts as though he's in a stupor, Pace glowers and barks orders by rote while Harris goes through her hysterical female officer routine as the lone woman up against the big boys—unfortunately, that doesn't include the big boy of the title.

Merlin and the War of the Dragons
Asylum 2008; 92 minutes; Director: Mark Atkins ***

In fifth-century Britain, young Merlin has to use his fledgling powers to fight off the Saxons and their dragon hordes.

Filmed among the bleak Welsh hills to impart an air of gritty authenticity, Asylum's version of the King Arthur legend isn't too bad, the type of movie kids used to sit down to at the matinee performance many years ago. Simon Lloyd-Roberts makes a personable, if inexperienced, Merlin; Joseph Stacey is his wicked young friend, siding with the enemy so that he can eventually rule Britain; Jurgen Prochnow plays the Sage, Merlin's tutor; and Carys Eleri and Nia Ann are the two bewitching denizens of the lake that is home to Excalibur, good and bad respectively. When Stacey joins with the Saxons and has at his command a legion of dragons, Lloyd-Roberts, under Prochnow's guidance and using the fabled Book of Spells,

UNDER TEN MILLION? ANYTHING'S POSSIBLE!

changes some of his companions into huge dragons, gets his hands on the magic sword Excalibur, and the scene is set for a final showdown in which, naturally, good triumphs over evil; Arthur is crowned king after the enemy, plus Stacey and his dragons, are defeated. Yes, the dialogue is straight out of the pages of a comic book and is that a tarmacked road Lloyd-Roberts gallops down at one point? Nevertheless, Atkins injects some life and energy into the familiar story, the CGI dragons are splendid and the actors seem to be enjoying themselves. A popcorn and Coke picture if ever there was one.

Nazis at the Center of the Earth

Asylum 2012; 89 minutes; Director: Joseph J. Lawson *****

Seventy years after the end of World War II, Auschwitz physician Doctor Josef Mengele, the infamous "Angel of Death," is alive and well and planning to resurrect a Fourth Reich from his hideout deep in the bowels of Antarctica.

What mad genius at Asylum thought this one up? Scientist Jake Busey and his team of researchers descend a shaft in the Antarctica ice cap to discover a vast cavern, home to Christopher Karl Johnson (as Mengele) and his storm troopers, kept in tiptop condition by regenerating their flesh with skin stripped from those captured from above. Johnson has constructed a huge Nazi UFO, to be piloted by none other than a robotic Adolf Hitler who will drop bombs full of flesh-eating bacteria over non-Aryan cities, thus paving the way for a fourth German Reich. Busey is in on the plan but his colleagues certainly aren't, particularly pregnant girlfriend Marlene Okner who, in one stomach-churning sequence, has her fetus vacuumed from her body to provide stem cells for the Hitler android. What with zombie-faced storm troopers in gas masks, flesh being ripped from Adam Burch's face, weapons that vaporize their targets, a bloody brain removal, the swastika-adorned Nazi UFO knocking fighter jets out of the sky and maniacal Hitler (James Maxwell Young) in his transformer-type suit pursuing Joshua Michael Allen and Dominique Swain ("Come on, you bobble-headed zombie Nazi son of a bitch!") across the ice, laser guns blasting, you won't have time to pause and consider how incredibly daft (and funny) Lawson's action-packed horror fantasy is, and how nobody but Asylum could get away with making it. John-

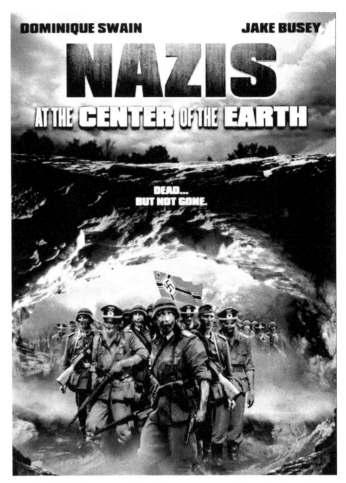

The Führer strikes again! James Maxwell Young is the robotic Hitler in *Nazis at the Center of the Earth*

son has his throat cut, there's a gruesome decapitation, Busey and Okner sacrifice themselves, disabling the UFO, and the Hitler android gets a dose of that lethal bacteria, sending the loony reconstructed Führer plummeting to the ocean depths. A German propaganda marching song is played over the credits, maybe to add a touch of gravitas, or should that be camp? Utterly insane, deliriously over-the-top nonsense but eminently watchable!

Oceans Rising

Asylum/SyFy 2017; 87 minutes; Director: Adam Lipsius *

Solar storms create worldwide destruction on Earth, the planet's magnetic field weakened, resulting in a 100-foot tsunami sweeping the globe.

"We were caught with our pants down" yells somebody in the first reel; those who purchased the DVD of *Oceans Rising* may well voice the same opinion. *Not* one of the company's better disaster "epics" as Jason Tobias, aware that a gigantic flood is imminent because of a "polarity reversal," builds a boat capable of holding around 20 persons, arguing with "I know everything" and "You've ruined my career" wife Summer Spiro of NOAA (the same NOAA that's in *Super Cyclone*?), a space weather outfit monitoring sunspot activity. Three years later, LA is under water and the warring couple meets in Galveston, heading to Boulder in Tobias' boat where Spiro takes command, bark-

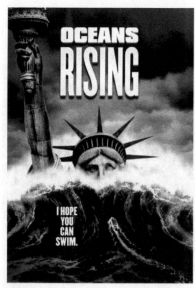

ing orders for workmen to construct a 60-foot sandbag/scaffolding barrier on top of NOAA's office block ("Someone's here. And she's pissed," is muttered out of her earshot). Tobias sails off in his craft on stormy seas with a few stalwarts ("I need three or four of you guys on the double. You're gonna save the world!"), making for the CERN Organization and Professor Paul Statman (plus his phony French accent) in France so that two black holes are prevented from destroying all life on the planet; Spiro, 3,000 miles away, plugs the NOAA electrics into a "particle collider" for the same purpose. The black holes consume themselves, green and red protons meet head-on, "jump-starting Earth's core," and the collider works, the "gravitational readings increasing" and the "magnetic fields re-engaging," rendering Spiro unconscious for a few minutes (thus giving us a break from her 100 mph squawk); Tobias receives a round of applause for his efforts in saving mankind and Spiro regains her senses, their rocky marriage back on an even keel. Cheapskate effects and a barrage of meaningless (and undoubtedly inaccurate) pseudo-scientific gobbledegook add up to the kind of remark that was written in one's end-of-term school report all those years ago: "Must try harder." On this lamentable showing, Asylum didn't try very hard at all.

100 Degrees Below Zero
Asylum 2013; 89 minutes; Director: R.D. Braunstein *

Seismic disturbances in Iceland cause a gigantic cloud of volcanic ash to drift towards Europe which will block out the sun and trigger a new Ice Age.

Place a bottle of whiskey in one hand, grasp the remote in the other and prepare to have the senses dulled as Jeff Fahey and new (much younger) wife Judit Fekete race from London to Paris to save his student son (Marc Ewins) and mouthy daughter (Sara Malakul Lane) from certain death in the French city battered by snowfalls, tremors, lowering temperatures and ice cyclones. Gasp at the number of times the kids fall down and bang their heads on the sidewalks without any side effects; splutter as the snow falls in sheets, then disappears, then returns; question scientist Iván Kamarás' jargon concerning glacial melt, chain reactions and tectonic shifts; wonder at the Euro Tunnel's English terminal manned by armed American commandos

and Eastern Europeans—not a Brit in sight; count how many times hysterical ex-Thai model Lane yells, "Oh my God! We gotta get outta here!" and "You okay?"; yawn with boredom during a 12-minute segment as Lane rescues Ewins and Ewins rescues Lane in different buildings; yawn again as Lane screeches, "It's cold! It's freezing! I don't wanna die out here in the street!"; stare in disbelief as Ewins, cracking his head for the umpteenth time, is resuscitated via a handy defibrillator; and marvel at the sight of the couple plus a French babe plucked from the toppling Eiffel Tower by Dad in a helicopter, the Arc de Triomphe smashed by the topmost portion of Paris' most iconic landmark. "Incredible, right?" grins action-lad Ewins inanely. Yes, it really *is* incredible! Colonel John Rhys-Davies, flying survivors to sunny Australia, is on hand to lend a touch of urgently needed gravitas (and sense), some of the disaster special effects are tolerable but, all in all, *100 Degrees Below Zero* is a headache to sit through, badly acted, poorly scripted, crammed full of implausible (and laughable)

situations and peopled by characters you don't have one iota of empathy with. By the time it grinds to a halt, that whiskey bottle will be drained of the very last drop!

100 Ghost Street: The Return of Richard Speck
aka **Paranormal Entity 4: The Awakening**
Asylum 2012; 84 minutes; Director: Martin Wichmann **

Paranormal investigators gain access to the building where serial killer Richard Speck murdered eight women and attempt to communicate with his spirit, with disastrous consequences.

On July 14, 1966, Richard Speck raped, strangled

and stabbed eight student nurses to death in one night of horror. Filmed in Los Angeles' abandoned Linda Vista Hospital, a bunch of paranormal researchers enter the building, set up cameras, walk into rooms shouting, "Let your presence be known," and wait for the inevitable to happen. A found footage exercise shot in grainy green night vision and monochrome (property of the Illinois Police Department!), *100 Ghost Street* at least gets on with the action from the outset instead of keeping us in suspense; team members squeezed into closets, crawl spaces and pipes, one decapitated, another sliced in half. But this whole *Paranormal Activity / Entity* subgenre is starting to wear a bit thin; we now know exactly what to see, what not to see and what to expect, so no surprises here as one by one, the hysterically terrified investigators are done away with by Speck's malevolent phantom, leaving Mike Holley and Jennifer Robyn Jacobs to try and find a way out of the hellhouse. Jacobs succeeds, but just as she says, "I beat you," something hits her from behind. We see a door open of its own accord, and then a blank screen. The movie is admittedly eerie in places and artfully pieced together, but remains derivative all the same.

Paranormal Entity

Asylum 2009; 88 minutes; Director: Shane Van Dyke ****

A young man arrested for the murders of his sister and a 52-year-old professor claims it was the work of a supernatural entity that had taken over his home.

Asylum's riposte to 2007's *Paranormal Activity* actually beats that movie by a whisker; perhaps the minuscule budget worked in the indie company's favor, something which they are well used to. So what we have here is a mock crime documentary (no cast or credits shown), supposedly

taken from police files: Footage from night vision cameras and camcorder, orchestrated by the youngster under arrest (played by Van Dyke himself), as both his mother (Fia Perera) and sister (Erin Marie Hogan) are convinced a spook inhabits their house and wish to catch any sign of it on tape. Forty minutes into the drama, paranormal investigator Norman Saleet turns up and announces that there *is* a presence in the house; it's an evil spirit called a Maron, entities that prey on young sleeping women, and it's after Hogan. Van Dyke eases in a succession of disturbing jolts to gradually raise the sense of supernatural dread—the effects are minimal (a falling cross; slamming doors; cameras moved; footprints on the ceiling; bells on a thread set off; bedsheets peeled back) and a total lack of music complements the goosebumpy events spread over 23 nights. The ending is a little feverish but overall, this makes for sweaty viewing, and you might want to leave the lights on when retiring for the night after watching it.

Paranormal Entity 2 aka 8213: Gacy House

Asylum 2010; 85 minutes; Director: Anthony Fankhauser **

Seven paranormal investigators set up their detection equipment on the site of the house once lived in by John Wayne Gacy, one of America's most prolific serial killers, responsible for the deaths of 33 young men in the 1970s. Their aim? To catch the psycho's spirit on film.

What a crashing disappointment after the spine-chilling *Paranormal Entity*. The same format applies here: Police files recording the deaths of six investigators on the old Gacy site, with the disappearance of one female. But director Fankhauser can't keep his camera still for a second and what you get is 85 minutes of frenzied camcorder footage showing the argumentative team, led by Michael Gaglio, descending into hysteria as doors slam, windows open, loud noises are heard, a girl is cut on her breast and a shadowy figure flits from one room to the next. Well, if you wander into a house where 26 bodies were found dismembered in the crawl space and 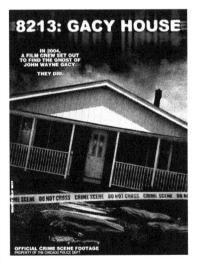 continually shout, "Gacy! Show yourself," what do you expect! Morgue notes detailing the cause of death for the six bodies (asphyxiation, hypothermia and cardiac arrest) add to the air of pseudo-realism, but in truth, Asylum should have come up with a far worthier sequel to *Paranormal Entity* than what is on offer here.

Paranormal Entity 3: The Exorcist Tapes
aka Anneliese: The Exorcist Tapes
Asylum 2011; 91 minutes; Director: Jude Gerard Prest *

A mock documentary utilizing alleged real-life footage detailing the demonic possession of young Bavarian Anneliese Michel.

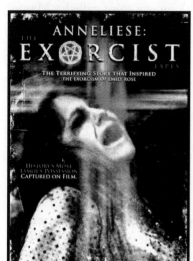

Coinciding with the October 2011 release of *Paranormal Activity 3*, Asylum's copycat take hit the DVD shelves the same month. Really, they should stop right here—if there is to be a *PA4* (there was, in 2012), let's hope there isn't a *PE4* to go with it (there more or less was in the guise of *100 Ghost Street*). Supposedly based on the 1976 *Emily Rose* case but more of an attempt at producing a sub-*Exorcist* thriller, Asylum's clueless excursion into possession has Nikki Muller in a short white nightie urinating, swearing, writhing and growling in a voice that sounds like Jimmy Durante with a bad head cold, while priests and doctors, headed by Kai Cofer and Robert Shampain, film her every move and debate endlessly over her condition. Some 50 minutes in, the movie practically grinds to a halt, relying on flashbacks to previous scenes, with everyone standing around doing nothing—40 long minutes pass before Cofer is stabbed in the back by the devil girl and we are then notified that Muller died of starvation a short time later. "The material contained in this film is real" states the pre-action (there are no credits) blurb, but if you can believe that, you can believe anything. Photographed in nicotine brown and monochrome, one fervently wishes that Asylum would get its act together and not get involved in tedious nonsense such as this.

Planet of the Sharks
Asylum 2016; 86 minutes; Director: Mark Atkins *

In a future where 98% of Earth is covered in water, sharks led by a huge alpha male hunt down the few human survivors.

Commencing with a shot of the Statue of Liberty under water, *Planet of the Sharks*, filmed in tandem in South Africa with *Empire of the Sharks*, is (like the planet) 98% scientific balderdash, 2% shark shenanigans. As screechy Lindsay Sullivan from the Vestron Oceanic Research Station attempts to send a rocket into the ionosphere to reverse global warming, first Junk City and then Salvation are wiped out by flotillas of sharks led by one giant specimen possessing a glowing blue snout. Like a cut-price take on Kevin Costner's disastrous 1995 soggy epic *Waterworld*, the non-action lurches from one protracted talkative scene to another, Angie Teodora Dick putting in the film's worst performance as a macho shark hunter speaking in a ludicrous Texas drawl. The climax has the cast detonating a volcano via an electronic device,

sending a laser beam into the atmosphere to cure the planet's problems and Brandon Auret's boat tackling cinema's worst-conceived tidal wave. That big "mother of all sharks" is finished off by Sullivan using electric rods (she's gobbled up for her troubles), the rocket is launched and, six months later, the Statue of Liberty is now *above* water (à la *Planet of the Apes*), the end of a deeply uninteresting shark feature that is a real effort to sit through.

San Andreas Quake
Asylum 2015; 82 minutes; Director: John Baumgartner *

A seismologist who has invented a method of predicting earthquakes forecasts dozens of micro-quakes hitting Los Angeles along the San Andreas fault line, with one monster quake all set to destroy the city.

San Andreas Quake will sorely test the patience of even the most ardent admirer of Asylum's work; it's tempting to simply say "steer well clear" and go no further. But here goes. In 1994, earthquake-mad geology student Allison Adams creates a minor tremor by lighting a fire cracker in a trench, resulting in the collapse of her house and the death of her

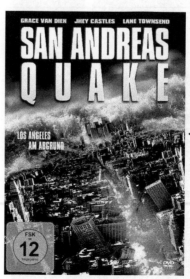

father. Thank the Lord that Adams doesn't figure in the rest of the action; you cannot understand a single word the girl is gabbling on about. Flash forward to the present: Adams is now Jhey Castles, a step-mom to Lane Townsend's pouting teen, Grace Van Dien (actor Casper Van Dien's daughter). As earthquakes hit Los Angeles, predicted by Castles, she rushes across town (and '70s disaster cliché-land) in hyperactive overdrive to rescue doe-eyed Van Dien from the Skyline Hotel before it collapses. The girl's boyfriend, Jason Woods, is behind the wheel, Townsend buzzing around in his 'copter carrying two bemused Asian tourists. You won't believe your eyes (or ears) as you take in the following: Castles continually squawking "Go, go, go," "Oh my God, oh my God, oh my God," "Gotta go, gotta go, gotta go" and "Drive drive, drive"; Castles staying glued to her red iPad through thick and thin, even finding time to video-message Townsend and Van Dien while lying in a shattered building wreathed in deadly hydrogen sulfide gas. The ubiquitous live electric cable swings, Castles stating the blindingly obvious, "Must have escaped from the zoo, huh?" when Woods' car is hit by a bad-assed hippo, Castles and Woods watching a giraffe strolling by, shoehorned into the scenario. Van Dien deals with an elderly couple celebrating their 40th wedding anniversary, being stuck in a jammed lift, coping with the old feller's heart attack and hindered by her gay, goofy workmate. Action-woman Castles hauls Woods *and* Van Dien to safety from a crumbling roof ledge; mass "I love you" cuddles when everyone is reunited; and more tear-stained group hugs as Townsend lands on the hotel roof, rescues wife, daughter and boyfriend and takes off just as the building collapses like a deck of cards, a tidal wave engulfing a Los Angeles in ruins. You could call it a one-woman show depending on how many drinks you have downed at the end of it all, but this cut-price version of 2015's $110,000,000 *San Andreas* is actually hindered by Castles' wild-eyed, over-exuberant, hell, just plain bad, performance; there's not all that much to boast about in the special effects department either. It's easy to be too over-critical at times, but it's certainly easy here. Come on Asylum, you can do a whole lot better than this grade A clunker.

The 7 Adventures of Sinbad
Asylum 2010; 93 minutes;
Directors: Ben Hayflick and Adam Silver ****

To save the world from an environmental catastrophe, a descendant of Sinbad must undertake to successfully perform seven extraordinary tasks.

The giant crab from *The 7 Adventures of Sinbad* resembles Ray Harryhausen's from *Mysterious Island*.

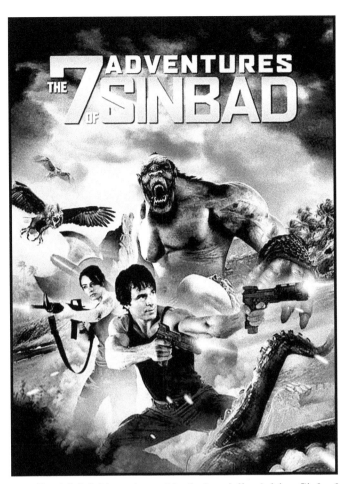

Patrick Muldoon is wealthy industrialist Adrian Sinbad (yes, that's right—Adrian Sinbad!) in a production that bears absolutely *no* resemblance to Columbia's 1958 classic *The 7th Voyage of Sinbad*, but you have to hand it to Asylum, they get away with blue murder when it comes to plagiarizing ideas from top-grade genre flicks. So here we have a Cyclops in a cave, a giant crab, Pterodactyls, sirens, an island perched on the back of a gigantic whale, a volcano, an earthquake and an *Apocalypto*-type tribe. Throw in a hot-air balloon and you can see a *Mysterious Island* influence as well! Muldoon's oil tanker has been hijacked by pirates and pulled underwater by a colossal squid. Stuck in a deep crater, a supernatural being residing there objects to its presence and Muldoon, plus pretty native girl Sarah Desage, has to recover the tanker intact before said being destroys the planet and thousands of gallons of oil are released into the ocean, meaning widescale pollution. Even without Ray Harryhausen at the helm, this particular *Sinbad*'s multitude of special effects are surprisingly delivered with lashings of style when considering the meager (by today's standards) budget of $500,000. It's bustling and action-packed, boasting colorful location photography, and Muldoon is more animated than usual in the role of the 21st-century swashbuckler with one almighty reputation to live up to. Highly recommended for fantasy buffs, showing just what Asylum are capable of when they put their minds to it.

Sharknado
Asylum 2013; 86 minutes; Director: Anthony C. Ferrante *****
Sharknado 2: The Second One
Asylum 2014; 95 minutes; Director: Anthony C. Ferrante *****
Sharknado 3: Oh Hell No!
Asylum 2015; 93 minutes; Director: Anthony C. Ferrante *****
Sharknado 4: The 4th Awakens
Asylum 2016; 85 minutes; Director: Anthony C. Ferrante ***
Sharknado 5: Global Swarming
Asylum 2017; 93 minutes; Director: Anthony C. Ferrante **
Sharknado 6: The Last Sharknado:
It's About Time
Asylum 2018; 86 minutes; Director: Anthony C. Ferrante **

Asylum are pretty good at doing disaster movies. Their shark features aren't too bad either. So why not combine the two and come up with six of the most insanely ridiculous slices of camp, cheesy and just plain *illogical* creature mayhem that should, and will, have you rolling about with laughter, all the time keeping one eye open for the countless movie references and in-jokes. Hell, if Paramount could successfully produce a spoof disaster picture in 1980 with *Airplane!* on a budget of $4,000,000, so can Asylum on a budget of one to three million per production. Serious moviegoers may well turn their noses up and look away in disdain and disgust, but the fact remains that Asylum's *Sharknado* sextet doesn't pretend to be high art, simply low-art entertainment for a good night in, so just relax and go with the flow. And let's not forget that these films are put together with oodles of panache, each backed by a raucous rock soundtrack: Special effects are imaginative, the gore level high, Ferrante directs with his foot planted firmly on the throttle, the cinematography (Ben Demaree) is top-notch and hero Ian Ziering (as Fin Shepard) gives all six his best shot. In their own mad, way-over-the-top fashion, these features represent both the best in indie moviemaking and quintessential Asylum, 100% cult classics that defy all serious critique *and* the natural laws of science. You've got to be a real sourpuss not to enjoy every single crazy second of them.

Sharknado: Santa Monica and Los Angeles are hit by storms and huge hurricanes that rain sharks on the population. See limbs chomped off; the sea turning red with blood; sharks flying through the air feasting on fleeing citizens; Santa Monica's pier wrecked, a Ferris wheel crashing into an office block; Los Angeles flooded; scenes of mass destruction; sharks swimming down the streets hitting pylons and emerging from storm drains; Ziering rescuing his estranged wife Tara Reid and daughter, the predators invading their waterlogged home; bodies gnawed on like dogs with a bone; debris crashing to earth causing havoc; action girl Cassie Scerbo and Chuck Hittinger dropping bombs into the eye of the shark-infested twisters from a

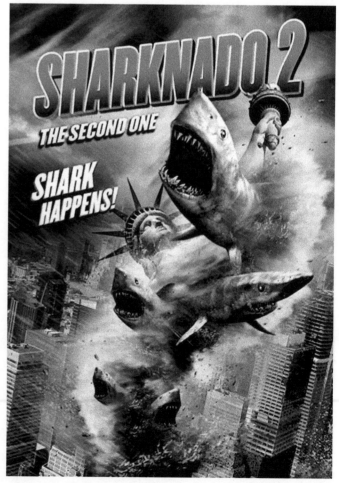

helicopter to stabilize them ("We need a bigger chopper!") and Scerbo swallowed whole but rescued when Ziering enters the shark's maw armed with a chainsaw and cuts her free. A frenzied hoot from start to finish.

Sharknado 2: The Second One: Now it's the turn of New York to receive a visit from those pesky sharknados—"This is a twister—with teeth!" Watch in amazement at the opening sequence on a jet liner attacked by flying sharks, Reid's hand bitten off, Ziering landing the plane himself; Kari Wuhrer and friends driving a refuse truck in an attempt to escape the Statue of Liberty's decapitated head which rolls down the streets, squashing pedestrians and coming to rest at the entrance to the Manhattan Tunnel; Reid up and about a day after having a prosthetic hand fitted; thousands of sharks in the Hudson River, towering waterspouts looming on the horizon; sharks *and* alligators in flooded subway tunnels; Ziering and ex-love Vivica A. Fox using a slingshot to catapult bombs into a double sharknado; Grand Central Station spectacularly destroyed; Reid with a circular saw, hacking sharks to shreds; New York's citizens taking to the streets, armed with shovels, pitchforks and sub-machine guns as sharks rain down in their hundreds; sharks in the TV newsroom; Ziering wielding a hefty chainsaw to good, and very bloody, effect; and our hero prizing the ring off a chewed hand, proposing to Reid again. And don't forget to sit around for the wacky end credits. Mind-boggling nonsense that comes at you like a whirlwind on dope—not to be missed!

Sharknado 3: Oh Hell No!: The fun and games continue as first Washington DC, then Orlando, Florida, is hit by a "sharknado wall," threatening all life on America's Eastern Seaboard. See Ziering being presented with the Order of the Golden Chainsaw, Jackie Collins offering her congratulations; Ziering and President Mark Cuban blazing away at flying sharks in gung-ho slow motion; a dead shark in the lap of President Lincoln's statue; George Washington's head between a shark's jaws; Ziering, Cuban and friends spearing a predator on a US flagpole in an Iwo Jima pose; the White House and Washington Monument reduced to rubble; Bo Derek putting in an appearance as Reid's mother; David Hasselhoff putting in an appearance as Ziering's father; busty Cassie Scerbo returning to the action in a battle truck, now a shark hunter; a twister and sharks decimating the Daytona race track; Ziering and Scerbo scrambling from their crashed jet fighter, she in bikini, he in swimming trunks; three TV presenters gobbled up on air; a shark attacking those trapped on a roller coaster at the Universal Theme Park; the Universal Globe tumbling down the streets; a brief guest appearance by Irish pop twins Jedward; a cinema screening *Shark Wedding*; Ziering, pregnant Reid and the Hoff heading into outer space to laser the sharknados to a watery hell; the NASA shuttle attacked by a predator ("Sharks in space!"), Reid swallowed, Ziering

Hell! What's this thing doing in outer space? From *Sharknado 3: Oh Hell No*

diving into the beast's jaws, plummeting to earth; Ziering hacking his way out of the scorched, bloody carcass and being presented with his baby son, Reid (fully dressed) following suit; a shot of savior-of-mankind Hasselhoff on the moon, treating his disbelieving audience to a cheesy grin; and Ziering's family reunited, or is Reid about to be sliced in half by that piece of falling debris? By far the craziest of the lot, *Sharknado 3* is 93 minutes of unadulterated shark lunacy; if only spoofmeister Leslie Nielsen had been on hand to top it all off …

Sharknado 4: The 4th Awakens: Tommy Davidson's Astro-X atmosphere stabilizer has meant no more sharknados

and the Grand Canyon, are wrecked by the sharknados, or sandnados, bouldernadoes, oilnados, cownados, hailnados, lavanados, firenados and lightningnados, as they are termed by a lunatic news reporter; in Kansas, Ziering's homestead is dragged into the shark-laden twister (*Wizard of Oz*, anybody?); Astro-X's quantum box sucks up the Niagara Falls, neutralizing an atomic-powered sharknado; and the whole kit and caboodle ends in laughable fashion, young Christopher Shone, armed with a chainsaw, cutting loose his family from a huge blue whale that has swallowed four sharks (one shark per family member); unconscious Ziering has to be revived with two shark defibrillators! The fourth in the series is amusing in parts and pretty gory, but the freshness, not to mention the novelty factor, is missing; like that gigantic ball of twine containing snapping sharks, the absurd shenanigans unravel to a point where you're waiting for the picture to finish; even the Hoff isn't in his usual self-deprecating mood. Surely, there wouldn't be a *Sharknado 5* in the offing, would there?

Well, there was: *Sharknado 5: Global Swarming*. Ziering's son (Billy Barratt) has been swept up into a vortex contained within a 500 mph sharknado. A stone artifact discovered by action girl Cassie Scerbo in a vast cave system bordering England's Stonehenge (whaaaat?) is responsible for the worldwide shark tornados that follow, decimating London, Tokyo, Rio de Janiero, Egypt, Sydney and Af-

for five years, and he's erected a shark-themed hotel in Las Vegas, a monument to his crowning achievement—until a sandstorm containing those annoying finned predators rolls across the city, causing Asylum-type chaos. Where do you begin to start in a spoof movie that's presented like a hurricane on speed? The first 18 minutes matches the previous three in the series in sheer looniness, from its opening *Star Wars* credits, to a cab driver stating to Ian Ziering, "Vegas is a great place to relax. Drinking, gambling, smoking, prostitution. Bring the kids, that's what I say," to the Chippendales warding off sharks, to Masiela Lusha continually screaming, "Go, go, go," to Ziering on board a pirate galleon, rescuing son Cody Linley and daughter-in-law Imani Hakim, every crazy stunt played at 100 mph among a welter of bad hair and facelifts, backed by that Ramones-type, infuriatingly catchy, theme song. Then cartoon credits roll, and *Sharknado 4* goes off the boil. It's a little *too* far-fetched, Anthony Ferrante's frantic camerawork and a barrage of incidents numbing the senses (as if they needed to be numbed!), hitting you over the head like a sledgehammer: Ziering's wife, Tara Reid, thought, dead, turns up as a bionic woman; David Hasselhoff wages war on the sharks in a mech-suit; Jedward appear for two seconds; one major city after another, plus the Hoover Dam

the Kid and the laser-spouting head of wife Reid, not to mention winding up 20,000 years in the future where a race of android Tara Reids are ruled by a despotic robotic queen resembling (yes, you've guessed it) Tara Reid. Jumping from one absurd situation to the next and shot in a chaotic, madcap style, the film climaxes with pregnant Reid suffering birth pains. You'll need the brain of an Albert Einstein to understand it all, if it's your wish to understand any of it, that is. "It's About Time" just about sums up the final *Sharknado* movie to a tee.

Sinbad and The War of the Furies

Asylum 2016; 90 minutes; Director: Scott Wheeler **

A descendant of Sinbad the Sailor has to prevent the Heart of Medusa, a gemstone containing awesome destructive powers, from falling into the hands of the Russians.

By stealing the fabled emerald from the Treasure of Perseus located inside a secret cave, John Hennigan (Sinbad) unleashes three angry Furies (Chloe Farnworth, Ashley Doris and Georgia Thompson) whose aim is to rip him to shreds rather than grab back the doomsday jewel. The reason? Apparently in times gone by, Sinbad, on the fourth

rica; meanwhile, Ziering (armed with a trusty chainsaw given to him by the Pope), bionic wife Tara Reid and Scerbo engage in one highly improbable stunt after another to rescue Barratt and stop the carnage. Jumping from James Bond mickey-takes to Indiana Jones' spoofs, from one of England's most important archaeological sites being destroyed ("A sharknado just took out Stonehenge!") to Sydney's Opera House morphing into a battle station, Asylum's $3,000,000 fifth outing in the franchise defies all cinematic logic (and the laws of physics)—you'll either laugh your head off or cry your eyes out. Dolph Lundgren turns up at the end, Ziering's son now older due to time travel (don't ask!), closing an utterly crazy exercise in filmmaking that has imaginative effects (a sharkzilla rampaging through Tokyo; an airship crashing through the sharknado hurricanes) but hardly anything else in the way of finesse—but is it really needed here?

The Last Sharknado: It's About Time (aka *Sharknado 6*) had Ziering, Reid and Scerbo time traveling from the Jurassic Age to the present in an effort to eliminate the first sharknado; the trio finally end their scatty quest in Fin's Bar surrounded by Ziering's extended family, the blue sky clear of sharks and storms, just where we were back in 2013 when the series first kicked off. Dumb and preposterous, our chainsaw-wielding hero encounters dinosaurs, Merlin, Camelot, Benjamin Franklin, George Washington, Billy

South Korean poster for *Sinbad and The War of the Furies*

of his seven voyages, was thrown into a deep tomb alongside the married woman he was dallying with. He used the jewel to bludgeon her to death for her food and committed a similar deed on two other women; the three Furies are on the revenge trail for these acts (so, the legendary sailor is both thief *and* murderer!). The only justification in giving this updating of the old Sinbad tale a two-star rating instead of one is Scotty Mullen's jokey script, containing plenty of references to 21st-century media devices, Cleopatra having "a nice asp" which Julius Caesar appreciated, Hennigan stating, "we're gonna explore the women of the world and screw the seven seas" and our muscular hero termed an "Arabian Chippendale." There's a magic carpet ride of the low-budget variety, a hyperactive genie from a lamp (Jennifer Dorogi), a one-eyed Russian thug called Cy (short for Cyclops!), chief villain Josh Fingerhut is a mincing gay while double-crossing heroine Jamie Bernadette resembles Rachel Weisz in a bad light. Bernadette turns wicked, siding with the Russians and desiring a cut of the $100,000,000 that the Heart of Medusa is reputedly worth, but ends up a shower of stone fragments after archaeology artifacts dealer Wayne Ward, two of the Furies plus the Ruskies have all been exploded into dust by the emerald's lethal blue beam. "We can go wherever we want," cries Hennigan as he, pal Terence Keith Richardson and Richardson's girlfriend, Sole Bovelli, set off in their motorized launch for more modern-day adventures (which hopefully won't make it onto the big screen). Unusually for an Asylum picture, the color is dull, not presented in their usual glossy sheen, while the acting ranges from school-pantomime level (the Furies, Fingerhut and Dorogi) to energetic-but-dumb (Hennigan and Bernadette). Nowhere near the fine standards set by the company's *The 7 Adventures of Sinbad*, Scott Wheeler's cheap-looking production, just falling short of an outright travesty, will have diehard fantasy followers reaching for their copies of *The 7th Voyage of Sinbad* in order to restore some level of sanity to their fevered minds.

Super Cyclone
Asylum 2012; 89 minutes; Director: Liz Adams *

Ultra-deep water oil rig Wilberforce 3 drills penetrates a magma/methane gas belt, the resulting rise in sea temperature producing a ferocious storm that threatens Southern California.

Given a few tweaks here and there and performed with tongues firmly in cheeks, *Super Cyclone* would have made a classic five-star disaster-type comedy, it's that hilariously dreadful. But no, writer/director Liz Adam's $200,000 calamity opts for the serious approach (or does it?); at the end of a jaw-dropping 89 minutes, you'll be saying to yourself: "Did I really *see* this?" Consider the facts: That rig is subjected to bouts of fire, explosions, boiling seas, destabilization, molten lava and even hit by a ship

tossed in the air, yet still remains virtually intact by the final reel; atmosphere specialist (?) Ming-Na Wen from NOAA drives from here to there in battered, oil-covered vehicles, one stolen from a guy with a gun—minutes later, she's trying to steal *another* truck from *another* guy with a gun; would anyone fly a helicopter into a cyclonic tornado, only for it to emerge unscathed; how come superwoman Wen is the only person around who suggests placing a payload of "Nano-Flakes" in the eye of the storm (it fails, the young F-16 pilot incinerated in a plume of flame) and then plumps for pumping the fiery well full of liquid nitrogen; how many times throughout the film does Wen shout, "A storm of this size"; and why does Wen stare at a tree uprooted in a hurricane and say to Andy Clemence, "What's going on with that tree?" Dylan Vox's one-note turn as the rig's stone-faced manager (matched only by Darin Cooper's stone-faced colonel) hits the deck, and two clumsily executed scenes are guaranteed to have you spilling your popcorn all over the carpet: Men in a dinghy, trapped in the scorching waters, crying, "Ah! Ah! Ah! Ah!" as someone yells, "Come back! God, they're boiling alive" and Wen's oil-drenched car picked up, flung around like a cereal toy and dumped on the ground, the gal scrambling out still clutching her shoulder bag. Whirlwinds, electrical bolts, roads torn up, volcanic eruptions, hailstorms, acidic water, a collapsing dam, a tidal wave, balls of fire and even a sinkhole sit side-by-side with crass dialogue of the Asylum variety: "You saved our ass back there." "Stop the truck! The car's on fire! Everything's on fire!" "Can you handle a storm with the power of five Katrinas?" "We gotta stop it! We must stop the storm!" and "We must evacuate." "To where?" are just some of the gems on offer to fans of the awful. Granted, there are a few moments of eye-catching mass catastrophe, but the dire acting, uneven continuity (Wen's vehicle is on the highway, then on dirt tracks, then the highway, and so on …) and a plethora of risible situations lets the whole enterprise down, big time. Leslie Nielsen would have had a field day with this hokey material to work on.

Supercroc aka Jurassic Croc
Asylum 2007; 85 minutes; Director: Scott Harper ***

A 60-foot-long crocodile lumbers out of a lake in Los Padres National Forest, heading for Los Angeles on a trail of destruction.

"The epic adventure of Godzilla and King Kong!" claims the DVD cover. Well, not on a $200,000 budget it

UNDER TEN MILLION? ANYTHING'S POSSIBLE!

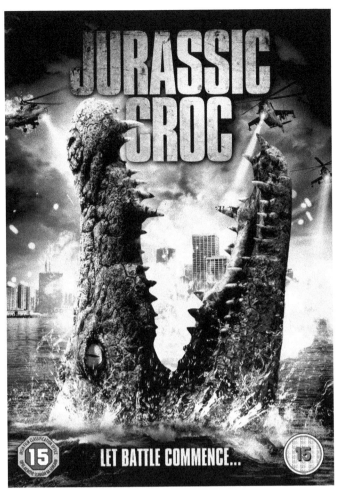

hell!"), the "panicking crowds" scene the ropiest you'll ever see in *any* movie. "We're gonna blow this fucker up!" roars Novak to no one in particular, the monster croc slumped unconscious across the freeway before continuing on its way. Novak throws a fit: "We need to move a few million people in 20 minutes. This is a fucking disaster. This isn't a war. It's a fucking animal!" The eggs are used as bait (Little wants their DNA to create a "military defense" of a different kind), heroine Hall plants explosives in its underbelly, the croc is dispatched (a pity; the beast was getting quite interesting) and as Hall treats Blashaw to a celebratory drink (and anything else!), one egg left in a trash bin starts to hatch, a cue for *Supercroc 2*? In a way harking back to the company's golden period (if ever it had one), Scott Harper's creature-feature is enjoyable nonsense for all the right/wrong reasons, one or two moments giving a hint of "what might have been" if the feature had been produced on a much larger budget.

The Terminators
Asylum 2009; 89 minutes; Director: Xavier S. Puslowski *

America is taken over by TR4 androids and it's up to a small band of resistance fighters to destroy them in their quest for world domination.

Terminator 3: Rise of the Machines minus the all-important machines—Asylum's blundering take on the *Terminator* series is one hell of a lame sci-fi movie, even though the

isn't! *Supercroc* is the kind of cheapo monster movie (think *King Dinosaur* and *The Giant Gila Monster*) you would catch in an English fleapit on a wet Sunday afternoon and reckon, at the time, that you had had your money's worth of monster entertainment. The CGI effects aren't *too* bad, Steve Bevilacqua's dialogue is ridiculous but funny (when you can hear it; the audio mix at times is terrible), the acting so-so and some of the photography (Stephen Parker) acceptable. Six minutes of credits drag by until, on the 8th minute, the giant croc appears behind a soldier, the green waters dissolving into a massive brown snout (a great shot, this). "Why is it on American soil?" questions General David Novak at LA headquarters, his team of grunts whittled down to one (Cynthia Rose Hall), a female with balls: "Run, run, shit, c'mon!" they yell as jaws closes in on them. A second squad is sent in, Hall bonds with hunky Matt Blashaw (her fiancé is eaten by the croc, the poor guy rapidly erased from her memory bank) and the creature's eggs are destroyed, three kept back by devious scientist Kim Little. A chopper is brought down by the monster, Little gabbles on about huge reptile bones from the Triassic period found after a recent hurricane ("A Sarcosuchus. It could eat a T-Rex!") and "the tank with an appetite" waddles along Santa Monica boulevard and into the streets of Los Angeles ("Blast that thing to

opening sequence on board a space station looks full of promise. Once the action is shifted to Los Angeles, however, we are stuck in shrieking female "Go! Go! Go!" territory. Sheriff A. Martinez and his motley bunch are on the run from identical-looking TR4s (all played by Paul Logan in tight vest top and combat trousers); the only way the androids can be stopped is to pilot a craft to the space station and turn off the robots' power source. Jeremy London appears to be the only human being sporting a gun that can bring down the TR4s, Martinez turns out to be an android himself and babes Lauren Walsh and Lucinda Rogers spend all of their available time shouting and screaming. By the time the team have shut down the station's power and disabled the androids, Rogers sobbing hysterically, "I did it. I did it. I did it" over and over again, you may well and truly have had enough of *The Terminators*, correctly classified by buffs as one of Asylum's worst features in recent years.

Titanic 2
Asylum 2010; 90 minutes; Director: Shane Van Dyke *

A melting glacier in Greenland releases an iceberg the size of Manhattan into the ocean, resulting in a tsunami of enormous proportions that threatens a global catastrophe—and the latest reincarnation of the *Titanic* is on her maiden voyage to America, directly in the path of the gigantic, 800 mph wave.

There's no two ways about it—this is a very bad effort from Asylum that, after 40 minutes, slides rapidly into farce. In fact, we have two tsunamis here: one that hits the big ship broadside on, the other that overturns it (à la *The Poseidon Adventure*). And both contain massive chunks of ice that can rip through metal. Yes, unlike the James Cameron epic, this *Titanic* begins to sink 40 minutes into the action, not 100 minutes. One of the engines overheats, exploding in a ball of fire, and mass panic sets in. Passengers run around like headless chickens, the lifeboats are useless and we are subjected to a protracted (and very tiresome) 50 minutes as Shane Van Dyke (the ship's designer), ex-partner Marie Westbrook and her mate, Michelle Glaven, become stuck below decks, faced with a variety of hackneyed cinematic disaster obstacles: Jammed hatches; an electrical cable dangling over a water-filled passage; and, finally, trapped in a fast-disappearing air pocket when the liner flips over. Westbrook's father (Bruce Davison) comes to the rescue in a helicopter that by rights should have run out of fuel at the beginning of this charade, and Van Dyke does a Leonardo DiCaprio at the end, drowning to save his ex-girlfriend. The effects showing two giant waves ramming the liner aren't too badly executed but *Titanic*'s interior is hilariously clapped-out (rusty pipes, concrete walls!) and surely those scenes of panic were filmed in a shopping mall somewhere. Perhaps Asylum were full of good intentions when they decided on producing a cheapskate, unofficial runner-up to Cameron's 1997 blockbuster. If so, those good intentions never made it into this shoddy, underdeveloped feature.

Transmorphers
Asylum 2007; 86 minutes; Director: Leigh Scott ***

Three hundred years after a race of alien machines has conquered the Earth, forcing humans underground, a military group decides to terminate their reign.

Asylum's $150,000 take on Michael Bay's $150,000,000 *Transformers* can only be enjoyed if you lower your standards and take it for what it is. So what if the acting (apart from Griff Furst) and dialogue is corny. You don't need to be a future Olivier in this kind of actioner. It's the visuals that count and considering the budget, they're quite striking. Eliza Swenson plays the general in what appears to be a rather bitchy female-dominated society, barking out orders to Matthew Wolf (he happens to be an android); Wolf and his squad have to venture outside in the relentless rain to destroy not only the robots but their main control center. After several colorful battles involving laser guns and Frisbee-bombs, both on the ground and in the air, the mechanical invaders are overthrown, Wolf sacrificing himself in order to bring about the collapse of the robots' headquarters. Quite a few Asylum movies suffer from an inconsistent audio track, a real annoyance, and *Transmorphers* isn't any different—loud one minute, muffled the next. But at least the film is far from pretentious and sci-fi fans might get a kick out of it, more so than they would like to believe.

Transmorphers: Fall of Man
Asylum 2009; 86 minutes; Director: Scott Wheeler ***

Robotic invaders attack Earth, transforming everyday objects into lethal killing machines.

UNDER TEN MILLION? ANYTHING'S POSSIBLE!

it, okay?" "Alright, let's do it." "Yes, I can do it." "Taste this, tin head!"). Action-wise, the movie scores highly, the kids will enjoy it and, hey, it does its level best to compete with *Transformers: Revenge of the Fallen*; let's face it, that wasn't high art, was it? Surely that's recommendation enough to watch.

Triassic World

Asylum 2018; 89 minutes; Director: Dylan Vox **

Two corporate bigwigs are shown the sights around a research facility cloning dinosaurs from DNA, unaware that one of the beasts has broken loose and is creating carnage.

Joel Berti and Jennifer Levinson quickly decide *not* to fund the project after dinosaur G32 embarks on a rampage, forcing the entire cast to decide on lockdown procedures and how to get out of the facility. Facility boss Hayley J. Williams wants to gas the creatures to death, while Shellie Sterling is hell-bent on saving her "babies." The prehistoric critters are being pumped full of human protein, bred for organ transplants for use in the human body, despite one bite from their slavering jaws releasing a deadly infection that turns their victims into crazed, zombie-like maniacs. After everyone has been made mincemeat of by several of the escaped monsters, the dinosaurs are gassed to oblivion, Sterling making it out alive courtesy of the LAPD

Right—once again, we are *not* talking Michael Bay and his pair of queue-forming *Transformers* blockbusters here. Accept the fact that Asylum have produced its own low-budget copycat versions, two of their many, now infamous, "mockbusters." It's a futile exercise comparing the two markets (major film studio vs. independent). By acknowledging this, you *might* enjoy this prequel to 2007's *Transmorphers* just that little bit more: Mobile phones transforming into spidery metal monsters; a satellite dish morphing into a robot; infra-red signals received from space; and a sat-nav firing a laser beam into a driver's forehead. Apparently, aggressive intelligent machines named Robotic Predator Drones (RPDs) *were* constructed by the military from information gleaned in July 1947 following the Roswell UFO incident (not that again!), but now they're being controlled by an extraterrestrial source, with orders to eliminate all human life. A band of survivors headed by Shane Van Dyke and Bruce Boxleitner decide to thwart their activities in modifying the planet by destroying Los Angeles' terraform plant but in doing so, a poisonous gas is released into the atmosphere, driving the human race underground. The special effects aren't all that bad considering this is Asylum, not Paramount and Warner Bros., but it's best to overlook numerous incongruities: Doctor Jennifer Rubin is walking perfectly after a metal spike has been removed from a bloody leg wound; and Van Dyke's team of seven somehow turns into six within the space of five seconds. The written-by-numbers script is also a headache ("I know I can do

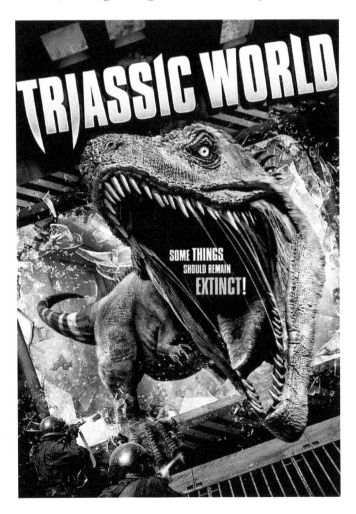

and revealing that she has rescued one dino egg for future experimentation. Similar in concept to 2015's *Jurassic City*, Dylan Vox's movie debut moves quickly through its paces but offers nothing new in the way of dinosaur thrills, although the effects are decent enough; and if monosyllabic Levinson (do corporate financiers *really* dress as shabbily as she does?) had spent less time burying her head in her cellphone, she might have stood a chance of breaking out of the complex alongside Sterling instead of being chewed to pieces in the final reel.

Troy the Odyssey

Asylum 2017; 90 minutes; Director: Tekin Girgin **

After the fall of Troy in 1184 BC, King Odysseus has to undergo many hazardous adventures on his 10-year return to Ithaca where his wife Penelope is being forced to take another husband because of his long absence.

Not Wolfgang Petersen's $175,000,000 blockbuster but Asylum's *very* modest interpretation on the siege of Troy. So, a cast of a hundred instead of thousands, Achilles (Eoin O'Brien) joining in the sacking of the city (he didn't, perishing a year before; but Petersen committed the same sin in his opus), a barely-glimpsed wooden horse and King Agamemnon played by "Mr. Australia of 2006," bodybuilder David Blazejko in a broad Aussie accent. Leaving a burning Troy in ancient mythology's smallest craft,

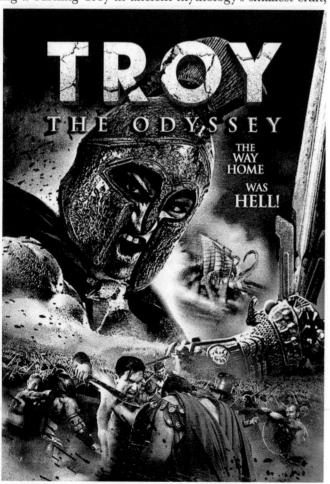

Dylan Vox (Odysseus), "Trojan bitch" Lara Heller (Circe) and assorted crew, pursued by the Kraken, come across an island surrounded by a pink mist, are enchanted by the sirens, manage to break the spell (the sirens are all old hags), negotiate the Path of the Dead (a single gloomy gallery), fight a beefy warrior wearing a Minotaur mask, meet the man-eating Cyclops in his labyrinth (an engaging creation from Asylum) and finally reach Ithaca. Once there, Vox reunites with his son, Telemachus (Dan Renalds) and proves his legitimacy by stringing his hunting bow, firing an arrow through five golden rings and defeating his rival for the hand of Penelope (Kelly B. Jones); he also, with Heller's assistance, slays the mighty Kraken as the tentacled terror of the deep storms up a beach, the movie closing with Heller's funeral. The clunky action sags in the middle when the bemused Vox is seduced by Calypso (Cecilia Belletti) on the Isle of Sirens, and the actor's wooden interchanges with Heller on board their tiny vessel are embarrassingly inept. The Thailand locations look attractive but, in all honesty, this cut-price version of Homer's epic poem *Odyssey* is for diehard lovers of Asylum only; others might well give up on it after half-an-hour.

2-Headed Shark Attack
Asylum 2012; 88 minutes;
Director: Christopher Douglas-Olen Ray *****
3-Headed Shark Attack
Asylum 2015; 89 minutes;
Director: Christopher Douglas-Olen Ray ***
5-Headed Shark Attack
Asylum 2017; 89 minutes; Director: Nico De Leon ***
6-Headed Shark Attack
Asylum 2018; 86 minutes; Director: Mark Atkins ****

What better than a gigantic shark, not with one head but with two, or even three, heads? That's the premise in Christopher Douglas-Olen Ray's double helping of mutated *Jaws*-type thrills, strong on blood and carnage, not so strong in the acting/script department. The first is classic Asylum, straight from the start: Two babes water skiing are picked off by a gargantuan doubled-headed super shark (one for each head!), the monster smashing the towing boat and its three dudes for good measure. Teeth, blood and mangled body parts, in full frame—that's the setting, admirably maintained right up to the final seconds. On board education vessel *Sea King*, Professor Charlie O'Connell and Doctor Carmen Electra are having difficulty in teaching a bunch of partying-on students the finer points of the sextant, that's when Electra isn't preening her well-honed body in front of the camera. The partying comes to an abrupt stop when the two-headed predator rams *Sea King*'s hull, forcing all on board to make for an atoll shaken by earth tremors to search for scrap metal to repair the boat. From then on in, it's colorful, extremely bloody,

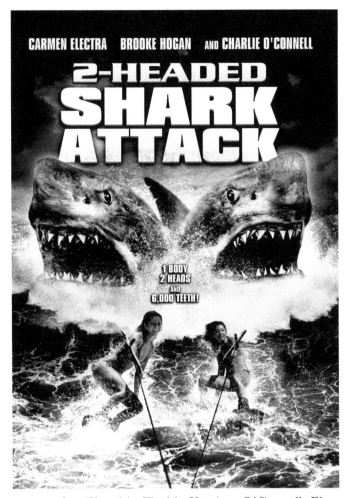

CARMEN ELECTRA   BROOKE HOGAN   AND CHARLIE O'CONNELL

2-HEADED SHARK ATTACK

1 BODY 2 HEADS AND 6,000 TEETH!

ing a group of scruffy activists) heading out to a "booze cruise" vessel in imminent danger of being capsized by the monster. Grizzled skipper Danny Trejo is also en route in his boat with two machine-gunners, determined to blast the thing out of the sea. The movie gets bogged down at this stage in a "who's going to escape, who's not and who's going to act as a decoy" scenario, a series of risible situations spoiling the mix: The vessel, head-butted and listing at a 45 degree angle, appears upright in the water in long-shot while Karrueche Tran's "It's only 10 miles" distance is covered in a few seconds—and would anyone in their right mind jump on the back of a 60-foot three-headed shark armed only with an axe? The beast's middle head is severed, but, like a hydra, it sprouts three more—we now have a five-headed shark! Eventually, the monster muta-tion is led into the garbage zone where it consumes tons of rubbish, destroying itself in a feeding frenzy. The shark

monster fun (filmed in Florida Keys) as O'Connell, Elec-tra, smart cookie Brooke Hogan, whiz-kid Paul Gallegos, mentally challenged jock Geoff Ward and company think of various ways to eliminate the shark and get off an is-land slowly sinking into the ocean. Following a welter of chewing, chomping deaths, both in the sea and on land (plus a tsunami), the creature has one head blown off; it's finally dispatched when it swallows a drum of gas which explodes, turning shark meat into mincemeat, Hogan and Gallegos the two survivors. *2-Headed Shark Attack* is packed with destructive gory incident, making you forget about Shannan Stewart's shrieking Minnie Mouse delivery ("We're all gonna get eaten! We're screwed!"), O'Connell's constant groaning as he hobbles around with a minor leg wound and the atoll that's supposed to be sinking but ap-pears pristine (and level) throughout. The shark's the thing, a terrific CGI monstrosity, one of indie's best, in a movie delivering gruesome shark shocks by the bucketload; the women aren't too bad, either!

3-Headed Shark Attack offers more of the same although in this case, the cast don't sparkle as much and the pace drags in the middle. It starts well, the triple-headed pred-ator gobbling up a bevy of teens on an island before we move to Jason Simmons' government research facility studying the effects of pollution on sea life. The center, battered by the mutated menace attracted by the floating pollution, explodes and sinks, a posse of survivors (includ-

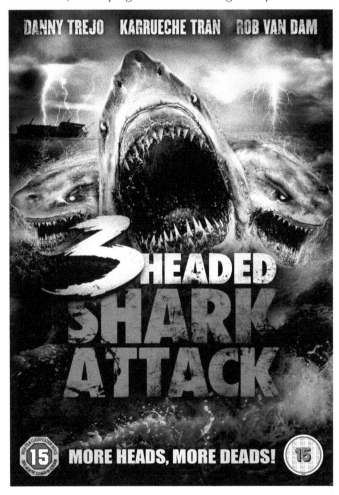

DANNY TREJO   KARRUECHE TRAN   ROB VAN DAM

3 HEADED SHARK ATTACK

15   MORE HEADS, MORE DEADS!   15

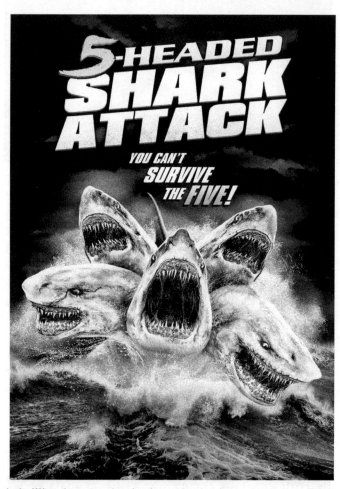

Holsman gets dragged by his feet into one of the mouths), Bruno asks Howard to marry him; after what he's been through, it's the least that he deserves!

The prolific Mark Atkins, one of Asylum's better directors, took over the helm for *6-Headed Shark Attack*, concerning a bunch of squabbling couples spending time out on the Isla Corazón near Mexico to reignite their stuttering relationships, a marriage boot camp of sorts. Those fragile relationships and incessant flirting are put to the test when a colossal six-headed shark, the subject of animal experimentation, makes its presence felt, chomping up swimmers in a sea of blood, wrecking boats and even managing to crawl ashore using its snouts in pursuit of its prey; if it loses a head, another grows in its place. There's plenty of grisly goings-on in Atkins' fast-paced confection, backed by a pulsating rock score from Christopher Cano and Chris Ridenhour; loads of busty beauties to feast your eyes on, Iggy Pop look-alike Jonathan Pienaar's demented performance (he gets ripped in two) and a decent CGI monster that finishes off the entire cast with the exception of Brandon Auret and black babe Thandi Sebe, who blow the creature to smithereens before getting up close and personal. It may have been made in 2018, but the Asylum folk were back to their vintage best and bang on form in this lively mutated shark offering.

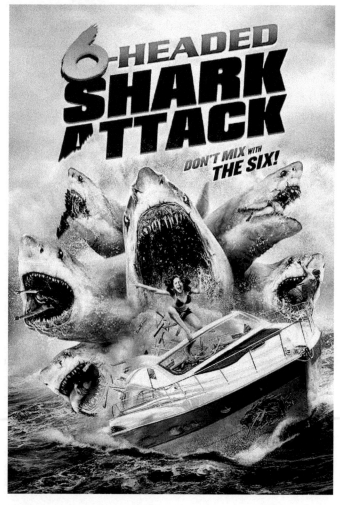

is brilliantly conceived, given the budget, the gory effects in-your-face; however, it's not the glossy thrill-ride that highlighted the first entrant, a lifeless cast seeming to go through the motions. Enjoyable in places but not in the same league as its two-headed cousin.

Shot around Puerto Rico in glossy color, *5-Headed Shark Attack* featured a mutated predator with four heads in front, one in its tail ("Is it possible for a shark to have more than one head?"). Aquarium project boss Jeffrey Holsman hires Chris Bruno's boat in an attempt to capture the beast, even though it's head-butted numerous yachts and eaten its way through several cast members during the first lively 20 minutes, including some of Holsman's young interns. Marine biologist Nikki Howard tries to talk her slimeball boss out of the insane scheme as the ocean fills up with blood and guts, but he wants the thing as the aquarium's prize attraction; dollars speak louder than multiple deaths in his book. After a fairly invigorating 50 minutes (the predator finishes off a humpbacked whale and a Great White Shark, as well as humans), the movie goes off the boil. Bruno and a couple of cops lay lines rigged with explosives and speakers emitting dolphin cries which sharks are afraid of, the monster leaps out of the sea, grabbing a helicopter in its jaws, Bruno jumps onto its back, burying a hefty hook into its flesh and depth charges reduce the thing to massive chunks of bleeding shark flesh. Mission accomplished (yes,

UNDER TEN MILLION? ANYTHING'S POSSIBLE!

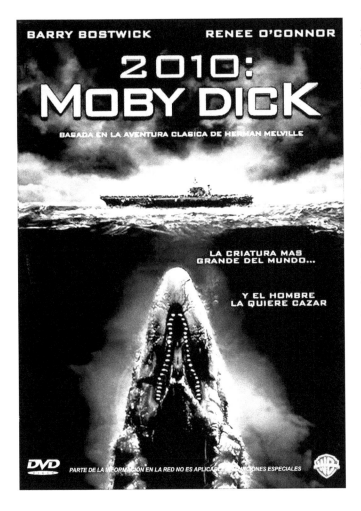

2010: Moby Dick

Asylum 2010; 87 minutes; Director: Trey Stokes *****

In 1969, young Captain Ahab loses his left leg on board USS *Acushnet* when the submarine is ripped apart by a 500-foot whale. Forty-one years later, as captain of USS *Pequod*, he's on a mission of personal vengeance, hell-bent on ridding the seas of the titanic cetacean that has caused him so much pain and torment.

Freely adapted by Paul Bales from Herman Melville's classic 1851 novel, even down to using character and vessel names direct from Melville's prose, Asylum's updated version, *2010: Moby Dick*, is (pardon the pun) a whale of a monster movie, scarred Barry Bostwick chewing the scenery as barking mad Captain Ahab, intent on exterminating the giant whale that caused him to lose his leg ("I want my revenge on Moby Dick!"). Now commanding USS *Pequod*, he's become such a security liability that ex-partner Matt Lagan (he lost a right arm in the 1969 incident) is ordered by Washington to terminate his activities, submarine USS *Essex* also sent to destroy Bostwick's vessel at present in the Pacific. To make up the party, marine biologist Renée O'Connor and pal Derrick Scott are on board the *Pequod*, their job to decipher Moby Dick's whale-talk, while second-in-command Adam Grimes has his work cut out trying unsuccessfully to hold Bostwick in check. Cue for masses of monster action: A whale tourist boat is upended by the behemoth; USS *Essex* is sunk; Bostwick homes in on the giant ("Chase him to hell! He took my leg. I don't intend to give him my ass!"); a harpoon is constructed from the steel hub of USS *Acushnet*, Bostwick dripping blood over the barbed end as an omen of good luck; a cruise liner is rammed; and the climactic standoff takes place on Tau Pi Atoll where Bostwick, replacing his lost prosthetic leg with a wooden cross, lures the Godzilla of the ocean into the heavily mined lagoon (*much* too shallow for a mammoth whale, but who cares?). After Moby Dick has battered the island and smashed up *Pequod*, everyone bar O'Connor perishes, including Lagan and Scott, Bostwick's body, entwined in harpoon rope and pinned to the whale's flank, disappearing into the inky depths as his gargantuan nemesis escapes the military (or is he dead?). From the exciting opening 1969 sequence to the explosive final showdown, *2010: Moby Dick* is a colossal guilty pleasure, free of the usual quota of Asylum bimbos, blessed with a decent nautical-based soundtrack from resident composer Chris Ridenhour and purposefully directed by Trey Stokes; years ago, it would have made a profitable double bill playing alongside *Bigfoot*. Those days are long gone, so enjoy the movie for what it is, a rollicking indie seafaring adventure boosted by more-than-adequate effects, a fabulous monster and a great star turn from Bostwick. You don't often get a performance like his within the indie genre, but on this occasion, you do. Thar she blows!

2012: Doomsday

Asylum/Faith Films 2008; 85 minutes;
Director: Nick Everhart *

A 2,000-year-old Mayan legend decrees that the end of the world will occur on December 21, 2012: Four strangers and a pregnant woman make for a Mayan temple where the birth of her child will bring forth a new kind of world for mankind to live in.

Take note of the outfit that produced *2012: Doomsday* in tandem with Asylum—Faith Films. There's an awful lot of faith spouted *ad nauseam* from the 45th minute onwards, enough to have even the most devout believer in God turning to the Dark Lord for enlightenment. Shot mainly in Belize, we begin 36 hours before doomsday: The Earth has shifted off its polar axis, its rotation slowing down, a distant black hole the culprit; Dale Midkiff and Caroline Amiguet have just unearthed a golden cross from a Mayan chamber that, if inserted in a certain

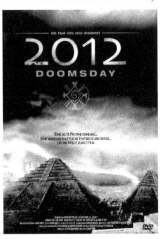

temple wall, will bring hope to all after the cataclysm takes place. The action flicks backwards and forwards from various Mexican locations to Baltimore and San Diego, counting down the hours: Cliff De Young is desperately trying to convince daughter Danae Nelson to return home before the earthquakes and eruptions start; naturally, she refuses, too intent on dragging pregnant Sara Tomko to a Mayan temple through earth tremors and falling snow, so Dad decides to fly out to meet her, notwithstanding cyclones that would tear his light aircraft to shreds—but is his unruffled pilot, who disappears on landing, a messenger from above ("This is your journey. Trust in God."). Meanwhile, Ami Dolenz and her mother, Shirley Raun, are heading towards the sacred pyramid; she doesn't believe in the Almighty ("The prophecy is a myth.") but Mum does, gabbling on about God's will. The car stalls; Dolenz gets out to find Raun gone, *another* of God's messengers? This happens in the 45th minute, a doomsday event in itself as from here on in, viewers of all denominations are subjected to a barrage of religious mumbo-jumbo accompanied by sobbing, pious face-pulling, a welter of "I love yous" and heavenly music, designed (perhaps) to convince atheists everywhere that there *is* a God after all (at least there are no shrieks of "Oh my God!" Now that *would* be deemed as blasphemy!). The message that "God has a reason for everything" is rammed home every single minute, right up to the sickly sentimental final sequence taking place in the Great Temple, Tomko producing a baby surrounded by De Young, Midkiff, Dolenz (who just happens to be a paramedic!) and Nelson, everyone crying and praying, Dolenz converted to Christianity, yells of "You did it! You did it!" to Tomko who has undergone the longest birth in indie cinema history and shouts of "No matter what happens, we have faith! This isn't the end, it's just the beginning, a miracle of life!" Glory hallelujah! As for the disaster aspect, it's brief and disappointing, but was Nick Everhart's movie really about a catastrophic event or simply an advertisement for God's mysterious and wonderful ways, religious propaganda stretched out to ridiculous lengths? Yes, it's very easy to be cynical, but after sitting through Asylum's bible-bashing opus, you will feel sorely tempted to reach for the nearest "18" rated splatter/gore feature to wash the sanctimonious taste from your mouth, wherever your religious beliefs may lie.

2012: Ice Age
Asylum 2011; 91 minutes; Director: Travis Fort **
Iceland's Mount Hekla erupts, pushing a gigantic glacier towards New York, with devastating results on global weather.
Patrick Labyorteaux, wife Julie McCullough and teen son Nick Afanasiev race across blizzard-hit America in the wrong direction to rescue student daughter Katie

Wilson and her boyfriend Kyle Morris from freezing to death in New York. A near carbon copy of *The Day After Tomorrow* (2004), Travis Fort's effort contains reasonable effects let down by the usual old "parents saving kids from disaster" storyline, particularly when said kids are as self-obsessed as Wilson. Still, Mum and Dad know best as they drive like crazy through a snow-covered wasteland, McCullough shouting "Get us outta here" nonstop while Afanasiev sulks on the back seat of the van, lost without his beloved internet ("I need to get online!"). Characters in these Asylum disaster actioners tend to come off a poor second best to the ongoing calamity and *2012: Ice Age* is no exception to the rule; you haven't got an ounce of sympathy towards any one of them and the problems they are all are facing. After a barrage of "Go faster," "Dad. Get us outta here!" and "Are you okay?" and negotiating several traffic jams, the family is reunited just as the glacier rams into the Big Apple, stopped in its tracks by bombs and missiles; the final shot is of the five peering out from the head of the Statue of Liberty, facing an uncertain future (and a sequel?), the remainder of the monument buried in ice and snow.

2012: Supernova
Asylum 2009; 87 minutes; Director: Anthony Fankhauser *
Two hundred years ago in the Lyra constellation, a star went supernova; now, a vast stream of radiation emanating from the star's collapse enters our solar system, threatening to turn Earth into a radioactive wasteland.
There was a time, not so long ago, when Asylum knocked out spiffy little horror movies: *The Beast of Bray*

Road, *Frankenstein Reborn*, *Legion of the Dead*, to name but a few. However, since jumping onto the disaster/mockbuster bandwagon, their output has steered a dodgy course between the truly sublime and the utterly ridiculous. *2012: Supernova* firmly falls into the latter category, for a host of reasons. Brian Krause plays a scientist charged with delivering atomic warheads to an international space station; once in position, the missiles can be launched and detonated, forming a barrier around Earth's atmosphere which will hopefully prevent the radioactive hurricane from wiping out the planet. While Krause, Chinese colleague Allura Lee and vodka-swilling Russian Alan Poe are ensconced in the base's command center, talking scientific gibberish, unsympathetic wife Heather McComb and sulky daughter Najarra Townsend are driving hell for leather down the freeway, coping with earthquakes, boulders, electrical storms, twisters and flat tires in an attempt to reunite with Krause; he takes off in the shuttle, is forced to kill saboteur Lee and then successfully launches the missiles from the space station, intoxicated Poe collapsing, as dead as a doornail (probably through too much alcohol). When are moviemakers going to realize that there is nothing dramatic whatsoever in watching actors staring into computer screens for what seems like hours on end, as Krause and his buddies do here. The crass dialogue also grates, Townsend and McComb incessantly squawking "We're gonna be okay," "We're not gonna be okay," "Oh my God! Oh my God!" "Go, go, go, go, go," and "C'mon, c'mon, c'mon," made all the worse by an erratic sound balance (the bane of many of Asylum's earlier films). And haven't back-projected shots from the inside of cars long-been consigned to cinema's special effects waste bin? The outer space CGI work is quite impressive but in no way makes up for a pretty poor excuse of an end-of-the-world disaster movie. It's almost impossible to say anything positive about *2012: Supernova*—sorry, Asylum, all those one-star internet ratings are fully deserved for this one.

Zombie Apocalypse

Asylum 2011; 87 minutes; Director: Nick Lyon ****

The deadly VM2 virus is responsible for a worldwide zombie plague, a handful of survivors battling their way through a Los Angeles populated by hordes of the living dead to reach the human zone on Catalina Island.

Zombies, let's be frank, don't do a lot. They stagger and lurch, blank eyes staring out from ravaged faces, only livening up when uncontaminated human flesh is at hand and hiding away at night in old buildings—they're also easy to dispose of, by a bullet in the head, axe, knife, hammer, sword, shovel, grenade and, in *Zombie Apocalypse*, arrow. In the main, they don't make for overly exciting horror cinema: It's up to directors to stir up the broth, to somehow raise the interest level in what can easily become boring and predictable fare; zombies, after all, are pretty much one-dimensional in their approach as monsters. So all credit to Nick Lyon for injecting life, soul and vigor into Asylum's spiffy zombie outing, imbuing the main characters with a degree of depth. Kicking off with newsreel footage showing various countries decimated by the

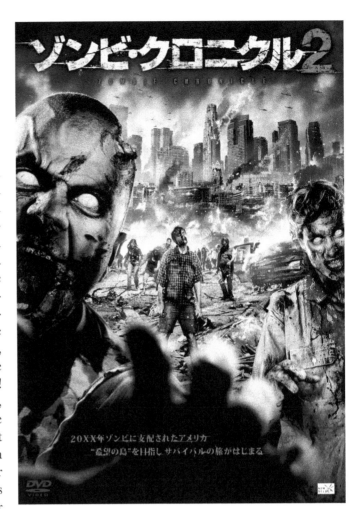

Japanese poster for *Zombie Apocalypse*

plague (London's Big Ben gets demolished by a crashing airliner), EMPs from space bombarding cities with lasers to control the living dead menace, Lyon then focuses on a group of survivors scurrying through battered Los Angeles in an attempt to reach the ferry to Catalina Island, a safe refuge. En route, they go head-to-head with the mangle-faced hordes, avoid a rabid dog and are joined by a couple of female archers; reaching the docks, they fight two ferocious mutated, zombified tigers ("Miaow, bitch!" yells Ving Rhames) and await the ferry which arrives at the allotted time. Three of their numbers are lost to the zombies, Johnny Pacar, Eddie Steeples and likeable hunk Rhames, the others making it to safety. Extremely gory for a UK "15" rating (decapitations; severed limbs; fountains of blood; chewed body parts), this is a well-made zombie flick which even those who are not really into zombie movies will find some satisfaction in. Taryn Manning and Lesley-Ann Brandt are particularly fine playing the female leads, macho boss Gary Weeks comes across as almost sensitive and caring while musclebound Rhames exhibits stony-faced charisma of a primeval kind. Vivid zombie entertainment from Asylum, as good as anything else similar that gets released on the major circuits by the big studios.

Full Moon

In 1989, B movie producer Charles Band formed Full Moon Productions (later changing to Full Moon Entertainment), the aim being to create low-to-medium-budget horror, fantasy and sci-fi pictures that had a more upmarket sheen than the competitors. Paramount was to be the major distributor. Capitalizing on Band's interest in devil puppetry, the company's first production in 1989 was *Puppet Master*, directed by David Schmoeller and budgeted at $250,000, a surprise hit on VHS and the long-forgotten laserdisc format. Ten sequels in the franchise were to follow, an eleventh, *Puppet Master: Axis Termination*, appearing in 2017, continuing with *Puppet Master: The Littlest Reich* in 2018, *Blade: The Iron Cross* scheduled for a 2020 release. In 1995, Full Moon was dropped by Paramount because of lack of interest in the straight-to-video market but continued releasing features under various labels including Pulp Fantasy Productions, Cult Video and Alchemy Entertainment up to 2000. In 2003, Full Moon Pictures was reformed (also branded as Shadow Entertainment/Films), its first production *Dr. Moreau's House of Pain*; Band later rechristened this to Full Moon Features and the company still carries on to this day under various guises, the indefatigable producer seemingly never giving up on his pet project, fantasy filmmaking. Band and his Full Moon retinue have produced some out-and-out classics over the years—*Castle Freak*, *Hideous!*, the *Dr. Moreau* outing, *Dark Angel: The Ascent* and *Vampire Journals* are imaginative, well-crafted excursions into horror fantasy cinema that are as good as anything turned out by the Hammer and Amicus studios in their formative years, while the enchantingly gruesome *Puppet Master* series has an idiosyncratic value all of its own. All Full Moon pictures come highly recommended to lovers of the cut-price bizarre.

Charles Band, founder of Full Moon

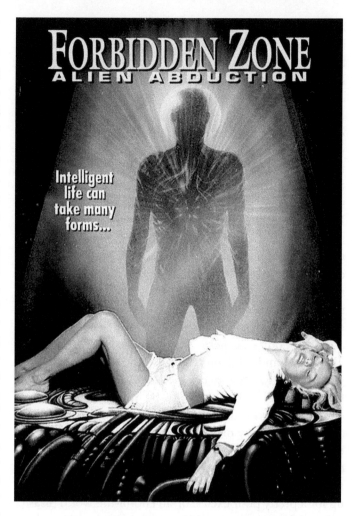

Alien Abduction: Intimate Secrets
Twilight Ent./Full Moon 1996; 90 minutes;
Director: Lucian S. Diamonde ***

Five women meet at a health spa—three of them slowly begin to realize that they may have been abducted by an alien from a dying planet whose purpose is to learn all about the female reproductive system and impregnate one of them.

An erotic sci-fi chick-flick by any other name—how could it not be, with ex-*Playboy* centerfold Pia Reyes one of the objects of alien Dimitrii Bogomaz's desires. Beside a pool in the spa's steam room, Meredyth Holmes has a fit, recovers and tells her disbelieving friends that she recently had an encounter with a UFO; what's more, herself, Reyes and Darcy DeMoss all engaged in sexual activity with an alien. Tapping into their deep-rooted sexual fantasies (as much for his own satisfaction as theirs), the good-looking alien (he's adopted human disguise) turns the women on to untold heights of orgasmic pleasure—in other words, he wants to discover what makes these babes tick. Following one soft-focus porn sequence after another, related in flashback, the women leave the spa, Meredyth positive that she is pregnant—but what with? Incorporating dialogue along the lines of, "They've been trying to make contact." "The only thing you need to make contact with is a vibrator," and a solitary scene inside the spaceship that is distinctly grade Z '50s in design, it's nigh on impossible to take this quasi-science fiction humbug seriously—just sit back and ogle the amount of scrummy female goodies on display and disregard the ridiculous plot.

Castle Freak
Full Moon Entertainment 1995; 90 minutes;
Director: Stuart Gordon *****

A family travel to Italy to view a 700-year-old castle left to the husband in a will, unaware that a deformed, flesh-eating lunatic has been interned in a dungeon cell for decades.

Echoes of '70s Hammer and Amicus, plus the continental horror genre (1964's *The Castle of Terror*, anyone?), abound in Full Moon's lively Gothic chiller; Jeffrey Combs, wife Barbara Crampton and blind daughter Jessica Dollarhide investigate an inherited castle that, unknown to them, houses tormented freak Jonathan Fuller, chained to a cell wall in the gloomy dungeons. Combs and Crampton have major problems—she blames him for the death of their five-year-old son and Dollarhide's blindness, caused by the car he was driving hitting a tree; he was drunk at the wheel. The housekeeper hints at the place being haunted and it's not long before a terrible family secret involving

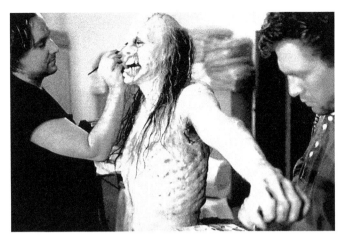

The make-up department gets to work on Jonathan Fuller in *Castle Freak*.

the fake burial of Fuller when *he* was aged five is let out of the bag; Fuller, revived after eating a cat, bites off his thumb, enabling him to slip through his manacles and menace the household, dressed in a sheet to disguise his fearsome appearance. There's a great deal of screaming taking place in the film's second half as Fuller hobbles about on a rampage, and the mutilation and near-murder of a prostitute by the maniac in a cell is extremely graphic, as is the sex scene that precedes it. The end sees a *Curse of Frankenstein*-type climax played out on the battlements: The family are cornered by the deranged Fuller, his disfigured features on show; troubled Combs redeems himself in the eyes of his wife by grabbing him and jumping from the walls—both die as a result. The company's usual high standard color photography, Richard Band's score and Gordon's fluid camerawork make for an engrossing thriller that involves right up to the tragic finale.

Dangerous Worry Dolls
aka **Dangerous Chucky Dolls**
Full Moon Features/Wizard Ent. 2008; 75 minutes;
Director: Charles Band ***

Bullied by all around her, a single mother serving time in a state penitentiary calls upon the supernatural power of five worry dolls (given to her by her daughter) to relieve her of her misery. After being given the tiny dolls, Jessica Morris places them under her pillow; during the night, they crawl inside her ear and turn her into a fearless fighter.

Another "killer dolls" movie from Band which entertains throughout its swiftly moving running time *if* you don't take it too seriously. In fact, you almost root for the transformed Morris as she eliminates chief tormentor Meredith McClain, electrocutes the sexually repressed warden (Deb Snyder) and straps on a dildo, "raping" transsexual guard Anthony Dilio in retribution for him/her assaulting her. With a grinning, green-eyed mini-skull face frequently popping out of an erupting spot on Morris' forehead, the

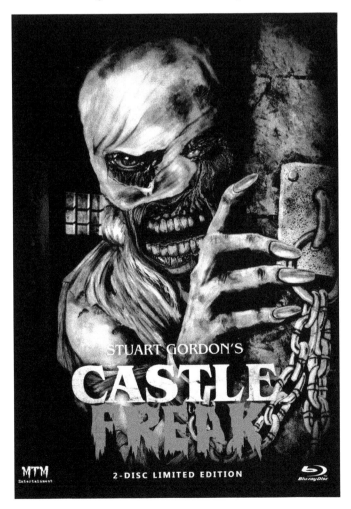

STUART GORDON'S
CASTLE FREAK

MTM
Entertainment
2-DISC LIMITED EDITION
Blu-ray Disc

es, Featherstone travels through a portal to the world of mortals ("I want to walk under the golden globe I have dreamed of.") and becomes enraged, disgusted and saddened, by watching TV news bulletins, at the amount of evil corruption tainting the planet. Befriended by caring ER medic Daniel Markel, Featherstone the avenging angel is soon stalking the streets with her dog Hellraiser when Markel is on night shift, using her unholy powers to rip apart those committing misdemeanors and feeding her pet body parts. Two cops trail her, convinced that she is somehow linked to a series of grisly slayings, but one lives to regret it, reduced to a quaking, incoherent wreck. When Featherstone homes in on the double-dealing mayor, Milton James, Markel finally realizes just who, or what, she is, and where she comes from, but by then, he's totally hooked. Following a trip to a cinema to watch a porn movie, she states seductively in his apartment, "I want to have sexual intercourse," which is what they do, her satanic appearance making its presence felt through lust but not putting him off one iota. A semi-tragic climax—Featherstone is shot in the back after scaring the mayor half to death, and has to return to her own world to bathe in the River Styx as a cure—is redeemed when she returns through Markel's bedroom mirror in full resplendent glo-

picture is undoubtedly comic book horror fodder at times and the fate of Morris is left in the air—she disappears from the scenario and the worry dolls are retained by timid Cheri Themer, who will obviously use them to vanquish *her* enemies. Like a '50s B movie, *Dangerous Worry Dolls* is short, sweet and tacky, but enjoyable.

Dark Angel: The Ascent
Full Moon Entertainment 1994; 81 minutes;
Director: Linda Hassani *****

A female demon living in the fiery pit of hell, where souls pay for their sins, decides to explore the world above and becomes emotionally attached to a young doctor.

Made on a budget of $350,000 with a cast of unknowns, *Dark Angel: The Ascent* must surely rank as one of Full Moon's finest hours, a B movie where the B stands for brilliant. Acting, direction, music, script, emotional depth, photography, ideas—all contribute to a telling minor horror fantasy that enthralls and moves throughout, the exemplary production held together by a truly spellbinding central performance from Angela Featherstone as alluring demon Veronica; little-girl-lost one minute, lethal killing machine the next. Her ice-cool beauty is hypnotic, even in demon mode—horns, wings, pointed ears, tail, flashing red eyes and long black nails. Against her parents' wish-

UNDER TEN MILLION? ANYTHING'S POSSIBLE!

Charles Band

ry to rejoin him in passionate love (shades of Jean Cocteau's *Orphée* here), Markel thanking God for allowing her to come back to him. A fantastical *Romeo and Juliet* meets *Death Wish* with one challenging thought put forward for debate—does heaven actually control what's taking place in hell? From the opening scenes depicting the pit of eternal damnation to the lovers reuniting, this is a superb example of low-budget filmmaking at its very highest peak; in its own unique way, quite unforgettable.

Decadent Evil aka Decadent Evil Dead
Full Moon Features 2005; 67 minutes;
Director: Charles Band ***

A female vampire whose victims total almost 10,000 requires just three more unwilling subjects which will make her invincible to all men.

Short, sweet and trashy sums up this lurid potboiler which mostly takes place in the confines of Debra Mayer's ornate mansion. The dark-haired bloodsucker has two delicious assistants (Raelyn Hennessee and Jill Michelle) and a red-skinned homunculus imprisoned in a birdcage. Michelle wants to take a break with boyfriend Daniel Lennox (he's unaware that she's a vampire) and when he turns up at the mansion to collect her with midget vampire hunter Phil Fondacaro in tow, the scene is set for Mayer's downfall. Straying into soft-porn territory at times, especially

in the opening pole-dancing sequence, Band's hokey little skit on the undead contains no flab, it simply gets on with things, albeit in a ramshackle kind of way. And the last few minutes showing the red male homunculus (Fondacaro's father) engaged in rough sex with the green female homunculus (Mayer, stripped of her vampire state, in a new guise) is worth the price of the DVD alone.

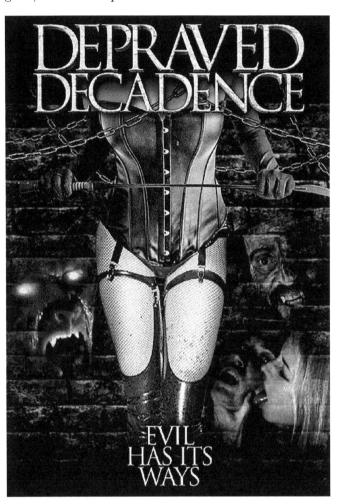

Decadent Evil 2 aka Depraved Decadence
Full Moon Features 2007; 82 minutes;
Director: Charles Band ***

A part-vampire and her boyfriend take up employment in a lap-dancing club with the sole purpose of slaying a master vampire who runs the joint.

A direct follow-on to 2005's *Decadent Evil*, Band's hammy vampire frolic isn't quite as inventive as the first outing but is fun all the same. In this second instalment, Jill Michelle and Daniel Lennox book into a motel, along with Marvin the horny homunculus, housed in a birdcage. The duo are on twin missions: To end the rule of king vampire Mike Muscat—the bloodsucker is three victims short of the magic 10,000 which will grant him invincibility and to obtain a sample of his blood to bring back to life midget vampire killer Ivan (played by Ricardo Gil, taking over Phil Fondacaro's role in the first movie) who died after dispatching vampiress Morella. Much skulking about in the Vision nightclub, trying to guess the identity of vampire number one, leads to the inevitable showdown in a garage parking lot; Gil, resurrected from the dead, slays vampire number two (James C. Burns) while Michelle does away with the bat-eared leader. As a reward for his unswerving devotion, Marvin the homunculus performs an act of unbridled lust on sexy vampire Jessica Morris, tied to a bed festooned with garlic. Vampire purists might find this all rather silly but the movie entertains, Marvin is a unique character in Band's idiosyncratic stable of puppetry and the gyrating lap-dancers will have many males needing a cold shower afterwards.

robot sporting zap guns; and a ferocious teddy bear. Tracy Scoggins is the cop, Daniel Cerny the Damien-like demon wearing green contact lenses who continually morphs into an adult demon, complete with horns, then back again. Robert Mitchum's grandson Bentley plays a delivery boy caught up in all the mayhem; the toys are eventually eliminated, the warehouse is blown up and a toy boy soldier vanquishes the demon. Made before the days of CGI, Band's array of mechanically manipulated devil dolls that populate his sometimes bizarre productions are endowed with far more flair, both zany and barbarous, than if they were conjured up in a computer; comic book in execution, and rather cheesy, *Demonic Toys* is great horror fun without being obviously funny, a lively addition to the Full Moon stable.

Dr. Moreau's House of Pain
Full Moon Pictures/Rednavel Filmworx 2004; 72 minutes;
Director: Charles Band *****

Searching for his missing brother, a boxer, his girlfriend and a reporter are taken to an abandoned asylum by a sexy stripper where a doctor is performing experiments on humans using animal DNA, producing hybrid creatures he terms "manimals."

Filmed in 1940s *film noir* fashion, the quirky set design attractively photographed in garish colors, Band's dazzling

Demonic Toys
Full Moon Entertainment 1992; 86 minutes;
Director: Peter Manoogian ***

After her partner has been killed, a pregnant cop pursues a group of arms dealers into Arcadia Toys' abandoned warehouse; a wounded villain's blood reactivates a 66-year-old demon who wants to possess the soul of the officer's unborn child and commands the discontinued toys to slaughter anybody who stands in his way.

Another Charles Band romp through evil-minded puppetry territory, boasting an atmospheric score by Richard Band and a collection of great little monsters: A sadistic, foul-mouthed baby doll; a clown jack-in-the-box; a plastic

UNDER TEN MILLION? ANYTHING'S POSSIBLE!

take on H.G. Wells' *The Island of Doctor Moreau* must rank as one of Full Moon's finest features and at 72 minutes doesn't outstay its welcome. Jacob Witkin plays a crazed doctor, eager for fresh supplies of human organs, assisted by dour Ling Aum whose daughter is horribly disfigured and requires urgent surgery. Pugilist John Patrick Jordan, girlfriend Jessica Lancaster and sassy reporter Debra Mayer are lured to Witkin's laboratory by Lorielle New on the pretext that she knows where Jordan's brother is—in reality, they are all being lined up as donors for Witkin's experiments. In a frenetic series of events, Mayer is butchered by Dogface, Pigface is killed by New because she has fallen for Jordan and objects to the creature cutting up his tethered body, and foxy New has animal DNA in her genes, hissing and snarling when aroused. Aum's daughter, one large green eye staring out of a mass of twisted flesh, also dies, as does Witkin, slashed across the throat after New has been shot. However, judging by the flickering forked tongue on that new stripper in the seedy joint, the doctor's creations live on. Fast-paced and bathed in lurid color, Band's effort appears like a cross between an early Hammer B film and a continental shocker from the 1960s, dripping in '40s atmosphere, a novel concept that produces, by indie standards at least, an exceptional, and rather unique, little horror movie.

Frankenstein Reborn!
Castel Film Romania/Full Moon 1998; 61 minutes;
Director: Julian Breen ***

A young girl visits her uncle in his castle and suspects that he is up to no good in the basement.

NOT Asylum's 2005 gore-fest of the same name but part of a series entitled *Filmonsters!* which apparently never got off the ground. Briefly, young Haven Burton meets her uncle, Jason Simmons (Baron Frankenstein), who, with the aid of right-hand man George Catlin, is creating a human being out of dead body parts. The monster (Ethan Wilde) escapes from the lab; Burton befriends it; Simmons finds out; there's a tussle in the castle; both creator and creature die; and the girl plus Ben Gould escape as the castle goes up in flames. This being a Charles Band production, the opening graveyard credits sequence features some peculiar puppetry and the movie is ridiculously short. Also, in what century is the action taking place? Burton (wearing trainers and modern-day clothing) looks like a college co-ed, Gould is kitted out in 1920s-style garb, while the backdrops are distinctly 19th-century. And this is the first *Frankenstein*

movie this author has ever seen sporting a PG (Parental Guidance) certificate, so not much in the way of scares here, obviously! A truncated version of the old tale which, despite decent sets and atmospheric photography, is something of a lukewarm oddity.

The Gingerdead Man
Full Moon Features/Talos Ent. 2005; 70 minutes;
Director: Charles Band **

The soul of a killer returns in the form of an evil gingerbread man, intent on claiming the life of a girl he once spared in a burglary.

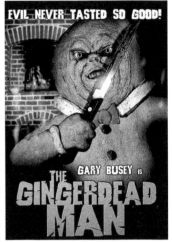

Gary Busey stars as the loopy killer in the opening five minutes—exit Busey (who's eventually executed) and enter the diabolical little devil of the title, another one of Band's fiendish (but original) puppets-turned-bad creations; Busey's ashes have been mixed with dough and blood to produce a homicidal cookie with attitude! Played out on virtually one set (Margaret Blye's dimly lit bakery), *The Gingerdead Man*, although short, drags: Robin Sydney is the object of the doughy one's hate, Ryan Locke the hunk coming to the rescue after the animated biscuit has mown down Blye's rival in a car (he wants to open an eatery opposite her). Bakery assistant Jonathan Chase finally bites the mini-monster's head off, Busey's spirit entering his body and transforming him into a zombie-like psycho with a black tongue. The end has Chase locked in the main oven, cooked to death. It's not very inventive and the gingerbread man himself resembles a dwarf-sized Golem that somehow manages to outwit the humans, despite its size. Played mainly straight, this is not one of Full Moon's better features, although it's hardly what you would term standard indie fare.

Gingerdead Man 2: Passion of the Crust
Full Moon/Transition Films 2008; 82 minutes;
Director: Silvia St. Croix ****

Cheatum Studios, specializing in low-budget horror movies, is in crisis: Their two back-to-back productions (one horror, the other science fiction) are plagued by staff differences and a homicidal gingerbread man is carving up key members of the crew.

Insanity rules in producer Charles Band's riotous, sharply scripted sequel to *The Gingerdead Man*, a zany pisstake stuffed to the rafters with witty one-liners, movie source references, in-jokes, bad taste scenes, self-mockery—you name it, Band (he surely must have been at the

Hideous!

Full Moon Features 1997; 82 minutes;
Director: Charles Band *****

Sewage workmen fish out of the sludge a deformed fetus which becomes the object of an all-out war between two fanatical collectors of human abnormalities, both of who wish to covet the specimen at a huge financial cost.

One of Band's more quality "insane puppets" offerings: An amusing script, bravura performances from larger-than-life characters and a quartet of cute but deadly baby monsters all add up to a frothy mix of camp shenanigans and horror, as only Band can achieve. Tracie May (head of International Medical Specimens) sells a four-eyed, twin-mouthed mutant to Mel Johnson, Jr. for $650,000. On his way home, Johnson is waylaid by a half-naked girl wearing a gorilla mask (Jacqueline Lovell) who pinches the fetus and takes it to her master, avid collector and "gourmet of the unusual" Michael Citriniti. May, dumb blonde secretary Rhonda Griffin, detective Jerry O'Donnell and Johnson then descend on Citriniti's castle to retrieve their prize. Unknown to them, the mutant has revived three others and the malformed foursome set about killing their captors before escaping from the castle. Agreed, this *is* comic book stuff but wondrously entertaining all the same: Griffin as the broad without a brain has some terrific lines ("I don't wanna go to jail. There's lesbians in there.") and so does

director's helm) has chucked it in somewhere. Getting off to a flying start with an artful '50s pastiche-style credits sequence, the gingerbread man, his gruff vocabulary littered with obscenities and armed to the teeth with all manner of weapons, sneaks around the (Full Moon?) sets, plunging knives into backs, decapitating with a cleaver, shoving a hair-dryer up an anus and using a chainsaw to slice off the chief puppeteer's hand. In a subplot of sorts, Kelsey Sanders pushes disabled Joseph Porter around the two movie sets, unaware that he isn't disabled—the guy is an out-of-work actor fired by the studio and wants revenge for his perceived mistreatment. In addition to the blood-spattered cookie monster, busty Michelle Bauer is on hand to stimulate certain senses, starring against type as a virgin sacrifice and, joy of joys, the Tiny Terrors put in an appearance, six devilish dolls in the true Band tradition: Haunted Dildo, Hemorrhoid and Shit For Brains, among them. After 80 minutes of helter-skelter absurdity, mass hysteria and bloody gore, Porter dies on the spaceship set, gasping "Rosebud!" (now where did that originate from?) and the serial killer biscuit is crucified by the Tiny Terrors. If there is one gripe about the movie, it has to be that noisy soundtrack which doesn't let up for a single second, but don't let that put you off; *Gingerdead Man 2* is a superior follow-up that will have you grinning from ear to ear if you're in the mood for such tongue-in-cheek unbridled nonsense.

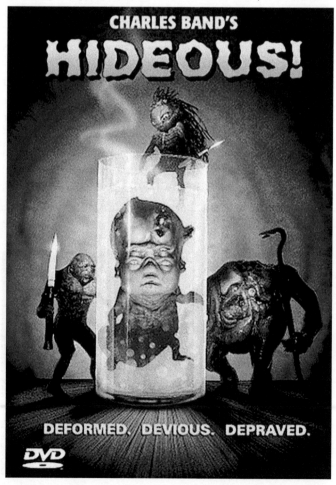

Citriniti ("I want my babies back!"); the sight of one of the mini-monsters sucking Griffin's right nipple has to be seen to be believed; the mutants are endearing in a sick kind of way; and how Johnson and Citriniti manage to keep straight faces in this sub-Gothic setup is a miracle. Despite nearly everybody tumbling into a tank of acid, O'Donnell and Lovell drive off in the end with a couple of the little devils in the car's trunk. Cheesy but great fun.

Huntress: Spirit of the Night
Castel Film Romania/Full Moon 1995; 86 minutes;
Director: Mark S. Manos ***
Attending her father's funeral in Brecon, North Wales, a young woman comes under the curse of lycanthropy.

Latin erotic cinema meets Edgar Allan Poe in a sexploitation picture that has little to do with werewolves but more to do with women pleasuring themselves. The lightweight plot features flame-haired Jenna Bodnar inheriting her father's grand mansion—unfortunately, friend Blair Volk and her lover (David Starzyk) are desperate to own the swanky place and resort to devious methods (including sexual manipulation) to procure it. Throw in a family friend (Ty Cooper) who warns Bodnar about an ancient prophecy concerning a "beast," a photographer who lives in a cave and local villagers prowling the woods with torches, looking

for something that has been on a killing spree, and what you appear to have is an extremely rum take on Val Lewton's *The Cat People*. Bodnar develops animalistic tendencies after a young girl found naked and cowering in her wine cellar transmits a ball of spiritual light which enters Bodnar's body. The open-ended coda has the heiress running through dark woods, apparently in the middle of a "change," but the only transformation on show is Bodnar's eyeballs turning a glowing black. A near-the-knuckle threesome sex frolic on a piano between the two female leads and Starzyk (lucky man!) and an even more salacious masturbation episode uses up a good 15 minutes of the film's short running time, leaving you with a rather arty-farty excuse for a werewolf movie (if that was the intention). One major gripe (for British viewers): The Romanian locations are a totally unrealistic substitute for Brecon in Wales, as are those atrocious attempts at a Welsh accent—and you *never* hear Irish folk music being played in Welsh pubs!

Lurking Fear
Full Moon Entertainment 1994; 76 minutes;
Director: C. Courtney Joyner **
A man sets off for the town of Leffert's Corners to unearth a fortune in cash that is buried on a corpse, unaware that the town has long been plagued by demonic ghouls.

Based on an H.P. Lovecraft story, *Lurking Fear* has a neat opening sequence: Two women are trying to protect a baby from a long-taloned ghoul hiding behind a grill; the baby is saved, but one of the girls is dragged to her doom. After that promising start, the movie quickly goes downhill—Blake Bailey travels to Leffert's Corners to claim his inheritance, a corpse stuffed with dollar notes, meets gangster Jon Finch who is also after the money, and finds himself in a church where priest Paul Mantee is trying to rid the town of the underground-dwelling demons. Most of the non-action takes place inside the church, the cast standing around doing very little, punctuated by swift bursts of creature mayhem as the ghouls reach through the windows in search of their prey.

Jeffrey Combs' intoxicated doctor is mildly amusing, a fiery finale rounds it all off, but there are several gaping plot holes (particularly concerning the two women in the first reel—and what became of the baby?) and this, together with some jumbled editing, may well leave you wondering what the hell is going on. A muddle-headed horror movie lacking fright appeal.

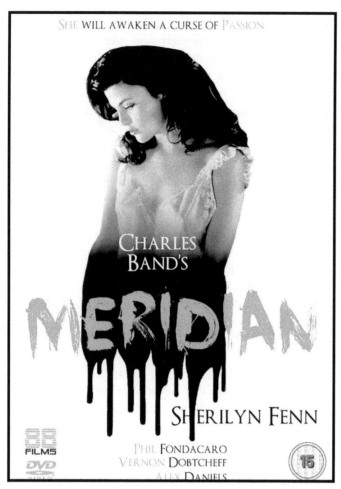

Meridian aka **Phantoms**
Full Moon Features 1990; 85 minutes;
Director: Charles Band ***

Two girls on holiday in Italy become involved in a 15th-century curse centered on twin brothers, one good, the other evil.

Charles Band temporarily deserted his favorite "killer puppets" movies and came up with this soft-porn variation on *Beauty and the Beast*. Busty Sherilyn Fenn invites friend Charlie Spradling over to her castle for the weekend; the two attend a sideshow, invite the troupe back to dinner and are drugged and raped by twin brothers (Malcolm Jamieson in both roles). The rape scenes are filmed for maximum impact, mainly to exploit Fenn's delectable curves, and go on for around 10 minutes; however, there *is* a story. The good twin changes into a hairy monster at intervals, the penance he must pay for seducing the lady of the castle centuries ago, who subsequently died at the hands of his brother; he can only be freed of the curse by the woman he loves killing him. The bad twin, an illusionist, is against this, wanting immortality. In true fairy tale fashion, the baddie is done away with and the beast becomes a complete man again, leaving him and Fenn to walk together hand in hand to a magical world between the jaws of a giant statue. How this rather twee fantasy earned an "18" certificate in England is a mystery, although the groaning nude sex sequences leave very little to the imagination. All the same, a novel take on the old theme of beast loving a beauty.

The Pit and the Pendulum
Full Moon Entertainment 1991; 97 minutes;
Director: Stuart Gordon ****

1492: A fearsome Spanish Inquisitor lusts after a young woman he has imprisoned for heresy.

Featuring a best-ever performance from Lance Henriksen as the sado-masochistic torturer (looking uncannily like Klaus Kinski in *Nosferatu the Vampyre*), Full Moon's interpretation of the Edgar Allan Poe story is nowhere near the standard of Roger Corman's 1961 classic (but then, what other version is); nevertheless, it remains one of this company's finest, most colorful, pictures. Henriksen is in unbelievable, eye-rolling form, bald and cloaked, at odds with his religious beliefs when he hauls in Rona De Ricci for interrogation and sets his sights on her voluptuous naked body (and *what* a body). Husband Jonathan Fuller languishes in a cell while the Inquisitor does a trade-off—sex with De Ricci on condition he releases Fuller. Trouble is, the torturer is impotent, needing regular lashings of the whip to gain sexual gratification. You get a witch eating gunpowder and exploding at the stake, a desiccated corpse strung up and whipped, then ground into dust and placed

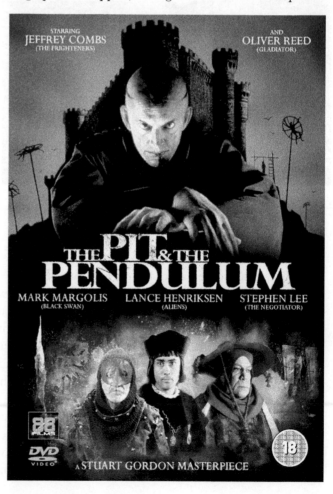

in an hourglass and of course the infamous swinging pendulum finale in which Henriksen meets his doom, falling into a pit full of spikes. Granted, some of the swordfight bouts are straight out of a Saturday night pantomime and Gordon infuses one or two scenes with an unwelcome comic element, but overall, the movie harks back in many ways to the period horror flicks of the 1960s. Oh yes—none other than Oliver Reed makes a guest appearance as a cardinal sent by the Pope to put a halt to the Inquisition's diabolical methods. For his pains, Henriksen, in true Poe style, bricks him up behind a wall.

Puppet Master
Full Moon 1989; 85 minutes;
Director: David Schmoeller ****

Four psychics meet at the abandoned Bodega Bay Hotel where, in 1939, puppeteer/alchemist André Toulon kept hidden the secret of imbuing life to his puppets by blowing his brains out, his demonic toys packed away in a closet behind a wall panel.

The first of executive producer Charles Band's horror fantasies surrounding a posse of murderous puppets is violent stuff (and contains a raunchy sex scene), notwithstanding the diminutive size of the movie's protagonists (British DVDs come with an "18" rating): Tunneler, Pinhead, Leech Woman, Blade and Jester. Opening in 1939 with the death of Toulon (William Hickey), we move to the present day: Paul Le Mat, Irene Miracle, Matt Roe and Kathryn O'Reilly converge on the hotel, each possessing a specific psychic power, where they find owner Jimmie F. Scraggs in a coffin, not-so-grieving wife Robin Frates by his side. Unknown to them, corpse-faced Scraggs, an evil magician, isn't really dead; he's lured the four there to finish them off, seeing them as rivals in gaining access to Toulon's secrets of life, obtained from the Egyptians. Scuttling around the hotel corridors to the sounds of Richard Band's carnival-based score, Tunneler, Pinhead, Blade and Leech Woman, under the guidance of Jester, carry out their grisly work, drilling into flesh, slicing throats, bashing heads with a poker and vomiting giant black leeches, Le Mat the sole survivor, staggering from the building half-alive. Scraggs meets a particularly nasty end, his fingers cut off, spouting green blood, then tortured by the tiny devils in an elevator. It's Frates who appears to have discovered Toulon's secret, Miracle's stuffed pooch suddenly coming alive in her arms as she walks back into the hotel. Full Moon's *Puppet Master* features are unique in so much that the unholy puppets themselves possess a deadly charm, endearing but vicious, manipulated by the special effects department to take full advantage of each one's lethal abilities. A minor hit when first released, the quirkily different *Puppet Master* gave birth to nine sequels (and another in the making) and on this showing, it's not too difficult to understand why.

Puppet Master: Axis of Evil
Full Moon Features 2010; 83 minutes;
Director: David DeCoteau **

1939: The Nazis have teamed up with a Japanese sect, their aim to steal the secrets behind André Toulon's animated puppets and also to destroy a military facility, thus thwarting America's war effort.

Charles Band's murderous marionettes—Ninja, Blade, Pinhead and Tunneler—feature in a distinctly empty looking addition to the *Puppet Master* series; there's little in the way of puppet action, the gore is kept to a minimum and the movie lacks Full Moon's customary flair. Levi Fiehler plays a young guy entrusted with Toulon's puppets after the old man, threatened by the Germans, shoots himself. When two Nazis murder Fiehler's mother and brother and abduct girlfriend Jenna Gallaher, he injects each doll with a green fluid and tracks the killers to Ada Chao's hideout, a Japanese opera house in Chinatown. Unleashing the little devils, Chao, her acolytes and the Nazis are done in one at a time before they can make plans to bomb America, leaving Fiehler to rescue Gallaher from their clutches. Band's distinctive devil-doll pictures are always a joy to watch solely because he's the only producer/di-

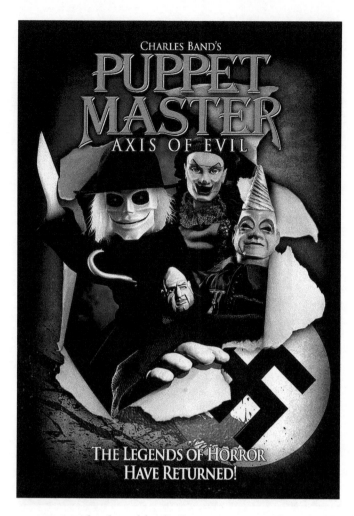

rector around to base his plotlines on puppets blessed with cunning and malevolence. This latest excursion, however, seems hurried and poorly conceived, the puppets not their usual fluid self (apart from Blade), although the muted color photography is a bonus.

Puppet Master: The Legacy
Shadow Ent./Shadow Films 2003; 78 minutes;
Director: Charles Band (as Robert Talbot) **

A rogue agent holds André Toulon's adopted son prisoner in his workshop, determined to terminate the puppets' diabolical lives, thus ending their suffering as tormented souls trapped inside wooden bodies.

In what virtually amounts to a "Best of *Puppet Master*" compendium, Kate Orsini, after reading André Toulon's journal but gaining no information about his secrets, bursts into Jacob Witkin's workshop, intent on discovering the ancient methods of imbuing puppets with eternal animation handed down by Toulon. Cue for almost 50 minutes of footage from previous *Puppet Master* outings to pad out the narrative, most notably *Puppet Master 3: Toulon's Revenge*, taking place in Nazi Germany, and *Puppet Master: Axis of Evil*, the aim to relate the life of Toulon and his various adventures to Orsini (and the viewer). It's a cheapskate method of introducing newcomers to the wild and wacky world of Toulon and his deadly dangerous puppets, even if very little makes sense; chronological order wasn't the series' strong point, confusion the norm. Orsini is shot dead at the climax, but not before revealing that her intention was to release the tortured souls trapped inside the puppets' wooden bodies ("I wanna know what makes them die—for good!") by reversing Toulon's secret of everlasting life. In revenge, Blade, Pinhead and company make Witkin pay for doing away with their possible benefactor, the film ending abruptly.

Puppet Master 4 aka
Puppet Master 4: The Demon
Full Moon Entertainment 1993; 79 minutes;
Director: Jeff Burr ****

In revenge for André Toulon stealing his secret formula on reanimation, Egyptian God Sutekh summons his minions, the Totems, to enter the upper world and kill a young scientist who is in possession of the magic liquid.

More puppet-filled frolics from Charles Band and his team, this episode containing a lot more inventive action than some others in the series. Gordon Currie unlocks Toulon's trunk, dumped in a storage room, and discovers the man's journals, an Ouija board, two bottles of green liquid and four dolls—Tunneler, Jester, Pinhead and

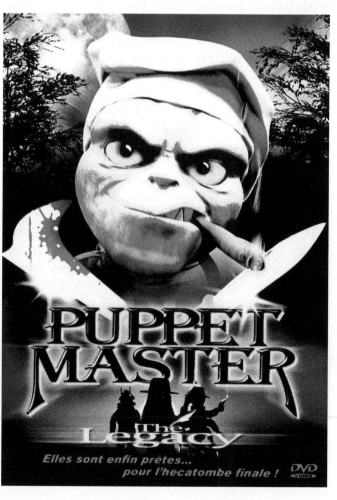

When bad puppets turn good

PUPPET MASTER 4

Six-Shooter; Blade is already there, lurking in the background. When Currie's Gothic mansion is invaded by the *Gremlin*-type Totems, the scientist injects all five dolls with Toulon's elixir and the scene is set for a battle between the living puppets and Sutekh's scaly assassins. Currie and pal Ash Adams come off second-best in the acting stakes to girlfriends Chandra West and Teresa Hill—Currie is a bit on the wet side, while Adams is too much in love with himself (thankfully, he's bumped off midway through the movie). Guy Rolfe puts in a fleeting appearance as Toulon, his spirit causing a new creation, Decapitron, to vanquish the Totems with bolts of electricity, leaving Currie to take on the mantle of the new puppet master. Skeletal Sutekh's bone-strewn underworld kingdom is imaginatively realized in the opening credits and the puppet effects (stop-motion and mechanized) are endearingly cute. If you've never experienced one of Full Moon's puppet features, you're probably wondering what on earth this is all about; for devotees of the series, *Puppet Master 4* is fast-paced with colorful production values.

Retro Puppet Master
Full Moon Pictures 1999; 83 minutes;
Director: David DeCoteau ****
1944: An elderly puppet master, holed up in a deserted inn four miles from the Swiss border with his creations in a trunk, reflects on the origins of his animated puppets.

Those origins date back to 1892 when three Egyptian High Priests are reactivated, their task to hunt down a sorcerer (Jack Donner) who has stolen a scroll containing God's Secrets of Life. In Paris, 1902, the young puppet master Toulon (Greg Sestero), working at the Theatre Magique, obtains the scroll after the sorcerer is killed and so begins the saga of the animated dolls—Blade, Cyclops, Pinhead, Six-Shooter, Ninja and Dr. Death feature in this telling of the story. Brigitta Dau plays the love interest, Guy Rolfe the older André Toulon. Needless to say, the three mummy-assassins are polished off by Blade and company by the end credits; Rolfe finishes relating his story and that's it, the climax a whimper instead of a bang. Cutting down on the gleeful violence that hallmarks the other entrants in Full Moon's *Puppet Master* franchise (Viorel Sergvici's warm color photography is a plus) and slightly hampered by atrocious, hammy acting from the three assassins, those ingenious dolls themselves are the real stars of this flick, as they are in most of producer Charles Band's other "killer puppets" productions. Given this, fans will not be all that disappointed in *Retro Puppet Master*, the seventh chapter, the movie counting as one of David DeCoteau's better directorial achievements.

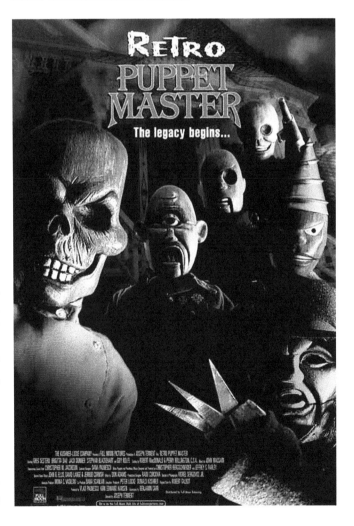

RETRO PUPPET MASTER
The legacy begins...

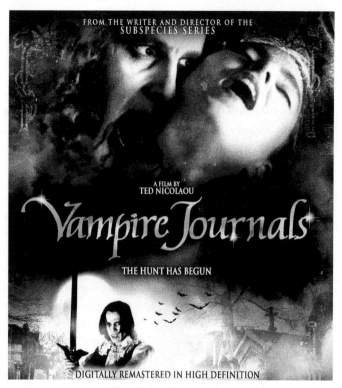

Vampire Journals

Castel Film Romania/Full Moon 1997; 82 minutes;
Director: Ted Nicolaou *****

A part vampire/part human is set on slaying a master vampire who murdered his one and only true love.

Sumptuous, elegant, moodily Gothic, beautifully shot, acted with conviction and intelligently directed—words of praise not readily associated with indie vampire features, yet *Vampire Journals* is all of these and more, as good as any continental horror film of the 1960s and, dare I say it, even a Hammer feature from the same decade. David Gunn plays a vampire with a mortal soul who tracks down Jonathon Morris and his followers to an ornate mansion known as Club Muse; Gunn is resolved to ending the vampire's reign for causing the death of his partner in an act of vampiric lust. Morris has abducted elfin concert pianist Kirsten Cerre—he's totally infatuated with the girl and wants to initiate her into his unholy clan. Jealously rears its ugly head in the delectable shape of headstrong vampiress Ilinca Goia while acolyte Starr Andreeff, who ensures the vampires' safety during daylight hours, is herself at loggerheads with Morris over his latest infatuation. Making splendid use of the opulent Romanian locations and filmed mostly at night, Nicolaou serves up a bewitching brew that adds to the long history of the undead on celluloid, with all the expected bloodsucking set pieces expertly rendered to full effect. Even the ending is bravely downbeat, both Gunn and Cerre cursed to centuries of living in the dark after Morris and Goia have been defeated. Similar in some ways to *Interview with the Vampire* (but minus the A-listers), *Vampire Journals* is solidly crafted fare which doesn't disappoint, a minor gem of low-budget horror cinema.

The Werewolf Reborn!

Castel Film Romania/Full Moon 1998; 62 minutes;
Director: Jeff Burr ***

A young woman travels to an Eastern European country to see her uncle who is a werewolf.

The second of Full Moon's *Filmonsters!* series is watered-down werewolf fodder for the *Harry Potter/Twilight* generation; PG-rated, handsomely photographed but way too short, a companion piece to Full Moon's *Frankenstein Reborn!* issued the same year. The standard lycanthrope plot, harking all the way back to Universal's *The Wolf Man* (1941), is this: Winsome Ashley Tesoro alights at a railway station but nobody will take her to her uncle's (Robin Atkin Downes) overgrown Gothic mansion; two Gypsies give her a guarded warning about the place; Downes locks her in a room overnight as the full moon is about to rise; a Gypsy grandma states that Downes inherited the curse from her brother; police inspector Len Lesser is skeptical and shuts Downes in a cell; Downes does an Oliver Reed, breaks out, and is shot with a silver bullet by his niece, who then goes home. It's cheap and cheerful, boasting atmospheric lighting in some scenes, but really comes down to a potted version of the old legend, a kind of textbook "How to Make a Werewolf Movie in Six Easy Stages" lesson in filmmaking. You even get the obligatory "villagers with torches" sequence! Offbeat to say the least, but not all that scary.

UNDER TEN MILLION? ANYTHING'S POSSIBLE!

The Sandler/ Emenegger Productons

The production team behind Gold Key Entertainment, UFO conspiracy buffs Allan Sandler and Robert Emenegger, were the men responsible for 10 low-grade, quirky (but entertaining) science fiction movies made in 1980/1981 on a shoestring budget, each film knocked out in two weeks utilizing a former Bank of America building in Los Angeles as a makeshift studio, all exteriors shot in the surrounding LA hills. Amateurish acting (even from well-known stars), engaging outer space electronic/synthesized scores (composed by Emenegger himself), washed-out fuzzy color, wobbly interstellar effects, plastic-looking spacecraft, *Dr. Who*-type aliens, hammy scripts, unusually involved storylines—these were the traits that characterized Sandler and Emenegger's uniquely weird output. In their own cheapskate fashion, these oddball titles, belonging to a completely different kind of sci-fi celluloid universe than anything else out there, hark back to the '50s and '60s in looks, feel and execution, when plot took precedent over special effects. They're worth seeking out for their sheer rarity value alone—a few are available on VHS (or were) but only four have been officially released on DVD by VCI Entertainment, in 2007: *The Killings at Outpost Zeta*, *The Perfect Woman* and a double bill of *Time Warp* and *Warp Speed*. Be prepared to be entertained on a very low-brow, wholly idiosyncratic level, the unique likes of which you'll never experience elsewhere!

Robert Emenegger

Beyond the Universe
Sandler/Emenegger Prods. 1981; 90 minutes;
Director: Robert Emenegger ***

In the year 2081, Earth's oxygen is depleted following a devastating atomic war which has caused widespread catastrophes; a scientist has the idea of communicating with the universe's "Ultimate Being" in order to save mankind, but his enemies have other ideas.

Extraordinary ideas abound in Emenegger's jolly little sci-fi jaunt: Earth is on the verge of extinction and the World Emergency Council has rejected David Ladd's proposal (The Miracle Project) that they try to contact the cosmic intelligence that controls the universe for help by projecting a powerful thought transmission into the far reaches of space. The Council's agenda is to ban all births, exterminate all animals and to take care of the sick and dying (who are dosed up on dormant capsules to keep them asleep) by shunting them off to an asteroid and then jettisoning them into space, thus freeing up Earth's fast-vanishing oxygen supplies. Ladd's lab is on board the spacecraft *Oracle* and includes girlfriend Jacqueline Ray plus ex-*High Chaparral* star Henry Darrow. When his mentor (a heavily bearded Christopher Cary, looking like a cross between Moses and an Olympian god) is abducted by John Dewey-Carter and his goons and taken to an asteroid for termination, Ladd and company come to the rescue. Using Cary's futuristic ray machine, they project a signal into space; Earth dies, a Black Hole is formed and the planet, now cleansed, is reborn, a new world to populate for future generations. The budget is obviously rock-bottom but there's a lot going on here that in bigger and more financially able hands might have achieved something special—as it stands, *Beyond the Universe* is obscure enough for diehards of the unusual to seek it out and revel in its plastic-looking tackiness. And see if you can spot Steven Spielberg's sister Anne on the production credits.

Captive aka **Prisoners of Styrolia**

Sandler/Emenegger Prods. 1980; 90 minutes;
Directors: Allan Sandler and Robert Emenegger ****

In the distant future, Earth is at war with the planet Styrolia over control of the precious Dirathium crystals; during a space skirmish, two Styrolians are forced to land their ship on Earth and take cover in a farmhouse, holding the occupants captive.

The most violent of all the Sandler/Emenegger productions, thanks mainly to burly Cameron Mitchell's performance as a brutal alien, bashing and half-strangling Dan Sturkie's family into submission—in fact, the UK video release was certified "18." Fortunately, nicer alien David Ladd (conceived in a test-tube on his home planet) is on hand to curb his partner's callous tendencies. A fast-moving little sci-fi movie with reasonable effects (the Styrolian fighters resemble yellow/pink stealth bombers), a philosophical script highlighting the social differences between Earth and Styrolia, a doom-laden, sparsely utilized electronic score and a bullying, mean turn from ex-Western heavy Mitchell as the alien who prefers to speak with his fists. The ending is downbeat as well—Ladd falls for Lori

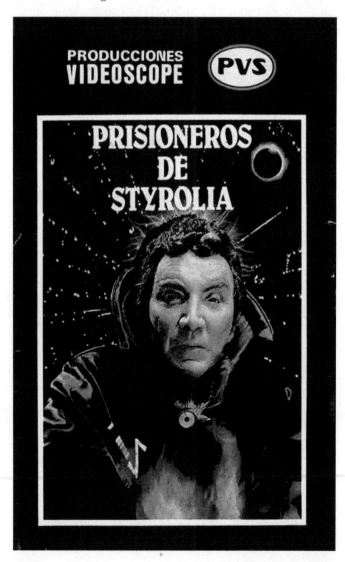

Saunders, realizing that he can experience both love and family life as a concept, but decides to go it alone as agents are on his trail, leaving Saunders in tears. Never released on DVD (the VHS version disappeared years ago), *Captive*, if you can track it down, won't disappoint; like the title, it captivates.

Escape from DS-3

Sandler/Emenegger Prods. 1981; 90 minutes;
Directors: Allan Sandler and Robert Emenegger *****

Year 2045: Falsely accused of both treason and sabotage, an agent is sent to space detention satellite three which orbits the Earth for life imprisonment but is soon making escape plans.

Yes, the special effects may date back to sci-fi's Dark Ages (*DS-3* itself resembles a giant microphone suspended in an inky blackness) but there's a lot of enjoyment to be had in sitting through the best of Sandler and Emenegger's dual efforts—the script is believable, Jackson Bostwick handles the "wronged agent" role competently, a measure of suspense is generated in the mechanics of the escape attempt and Robert *The Thing from Another World* Cornthwaite puts in a guest appearance. As for those effects, think *Dr. Who* and British TV's 1961 *Pathfinders in Space* series, not the latest million-dollar blockbuster showing down the road. Bostwick, Bubba Smith and two other prisoners hatch a plan to board a space freighter due to dock in two weeks, overwhelm the crew and fly the ship not to Earth but to Altair 6, an outlaw planetoid. How they go about their task without being detected by the sadistic guards makes up the bulk of the 90-minute running time; in between, we have sex-droids named Pen-Pals, built to satisfy the prisoners' lust, prescription drugs on offer and an execution, expedited by ejecting the convict into space through an airlock. Bostwick and accomplices eventually make it, the final shot showing their ship heading towards a blue planet and refuge as a signal from Earth declares that the agent is innocent after all. A nifty little space opera which shows just what can be attained on the meanest of budgets.

The Killings at Outpost Zeta

Sandler/Emenegger Prods. 1980; 92 minutes;
Directors: Allan Sandler and Robert Emenegger **

Starfleet sends a mission to the volcanic planet of Zeta to find out why 12 astronauts have died there in the space of three months.

They don't come much cornier than this. Mixing elements of *Star Trek*, *Dr. Who* and *Space: 1999*, *The Killings at Outpost Zeta* is cardboard-ness personified. The original *Pathfinder* team on Planet Zeta has been wiped out by an

alien species they were cultivating by feeding it human blood. When Gordon Devol (also Gordon De Vol) and company arrive on the barren planet in their gimcrack spaceship, two volcanic monsters begin to terrorize the astronauts. The unprovoked attack is the signal for the customary "let's get the hell off this planet" routine, the squad, donning motorcycle crash helmets and moon boots, arming themselves with red plastic tubes and firing laser beams at the creatures. And the aliens themselves? Vaguely seen gray rocky forms that move slowly and growl. Devol and Jacqueline Ray manage to take off in the end after destroying one adult monster by pushing it into a volcanic vent; the other, plus a dozen eggs, is blasted with oxygen, a gas poisonous to the aliens' biological systems. Very, very cheap and not all that cheerful summarizes this bargain-basement space adventure, but somehow along the line, it manages to be strangely addictive. The picture's one saving grace is Emenegger's discordant (but effective) electronic soundtrack, curious indeed given the shortage of production values on show here. But then, it worked in *Forbidden Planet*, didn't it!

Laboratory

Sandler/Emenegger Prods. 1983; 90 minutes;
Directors: Allan Sandler and Robert Emenegger ***

Aliens abduct three men and three women, beaming them into an abandoned desert research facility in order to experiment on their mental state.

A weird little movie indeed which, if you are able to ignore the overall economical style, grows on you ever so gradually. An ominous electronic score pulses away in the background as Martin Cove, Ken Washington, Camille Mitchell (actor Cameron Mitchell's daughter) and three

others are enveloped in a ball of red light while they are going about their daily tasks, waking up to find themselves imprisoned in a derelict laboratory complex. A group of aliens (dressed in glittery suits and talking like Daleks) probe their bodies and minds, basically to see what makes humans tick. Washington and Cove attempt to escape by blowing the place up but Mitchell finally manages to communicate with her captors via a primitive computer-type machine, determining that they have friendly intentions. All six are beamed

back to their respective homes in the end, unharmed with memories erased, and the aliens fly off in their glowing spaceship. There's a lot of strolling around from room to room by the two principal male leads and 50 minutes in, that doleful music suddenly changes to the sort of electronic beats that Kraftwerk perfected during the 1970s, adding to the overall quirkiness. Very easy to dismiss out-of-hand, *Laboratory* will be enjoyable in a totally left-field way to fans thirsting for the rare and unusual.

Lifepod

Sandler/Emenegger Prods. 1981; 90 minutes;
Director: Bruce Bryant ***

A highly advanced computer that controls a luxury interplanetary space vessel tells all personnel to abandon ship in the vicinity of Jupiter as it has its own secret agenda.

A classic example of one of the Sandler/Emenegger unique brand of sci-fi features: Dodgy acting, muted color, shaky model work, passable script and that ever-present electronic music bleeping and popping away in the background. Ordered to leave the *Arcturus* in lifepod LPA3 by the HAL-type Cerebral computer because of a fictitious disaster, Joe Penny, Kristine DeBell, Carl Lumbly, San-

dy Kenyon and Jordan Michaels head towards one of Jupiter's moons for safety, but the giant vessel then decides to pursue them. Why? It's after designer/owner Kenyon who originally fused DNA with the computer in order for *Arcturus* to be the first starship to explore the universe; he then ran out of funds and converted the craft into a luxury space liner instead. The Cerebral wants to explore the stars and is annoyed that Kenyon prevented it from doing so. After a great deal of talk and argument, Kenyon dies after attempting a mind-meld with the computer, the *Arcturus* rectifies a life-threatening fault on the LPA3 and steers a course for interstellar space with the captain on board (Christopher Cary), Penny canoodles with ex-beauty queen DeBell and the pod makes for the moon of Hades. *Lifepod* is harmless fun in a '60s second-feature kind of way and will probably make a welcome change (for some buffs, anyway) to all those noisy million-dollar CGI effects seen at your local multiplex. Like the robots that inhabit the ship (the "mechanicals"), it's all rather cute.

The Perfect Woman
Sandler Inst. Films/Emenegger Prods. 1981; 90 minutes;
Directors: Allan Sandler and Robert Emenegger ***

King Kroger from Planet Zuko requires a queen to carry on his dynasty, so sends two emissaries to Earth to

search out the perfect mate, not appreciating the vast differences in social outlook between the two races.

"I enjoy being a bachelor" sighs King Fred Willard, relaxing in his bubble bath and watching Hollywood glamour girls from the 1930s strutting their stuff on old movies, but council leader Marie Windsor has other ideas. If the lazy dolt doesn't produce a legitimate son and heir soon, his dastardly cousin will take control of the royal throne and ruin everyone's ambitions, including General Cameron Mitchell's warlike intentions ('30s crooner Rudy Vallée sits on the council). Therefore, outer space's answer to Abbott and Costello, dunderheads Peter Kastner and Barry Gordon, fly to Earth in their pear-shaped spacecraft on a female-finding mission, befriending Joanne Nail. Intrigued at the offer of queen-ship, she eventually agrees to go back with the two idiots, marries Willard and starts laying down a few Los Angeles-type house rules: No more television, no more pictures of pinups on the walls, proper meals (spaghetti) instead of food pills, a water bed to add spice to their sex life and, most important of all, women allowed to proudly display their pregnancies, not pass the problem on to a "mechanical mother," the custom on Zuko. Willard huffs and puffs and wants the marriage dissolved but eventually gives in; after all, who can resist Nail's shapely legs and body (seen *very* briefly naked behind a shower curtain), *and* she's now pregnant. Unfortunately for clowns Kastner and Gordon, they're back on Earth looking for *another* mate for Nail, unaware that, 28,000 light years away, Zuko's latest queen is making it up American-style with love-struck Willard between the bedsheets. Backed by Robert Emenegger's squiggly electronic synthesized tones, *The Perfect Woman* is a low-budget riot of bad haircuts, over-the-top mugging, men in yellow tights, outlandish *Star Trek*-like costumes, tacky sets, tongue-in-cheek dialogue and a black/white patterned planet resembling a giant bullseye in space (the spacecraft is actually quite good). If you've never experienced a Sandler/Emenegger production before, you will be completely baffled by the whole package and concept and won't have a clue as to what the hell is going on, or why; if you're au fait with the duo's work, you'll know what to expect, extraterrestrial high jinks of the visually primitive kind but quirkily entertaining all the same.

PSI Factor
Sandler/Emenegger Prods. 1980; 93 minutes;
Director: Bryan Trizers **

An astronomer at a NASA base, working on project Deep Probe, is convinced that strange signals received via radio telescopes emanate from aliens intent on invading the Earth.

A long-forgotten cheapo with effects that wouldn't have looked out of place in a 1950s grade Z sci-fi feature the aliens are nothing more than balls of glowing orange

UNDER TEN MILLION? ANYTHING'S POSSIBLE!

THE PSI FACTOR

light emitting odd noises. Peter Mark Richman and Gretchen Corbett play the couple who ascertain that the signals are coming from a planet called Sirus B in the Andromeda galaxy. Stealing confidential files, they attempt to track down a previous employee at the NASA base who was dismissed on the grounds that "he knew too much." Not a great deal happens as the duo cross country, pursued by both agents and a glowing ball of light. The end has Richman, Corbett and Tom Martin in contact with a host of alien globes, trying to communicate with them—it transpires that they are a benign race with a childlike curiosity of our planet. The muffled soundtrack and fuzzy color gives *PSI Factor* the look of a home movie on occasions and only hinders matters, and with dialogue along the lines of "I gotta response from outer space," it's hard to take this feature seriously. A lost rarity that deserves to be ferreted out because of its sheer amateurishness.

Time Warp

Sandler/Emenegger Prods. 1981; 88 minutes;
Directors: Allan Sandler and Robert Emenegger *

An astronaut flies his ship through a time warp in the vicinity of Jupiter and lands on Earth a year after he was supposed to, rendering him invisible to those around him.

Was Adam *Batman* West intoxicated when he starred in this tacky sci-fi comedy? Was the whole crew also under the influence? Resembling an early 1950s B movie, *Time Warp* will amuse the under-eights—anyone older might just as well add the figure "one" to the running time because the movie *seems* like 188 minutes long. Astronaut Chip Johnson and his speaking computer MUD land on Earth in 1986, not 1985. It's all slippery West's fault—he reprogramed the *Solo 1*'s computer so that it deviated course and was swallowed up by a space anomaly, knowing that Johnson would disappear, thus enabling him to get his dirty hands on Gretchen Corbett, Johnson's wife. The tables are turned when the astronaut discovers he can communicate with his pet dog and parrot who in turn relay his messages to Corbett and her son; he inveigles his way on board the

Solo 2, which is heading out to Jupiter with unwilling West as commander, its mission being to discover the whereabouts of *Solo 1*. West is lured off the ship by Corbett's sexual enticements, Johnson takes off, zooms through the time warp and emerges in the correct year, tearful because his faithful computer has imploded. It's not remotely funny, it's badly acted (West looks vacant throughout), it's corny and the cardboard effects could have been conjured up in any kid's bedroom in 1956. Low-budget or not, *Time Warp* is one helluva space turkey, easily the worst of the Sandler/Emenegger productions.

Warp Speed

Sandler/Emenegger Prods. 1981; 92 minutes;
Director: Allan Sandler ***

Space vessel *Atlas*, lost after a mission to Saturn went awry, appears drifting in space with no one left on board; a psychic boards her from a Starfleet recovery ship to find out what became of the crew.

Cheap and cheerful sums up this thoughtful minor space opera: Attractive psychic Camille Mitchell (Cameron Mitchell's daughter; Mitchell, Jr. also has a small role), sensors implanted on her body, enters the derelict ghost hulk and " hears and sees" various uncoordinated events taking place, most involving mutinous David Chandler's confrontations with the ship's ineffective captain, Adam West. Slowly, the pieces of the jigsaw slot together: Following an explosion in the fuel tanks resulting in the loss of one engine, the *Atlas*' mission to Saturn had to be aborted. In order to reach Earth, items were jettisoned to lighten the load and the

crew, each giving way to their troubled psychosis, played cards Russian roulette-style, the loser also jettisoned. Monitored by the rescue ship, Mitchell comes under the evil influence of Chandler, the sole survivor after stabbing Joanne Nail, who won the final card game and was therefore earmarked as the person who would return to Earth, to death; the psychic is murdered by him in the closing hurried seconds. An eerie electronic soundtrack adds to the gloomy atmosphere of a production which comes across more like an extended *Star Trek* episode minus the talents of Kirk, Spock, Bones et al., and even if the *Atlas* bears a passing resemblance to the Jupiter mission vessel in *2001*, that's all it is—a passing resemblance. We're talking '50s-type effects here, not Stanley Kubrick-type effects.

Aliens

Alien Cargo
Wilshire Production 1999; 90 minutes;
Director: Mark Haber ****

Two of the eight crew in hypersleep on board space freighter *SSS17*, transporting cobalt ore from Saturn's moon Titan to Mars, waken after 10 months, not their scheduled 56 days, to find that the ship has been wrecked and the two crew members whose shift they were due to take over have disappeared.

Not only that, but the ship is nowhere near Mars, heading out towards deep space. What could have gone wrong in those intervening months? That forms the backbone of Mark Haber's suspenseful, claustrophobic space drama boasting excellent model effects for a TV production (it was distributed by Paramount Television in America). Jason London and Missy Crider are the lovers investigating the mystery with the aid of computer Shoshone, 98% of their fuel used up. A log kept by astronauts Simon Westway and Warwick Young shows space junk being retrieved, both men's bodies discovered in a horrible condition. When the object retrieved by Young is approached, it emits waves of energy and soon, London and Crider bleed blue blood and are on the verge of killing each other, infected by a bio-agent inside the large lump of metal. Finding that lowering the temperature brings the contagion under control, *SSS17* makes contact with research vessel *Dolphin*, busy tracking a comet. In a series of unexpected events, *Dolphin*'s captain, Elizabeth Alexander, decides to take the six "sleepers" on board against the advice of second-in-command Alan Dale—but not London and Crider. The thing that Young brought back to ship is an old NASA probe that has been corrupted by an unknown species as a warning to "keep away," the agent triggered by human contact The risk of contamination is too great, so *Dolphin* departs with the six sleepers, now awake, leaving London and Crider, still infected, to drift towards the sun with two hours of life support left where they'll burn up and destroy the deadly disease, the *SSS17* bio-coded "DO NOT ENTER." A taut little sci-fi outing with shades of *Alien* without the alien, *Alien Cargo* is a suspenseful sleeper showing just what can be achieved with this kind of material on minimal funding.

Alien Dawn
Halcyon International Pictures/Morphius Films
2012; 86 minutes;
Director: Neil Johnson *****

Martians invade Earth, their huge war machines decimating cities, the aliens terraforming the planet and living off human blood.

Let's begin by giving these indie filmmakers *some* credit, for all those comparing Neil Johnson's *Cloverfield*-inspired $1,850,000 alien invasion outing to Steven Spielberg's $130,000,000 *War of the Worlds*. The effects are, on the whole, commendable, giant machines on tripods evaporating humans with laser beams, a domed Martian city

A.D. 2012

rising above the rubble, massive cylinders falling from the sky, clouds of black poisonous gas released in an attempt to eradicate the invaders, streets littered with corpses, severed limbs and wrecked vehicles—and no skimping; you get to see a lot of what's on offer. One Martian is viewed close-up, a tentacled, clawed monstrosity straight out of the '60s school of sci-fi. The execution is a workable mix of shaky camcorder, semi-documentary and found footage, conveying a real sense of mass destruction and panic, the downside being a poor audio track where dialogue is virtually inaudible in places. Alex Bell, Rachelle Dimaria and Michael Abruscato are the three central characters fighting to survive, the two men arguing most of the time over what course of action to take, Dimaria recording a video diary of events on her cellphone. Combined with sporadic news broadcasts, there's a genuine "end of mankind" ambience as the ragbag trio construct bombs, note strange red weed springing up in the desert and realize that the invaders are feeding off human flesh. The action taking place over a 10-day period, *Alien Dawn* climaxes on a downbeat note, Dimaria joining armed citizens in forming a resistance movement to rid Earth of the Martians after a city has finally been nuked. One point of interest: The sound of the Martian machines firing green rays has been filched from George Pal's classic 1953 production; was permission sought to do this? Amateurish but effective, Johnson's *Alien Dawn* has much in common with Asylum's 2005 *War of*

the Worlds, two worthy examples of low-budget companies giving the big boys a run for their money when it comes to movie adaptations of the H.G. Wells novel.

Alien Encounter
1066 Films 2008; 82 minutes;
Director: Andrew Mackenzie **

Purportedly based on fact, five teenagers become caught up in alien activity in Phoenix Arizona, 1997, when they encounter a mile-wide space vessel while on a camping trip.

No amount of time-lapse photography, scratchy newsreel-type editing and fast forward/rewind trickery can disguise the fact that this poorly conceived *Close Encounters of the Third Kind* effort is a bit of a bore. Ossie Beck, Matt Mercer and three pals go hiking in the desert, unaware that the military is monitoring a huge alien ship in the area. When Beck and Mercer go for a drive and wake up on a beach outside of Los Angeles two days later next to a strange girl, Terin Alba,  having no recollection of what has happened to them, the scene should be set for an intriguing alien abduction story. What we get instead is a jumble of half-visualized ideas that refuse to gel: Beck hands a mysterious glass rod made of an unknown element to a United Nations scientist for analysis; Mercer suffers from visions of being held captive on the ship, with gray-faced aliens hovering over him; a tarty TV reporter is beamed aboard the vessel in a flash of light; and Beck becomes ill with an other-worldly virus after sleeping with Alba. The movie ends abruptly, as though funds for the project had run out, with outtakes showing over the closing credits. Cheap and far from cheerful, *Alien Encounter* has one or two flashes of imagination (the spaceship showing as a circle of separate lights looming over the landscape) but the PG (in Britain) rating speaks volumes—this is sci-fi for undemanding kids.

Alien Hunter
Nu Image 2003; 92 minutes; Director: Ron Krauss ****

Scientists extract an object from deep within the Antarctic ice that is emitting a mysterious signal relating to the alien landings at Roswell, New Mexico in 1947.

The Thing meets *Close Encounters of the Third Kind* meets … well, all kinds of genre sci-fi flicks, no bad thing; filmmakers have to get their inspiration from somewhere, so why not the pick of the crop. Forget the clumsy title—*Alien*

is swallowed up in a vast multicolored vortex that descends from the sky, an alien ship that takes Spader, Eser, Nikolai Binev and Leslie Stefanson off to another world, just as the facility is bombarded by missiles. Another cover-up follows, news from Washington stating that the center was destroyed by its nuclear reactor going into meltdown. Produced on a budget of nearly $7,000,000, *Alien Hunter* is involving, at times suspenseful, fare, the Antarctic research sets suitably claustrophobic, even though fans can detect all manner of plagiarism going on, and Spader is his usual floppy-haired, engaging self.

Alien Terminator
Calibre Films 1995; 80 minutes; Director: Dave Payne *

Five miles beneath the Earth's surface, a mad, coke-snorting scientist has created an alien being from genetically tampered DNA.

Of all the *Alien* rip-offs foisted upon sci-fi buffs since the 1979 release of the Ridley Scott classic, *Alien Terminator* ranks as one of the worst, if not *the* worst. Six stereotypes battle a little-seen flesh-eating creature, attempting to reach the surface via an elevator shaft before the power is cut off. You have the cat scene ("Here, kitty, kitty"), the bursting out of the body scene, the scuttling face-hugger scene, the complex's computer counting down the minutes to destruction scene and the Sigourney Weaver tomboy figure, played by Maria Ford wearing a *very* skimpy top. The monster, when you are afforded a glimpse (and *only* a glimpse), appears to be a man in a baggy Yeti suit with claws, roaring its head off. Never has 80 minutes seemed so long. Lamentable is too mild a word in describing this cheapskate turkey; an Ed Wood film for the 1990s, if ever there was a need for one!

Almost Human
Channel 83 Pictures/Ambrosino/Delmenico 2013; 80 minutes; Director: Joe Begos ***

A man's best friend disappears in a flash of blue light following freakish disturbances over Maine. Two years later, he returns as a murderous alien in human guise, impregnating his victims to form a new species that will conquer the world.

"I'm different now." Words spoken by Josh Ethier to one-time fiancée Vanessa Leigh as he prepares to rape her

Hunter is an intelligently scripted alien movie that holds the attention throughout; there's nothing like a big block of ice containing a vague shape to set the imagination into overdrive, and that's what we have here, languages and signals expert James Spader (a former S.E.T.I. boffin) traveling to the Axxon Resources Study Group Center at the South Pole to decipher what lies inside that block, and what those signals translate into. "Do Not Open" is the alarming message, but too late: The ice melts, revealing a shell-like cocoon composed of a carbon-based alloy; when opened, a being emerges that kills two of the team and scuttles off. Spader tracks it down and communicates with it, by speech and thought waves, but the visitor is shot to death, dissolving into sticky goo. However, that's not the end of the story, the plot shifting into a different gear. Is the base, and those inhabiting it, contaminated? In Washington, Keir Dullea (of *2001: A Space Odyssey* fame) reckons that the alien's signal was a distress call to its companions who crashed at Roswell; their intention was to render mankind extinct by releasing deadly pathogens, so why should this specimen be any different. The Russians are invited, on behalf of the USA, to obliterate the base, even though Spader, ex-girlfriend Janine Eser and a few others are clear of any contamination. However, the center's cornfield withers and dies, so someone must be affected. Disbelieving scientist John Lynch tries to escape but

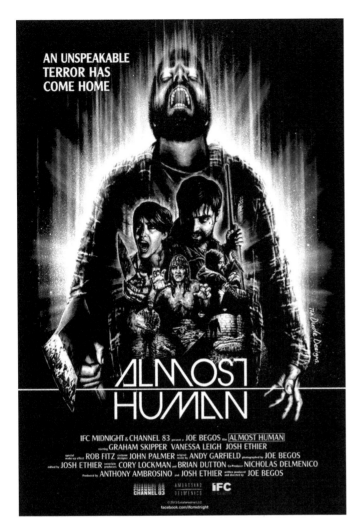

The Dark Lurking

Filmwerx77; 2009; 97 minutes;
Director: Gregory Connors **

In a research facility a mile underground, staff are attacked by flesh-eating mutant alien beings created from ancient DNA.

Following a beautifully constructed opening space sequence, *The Dark Lurking* plunges into a sea of gobbledegook as military personnel combat an army of mutated humans in the style of both *Alien* and *Aliens*, a strange girl tagging along who is not all that she appears to be. Shot mainly in dark corridors, Gregory Connors' gung-ho sci-fi feature is lumbered with a truly dire script and an abundance of flashy editing that renders the spiky, fanged monsters with faces like mashed-up pizzas almost invisible at times. Dirk Foulger plays a doctor who spills the preposterous beans to grunts Bret Kennedy and Ozzie Devrish: During World War II, a fossilized relic called "The Dark Angel" was discovered by troops. The artifact was locked away but scientists implanted its evil DNA into humans, the result being the creatures they are now up against. And one of the humans among them is the original host. Lithesome Tonia Renee is that host, metamorphosing into a monster after leafing through the blood-soaked pages of the Book of Souls. Then the rescue ship they have board-

with a slimy phallus-type tube emerging from his mouth, one of the many sickening scenes on display in Joe Begos' alien splatter-fest (he also produced and wrote the script). Others include heads being shot from bodies, throat-cuttings, an axe in the head and back, necks broken and the gruesome sight of a bloody, decapitated Ethier attempting to shove that pulsating tube down Leigh's protesting throat. Supposedly based on true events, this cheapo effort shot in dingy color delivers the goods from a gore point of view, if not a sci-fi one. After a promising start, butchery takes precedence over plot: Ethier, having been "tampered" with (shown in black-and-white flashes), returns as a killing machine, stunning his prey by emitting a high-pitched hooting noise, corpses emerging from sticky cocoons à la *Invasion of the Body Snatchers*, the audience left wondering exactly who will survive this low-budget bloodbath. Nobody does. Ethier is dispatched, pal Graham Skipper driving off with Leigh who has become infected. Screeching to a halt when Leigh starts going berserk, Skipper flags down a passing motorist; Leigh attacks the pair of them; Skipper reverses over her in his car and, as he smashes the girl's head to pulp with a rock, the police (where did they come from?) gun him down. The end to an alien takeover outing that is short, violent and not all that sweet.

ed blows up, killing both humans and creatures in one go. Mixing sci-fi horror with the Devil and all his works makes for uneasy bedfellows, and this noisy Australian sci-fi actioner doesn't have the expertise to pull it off.

Dark Skies
Alliance Films/Blumhouse Pictures 2013; 97 minutes;
Director: Scott Stewart ****

In the American suburbs, a family, unknown to them, has been targeted by the "Grays," aliens who eventually plan to steal their youngest son.

It makes a change to have an alien movie presented in *Paranormal Activity* fashion with an added pinch of horror, but that is just what Scott Stewart has achieved in his $3,500,000 feature. The pace is sluggish at first, a sign perhaps of the modest budget, picking up after 40 minutes when argumentative parents Josh Hamilton and Keri Russell realize that there may be more than meets the eye to six-year-old son Kadan Rocket's unusual behavior and talks of "Sandman" visiting his room at night. The fridge is raided, ornaments are found stacked in geometric formation, hundreds of birds crash into the house and photographs are stolen; Rocket develops livid bruises on his body, brother Dakota Goyo baffling symbols branded on his abdomen while Hamilton contracts an odd rash behind his right ear, his wife suffering a six-hour blackout.

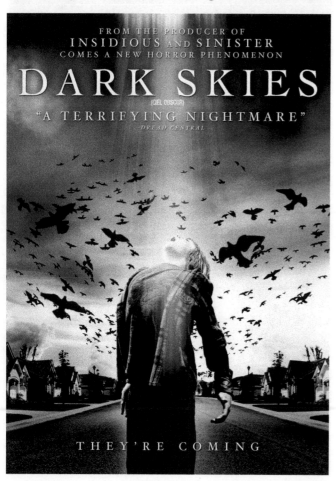

FROM THE PRODUCER OF
INSIDIOUS AND SINISTER
COMES A NEW HORROR PHENOMENON

DARK SKIES
(CIEL OBSCUR)

"A TERRIFYING NIGHTMARE"
DREAD CENTRAL

THEY'RE COMING

CCTV cameras pick up an unearthly figure in Rocket's bedroom, so UFO conspiracy buff J.K. Simmons is consulted, his apartment walls covered in cuttings relating to alien child abduction. "You've been chosen," he tells them. "You are experiencing an encounter. You are not alone in this." "Why have they chosen us?" The answer is that Simmons doesn't know; the Grays, one of three species of alien life (the Insectoids and the Reptilians are the other two) have been among humans for decades, he states, picking families at random to study and living off people's fears before taking a child to where they originate from; and that rash behind Hamilton's ear is an implant which cannot be removed. Simmons suggests fighting the intruders ("Make it difficult so that they move on to someone else."), so a shotgun and guard dog are purchased. The alarming, tension-fueled climax, giving a nod in the direction of *Close Encounters of the Third Kind*, has the spindly beings infiltrating the boarded-up house in force on July 4, Independence Day, and in a cruel twist, it's 13-year-old Goyo who vanishes, not his younger brother; Simmons is seen posting another missing persons report to his wall to join the others. Three months later, as Hamilton and Russell are packing to move house, Russell discovers drawings of alien figures that Goyo drew as an infant, a premonition of things to come; Rocket hears noises from his walkie-talkie, presses "receive" and hears the crackling voice of his brother on the other end, from where no one knows, repeating one word over the static, "Sammy," a chilling conclusion to what could be termed an Alien/Ghost film, and one that delivers in style.

Deep Evil
Regent Ent./Insight Film Studios 2004; 90 minutes;
Director: Pat Williams **

An alien microbe termed PB3, nurtured in an Alaskan facility, breaks out of the lab, threatening all life on Earth, so a crack team is sent in to destroy it.

This particular alien organism is water-based, the liquid morphing into spiders, beetles and, in the closing stages, humanoid creatures, unusual to say the least. The story is told in flashback by survivor Jim Thorburn, interrogated by the military: He-man Lorenzo Lamas, among a squad led by Ona Grauer, enters the underground laboratory and after a great deal of wandering around, the group spots one lab worker erupting in red and orange blisters, infected by the organism. From thereon in, we enter "let's get the hell away before they nuke the place" territory as the team are picked off by the watery spiders/humanoids, Grauer escaping but shot dead to prevent the base's secret from leaking out. And as for Thorburn, we know after 30 minutes has gone by that *he's* not human; he proves it in the end by breaking his cuffs and demanding to be taken to the White House. Nu Image's *Alien Lockdown* (2004) explored this plot setup far more

UNDER TEN MILLION? ANYTHING'S POSSIBLE!

successfully because at least it had a monster for the cast to contend with—here, we are left waiting for an hour before the action hots up, and then the effects are marginal, with over-emphasis on military-speak and gung-ho dramatics plunging the movie into cliché-land. Although diverting at times, *Deep Evil* is only one-star away from being a very boring sci-fi flick.

Earth Alien aka Endangered Species
MBP/Drotcroft Productions 2002; 94 minutes;
Director: Kevin S. Tenney **

Two aliens arrive on Earth: One embarks on a killing spree, targeting health spas and gyms, the other is out to destroy him.

Shades of Nu Image's *Alien vs. Alien* (2007) feature here, as well as *The Terminator*. Saulis Siparis is the baddie, bursting into health clubs, slaughtering the customers by shooting them in the eyes or ears and disappearing with the bodies of the super-fit, each equipped with an implant that acts as a homing beacon. Meanwhile, goodie Arnold *The Mummy* Vosloo (known as the Warden) teams up with cop Eric Roberts to bring the alien's reign of terror to an end. *Earth Alien* is hard-going most of the time, with a succession of vehicle chases, explosions, shoot-outs and little else. Apparently, Vosloo informs Roberts, Earth's wildlife has been studied for aeons, teaching his race a few tricks, and they don't want Siparis upsetting the balance: The killing machine is there to make body armor out of human skins, picking only perfect specimens. Vosloo communicates with his home planet via a teleporter machine straight out of an old episode of *Star Trek*, both aliens use cloaking techniques to remain hidden, there is an attempt at dark humor between Roberts and his fellow officers (John Rhys-Davies is utterly wasted in his role as an unhygienic cop) and there's a surfeit of full-frontal female nudity on display. And yes, in the final few minutes, Siparis peels off his human face to reveal alien features. Oddly unsatisfying, this pedestrian sci-fi effort seems to go on forever—only the world-weary Roberts makes it watchable.

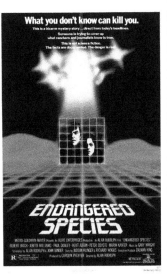

Independence Daysaster
Cinetel Films/Reel One Ent. 2013; 90 minutes;
Director: W.D. Hogan ***

Mankind comes under attack from thousands of alien globes and huge drilling machines that release a toxic gas into the atmosphere which will eventually kill all life on Earth.

Independence Day, July 4: Americans are at play when suddenly, tremors shake buildings; gigantic drills surface from deep underground and create havoc, the sky seething with mechanical razor-toothed globes that appear indestructible to everything thrown at them. President Tom Everett Scott's helicopter is brought down but he survives, reaching a farm where computer hackers Iain Belcher and Grace Sherman help him contact the White House to prevent loose cannon Vice President Garwin Sanford from nuking the aliens' 12-mile-long mother ship, in orbit around the moon. Meanwhile, S.E.T.I scientist Emily Holmes, Scott's son Keenan Tracey, his girlfriend Andrea Brooks and Scott's brother, Ryan Merriman, have disabled one of the projectiles. Teaming up with Scott and his new whiz-kid pals, they hit on a way to eliminate the vast alien vessel when all else has failed (including a mass missile strike), getting one of the globes to carry a device back to the ship where it allows a nuclear warhead to hit its target, blasting the giant spacecraft to bits; the human race is saved. Cinetel's Canadian-produced *Independence Day* mockbuster contains expert effects (budget was $1,800,000) and nicely done sequences of destruction, although W.D. Hogan's frenetic camerawork might induce a feeling akin to seasickness, so intent is he on conveying a sense of hysterical panic. The movie also sags in the middle, the alien machines notable by their absence, but picks up in the latter stages. And, as is the case in a lot of these alien sci-fi actioners, it ain't all over, the final shot showing more silvery globes hurtling towards Earth.

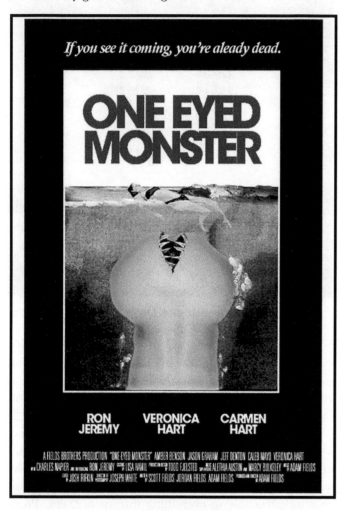

One Eyed Monster
Fields Brothers Prods. 2008; 84 minutes;
Director: Adam Fields ***

A group of hardcore-porn moviemakers heads for a cabin in the woods to shoot their latest epic; the leading man, a well-endowed stud, is impregnated by an alien on a shooting star and one part of his body takes on a life of its own, sexually killing the film crew.

Well, alien life forms have taken over much of man's body in countless other features, so why not his penis. Vulgar and tasteless in the extreme, *One Eyed Monster* works remarkably well as a spoof because the entire 84 minutes is played dead straight, the poker-faced delivery providing a distinct contrast to the mind-boggling sight (most of it

off-camera) of Ron Jeremy's detached (and rather enormous) member bobbing around and performing unmentionable acts on the porn starlets (think *Deep Throat* and you'll get the idea). Also unprintable is 90% of the hilariously lewd dialogue, much of it pointedly aimed at the porn industry, but here's a couple of tasters to whet the appetite: "There's a d—k in Angel's mouth and it's not attached to anyone!" "Circumcise it to oblivion with an axe!" Fields directs with authority, almost as if he's engaged on a more serious piece of work, while Jason Graham (the sensible black guy) seems to be caught up in a schlock remake of John Carpenter's *The Thing* in the closing minutes as both he and Amber Benson escape through frosty tunnels, the thing (well, what else can you call it) chasing after them. Together with an inventive orgasm machine developed by Caleb Mayo (a sex toy *par excellence!*) and Graham and Benson caught in a sperm shower at the end, *One Eyed Monster* is *not* for the prudish, but it *is* very funny if you let your hair down after a couple of drinks.

Plaguers
Nightfall Pictures 2008; 86 minutes;
Director: Brad Sykes **

Spaceship USS *Pandora* answers a distress signal from USS *Diana*, only to be boarded by female space pirates when the vessels dock. Unknown to them, *Pandora* is taking an alien power source harboring unnatural powers (discovered on Thanatos) back to Earth; when the glowing green globe is tampered with, it transforms the crew into ravenous mutants.

Sykes' *Alien*-type rip-off features some impressive space shots; the same cannot be said about the rest of the movie. Both sexy pirates and ship's captain Alexis Zibolis' crew turn into flesh-eating mutations with faces like mangled spaghetti when an alien virus breaks out of the globe and infects the humans. Steve Railsback is immune to the contagion—he's the ship's android and ends up fending off the creatures, some of whom have undergone a complete transformation into an alien being, as Zibolis heads off to Earth in a pod, the *Pandora* blowing up behind her. But hang on, what is that growling, moaning sound emanating from the pod as it enters Earth's atmosphere. Like a 1980s sci-fi production in looks and design (*not* the genre's finest decade), *Plaguers* is hoary old tosh containing one or two moments of excitement to prevent it from drowning in a sea of tedium.

Roswell: The Aliens Attack
Credo Ent. Group/Future Films 1999; 96 minutes;
Director: Brad Turner ***

During the UFO crash-landings at Roswell New Mexico in 1947, a male and female extraterrestrial emerge from two saucers, their mission to detonate a massive bomb housed at the nearby army base that will annihilate Earth by creating a 10-year nuclear winter.

Shades of *Starman* (1985) in Brad Turner's low-key exposé of the alleged military cover-up that took place at Roswell just after the end of World War II; alien Steven Flynn falls for widow Kate Greenhouse while partner Heather Hanson despises the human race, wanting to obliterate our species. Distributed by Paramount (hence the opening snippet from 1953's *The War of the Worlds*), this is one sci-fi movie which can be described as twee. Lonely Greenhouse comes on to reticent Flynn, setting his eyes flashing green as he records everything around him on a disc, her young son Ben Baxter, mad on space comic books, sussing out the stranger's true origins from the start ("Are you a spaceman?"). At the base, chain-smoking officer Brent Stait accuses Flynn and Greenhouse of spying for the Russians, two alien corpses, the "gray ones," are dissected and Hanson, dressed like a fashion model and rather taken with Hollywood's glamour lifestyle (she's read a movie mag) primes the huge bomb, standing in a hangar, for explosion. In a showdown between the two aliens, a reinforcing chain snaps, crushing Hanson under the bomb which Flynn deactivates. "I came to destroy the planet. I changed my mind because of you," Flynn tells besotted Greenhouse, informing her he lives "to the left of Venus, only a million light years away." "I will come back," he promises, Colonel Sean McCann allowing him to leave Earth in his saucer after all evidence of an alien landing has been swept under the carpet. Decades later, he hasn't returned, an elderly Greenhouse and her son peering into the heavens, she mourning her lost love. Jim Makichuk's script steers just this side of over-sentimentality, even touching in places, particularly when Greenhouse takes Flynn to a dance; and the spaceman/young boy relationship has been ex-

plored many times before, notably during the 1950s. A charming, low-budget examination of the never-fully-explained facts behind the infamous Roswell UFO sightings.

The Salena Incident aka Alien Invasion Arizona
Newbold Pictures/Temple Hill Ent. 2007; 87 minutes;
Director: Dustin Rikert *

An alien prison ship crashes in the Arizona Desert near the mining town of Salena, unleashing a pack of bloodthirsty creatures on the local populace.

Plot? UFO crashes; military are decimated in mining tunnels; two hot chicks release hardened criminals from a prison bus; criminals plus chicks plus three prison officers and one marine survivor (Dan Southworth) fight aliens in Salena; the buried alien ship is discovered in the mine; the aliens produce green eggs; their aggressive blood causes humans who come into contact with it to mutate into flesh-eaters; the mine workings are blown up, leaving four humans intact; Salena is bombed by the military; a conspiracy (Roswell-style) is hinted at; and a fleet of alien craft leaves Earth at the end. Execution? Amateurish verging on the diabolical. Kicking off with a badly conceived UFO crash and concluding with a space scene not too far removed from what one views on a games console, this "the aliens have landed" flick is a fiasco from start to finish. Its one cardinal mistake is to leave the audience wondering what the aliens actually look like. In the 1950s and 1960s, you could leave a cinema after catching a monster/alien feature and describe *exactly* what said monster/alien resembled; even low-budget efforts had a fully seen creature as the protagonist. Nowadays (and some big-budget motion pictures are just as guilty of this), you can't. Dustin Rikert presents us with a flurry of shots taking in a fanged mask here, a tentacle there. A brief glimpse of a man in a rubber suit doesn't help, and neither do the distorted monster-perspective shots. Hampered by a plethora of shouty-shouty acting, a jumbled conclusion and a Michael Madsen look-alike in the form of Mafia boss James Luca McBride, *The Salena Incident* is so poorly done that it cannot even be viewed (or classed) as a guilty pleasure.

Sea Ghost aka The Thing Below
Hellfire/Insight Film Studios 2004; 94 minutes;
Director: Jim Wynorski *

A radioactive alien life form enclosed in a meteor that fell to Earth two million years ago is dug up from the ocean floor by an oil rig with calamitous results.

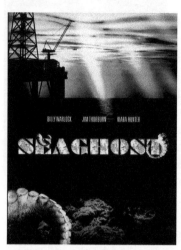

Look, if you must plunder your main ideas from *The Thing from Another World*, *The Thing*, *Alien*, *Deep Rising* and even Fearnort's indie *Parasite*, make sure the final product is worth all the effort; if you don't, you'll end up with a stinker, which the Canadian-produced *Sea Ghost* is, in spades. Kicking off on a ship where a tentacled monster breaks out of a canister before the vessel is blown to pieces, the action then switches to the oil rig *Sea Ghost*, awaiting supplies from Billy Warlock on board the *Sea Star*. Warlock and his crew dock with the rig and find the place under siege from an alien identical to the one seen in the opening ten minutes. Fifty minutes into the movie, everyone is referring to the creature as that "Thing," dialogue from Howard Hawks' much-revered picture is used ("What if it can read our minds?" "It'll be awfully mad when it gets to me.") and Warlock even resembles Dewey Martin from the RKO classic. What's more, this alien can be whatever you want it to be: A sexy stripper one moment, a long-dead grandfather the next, then a gunslinger in a Wild West frontier town (Sergio Leone this isn't!) and finally a two-minute segment showing a covert operation in Iraq. Everything is monitored by two agents in Washington and although the rig is destroyed, that "Thing" isn't, changing from professor (Catherine Lough Hagguist) to agent (Peter Graham-Gaudreau) in the blink of an eye in front of Warlock and his brother. Unacceptable CGI effects (the tentacles look like something out of a Disney cartoon), long periods where nothing happens, mawkish scenes involving Warlock's grandpappy, ideas and dialogue used in a hundred other (and much better) sci-fi features—*Sea Ghost* will test the patience of all those who are addicts of films so awful that virtually no one else watches them. At one point, one of the Washington agents states "This is turning into a circus." How right he is!

Thirst
Cosmic Entertainment 2015; 87 minutes;
Director: Greg Kiefer ***

Five troubled teens and their guides, on a field trip in the wilderness to iron out the kids' behavioral problems, are attacked by a ferocious alien that feeds on bodily fluids.

Shot in Utah in muddy color, the alien's the thing here, a splendid (for the budget) biomechanical mini-Godzilla displaying rows of fangs that has hatched from a large outer space egg, hides in a cave and decimates the cast, leaving only John Redlinger, Clare Niederpruem and Ryan Zimmer the survivors. Zimmer and Niederpruem are two of the five disagreeable youngsters whose parents "don't understand us," having to bond when the fearsome creature homes in on obnoxious dude Cardiff Gerhardt as he's about to "take a dump." Jes Macallan and Karl Makinen's base camp becomes a refuge, static electricity announcing the arrival of the beast, helicopter pilot Mike Law, on a rescue mission, ravaged in his cockpit when the monster clings onto the chopper which crashes into a cliff face, the alien crawling unscathed from the burning wreckage. Eventually, Redlinger's tomboy aunt, Christina Thurmond, becomes the sacrificial lamb, blowing the alien (and herself) to smithereens by driving a bulldozer at it, propelling the creature into a barn stacked full of gas tanks which ignite. Decent alien shenanigans (the victims are sucked dry, turned into human husks) compensate for sloppiness in the dialogue department: Redlinger is either Ross, or Roth or in one instance, Chad; dope addict Bryan Dayley becomes Dick or Wes; and Makinen plays Uncle Berk or Uncle Bert (this is a common fault in many low-budget capers). *Thirst* is straightforward, no frills "alien hunting humans for food" fodder presented with plenty of vigor—and, as stated, that stomping, armor-plated visitor from another world, which you get to see a great deal of for a change, is the real star of the show.

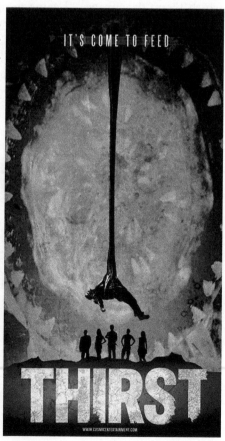

IT'S COME TO FEED

THIRST

WWW.COSMICENTERTAINMENT.COM

UNDER TEN MILLION? ANYTHING'S POSSIBLE!

Disaster

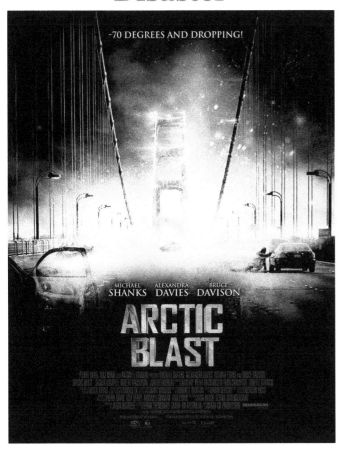

-70 DEGREES AND DROPPING!

MICHAEL SHANKS ALEXANDRA DAVIES BRUCE DAVISON

ARCTIC BLAST

Arctic Blast
FG Film Prods. 2010; 92 minutes;
Director: Brian Trenchard-Smith ****

Following a solar eclipse, sunspot activity tears a massive hole in the mesosphere, creating a vast cloud of ice that freezes everything in its path.

Forget all those scientific inaccuracies (and there are an awful lot of them), sit back and enjoy this Australian disaster fantasy which thunders along nicely with no lulls in the action. A monstrous fog-bank with a temperature of 90 below zero heads towards Hobart, Tasmania, and it's down to weatherman/scientist Michael Shanks (under pressure from boss Bruce Davison) to figure out a way of repairing the gaping hole in the mesosphere, itself 140 degrees below freezing. Two other things Shanks has to work out is how to stop wife Alexandra Davies from divorcing him and how to win over rebellious daughter Indiana Evans. With a human drama of sorts set firmly in place, it's up to the special effects people to work their magic and they do, handsomely; the mighty cloud of ice particles freezes ships, people, planes, buildings and cars as it rolls inexorably onwards. Furthermore, several other clouds appear; Tokyo, London, Rio de Janeiro, Moscow and Sydney crackle under that frigid air mass. After dozens of balloons filled with magnesium fail to close the rifts, Shanks fires off three rockets above the mesosphere, they explode, the gaps seal and Earth returns to normality. One or two human touches and a chilling (in more ways than one) scene showing a woman in a bar awaiting certain death as white vapor seeps under the door make this an above-average indie disaster flick. As I said, ignore the implausible science; even big-budget movies contain them. This *Day After Tomorrow*-type effort is a bit of a chill-thrill all round.

Atomic Twister
TBS Superstation 2002; 91 minutes;
Director: Bill Corcoran *

A nuclear power station stands in the direct path of a trio of tornados and staff must somehow shut down the reactor to avoid a cataclysmic explosion.

A cataclysmic waste of 91 minutes is more apt in a disaster movie that patently fails to deliver a disaster of any description: At least 80 minutes of the running time is given over to Sharon Lawrence's frenzied attempts to prevent water evaporating over the reactor's fuel rods, hampered by three blundering colleagues who don't appear to have a clue what they're up to. Meanwhile, pretty-boy cop Mark-Paul Gosselaar dashes around in a patrol car, dodging flying debris and his jealous ex-girlfriend, while police chief Corbin Bernsen wears a look of total resignation, as well he might with this cock and bull script to work on. Vest-wearing Lawrence, the only one with her head screwed on, prevents the impending nuclear catastrophe, ending up looking like a female Bruce Willis from *Die Hard*. *Carry On Twister* would have been a suitable UK title for this inexpensive bunkum (the *Carry On* comedies were a big hit in

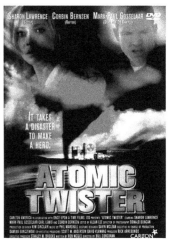

Britain's cinemas during the 1960s)—how on earth did the cast manage to keep straight faces making it?

Dark Storm
Cinetel Films/Insight Film Studios 2006; 89 minutes;
Director: Jason Bourque **

Scientists invent a machine that can store dark matter, but one of them decides to use this knowledge to destroy the world.

If you can manage to tear yourself away from the bizarre sight of chubby Stephen Baldwin's floppy haircut, you might be able to obtain a smidgen of satisfaction from Cinetel's scientific disaster outing, blessed (thankfully) with polished indie effects as befits this particular company's

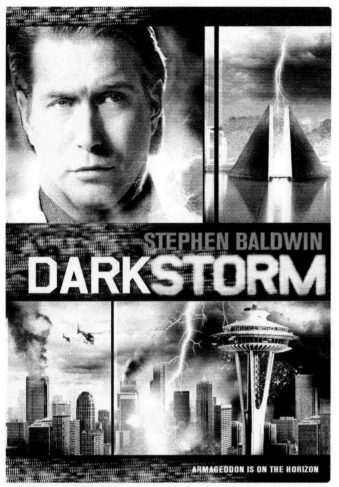

STEPHEN BALDWIN

DARKSTORM

ARMAGEDDON IS ON THE HORIZON

output. There's a lot to take in here: A damaged space satellite leaking dark matter, causing worldwide destructive magnetic storms; scientist Baldwin catching his own dose of the swirling matter, turning him into an electrically charged superhuman; Baldwin's reptilian boss (Gardiner Millar) selling the blueprints to a rival power but planning, behind their backs, to turn himself into an indestructible being; terrorist shoot-outs; funnels of matter writhing around buildings; and a stern-faced general (William B. Davis) mouthing one military cliché after another. An inordinate amount of screen time is spent on people in white coats peering at computer monitors, a curse of the modern-day science fiction movie, be it low-budget or high-budget—no tension, no drama, just time filling for the sake of it. The finale sees Baldwin and Millar engaged in an electrical-cum-dark matter tussle, the floppy haired one coming out tops as another rogue satellite is blown to smithereens by a machine known as an Erupter, Millar disintegrating and the storms dispersing. Baldwin was reasonably okay in Nu Image's *SnakeMan* (2005) but in *Dark Storm* the man is virtually comatose. Check the man's expression when he's informed by Millar that his wife (Camille Sullivan) has been abducted—it doesn't register a thing; there's simply no spark. Obviously, being in contact with dark matter didn't liven him up, not one iota! Baldwin aside, the rest of the cast are efficient enough but *Dark Storm* is all

about effects—take those out of the equation and you are left with a bit of a clunker, to be honest.

Fire From Below

Black Chrome Prods. 2009; 89 minutes;
Directors: Andrew Stevens and Jim Wynorski *

Miners disturb a rich vein of L6 lithium which reacts with liquid, resulting in fire tornados that appear from deep underground and torch everything and everybody in their path.

Seismologist Kevin Sorbo and girlfriend Maeghan Albach are hero and heroine respectively, trying to devise a sensible plan to stop a rogue lithium lode with a mind of its own from destroying the planet by ejecting huge geysers of flame and releasing ammonia gas. Jim Wynorski should have chucked in one of the monsters that feature in a lot of his Cinetel Films releases to liven up this turgid movie in which nobody gets burned alive: A brash, discordant score; clichéd military-speak ("Go! Go! Go!"  "Let's go people."); lame effects; a tired "let's get it all over with" performance from Sorbo; and a protracted climax in caverns that has the cast running backwards and forwards through the same tunnels *ad infinitum*. Two bombs put pay to the fiery menace (only two bombs?), Sorbo and Albach engage in lip action, Sorbo's ex-partner GiGi Erneta gives him a frosty stare and that's it. Eighty-nine minutes of poorly conceived disaster thrills, about as flat as an unrisen soufflé.

Frozen Impact

Porchlight Entertainment 2003; 96 minutes;
Director: Neil Kinsella *

A family whose 12-year-old son requires an urgent liver transplant is caught up in a race against time when their town is hit by America's worst-ever hailstorm.

Medusa is the name given to the storm as it hurls hailstones the size of baseballs from glowering skies, smashing glass and demolishing buildings. In a plot straight out of a woman's magazine, Linda Purl is a

UNDER TEN MILLION? ANYTHING'S POSSIBLE!

hard-working nurse, at loggerheads with a cold-eyed administrator who puts hospital finances before lives; Ted McGinley plays her husband, locating the donated organ in a plane crash; organ safely on board, McGinley has to drive like the clappers through hail, stopping en route to collect errant daughter Nicole Paggi from a rock face; and Stacy Keach's auto auction is totally wrecked, leaving him to bemoan the loss in revenue. The saccharine-coated finale has the entire cast kissing and cuddling one another following (of course) a successful transplant operation on young Myles Jeffrey. Okay fodder for the Hallmark Movie channel perhaps, but a dramatic sci-fi disaster thriller? No!

Ice Quake
Cinetel Films/Reel One Ent. 2010; 90 minutes;
Director: Paul Ziller **

A massive ice shelf collapses in Russia causing tremors in the Mount Phaeton region of Alaska; the ice cracks and a vast lake of methane gas threatens to decimate the Earth.

One of Cinetel's lesser offerings, mainly because the scenario has been done so many times before in previous indie movies and is starting to look a little tired. A bog-standard storyline has scientist Brendan Fehr, wife Holly Dignard, plus their two kids trekking up Mount Phaeton, overlooking Fairbanks, to investigate tremors in the area and the disappearance of two engineers. A chasm opens up at their feet, methane geysers shoot into the atmosphere, the family is separated, a rescue helicopter crashes, frozen corpses are found, a geophysics team gets wiped out and a military squad are thrown into the action. There's an avalanche, several icy earthquakes and, for a change, a colonel (Victor Garber) who *doesn't* mention using the ubiquitous atomic bomb as a means to an end. It all concludes happily-ever-after—two explosives steer the methane gas towards an oil well, resulting in the mother of all explosions, and the townsfolk are left to get on with the Christmas festivities. Even by these standards, this is uninspired fare with lifeless performances to match. The gleaming cinematography, making full use of the picturesque Canadian mountain scenery, is the film's one major asset.

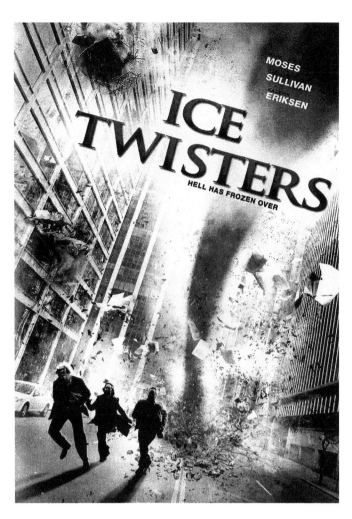

Ice Twisters
Cinetel Films/Insight Film Studios 2009; 89 minutes;
Director: Steven R. Monroe ****

Scientists create mechanical machines called seraphs that have the ability to form rain in areas of drought; when they malfunction, ice-laden tornados wreak havoc.

A cross between *Twister* and *The Day After Tomorrow*, *Ice Twisters* (like most of Cinetel's movies) contains decent special effects and crystal-clear photography. Mark Moses, who writes fictional stories on disasters, is caught up in the real thing when his book-signing stint is rudely interrupted by a vicious ice-tornado that rips through the town, freezing everything in its path. From thereon in, we're quickly into goodies versus corporate baddies territory: Camille Sullivan wants her weather-changing experiment, which has created these abnormalities of nature, aborted, against reptilian boss Robert Maloney's wishes; he's in it for profit and domination. Only by blasting a hole through the ozone layer and heating Earth's upper atmospheric layers can the ice-laden twisters be stopped. Fast-moving and overflowing with incident and action, containing stronger-than-usual characters, Steven R. Monroe's entry into the indie disaster flick zone is okay disaster filmmaking that doesn't let up for a single second.

Icetastrophe aka **Christmas Icetastrophe**
Cinetel Films/Ice Cap Pictures 2014; 86 minutes;
Director: Jonathan Winfrey ***

On Christmas day, a meteorite enters Earth's atmosphere and splits into two, one lump causing "flash freezing" in the Montana town of Lennox.

A standard Cinetel Films' disaster flick, so you know what to expect by now: Good guy Victor Webster and physics student Jennifer Spence racing against time (and instant freezing) to join the hot meteorite fragment with the cold specimen in the hope of ending the icy catastrophe; Webster's son Richard Haman and girlfriend Tierra Skovbye trekking through the snowy wastes in search of safety; Haman's lily-livered father, Mike Dupud, not lifting a finger to help anyone; wives Boti Bliss and Johanna Newmarch fretting over their spouse's well-being; and half the population of Tannen huddled in the town school as the walls and ceiling freeze over. Cinetel's effects are a cut-above the rest of the pack when it comes to this kind of fare, the giant ice crystals erupting from the sidewalks reminiscent of the huge alien crystals on the march in Universal's classic 1957 feature, *The Monolith Monsters*, and the frozen solid victims disintegrating into shards is also conincingly put across, as is the hospital sequence, the wards full of frosty human statues; Webster and Spence negoti-

ating old mine workings under Lennox and confronting those deadly attractive crystals is another decent moment to enjoy. Unfortunately, the loathsome Dupud survives, despite his confession that, "I didn't save anyone. I closed the door on them," but at least the rat's reconciled to the fact that Skovbye and Haman are dating. Filmed in Hope, British Columbia, the film manages to convey a sense of bitter coldness and jettisons stupid dialogue in favor of a slightly more meaningful script; the acting is also above-average. Of its type, it's okay fodder for a younger audience.

LA Apocalypse
Cinetel Films 2014; 80 minutes;
Director: Michael J. Sarna **

The Earth's inner core collapses, leading to violent earthquakes, widespread volcanic activity, poisonous gas in the atmosphere and worldwide destruction.

The superb effects present in *LA Apocalypse* count for little when propped up by a wafer-thin plot that could have been sketched out on the back of an envelope in under a minute. David Cade, aided by Lieutenant Christopher Judge, attempts to rescue fiancée Gina Holden twice, from a smashed-up office block and then from the hands of crime lord/terrorist Kamar de los Reyes while all around him, Los Angeles is in a ferment of cataclysmic destruction.

And that's it. Reyes' hostages are eventually rescued, the smirking criminal is shot in a revenge killing and LA (or what's left of it) is obliterated by missiles, creating a vortex that prevents the Earth's crust from breaking up and destroying what's left of the planet. "Marry me," says Cade to Holden as they cuddle amid the rubble, Judge and his fellow grunts whooping with joy, although judging by the ruined state 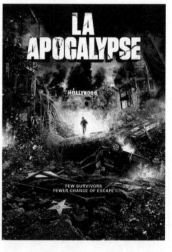 of the city in the aftermath of that missile strike, there's not much cause for celebration. Even at 80 minutes, the film is tedious to watch; those very special effects are completely wasted on this occasion.

Lightning: Bolts of Destruction
Porchlight Ent./Legacy Filmworks 2003; 95 minutes;
Director: Brenton Spencer **

A super-storm appears over Earth, firing lethal bolts of lightning that are so destructive in nature they could trigger off a new Ice Age.

Melodramatic soap opera is no substitute for ace special effects, which is the movie's downfall. Who cares a

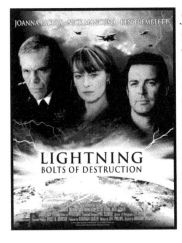

jot about weather woman's (Joanna Pakula) problems with her drippy student son (Noel Fisher), or her "never at home" husband (Ken Tremblett). What you need in a film of this sort are expertly conceived scenes of disaster to maintain the interest; Brenton Spencer's flick suffers from a paucity of such scenes. So sandwiched between all the family angst, Pakula scurries here, there and everywhere, telling General Nick Mancuso *not* to nuke the storm (!) but to allow Tremblett (stationed at the North Pole) to reverse the planet's polarity with a machine that would not have looked out of place in a 1930s *Buck Rogers* serial. This, she states, without batting an eyelid, will dissipate the storm. Naturally, her husband achieves it and the loved-up family is reunited in the closing frames. If 15 minutes shorter, *Lightning: Bolts of Destruction* would have been tolerable. At 95 minutes, it's far too strung out and becomes a chore to sit through.

Meteor Storm

Marvista Ent./Unity Pictures 2010; 90 minutes;
Director: Tibor Takacs **

Four meteor showers successively rain down bullet-sized lumps of glowing rock on San Francisco, but nowhere else.

Tibor Takacs' Canadian feature, filmed in British Columbia, boasts one spectacular scene in which the Golden Gate Bridge collapses—and really, that's all you get for your buck. We're in disaster cliché-land here: Feisty female scientist (Kari Matchett); ex-husband (Michael Trucco); two brat kids (Kirsten Prout and Brett Dier); and stern-faced military "let's nuke the sonofabitch" leaders. As the residents cower in terror from repeated meteor bombardments, Trucco bombs around the city on a motorbike, looking for his straying offspring, while Matchett expounds her theory: The meteors are attracted to the city's bay area because, millions of years ago, a massive asteroid landed there and it's still giving off electromagnetic signals. Jam those signals, nuke the main meteor and, wonder of wonders,

everything will be fine and dandy. Takacs has a commendable roll call of indie movies to his credit (*The Black Hole, Deadly Water, Mosquito Man*) but regrettably, *Meteor Storm* is one of his lesser efforts.

Polar Storm

Cinetel Films/Insight Film Studios 2009; 92 minutes;
Director: Paul Ziller **

A comet passes close to the Earth, a fragment breaking away which hits the planet, creating a polar shift and huge magnetic storms.

A lot of Cinetel Films' disaster features open with a pre-credit sequence of events to come, repeated later on, a taster of what to expect (or what *not* to expect): Here, Tyler Johnston and stepmother Holly Elissa get separated by a huge crevasse that splits the road in two, the lady tumbling to her doom—or does she? Husband Jack Coleman, a doctor in physics, dashes from one locale to the other as waves of electrical energy sweep the countryside, dust clouds plow through the forests, the sky is lit with a purple polar aurora and earthquakes crack up the roads; the Earth's axis is out of alignment due to that pesky comet, Coleman trying to figure out a way to cure the problem while sulky Johnston moons over frisky Emma Lahana and refuses to bond with Elissa, one more in a long line of indie/low-budget "I hate my stepparent" teenagers who deserve a good spanking. Johnston then becomes a man, hauling stepmom out of the crevasse seen at the start, Coleman informing President Roger Cross that "there's been a geo-magnetic reversal, resulting in a misaligned crust. We're gonna lose our protective shield. Solar radiation will burn us to a crisp," at the same time resuming relations with his grumpy dad, General Terry David Mulligan. Yet another piece of scientific balderdash is thrown into the broth

(mini pulse sites) before superman Coleman rejects the idea of nuking the atmosphere in favor of detonating a number of warheads in the Mariana Trench ("Polar reversal completes in 48 hours and it's then bye bye planet!"). In the time it takes to brew a cup of coffee, Coleman rustles up an old diesel-powered Russian sub complete with Russian crew ("Ve vork together to save world, no?"), reaches the six-mile deep trench in record time, plants his warheads and hightails it out, the explosions correcting the tilting axis—Earth is saved! Back home, Coleman, Elissa and Johnston engage in a group hug, Johnston no doubt sure of a date with Lahana, now that he's proved himself a hero. A mediocre entrant in Cinetal's long list of modest "end of days" epics shot in Canada (many directed by Paul Ziller, including the "paranormal storm" opus *Ghost Storm* in 2011), everybody going through the well-worn paces with a modicum of conviction; the effects, as ever with this company, are above average.

Quantum Apocalypse
Nu Image/Bullet Pictures 2010; 93 minutes; Director: Justin L. Jones *

A massive comet is diverted towards Earth via a gravitational vacuum, threatening to end all life on the planet.

A rare misfire for Nu Image—there are a plethora of "Earth in danger of destruction from comet" indie movies on the market, but *Quantum Apocalypse* is near the bottom of the heap. Reason? Bad acting, cheap effects and a definite seen-it-all-before air. A massive comet is due to hit our planet in what scientists term an "extinction level event." What's the solution? Bring in two young theoretical "rock" physicists (Gigi Edgley and Colin Galyean) and let them figure out what to do. Except all the girl does is jump up and down, annoyingly rolling her eyes and screaming, "It's all gonna end," and, "It doesn't look good," while her silent partner scratches his stubble in utter bemusement, not having a clue what to do. Autistic Rhett Giles then appears on the scene in the hope that his wacky brain patterns can achieve something of value where others have failed. Wrapping up a tiresome scenario, a solitary missile diverts the comet from its intended course, a wormhole is opened, time is reversed and we are back where we started, right at the beginning of a very forgettable sci-fi/disaster excursion. *Deep Impact* has a lot to answer for!

Snowmageddon
Cinetel Films/Reel One Entertainment 2011; 89 minutes; Director: Sheldon Wilson ***

In the lead up to Christmas festivities, a family receives a mysterious present in the form of a snow globe that, when activated by its mechanism, causes a series of catastrophes in and around their small Alaskan town.

Quirky Christmas disaster frolics laced with a smidgen of tension as youngster Dylan Matzke activates a myriad of cogs and wheels at the base of an antique snow globe containing a mirror image of his town and the surrounding mountains. Once set in motion, the image wobbles, fissures belching flames open in the streets, giant ice balls

rain down from black skies and the mountain peak takes on all the aspects of an erupting volcano. Antiques dealer Michael Hogan is at a loss as to where the "globe from hell" originated from while David Cubitt races up into the snow-covered mountains in his snowcat to rescue wife Laura Harris and daughter Magda Apanowicz whose helicopter has crashed after giving two snowboarders a lift. True, there's nothing on show here we haven't seen a dozen times before, but Cinetel Films' special effects are usually a tad more skillful than most: Deep fiery crevasses, an avalanche, rocky spikes emerging from the road, vehicles wrecked and fearsome-looking storms add to the broth with a degree of expertise, the globe finally tossed into a volcanic crack in the ice whereupon everything returns to normality, Cubitt and family falling and sobbing into each other's arms—but that's the norm in today's movies, whatever the genre!

Stonados
Marvista Entertainment 2013; 88 minutes; Director: Jason Bourque **

Gigantic waterspouts appear off the coast of Boston, emanating from undersea volcanic activity, bombarding the city with exploding balls of rock.

"Are we done with the family trauma here?" says weather reporter Sebastian Spence to college lecturer

UNDER TEN MILLION? ANYTHING'S POSSIBLE!

Paul Johansson at one point. Unfortunately no—for the first of two occasions, Johansson, a widower, is dashing around a Boston bombarded by exploding rocks in search of son Dylan Schmid and self-obsessed daughter Jessica McLeod; why can't these kids *ever* do what Dad tells them to do? Meanwhile, in between all the chaos and destruction, Spence is trying his hardest to goad Johansson's cop sister, Miranda Frigon, into going out on a date, as he has been doing for the past 10 years—surely, there are limits to how long a girl can play hard-to-get! "Gotta check out my kids," mumbles Johansson for the umpteenth time; having rescued them once, sulky McLeod, ignoring storm warnings, has decided to drag her brother along to a baseball game, even though her father has expressly forbidden it. "We'll do this together, as a family," states our hero at the end, stern-faced Federal Oceanic Agency boss Thea Gill having produced at the drop of a hat a lethal warhead device, something which youngsters should never be near (but these two are). Their rocket launcher malfunctioning, Johansson and Spence set the bomb's timer (for one minute only!), drive their vehicle into the path of a massive waterspout and leap out; the car is sucked into the vortex, there's a huge explosion and the rock-laden twister van-

ishes. Cue for Dad to hug his kids, and for Spence to finally get to kiss Frigon. The opening scene of the Plymouth Rock being plucked from its resting place, plus tornados raining boulders down onto buildings and crushing the screaming populace, are fairly effective in a stereotypical "let's rescue the kids in peril" Canadian disaster offering that's far too sugar-coated for its own good. *Sharknado* it ain't!

Stonehenge Apocalypse
Cinetel Films/Reel One Ent. 2010; 92 minutes;
Director: Paul Ziller ****

Archaeologists investigating the Chamber of the Sun in Maine trigger off a number of worldwide catastrophes, the catalyst being Stonehenge in England whose weather-beaten stones conceal a terrifying magnetic-electrical force field.

Packed full of incident, *Stonehenge Apocalypse* moves like an express train through a (sometimes) implausible and over-ambitious plot. When the megalithic monuments (alien in origin? That theory has been discussed for decades!) start to turn clockwise, emitting discharges into the central altar stone, paranormal radio presenter Misha

Collins is flown to Salisbury Plain where England's most famous Neolithic circle of standing stones is under military jurisdiction. Every 10 hours, the force pumped out by Stonehenge destroys various well-known structures (Mexico's Yucatan pyramid; Egypt's Giza pyramids). Collins deduces that Stonehenge is an alien nuclear reactor (!) and that his rival, Hill Harper, has his hands on an ancient key that has the power, if inserted into Stonehenge's central altar stone, to prevent the world from being annihilated and then terraformed. From then on, it's a race against time as Collins (plus token female Torri Higginson) flits backwards and forwards between England and America to grab this mechanism off Harper who has set himself up as one of

Canada's answer to England's Stonehenge becomes an alien nuclear reactor in *Stonehenge Apocalypse*.

the chosen survivors should the world end. If you're English, the movie's major faux pas lies in the depiction of Stonehenge itself. Since when has Salisbury Plain been surrounded by mountains and thick forest? And if the authorities want to nuke the stone circle, giving everyone 30 minutes to evacuate, such a blast would affect not only every major town and village in the area but London itself with a population of millions! Shooting the production in Canada is the answer here, one of England's major heritage sites created in a computer. Putting that aside (and those fake Limey accents), *Stonehenge Apocalypse* is edge-of-the-seat fodder put over with real zest.

Super Eruption
Marvista Entertainment 2011; 88 minutes;
Director: Matt Codd *

A mighty volcano underneath Yellowstone Park threatens to erupt, triggering hundreds of other eruptions that will extinguish all life on Earth.

Matt Codd's tawdry effort makes *Dante's Peak*, and even the risible *Volcano*, look like multi-Oscar contenders. Park Rangers scamper around giving out warnings, people are scalded in hot rivers, scientists spend most of the screen time in control rooms, tearing their hair out, and it's left to Juliet Aubrey and Richard Burgi to save the planet; they descend into the  main crater and neutralize the threatening lava with two metal devices. The effects are poorly conceived and Aubrey should return to drama school forthwith; it's no good producers expecting actors to mouth streams of scientific mumbo-jumbo if said actors give no indication that they know what they're talking about. Aubrey's shrieking delivery

is just that—a shrieking delivery guaranteed to raise the blood pressure of most seasoned moviegoers. A disastrous end-of-the-world flick that even the under-10s will fidget through.

10,000 Days
Bahr Productions 2014; 91 minutes;
Director: Eric Small **

Twenty-seven years after Comet 23 hit the Earth, causing a new Ice Age, two rival clans fight for supremacy in a frozen world.

Once again, as so often happens in these end-of-days movies, the human race has reverted to a kind of hippiedom following a worldwide cataclysm, John Schneider's clan, holed up in an observatory high in the Rocky Mountains, warring with former friend Peter Wingfield and his bunch, living in igloos. When the fuselage of presidential aircraft Air Force One is discovered in a vast ice cavern, complete with frozen corpses and high-tech weaponry, the race is on to retrieve a nuclear device that, when detonated, might bring about global warming and melt the ice; twisted Wingfield, however, would rather use it to destroy his enemies and become master of a new world. A talkative post-apocalyptic disaster-cum-fantasy that appears much longer than its 91 minutes (it originates from a 2010 TV series which ran for one season), *10,000 Days* encompasses

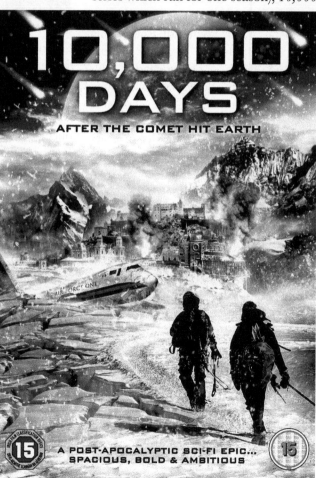

the usual conflict of love interest (Lydia Look fancies James Harvey Ward from the opposing faction), woolly-hatted women tending plants and wobbly CGI snowscapes—the production also ends abruptly, Romeo and Juliet lovers Look and Ward heading off to those greener climes spotted on the horizon as Wingfield, armed with bombs, prepares to carry out his own private war, the outcome of which, thankfully, we will never be privy to.

Fantasy

Avalon: Beyond the Abyss
Viacom Prods./Waterworks BHS 1999; 92 minutes;
Director: Philip Sgriccia **

In the Gulf of Mexico, a vast black toxic tide is ejected from the ocean depths during a seaquake, poisoning everything in its path as prophesied in ancient Mayan legend.

Distributed for TV/DVD release by Paramount,  *Avalon: Beyond the Abyss'* template is 1989's *The Abyss*, sourcing James Cameron's underwater epic for material and winding up a terminal, talkative bore, with little on offer in the way of drama, effects or plot cohesion. Following the destruction of an island in the Gulf of Mexico, Parker Stevenson and his crew from the Oceanic Institute investigate the ocean bottom in their submersible *Scorpio* while anthropologist Krista Allen discovers Mayan paintings in a cave, depicting Earth's destruction in a series of cataclysmic events related to the meteorite that hit the area 65,000,000 years ago. Yes, not only did it kill off the dinosaurs, the catastrophe also created parallel worlds (and a black hole?) that have now shifted and opened, resulting in chaos. People start changing: Matt Battaglia dives deep and returns minus his tattoo (he's now "a visitor"), Stevenson's vision and memory becomes blurred and techno-kid Billy Rieck's sugar intake escalates in between him blubbering every time someone gets into difficulties. Mehgan Heaney-Grier is the resident scientific babe who loses boyfriend Battaglia to those inscrutable Mayan forces, disbelieving Stevenson ("A Mayan god didn't cause this.") donning an armored diving suit, plunging 3,000 feet down and encountering three other clones of himself. After a lengthy discourse, the undersea trench closes, rendering the black tide harmless, mankind is saved and Stevenson, back on board, gets to play house with Allen. Science meets mystic legend in a mundane production lumbered with too much gobbledegook and not enough eye-catching action to maintain the interest.

Ba'al: The Storm God
Cinetel Films/Insight Film Studios 2008; 90 minutes;
Director: Paul Ziller **

A terminally ill archaeologist hunts for four magical amulets which he thinks will cure him of cancer; once

found, they unleash an ancient storm god that threatens to devastate Earth's climate.

There's plenty of pace and stormy effects in this fantasy as Professor Scott Hylands steals some ancient scrolls from a museum and sets about locating four Sumerian amulets representing earth, air, water and fire—in doing so, Ba'al, the storm god, returns in all his fury, his red-eyed face glowering among the black clouds. Each amulet, when located, sends a shaft of light into the heavens and soon the Van Allen Belt is creating dangerous electromagnetic storms. Only by inserting all four amulets into the statue of Ba'al's rival, El, can the giant storms dissipate. A good-enough idea is let down by Jeremy London's middling Brendan Fraser takeoff, Stefanie von Pfetten's pretty-but-dumb archaeologist, Lexa Doig's expressionless face (she plays, or tries to, a doctor studying weather patterns) and clichéd dialogue ("Let's nuke the sonofabitch!" barks a general, the army's dubious methods of dealing with a cloud mass). References to Inuits, stone tablets, priests and mystical ley lines crop up in the script, Doig spouting off streams of scientific jargon with the look of someone who hasn't a clue what they're talking about. The sequences depicting the storms wreaking havoc are adequate but really, *Ba'al* is sub-*Indiana Jones* fodder which could have turned out far better than it did.

Beyond Sherwood Forest
Front Street Pictures 2009; 93 minutes;
Director: Peter DeLuise ****

In 1174, Robin Hood and his band of Merry Men not only have to contend with the devious Sheriff of Nottingham but also a mysterious woman who can transform herself into a giant flying reptile.

England's Sherwood Forest goes Canadian (shot in North Vancouver), Peter DeLuise combining elements of both the Robin Hood and King Arthur legends and chucking in a monster dragon for good measure. Robin Dunne and Erica Durance play Robin and Marian like a couple of New Yorkers out on a first date, elfin Katharine Isabelle shines as the tormented, shapeshifting damsel without a heart (literally!) while snarling Julian Sands chews the scenery as the blond-haired Sheriff. Actually, *Beyond Sherwood Forest* is a well-crafted fantasy that will appeal to all age groups, packed to the green forest treetops with sword and sorcery-type incident, a mysterious dark wood where a race of elders called the Sylvans and huge wolves lurk and a fantastic CGI rampaging winged serpent, expertly conceived—and rotund Friar Tuck dies, savaged by the dragon! Cursed Isabelle also succombs, dying in the sun's rays after Dunne has plunged a dagger into his adversary's ribs; he's then given a pardon by a rather piqued King John. Entertaining and imaginative fare, an unusual take on the old yarn; just ignore those suspect English accents!

Carnivorous aka **Hell's Labyrinth**
Lightning Rod Studios 2007; 90 minutes;
Director: Drew Maxwell **

Several people wake to find themselves imprisoned inside a vast edifice whose labyrinthine passages are the home to flesh-eating dragon-like demons.

A video game passing itself off as a feature film—shot in an abandoned warehouse on tape against a green screen backdrop, the elaborate details later filled in by computer, this soulless, badly acted exercise in *Dungeons and Dragons*-type thrills might appeal to those who enjoy manipulating their characters on handsets through one maze and obstacle after another as spiky creatures hunt them down; for discerning buffs brought up on more traditionally crafted special effects, the very nature of how all this was conceived will rankle. In many scenes, the actors don't appear to be making contact with the ground; in others, they look for all the world what they are, tiny miniatures inserted into a CGI-envisaged roomscape. There *is* a plot: A servant (Chris Flieller) is entrusted with the task of abducting people and transporting them to this dark underworld so that the monsters can feed on them. This will prevent said monsters from entering into our world, searching for human prey. Leah Rose takes on the mantle of servant/protector of the human race after she kills Flieller and manages to escape from the otherworld with Ryan Schaufler and another girl. Admittedly, some of the computerized set design is imaginative and Rose's all-action, feisty female is as good as most (her well-defined cheekbones help!), but CGI-produced fantasy/horror fare like this, lacking warmth and depth, really belongs to the games market, not cinema; after all, the big-budget *Sky Captain and the World of Tomorrow* was a box-office flop and *that* used identical technology.

Cyclops
Concorde/New Horizons 2008; 88 minutes;
Director: Declan O'Brien ***

A one-eyed giant is captured and brought to the Roman arena to do battle with gladiators as part of the emperor's victory games.

The Roger Corman-produced *Cyclops* is an absolute hoot for all the wrong reasons, coming across like a cheapo Italian peplum fantasy: Eric Roberts starring as a smirking Emperor Tiberius? I don't think so!; "Tell them the Cyclops is loose and is killing people. Run!" shouts

the guy in charge of the slaves in a thick Australian accent; did the expression "Face-Off" *really* exist in ancient Rome?; Roberts' tatty main arena, the perceived glory of Rome, seats about 100 persons; no sign of any Mediterranean warmth here—breath vaporizes in the air when the actors speak; genre references copied from *Gladiator* and *Spartacus* are in the mix somewhere; and *this* particular Cyclops is eight-foot-tall, can grunt one word at a time and turns into a good monster. Craig Archibald hams it up to the hilt as Roberts' campy, devious deputy, clashing with Kevin Stapleton's centurion-turned-gladiator, while statuesque Frida Farrell provides the lust interest. Kids will love this corny balderdash—older hands will sigh heavily and agree to a man; Harryhausen's Cyclops from *The 7th Voyage of Sinbad* towers head and shoulders (literally!) above all others.

Dragon Storm
UFO/Sci-Fi Pictures 2004; 96 minutes;
Director: Stephen Furst **

Carpathia in the year 1190: Alien dragons arrive in meteorites, laying waste to the countryside, thus prompting two rival kings to join forces in defeating them.

Nice dragons—shame about the rest of this panto-mime-looking production shot in wintry Eastern European locations. John Rhys-Davies throws his considerable weight around as a cowardly king trying to make it up with rival king John Hansson after his castle is burnt to the ground by a host of fire-breathing dragons from outer space. Hansson begrudgingly allows his enemy to stay in his castle on certain conditions and instructs hunter Maxwell Caulfield

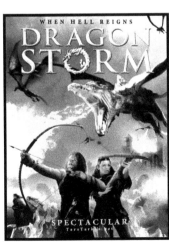

to enlist the aid of an elite group of men to go forth and slay the winged menaces, with his daughter Angel Boris Reed (gorgeous but wooden) tagging along with her crossbow. However, when they eventually leave on their mission, dastardly Rhys-Davies plots to overthrow Hansson and claim the castle as his own. The climax involves the two warring factions tussling with one another *and* a large dragon that has flown in to reclaim her egg, stolen by Caulfield. Rhys-Davies aside, the acting here is pretty rudimentary to say the least, matching the drab sets, the hammy kid's-own swordfights and lethargic direction. If you leave out the CGI dragons, this is very lumpy fantasy fare indeed, even for the younger set.

Journey to the Center of the Earth
High Productions 1993; 90 minutes;
Director: William Dear *

A professor invents a boring machine and disappears down an active volcano in an attempt to discover the secrets below us. Ten years later, his nephew and a team of seven undergo the same journey in the *Avenger* which is capable of sonically blasting a pathway through the Earth's crust.

One of the worst adaptations of Jules Verne's legendary novel, even with Oscar winner F. Murray Abraham appearing fleetingly during the opening minutes as the professor. Several hundred kilometers underground, leader Jeffrey Nordling and company stumble across green-eyed manta ray monsters controlled by a disfigured humanoid, a non-aggressive, white-haired Yeti and a tribe of grotesque missing links in panto-mime-looking underground

sets straight from the 1960s. The dialogue is undeniably forced ("We are the descenders." "Sounds cool.") and only John Neville emerges unscathed with any credit to his name in the acting stakes, starring as a legendologist (?) who holds the missing piece to The Book of Knowledge (whatever that might be, but the humanoid is after it). To cap it all, the disembodied head of actress Justina Vail floats around in a blue bubble, the vessel's on-board HAL-type computer. There's much talk of Atlantis and cosmic forces before Nordling and his stereotypical group decide to explore their strange new world instead of returning to base. The producers appeared to be bent on updating the Verne novel for a younger generation (hence the ghastly synthesizer soundtrack) but by doing so completely destroyed the Victorian ambience essential to the story. Pinching many of its ideas from 1950's *Unknown World* (the underworld an escape from Earth's polluted surface), this was originally to have been a TV two-parter (the reason, no doubt, for the unresolved ending) but the idea was hastily dropped, and a good job too! 20th Century Fox's benchmark 1959 version, starring James Mason and Pat Boone, has still, after all these years, to be bettered!

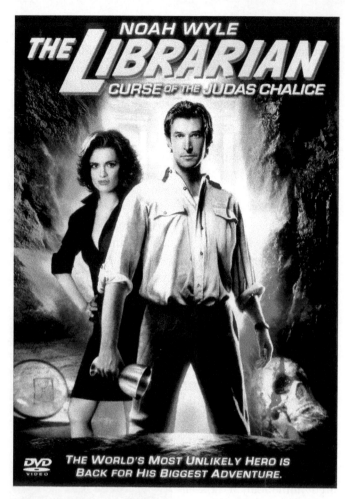

NOAH WYLE
THE LIBRARIAN
CURSE OF THE JUDAS CHALICE

DVD VIDEO
THE WORLD'S MOST UNLIKELY HERO IS
BACK FOR HIS BIGGEST ADVENTURE.

The Librarian 3: The Curse of the Judas Chalice
TNT/Electric Entertainment 2008; 90 minutes;
Director: Jonathan Frakes ***

Ex-KGB Russian agents are hunting for the goblet made out of the 30 pieces of silver given to Judas Iscariot for betraying Jesus; the vessel will enable them to revive Vlad the Impaler, who will command an army of the undead and revive Russia's former glories.

Noah Wyle returned as Flynn Carson in the third and final part of the *Librarian* trilogy (it ran as a TV series in 2014/2015), a super-intelligent, accident prone clone of archaeologist Indiana Jones employed by Bob Newhart, custodian of a cavernous New York museum housing fabulous artifacts from antiquity. Like the previous two (*The Librarian: Quest for the Spear* and *The Librarian 2: Return to King Solomon's Mines*), the accent focused on lighthearted frolics rather than out-and-out horror, even though Wyle's new love interest, bewitching singer Stana Katic, was a 403-year-old vampire, out to put an end to Bruce Davison's Vlad, posing as a college professor; it was he who bit her neck in Paris way back in 1628. Shot around Baton Rouge, director Frakes piles on the action and incident, including a derelict galleon, markers and coins that have to be deciphered, vampire transformations (not scary enough to upset the kids) and Wyle falling head-over-heels in lust with tigress Katic. The ending is quite moving for this kind

of fare—having dispatched bloodsucker Davison with a stake made from the tree on which Judas hanged himself, Wyle and Katic sit on a bench, overlooking the sea. "I loved you," she whispers to Wyle as the sun comes up, dissolving her into pinpoints of radiance, her soul finally at rest. And is Newhart, who takes possession of the fabled chalice, *really* 2,000 years old as suggested in the closing seconds? A vampire fantasy adventure not to be taken seriously, with Wyle on top form; even under-10s could watch it without being too much disturbed.

The Lost City aka The Legend of the Hidden City
Dandelion Productions/Wehemeyer 1997; 91 minutes;
Director: David Lister *

An archaeologist escapes from the lost city of At-Bara in South America and drowns in a river—50 years later, his skeleton is unearthed in a dig, along with a sacred medallion and crystal globe.

The Arabian Nights meets *Road to Morocco*—yes, midway into David Lister's supremely ridiculous (and hard to obtain) adventure fantasy, cobbled together from an obscure South African TV series, you half expect Bing Crosby, Bob Hope and Dorothy Lamour to walk on set, followed by Anthony Quinn in a turban. Flown by helicopter into the jungle by devious Andre Jacobs, two guys and a gal find themselves captured by Egyptian-looking warriors after the chopper crashes on a mountain ledge. Taken to the fabled lost city, Gina Borthwick is imprisoned but the men (Brendan Pollecutt and Fezule Mpela) are worshipped like gods as prophesied in ancient legends, arousing jealousy in the evil queen and her equally evil son; Jacobs is only interested in the gold. Umpteen escape attempts later, plus three sacred tests to prove his worth and several fights, Pollecutt defeats the power-mad son and this peculiar kingdom winds up being ruled by a beautiful, virginal princess. Presumably, the scatty "intruders" manage to get free and walk off to freedom, although this isn't made very clear as the movie ends suddenly without warning (apparently, the

Danger
Beyond
Imagination -
In a City
Lost in Time!

Legend of the HIDDEN CITY
ACTION - ADVENTURE SERIAL
26 x TV HALF HOURS AVAILABLE WORLD-WIDE

series only lasted for three episodes). Saddled with artificial sets, laughable dialogue and tinsel costumes straight out of a cheapskate 1950s sword and sandal co-feature, even the high quota of camp can't save the ultra-rare *The Lost City* from being a one-star disaster, a kind of *She* for kiddies; however, even those under the age of 12 will find it as heavy-going as adults, *if* they can locate a DVD/VHS copy.

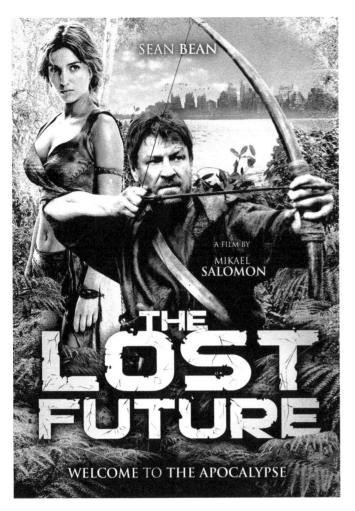

scenery overlaid with CGI ruins adds to the movie's mystique and tough-guy Bean is as dependable (and morose) as ever, bringing some much-needed gravitas to what may be a comic book futuristic romp, but an entertaining one.

Pegasus vs. Chimera aka **The Blood of Pegasus**
Chesler/Perlmutter Productions 2012; 90 minutes;
Director: John Bradshaw ** (**** for the Chimera)

A tyrannical ruler and his warlock assistant conjure up the legendary monster Chimera to destroy the local population; only the fabled winged horse Pegasus can help in defeating the beast.

Filmed in forests near Toronto, this Canadian semi-mythological romp has one thing going for it—the Chimera. Its lion's head sprouting four spiral ram's horns, the tail topped off in a spiked club, the ferocious predator puts the rest of the cast to shame: Sebastian Roche's limp blacksmith hero, Bellaros; Nazneen Contractor's cute but dim Princess Philony; James Kidnie's bullyboy warlock, General Actae; Carlo Rota's whining, self-obsessed King Orthos; and Rae Dawn Chong's hammy witch, Mayda. Roche's father is murdered by Kidnie; years later, he teams up with Contractor in an effort to overthrow Rota, Kidnie and the rampaging Chimera, Chong summoning Pegasus from the heavens ("A war horse from the Gods!") to as-

The Lost Future
Film Afrika/Tandem 2010; 90 minutes;
Director: Mikael Salomon ***

In a post-apocalyptic world, a small band of survivors travels to a ruined city on an island to obtain a yellow powder; the ingredients can prevent humans from mutating into zombies.

Why is it that following a worldwide catastrophe, mankind always (in the eyes of filmmakers) reverts to a kind of Stone Age savagery? Shades of *One Million Years B.C.* (minus the dinosaurs), *Teenage Caveman* and *World Without End* crop up in an energetic German/South African/US little-seen fantasy that contains one monster, a huge malformed bear that Corey Sevier and his clan slaughter at the beginning. When mutated cavemen attack their village, Sevier, Sam Claflin (the only tribe member who can read) and Annabelle Wallis head towards a city where the despotic leader (Jonathan Pienaar) has his greedy hands on a powder that combats the man-into-zombie disease; Claflin also wants his father's notes on how to concoct the powder. British tough guy actor Sean Bean (always a good bet in any film he appears in) and his group help them out, the powder is eventually spirited away, Claflin administers the cure to the tribe (who have been holed up in a cave) and Bean's mob defeats the zombies. Filmed in South Africa, the striking

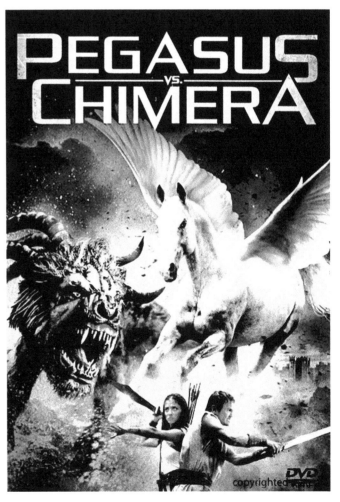

sist them in their task. Empire-builder Rota wants to drink the blood of the winged horse to achieve immortality as Kidnie's potions are only temporary ("I will live one thousand years!"), but there's a major obstacle; if Pegasus isn't returned to the stars by the next full moon, the world will end. Cue for a wealth of lackluster sword fighting, a smattering of blood and gore after the monster has attacked villages and Pegasus looking a tad cartoonish as he takes to the skies. Roche plunges a blade into Kidnie in a waterfall duel, Pegasus tramples Rota to death and Roche, his sword dipped in the horse's magical blood, slays the Chimera. Mission accomplished, Pegasus rejoins his friends in the firmament while we're left to ponder whether or not Roche will get it together with Contractor; at least it might remove the glazed expressions from their faces. Overall, *Pegasus vs. Chimera* is a dull-looking fantasy adventure; the monster of the title makes it all marginally watchable.

Riverworld
Tasman Films/Alliance Atlantis Comms. 2003; 86 minutes;
Director: Kari Skogland **

An American astronaut who dies when his space shuttle crashes after being hit by meteor debris is reincarnated and washed ashore with hundreds of other people on a mysterious planet called Riverworld, which provides a hereafter existence for varying civilizations and life forms.

You're either an ardent fan of this kind of high-blown, scatterlogical fantasy filled to the brim with gibberish or you're not. A bizarre cast of characters includes a Neanderthal Man, an alien (who died on Earth in 2039), Emperor Nero, a Holocaust survivor, Alice (from *Alice in Wonderland*, played by Emily Lloyd) and a native princess; all inhabit an afterlife presided over by hooded aliens (and we thought the hereafter was Heaven, presided over by angels!). Riverworld is ruled on the lines of a tribal fiefdom, a power struggle taking place, so it is left to hunk Brad Johnson to stage a revolt against the despotic leaders, steal a Mississippi-style riverboat and explore this strange new planet. Apparently mooted as a possible TV series which never got off the ground,

the pilot to the series, a collaboration between Canada, New Zealand, America and Britain, sinks under the weight of its own over-fertile imagination; in tone and looks, it's curiously similar to Kevin Costner's disastrous undertaking, *Waterworld*—those who prefer their fare straightforward with a beginning, a middle and an end will do well to give this frothy nonsense a wide berth.

Treasure Island in Outer Space
aka **L'isola del Tesoro**
Bavaria Film/Sagis Intl. 1987; 152 minutes;
Director: Antonio Margheriti *****
Robert Louis Stevenson's classic yarn transposed to a futuristic setting in outer space.

We all know the story, of course, so how does this hard-to-find Italian version add up to all the others. Brilliantly done is the answer. Originally an eight-hour mini-series broadcast on Italian television, a 150-minute edited print was released on VHS in Europe in the 1990s, but little has been seen of it since. Among a bevy of character actors (mostly Italian), Anthony Quinn is a robust Long John Silver, Ernest Borgnine puts in a brief appearance as Billy Bones and 12-year-old Itaco Nardulli makes a lively, tousled-haired Jim Hawkins, living in the ruins of Romeopolis. The treasure is located on a remote desert planet called Hibiscus, so everyone a third of the way into the movie sets off from an Earth devastated by radiation in the disc-shaped *Hispaniola* to find it, leading to mutiny, an encounter with a wrecked cargo vessel and battles on the planet itself. An imaginative final segment sees the treasure discovered in a bog and the mutineers trapped in a valley filled with gigantic

bones dating back to Hibiscus' prehistoric period. Hawkins, Captain Smollett, Ben Gunn, Doctor Livesey and Squire Trelawney win the day and Long John Silver swaps sides (again!); he joins the goodies and off they depart for Earth, leaving the pirates behind. *Treasure Island in Outer Space* is a long way off from those garish X-rated horror movies Margheriti made in the 1960s (*The Castle of Terror*, *Castle of Blood*), but the director's continental flair shines through in practically every scene. The space sequences are excellent, the pace quick and the acting top-notch. Adults and children alike will enjoy this ripping, colorful space adventure *if* they can lay their hands on a copy—unavailable on DVD (legally that is), the video is a rarity that deserves tracking down.

Ghosts/Hauntngs/ The Supernatural

The Awakening

BBC Films/Creative Scotland/Origin Pictures 2011; 102 minutes;
Director: Nick Murphy ***

In 1921, a skeptic in the paranormal is assigned to investigate the apparition of a small boy that is frightening pupils at a boarding school in Cumbria.

Author Rebecca Hall, first seen debunking a clairvoyance session in London ("You're all charlatans!"), travels at Dominic West's request to an isolated boarding school to discover for herself whether or not the specter of a boy with twisted features is inhabiting the dim corridors (filming took place at East Lothian's Gosford House and Berwickshire's Manderston House). Setting up her ghost-finding equipment, she quickly flushes out the two culprits responsible for the supposed prank, but then a disturbing series of incidents causes her to question her non-belief in the hereafter. Hall, guilty over the loss of her fiancé in the 1914-1918 conflict (she jilted him and he died in combat), befriends Isaac Hempstead Wright, the only lad left alone in the school at half term with housekeeper Imelda Staunton, but is he all he appears to be? And how is it that West never acknowledges the fact that he's there. Ultimately, *The Awakening* is all about loss: It transpires after a run of sinister shenanigans that Hall once lived in the place as a child but suppressed the memory of her father shooting dead her mother and his illegitimate son before turning the shotgun on himself, the scenes presented as an intermingling of past and present events. Wright, his face disfigured one minute, normal the next, is the phantom of her step-brother; he wants her to stay, Staunton (Hall's old nanny and Wright's real mother) poisoning herself and Hall so that they can all be together in the afterlife. However, West revives Hall and she departs, convinced that the spirit world presents itself to those who are lonely and missing their loved ones. Although featuring far too many red herrings in its twisty-turny scenario, the tale is elegantly woven in the manner of *The Others* and *The Orphanage* (Eduard Grau's photography is superb), yet the film ends up as cold and empty as the vast building where it all happens; it lacks warmth. The gratuitous assault/rape on Hall by demented groundkeeper Joseph Mawle is superfluous to requirements, as is Hall's masturbation moment (these contributed towards the UK "15" rating). At the end of the day, you feel nothing for the characters involved, and the genuinely scary interludes are very few and far between; a glossy supernatural presentation that just misses the mark.

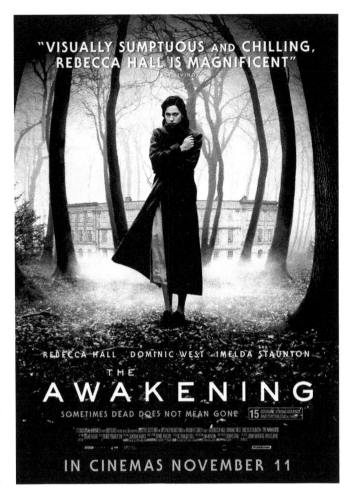

The Borderlands aka Final Prayer

Metrodome Distribution 2013; 89 minutes;
Director: Elliot Goldner ****

Three men are sent by the Vatican to a 13th-century church in Balcombe, Devon to investigate supernatural activity that has been reported by the local priest.

The Borderlands was filmed in rural Devon in England's far south west: Skeptical priest Gordon Kennedy, layman/technology expert Robin Hill and Father Aidan McArdle set up their cameras and microphones in a church run by Luke Neal. At a recent christening, the altar shifted, a candle fell to the floor and weird growling noises were heard. McArdle and Hill reckon Neal is messing around in the name of publicity; however, Kennedy, who attended a similar occurrence in which seven priests died, isn't so sure. The "found footage" scenario switches from the cottage where the three are staying to the dark, eerie church; at night, Neal is seen praying and whimpering, odd rumbles emanating from the walls. The next morning, scraping sounds are detected traveling from one side of the nave to the other and along the walls and, raising their goosebumps (and ours), they hear a baby crying. Out of his mind because he experienced a "dark miracle," Neal throws himself off the bell tower to his death. McArdle then wants to terminate the investigation but Kennedy vis-

FINAL PRAYER

EVIL HAS A NEW FORM

nents of the "antiquarian haunted church/old house" tale and Elliot Goldner's fast-paced chiller does the author's classic English supernatural prose, and themes, proud.

The Cradle
235 Films/Peace Arch 2007; 90 minutes;
Director: Tim J. Brown ****

A couple and their baby son move into a neglected house and soon the infant is under threat from an unseen force that wants to harm it.

Very, very slow is how to sum up the first hour of Brown's carefully wrought Canadian ghost story, but that's no bad thing in today's effects-driven cinema, and a welcome lack of blaring music adds to the musty atmosphere. Emily Hampshire suffers from post-partum depression, leaving worn-out writer Lukas Haas to cope with their fretful baby. Setting up monitors in the nursery because his wife refuses to go near the child, Haas wanders through the dark, gloomy woods and, after a great deal of time and effort, befriends crotchety neighbor Amanda Smith who has a startling tale to tell: When she was a young girl, her father inadvertently buried her baby sister alive, thinking she was stillborn. The spirit of the girl now haunts the surroundings, focusing its evil intentions on any baby brought into the vicinity. As if that wasn't upsetting enough, why

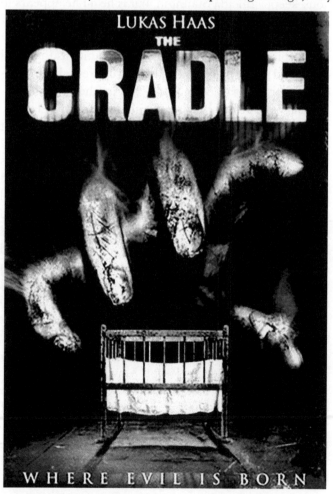

LUKAS HAAS
THE
CRADLE

WHERE EVIL IS BORN

its the church after dark, hearing both the crying infant and Neal screaming in the distance. Vatican exorcist Patrick Godfrey is brought in to perform a banishing ceremony: The four ministers gather in the church and, under the glare of flashlights, spot pagan signs on the floor. Kennedy recalls a quote in a journal written by the church's original deacon in the 1880s ("He lies beneath, waiting for souls."); suddenly the lights explode, bells ring, Godfrey vanishes and the door slams and locks, leaving Kennedy and Hill to descend a steep flight of worn steps in pursuit of whom they believe to be McArdle down endless labyrinthine passageways (shot in Kent's Chislehurst Caves), stumbling across a carved altar stone, small wooden cages and the tiny skeletons of dozens of children, sacrifices from a former orphanage—but sacrifices to what? After running down more galleries, Deacon and Hill squeeze through a membranous, unnatural-moving pipe coated in sticky secretions and become trapped, both men shrieking in agony as something holds them fast, its digestive juices getting to work, the pair coughing up blood in their death throes; the ancient deity that the locals worship to this day has claimed its latest victims. A worthwhile British found footage exercise, only marred in places by Hill's incessant swearing, *The Borderlands* is presented very much in the vein of an updated M.R. James ghost story; James still preserves the reputation of being one of England's greatest expo-

does Haas come back from his wanderings to find the door open, why is there the sound of a baby crying far off and why does the increasingly neurotic Hampshire keep disappearing, then reappearing. In a series of revelatory flashbacks going right back to the movie's first 20 minutes, the truth hits home—Hampshire, in a depressive state, followed Haas into the woods, fell down a slope, hit her head on a rock and died. The baby is also dead, killed by either Hampshire or the evil-minded spirit. A bleak ending, maybe, but *The Cradle* is a pretty bleak little supernatural chiller of the old-school variety, decently acted and conveying an air of unnatural suggestion rather than full-on shocks. Admirably done.

The Cycle aka The Devil's Ground
North American Pictures/H30 Ent. 2009; 89 minutes;
Director: Michael Bafaro ***

A woman driving through the night to Bangor picks up a distraught, blood-covered young female who tells her a horrifying tale concerning the brutal deaths of her four student friends.

In 1967, 239 men died in Pennsylvania's worst mining accident, but what caused this? Leah Gibson, Luke Camilleri, Jeb Beach, Lee Tomaschefski and Marcia Gruending are students investigating an accursed Indian burial ground in the Bradford area where the disaster took place, their aim to establish whether or not the site actually ex-ists; if so, does it pose an environmental stumbling block to planned future mining operations? Gibson relates her garbled story to Daryl Hannah, the events unfolding in flashback: After they stopped at a gas station for fuel and were told that many locals suffered from a deformity of some sort (the attendant had no hands), the students, ignoring warnings, drove over to the forest; remains dating from the present day were dug up along with Indian bones, indicating foul deeds, and a masked maniac appeared out of nowhere, armed with a machete and rifle, killing her friends after a series of narrow escape attempts. The savage twist in this particular tale is that Gibson turns out to be a ghost; Hannah is now at the mercy of the facially disfigured lunatic who dispatches her in the closing seconds. Short on interpretation, Bafaro's movie has wintry atmospheric photography to complement the tense action; the gore quota is surprisingly low, but the "what's going to happen next" quota is high enough to compensate for the lack of blood and guts.

Death of a Ghosthunter
Ominous Productions 2007; 107 minutes;
Director: Sean Tretta ****

A paranormal investigator is asked by the owner of a house to determine whether or not it is haunted by members of his family who were murdered there in 1982.

An American Haunting meets *Paranormal Activity* in an unnerving supernatural thriller that has decent acting, ar-

ticulate dialogue, creepy effects and a sting in its tail. Patti Tindall sets up her stall in the Masterson house where, 20 years previously, a couple and their two children were found shot and stabbed to death. Accompanying Tindall on the instructions of the owner is cameraman Mike Marsh, writer Davina Joy and religious ghost skeptic Lindsay Page. Filmed as a video journal (Day one, Night one), with a two-note piano the only music, Tretta builds up a chilly atmosphere of unease as chairs move, a figure is half-seen and voices are picked up on magnetic tape. When on Day three the owner informs Tindall that he has no idea who Page is and didn't hire her, events take an even more sinister turn—is the young church-going fanatic anything to do with a baby discovered by police at the murder scene, and if so, what is she doing in the house now? The past blends with the present, leading up to a tragic climax as the Masterson household's perverted secrets are let out of the bag; Tindall and her team are slaughtered by the deranged Page, who then commits suicide. The house now has a second set of ghostly residents! A commendable haunted house feature that keeps the interest going right up to the end.

11:11 aka Hell's Gate
Evolution Pictures 2004; 95 minutes;
Director: Michael Bafaro ***

A terrifying journey into the Paranormal...

HELL'S GATE

A seven-year-old girl sees her parents gunned down by two bank robbers and then shoots dead both assailants with the assistance of her mysterious playmate: 18 years later, on medication for depression, she is haunted by an iniquitous guardian who refuses to leave her side and murders those who cross her path.

Bafaro is responsible for a number of low-budget, commendable Canadian thrillers (*The Barber*, 2001; *The Covenant: Brotherhood of Evil*, 2006) and *11:11* gets off to a fine start, depicting the callous murder of Laura Mennell's parents combined with a ghostly element in the shape of a pale-faced girl flitting across the fields who the youngster has befriended. Years later, Mennell, now a student, attends lectures on the paranormal at college. When her aunt is brutally killed following a fling with the college jerk, the movie becomes bogged down in supernatural mumbo-jumbo; that strange little girl in the fields has matured into a red-haired malevolent being (Christie Will), arranging the deaths of those who come between her and Mennell. But why isn't made clear: An impending apocalypse is mentioned, as is the 11 gates to hell, and supposedly Mennell (she keeps receiving visitations from her dead mother) is prophesied as being a chosen one. But chosen for what? And what motivates the cold-eyed Will into making a lesbian pass at Mennell. Granted, there are one or two disquieting moments: Will appearing from nowhere, hounding her chosen victims and, at intervals, a general air of the unnatural, but that's all down to Will, a nasty, manipulative piece of work if ever there was one. In fact, the highly watchable actress is the best thing around in this fanciful offering, her performance elevating the material to must-see status; Mennell, on the other hand, resembles an anorexic Goth and mugs furiously throughout, while boyfriend Paul Dzenkiw is simply a lamb for the slaughter. With a bit more cohesion in certain departments, *11:11* could have been a neat little mystical thriller of some note; as it stands, the picture might give you a headache trying to fathom out what it's trying so hard to say. Will is the main reason to catch it.

The Ferryman
Atlantic Film Productions/Revolver Ent. 2007; 100 minutes;
Director: Chris Graham ***

Two couples hire a charter boat to take them from New Zealand to Fiji; two days into the crossing, they answer a distress call and sail into a dense mist, meeting an evil spirit that requires their souls to achieve immortality.

A New Zealand horror film that delivers the shocks, the gore and some fairly vicious scenes involving the abuse of women. Captain of the *Dionysius* Tamer Hassan and wife Kerry Fox set out for Fiji with preening jerk Craig Hall, bimbo girlfriend Sally Stockwell, enigmatic Kiwi Julian Arahanga and his girl, nurse Amber Sainsbury. By picking up Greek John Rhys-Davies from his stricken vessel, they set off a chain of disasters: Rhys-Davies, sporting a figure-of-eight tattoo on his back, starts coughing up blood during a card game, draws an ornamental dagger from his belt and stabs Arahanga in the chest. In doing this, he transfers the demon within him to another person; Arahanga is possessed (the tattoo appearing on *his* back), stabs Hall and so the vengeful spirit of "The Ferryman" passes from one body to another until the only ones left alive are Sainsbury and a horribly scarred Rhys-Davies. It's well-directed by Graham and looks good (similar to John Carpenter's *The Fog*), but one or two scenes leave a nasty taste in the mouth (the prolonged death of Hassan's dog is quite unnecessary) and blonde Stockwell plays the hysterical, foul-mouthed tart with a little too much vigor. And if you enjoy happy endings, *The Ferryman* hasn't got one. Nevertheless, this is a decent-enough horror flick from

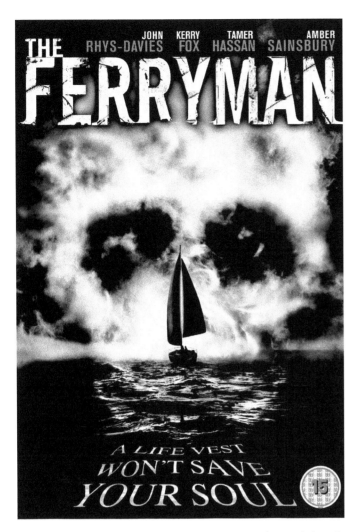

an illicit romance between vicar Roshan Seth (his wife is seriously ill) and Henderson, a sex-pest and the missing girl's shifty boyfriend. Have no fear, the payoff doesn't disappoint; it's a belter in the moving tradition of *The Others*, leaving viewers shocked, saddened and enlightened in a final shattering few minutes. The entire cast is exemplary, Henderson's vulnerable but dogged tomboy a standout turn. *Frozen* goes to prove that when they put their minds to it, the British can do indie as well as any other nation. This is definitely a picture to savor over and over again—and that very final fade-out frame takes some beating.

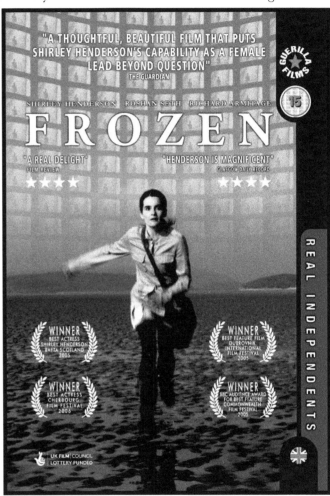

Down Under and the title demon, seen at the end, is suitably leprous in appearance.

Frozen

Guerilla Films 2004; 86 minutes; Director: Juliet McKoen *****

A young girl, obsessed with locating her sister who has been missing for two years, convinces herself that the girl's spirit is leaving clues to the reasons behind her sudden disappearance.

Northern England's bleak Morecambe Bay provides a fitting backdrop to this mournful, low-key supernatural drama, a first-rate debut by Juliet McKoen who also co-wrote the incisive script. Shirley Henderson works in a fish market, haunted by the disappearance of her kid sister. On being allowed to study CCTV footage of the girl's last sighting in a dockyard alley, Henderson states to cynical cop Richard Armitage that blurred images on the footage from both cameras *could* be the face of her sister, apart from one odd anomaly. Spurred on in her belief, Henderson repeatedly visits the alley, hearing loud rumbling sounds and experiencing strange sensations. Out on the desolate mudflats, she also spots a mysterious boatman and a figure dressed in a red raincoat. What can all this mean? McKoen litters the scenario with red herrings, false trails,

Furnace

Swirl Films 2007; 86 minutes; Director: William Butler *

The old south wing of Blackgate prison is opened to house new inmates, but vengeful spirits kill all those who enter the long-abandoned corridors.

Butler did much better with 2004's *Madhouse* than he does here; the credits sequence, detailing the horrific history of the prison dating right back to 1850, promises much, but these promises aren't fulfilled. One of indie's oft-used actors, Michael Paré, plays a detective investigating the possible suicide of a man who was engaged on clearing out the prison's gloomy south wing in preparation for a new batch of inmates. Ex-colleague Tom Sizemore, now a corrupt prison officer, objects to Paré poking around the prison, convicts Ja Rule and Danny Trejo hint at something lurking in the vicinity of the old furnace, psychiatrist Jenny McShane wants to play house with Paré who is apparently grieving over the death of his family at the hands of a gunman, and the charred-looking manifestation of a young girl pops up at intervals. When the remains of said girl are

retrieved from the furnace, all hell breaks loose and soon the whole cast—prisoners, cops, doctors—are dying like flies as the venomous spirits once contained in the south wing wreak havoc. Butler's erratic direction lurches from one disjointed scene to the next, with little in the way of plot development or cohesion, Paré is his usual wooden self, all Sizemore does is throw his weight around and glare and the roasted ghosties are barely glimpsed. There's no doubt about it—*Furnace*, based on those credits, had the potential to be better than it turned out to be.

Ghost Writer aka Suffering Man's Charity
Now Pictures/Scoosh 2007; 93 minutes;
Director: Alan Cumming *

A narcissistic music teacher murders his lodger over rent arrears, steals his ideas for a book, becomes a best-selling author and is then visited by his ghost, bent on revenge.

There are movies which are bad, and those movies which are irritatingly bad. *Ghost Writer* is *extremely* irritating and it's all down to one person—British actor/director Alan Cumming. His preening, simpering, camera-hogging, emoting portrayal of a gay tutor, like a drag queen on heat, screams, "Me! Me! Me!" in every scene he appears in, which unfortunately is about 99% of the running

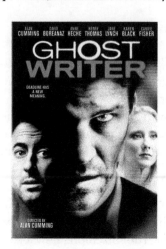

time. Yes, David Boreanaz is allowed a look-in as the impoverished writer who Cumming imprisons, dresses in sequinned bra and panties, tortures and then kills, but one wonders what on earth Anne Heche, Karen Black and Carrie Fisher are doing appearing in such over-dramatized camp twaddle: Heche has lost the fresh-faced appeal that characterized her role in *Six

Days Seven Nights, Black gives a horrible performance as an over-the-hill sex-starved tramp and Fisher looks old and shop-worn. This is Cumming's show, no doubt about it, but the sheer self-indulgence of it all will turn many viewers away. Black ghost/horror comedy? Black *camp* ghost/horror comedy? *Intolerable Suffering* would be a far more apt title here.

Grave Encounters
Twin Engine Films/Digital Interference Prods. 2011; 92 minutes;
Directors: Colin Minihan and Stuart Ortiz (The Vicious Brothers) ****

Unseen found footage from the *Grave Encounters* ghost-busting television program *The Haunted Asylum* points to the fact that the derelict Collingwood Psychiatric Hospital, closed in 1963, does indeed contain spirits and ghouls of the malevolent variety.

With a mad neurosurgeon practicing illegal brain surgery, murdered by six of his patients, and 80,000 individuals incarcerated within its forbidding walls over a 65-year period, what fool would be brave or stupid enough to enter that vast empty edifice during the night to investigate possible supernatural phenomena (the abandoned Riverview Hospital at Coquitlam, British Columbia, was used for location filming). Sean Rogerson and his skepti-

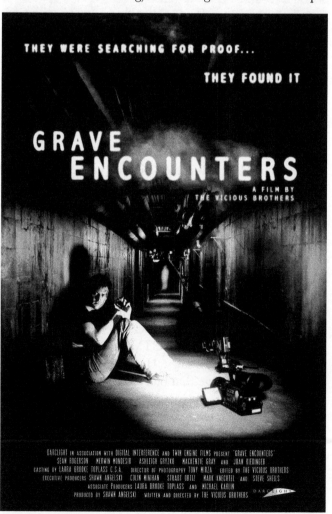

UNDER TEN MILLION? ANYTHING'S POSSIBLE!

cal crew step through the doors with instructions to the janitor to be left alone until six the next morning. Setting up their cameras and equipment on different floors, they sit back and wait for things to happen. And happen they do, big time, in The Vicious Brothers' clever reworking of the whole *Paranormal Activity*/*Blair Witch* schtick, mostly shot through shaky, green night vision lenses. After a careful buildup to heighten the claustrophobic tension, the walkie-talkies pack up, dark-eyed ghouls and deformed mental patients are spotted, noises heard, windows open, doors slam and technician Juan Riedinger is the first to vanish, reappearing later as a blabbering wreck attired in a white surgical gown and throwing himself down a lift shaft. Time mysteriously shifts, as does the institution's inner dimensions—forced exit doors open, not to the outside but to other endless corridors, the place becoming a prison, its new inmates, steadily growing crazy with fear, unable to break out. Ashleigh Gryzko has "Hello" carved on her back, that evil doctor and his hellish team put in an appearance and Rogerson, no longer cynical, having been tossed into the air like a rag doll, winds up a quivering idiot deep in the gloomy confines of the underground service tunnels, munching on a dead rat. Made on limited funds, *Grave Encounters* is spine-tingling fun, almost as good as what many fans reckon to be the ultimate in indie haunted insane asylum movies, USA Films' 2001 *Session 9*. The slightly inferior *Grave Encounters 2* followed hot on its heels in 2012.

Grave Secrets: The Legacy of Hilltop Drive
Hearst Entertainment 1992; 97 minutes;
Director: John Patterson ***

A couple and their young granddaughter move into a house that has been built over a 60-year-old negro cemetery named Black Hope and come under attack from unseen forces.

Yes, it's been done many times before (*Poltergeist* and numerous others) but this made-for-TV effort is more effective than most low-budget "cursed houses" flicks. Patty Duke and David Selby play the harassed couple, granddaughter Kiersten Warren experiencing eerie shadows on the walls. It's all here: The self-flushing toilet; people becoming seriously ill; flickering lights; mysterious black stains; an uncanny tree; and a writhing serpent. Based on fact, the other residents on the Hilltop Drive estate were similarly troubled, the first being neighbor David Soul: Two bodies

were discovered on his plot while excavating for a pool. Given short shrift by the building company who denied all knowledge of a burial site and refused compensation, every family eventually upped sticks and moved out, at considerable financial loss. If you enjoy the likes of *The Amityville Horror* (the 2005 remake!), this well-paced, decently acted supernatural chiller will be right up your street.

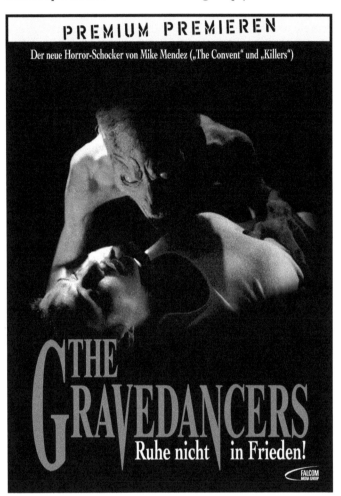

The Gravedancers
Darclight/Code Ent. 2006; 95 minutes;
Director: Mike Mendez ****

To celebrate the burial of a mutual friend, three pals throw an impromptu party in the cemetery; mildly intoxicated, they dance on three gravestones while reading the script of a strange card found beside their friend's grave and in doing so conjure up three malevolent ghosts.

With *Poltergeist*-type effects near the end and plenty of scary shocks in between, Mike Mendez's supernatural thriller keeps us involved from start to finish, expertly jangling the nerves and raising the goosebumps. Following a funeral reception, Dominic Purcell, Marcus Thomas and Josie Maran drive out to the cemetery, get drunk and disturb three thoroughly evil spirits who are determined to terminate their lives. Mendez artfully goes for a slow, icy buildup in the first hour: Purcell and wife Clare Kramer disturbed by creaking doors, rattling pipes, voices, a piano playing and the vision of a hag in a white shroud; Maran plagued by similar manifestations; and Thomas experiencing small fires breaking out in his house. When a team of paranormal investigators is called in (Tchéky Karyo and Meghan Perry), they discover that the trio of phantoms on their tail comprise a boy arsonist who wiped out his family when he set the house ablaze, a demented female axe-murderess and a judge who imprisoned young girls, tortured, raped and killed them—certainly *not* your average spooks! Karyo reckons that by digging up the remains and re-burying them in new graves, they will be laid to rest, but when they do so (in the grounds of Karyo's house), all hell breaks loose; massive railings rise up to enclose the building and the three ghouls begin a rampage of terror. There's enough incident here to flesh out half-a-dozen movies and the resurrected dead, grinning ear to ear from skull-like faces, are truly creepy creations, which means you *don't* scoff when Purcell is pursued in his car by a giant floating skull. Played straight, directed with finesse and not ruined by an over-loud score, *The Gravedancers* cuts the mustard as far as indie ghost flicks are concerned. See it with the lights on!

Grim Reaper

MRG Ent. 2007; 82 minutes; Director: Michael Feifer **

On her way home from a pole-dancing session, a woman is hit by a cab but somehow emerges unscathed; however, she then finds herself imprisoned in a derelict asylum, St. Joseph's, where death awaits her.

In other words, Cherish Lee's time wasn't up, but it should have been—she and several other inmates have broken the "circle of fate" and are existing in a kind of netherworld, according to chain-smoking doctor Brent Fidler who claims to be experimenting in mass hypnosis, a cover-up for what's really happening. To return to normality, Lee, with the help of trainee medic Benjamin Pitts, has to go into a self-induced coma, confront the Grim Reaper, and then be revived. A rehash of the "lost souls in limbo" framework, it's difficult to see how any moviemaker can offer a fresh slant on this particular theme. Filmed at night in dingy surroundings, *Grim Reaper* is something of a slog, although the cloaked, scythe-carrying phantom stalking the cold corridors is a scary creation and the numerous plot

twists are wrapped up neatly by the time Lee vanquishes the demon in a flash of blinding light. But the overall feel is one of drabness; it lacks the vital spark to lift it from the ordinary to the acceptable.

The Hearse

Crown International 1980; 95 minutes;
Director: George Bowers **

A woman stays at her deceased aunt's house, left to her own devices by her mother, and finds herself continually harassed by a mysterious black hearse that chases her down country roads.

Featuring Joseph Cotten in his last major role, *The Hearse* is a low-budget formulaic haunted house thriller burdened by a busy score that borrows from every supernatural/horror movie ever made—it tinkles, it shrieks, it roars, it's all over the shop and sets the teeth on edge. The veteran actor plays a grizzled estate agent trying his damnedest to put off Trish Van Devere moving into her aunt's spooky house; the aunt practised black magic years ago and her evil presence haunts the place. When handsome David Gautreaux shows up, bearing an uncanny resemblance to her aunt's boyfriend, and a hearse appears at night driven by a cadaverous-looking man, the film enters into stock "slamming doors and windows/flickering lights/dream sequences/barely glimpsed figure" mode, backed by that annoying soundtrack. A priest (Donald Hotton) gives more dire warnings about the house, Van Devere discovers that Gautreaux died in 1952, Cotten and young Perry are slaughtered by the phantom witch and the movie ends on a vague, unsatisfactory note, as if everyone concerned had thrown in the towel, or at least were unable to come up with a logical explanation as to what the heroine had been put through. Some moments of unquiet and Van Devere's measured performance are let down by the woeful wrap-up; *The Hearse* will provide mild shocks for the under-12s only.

House of Voices aka **Saint Ange**
Castel Film Romania/ Eskwad-H Factory
2004; 98 minutes;
Director: Pascal Laugier **

Hired to clean Saint Ange, an orphanage in the French Alps that is closing down, a young woman falls prey to the baleful presence of 300 children who mysteriously disap-

peared from the premises at the end of World War II.

Beautiful to look at (cinematography: Pablo Rosso), French-produced *House of Voices* is ultimately a dull "haunted orphanage" supernatural offering lacking in dramatic impetus and static for its opening 50 minutes: Virginie Ledoyen simply wanders the empty corridors looking distressed while young adult Lou Doillon, the only orphan left

and behaving like a retarded Goth, talks of the "scary children," housekeeper Dorina Lazar is too motherly for her own good and severe governess Catriona MacColl is covering up secrets best left undisturbed. Ledoyen is pregnant; MacColl knew this when she hired the girl and allows her to stay, but why? Full marks to composer Joseph Loduca for throwing everything including the kitchen sink into his score to prevent us from drifting off: His music blasts away without pause, highlighting every single plot nuance; just when you thought Laugier's handling of the narrative couldn't get any slacker and you're screaming for something to happen, in comes Loduca to jolt us out of our torpor (Laugier fared much better with the sadistic *Martyrs* in 2008). Yes, the enigmatic closer, taking place in a white sterile ward deep beneath the orphanage, is a puzzle, shaven-headed zombie children appearing and watching Ledoyen giving birth; mother and child die, to join the ranks of those ghostly orphans, her blank-eyed phantom spotted by Doillon as she leaves the place with MacColl and Lazar. Were these kids the subject of Nazi experimentation, hinted at when Ledoyen discovered a box of case records and photographs in an abandoned chapel? Was the clinic scenario a figment of her fevered imagination? What was behind those scars on Ledoyen's back? Why was irritating Doillon on medication? Who drowned those kittens, and why? Who knows (and many will say who cares), a clear case of too many unanswered questions. Filmed in Romania, *House of Voices* had an unsuccessful run in some European theaters, going straight to DVD in other countries. In this instance, the actors and direction come off second-best to that splendid old building which Pascal Laugier should

have made more use of, a distinctly fidget-inducing exercise in haunted orphanage non-thrills.

Imaginary Playmate
Ardmore Prods./CanWest 2006; 93 minutes;
Director: William Fruet ***

A couple moves into an old house and soon, their 10-year-old daughter has an imaginary friend connected to the building's dark past.

There's nothing quite so nerve-tingling as when an innocent child hooks up with a not-so-innocent invisible buddy. The trouble is, Cassandra Sawtell's buddy, Candace (Nicole Muñoz), was abused by her mentally retarded father and then hanged from a tree 100 years ago when her mother died in childbirth; her restless spirit now wants a "proper" family to love her and that includes Sawtell's pregnant stepmother, Dina Meyer. Needless to say, boneheaded hubbie Rick Ravanello doesn't believe a word when Meyer voices her concerns over Sawtell's disturbing behavior, not even when interfering doctor Nancy Sivak is killed in a car crash by the demon girl and Meyer miscarries in another ghostly accident. A moderately creepy thriller containing a few minor shocks, shot in Canada and directed with pace by William Fruet, crams it all in: A sealed, cobwebby bedroom in the attic; a faded photo-

graph, the man's head missing; elderly care resident Marilyn Vance seeing the presence of Muñoz standing beside Meyer; Sawtell bombarded by dolls in her bedroom after upsetting Muñoz who is buried in unhallowed ground; and a moving swing with no occupant. Sawtell puts in a bravura performance for one so young, chatting, playing and then fending off her increasingly unfriendly playmate, while Meyer, as the tormented mother, is totally believable. The climactic twist? Vance happens to be Muñoz's long-lost sibling, an orphan abandoned on the church steps; after the blue-faced specter has forced Meyer and her family to flee, another family moves in, Vance asking the couple, "Have you seen my sister?" as their son spots that ominously moving swing in the garden.

KM31: Kilometre 31
Santodomingo Films 2006; 103 minutes;
Director: Rigoberto Castaneda ***

On a stretch of the Desierto de los Leones road, at junction KM31, a spate of supernatural accidents resulting in injury or death is attributed to the shades of a small boy and his mother.

Almost identical in subject matter to Fidelity Films' 2007 *The Cry*, *KM31* is based on a Mexican urban myth concerning a woman wronged centuries ago by a colonial

who used her to procreate children, even though he was married; in anguish at his cruel treatment, she drowned herself and her son. Their vengeful spirits use waterways to trap their victims, and also the road which was once a river. For 75 minutes, this Mexican thriller grips the attention as Iliana Fox plays the sister of a woman seriously injured on the road; both her legs are amputated, and she's in a coma to boot. Into the picture appears boyfriend Adria Collado and her sister's boyfriend, Raul Méndez, plus cop Carlos Aragon who's investigating 25 incidents at this site and the identity of the scary little kid seen there. Lulling the viewer into thinking that what they are being served up with is a finely crafted platter of psychological ghostly shocks, Castaneda then goes down the Asian horror route and gets all arty-farty: An old woman meets Fox, telling her of the legend and that her sister, hovering between life and death, is trying to communicate with her; can the sister (also played by Fox) defeat these evil spirits; what is the relevance of the family tragedy involving the death of their schizo mother—did the sisters drown her? Misty roads, whisperings, half-seen figures, dark woods, gloomy underground passages—the director throws it all in, including a confusing climax in the sewers whereby Fox sacrifices herself to the ghoulish phantom to save her sister—or does she? Great cinematic ghost stories are those kept simple—here, it's a case of too much plot spoiling the broth. However well the film is directed, photographed and acted, *KM31* comes across as a Mexican ghost story masquerading as an Asian ghost story and the format, by now, is becoming ever-so-slightly stale.

Lake Mungo
Mungo Productions/SBS Independent/Screen Australia 2008; 87 minutes; Director: Joel Anderson *****

A 16-year-old girl is drowned in a dam near the town of Ararat in South West Victoria, Australia; after her body is recovered, a series of inexplicable incidents occur at the family home.

There are paranormal features; and then there are *exceptional* paranormal features. *Lake Mungo* falls firmly into the second category, a superior Australian exercise in grief, loss and fright from writer/director Joel Anderson that will hold you in its clammy grip right to the very end; and *don't* skip the final credits! Presented in found footage/documentary-style (interviews with friends, video and home cine footage, camcorder/cellphone footage), combined with "normal" filming (an artful blend from Anderson and editor Bill Murphy), the cast give commendably realistic, almost one-dimensional performances (which work here; no silly histrionics), the involving plot (based on fact, as most Aussie films are) commencing with the discovery by police divers of Talia Zucker's body in a dam on December 21, 2005. Dad David Pledger identifies her decom-

In 2008, Alice Palmer died...
Her nightmare didn't.

LAKE
MUNGO

night, she buries her cellphone, rings, bracelet and necklace by a tree in the dry lake bed, a form of ritual, but for what? The family drives to the lake, retrieves the buried items and watches her cellphone footage in mounting horror: Zucker was running from *something*, a corpse-like doppelgänger of herself, the final freeze shot depicting her agonized face, "the same face I identified on her body," Pledger mutters, trembling. "I think Alice saw a ghost, her own, a glimpse of the future coming together," and this is confirmed in parallel interviews with Jodrell; Zucker's in July 2005 and Traynor's in February 2007. In the first, Zucker, eyes closed, relates how she walks into the house, her mother's there but leaves without acknowledging her; in the second, Traynor, eyes closed, says she goes into the house and sees Zucker on a wicker chair in her bedroom; then she vanishes. "She wanted us to find out who she really was before she could leave," declares Traynor, the family moving away from a now calmer dwelling. During the end credits, those photographs faked by Sharpe show the ghost of Zucker *but in a different position* to those previously seen, and her image is visible in the window of the family home as Mum, Dad and son line up for a group photo—she was there all the time, a chilling denouement to a supernatural mystery thriller that gets right under your skin and leaves an indelible impression. You won't forget it in a hurry.

Nazi Dawn aka Deadwater aka Black Ops
First Look Studios/Rebel Films 2008; 90 minutes;
Director: Roel Reiné (Rebel Wan) *

A 60-year-old ship adrift in the Persian Gulf houses the evil entity of a genetically altered Nazi SS officer from World War II.

For SS, substitute SSSS: Soggy Seafaring Supernatural Saga. A jaded-looking Lance Henriksen, looking as worn-out as the plot, abseils aboard a floating rust-bucket with his militia, only to find dismembered bodies cluttering up the galleys. Son Gary Stretch has survived, along with a few others, and soon all are at the mercy of a Nazi who was captured in 1945: Experimented on and genetically messed up, his essence has fused with the ship to form a type of murderous entity that dismembers, decapitates and electrocutes—the ultimate killing machine,

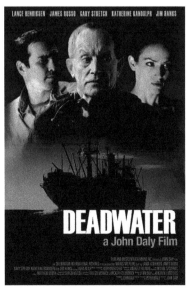

posing corpse: 10 days on from the funeral, the house is subjected to doors slamming and other unsettling noises, Mum Rosie Traynor having distressing visions of Zucker standing at the foot of her bed; Pledger states that he was in Zucker's room when she wandered in, froze, then screamed "Get out!" In April 2006, Zucker's brother, budding photographer Martin Sharpe, sets up cameras in key spots, footage revealing his sister's indistinct ghost which he later admits were faked to ease his mother's pain. A photograph taken at the dam shows Zucker standing in the background; again, Sharpe claims he doctored the picture. Is she still alive? DNA samples taken from her exhumed remains prove she did die. Psychic Steve Jodrell is called in, two séances are held and in August, while Sharpe is on a road trip with Jodrell, his camcorders pick up Tucker's image in the hallway—and he wasn't around to fake them! In September, Zucker's diary is found, the words LAKE MUNGO written three times on one page. It also comes to light that not only was the secretive teenager indulging in group sex with her neighbors, who moved out of the district following her death, but had visited Jodrell in July 2005 so that he could interpret vivid nightmares she was suffering in which she felt "scared, cold and wet." Through a series of chilling cellphone images, we see Zucker on a school trip to Lake Mungo in August 2005; during the

which is why the top brass want the entity captured in an "ectoplasmic reader." Katherine Randolph is the only person to step ashore in the end but judging by the glint in her eye, she isn't what she appears to be either. After an interesting, and very gory, initial 20 minutes, *Nazi Dawn* drops away into horror-cliché land and becomes turgid viewing. Henriksen's pained expression says it all!

Return to House on Haunted Hill
Dark Castle Entertainment 2007; 79 minutes;
Director: Victor Garcia **

A woman seeking the statue of evil god Baphomet is murdered by a criminal gang; her sister is taken hostage by them and they drive to the haunted Hill House to search for the idol.

In the late 1950s/early 1960s, Allied Artists' 1958 *House on Haunted Hill* was staple fare for horror fanatics in England, running for years on the Sunday one-day/late-night circuits. The 1999 remake was a blood-soaked disappointment and now comes this straight-to-video instalment which would probably have William Castle and Vincent Price turning in their graves. John Travolta look-alike Erik Palladino and his toadies kidnap Amanda Righetti and boyfriend Tom Riley. The smarmy criminal has been offered five million dollars by a collector for the idol which is believed to be hidden deep in the bowels of the accursed house, and Righetti is in possession of an old journal detailing its whereabouts. When they arrive, professor Steven Pacey and two students are also looking for the artifact. The presence of both parties triggers off a host of manifestations, including two lesbian ghouls and the appearance of Jeffrey Combs, the original mad owner. A cliché-ridden ride on an empty ghost train that has lashings of gore but little else; it's competently acted, and babes Cerina Vincent and Righetti are suitably attractive; that lesbian scene is included for sheer voyeurism purposes only. The script, however, is a letdown, littered with four-letter profanity. Only Righetti and Riley make it to the final reel after the idol has been flushed down a sewer; Combs is ripped to pieces by his phantom patients while the loathsome Palladino is fried in a crematorium. Hopefully, the curtain has now come down on this particular franchise because there is nowhere else left to take it.

Sarah Landon and the Paranormal Hour
Sunset Creek Productions 2007; 81 minutes;
Director: Lisa Comrie **

A 17-year-old girl goes to stay in Pine Valley with the grandmother of her best friend who was killed by a drunk driver, and becomes enmeshed in a supernatural mystery involving two brothers.

A mild ghost story for the younger set—the plot may be involved, but it's put over as family friendly. Rissa Walters stays at the house where she played with her deceased buddy as kids, bumps into old flame Matt (Dan Comrie) and learns that his brother David (Brian Comrie) is living in fear of his life. The reason? Their uncle (Rusty Hanes) had an only son who was a promising sports star. On his 21st birthday, he was killed in a road accident and Hanes blames the boys' mother, Nicole Des Coteaux (the driver), swearing that he will kill David on *his* 21st in revenge. Dead from a heart attack, Hanes' troubled phantom stalks Pine Valley and David is convinced the phantom will carry out this threat, even from the spirit world. Lots of breaking into houses you should stay clear of, creepy happenings (is Walters being haunted also, by her best friend?) and two mediums chucked into the mix, with a silly ending involving a Druid circle and reincarnation—it's a rum blend but a little too innocuous; none of it will raise the goosebumps. Walters looks nice but you can't understand a word she is saying. Really, this will only be of interest to kids looking for their very first cinematic supernatural thrill; the UK "PG" rating says it all.

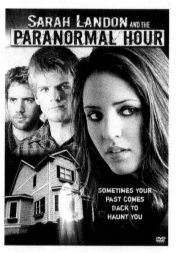

Satanic
Psycho Studios/Barnholtz Ent. 2006; 88minutes;
Director: Dan Golden ***

Following a fatal car accident, a young woman is admitted to hospital to have reconstructive surgery on her shattered features and is plagued by nightmarish visions involving death and black magic.

There are plenty of flashbacks and red herrings in this intriguing little supernatural conundrum: Annie Sorell (nicknamed "Bride of the Mummy" by hospital staff) has her broken face rebuilt by surgeon Angus Scrimm and sent to a home for disturbed delinquents, run by objectionable Rick Dean and his harridan of a wife, Diane Goldner. The girl has constant dreams concerning her dead father, a hooded hitchhiker, a ghoulish monster and of dabbling

in the occult. When a mysterious figure enters the home and starts slaying the residents, Sorell, who has been using an Ouija board with punk roommate Eliza Swenson after reading a journal full of demonic script, thinks she's responsible for the murders. The conclusion is slightly messy, verging on the illogical, revealing that Sorell's features were rebuilt using a set of incorrect photographs. She, in fact, is the hitchhiker while Lauren Emmel is the rebellious teen wanting immortality and causing the car accident; she jumped from the door just before the vehicle crashed, killing her father and *almost* killing Sorell. A fairly compelling excursion in devil-horror which is played out relatively low-key for once.

Static
New Arts Alliance/Divide Pictures 2012; 83 minutes;
Director: Todd Levin ***

Following the death by drowning of their three-year-old son in a lake, a couple suffering marital problems is terrorized in their home by mysterious hooded figures wearing grotesque masks.

An old indie favorite scenario—is writer Milo Ventimiglia dead? Is wife Sarah Shahi dead? Is the girl who visits them one night, Sara Paxton, claiming she is being pursued by murderous masked men, dead? Are they *all* dead? Take note of the two bodies briefly glimpsed at the beginning, and the boy's grave in the woods, and you can probably work it all out by the 70th minute. But that won't stop you becoming involved in Todd Levin's spirited, spook-ridden thriller (his debut feature film; he also wrote the script) as intruders in frog-like masks prowl the gardens near Ventimiglia and Shahi's property, seemingly up to no good. Why does Paxton know more about the boy's death than she should? Why, in an adjoining neighbor's house, are pictures of the drowning and newspaper cuttings plastered all over the walls as in a crime scene? Why is the couple's home under surveillance? Why do the lenses of those masks illuminate dark, unseen objects? All is revealed in the final five minutes—after the boy drowned, Shahi, deranged, shot Ventimiglia and then turned the gun on herself. Paxton and her so-called pursuers are ghosthunters: Only by making contact and scaring the couple into seeing what they have done and confronting the issue can their spirits be at peace; and yes, there are *three* graves in that wood! A worried estate agent is informed that the house is now "clean" as the spirits of mother, father and son disappear into the sunlight, rounding off a satisfactory tale of the supernatural containing a nice climactic twist.

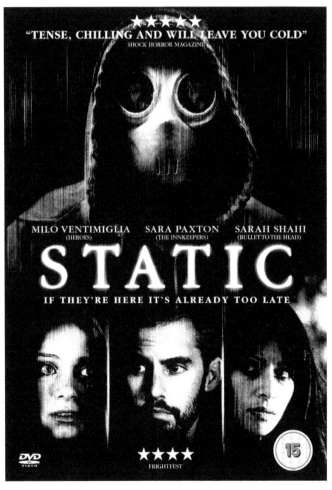

Superstition
Movie Masters 2001; 95 minutes;
Director: Kenneth Hope **

A British au pair working in Italy is accused of murdering the infant in her care by starting a fire, but she denies all knowledge of the act.

Part supernatural puzzler, part courtroom melodrama, part romantic thriller—even the presence of a sterling cast that includes David Warner (judge), Frances Barber (prosecuting counsel), Charlotte Rampling (psychiatrist/mother superior) and David Schofield (professor) can't save this joint British/Netherlands feature from being just plain uninteresting, a soulless exercise with no real depth. The main problem is Sienna Guillory as the girl with a troubled childhood who apparently can cause fires without realizing it. Her elfin features and dumb South London accent bring little conviction to the role; she's certainly no match for David Strong's sympathetic defense counsel and the only one around who believes in her. Flashing backwards and forwards from courtroom spats to Guillory's visions of previous disasters, with a raven and religious motifs inserted at

irregular intervals, *Superstition* spins round and round in ever-decreasing circles and the hurried ending, whereby Guillory rescues Strong from a blazing car which she subconsciously instigated, thus expunging her hidden demons, doesn't make much sense. Based on a true series of events, Hope's sub-supernatural mystery is heavy-handed and dull.

They Come Back
Chesler/Perlmutter Prods. 2007; 90 minutes;
Director: John Bradshaw **

After losing both parents in a car crash, a 10-year-old girl starts seeing a ghostly figure somehow connected to the fatal accident.

A low-key Canadian made-for-TV supernatural thriller that, in its own quiet way, delivers a few mild jolts, probably more appreciated by a younger audience rather than older buffs brought up on a diet of X-rated ghostly shockers such as *The Haunting*. Angst-ridden Mia Kirshner plays a psychologist attempting to unravel the apparently disturbed mind of Niamh Wilson; the girl claims that since her parents died, a presence from beyond is endeavoring to communicate with her, water a significant motif in the messages. Jonathan Watton, Wilson's uncle, hires Kirshner to solve the inexplicable manifestations, even though he

remains unconvinced, while grim-faced Rosemary Dunsmore, Watton's housekeeper, hovers like a dark angel in the background, her intense dislike of the attractive doctor all too evident, but why? *They Come Back* is one of those movies where you're left trying to work out who, and who isn't, a ghost, and the final revelation, which links a missing 16-year-old (Charlotte Arnold) to the odious Dunsmore, won't come as that much of a surprise if you've been closely following the plot. Nevertheless, it has its unsettling moments, and young Wilson is captivating as the 10-year-old with the weight of the world on her shoulders.

They Wait
Brightlight Pictures/TVA 2007; 99 minutes;
Director: Ernie Barbarash **

Returning from Shangai to Canada to attend the funeral of a family member, a woman and her son are caught up in a 50-year-old mystery during the Chinese Festival of the Hungry Ghost.

Plot: One of Terry Chen's uncles was a bone collector; that is, he was responsible for ensuring the bones of deceased immigrants were safely interred in their homeland. If not, the spirits became restless. The movie goes into *Sixth Sense* mode when Chen's young son, Regan Oey, starts seeing disfigured wraiths on the streets, all connected to a disused clothing factory that was once a cover for drugs and other illegal activities. Execution: *They Wait* is recycled Asian ghost/horror and the genre is looking decidedly predictable nowadays. Jaime King is fine as the anguished mother trying to unlock the factory's dark secret, but the shock tactics involving the spooks are leftovers from

The Grudge, *The Eye* etc. and you can predict the ending without too much hassle. If made five years earlier, this would have been quite novel, but the novelty is now getting to wear increasingly thin. Despite the atmospheric photography and good performances, *They Wait* is bland supernatural fare. And what is that opening scene showing a tree leaking blood all about?

The Uninvited

Canal Street Films 2008; 91 minutes;
Director: Bob Badway *

A young woman's phobia (a fear of enclosed spaces) is tested to the limits when she goes to recuperate in a remote cabin where, 30 years ago, seven people died.

Viewers will also be tested to *their* limits when sitting through this incoherent psychological claptrap, no doubt with one question on their minds: What on earth is this all about? Marguerite Moreau plays the woman under stress, married to therapist Colin Hay who spends most of his time away, recording his own cases. Moreau spends most of *her* time hiding underneath her bed, a permanent frown on her features (and has anybody ever noticed that all the brunette leading actresses in these movies look the same), probably trying to escape from an unfathomable plot that includes a stolen baby (hers or the demented young girl's who turns up out of the blue on her doorstep); husband Hay involved in shady dealings with the girl, but what is never explained; a bulky fellow in chains who stomps around like the Frankenstein monster, wielding a huge knife; the ghost of an old woman seen in a window; and bloodstained sheets in the cellar. If the intention was to lace the story with hidden meanings, they remain well and truly hidden, and the damp-squib climax resolves nothing—Moreau walks out of the lodge cradling the baby, leaving behind a room full of mysterious dark forms mumbling among themselves, and is followed by the young girl, drooling blood from a cut throat. In a lifetime of watching psycho thrillers of all shapes and sizes, *The Uninvited* is one of the worst this viewer has ever encountered; you may lose the will to live (or need a psychoanalyst) after watching it.

When the Lights Went Out

Kintop Pictures/SC Films Intl. 2012; 86 minutes;
Director: Pat Holden ****

March 1974: In West Yorkshire, a family moves into a council house harboring two entities: the benign spirit of a dead girl and the malevolent poltergeist that originally murdered her.

In August 1966, the Pritchard family became the topic of much media attention due to poltergeist activity in their Yorkshire home, attributed to the fabled Black Monk of Pontefract. Director Pat Holden, nephew of

Jean Pritchard, moved events forward eight years and had 13-year-old Tasha Connor terrorized by not only the pernicious monk but the manifestation of a young girl who was raped, strangled and had her tongue cut out by the hooded killer in the reign of Henry VIII, the madman hanged for this and other similar crimes. Holden's eye for all things "tacky 1970s" is spot-on, as is his careful buildup to the sinister events that unfold and plague Connor and her parents, British TV regular Steven Waddington and Kate Ashfield: Swinging lights, drops in temperature, bedclothes pulled back, furniture moved, crashing and rattling, shadows on walls, someone sobbing, doors slamming and the grandfather clock plummeting down the stairs. Connor tries to communicate with the phantom lass ("What do you want?"), the newspapers take up the case after a disbelieving reporter is punched in the face by an invisible fist, greedy Waddington charges a pound a head for the public to view his home, Connor's terrified friend, Hannah Clifford, is locked in the toilet, Ashfield is badly stung by a swarm of wasps and paranormal investigator Tony Pitts fails to contact anything unusual. Priest Gary Lewis, busy having a fling with his housekeeper, is blackmailed by Waddington and pal Craig Parkinson into performing an exorcism, holy water sprayed in the rooms which drives the poltergeist away—but only temporarily. Normality returns

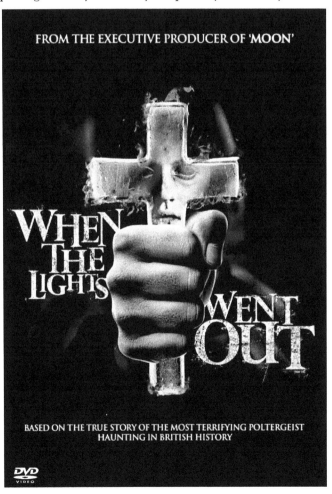

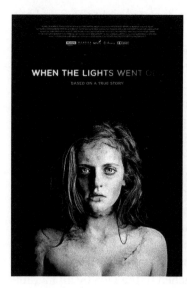

for a short time until one night, the monk materializes in wreaths of black smoke to claim Connor, almost throttling her to death; the vengeful wraith of his former victim drives him back into the dark regions in a blast of blue light; she is last seen as a faded, smiling image in Connor's bedroom mirror, finally at peace—and so is the family home. Very much a British-looking supernatural offering, low-key and gritty, Holden's feature is a solid, well-acted "based on facts" ghost drama that you feel should have been 10 minutes longer to develop more fully one or two plot strands.

Whispers
Tower Bridge Films 2015; 90 minutes;
Director: Tammi Sutton **

Grieving over the loss of their daughter in a drowning accident, a couple goes on vacation to a large country house, the woman tormented by visions of a demonic entity connected to her childhood.

Concentrate hard on the opening 14 minutes of this hit-and-miss supernatural offering; if you don't, nothing that follows will make much sense. Young Catherine (Lilja Johnson), whose mother is one step away from being a child-bully, unearths a raggedy doll in the woods; her brother burns it, he's drowned in a bathtub ("Marie did it," sobs Johnson) and her distraught parent (heavily tattooed model Nina Kate) commits suicide. Flash forward 20 years: Keeley Hazell (grown-up Catherine) and husband Craig Rees stay at a large country house to repair their fractured marriage after the death of their daughter Lily (filming took place at Chulmleigh Village in Devon). Hazell, dosed to the eyeballs on medication by her doctor/therapist Diane Ayla Goldner, starts hearing "Mummy" and "Catherine, I see you" echoing through the rooms, suffers repeated visions relating to a childhood trauma, doors slam, a gray specter is seen in reflective surfaces, sex with Rees is off the menu and when friends Ramon Estevez and Barbara Nedeljakova arrive, the edgy atmosphere drops several degrees, the buxom Slovakian actress blithely announcing she's pregnant. "Where is your crazy wife?" storms Nedeljakova to Rees after she's locked in a sauna. "She hates me 'cos I'm having a baby." An infant's crib mysteriously appears and disappears, the spirit of Lily turns up, Nedeljakova is dragged under the swimming pool, Estevez

falls off a chair and Hazell stabs her husband. Cue for an ending blatantly stolen from *The Others* as another couple moves into the house (she's pregnant!), the woman stating that the previous occupant killed her husband and friends before doing herself in. Yes, Hazell and company were ghosts all along; "Mummy, it's time to go," says Lily as she and Hazell skip into the garden in blazing sunshine. The acting for the most part is dire, Kirk Douglas' (no, not that one!) photography lurches from iPhone standard to garish and the overall execution, constantly interrupted by marriage guidance/therapy sessions, verges on the amateurish. Ambiguities abound: What was the purpose/reason behind young Catherine's mother rising up from an elevator in the floor? Was it *Grudge*-like Marie who was haunting Hazell, or Lily, or both? Who *was* Marie and why was she tormenting Hazell year after year? On a larger budget and given a more professional treatment by producer/writer/director Tammi Sutton and her team, *Whispers* might have made the grade and been more structured; however, after that relatively promising pre-title appetizer, the end result comes across as being concocted by a bunch of student moviemakers engaged on a project for their film degree.

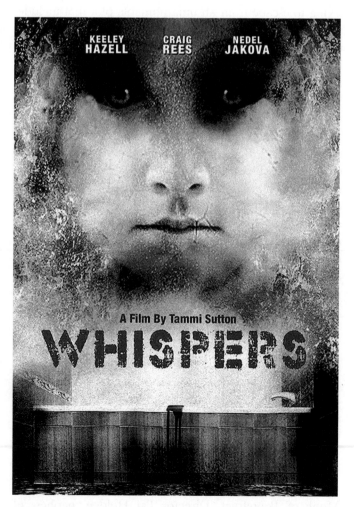

UNDER TEN MILLION? ANYTHING'S POSSIBLE!

The Giants

In time-honored fashion, an explosion in a disused power plant finishes off the snakes and their offspring; Allen then burns her research notes after stabbing the ex-*Baywatch* star in the stomach for his act of treachery. One burning question—where was the action supposed to be taking place? Africa? South America? The filmmakers forgot to address this issue, although the movie was, as a matter of fact, shot in Romania.

Anacondas: Trail of Blood aka Anaconda 4
Stage 6 Films/Castel Film Romania/Hollywood Media
Bridge Prods. 2009; 89 minutes;
Director: Don E. FauntLeRoy ***

A dying pharmaceuticals mogul hires a group of assassins to obtain a vial of the Blood Orchid serum so that he can be cured; anyone standing in their way is to be eliminated.

In the Carpathian Mountains, scientist Zoltan Butuc is treating a baby anaconda with the serum from the Blood Orchid to test its regenerative powers; growing in size, the huge snake escapes from the lab and gobbles him whole as he's tending his orchids in old mine workings. Billionaire John Rhys-Davies, suffering from bone cancer, pays hitman Emil Hostina $1,000,000 to kill Butuc (who's already dead), finish off Doctor Crystal Allen

Anaconda 3: Offspring
Stage 6 Films/Castel Film Romania/Hollywood Media
Bridge Prods. 2008; 91 minutes;
Director: Don E. FauntLeRoy **

A synthetic serum produced in genetically enhanced snakes to cure cancer and Alzheimer's disease leads to the escape of two 60-foot-long anacondas from the lab.

Anaconda 3 is more gruesome than its two predecessors (*Anaconda* and *Anacondas: The Hunt for the Blood Orchid*), just as fast-moving and daft. Super-rich John Rhys-Davies, corrupt head of Wexel Hall Pharmaceuticals (he wants to sell baby anacondas at a hefty $10,000,000 apiece) looks positively apoplectic when his two prime specimens break out of the establishment; Crystal Allen, the blonde super-bitch scientist with a conscience, leads a team to hunt and destroy the serpents; and David Hasselhoff plays a mercenary who sides with Rhys-Davies, those millions of dollars too hard to resist. Heads get bitten off, bodies are swallowed whole, spiked tails skewer torsos and the dialogue will have you wincing in toe-curling embarrassment ("I think my leg is broken," states one of the hunters, staring at her shattered left leg, bone protruding through the skin).

("She knows too much. Remove her.") and bring back the serum. Also converging on the wooded site is Linden Ashby and his team, undergoing research into ancient excavations, plus backpacker Călin Stanciu. Director Don E. FauntLeRoy cuts down on the silliness prevalent in *Anaconda 3* and gets down to the nitty-gritty, the entire cast of disparate characters on the run from each other and the 50-foot anaconda who chomps off heads and limbs with abandoned relish. Hostina (like all paid thugs) gets greedy ("I want 10 million!"), blonde Allen looks great in a skimpy vest top and Rhys-Davies hobbles into the camp, injecting himself with the crimson fluid ("It works! It works!") before being crushed and decapitated by the massive slithering predator. Ashby, Allen, Stanciu and Ana Ularu make it out in one piece, everyone else devoured or gunned down by the gangsters; the anaconda is blown into meaty chunks at the end, yet still manages to regenerate as the final credits appear. The action moves at a clip, Allen and Rhys-Davies steal the acting honors and the anaconda itself is a tolerable CGI creation; yes, it's samey, but lovers of giant reptile movies won't be all that disappointed in the gory action.

Behemoth
Cinetel Films/Reel One Ent; 2011; 90 minutes;
Director: W.D. Hogan **

A colossal mythical monster, asleep for centuries inside a dormant volcano, is disturbed by tremors and awakes, causing worldwide earthquakes.

A disappointing monster yarn from usually dependable Cinetel—the creature (vaguely resembling the Kraken from 1981's *Clash of the Titans*) is only really seen near the end, so in effect we have 80-odd minutes of the cast working their socks off in attempting to generate some excitement, whereas fans will want a glimpse of the beastie sooner rather than much later—all we are afforded is a huge eye and some tentacles. Not good enough! Logger Ed Quinn, daughter Cindy Busby, ex-wife Pascale Hutton and secretive agent Ty

Olsson find themselves, for a variety of reasons, on the wooded slopes of Mount Lincoln, a dormant volcano that is fast becoming unstable, while Quinn's professor father (William B. Davis) and Jessica Parker Kennedy are trapped when Kennedy's diner collapses into a crater. *Behemoth* is a shade too frenzied and po-faced, with lots of scurrying around on the mountain and little else, and the ending (Quinn fires off a missile into the monster's gaping jaws) seems rushed; naturally, after saving the planet, he falls into the arms of Hutton, divorce or no divorce. The rugged mountain scenery is a plus and so is the creature *when* it finally appears—the trouble is, the thing has so little screen time that most will have lost interest long before it clambers into view over the mountain top.

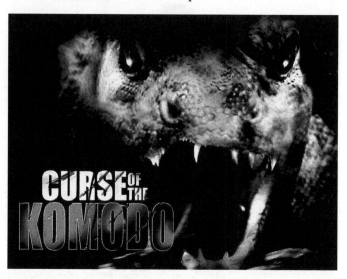

The Curse of the Komodo
Royal Oaks Ent. 2004; 92 minutes;
Director: Jim Wynorski (as Jay Andrews) **

Giant Komodo lizards prowl an isolated Pacific Island, their septic saliva turning humans into infected zombies.

Trapped on the island is Professor William Langlois and friends; landing on the island (by helicopter) in a storm, a bunch of criminals appear, lead by Paul Logan, who have just robbed a casino. The two groups accidentally meet up and then it's every man for himself as they all try to get away from the place, pursued by a posse of colossal CGI reptiles. Meanwhile, on Hawaii, the military are planning to napalm the island, fearing that Langlois' experiments in turning animals into biological fighting machines (Project Catalyst) have gone haywire. Halfway through this no-brainer, you might experience a sense of déjà vu, that what you are suffering through, you have suffered through before. Well, if you've caught Cinetel Films' *Komodo vs. Cobra* (2005), you have! Same plot, same monster (minus the big cobra), same climax (a few survivors get clear in the chopper; the island is bombed; the general responsible for sending in the planes shoots himself); and what's more, the ubiquitous Jim Wynorski, aka Jay Andrews, directed *that* movie as well. Actually, *Komodo vs. Cobra* is the safer bet between the two, but only by an inch or so; the visuals are more striking. Wynorski shoots at a nifty pace, but the inane characters, dumb females (especially Logan's moll, Melissa Brasselle) and hackneyed situations make for an unimaginative monster flick that doesn't engage or excite.

Dinocroc
Concorde/New Horizons 2004; 90 minutes;
Director: Kevin O'Neill **

DNA extracted from the fossilized remains of a pre-historic crocodile discovered in North Africa results in a 40-foot-long modern-day counterpart running amok.

Fifty years on from Universal's classic *Tarantula*, movie scientists are *still* meddling with accelerated growth hormones in order to come up with a solution to the planet's dwindling food supplies. Trouble is, all these similar-themed movies fall a long way short of Jack Arnold's seminal 1955 masterpiece, so veteran producer Roger Corman must have been fully aware of the pitfalls in regurgitating yet another example of science gone wrong. Here, we are presented with Godzilla's little brother; the scaly creature escapes from the lab after eating its sibling, goes on a rampage, is gassed in a tunnel, revives and is then hit by a freight train, although

it appears to have survived, judging by the closing shot. Charles Napier plays the mandatory grizzled sheriff, Costas Mandylor turns up as an Aussie croc killer and the love interest is supplied by animal activist Jane Longenecker (feisty) and beau Matthew Borlenghi (impassive). A few savage attacks liven things up in what is, to be honest, a very ordinary monster offering lacking in originality.

Dinocroc vs. Supergator
Concorde/New Horizons 2010; 87minutes;
Director: Jim Wynorski (as Rob Robertson) ***

On a tropical island, two genetically altered giant reptiles break loose from their cages and go on a rampage.

David Carradine pops up as the shady head of a biotech research center on an island near Hawaii that is supposedly conducting experiments in growth nutrition on plants, not animals. When the two titanic saurians escape from the lab and head for a holiday resort, it's up to sheriff John Callahan, FBI agent James C. Burns, Callahan's daughter, wildlife officer Amy Rasimas, undercover agent Corey Landis, redneck hunter Rib Hillis plus the military to stop them in their tracks. Another energetic monster-fest from the ever-present Jim Wynorski: Following in the footsteps of *Komodo vs. Cobra*, *Piranhaconda*, *The Curse of the Komodo* and other Wynorski "classics," this is entertaining "giant reptile" fodder for the undiscriminating. Simply disengage the brain, sit back and wallow in the crass dialogue, cardboard characters, CGI monster mayhem, done-to-death

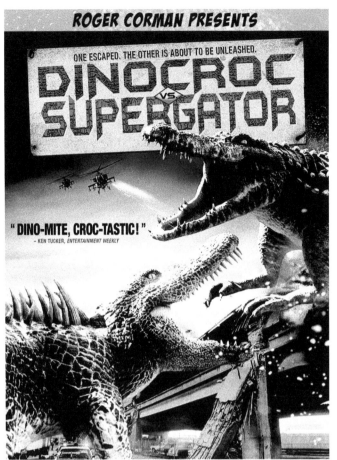

plot and predictable ending, and take time to ponder how grizzled-looking Carradine, in one of his last screen roles, could lend his talents to a production such as this. Actually, the big reptiles look pretty good (Dinocroc eats Supergator and is then blown to bits—but they've produced offspring!), appearing as soon as the title credits are finished which is a bonus, and the sunny tropical settings are well-photographed. It's nowhere near as awful as it sounds.

Mega Snake
Nu Image 2007; 90 minutes;
Director: Tibor Takacs ***

In Hicksville, USA, a man steals a rare snake from an Indian snake breeder but the reptile escapes from its crate, growing to an enormous size and terrorizing a local county fair.

Ranger Michael Shanks' complicated love-life—he's going out with Siri Baruc; she's jealous of local tart Michal Yannai's attentions to-

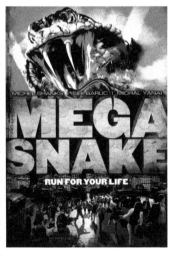

wards Shanks, so she flirts with smarmy Todd Jensen—is rudely curtailed when a snake brought back to the family home breaks free, eats the cat and chickens, feeds off his mother, swallows his brother and slithers through the woods, all 60 feet of it. Indian Ben Cardinal reckons the only way to kill the serpent is to get inside its body and cut out the heart, which is what Shanks and Baruc achieve after the colossal snake has wreaked havoc at the fair. Takacs, somewhat of a veteran of independent monster movies, directs with pace and no one is left guessing as to what the enormous CGI serpent looks like—it's there from reel one, and you get to see plenty of it. The snappy script and lively performances ensure that nothing is really taken all that seriously; all in all, *Mega Snake* is one fast-moving, enjoyable indie giant creature flick.

Megaconda
Retromedia Ent./Babysteps Ent. 2010; 86 minutes;
Director: Christopher Douglas-Olen Ray ****

Construction workers disturb a 100-foot prehistoric anaconda in its underground lair, awakening the monster which embarks on a feeding spree.

Only available (as I write) on obscure DVDs from Thailand, *Megaconda* is one of those indie rarities that contain a memorable score, in this case from composer Chuck Cirino; it sticks in the mind throughout, refusing to budge long after the closing credits. One-time Hollywood glamour puss (*Playboy*'s Playmate of the Month, January 1960) Stella Stevens is on hand playing a diner owner, 74 at the time of filming. Corrupt developer Greg Evigan is building on rural land treasured as a walking area by locals, not the most popular person in town. Flirty wife Brianna Lee Johnson has the hots for foreman Dylan Vox, while Sheriff Ted Monte is investigating the disappearance of two men in the hills, the very same hills that son Christopher Russell Yocum, girlfriend Jessica Irvine and nerdy pal Matthew T. Chandler are conducting a camcorder exposé on, to be handed to TV reporter Angela Landis. Indie regular Michelle Bauer appears midway through, an attractive drifter living in a cave. That's the cast: The main character is that mighty reptile, emerging from its crater home, slithering here, there and everywhere and gulping down human prey with relish; it even gets to drag a chopper out of the sky. Steve Latshaw's script admirably stays on the side of sensible but with a few hilarities chucked in to appease dialogue-lovers ("It looked to me like a big-assed snake!" "It likes people." "It likes to eat them!"), Christopher Douglas-Olen Ray (his father, Fred Olen Ray, was producer) keeping things moving amid sunny, rocky scenery. Needless to say, only Monte, Bauer, Yocum and Irvine make it out alive after poacher Michael Gaglio has blown the creature into three segments ("You're gonna make one helluva pair of boots!"), the foursome outlined against a vivid blue sky, an arty parting shot if ever there was one. And judging by the way Bauer is gazing up at him, widowed Monte is soon going to have a new playmate of his own! Colorful, entertaining monster hokum produced on a $200,000 budget, a tad more intelligently worded and handled than most.

Piranhaconda
American World Pictures/New Horizons 2012; 86 minutes;
Director: Jim Wynorski ****

Shooting their latest horror masterpiece, *Head Chopper 3*, on Hawaii, a film crew meets a new kind of horror—a mutated, 100-foot anaconda sporting the head of a piranha.

Shot around spectacular Kaua'i, Hawaii in dazzling color (cinematography: Andrea V. Rossotto) with old hand Roger Corman executive producer at the helm, a rocky title track (Jasmin Poncelet), an eye-catching CGI creature and briskly directed by monster movie specialist Jim Wynorski, what's not to like about AWP's $1,000,000 budgeted *Piranhaconda*? Fair enough, gruff scientist Michael Madsen does a reasonable impression (once again—see 1998's *The Sender*) of sleepy-eyed Robert Mitchum in a straw hat, blonde Shandi Finnessey is a cute *and* dumb bikini babe while square-jawed Rib Hillis plays a one-dimensional stuntman, romancing standoffish Terri Evans, but these aren't detractions, rather playthings for that enor-

50 TONS OF BONE CRUSHING TERROR

MEGACONDA

> *Piranhaconda* and *Dinocroc vs. Supergator* director Jim Wynorski told us: "The greatest thing about these two films was they got me over to Hawaii twice for wonderful 'working' vacations. On the island of Kaua'i, you can point your camera in almost any direction and get a beautiful shot.

UNDER TEN MILLION? ANYTHING'S POSSIBLE!

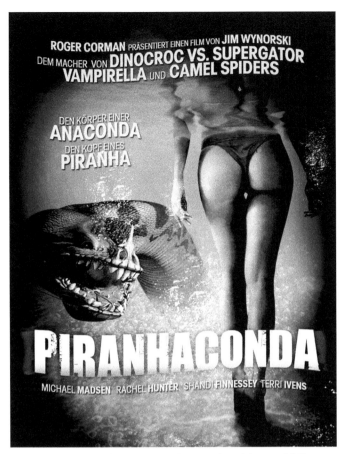

mous yellow reptile to hunt down, the thing gobbling up all and sundry amid breathtaking scenery. Chris DeChristopher and his crew are kidnapped by gangster Michael Swan's mob and held for ransom in an abandoned works, Madsen (carting around an egg which he terms an "evolutionary weapon") warning everybody of the mighty "river devil" lurking in the rainforest. By the finish, everyone bar Hillis and Evans has been bitten in half, dismembered or swallowed, or all three, the snake blown to bits in a pool but a second ready to fill its skin as Hillis and Evans walk off to play house. Red perspective monster views, the reptile grabbing a helicopter out of the air, severed torsos, gunfights, Poncelet's rockin' soundtrack, truly wonderful location work plus plenty of giant monster action; *Piranhaconda* is an enjoyable exercise in good, old-fashioned, creature-feature thrills which fans of all ages will lap up.

Poseidon Rex

Titan Global Entertainment 2013; 81 minutes;
Director: Mark L. Lester **

Divers searching for Mayan gold off a Caribbean island, the "Lost Gold of Cortez," detonate the seabed, disturbing a colossal T-Rex-type sea monster that goes on a rampage.

Grizzled treasure hunter Brian Krause, busty blonde marine biologist Anne McDaniels, beefy boat owner Berne Velasquez and tourist Steven Helmkamp battle both the titan from the depths and local drug dealers in this glossy-to-look-at (filmed in Belize) monster romp that manages to

pass the time in unmemorable fashion. CGI effects in indie cinema have come on in leaps and bounds over recent years, so scenes of the big web-footed reptile smashing boats, gobbling humans and stalking its prey on shore, plus a newly hatched baby monster running loose in the lab, are quite well executed, considering the budget. A couple of severed limbs, the army wanting to blast the island to bits despite loss of human life and McDaniels dragging Krause into bed, regardless of all the mayhem taking place, ensures that the movie isn't quite inane fodder for the kiddies (15-rated in Britain), and after hot dish McDaniels blows the creature's head off, we are left with the sight of eggs littering the ocean floor, one hatching to reveal a snarling, fanged face, something which everyone concerned evidently forgot about—*Poseidon Rex 2*, anybody? Reasonable giant monster shenanigans, suitable for a wet night in.

Xtinction: Predator X aka Alligator X

K2 Pictures/Marvista Ent. 2010; 89 minutes;
Director: Amir Valinia *

A cloned 50-foot-long marine dinosaur causes havoc in the Louisiana Bayou.

Great title—not-so-great movie. In fact, it's a complete and utter dud. Something is chomping up the residents of a swamp community and Elena Lyons, who with her father runs sightseeing trips in their battered boat, soon finds out that her ex-husband, scientist Mark Sheppard, is behind it all: He's created a monster from prehistoric DNA and the creature, resembling a scaly plesiosaurus with fangs, is out of control, and pregnant. Sheppard wants to buy up all the land to breed these things, Lyons and blonde babe Lacy Minchew are abducted by two of Sheppard's redneck thugs, sheriff Lochlyn Munro (who fancies Lyons like mad) comes to the rescue and the beast is blown to smithereens by Lyons' mammy after it has eaten its cre-

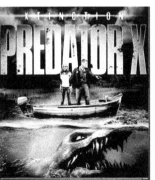

ator. Naturally, the final shot sees the dinosaur's eggs hatching on the swamp bed. Dull talkative interludes, hammy acting and a poorly executed CGI monster all contribute to an unimaginative creature-feature that, in the context of a "something is lurking in the swamps" thriller, is way, way down on the list.

Horror/Psychological/ Possession

The Abandoned
Filmax Intl./Castelao Prods. 2006; 99 minutes;
Director: Nacho Cerdà ***

A woman travels to the backwoods of Russia to view the house she inherited from her mother who was murdered when she was a baby, and meets the phantoms of her disturbing past.

A joint Spanish/UK/Bulgarian production filmed in the bleak forested wastes of Bulgaria, featuring a nightmarish house in the middle of nowhere, the kind of place you wouldn't want to take on in a million years—but neurotic Anastasia Hillie does just that. After a fraught journey, she meets her twin brother (Karel Roden) at the rundown house, encounters their ghoulish doppelgängers and gets caught up in a 42-year-old supernatural time loop revolving around the brutal murder of their mother by Valentin Ganev, their deranged father. His presence, and the house itself, wants the siblings to stay put, thus completing the cycle of events ("We were never meant to leave this place."), so any attempt at escaping the house and its remote environs is doomed to failure as the trick ending proves (Valentin is both the evil father *and* the estate agent passing the property on to Hillie). Expertly directed and photographed, an electronic background drone adding to the mood of haunting desolation, *The Abandoned* comes unstuck in its final section by piling on far too many false endings; just when you think it's all over, it isn't, and so on, and so forth, to the point when you wish the film would wrap up and finish. The picture eventually closes with the voice of Hillie's daughter declaring that, in her opinion, she doesn't want to know anything of her mother's disappearance; it's best to remain abandoned (as, indeed, Hillie herself was). There are several interludes of sweat-inducing terror that take place in Hillie's moldy, decaying inheritance, including a dose of harrowing poltergeist activity, but those protracted multiple climaxes spoil what could have been a real devil's brew if edited down by a few minutes.

Airborne
Press On Features/Black and Blue Films 2012; 81 minutes;
Director: Dominic Burns ****

A flight from East Midlands Airport to New York goes horribly wrong when the evil spirit of a dark Chinese Lord escapes from an ancient cursed vessel, forcing those he possesses to murder the other passengers.

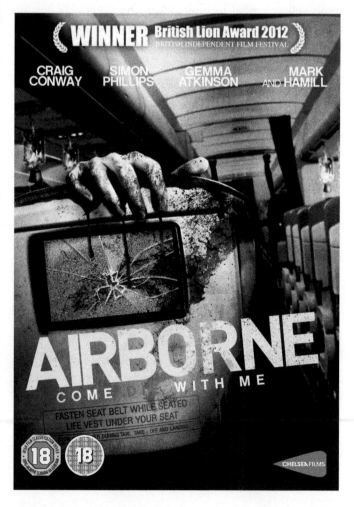

UNDER TEN MILLION? ANYTHING'S POSSIBLE!

Was it the intention to make this scatty, foul-mouthed British movie a horror sendup of 1980's glorious *Airplane!*? From an English point of view, it's very, very funny—every time tough guy actor Alan Ford opens his mouth, a stream of expletives pours forth, most not suitable for publication ("One of you c..ts is a killer," he barks). Controller Mark *Star Wars* Hamill, on the point of retirement, has his work cut out as Flight 686 veers off course in a storm, heads towards South America, then disappears from the radar screens: Onboard, Ford, his two heavies, a couple of soldiers, a doctor, a geography teacher, a secretive steward, a couple determined to join the mile-high club, a lone woman, two sexy stewardesses, a guy yearning for some peace and quiet (he won't get it on this flight!) and a professor fight and squabble, that creepy crate in the hold emitting high-pitched soundwaves that send them all crazy, as if they weren't crazy enough already. People go missing, found butchered in the hold, Julian Glover tells all about the crate's supernatural hidden secrets, the Chinese vase is smashed and the two pilots are shot dead. It turns out stewardess Gemma Atkinson is in league with thug Craig Conway, planning to sell the vase for millions to a South American dealer; however, the possessor of human souls has other ideas. Back on dry land, Hamill receives a visit from Billy Murray and his gun-toting agents who arrest him and his team ("No one must ever know.") as a missile strike is called off, the plane now in American airspace. It crashes into the Atlantic, but whatever entity was inhabiting the urn now inhabits Hamill, judging by his malicious grin and glowing blue eyes. An utterly bonkers UK horror/possession cheapo effort that gallops along on a wave of mounting paranoia, almost a one-off, ludicrous, hammy, hilarious, coarse and illogical but criminally tasty, a real guilty pleasure of the highest order.

Apartment 143 aka Emergo
Nostromo Pictures 2011; 80 minutes;
Director: Carles Torrens ***

A father who has moved his family into an apartment calls in a team of parapsychologists, convinced that the spirit of his dead wife is haunting the place.

A Spanish camcorder "paranormal entity" effort shot in Barcelona that has Doctor Michael O'Keefe and assistants Fiona Glascott and Rick Gonzalez setting up their cameras in Kai Lennox's apartment, hopefully to catch on tape the cause of all the disturbances plaguing the family. Is it the restless ghost of his recently deceased wife who died in a car accident? O'Keefe reckons not. "It's unexplained phenomena," he announces. Stroppy teen daughter Gia Mantegna blames Lennox for her mother's death, while five-year-old Damien Roman has spoken to his invisible mummy. In a subgenre packed to the rafters with this kind of supernatural fare, *Apartment 143* isn't all that

bad, producing a few eerie interludes (crashing sounds; flickering lights; moving furniture; the vague outline of a spectral figure) before Lennox reveals that his wife was, "A fucking whore. She was wicked. Never washed. Lost her job. I looked after the kids," and Mantegna, "found her in bed with another man. I beat him up." Not a happy household, then, and, to cap it all, Mantegna has inherited her mother's schizophrenic traits which a poltergeist has latched on to (O'Keefe admits he was aware of this the moment he entered the building), possessing the girl and turning her into a blank-eyed, obscenity-spouting devil in the *Exorcist*-type climax. A psychic storm wrecks the apartment, the equipment is packed away, everyone departs (Mantegna is carted off to hospital) and the final minute shows the one remaining camera focusing on a room. A picture falls off the wall, the camera swivels upwards and a ghoul on the ceiling scuttles towards the screen, an effective ending to a better-than-average paranormal horror outing that, although treading familiar ground, might produce the odd shiver or two.

The Appearing
KK Ranch Prods./Sean Roberts Ent. 2014; 92 minutes;
Director: Daric Gates **

A couple whose daughter drowned in an accident starts a new life in secluded Glenwood Bay; the wife soon comes under the influence of a malevolent spirit inhabiting a nearby derelict house.

First, the good news: The old Bates Motel from *Psycho* was brought out of mothballs and given an airing, like seeing an old friend from times gone by. Secondly, the bad news: *The Appearing* is just one more in a series of modern-day possession movies involving ghostly devil-children, all of which culminate in a protracted, *Exorcist*-type climax. The effective opener has Abigail Cooper and randy boyfriend Payton Wood investigating the alleged haunted building; Cooper disappears, later found with mystical letters carved on her corpse, Wood winding up in a psychiatric ward run by Dean Cain. Morose Will Wallace and neurotic wife Emily Brooks turn up, Wallace to take on the role of Sheriff Don Swayze's deputy and as quick as a flash, Brooks spots a young girl flitting about in the woods, has nightmares involving her dead daughter and enters the cobwebby house, witnessing a girl stabbing another to death. Is it all in her fevered imagination, or related to past

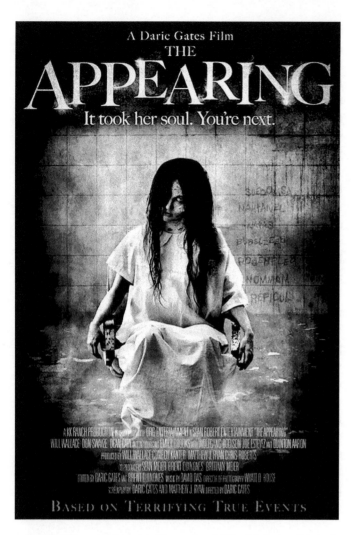

by unexplained supernatural events linked to the father's disturbed mind.

Canadian-produced *Barricade*, at the conclusion to 82 minutes of queer occurrences and flashbacks to happier times—mysterious coughing fits, a ghastly face at the frosty window, handprints on glass, the sheriff appearing, then disappearing, then appearing again, noises in the attic, lights flickering on and off, shadowy figures in the snow and his son and daughter dead, then alive—appears to be all about guilt; Eric McCormack's guilt. When wife Jody Thompson was alive, she criticized him for not taking enough notice of his children's needs. "You're the Dad and you have to look after us," says terrified Connor Dwelly as the banging on the doors and window frames increase in the darkly lit house; "Daddy, please help," moans Ryan Grantham, burning up and feverish, McCormack replying, "I can be a good Dad." Is it all a manifestation of the man's tortured psyche, a product of his guilt and the medication he's on? The end has us believe that Sheriff Donnelly Rhodes passed on a fever to the family who eventually recovered after 48 hours of delirium and were taken away by ambulance. So was everything they experienced a supernatural occurrence or not, particularly when the curtains are drawn aside by "someone" as the ambulance drives off in the snow. One thing's for sure; fathers everywhere will pay just that bit more attention to their kids af-

events? What is the significance of "Sad Mouse Lives in this House" that keeps cropping up time and time again? Amid a deluge of psychological chat concerning fallen angels, guilt, possession, suicides and tortured spirits, it's just about possible to figure out that Swayze is in on Brooks' little secret: As a youngster, she murdered her sister and was a patient in Glenwood Bay Hospital, burying the facts from Wallace. Now, as legendary demon Asmodeus, she grunts, screams, salivates and tries to seduce the local priest Linda Blair-style in a noisy, hysterical sequence that drags its heels; she then recovers, cold-shouldering Wallace as Swayze languishes behind bars for the murder of his wife who was also possessed years ago. A disappointing possession outing that is far too muddled, lacking cohesion and going all-out for a shouty-shouty conclusion that irritates rather than raising the goosebumps.

Barricade
WWE Studios 2012; 82 minutes;
Director: Andrew Currie ***

A year after the accidental death of his wife, a psychologist takes his two children for a week's break at a remote house in the woods where his wife used to go on holiday as a child. Bad weather sets in, and they're menaced

UNDER TEN MILLION? ANYTHING'S POSSIBLE!

ter sitting through this clever little nailbiter that manages, once or twice, to raise the hackles, McCormack turning in a solid, believable performance throughout.

Blackwater Valley Exorcism
Psycho Studios/Wiseacre Films 2006; 90 minutes;
Director: Ethan Wiley **
Against his religious beliefs, a priest, on being contacted by a family, performs an exorcism on a young girl possessed by a demon.

Three decades on from Linda Blair's vomiting, head-revolving performance in *The Exorcist*, we have Kristin Erickson writhing half-naked on a bed, shouting obscenities in a gravelly voice and somehow coming up with a few unpalatable home truths: The local doctor had sex with her mother; the not-so-saintly priest caught her in the shower and what's more enjoyed it; one of the hired hands lusts after her; and the sheriff performed an indecent act with a female prisoner. Unfortunately, horror plus soap opera doesn't add up to much and the continuity is deplorable—characters are seen for a few seconds, then disappear, then reappear; in addition, the dialogue is, in places, totally inaudible. To cap it all, Erickson's sister (Madison Taylor) was/is in love with the priest (Cameron Daddo) and *may* be the catalyst behind the demonic control as she performs a devilish ritual near the end and *might* be possessed herself. The sight of the doctor attempting to inject Erickson with horse tranquilizer from a syringe the size of a rolling pin is nothing short of ludicrous and the end shot, both girls normal and Daddo carrying off Taylor into the sunset, is weakly handled. Erickson saves the day here, her bravura turn lifting the movie from a farrago to a near-farrago.

Blood Snow aka Necrosis
American World Pictures/Two Meter Prods.
2009; 90 minutes;
Director: Jason Robert Stephens ****
Six friends spend a weekend vacation in a snowbound mountain cabin and one of their number begins to see the specters of dead settlers, the Donner party, who, trapped on the mountain in 1846, resorted to cannibalism to survive.

A psychological essay into the effects of cabin fever? The horror is minimal in this capable little chiller—yes, you see gray-faced ghouls in the snow, but the movie is more about isolation and the tricks it can play on your mind.

James Kyson-Lee is the guy who starts to see corpse-like figures among the snowdrifts that whisper "save yourself." But Kyson-Lee has a history of schizophrenia, so is he *really* experiencing ghostly manifestations, or are the back-of-beyond settings playing tricks on his mind? A scrapbook discovered by Penny Drake contains newspaper cuttings detailing a history of murder connected with the cabin and Kyson-Lee finally flips, shooting pregnant girlfriend Danielle De Luca before Drake guns him down. Alone in the cabin, Drake and admirer George Stults face an uncertain future as the bad weather closes in (couple Robert Michael Ryan and ex-pop singer Tiffany have apparently perished in a snowcat accident). Boogeyman Michael Berryman (from Wes Craven's *The Hills Have Eyes*) guests as a local who tries to warn the six off but pays with his life; Stephens makes imaginative use of the wintry landscapes; and the discordant nursery rhyme score matches the bleak surroundings. All things considered, *Blood Snow*, by cutting out the usual bloodshed and teen melodramatics, is rather tasty fare.

The Breeder
Gute Filme/Killing Woods Productions 2011; 91 minutes;
Director: Till Hastreiter ***
Two American girls hike through the mountains of Georgia, on the Russian border; one is abducted by a madman who is after the perfect mate.

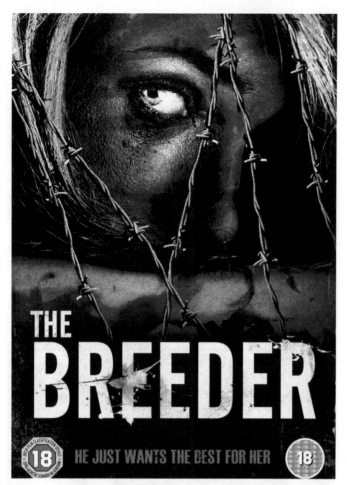

HE JUST WANTS THE BEST FOR HER

A German/Swiss production not released until 2013, *The Breeder* was filmed in Switzerland and, from a scenic view, looks splendid. Perhaps the depiction of Georgia's backward, wall-eyed peasants isn't too accurate, but Peter James Haworth's bunker laboratory (a disused mine was used) is icily menacing; it's here that he drags Julie LeGal, subjecting her to the kind of medical abuse and graphic internal examination you would normally expect to witness in a hospital, and nowhere else. Female watchers will be discomfited by these drawn-out sequences while others will have difficulty in understanding a word the psycho is grunting about under his mask. What the man (a deranged US Major, requiring repeated shots of gas) is looking for is never made clear. The unblemished, perfect sexual partner? No chance with LeGal who has already had a lesbian fling with her buddy, Theresa Joy. Joy and Giorgi Kipshidze (his girl, Tamara Phaliani, has also gone missing; she's in the bunker with LeGal) eventually negotiate the minefield surrounding Haworth's center of operations and save LeGal from possible rape, a priest hanging Haworth up by the thumbs and slitting his flesh, blood dripping into a bucket. Full of cryptic, superstitious warnings and hidden agendas, both from the villagers *and* Kipshidze (what's the mystery behind that lake?), *The Breeder* is obscure and unusual enough to seek out, if only for its atmospheric, very different, setting.

Cassadaga
PoilyWood Entertainment 2011; 108 minutes;
Director: Anthony DiBlasi **

In Cassadaga, a deaf art teacher moves into rented accommodation following the death of her younger sister and is haunted by the apparition of a missing girl who may have been abducted by a serial killer specializing in transforming his victims into marionette dolls.

A case of too much plot spoiling the broth: Everything is crammed into Anthony DiBlasi's horror/supernatural thriller but what finally emerges is a hodgepodge of genre tropes that ultimately refuses to gel into a satisfactory whole. Kelen Coleman plays the deaf teacher, her sister (Sarah Scuko) hit by a car outside her school; Kevin Alejandro is the guy she meets, busy fighting a custody battle over his daughter; Louise Fletcher plays the pot-smoking lady whose mansion Coleman goes to stay in; Lucas Beck is her grandson, spending all his time upstairs watching porn movies with his hand down the front of his pants; and Russ Blackwell is the handyman. Coleman, after a visit to a medium, is plagued by visions of a teenager missing for four years and has a conversation with Scuko *after* she has been killed. We then witness a jogger kidnapped, taken to a workshop, her arms and legs severed and turned into a

human string puppet before stabbed with scissors (linked to the opening scene of a young puppet-obsessed boy murdering his abusive mother) and wonder if Blackwell is as innocent as he looks. Shifting backwards and forwards from one disjointed incident to the next and padded out to knock up the running time (foul-mouthed Alejandro, after assisting Coleman and indulging in sex with her, drops the teacher like a hot brick, stating their relationship is affecting his custody battle and that's she's a schizo, vanishing abruptly from the scenario; why was he ever included in the first place?), *Cassadaga* moves towards its convoluted finale—Blackwell's the psycho, imprisoning mutilated women in an underground bunker inside the greenhouse where Coleman discovers the mummified corpse of the missing girl; loony Beck only uses the greenhouse to grow cannabis. The film ends with a return to the sequence where Coleman talks to Scuko (a spirit) in her car, but why is not quite clear (is it anything to do with that Eiffel Tower pendant containing a hidden blade?). A puzzler of a horror movie that, in the long run, is not worth scratching your head over, despite one or two gruesome highlights and Kelen Coleman's personable performance.

Cherry Tree
Fantastic Films/House of Netherhorror 2015; 85 minutes;
Director: David Keating **

In order to save the life of her terminally ill father, a schoolgirl has to sacrifice her newborn baby to a coven of witches.

Produced by the same team behind Hammer's *Wake Wood*, *Cherry Tree* is an update on the much-used *Rosemary's Baby* theme of a child born through the intervention of the black arts, governed by the Lord of the Underworld. Anna Walton plays the attractive, devious witch, accompanied by her centipede familiars, whose Gothic house contains an underground chamber directly below the roots of an ancient cherry tree. In exchange for sacrifices made to the tree's fruit, her coven is granted satanic powers; in fact, they're all horned demons in human guise, revealed in the final 10 minutes. Naomi Battrick is the 15-year-old getting pregnant in double-quick time by Patrick Gibson; the lad, possessed by a demon, morphs into something not quite human when they have sex. She's pregnant, Dad Sam Hazeldine is cured of cancer (recovered enough to have a romp with Walton) but when the child is born, Walton turns the tables by snatching the baby and throwing father and daughter into a car which is set on fire; Battrick escapes, Hazeldine burned to death. In revenge, the girl dons one of the sect's masks and, in the chamber, sees Walton knife the infant, blood spilling into a bowl of cherries. Walton is strangled to death by living tree roots ("Enjoy hell!") when Battrick grabs the baby back in her arms and Gibson, now transformed into a fiendish monstrosity,

slaughters members of the clan, allowing Battrick to escape. Performing a ritual under the tree's branches, the baby is brought back to life and in the climax, three trick-or-treaters discover that Battrick, in white make-up and crimson lips, now owns Walton's old house. "Are you a witch?" asks one little girl. "No," replies Battrick, smiling wickedly, "but my son is the Devil," and we close on the hideous features of her black-robed toddler as it approaches the door. Filmed in Ireland, *Cherry Tree* has pace, is gory but lacks style, appearing clumsy in some quarters and not very attractive to watch in others. Overall, it fails to impress as a modern-day witchcraft thriller, perhaps because of its young, relatively inexperienced supporting cast.

The Children
Vertigo Films/Barnscape Films 2008; 84 minutes;
Director: Tom Shankland ****

Two families at a Christmas get-together find themselves at the mercy of their young children who suddenly change into homicidal killers.

The first part of Tom Shankland's grim British horror outing is the cinematic equivalent of contraception: Eva Birthistle, husband Stephen Campbell Moore and their kids, moody teenager Hannah Tointon, William Howes and Eva Sayer, descend on Birthistle's sister, Rachel Shelley, her husband Jeremy Sheffield and their two offspring, Rafiella Brooks and Jake Hathaway. Cue for a barrage of screams, shrieks, shouts, tears, tantrums, adult hysteria and noisy shenanigans at the meal table, the children misbehaving big time. Next morning, matters haven't improved as snowball fights turn vicious, the two sets of kids eyeing each other up as though they're set for all-out war. Sweet little darlings they're not! Shankland includes, at intervals, shots of the surrounding, misty, snow-laden woods. Why is made relatively clear at the end after Brooks and Hathaway, suffering from a strange sickness (she vomits up blood), have gone on a rampage, dispatching Sheffield and Shelley and masterminding the gruesome death of Howes. Moore and Sayer manage to drive away, leaving Birthistle (she has a shattered leg) and Tointon at the mercy of satanic Brooks and her equally evil brother. Birthistle kills Hathaway with a poker, drives off with Tointon and encounters Moore's wrecked car in the woods. Moore lies dead in the snow, butchered; Sayer, now a malevolent demon, is finished off by Mum as a group of pale-faced children appear among the trees, Brooks with them. The film closes with Birthistle and Tointon driving hell for leather away from the accursed place. The premise, that under certain conditions, kids would murder their parents and vice versa, is a twisted one that works effectively in this occasionally stomach-churning thriller that may put you off young children, or even *having* children, for life!

Coffin Rock
Bankside/Screen Australia 2009; 92 minutes;
Director: Rupert Glasson ***

A young drifter becomes fixated with a married woman who is trying to conceive by IVF treatment.

Fatal Attraction in reverse—this time, it's a woman (Lisa Chappell) who, after a bout of heavy drinking, gives herself to young Sam Parsonson and then lives to regret the day when he changes into a raving lunatic. Filmed on a tight budget in a dreary looking Australian fishing community, *Coffin Rock*, after an inauspicious start, steps up a gear once Chappell realizes what a blunder she has made in allowing the odious Parsonson to have sex with her. Husband Robert Taylor, full of the joys of spring on learning that his wife is pregnant, can't stop talking about it, unaware that the baby isn't his. When the news of the pregnancy reaches Parsonson, he flips his lid and goes all out to possess Chappell body and soul, violently disposing of anyone who gets in his way. It's a tried and tested formula but presented with vigor; Rupert Glasson only

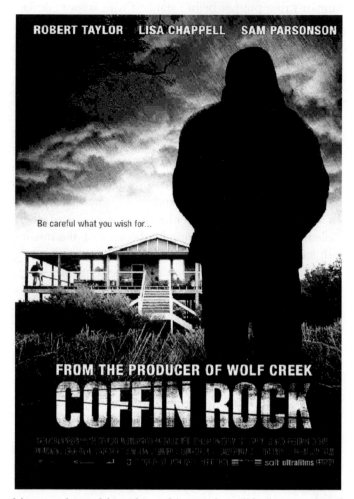

hints at the unhinged youth's previous life (he murdered his father) but one scene, in which Parsonson savagely kills his pet baby kangaroo, is totally unnecessary and extremely distressing to animal lovers—couldn't the director have found a more subtle way to focus on the kid's uncontrollable rage than by showing this? The downbeat ending sees Chappell surviving but ostracized by the close-knit community, and that includes her insensitive husband. Parsonson is truly terrifying as the baby-faced psycho who won't let go and Chappell is equally fine as the wife with no one to turn to. Another low-budget gem from the state-funded Australian indie cinema and a contrast in many ways to the more hyperactive counterparts produced elsewhere.

Cradle of Fear
Pragmatic Pictures 2001; 120 minutes;
Director: Alex Chandon **

Locked away in an asylum, a hypnotist-cum-child killer sends out his demonic emissary to dispatch all those responsible for his incarceration.

Shot on digicam, Chandon's homage to the Amicus compendium horror thrillers of the 1970s plays like a death metal song on celluloid; it's shoddy beyond belief, the four tales constructed haphazardly, the acting poor, the

UNDER TEN MILLION? ANYTHING'S POSSIBLE!

repeated scenes of vomiting too much to stomach (literally!), the bloodletting laid on with a trowel to the point of monotony. David McEwen plays the bearded psycho, Dani Filth (metal group Cradle of Filth's frontman) his Goth shape-changing acolyte, while Edmund Dehn is the world-weary cop out to nail the pair of them. We kick off with two Goths having a sexual encounter with Filth that ends in carnage (dig that baby with the spidery legs that crawls out of one of the girls' abdomen); next on the menu is the story of two female robbers whose double-crossing leads to bloody violence; then we have a one-legged guy who murders his friend so that he can pinch one of his legs to use as his own; and lastly, an internet freak who gets caught up in a snuff website. The movie climaxes with a frenetic bloodbath taking place in McEwen's cell, the de-

praved hypnotist shot dead but Filth surviving as a malformed being. Overlong (especially story number four) and disjointed, this drab British effort has snatches of originality in the first half (plus those sexy Goth chicks) but constant sickening close-ups of blood squirting out of decapitated trunks and of people puking destroy any artistic merit *Cradle of Fear* may have entertained.

Crazy Eights
American World Pictures/IKM Prods. 2006; 80 minutes;
Director: James K. Jones **

Six friends find themselves trapped in a clinic that once carried out unethical studies into children's behavioral problems—were they themselves incarcerated there many years ago?

Starting off with a disjointed, clumsily conceived opening 15 minutes, *Crazy Eights* is a turgid mystery-cum-supernatural drama, hampered by a melancholy soundtrack that adds to the overall dour mood—inaudible dialogue is another drawback. The plot concerns six friends attending the funeral of a seventh who has left them instructions to open a crate hidden in the attic of a dilapidated house. The crate is located and duly opened—inside are children's toys and a small skeleton. Then the six drive off to Entonsburg where a young girl is spotted running into a large derelict building; they follow her, become locked in, Dan DeLuca breaks his right leg in the cellar and it slowly dawns on all six that *maybe* they were all patients in the place many moons ago, and that the institution's malignant soul means to destroy them (why isn't really elucidated upon). Burning the toys will put to rest the building's demons but, one by

one, five of the friends perish; finally, Dina Meyer stabs herself with a glass shard and the movie ends. Perhaps there were supposed cryptic implications appertaining to childhood psychosis in *Crazy Eight*'s setup but if so, they remain open to question in an uninvolving outing that will leave you exasperated at the inconclusiveness of it all.

The Daisy Chain
ContentFilm/Screen Ireland/Wales Creative IP Fund
2008; 89 minutes; Director: Aisling Walsh ****

A heavily pregnant woman, mourning the loss of her baby, sets up home with her husband in a remote coastal community and cares for a shunned child possessing disturbing powers.

Angelic Mhairi Anderson stars as manipulative devil-child Daisy, responsible for a catalogue of disasters: She drowned her baby brother, caused a neighbor's son to fall over a cliff, set fire to her parents in a fairy ring, brought about the death of a social worker in a car accident, willed farmworker David Bradley to burst into flames after she's spat in his face and may be responsible for three children contracting meningitis. According to the superstitious locals, Anderson's a fairy changeling; only on Halloween night can she be reclaimed by the world from which she came. The gossip doesn't prevent morose Samantha Mor-

rubic, slightly demonic, features. A gritty drama to match the cold, hostile landscape, *The Daisy Chain* is a low-budget gem, boosted by Anderson's unforgettable changeling, a little girl who will really put shivers up and down your spine; cute one minute, radiating pure malevolence the next.

Dark Circles
After Dark Films 2013; 87 minutes;
Director: Paul Soter *****

A husband and wife move into a secluded country house with their newborn son and begin seeing a mysterious girl who commences a campaign of terror.

Sleep deprivation plays a major part in *Dark Circles*: A constantly crying baby, noisy construction workers at a nearby site and a ragged-looking girl (Lucresha Wells) who comes and goes, playing havoc with Pell James and musician Johnathon Schaech's lives, reducing them to shambling stressed-out wrecks constantly bickering with one another. Paul Soter's semi-psychological, semi-supernatural thriller is a rarity, a modern-day "haunted house" outing that actually succeeds in chilling the marrow. The couple's physical decline and fragile relationship is worsened by increasing visions of a malevolent female who focuses her attention on the infant, leaving a fire-blackened doll in the house to

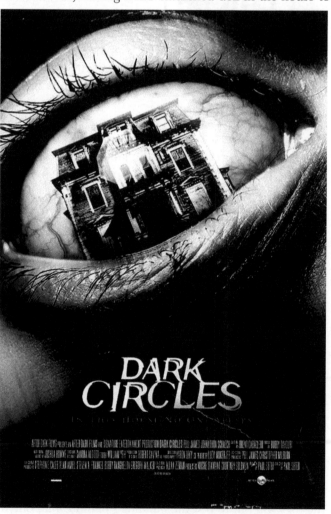

ton from becoming infatuated with the girl, despite husband Steven Mackintosh, the police, the doctor, friend Eva Birthistle (Anderson nearly drowns her daughter) and everyone else strongly advising her to leave Anderson for the authorities to look after (before he perished, Bradley had warned, "Don't say "no" to her. She is marked."). Filmed around the stark, bleak clifflands at Achill, County Mayo in Ireland (superb photography from Simon Kossoff), *The Daisy Chain* is yet another slant on the "mother grieving for lost child" syndrome popular in modern-day horror cinema. Morton sees in Anderson, forever dressed in a fairy outfit, her three-week-old baby who died and what she could have grown up into, ignoring the fact that she's soon to give birth. Possible autism is one reason given for Anderson's erratic behavior; she repeats words over and over, especially "Play with me! Play with me!" when children have no intention of playing with her and, at times, either remains silent or screams nonstop when she's not getting her own way. There's no happy ending: During a bath time session, Morton slips on the floor, blood seeps from between her legs and the next thing we see is Anderson singing "Rock-a-bye baby," the new baby in his crib; "What shall we call him?" asks the girl innocently to a broken Mackintosh, his wife lying dead on the bathroom floor, Aisling Walsh's camera closing on Anderson's che-

push them further over the edge. Babysitter Jenn Foreman, hired to enable the couple to catch up on urgently needed rest, spots the weird girl and vanishes, James and Schaech sleeping a full day before noticing she's gone. But is that unwelcome visitation an evil visitation, an hallucination, the product of nightmares or something even more sinister? When visitor Philippe Brenninkmeyer has his throat slashed, we are left to wonder. James then struggles with her unholy, knife-wielding house guest, strangles her and all is revealed in the closing minutes: A radio news bulletin tells of deranged Wells' escape from a mental institution after her eight-month-old baby was killed in a fire, and of the disappearance of Foreman whose body James has discovered in the basement. Alone at last, James, Schaech and their infant curl up on a motel bed, away from that accursed building, bathed in sunshine, sleeping the sleep of the dead and boy, do they deserve it! An excellent journey into spooky madness that grips right up to the final revelatory seconds.

Dark Corners
Matador Pictures 2006; 92 minutes;
Director: Ray Gower *****

A young woman undergoing IVF treatment has recurring, violent dreams in which she appears to be another person continually terrorized by an insane serial killer.

You'll need to have your wits about you to figure out all the tantalizing twists and turns in Ray Gower's brainstorming psycho thriller which, if you're in the mood for it, requires 100% concentration; nothing less will do. Thora Birch and hubbie Christien Anholt have been trying (unsuccessfully) for a baby over a three-year period. Plagued by disturbing visions of an alter ego and a hooded killer named the Night Stalker who eviscerates his victims, Birch visits psychoanalyst Toby Stephens and agrees to undergo hypnosis to ascertain the root problem of her fears. But is Stephens all that he appears to be? What is the significance behind the frequently shown number 618? Then you have the two women: Blonde Birch (in duel roles) lives in a brightly lit, pure environment; her brunette doppelgänger inhabits an ugly wasteland of filth and decay, populated by deviants. "What hell is. It's having your sins pulled out from the dark corners of your soul and served up to you in this endless loop of torture" intones Birch at one point. Take heed of those words. They're a major clue to unraveling this surrealistic essay into a disturbed mind which messes with *your* mind; the cryptic, bloody climax itself has to be scrutinized at least twice, allowing viewers to draw their own conclusions on what has occurred over 90 minutes. Relying on multiple flashbacks, repeat scenes and Freudian symbolism, *Dark Corners* has a touch of the David Lynch about it, which is no bad thing. As far as indie shockers go, Gower's tortuous offering, artfully edited for full impact, is truly outstanding.

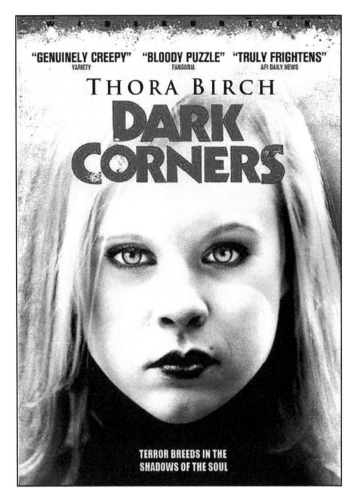

Dark Feed
Sinister Siblings Films 2013; 86 minutes;
Directors: Michael and Shawn Rasmussen **

A film crew shooting a movie inside an abandoned 100-year-old Boston psychiatric hospital falls prey to the building's malignant influences, slowly becoming as murderous as its former inmates.

Horror films taking place in real-life asylums are *de rigueur* these days, some good, some bad. *Dark Feed* exhibits both good and bad traits, the building (an actual sanitarium in Boston) the real star of the show, the cast coming off second-best. Scriptwriter Andrew Rudick turns up for a shoot and wishes he hadn't, most of the crew ignoring his friendly overtures. Taking place over one night, we have the sinister hydro-therapy room, the empty wheelchair, an array of operating apparatus, a portrait of the psychopathic owner, the icy morgue, lifts that jam, flickering lights, black water/blood oozing through pipes and mold creeping up walls, plus

an occasional glimpse of a ghostly former patient, all very goosebumpy. Then the effects ace blows an extra's brains out, followed by Michael Reed, the leading man, shaving off his hair, butchering lead actress Rebecca Whitehurst in the shower (straight from *Pyscho*) and dressing up in her clothes, a cue for the rest of the team to suddenly go berserk and revert to a homicidal zombie state, including mild-mannered Rudick. Presented in a dingy color wash to match the decaying, dank interiors, the Rasmussen Brothers' "loony asylum" offering conjures up the requisite air of insane menace (how could it not in a place such as this?), but as soon as the crew begins to go off the rails, so, unfortunately, does the movie

The Darkroom
Starz Prods./Mindfire Ent. 2006; 83 minutes;
Director: Michael Hurst ****

Having spent 15 years in an institution, a man suffering from amnesia walks out after being administered an experimental drug and is befriended by a shy youth whose stepfather is a certifiable bully.

Halfway through Hurst's mesmerizing psychological puzzler, you may wonder whether or not you are watching two separate movies running in tandem. We have patient Reed Diamond, found wandering in the road as a teenager covered in blood, locked away ever since, his memory of events leading up to his hospitalization blanked out. Then

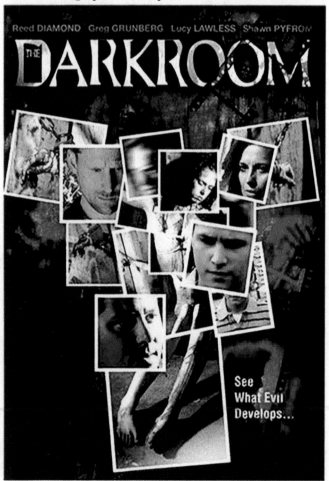

there's young Shawn Pyfrom, lumbered with the stepfather from hell (Greg Grunberg), a bullying Neanderthal who slaps his wife around (an excellent Lucy Lawless), lies about the fact that he has lost his job and disappears every night with a camera. What, if anything, have these two storylines got in common. Why does Diamond suffer from visions of a nightmarish beast with dagger-like claws, emerging from mud and slashing the throat of a chained-up girl. Workmen excavating land for a new housing estate unearth the mummified body of a woman, buried for five years—is this connected to Grunberg's nocturnal activities? Is Grunberg a peeping tom (photos in his darkroom bear this out). The director intricately weaves an involving series of brain-teasers that will keep most viewers scratching their heads right up to the *Sixth Sense* disclosure which packs quite a punch, and the ending satisfactorily ties up all the loose ends without cheating the audience. A cast of unknowns breath new life into what is fast becoming a seen-it-all-before framework (Bruce Willis realizing that he is a ghost has a lot to answer for!) so all credit to this low-budget feature for accomplishing it in style; you will have to watch more than once, though, to winkle out the many pointers scattered throughout its running time.

The Day
Guy A. Danella Prods./Faction M 2011; 87 minutes;
Director: Douglas Aarniokoski (Arnold Cassius) ***

In a post-apocalyptic wasteland, three men and two women, immune from a virus that turns humans into blood-drinkers, seek refuge in an abandoned house, not realizing the place is booby-trapped and that they are earmarked as the next victims.

Apart from brief flashbacks, *The Day* is shot in a grainy monochrome wash to reflect the planet on its last legs and has a brilliant opening spell. Dominic Monaghan (the group's leader), Shawn Ashmore, Cory Hardrict, Shannyn Sossamon and Ashley Bell trek along railway tracks and woodland trails in a cold, wet bleak landscape (Canada was the location), discover an isolated house and escape the rain, cleaning themselves up and taking stock of their dire situation. There's not much group unity here: Hardrict is sick with fever, continually coughing, Ashmore has withdrawn into his own private world and the two women mistrust one another. When the girls embark on a foraging expedition, Monaghan discovers a chest crammed full of cans in the basement. Food? No! The tins contain rocks. Alarm bells ring, a spike plunges into Monaghan's back, the women rush to the rescue and people appear, normal looking but existing on a diet of uncontaminated blood. From that carefully orchestrated beginning, we are plunged into "who's gonna get out alive" territory, with a big question mark hanging over secretive Bell's head—is she one of them? After all, her left thigh bears an unusual mark-

the cash from her death will then be forthcoming. What *is* forthcoming, however, is a spate of hallucinations and visitations from people killed on the site, including Bates who refuses to stay dead gracefully. Throw in a horny constable (Gillian Shure), anxious to play house with the dark-haired hunk, a couple of hillbillies who antagonize Jones and pay with their lives and the decaying ghouls of the family murdered all those years ago and you are presented with a gory supernatural outing where the atmosphere is diluted every so often by the proceedings nosediving into unnecessary farce (a decapitated head asking mottled-skinned Bates for a cigarette). The ending is open to interpretation (or did the producers simply run out of ideas)—for example, is Shure all that she cracks up to be, and why did she stab Jones to death *after* he was handcuffed—but this doesn't disappoint; *Dead and Gone* is a pared-to-the-bone thriller, acted with assurance and directed with spirit.

ing, the sign of those others. During a battle for survival, the sect's leader and son are killed, Sossamon carved to pieces in the woods, Hardrict bludgeoned to oblivion with a hammer, Ashmore fatally beaten and the blood-drinkers wiped out. A pessimistic ending sees Bell tramping off into the unknown, having slashed the throat of the leader's daughter who unwisely wanted to tag along with her. An atmospheric end-of-world thriller that could have been a classic if it had maintained the claustrophobic tension built up in that superb curtain raiser right to the end.

Dead and Gone
IM Global/Dark Haze Prods. 2008; 89 minutes;
Director: Yossi Sasson ***

A struggling actor and his invalid wife take up residence in a remote cabin where, 40 years earlier, a man shot dead his wife and daughter and then committed suicide.

An odd little horror movie that in its own low-budget way is quite diverting. Quentin Jones is an out-of-work actor up to his eyes in debt, his comatose wife (Kathrine Bates) connected to a life-support machine. Needing money urgently to ward of his creditors, Jones, with the help of mistress Felissa Rose, is attempting to lay his hands on his wife's insurance policies. Losing patience, he decides to end Bates' life and switches the machine off, hoping

Dead Hooker in a Trunk
Twisted Twins Prods. 2009; 92 minutes;
Directors: Jen and Sylvia Soska ****

Twin sisters, a junkie and a religious freak have a series of bloodthirsty adventures while trying to dispose of a prostitute's corpse found in the trunk of their car.

A cult classic, or wall-to-wall trash? This distant relative of Hitchcock's *The Trouble with Harry* (1954) goes for all-out grossness as sisters Jen Soska (the geeky one), Sylvia Soska (Jude, the macho one), a junkie rock singer (Rikki Gagne) and a wimpy church youth group leader (C.J. Wallis) embark on a road trip to hell; the body of a hooker has turned up in their car's trunk and they want rid. Cue for a series of stomach-churning vignettes: Gagne has her right arm nearly severed by a gang of thugs wielding a chainsaw, then it's ripped out of its socket by a truck, then Wallis stitches it back on; Jen Soska has her right eye gouged out; a drug dealer rummages through a guy's exposed intestines; the Hooker's murder by perverted priest Loyd Bateman is prolonged and vicious; and Wallis throws up every 10 minutes at the sight of blood (and there's a lot of it). Bad language, rough sex with two cops, a thumping metal soundtrack, graphic violence, garish color, in-your-face direction—you'll either lap up every outrageous second of this Canadian grindhouse horror flick that includes an array of ugly (by nature) people, or loathe it. One very important question: What is a beautiful piece of classical music—Saint-Saëns' "Aquarium" from his Carnival of the Animals suite—doing featured in a film of this nature?

Deadline
KRU Studios/Enso Entertainment 2009; 85 minutes;
Director: Sean McConville **

A writer takes up residence in a mansion to complete a play, but her work is interrupted by the tormented spirit of the former occupant who was murdered by her possessive husband.

One of Brittany Murphy's last films before she died at the age of 32, *Deadline* commences in splendidly creepy fashion, considering the formulaic material. We have the old dark house, the crib in a child's room, the dark, dusty attic, cries heard in the night, a piano playing and the obligatory bath with a dripping tap. McConville's camera prowls slowly around this gloomy edifice, building up layers of suspense: In the attic, Murphy discovers a batch of camcorder tapes relating to the previous couple who disappeared, Thora Birch and Marc Blucas, her concentration on these taking precedence over her play. Blucas is a control freak, obsessively filming Birch's every move to the point where she's sick of it all, urgently needing her own space. Murphy's troubled life, in fact, appears to run parallel to Birch's—both had abusive partners, both had miscarriages and both have/had secret lovers (in Murphy's case, lesbian Tammy Blanchard). But, like Blucas, Murphy has also been videoing Blanchard's movements nonstop. Role reversal takes over as Murphy dresses in Birch's clothes, the careful, psychological buildup giving way to standard, rather dull, shocks (although the moment when Murphy encounters Birch at the piano, only for the ghoul to turn suddenly and yell "Stop following me around!" will make you jump). The murdered woman's phantom prevents Murphy from being killed by Blucas who returns to the house (a ghost? His mother apparently saved

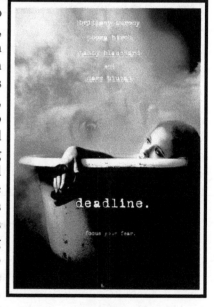

him from hanging himself) and as Murphy recovers from drowning in the bath, Blanchard, oddly unsympathetic to her girlfriend's plight, sees a video of herself on Murphy's camcorder, the girl's completed script an uncanny version of what she has just been put through. But was it all in Murphy's mind, a product of her disturbed psyche through not taking her medication? Will it happen all over again? We will never know.

hardened to so much splatter and gore to the point where it has little effect on the gastric juices. An overworked format that lapses frequently into tedium.

Devil's Den
IDT Entertainment 2006; 84 minutes;
Director: Jeff Burr **

A pair of drug-dealing dudes decides to try out their stash of aphrodisiac pills on the strippers at the Devil's Den joint, unaware that the gorgeous females are in fact flesh-eating ghouls.

The cinematic world is divided into two camps on this type of semi-humorous, tongue-in-cheek horror fare—those who lap it up, and those who give it the cold shoulder. Yes, the dialogue is darkly witty at times and the cast engaging, but the martial arts element grows tiresome after a while, as does the drawn-out fight sequences between ghouls and goodies in the misty passages. Basically filmed in two rooms, a tunnel and a cavern, Devon Sawa and Steven Schub enter a club populated by deliciously honed babes. Sawa tries it on with Dawn Olivieri, she bites his neck, Schub has his liver ripped out from his back and uproar ensues. These delectable strippers now sport faces like Halloween masks, acting like a pack of ravenous dogs; yes, it's Richard Cunha's notorious schlock classic *She Demons* (1958) brought up-to-date for a new audience! Big

Death Row aka Haunted Prison aka Prison of Death
Starz/IDT Ent. 2006; 92 minutes;
Director: Kevin VanHook **

A gang of jewel thieves and a group of young filmmakers find themselves trapped in a deserted prison on the Isla de la Roca, at the mercy of the evil phantoms of former inmates.

One of those horror movies where you can virtually tell exactly what's going to take place, who gets killed, who escapes—a tired framework acted out in scores of more recent genre pictures, the only thing different being what kind of death can be devised to bring more shock value to the subject. So, criminal Jake Busey, his floppy blonde mop drooping over his eyes, plus his gang, are electrocuted, cut in half, incinerated, sliced up into little pieces and squeezed through cell bars like mincemeat as the prison's ghoulish, ghostly inhabitants run riot. Likewise, only three of the five moviemakers make it out alive. Stacy Keach puts in an early appearance as a guard who had to hack off both legs to avoid being trapped in the prison's gas chamber, and there's mention of Busey's grandfather, a former inmate and occultist, the man probably responsible for the place being cursed. The performances are so-so, Busey clumsily hams it up and by now, audience's stomachs have become

black dude Ken Foree is on hand to help out, wielding a samurai sword (decapitation is the only method of dealing with these creatures), while kick-boxing Kelly Hu plays an assassin whose mission is to eliminate Sawa for dallying with a senator's wife. Once the queen of ghouls has been beheaded, our intrepid trio, six months later, have formed an extermination squad of a different kind, targeting a house full of werewolves. Funny in parts, gory in others, *Devil's Den* will probably have little attraction for older buffs; it's a reasonable bet that younger fans will revel in its blood-spattered silliness.

The Disappearance of Alice Creed
Cinemanx/Isle of Man Film 2009; 100 minutes;
Director: J. Blakeson ****

Two criminals kidnap a young woman and hold her hostage for a £2,000,000 ransom, each man nursing his own hidden agenda.

Made for £800,000 and shot around Douglas on the Isle of Man, writer/director J. Blakeson's sinuous psychological thriller throws up one surprise after another and comes highly recommended for lovers of lean, taut essays into human greed and treachery. It's a three-hander, Eddie Marsan (Vic) and Martin Compston (Danny) holding Gemma Arterton (Alice) captive in a reinforced flat, while Marsan sets the demands in motion for her release in ex-

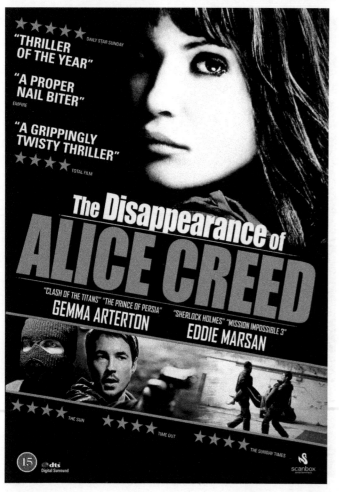

change for cash. Surprises and plenty of table-turning come thick and fast: Marsan, a vicious bully, is gay, hoping to go abroad with Compston when the deal is done so that "we can fuck each other's brains out." But Compston, unknown to his psychotic pal, is Arterton's on/off boyfriend; he initiated the plan of action to enable the two of them to escape together, leaving his accomplice in the lurch. Marsan, ever suspicious and growing angrier by the second, slowly unravels the truth behind Compston's deception after collecting the £2,000,000. Arterton is taken to a derelict workshop and padlocked to railings: Marsan's intention of finishing the job by murdering Compston in the woods backfires (he only wounds him) and, back in Arterton's cell, he's fatally shot by his injured partner who drives off with the money. Arterton manages to grab the keys from dying Marsan, unlocks her cuffs, staggers out of the building and finds the getaway car on a grass verge, Compston dead at the wheel. Hauling his body into the road, she eyes the two holdalls stuffed full of untraceable banknotes and pauses only for a second before driving away—Daddy ain't gonna get that fortune back, not after all that she's gone through. A gripping, stripped-down drama, incisively directed and acted by all concerned; full marks go to Arterton for *not* employing a body double in her numerous (and frequently distressing) nude scenes, and for actually being manacled to the bed in the name of art. Not many actresses would have the guts to put up with it all in front of the cameras.

11-11-11 aka 666: The Prophecy
Canonigo Films/Black Flag 2011; 90 minutes;
Director: Darren Lynn Bousman *

A writer and atheist whose wife and child died in a fire is haunted by the number 11-11, convinced that on November 11, 2011, he will fall prey to an infernal force that has taken exception to his non-belief in God.

Darren Lynn Bousman's exploration of one man's religious beliefs and faith (online sources state that the director was exploring his *own* beliefs) is like an out-of-control train, careering merrily along before coming apart at the joints and crashing in spectacular fashion. What, one will ask after the movie fades, was it all about? Divine retribution for bad-mouthing the Almighty? Guilt because Timothy Gibbs never got on with his brother? Guilt over his family's deaths? Gibbs puts in a good performance in a film that ends up a complete shambles: He meets Wendy Glenn at a support group for people who have suffered tragic loss, is plagued with vivid nightmares involving a winged angel/demon, somehow survives an automobile accident, travels to Barcelona where Dad Denis Rafter is on his deathbed and attempts to mend broken fences with wheelchair-bound brother Michael Landes: "Whatever happened to Mum wasn't your fault," he says to Lan-

des. Well, what *did* happen to her, apart from expiring on November 11? "They're watching you. They are here. Are you scared yet, Son? Do not answer the call!" croaks Rafter before passing away, nurse Ángela Rosal dragging Gibbs off to a church service in an effort to convince him that God isn't a "myth and does exist." Glenn appears on the scene, there's much mumbo-jumbo concerning those 11-11 numerals ("A gateway will open."), an armed local, Lluis Soler, hunts Gibbs in a maze (why?), video footage shows shadowy figures moving around the backyard, Glenn retrieves photos developed from Gibbs' camera which she looks at and then burns (we never see them) and the whole muddled shebang ends up *Exorcist*-style in Gibbs' ghoul-infested room, about as scary (and well-presented) as a ride on a fairground ghost train. Bousman concludes on the same hysterical note, more prolonged, frenetic shots set in a rainswept graveyard, Gibbs stabbed and dying, Landes now able to stand unaided. And that's where it finishes, Landes, restored, in front of his congregation, preaching the word of the Lord. "My purpose was to protect my brother. You're the apostle," states Gibbs in his final video message, the director hitting us with a barrage of flashbacks from previous events in the hope that everything we've witnessed will all make sense and fall into place—it doesn't. Notwithstanding sharp cinematography and Gibbs' solid turn, *11-11-11* reeks of a director embarking on his own personal crusade at the expense of the paying audience; unfortunately, the end product is an indigestible slice of pseudo-religious twaddle that would insult any believer, or even non-believer, in God the Almighty.

Elfie Hopkins: Cannibal Hunter
Black and Blue Films/Size 9 Prods. 2012; 89 minutes;
Director: Ryan Andrews ***

In the Welsh village of Thorntree Valley, amateur sleuths Elfie Hopkins and her boyfriend Dylan come to the conclusion that the new residents across the road are cannibals, responsible for a spate of murders stretching back years.

British tough guy actor Ray Winstone's daughter, Jaime, took on the role of college slacker Elfie whose obsession with detective stories and spying causes her to believe that smoothy Rupert Evans, wife Kate Magowan, son Will Payne and daughter Gwyneth Keyworth are meat-eaters of the human variety. The trouble is, the girl's so unpopular that nobody will believe her. A low-budget Brit-flick with Ray Winstone as one of its backers, *Elfie Hopkins* takes time getting into gear; it's a talkative, subdued 50 minutes before we enter horror territory, Winstone and boyfriend Aneurin Barnard arguing over the merits, or otherwise, of animal hunting (her mother was accidentaly killed during a hunt) while probing into Evans' tourist company; exotic hunting holidays are on offer, those going never arriving at their destination, butchered and eaten instead. Following the death and dismemberment of Kimberley Nixon (the family literally makes a meal out of her!), things liven up. Hopkins, armed with a shotgun, breaks into Evans' home. Payne is shot dead; Magowan's head is crushed by Winstone, wielding a glass skull; Barnard, the object of Keyworth's sexual fantasies, slashes the girl's throat with a sword; and Evans is blasted in the back by Winstone, Snr. after receiving a scythe in his neck. Now alone in the world (Hopkins and Barnard's parents have been murdered), the two dropouts drive off to pastures new. Not overly gore-laden like its American counterparts, *Elfie Hopkins* is more of a slow-burner, containing believable, almost cute, performances from its two young leads and vivid color work; it grows on you after a couple of viewings without being too exceptional.

VING RHAMES   AVA GAUDET

EVIL ANGEL

18   KILLING HER ONLY MAKES HER ANGRY   18

Evil Angel
Main Street Movie Co./Zion Films 2009; 123 minutes;
Director: Richard Dutcher *****

A vicious, evil spirit possesses the bodies of young women on the verge of death, brutally slaying anyone who takes her fancy, male or female.

The spirit is Lilith who was the first wife of Adam; cast out of the Garden of Eden as a fallen angel, she has lived on for centuries, satisfying her unquenchable bloodlust. Coming in at just over two hours, Dutcher's stunning horror movie is thrown together at a cracking pace, involving the viewer from the rather puzzling initial 15 minutes right through to the bloody finale. Kristopher Shepard plays a young paramedic attempting to unsuccessfully resuscitate a dying girl—when she expires, another woman in the hospital is miraculously revived (J.J. Neward) and embarks on a killing spree. At the point where the bloodthirsty Neward is defeated by a prostitute, you might be forgiven for wondering what's going on, but stick with it: Shepard's unfaithful, angst-ridden wife (Ava Gaudet) is the spirit's next target; she tries to electrocute herself in the bath but is revived as a vamped-up harpy, determined to eventually murder Shepard after she has sexually satisfied herself with him. Big boy Ving Rhames adds gravitas, an investigator on the trail of the female monster, while Marie Westbrook is the medic who falls for Shepard and ends up being taken over herself. "If I were you, I'd shoot her, I'd put a stake through her heart, cut her fucking head off, I'd put garlic in her mouth and I'd bury her 100 feet deep" is the advice given to a worried Shepard on how to deal with his wife who is not-a-wife! Lilith in non-human guise resembles Ray Harryhausen's Medusa in *Clash of the Titans* with bat wings (minus the serpents in her hair), a startling vision from hell, there's a surfeit of sexual antics and honed female bodies to add sauce to the mix and a score that delivers in all the right places. For an independent production, *Evil Angel* is fast-moving, gripping horror, right up there with the best of them.

Experiment
Magician Pictures 2005; 95 minutes;
Director: Dan Turner **

A husband, wife and their small daughter are abducted and programed with the ultimate purpose of assassinating a high ranking Russian diplomat.

A mediocre thriller on *Manchurian Candidate* lines set in picturesque Prague; Georgina French finds herself staggering around the streets suffering from loss of memory, as does husband John Hopkins. Their minds are being controlled by David Gant, Nick Simons and Andrew Byron who can, at the push of a laptop button, activate violent mood swings. Quite what this "experiment" is in aid of is not fully explained and when it is revealed that the couple's daughter (Molly Ewins) has also been programed to kill an important diplomat, the comings and goings of French and Hopkins as they try to cope with their erratic behavioral patterns appears to be superfluous to plot requirements. The contrived ending has Simons (who turns from baddie to goodie) being shot, then stabbing the perpetrator dead, French hurling herself under a subway train, Hopkins knifing Gant and, lastly, the zombie-like daughter stabbing Hopkins before (cue for twist ending) Byron (on the side of the Ruskies all along) leads the little girl

John HOPKINS   Georgina FRENCH
EXPERIMENT
WHO AM I? WHAT AM I?

off with the minister she was supposed to kill. The movie contains good performances, fine Eastern European locations and moves at a quick pace, but unfortunately the material is stale and doesn't really hold the interest as it should.

UNDER TEN MILLION? ANYTHING'S POSSIBLE!

Fertile Ground
After Dark Films/Signature Pictures 2011; 95 minutes;
Director: Adam Gierasch ***

Traumatized by a miscarriage, a woman and her husband move into his family's ancestral home where she starts to experience disturbing incidents related to the house's former murderous residents.

An unusually non-violent offering from the usual blood-soaked After Dark Films' roster; why it received a UK "18" classification on DVD release is a mystery. Clothes designer Leisha Hailey, suffering from depression, and artist Gale Harold set up home in an isolated, rambling edifice that harbors a terrible legacy: The place was built in 1813 and has a macabre history of pregnant wives being slaughtered by their husbands; as if that wasn't bad enough, two mass murderers once lived there and a teacher was pushed to her death out of a second-floor window. Carefully paced over seven chapters (Starting Over, Moving In, New Life, Old Secrets, Strange Happenings, The Gathering, Revelations), we're in romcom mode up until the 25th minute when the expected creepy happenings kick-in: A 150-year-old skull is found blocking water pipes, Hailey delves into the house's lurid past, a woman in an old soiled dress stalks the corridors, the new sapling that

Hailey plants withers and dies and Harold, spending day and night in his studio, acts strangely, cold and indifferent to his wife's needs, especially when Hailey announces she's pregnant again despite doctors previously informing her she couldn't conceive. Ordered to take things easy, Hailey, bored and restless ("I can't stand being alone in this house. I need my friends."), begins seeing ghostly visitors and convinces herself that Harold is having an affair with Stephanie Ross, his agent; the woman is shoved out of a window during a party and hospitalized. It all ends in a rooftop struggle after Hailey has accidentally plunged a knife into friend JoNell Kennedy's throat; grappling with Harold who resembles William Weaver, one of his 19th-century ancestors, they tumble to the ground, Hailey ferociously stabbing her husband to death. But the visitations and suspicions were apparently all in Hailey's tortured mind: At a mental hospital, a baby scan reveals nothing; she was never pregnant, the nightmare she has been living through a result of psychosis brought on by her miscarriage, depression and the morbid atmosphere of the house. She's last seen in a padded cell, cradling an invisible baby. The one drawback to this well-crafted chiller is Hailey's Minnie Mouse delivery; you cannot understand at least 30% of what she is saying, a sign that by and large, voice coaches have disappeared from modern-day cinema; on this showing, the actress was in urgent need of one.

Flight 7500
CBS Films/Ozla Pictures 2014; 97 minutes;
Director: Takashi Shimizu ****

Passengers on board Vista Pacific flight 7500 from Los Angeles to Tokyo encounter violent supernatural forces which could be connected to a curious passenger and his mysterious cargo.

But is the cold-eyed weirdo (Rick Kelly), who coughs up blood and expires midway into the movie, the catalyst for what follows? He's heard muttering, "Tear the eyeballs out," and his case plus an old ornate box contains not only the hair of numerous women in glass phials but a creepy doll, a Shinigami, that collects people's souls. Is this all a gigantic red herring put in place by director Takashi *The Grudge* Shimizu to fool the audience? It would appear so after the shock ending. Taking off from LA, we're presented with a quirky bunch of characters to get to grips with: Loved-up newlyweds Nicky Whelan and Jerry Ferrara; bickering couple Ryan Kwanten and Amy Smart; death-obsessed Goth Scout Taylor-Compton; small-time thief Alex Frost; "Am I pregnant?" gal Christian Serratos; air stewardesses Leslie Bibb and Jamie Chung; and pilot Johnathon Schaech, among others. An hour or so into the flight, there's turbulence, Kelly spits up blood, paramedic Kwanten and Ferrara attempt to revive him but the man flatlines, his body placed in business class upstairs. "You

FROM THE DIRECTOR OF THE GRUDGE

LESLIE BIBB JERRY FERRARA RYAN KWANTEN AMY SMART

FLIGHT 7500

THERE ARE FORCES MORE TERRIFYING THAN TURBULENCE.

black. Then we see Whelan, sobbing, slowly walking down an empty aisle towards a brilliant light outside. Suddenly, a gray hand emerges from a trash bin; by refusing to accept her tragic situation, she may well have placed herself in more danger. A nice touch is Kwanten watching The *Twilight Zone*'s 1963 episode *Nightmare at 20,000 Feet*, William Shatner staring at something not quite human on the plane's wing. But, in the context of *Flight 7500*'s surprise conclusion, that could be just *another* red herring to throw us off track!

The Frankenstein Experiment
aka The Prometheus Project
American World Pictures/NWR Prods. 2010; 88 minutes; Director: Sean Tretta *****

In a covert medical facility, scientists working on illegal stem cell tissue experiments create an intelligent but homicidal being from the corpse of a murdered security guard.

A thought-provoking modern-day reimagining of Mary Shelley's novel and the whole *Frankenstein* myth, combined with elements of 1985's *Re-Animator*, as cold and clinical as the surroundings in which the story unfolds via flashback. Tiffany Shepis, her features hidden behind a mask straight out of Georges Franju's classic *Eyes With-*

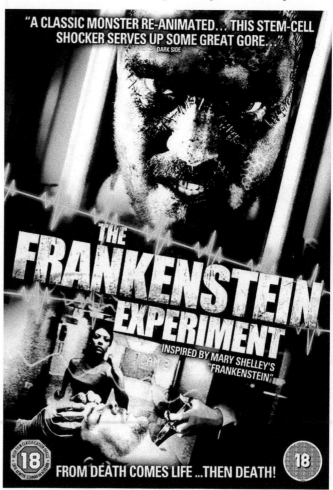

"A CLASSIC MONSTER RE-ANIMATED... THIS STEM-CELL SHOCKER SERVES UP SOME GREAT GORE..."
DARK SIDE

THE FRANKENSTEIN EXPERIMENT
INSPIRED BY MARY SHELLEY'S "FRANKENSTEIN"

FROM DEATH COMES LIFE...THEN DEATH!

gave CPR to a man with blood all over his mouth," yells ultra-fussy Whelan to Ferrara. "I can smell him already. Was he contagious? We're trapped with a dead body for six hours!" As Bibb discovers one of the dead man's teeth on his seat, the turbulence returns, cabin decompression forces water out of bottles, the aircraft plummets, oxygen masks are donned, smoke billows through the aisles and panic erupts. When things settle down, Frost decides to steal Kelly's Rolex watch from his corpse, communications with Tokyo are down, Kelly's body goes missing, the phials and doll are discovered after ransacking the luggage hold, Kelly's face is seen on laptop screens, Bibb spots a jet outside tailing their plane and clutching hands materialize from overhead storage compartments. The payoff is that everyone on board flight 7500 died in the second bout of turbulence; realization sinks in as, horrified, they stare at their own lifeless bodies, the TV monitor broadcasting the news that there was a malfunctioning of the oxygen supply masks during decompression and that the jet that Bibb spotted was there to ascertain if any survivors were on board; the aircraft has been on autopilot for five hours and is due to crash into the Pacific at any time. "Don't let me go," sobs Smart to Kwanten and the screen fades to

out a Face, relates her story to two FBI agents investigating rumored malpractices taking place in Doctor Ed Lauter's spartan, 300-roomed fortified clinic, and what an involving tale it is. Molecular biologist Shepis has been recruited as part of a small research team attempting to regenerate tissue growth by developing a serum composed of stem cells extracted from the embryos of artificially inseminated women who reside in the building's basement. She's soon at loggerheads with sour-faced Patti Tindall over which of them is top dog (or bitch!) in this setup. The serum, termed a universal healing system, reactivates a dead brain; brutal security guard Scott Anthony Leet, enraged that his pregnant girlfriend's embryo has been plucked from her body, threatens to sue for half a million bucks and is shot by Louis Mandylor, Lauter's right-hand man. Shepis decides to repair the brain damage, pump the body's head full of serum and see what happens, with disastrous and very gory consequences. The team squabbles over medical rights and wrongs, one member already murdered after trying to leave (nobody gets out of this place alive); Leet, childlike at first, quickly develops into a super-intelligent being exhibiting violent traits, able to read minds and open doors by thought alone. "Are we playing at being God?" the medics query as Leet, shot for a second time, is stitched up in *Frankenstein* mode and runs riot, ripping the flesh off Jonathan Northover's face, slaying the terrified stem cell donors and homing in on Shepis, severing her spinal cord and skinning *her* face. The climax to this powerful stem cell shocker has Tindall, mother to Leet's monster, demonstrating to a priest that her creation can change water into wine (she wants the church to fund further experiments) while alone in her home in front of a mirror, Shepis removes that mask, revealing features every bit as grotesque as we expected them to be. Scripted by director Tretta, *The Frankenstein Experiment* is up there beside Asylum's *Frankenstein Reborn* (2005) as independent cinema's most vital retelling of the old legend, a disturbing foretaste of possible medical procedures to come.

From the Dark

Workshed Films/Abandoned Films 2014; 90 minutes;
Director: Conor McMahon ***

A farmer digging for peat unearths an ancient grave, unleashing a creature that emerges at dusk, terrorizing two young tourists who have sought refuge in a remote farmhouse after their car has become bogged down in mud.

Irish horror films tend to be very dark and grainy in presentation and *From the Dark* is no exception to the rule. Shot mostly at night, Conor McMahon's exercise in survival horror focuses on Niamh Algar and Stephen Cromwell's attempts at evading a cloaked, clawed phantom that changes its victims into similar beings when it tears their flesh. Looking like Nosferatu in silhouette, the vampiric

creature shuns bright light—too much radiance (matches; candles; lamps; fire) will cause it to crumble into dust. The director opts for the *Blair Witch* approach, his camera shaking all over the shop, relying on an abundance of frantic close-ups shot in green night vision to raise the tension as Cromwell is ravaged and morphs into something sinister, leaving Algar to figure out a way of escaping the farmhouse and making it back to their abandoned car, stuck in a ditch. In open countryside, the bloodied, disheveled girl finally plunges a stake into the ghoul's heart but, as dawn breaks, she flinches at the sun's rays … the curse has been carried on! Obviously made on a micro-budget, *From the Dark* is an enterprising minor horror outing that stays within its limitations yet still manages to pack quite a punch.

Ghostquake aka Haunted High

Active Ent./SyFy 2012; 84 minutes;
Director: Jeffrey Scott Lando * (*** for the effects and score)

At Halloman High School, the demonic spirit of the former principal materializes from a secret chamber in the boiler room and hunts down the students as they prepare to celebrate prom night.

Andrew Morgan Smith's quirky score bubbles along merrily, completely out of place in this half-jokey ghost/possession/teen horror concoction that veers from silliness to just about watchable, hindered by M.C. Gainey's ridiculous maniacal laughing, reincarnated cult leader/ mass murderer and Jonathan Baron's wimpy jock hero. Only Danny Trejo brings any sense of balance to the haphazard narrative, playing the school janitor reading spells from Gainey's old notebook in an attempt to lay him and his ghoulish assistant, fanged Misty Marshall, to rest; Trejo also has a helper in the form of Amanda Phillips, his pure-white phantom sister. Baron is Gainey's grandson, holding a number of archaic coins inscribed with the pentagram; if destroyed, along with rings worn by Gainey's cult members who committed mass suicide, Gainey himself will perish. Gainey prowls the corridors, causing earth tremors (hence the clumsy title) and killing off students in a number of horrible ways (one is throttled by a trombone; another's head explodes), specimens of dead frogs coming alive zombie-fashion ("Frankenfrogs!") and even an activated suit of armor joining in the fun. In a climactic head-to-head battle of wills, the coins and rings are melted by nitric and hydrochloric acid, Phillips vanquishes Marshall, Baron is possessed by his grandfather, then isn't, and Trejo's ghost battles Gainey's in the netherworld, the school enveloped in flashes of green/white light before everything returns to normality. "What do we do now?" says Lauren Pennington to a bemused Baron. "Graduate," is the short answer. Tongue-in-cheek perhaps, yet *Ghostquake* remains one of those annoying features, falling between too many stools, where you wish it would all end quickly to enable you to get on with other matters.

Hallowed Ground
Grodfilm/Reel Entertainment 2007; 89 minutes;
Director: David Benullo **

A young woman making an unscheduled stop at the town of Hope is menaced by a reincarnated killer scarecrow who wants to make her pregnant in order that his spirit lives on through her child.

After a bright kickoff outlining Hope's devilish past—people were sacrificed in order to produce a bumper harvest and the place is cursed—*Hallowed Ground* spins into absurdity once Jaimie Alexander and dizzy journalist Hudson Leick venture out into the cornfields to see where the mad preacher who organized all those crucifixions a century ago is buried. Erecting a mock-up of a cross complete with scarecrow to use in a newspaper article, the raggedy monster comes alive, nails Leick to the cross and then we're in "can Alexander escape before the townsfolk/

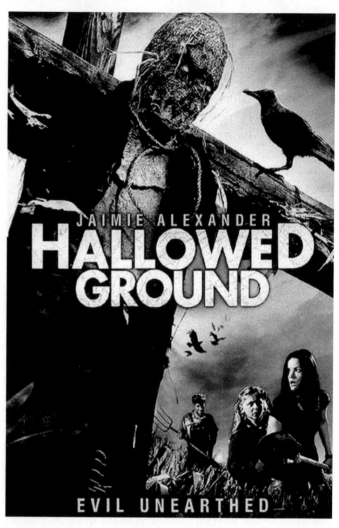

scarecrow catch her and use her as a host for the scarecrow's spirit" territory. Coming across like a hybrid mix of *Children of the Corn*, *The Wicker Man* and *The Texas Chainsaw Massacre*, with a *Birds*-type climax thrown in as masses of crows attack and wipe out the scarecrow's followers, this picture hasn't an ounce of originality in it; Alexander does her best as the frightened heroine on the run and actually makes it to safety in the end with would-be victim Chloë Grace Moretz (the vampire girl in *Let Me In*), but the actress is firmly rooted in horror cliché land, particularly in the final 20 minutes which is nothing more than a boogeyman chase movie, lacking in thrills and suspense. Direction-wise, Benullo does a good-enough job and the color photography is a notch above the average, but all in all, this is very uninventive fare indeed.

Haunted aka It's in the Blood
Monomyth Films 2012; 81 minutes;
Director: Scooter Downey **

A sheriff and his son head off for a trek in the wilderness, only to be confronted by demons connected with a disturbing incident in their past.

In that past, young medic Sean Elliot witnessed the rape and murder of stepsister Rose Sirna by Sheriff Lance

Henriksen's perverted deputy, Jimmy Gonzales, who then blew his brains out. Or so we are led to believe—nothing is quite what it seems to be in director Scooter Downey's murkily shot supernatural/horror thriller, a degree of uncertainty hanging over the proceedings like those mists that appear in the woods, heralding the oncoming of a spindly sharp-toothed ghoul from the netherworld. What is this creature that's intent on tormenting Henriksen in particular, stranded with a busted leg? Whatever Elliot devises to vanquish the thing doesn't work, including using Henriksen's maggot-riddled amputated limb as bait. Throughout the 81 minutes, we are treated to a welter of flashbacks and end up where we started, Elliot pursued through dark woods by a ghoul (Gonzales?) and being manhandled by several others. A shot of a car flying down empty roads; a door in a field that opens to blinding light; Elliot claiming he's never had sex, but seen (in flashback) having sex with Sirna; Henriksen's cruel streak (he shoots Elliot's injured pet dog out of hand); Henriksen knifing himself, his body, floating down river, hauled under by a huge claw; hate, jealousy, guilt, love and feelings of unforgivingness in equal doses—are these the inner monsters lurking inside this foursome, manifesting themselves as ungodly beings? Are the two main players actually dead? Henriksen is always worth a look whatever he's in but here, he's up against a scenario so dense that after watching it and trying to fathom it all out, you'll give up, take an aspirin for your headache and go onto other, more cohesive forays into the human psyche.

Jori Gill have been transformed from sexy, skimpily clad chicks to blood-soaked, stapled-faced, wild-eyed harpies in a series of chaotically disjointed sequences designed to give you one almighty headache; and it's *not* a haunted house film as such. Throwing one gory, incomprehensible scene after the other at a shaky camera in dimly lit rooms does not a good horror film make; none of what goes

on makes any kind of sense as the girls discover a tape machine giving out dire warnings ("A malevolent presence wants to be your friend, alive or dead."), are possessed and change into *Evil Dead* mode; a strange man, Joshua Winch, fights a bald-headed, grunting brute with an axe and there's a fanged monster in the murk somewhere, growling its head off. Apparently, the creek the teens cross at the beginning is supposed to be the River Styx, leading to the netherworld, in this case the cabin. The four end up like badly stitched marionettes, moving convulsively on a stage to Saint-Saëns' "Danse Macabre." The speech is muffled and inaudible, the soundtrack loud one minute, indistinct the next, and what is the reason (if any) of inserting views of a shopping center at irregular intervals? Cheap as hell (no pun intended) with hardly a redeeming feature to its name: I have omitted the follow-up, *Lake Fear 3*, which came out in 2018 (*Lake Fear 2*, released in 2016, is not related to these features) in the event that viewing it might seriously damage your health. Possibly the worst film to contain the word "Haunting" in its title; you have been warned!

A Haunting at Cypress Creek
aka Lake Fear; Cypress Creek

MGI Films 2014; 89 minutes; Director: Michael Crum *

Four teenage babes go to stay in an isolated cabin for a bit of girlie fun; the fun stops when they realize that they could be vacationing in a dwelling not too far removed from Hell itself.

Is this what Hell is supposed to be like? Well, it's purgatory for the seasoned horror enthusiast to sit through. Michael Crum's $8,000-budgeted nightmare, shot in eight days, two lines of dialogue summing up this unholy fiasco: "Man, I wish I had a beer right now" and "Fuck you," accompanied by a one-finger gesture, in the closing seconds. You'll certainly need the beer (more than one!) *and* you'll be giving the movie the finger after Shanon Sneddon, Taylor LeeAnn Graham, Jessica Dawn Willis and

The Hide

Solution Films 2008; 82 minutes; Director: Marek Losey ***

Alone in a hide on the Suffolk mudflats, an ornithologist's vigil is interrupted by the arrival of a scruffy stranger who appears to be a dangerous criminal on the run.

Marek Losey shot this low-key British psychological thriller on the bleak mudflats of the Isle of Sheppey and it's a two-man star show; Alex MacQueen is the nerdy, obsessive "twitcher," unshaven Phil Campbell the disheveled stranger who invades his territory. Circling one another like tightly coiled snakes, this impeccably acted conversation piece, interrupted by Campbell's memories/visions of crows pecking at human flesh, takes a sinister twist midway through as it transpires that the seemingly inoffensive MacQueen is not so inoffensive after all. Those police helicopters circling overhead may *not* be searching for Camp-

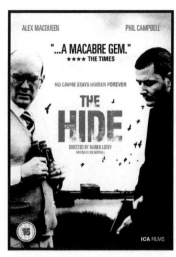

bell—the bird watcher has gassed his ex-wife and her lover and fed their corpses to a meat grinder. The swift ending has Campbell shooting MacQueen dead with the one bullet in his gun that he had reserved for himself—but why? This tense battle of wills between two psychotic killers set in a landscape so windswept that you can feel the cold comes with its own special health warning—do *not* eat any paste sandwiches prior to or during the watching of this film!

The House Next Door

Barbara Lieberman Prods./Muse Ent. 2006; 86 minutes; Director: Jeff Woolnough ***

A new house built on modernistic lines suffers from a murderous curse, bringing tragedy into the lives of all those who inhabit it.

A serviceable TV horror movie that is good for the odd shudder or two. Lara Flynn Boyle and Colin Ferguson watch in dismay as a new house is constructed adjacent to their land, three couples who go on to purchase the property regretting it big time. During a house-warming party, the first buyer, pregnant Charlotte Sullivan, is apparently pushed down the stairs by hubbie Stephen Amell; she loses the baby, he's arrested for murder. Next to appear on the scene are Julie Stewart and Aidan Devine; she starts seeing her soldier son, killed in the Iraq war, on television while Devine decides to play sex games with Heidi von Palleske; Stewart, out of her senses, hangs herself, Devine disappears. Then it's the turn of Emma Campbell, Noam Jenkins and their young daughter, Niamh Wilson. Jenkins changes into a manipulative bully, insulting guests and verbally abusing his terrified wife, resulting in Campbell pumping him full of bullets. When the

building's architect Mark-Paul Gosselaar arrives with his partner to claim the house for his own, Boyle and Ferguson confront him over the series of disturbing events: "That house is evil. It finds a weakness and preys on it. It corrupts and destroys. You move into that house, it'll kill you. Tear it down!" "This house will always be mine," he replies, agreeing that "there's something wrong with the house. There's something in there I didn't put in. I can't draw anymore." Sneaking round one night to erase the poisonous edifice from the face of the earth, Boyle and Ferguson are caught in the act by Gosselaar (who's just as creepy as his creation); an electrical fault combined with leaking gas blows the place up, the architect perishing in the inferno. Boyle and Ferguson are last seen on a beach with Wilson who they've adopted; meanwhile, a fourth couple is being offered the chance to have a new home built from scratch, based on original plans drawn up by none other than Gosselaar, a surefire recipe for disaster! A smoothly shot horror/ghost drama for the afternoon television audience that finds its mark in a few moments of nervy tension.

It's Alive

Signature Pictures/Foresight Unlimited/Millennium Films 2008; 80 minutes; Director: Josef Rusnak *

A college student gives birth to a fast-growing, murderous infant.

A truly appalling remake of the 1974 Larry Cohen schlock classic that boasts a hard-to-believe $9,000,000 budget, near the top end of the budgets featured in this book. The movie wasn't afforded a release in England (or most other major markets), going straight to DVD, so where was all that money spent,

and what on? A wintry Bulgaria, of all places, stands in for New Mexico—Bijou Phillips is rushed into hospital and undergoes a Cesarean operation to free her of her rapidly growing baby; the thing is only seconds old before it somehow manages to wipe out the entire medical crew. Back home with nice-but-dim architect husband James Murray and stepson Raphael Coleman, Phillips is besotted with her newborn, even though it has a habit of biting her breasts and scuttling off to eat wildlife, and at this point the picture then becomes rather messy and disjointed: Various people (Phillips' college pal and her boyfriend, a psychologist and two cops) visit the house and are subsequently ripped to shreds by the mutant infant. And how is it that wet-behind-the-ears Murray thinks the baby "looks like an angel" when it has two rows of pointed teeth and talons. That's when you are allowed to see it, of course—one quick glimpse of that clawed hand and about a second of the baby's scowling face is all that you're offered here. The rushed climax sees Phillips and her child perishing in a conflagration while Murray and Coleman live to tell the tale. From the opening scenes featuring Phillips' high-pitched, grating drawl to that below-par Hammer-type climax, the 2008 *It's Alive* fails miserably to live up to the illustrious original.

The Last Lovecraft: Relic of Cthulhu

Outlaw Films 2009; 79 minutes; Director: Henry Saine **

A descendant of H.P Lovecraft has to prevent one half of a sacred relic he owns being joined with the other half, discovered in an Egyptian archaeological dig: If it is, the world will be taken over by the "Old Ones."

Do the fabled texts of Lovecraft, mostly dealing with the Cthulhu Mythos, really deserve the *Bill & Ted's Excellent Adventure* treatment? Lovecraft's masterly prose drips with unearthly, eldritch horror and many would say that to present it in the form of a semi-comedy is sacrilegious to say the least. Gormless Kyle Davis is the last in the Lovecraft bloodline who sets off with equally silly pal Devin McGinn and dopey Lovecraft enthusiast Barak Hardley to defeat the Starspawn and his minions, and to retrieve the artifact, thus putting paid to the resurrection of the mighty Cthulhu. As a nod to the extraordinary monstrosities conjured up in Lovecraft's fevered imagination, there are a wealth of weird creatures on display plus a tentacled "thing." Unfortunately, the Starspawn wears a Darth Maul mask (from *Star Wars: The Phantom Menace*) and the comic book interludes depicting the Old Ones inhabiting the planet during the age of the dinosaurs are slightly infantile. To add insult to injury, the final few minutes has Davis and McGinn trekking towards the Mountains of Madness in Antarctica, the Old Ones' retreat (and why hasn't anyone yet made a movie out of the author's most riveting piece of fiction, *At the Mountains of Madness*? Director Guillermo del Toro's negotiations with Universal have broken down over the subject). For purists, this mercifully short exercise will have them throwing up their hands in disgust. For the youngsters, it may offer a few moments of amusement.

Lizard Woman

Edko 2004; 98 minutes; Director: Manop Udomdej *

A caving team discovers an ancient wooden box containing the wax model of a gecko lizard, but loses the artifact—weeks later, a writer comes across the box and is possessed by the gecko's evil spirit.

It's not often you spot a relatively recent Asian horror movie lying in England's bargain-basement bins selling for a measly pound (around $2), but this is where this terribly disappointing Thai effort has ended up in double-quick time. Reason? After a promising opening 15 minutes in underground settings, the film veers all over the place, becoming totally incomprehensible. Writer Rungrawee Barijindakul is transformed into the she-creature of the title,

geckos crawling out of her mouth along with quantities of gushing black slime. Meanwhile, boyfriend/doctor Pete Thongchua hovers in the background, trying to make sense of it all, as will the audience. Darkly lit photography, sloppy editing, deadly slow pacing where nothing of any consequence happens, a baffling storyline, over-emphasized acting—*Lizard Woman* represents the very worst in Asian horror. The one decent shot is of Barijindakul perched on top of a street light at night, flicking out her tongue to trap flying insects. One or two scenes of gore and a nude shower interlude do nothing to compensate for a paucity in originality which, given the general excellence of the Asian horror genre, comes as a hell of a surprise, and a depressing one at that. Perhaps it was the low budget—all the same, this is one to avoid.

Lovely Molly

Haxan Films/Amber Ent. 2011; 99 minutes;
Director: Eduardo Sánchez ****

A newlywed couple moves into the house once owned by the girl's deceased parents, but the building's malignant atmosphere results in her spiraling into drug addiction and murder—or is it all in her mind?

Yet another contemporary cinematic casebook on the workings of a fractured psyche, as witnessed in the opening shot where Gretchen Lodge, filming herself, holds a knife to her throat and whispers, "Whatever happened, it wasn't me." Sánchez, co-director of 1999's *The Blair Witch*

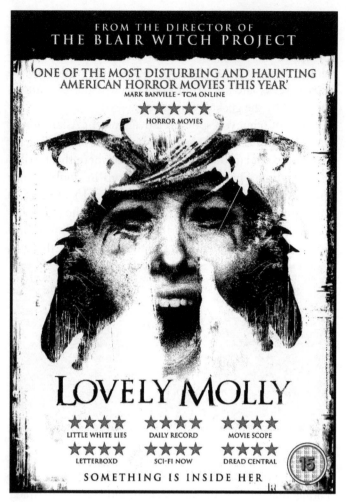

Project, elicits an outstanding performance from Lodge in a picture that combines the girl's camcorder footage within its tortured framework. Husband Johnny Lewis works as a long-distance truck driver, so ex-junkie and ex-psychiatric patient Lodge is alone in the house for days on end, her imagination working overtime; doors creak, windows rattle, she swears that her abusive father is lurking in the shadows ("He's alive!"), the alarm goes off for no apparent reason, a deep voice chants "Lovely Molly, I'll return" and sobbing emanates from a dark closet. Even her sister, Alexandra Holden, seems unable to help, especially when Lodge starts shooting dope to help her through the day ("Mum wanted to leave the house so badly. Why don't you leave?"). At work (she's a cleaner), an imaginary force caught on CCTV appears to rape her against a wall, she begins to look rough, savagely bites Lewis' lips during a frenzied bout of sex and even tries to seduce Field Blauvett, a priest who should know better (you can't blame the guy; Lodge has a great figure, posing full-frontal naked in a couple of scenes). But there are an awful lot of questions to be mulled over: What is causing the deterioration in her behavior? What is the significance of the horses in those old sepia photographs: What is a rotting, maggot-infested animal doing in the cellar? Who is filming another family, and why? Most remain unanswered—Blauvett is left

carved to ribbons in the bath following a sex session with Lodge, Lewis (discovered having a fling with another woman) has a screwdriver plunged into the back of his head and police unearth a man's body in a nearby garden. Indoors, pictures of horse's heads are stuck over photos of Lodge's father; naked, she steps out into the night, a shadowy figure waiting to embrace her. The house is then put up for sale; Holden, looking around upstairs, opens that spooky closet door and stretches out a hand to—what? Like so many of today's horror fare, it's left for the audience to decide what's taken place, a cop-out viewed by those demanding a satisfactory conclusion, others shrugging and thinking, "Well, if that's the way it is …" Notwithstanding the enigmatic payoff, *Lovely Molly* is a tense, scary and at times shocking journey into one person's psychosis, Lodge pulling out all the stops as a young woman descending into depravity of a mental kind.

Nailbiter
SenoReality Pictures/Ministry Machine 2013; 82 minutes;
Director: Patrick Rea **

A mother and her three daughters take shelter from a tornado in the cellar of a house, only to find themselves barricaded in, prey to mutant beings that appear during storms.

Why are we shown a meeting of recovering alcoholics, Mum Erin McGrane in attendance? Why does the film begin with morose teen Meg Saricks turning down an offer of sex from her boyfriend? What exactly are those fanged creatures that inhabit farmland on the outskirts of Kansas City, and why do their human carers turn into mutants when tornado sirens start wailing? What is the significance of the diary mentioning quadruplets born in 1865? Why does another couple harbor a room full of chained monstrosities, a metal muzzle on standby for her screaming infant? A lot of unanswered questions in a movie that develops well but finishes unsatisfactorily, one more in a long line of modern-day horror thrillers that steadfastly refuse to offer any explanation on what the audience has just sat through, as if all creative ideas had suddenly dried up. McGrane, Saricks, Emily Boresow and Sally Spurgeon are the foursome trapped in a grimy cellar with something evil connected to the old lady upstairs (Joicie Appell) who keeps talking about her "Dad." The setting is creepy, the creatures (only partly glimpsed) fearsome, the twister sequences

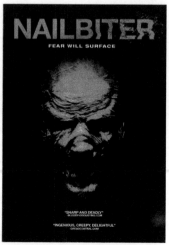

striking but none of it makes much sense and again, we have a rushed conclusion, McGrane's husband alighting at the airport and staring at all the text messages Saricks has been frantically trying to get over to him in the last 24 hours. Blighted by a poor audio track (can anyone understand a word McGrane and Saricks are mumbling about?), *Nailbiter* falls into the category of "could have been a whole lot better."

Necromentia

G2 Pictures/Compound B 2009; 82 minutes;
Director: Pearry Reginald Teo **

Three men journey into a hellish netherworld, each for different reasons.

A badly structured take on *Hellraiser*, shot in grim *Se7en* mode, concerning three men: Santiago Craig is a necrophiliac, performing obscene acts on his dead girlfriend's corpse—he wants to reunite her soul with her body by entering a version of Hell, even if it means he has to die to achieve it; Chad Grimes plays a drug addict who also wants to retrieve his dead brother's soul from Hell and is willing to help Craig get his girlfriend back; and Layton Matthews thirsts for revenge on those who sent him to Hell. Any shape the plot may have had is thrown out of the window as Teo assaults the viewer with a barrage of grainy, bloody images: A Cenobite-type creature; an Ouija board carved into a man's back; a woman paying for the privilege of being tortured; a man in a grotesque pig mask tormenting a disabled youth; and a pale human wearing a gas mask slurping on raw flesh. Hell is depicted as a long gloomy corridor lined with utility pipes, the dominatrix-style creations its inhabitants. Constantly switching backwards and forwards between the three male leads, *Necromentia* is an unpleasant mess that steadfastly refuses to make sense, and that goes for the closing minutes in which Matthews changes into the lumbering Cenobite monster. For masochists only.

No Man's Land: The Rise of Reeker aka Reeker 2

CMG/The Institution 2008; 88 minutes;
Director: David Payne ****

In 1978, a killer dubbed the Death Valley Drifter is sent to the gas chamber; 20 years later, his satanic entity lives on, claiming the souls of a disparate group trapped in limbo at a desert diner.

Director Payne virtually remade Primal's *Reeker* (2005), which he also directed, so if you've caught that ingenious

little horror mystery, you know what to expect very early on. The grisly prelude to events shows a hiker crushed under a car's wheels, his tongue cut out—this leads to the killer's arrest in a shack stuffed full of body parts. We then flash forward to the present: In a desert diner, Sheriff Robert Pine, the officer that apprehended the psycho, passes the reins of command to his son (Michael Muhney); two casino robbers arrive on the scene (Stephen Martines and Desmond Askew); the waitress (Mircea Monroe) happens to be Martines' ex-girlfriend; and also in on the picture is Valerie Cruz, a doctor. All the main characters in place, Payne kick-starts the action, getting the ball rolling with a shoot-out between cops and criminals and an exploding vehicle. But something is not right here: There's blood in the toilets; phone signals are down; Askew drives away, hits an invisible barrier, slices off the top of his head, yet still survives; an old man staggers out of the diner minus his heart; a headless body runs into the desert; a strange burning object floats through the air; the smell of rotting flesh pervades the atmosphere; and a hideous, refractive figure wielding butcher's tools finishes off most of the cast in all manner of grisly ways, each one experiencing a flashback over their lives before they expire. Are they all dead? Are only *some* of them dead? Payne keeps you speculating and neatly clarifies everything near the closing minutes, just in case you haven't figured out what's going on, and caps his movie beautifully with a "you thought it was all over but it isn't" ending. *Reeker* had a cast of teens—here, they're adults, so the approach is more adult-orientated, the result marginally superior, making for a classy supernatural horror thriller all round. (That burning object floating through the sky? All is cunningly revealed at the climax.)

Nude Nuns with Big Guns
Freak Show Entertainment 2010; 91 minutes;
Director: Joseph Guzman *****

Drugged, beaten, abused and raped, a nun turns psychotic killer, making all those responsible pay big time for her harrowing ordeal.

Filmed in blatant Quentin Tarantino fashion, Joseph Guzman's sexually gratuitous, over-the-top "Nunsploitation" B skin-flick hasn't an ounce of subtlety or finesse in it's bones, but doesn't pretend to be otherwise: Multiple rapes (two from behind), full frontal nudity (men and women), lesbian romps, drugs, a bar full of naked cocaine-packing beauties, bloody violence and nonstop bad language ("Lying fucking bitch" in subtitles) litter a production up to its neck in gross behavior, its tongue firmly in its cheek. Asun Ortega plays the abused nun, forsaking her vows in favor of two silver pistols, a machine gun and a shotgun ("God told me to kill."), hunting down garage/bar owner David Castro and his gang of boneheads who are busy laundering drugs through Father Perry D'Marco's church. Ortega's winsome lesbian pal Aycil Yeltan (they share a bath together) is raped by hulking Xango Henry (one of three such acts he commits: "Hey, Kick-Stand. Get your

dick over here now," orders Castro) and ends up smooching in Ortega's arms after every other cast member has been blasted to hell by the avenging nun with the curvaceous figure (which you get to see a lot of) except Mother Emma Messenger—she's throttled to death. For good measure, Castro's penis is shot off, Guzman's camera closing in on the severed organ, the bemused owner holding it up to his face before receiving a bullet in the head. "I will kill the bitch," snarls surviving priest Bill Oberst, Jr. in the final seconds—this ecclesiastical bloodbath's far from finished. A glorious example of celluloid bad taste taken to extremes, like a 21st-century Ed Wood art-house movie in parts, *Nude Nuns with Big Guns* is undiluted, 100% trash cinema, and funny to boot, *not* suitable for those easily offended. Enjoy it—if you can!

The Nun aka La monja
Fantastic Factory/Future Films 2005; 101 minutes;
Director: Luis de la Madrid ***

The wraith of a devilish nun, using water as a medium to gain entry into this world, murders the teenagers who put her to death 17 years ago.

In 1988, five 17-year-olds drowned Sister Ursula (Cristina Paget) in a bath, dumping her body in the lake in the grounds of their Catholic boarding school. Paget was evil incarnate, wanting to rid the world of sin, and tormented

her pupils to the point of brutality. Now she's back, slaying the girls one-by-one by enacting scenes from paintings showing the demise of patron saints; decapitation, burning, limbs torn from bodies. Anita Briem witnessed her mother being slaughtered by the fanged white-faced ghoul who announces her presence by water bursting up from the shower, baths, faucets, walls and flooring, traveling to the abandoned boarding school on the outskirts of Barcelona to uncover the mystery. Accompanying her is young priest Manu Fullola, Belén Blanco and her boyfriend Alistair Freeland. The action for the most part takes place in the creepy old school where two survivors of the group of five, also on a visit, meet their grisly ends. The twist here is that Briem's mother had an affair with a priest, giving birth to Briem who, mentally deranged, has developed a split personality, taking on the role of the nun herself in a form of a possession. Flooding the lower rooms (the thing can only be vanquished in water), Briem confronts the nun and fires an arrow through her heart; when Freeland and Blanco arrive on the scene, Briem's body is floating in the water, pierced by that arrow. A Spanish/British venture that contains a terrifying specter, some gruesome murders and startling water-based effects; however, it's let down somewhat in the acting stakes by a young inexperienced cast who seem at odds with the scary material.

Outcast
Irish Film Board/Bankside Films/Fantastic Films 2010; 98 minutes;
Director: Colm McCarthy ★★★★

Two Irishmen versed in ancient rituals travel to Scotland to exterminate an age-old beast that is slaughtering residents on an Edinburgh housing estate.

Irish horror movies are always grittier and a tad more realistic than their counterparts and *Outcast* is no exception, the action taking place in the dingy environs of an Edinburgh council estate, complete with trash-filled alleys and bored youths seeking nothing but trouble. British TV regular James Nesbitt, heavily tattooed with cabbalistic symbols, and Ciarán McMenamin go to Scotland, their mission to kill Kate Dickie's son (Niall Bruton). She's a witch, he's a teen who materializes into a demon at the first signs of sexual desire, butchering women and feasting on their intestines. Granted permission by Gypsy king James Cosmo to "hunt" on his property, Nesbitt has to first break down Dickie's psychic powers in order to discover where she's living; this entails him stabbing birds and spilling their viscera into jars. Meanwhile, Bruton has got himself involved with sexy lass Hanna Stanbridge who wants nothing better than to bed the shy lad despite Dickie's disapproval ("Stay away from him. I warned you—remember that."). There are mystical issues at stake here that are not fully expanded upon, only hinted at; for instance, how old is Dickie and her grotesque offspring, what underlying mo-

tive drives Nesbitt in his relentless search for the pair, who exactly is Cosmo apart from being called "The Laird" and who made Dickie pregnant with this monstrosity? Was it Nesbitt? If so, how old is *he* supposed to be? Bruton's leprous skinned, taloned other-self is a hideous freak, the boy morphing into the fanged beast as Stanbridge straddles him to have sex. Nesbitt has his neck ripped open in a confrontation after murdering Dickie in her flat and Stanbridge plunges a sacred knife into the thing's throat, the creature dying and changing back into Bruton. The final scene has Cosmo taking Stanbridge to lunch after giving her a "wee charm"; the girl's pregnant with Bruton's child, whatever *that* may turn out to be. *Not* a fun horror movie by any stretch of the imagination, Colm McCarthy's grim urban horror displays the dirtier side of black magic and must be applauded for its change of direction; glossy it ain't!

Outpost
Black Camel Pictures 2008; 90 minutes;
Director: Steve Barker ★★★★

An ex-marine and his six-man squad is assigned to check out a WWII bunker for real estate purposes, unaware that it was once the site of Nazi scientific experiments on the dead.

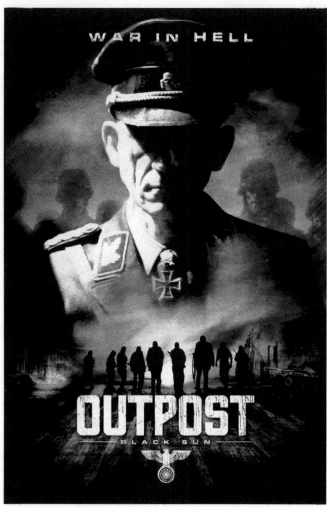

two survivors meet their end at the hands of Meres' blank-faced troops; a second team arrives three days later, Meres instructing his men by thought waves to form an attack formation and ensure no one gets out alive. A tough little horror flick containing sci-fi undertones, *Outpost* is one of the better of numerous independent movies to feature sinister old war bunkers and the monsters that inhabit them.

Plague Town
Dark Sky Films/Severin Films 2008; 89 minutes;
Director: David Gregory ***

A dysfunctional family on a bonding holiday in Ireland encounters a race of mutant children inhabiting remote woodlands.

Why these masked children, and some of the adults, resemble gray-skinned corpses isn't fully explained. What the grown-ups are after is fresh "seed" to cleanse the community from disease and hopefully continue their bloodlines, albeit in a more human-looking form. Along comes American David Lombard and his squabbling family; soon-to-be second wife Lindsay Goranson, two petulant daughters (Josslyn DeCosta and Erica Rhodes) and Rhodes' cocky English boyfriend, James Warke. It doesn't take long for the group to become separated in the dark—Warke is badly injured by a shotgun blast, Lombard has the top of his head sliced off by cheese wire

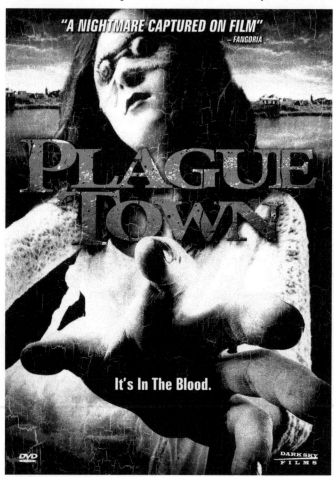

Filmed in Scotland, Gavin Struthers' washed-out color photography imbues this British horror outing with the necessary grit and grime as Ray Stevenson, shady businessman Julian Wadham and six hardbitten soldiers drive through war-torn Europe to locate an isolated bunker in woodlands. When Brett Fancy and Julian Rivett are killed by shadowy assailants in the surrounding trees, their bodies found fused at the heads, Stevenson demands answers to this and other questions: What is a pile of naked dead bodies doing in one of the rooms, and who is the silent, scarred living man among them (Johnny Meres)? It transpires that during the war, Hitler's SS were dabbling in occultism and experimenting in space and time physics by creating a revolutionary machine. Wadham has been tasked by his backers to recover and restart that generator which has the power to merge reality with reanimation, creating an army of "unstoppable soldiers, an invincible army," a very useful device to own in the current warfare situation. The generator, once activated, can control the undead by blasting out bolts of blue electrical energy, rendering them senseless, and does so after everyone except Wadham and Stevenson have fallen foul of the reactivated Stormtroopers, Meres commanding his ranks wearing a pristine SS uniform. When the machine breaks down, the

and Goranson is beaten to death with a hub cap, a sickening sequence that will have many diehards flinching in revulsion. The movie then enters the formulaic "who will escape from the spooky kids" scenario, which in this case is nobody. Shot mostly at night, *Plague Town* is an efficient chiller let down in the first half by a profanity-strewn script (foul-mouthed Rhodes is the main culprit) and some dim photography. But there are several eerie moments: Warke imprisoned in a cottage as a cadaverous, masked girl with doll's eyes approaches him in order to procreate; the same girl (Kate Aspinall) wandering out into the woods (a direct steal from the final moments in Georges Franju's classic medical horror film *Eyes Without a Face*); Warke gruesomely sacrificed; the noises of crying children in the woods; and the closing scenes showing a mutant infant in a crib. Yes, the mask is still a potent device in the horror genre and *Plague Town* uses that potency to good effect for most of its short running time.

Population 436

Destination Films/Pariah 2006; 92 minutes;
Director: Michelle MacLaren ****

A census officer arrives from Chicago in the Kansas community of Rockwell Falls and becomes puzzled by the fact that, according to town records, the population hasn't risen above 436 since 1860.

If you venture down to the boondocks today, beware of a big surprise and heed the following: An over-friendly town mayor and shifty-eyed cops; children and adults chanting, "We are the union of the divine"; all clocks stopped at 4:36 precisely; rusting cars littering a vehicle graveyard; protesting citizens suddenly suffering from a mysterious fever, then "cured" by electric shock treatment plus a lobotomy, converting them into Stepford-like clones; mumblings of "436. It must remain. It's God's law. We've been chosen"; some townsfolk desperate to escape but unable to do so; and, on Festival Day, a woman hanged in front of an admiring crowd with a smile on her face, sacrificing herself to preserve that all-important population figure. "Are you all out of your fucking minds?" screams Jeremy Sisto, staring at the dangling corpse. Yes, no doubt about it, this bunch of narrow-minded hick religious nuts *are* all out of their minds and Sisto has just woken up to the fact. But what can he do about it and avoid becoming a victim himself, the subject of a 19th-century curse these deluded inhabitants obey to the letter of the law—after all, he's now number 437 and upsetting the balance. After a sex romp with Deputy Fred Durst's winsome girl, Charlotte Sullivan, Sisto decides to flee to Chicago and take her with him but too late; she's caught and lobotomized, last seen vacantly washing dishes, tears rolling down her cheeks. Sisto manages to rescue young Reva Timbers from Doctor David Fox's lab, pinching a tow truck and reach-

ing the highway, but as soon as those storm clouds gather, you know that they ain't gonna make it; the truck smashes head-on into a juggernaut, wiping out the pair (in the alternate ending, they swerve and survive). The closing scene sees Sisto's colleague, his car disabled with two flat tires, on the town's outskirts, greeted by Sheriff R.H. Thomson in the same friendly but underlying sinister fashion. A tense low-budget supernatural/horror thriller, *Population 436* contains a believable central performance from Sisto and a "will he or won't he get out" storyline that is real edge-of-the-seat stuff, crammed with suspense, an indie gem.

Portal

Wind Chill Films 2009; 92 minutes;
Director: Geoffrey Schaaf **

When their car becomes stuck in an impenetrable fog, two musicians on their way to a gig head towards a motel and find themselves trapped by a coven of witches.

Chris Conrad and Alexander Martin play the two dudes who spend the night at a fog-bound motel, go down to breakfast, find that it's actually 6:15 in the evening, and partake of a dinner consisting of raw steak, uncooked vegetables and strong wine. Conrad, however, refuses the meal and by doing so slowly realizes that he and his pal

are stuck in a "Groundhog Day" situation—the food given to the guests by Kevin Dobson and his ghoulish staff deadens their minds, and Conrad and Martin have been reliving this scenario without knowing it for six months. Why? Apparently, these witches have a bevy of pregnant women locked up in cages, hoping one of them will produce the perfect child; they also require human sacrifices every so often to appease "Him." Director Schaaf's extended *Twilight Zone*-type horror outing is murky beyond belief and makes little sense, even with a trick ending tagged on. Poorly acted and directed, the germ of a decent idea is buried in that dense mist that renders most of the action a muddy blur.

Retreat
Ripple World Pictures/Magnet Films 2011; 90 minutes;
Director: Carl Tibbetts ***

A couple travels by boat to the isolated Blackholme Island to repair their shaky marriage; trouble presents itself in the form of a psychotic soldier who states that a global flu pandemic threatens all life on Earth.

You'll need the Prozac tablets at your side to view UK-produced *Retreat*, 90 minutes of unrelieved gloom and doom from start to finish: In the opening scenes, it's quite obvious that Thandie Newton has little time for hubbie Cillian Murphy; at the end, Newton, after shooting Murphy in a mercy killing, gets a bullet in the head from a helicopter marksman. Filmed at Gwynedd, North Wales, the gray, windswept barren landscape, highlighted by Ilan Eshkeri's funereal violin-based score, sets the somber mood

as Newton (she lost their unborn child) and Murphy's edgy relationship is rudely interrupted by Jamie Bell. He's a soldier, claiming that a contagious virus is sweeping the land; they must seal all the windows and barricade themselves in as protection against the outbreak. But is Bell telling the truth? His violent, bullying presence fuels further unrest between husband and wife, and when boat owner Jimmy Yuill is found dead on the beach with a bullet hole in his head, Murphy develops a backbone and turns the tables on their self-imposed gaoler. In the final 15 minutes, all is revealed: Bell, a former prisoner, is the main carrier of the virus, experimented on, a "military guinea pig," and then foolishly released; the authorities are now after him. In addition, he's tormented by the fact that he passed on the disease to his wife. Murphy starts coughing up blood and gunge, Newton puts him out of his misery with a shotgun but when she hears on the radio that an anti-viral vaccine has been developed ("It's not true!" Bell shouts) she blasts Bell for suppressing the fact; he told them the CB radio wasn't working when, in fact, it was. Loading Murphy's body into a wheelbarrow, Newton takes it to the cove where she's shot dead by the military who have tracked down their target. Newton struggles in some places with her "wronged woman" role, Murphy appears strangely uncomfortable and it is left to the excellent Bell to liven things up and chew the scenery as the demented soldier whom we finally come to sympathize with, more so than the morose couple he disturbed on their island retreat.

Rites of Spring
Red Planet Ent./White Rock Lake Prods. 2011; 80 minutes;
Director: Padraig Reynolds **

Over a period of 24 years, numerous women have gone missing on the first day of spring, the 21st of March, abducted by a maniac who feeds their bodies to a legendary creature associated with the new harvest.

Two stories are interwoven in Padraig Reynolds' so-so horror outing: In the first, teens Anessa Ramsey and Hannah Bryan are kidnapped by hooded old-timer Marco St. John and strung up in his barn, Bryan stripped, cleaned and decapitated, while in a chamber below, something ungodly stirs. In the second, a gang led by ruthless Sonny Marinelli abducts rich guy James Bartz's young daughter Skylar Burke, murders his wife and takes the girl to a disused factory, held for $2,000,000 ransom. Ram-

sey breaks loose from her tethers, takes off through a cornfield pursued by a figure resembling a badly bandaged mummy wielding an axe, and heads for that same factory where all hell breaks loose. What started out as two intriguing tales plunges into cliché-land as the thing from the barn slices its way through the cast, gun-happy Marinelli shooting his not-so-willing partners-in-crime and Bartz joining in on the bloodletting. Plot-holes abound: What exactly are those sticky objects in the monsters lair? Why does the gas station attendant lock the door on a terrified Ramsey? Why does the abducted nanny join forces with Marinelli—was she in on the kidnap? What are the meanings behind St. John's ramblings of "It has started again. I ask you for forgiveness. I will not let you down." Where did Burke disappear to once the climactic carnage began? The final shot is of bruised and battered Ramsey running for her life from that shambling menace whose face she has just slashed, and that's it, a "seen it all before" shocker featuring a tatty-looking killer who is never really given a full explanation.

The Room aka La habitación siniestra
Title Films/Bad Fourteen Pictures 2006; 80 minutes;
Director: Giles Daoust ***

Trapped in a dysfunctional family from hell, a pregnant woman seeks solace in the arms of her paralyzed, retarded brother.

An art-house psychological thriller from Belgium that kicks off with a splendid, Hitchcockian one-take shot of every room in the house where the action takes place. Residing in the house is wheelchair-bound Pascal Duquenne, sister Caroline Veyt, mother Francois Mignon, musician father Phillipe Résimont, their young son and his friend. Résimont is a demented no-hoper, Mignon sick of her lot and Veyt is pregnant after allowing her mentally retarded brother to experience the joys of sex—with her! They shout, they argue, they lash out at each other as one family secret after another tumbles out of the closet, all observed through the watchful eyes of Duquenne who is obsessed with his sister. When a forbidding door covered in inscriptions suddenly appears upstairs, and those who manage to open it are dragged screaming into a dark, unwelcoming netherworld, Daoust strips his film of color and shoots in blue monochrome, going all out for symbolism; luminaries such as Bergman and Hitchcock were undisputed masters at visualizing this kind of mind-bend-

ing framework so all credit to Daoust for at least having a stab at it himself. Unfortunately, the dreadful dubbing, combined with Résimont's overstated mugging performance, makes *The Room* look like the type of continental psychodrama you could catch up in London in 1968 and the denouement, that what we are witnessing lies in the twisted mind of the baleful Duquenne who has created a warped world of his own, will come as no surprise to those who have sat through *Spellbound*, *The Cabinet of Caligari* and many, many others. Nevertheless, *The Room* is not your average horror movie; it's quirkily different enough to engage the interest for much of its brief running time.

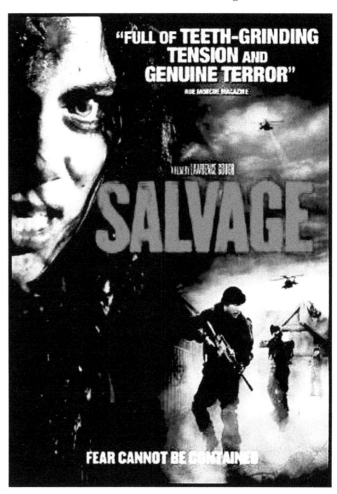

Salvage
Northwest Vision Media/Hoax Films 2009; 79 minutes;
Director: Lawrence Gough ****

A container washed ashore unleashes a mutated terrorist who brings terror and paranoia to a housing estate on the Wirral.

Filmed on Channel 4's old *Brookside* set, *Salvage* expertly combines terrorism and zombie-type thrills and is a classic example of what can be achieved on the lowest of low budgets (in this case, funded by England's National Lottery). Virtually a two-star show, Neve McIntosh (estranged mother of daughter Linzey Cocker) and part-time lover Shaun Dooley find themselves caught up in a nightmare scenario; the cul-de-sac she lives in is sealed off by the military, soldiers appear, helicopters buzz overhead, panic ensues, residents are gunned down at random, houses are plastered in blood and gunge and it's obvious that something dangerous is on the loose. Most of the plot involves McIntosh creeping from house to house under threat of being shot, desperately looking for her daughter—when she does locate her, she faces the mad thing that escaped from the crate. Don't expect a happy ending or any real explanation as to what's taking place; you get neither, although there is talk of a biological experiment on a Middle Eastern terrorist going terribly wrong. Gough's horror essay is all about the fear of the unknown, of being trapped in a situation out of your control. It looks cheap and gritty, but that adds to the tension. A smart little British horror feature to be sure, brilliantly acted by the two leads; those regional accents, though, might prove to be a real hurdle for those born outside the United Kingdom.

Seventh Moon
Haxan Films 2008; 87 minutes;
Director: Eduardo Sánchez **

A couple honeymooning in China during the Festival of the Hungry Ghost is earmarked as sacrificial offerings to a legion of flesh-eating demons.

Erratic camerawork and editing, murky photography and hyperactive performances from Amy Smart and Tim Chiou spouting one profanity after another make for an unattractive horror excursion into Chinese legend; zombie/slasher freaks may get a kick out of it, but many won't. After a colorful opening, Smart and Chiou taking in the sights, scheming guide Dennis Chan drops the pair off at a remote village at night under a menacing full moon, claiming he's lost; cue for the newlyweds to start acting as though they're heading for the divorce courts, not the bridal suite ("We're in China and it's all your fucking fault," screams Smart to her clueless, oversexed husband). Chan fails to come back, various animals are discovered tethered to stakes and in cages and, making off in the vehicle, a

bloodied man is picked up from the road, sparking a fight for survival from a tribe of gray-skinned ghouls. Like a zombie chase movie, Smart, Chiou and the man run through fields and woods, are attacked by the demons in the car (the old Chinaman is dragged to his death), hide in a tomb and end up at a candlelit temple. Drugged, Smart wakes to discover Chiou missing; she's turned loose, Chan, who emerges at a deserted house, informing her that her husband was offered as a blood sacrifice to prevent local villagers from being slaughtered and devoured; but he *can* be saved if she's willing to risk her own neck. Negotiating a waterlogged cave system, Smart finds Chiou chained to a slab, now morphing into a ghoulish state ("You have to go. They'll kill you," he mutters through blue-tinged lips). Placing his wedding ring on his gray, wrinkled, black-nailed finger, she flees the tunnels in terror, the creatures dispatching Chan and then pursuing her. As the moon sinks, dawn breaks and the welcoming sun comes up, the demonic hordes dissolve into dust; Chiou appears in the trees and as Smart watches, he too fades into nothingness, leaving her on her own in the middle of nowhere, no doubt cursing the day she ever became betrothed to a guy with a Chinese background.

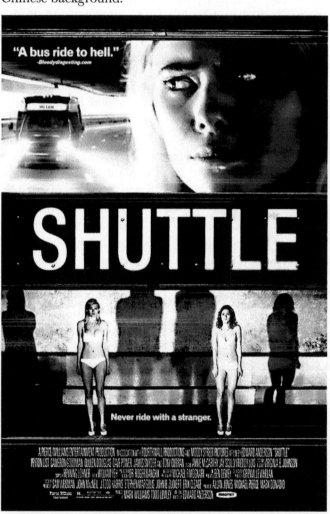

Shuttle
Moody Street Pictures 2008; 107 minutes;
Director: Edward Anderson ****

Two girls, fresh off a plane, are joined by a couple of young men and an accountant on an airport shuttle, unaware that the driver has devious motives in picking them up.

UNDER TEN MILLION? ANYTHING'S POSSIBLE!

Dingy photography, minimal music, tiny budget—but Edward Anderson's tension-fueled thriller beats many similar big-budget efforts hands down in the terror stakes. Chicks Peyton List and Cameron Goodman board a shuttle with two guys who have been hitting on them, a geeky man (Cullen Douglas) sitting in the rear. Once on the road, it soon becomes blindingly obvious that the nondescript driver (Tony Curran) has a hidden (and disturbing) agenda; the males are expendable in his plans, but the girls have to be prevented from harm at all costs. Why? All is made clearer when, halfway through, director Anderson delivers a chilling sucker-punch—that cowardly Douglas who has been trying his best to avoid being injured is totally deranged, in cahoots with Curran over the girls' plight, whatever that may be. So what at first appears to be a standard sex killer shocker deviates into something far more sinister as List and Goodman are taken to an underground parking lot (after Douglas and the two men have died) where an unexpected fate awaits them. A gut-wrenching climax, plus that heart-rending final shot showing List's one item of lost luggage appearing on the airport conveyor belt, completes an incisively acted drama, blessed with an intelligent script, that fires on all cylinders and keeps you playing guessing games right to the finishing line.

Small Town Folk
Gumboot Pictures 2007; 90 minutes;
Director: Peter Stanley-Ward *

The inhabitants of a village called Grockleton murder all those who stray over its boundaries.

Chris R. Wright is the landlord of Beesley's Manor, a deranged despot ruling a gang of inbred retards (all sporting rotten teeth, a couple wearing scarecrow masks). When couple Greg Martin and Hannah Flint drive into this far-from peaceful rural retreat, Wright, with the assistance of his nauseous brothers, captures Flint and imprisons her. Martin escapes, bumps into Simon Stanley-Ward (his friends have all been slaughtered by a sword-wielding

masked lunatic) and, after a series of perilous confrontations, sets fire to the manor house and wipes out the retards. Comic book photography in the style of 2005's *Sin City* cannot disguise the fact that this cockeyed variation on *Deliverance* is as ugly as Wright, Warwick Davis, Dan Palmer and the rest of this ghastly crew. Shot mainly in three fields and a wood, there's a host of gory killings (by sword, axe and scythe) but the attempt at black humor misfires badly after the first five minutes and what you are left with is a very unattractive horror outing; once is definitely enough for *Small Town Folk*.

Splintered
Splintered Films/Not a Number 2010; 85 minutes;
Director: Simeon Halligan **

A teenager who was abused by her father when she was a small girl encounters a schizophrenic madman running loose in an abandoned boarding school.

Is it a werewolf that's running amok in the Welsh countryside, as the British-made *Splintered*, in its opening spell, would have us believe? No such luck: It's an insane former pupil at the abandoned St. Joseph's College whose equally demented sibling has returned to the place in the hope of trapping him before he causes any further damage. Stephen Walters plays both brothers in Jekyll and Hyde fashion, an over-

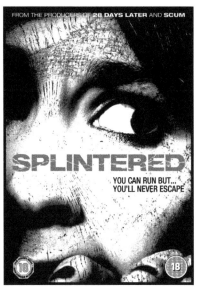

the-top, wild-eyed monster straight out of the 1950s school of psycho horror thrillers, but, as a whole, the film doesn't match his bravura performance. Instead, it becomes yet another "girl and buddies in creepy old house trying to escape a butchering maniac" exercise, lapsing into sameness. Holly Weston is the teen obsessed with the supernatural creatures of legend, ending up the lone survivor of her group, comprising of boyfriend Sacha Dhawan, soulmate Sadie Pickering, her detestable other half, Sol Heras and Pickering's young brother, Jonathan Readwin—all are slain by the rampaging loony, including a couple of police officers. Three lengthy dream sequences near the start hint at Weston's disturbed state of mind, an angle that's never fully developed (she finishes off Walters the madman by plunging a crucifix in his eye), Colin Tierney cropping up as a priest bent on revenge for the killing of his brother years ago by Walters who, when a pupil, was shoved in a room full of wolves as punishment. Shot on location at St. Joseph's College, Upholland, Lancashire (the imposing edifice was closed in 1991), *Splintered* is littered with psychological overtones but opts for "running, jumping and standing still" standard shocks which greatly lessens its potential impact.

any the less for this; as a matter of fact, it's a well-mounted shocker that will have you on the edge of your seat, no mean feat in today's cinema.

Straight into Darkness
Silver Bullet/Clan Cameron Cinema 2004; 95 minutes;
Director: Jeff Burr ****

Western Europe 1943: Two deserters from an American airborne division struggle through a harsh, war-torn landscape and meet a French couple who are in charge of a group of strange orphans.

Burr's engrossing (and macabre) mix of bloody war, visions, madness, horror and even *Freaks* is one of those strange little movies that can be viewed on several different levels. Ryan Francis and Scott McDonald (continually at loggerheads) wander through stark, snow-laden woodlands, encountering body-strewn ruins and scavenging dogs. Sensitive Francis suffers from repeated flashbacks of his prewar life and has visions of people killed in the ruins they stumble across. When they discover a large, apparently abandoned, house, David Warner and Linda Thorsen turn up and about a dozen little urchins, hidden in the house, show themselves. Most suffer from an affliction; one with no legs, another scarred, a girl hiding her ravaged features behind a doll-like mask. From this point on, the Americans plus Warner's retinue engage in a battle with 60 German troops, resulting in mass slaughter on both sides. The moving final moments sees the masked girl re-

Stag Night
Instinctive Film 2008; 84 minutes;
Director: Peter A. Dowling ****

Four guys out on a bachelor party disembark unlawfully from a subway train and find themselves running for their lives, pursued by a group of cannibalistic killers.

A rip-off of Christopher Smith's splendid *Creep* (2004), *Stag Night* is a breathless ride on a ghost train, and very gory with it. Kip Pardue, Breckin Meyer, Scott Adkins and Karl Geary, together with two women they pick up in the carriage (Sarah Barrand and Vinessa Shaw), force the doors open when the train halts at a junction, an act they soon live to regret; long-haired, bearded sub-humans dwell in the passages, feeding on raw human remains. Adkins and Barrand are the first to get chopped up; the others flee down the deserted tracks, desperate to find a way out as the hairy butchers and their savage dogs close in on them. Dowling stages the bloody set pieces in *Descent*-like fashion, making excellent use of the shadowy subway tunnels and the innate menace they harbor; the sudden ending is both uncompromising and tragic as sole survivor Pardue *nearly* makes it out, but doesn't. Fair enough, abnormal beings lurking in underground train networks (America, Britain and France are favorite locations) are nothing new in the horror field, but that doesn't mean to say that *Stag Night* is

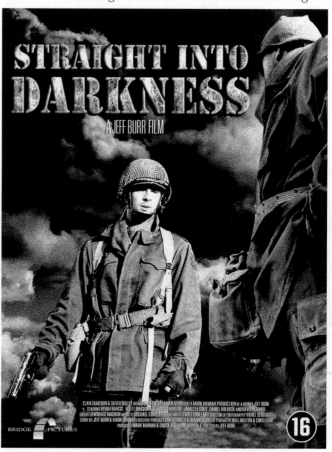

UNDER TEN MILLION? ANYTHING'S POSSIBLE!

moving her disguise and caressing Francis as he dies of gunshot wounds. *Straight into Darkness* is like a descent into some kind of World War II mystical hell with all kinds of filmic source references on offer, appealing to those buffs who like their fare rather more complex than usual. Even that haunting closing sequence has a whiff of *Eyes Without a Face* about it! A low-budget exercise in allegorical cinema that is well worth a look. It really does linger in the mind.

Them aka Iles
Castel Film Romania 2006; 77 minutes;
Directors: David Moreau and Xavier Palud ****
A French couple spending the weekend at their secluded country retreat in Snagov, Romania, are terrorized by unknown, and unseen, assailants.

High on white-knuckle, edge-of-the-seat suspense, this French/Romanian thriller will have you holding your breath for the entire 77 minutes—it's a classic example of not what you see but what you *don't* see as Olivia Bonamy and Michael Cohen find themselves trapped in their rambling old house by a person, or persons, unknown, bent on life-threatening mischief. Slamming shutters, banging doors, lights switched on and off, the car moving from its parking spot, torches shining through windows, vague hooded figures, the television on one minute, off the next, a running tap—what precisely *is* it that is reducing the pair

to nervous wrecks? Can it be tied up with the frenzied double murder seen at the beginning? Based on a true series of events dating from 2002, the payoff, taking place in a complex of storm drains, comes as much of a shock as to what has gone before and says a lot about the aimlessness and cheap values held by many of today's youths. Tautly directed with virtually no intrusive music and no flab, *Them* is almost worthy of Hitchcock himself; just don't expect a happy ending because you won't get one. And the phrase "I just want to play" will haunt you for a very long time afterwards.

Tourist Trap
Compass Intl./Charles Band Prods. 1979; 90 minutes;
Director: David Schmoeller ***
When their two vehicles break down, five teenagers chance upon Slausen's Lost Oasis, a run-down wax museum that houses malefic mannequins.

Charles Band's puppets strike again, 10 years before he formed Full Moon productions. Band was executive producer and it shows, his puppetry life-sized here instead of miniature, but just as evil. Crazy Chuck Connors stars as the museum's owner, controlling the dummies through telekinesis and adding to his collection by bumping off passing travelers and coating them in plaster. Connors (he killed his wife and brother for having an affair behind his back) murders four of the group but is willing to spare Jocelyn Jones the indignity of becoming a wax model because she reminds him of his dead wife; however, Jones escapes in the delirious climax, driving down a road, totally unhinged, her four friends, transformed into dummies, propped up on the back seat. Schmoeller borrows from all manner of movies connected with wax museums, corpses and masked loonies, notably *House of Wax* and even *Psycho*, successfully tapping into most people's inherent fears of wax figures housed in dusty museums; the director conjures up some truly scary moments showing the dummies coming to diabolical life, laughing maniacally as they jerkily close in on their victims. Pino Donaggio's quirky score is another bonus. Less impressive is the murky color and, like many other '70s horror films, *Tourist Trap* looks dated. Nevertheless, as is the case

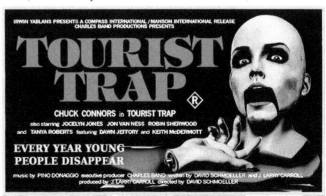

with other Band productions, the unorthodox style and those lifelike puppets make the film more interesting than it appears to be on the surface.

Triloquist
American World Pictures/Sawyer Levine Jones Prods. 2008; 85 minutes; Director: Mark Jones **

A brother and sister embark on a road trip to hell with their dead mother's ventriloquist's dummy that possesses an iniquitous intelligence of its own.

An 18-rated comedy-horror thriller of a vacuous kind: Disaffected blonde teenage slut Paydin LoPachin, her dim, goofy brother Rocky Marquette and a malicious, cowboy-clad dummy drive west to Vegas, murdering shop-keepers, car owners and police en route; the pair abduct a young woman (Katie Chonacas) so that Marquette can make her pregnant, thus producing an heir. Quite what the point was behind all this craziness is uncertain. Grainy monochrome images and a rock/country soundtrack point to some attempt at artistic merit, and the script is, in plac-es, crude, witty and funny. However, the splatter/murder/sexual abuse scenes don't sit well with this kind of hokey

material, and neither does the semi-serious attempt at explaining away the obvious theme of dual personality, the silent Marquette acting like his precious wooden pal while callous LoPachin has sup-plied the dummy's voice all along. That ghastly dummy baby gurgling in a crib in the final few seconds (the result of brother and sister coupling) is the wacky icing on an offbeat horror cake that only amuses in fits and starts.

Underground
Tax Credit Finance 2011; 83 minutes; Director: Rafael Eisenman; Rating: **

Following a fracas at a rave party, four men and four women take refuge in an underground military bunker, home to flesh-eating humanoid creatures genetically engi-neered by a mad disciple of notorious Nazi exterminator Josef Mengele.

The Descent meets *Wrong Turn* meets *The Cave* ... the opening sequence of a rave gig in full flow, foul-mouthed language matching the obnoxious antics of dudes and babes, has you hoping that all eight cast members meet their Maker sooner rather than later. Six do, but not before we've been treated to plenty of frantic pursuit through a dimly lit industrial subterranean complex, the fanged mu-

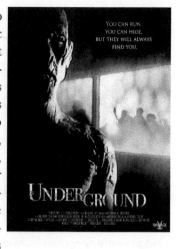

tants tearing their prey to shreds and surviving in toxic water, atmospherically put together by director Eisen-man although at times, it's difficult to figure out who's being chased, and who isn't. However, on the hour, with the body count at five, loony scientist Jack Donner turns up in a wheelchair af-ter gruesomely plucking the eyes from Christina Evan-gelista and the movie goes downhill fast. It turns out that Donner created these sub-human beings in tandem with the US military (a form of expendable soldier, his pet "Trogs") by abducting pregnant women and injecting their fetus' with "ferocious animal serum," including alligator fluid. Ross Thomas and Sofia Pernas make it out unscathed, both suffering from night-mares in which they change into monsters themselves, and the final shot is of Jeff D'Agostino on Thomas' cellphone, left behind and screaming in terror as he's tortured by the hideous denizens of that underground hellhole.

Unrest
Asgaard Entertainment 2006; 88 minutes; Director: Jason Todd Ipson ***

On her first day at the SUU School of Medicine, a new intern is convinced that the corpse she is dissecting in

a mortuary possesses a soul that is trying to communicate with her.

For almost an hour, *Unrest* is tremendously different scary horror fare: A leisurely, almost lethargic pace, disturbingly realistic pathology sequences, bright performances, with the one question, "What is this all about?" on the tip of your tongue. Intern Corri English and three guys are carrying out an autopsy on the corpse of a prostitute. English senses that she "feels something" emanating from the ravaged remains and decides to investigate the facts leading up to the girl's death. Ipson conjures up an icy atmosphere to match the sterile surroundings, and even the romance between atheist English and religious Scot Davis doesn't lighten the mood of impending doom as the girl delves deeper and deeper. Then the death toll starts to mount—those in contact with the cadaver die from excessive blood loss and what up until then was a careful exercise in freezing terror lapses into standard shock tactics. The deliberate slow pace becomes frantic, English's colleagues drop dead, teacher Derrick O'Connor is almost sliced to pieces and bodies turn up in a tank brimming with formaldehyde, all to the sound of weird chanting and thumping drums. It emerges that the corpse was that of an American tourist (Marisa Petroro) who discovered by chance a mass Aztec grave in Brazil (Aztecs in Brazil? Surely not!) and became possessed by the spirit of Tlazolteotl, the god of fertility and prostitution. Confined in an institution, she eventually committed suicide but the demons inside her lived on. English incinerates the corpse, yelling "Rest in peace, bitch," exhibiting a complete character change to that of her former mousey persona, a change that mirrors the film itself. If *Unrest* had stuck to its guns and continued in the vein of the first hour, it could have had the potential to become a five-star minor miracle. Instead, by pandering to the masses (as far as masses go in indie cinema) it winds up as being just another possession shocker, albeit a well-made one.

Vinyan
Backup Films/Wild Bunch 2008; 96 minutes;
Director: Fabrice Du Welz ***

Six months after their son was tragically lost in the 2004 tsunami, a couple is convinced that he is still alive after seeing his indistinct image on video footage.

Several independent film companies gave their financial backing to Welz's partly successful attempt to fuse Asian supernatural horror with Joseph Conrad's *Heart of Darkness* and Nicolas Roeg's *Don't Look Now*. Vinyan means disturbed spirit; the term is only mentioned once, so viewers may have a hard time fathoming out what is happening as Rufus Sewell and Emmanuelle Béart embark on an odyssey into hell: Petch Osathanugrah promises to locate their son in Burma (at great cost) but the journey develops into a nightmare of its own making: Mud-covered children appear everywhere resembling ghouls from the grave; corpses

and the living are stoned by the children; the couple's crafty Thai hosts demand more money at every stage; and they are eventually abandoned at a remote village with only those creepy kids for company. Welz piles on the portents of doom (Chinese lanterns in the night air, an offering to troubled spirits; the scabrous children exuding hate and malevolence; Béart whispering to skeptical Sewell "You let him go."); and the location photography is spot on, conveying a dark air of rain-drenched melancholia that affects the film's second half. The shattering last few minutes may or may not make much sense, but the two leads put in professional, though somber, performances to match the pessimistic mood. *Vinyan* runs against the grain of most mainstream Thai-based horror features—it makes you think, and in that respect, should be roundly applauded.

Wake Wood
Hammer/Exclusive/Vertigo Films 2009; 90 minutes;
Director: David Keating ***

A couple setting up home in Wake Wood agree to undergo a grisly ritual in order that they can be reunited, for three days only, with their nine-year-old daughter, mauled to death by a savage dog.

Veterinary Aidan Gillen and pharmacist Eva Birthistle, mourning the death of Ella Connolly, go along with Timothy Spall's plan to raise their daughter from the dead by performing a gruesome ritual involving the body of a

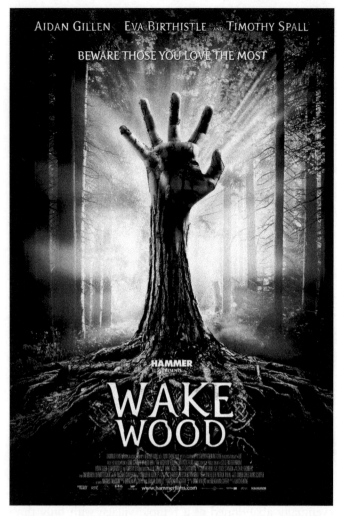

Hammer logo, this isn't a case of returning to past glories. It's left to Spall to steal the show, playing the wily landowner up to his neck in all things pagan, a telling performance from one of Britain's most versatile character actors.

Walled In
Indigomotion 2009; 91 minutes;
Director: Gilles Paquet-Brenner **

A newly appointed engineer is assigned the task of demolishing a vast building where, 15 years previously, 16 bodies were discovered within its walls, entombed in cement.

For 35 minutes, *Walled In* is riveting horror: Mischa Barton, employed in her father's engineering company, travels to a massive Gothic edifice built on marshland; her job is to compile a demolition report. Deborah Kara Unger greets her with son Cameron Bright and warns her to stay away from the eighth floor and the roof. They also put her into room 208, scene of the murder of a young girl. So far, so good. The director builds on the building's aura of doom and gloom, plus sheer size, and the fact that it was here that all those cement-covered corpses were found. Teenage Bright forms an unhealthy attachment to Barton, only two tenants remain on the site, Barton has disturbing visions of the small girl's death and phone signals are down. It is at this point that the movie's solid narrative takes a sudden turn for the worse, akin to a ball of string unraveling of its own accord—the building's architect (Pascal Greggory), presumed dead, is the killer, now imprisoned at the bottom of a deep shaft situated in the building's center; Barton joins him involuntarily, pushed in by the besotted, mother-fixated Bright who is determined that no one else can have her; Greggory designed the block on the principles of the Egyptian pyramids and wants Barton to kill him so that he can be entombed in cement like a pharaoh; Barton, from being a strong female character, changes into a cowering wimp; and when the demolition team turns up, Barton is still trapped in the shaft. Instead of flying off at all tangents, they should have kept things simple: The real star of the show, that huge ugly building, deserved a lot more than the highfalutin' exposition offered to the viewer; the movie would have worked far better as an uncomplicated horror-cum-ghost thriller. Take that monumental structure out of the frame and what you have is a one-star calamity; you can see why *Walled In* never made it onto UK circuits.

newly-deceased farmworker and bones from Connolly's hand, dug from her grave. Spall warns of dire consequences if the couple has lied to them about Connolly's particulars; they have, stating that she died 11 months ago when in fact it was over a year, one month beyond Spall's stipulated time limit. They can only have Connolly for three days and the girl must not wander outside of the town boundary lines, set by a row of wind turbines. Spewed forth in a welter of blood and gunge, Connolly is taken home and cleaned up, but Ruth McCabe, the dead farmworker's wife, senses something's wrong and after three days, Gillen and Birthistle refuse to relinquish hold on their daughter. Result? Connolly turns into a devil-child, hacking to death animals and humans before being dragged over the boundary line where she dies, hauling her mother down under the earth with her in a makeshift burial. However, Birthistle was pregnant; she's returned from the dead in another ritual and it's quite clear from the final scene of Gillen eyeing his surgical instruments that he plans to lay his hands on his newborn, whether his wife likes it or not. Shot in Ireland and Sweden, the newly formed Hammer's first production in 30 years made no impact at the box office on limited release and fans of vintage Hammer Horror pictures will say that although the movie bears the

UNDER TEN MILLION? ANYTHING'S POSSIBLE!

Killers/Serial Killers

Alone
Evolution/CFI-CYF Productions 2002; 89 minutes;
Director: Phil Claydon **

Tormented by a harrowing childhood, a psychotic killer obsessed with cleanliness and strict schedules befriends young women and then murders them.

Let's first of all get the climax (or anticlimax) out of the way. It's a cop-out, the film ending abruptly, leaving the audience to play guessing games. A low-budget British psychological thriller that never made it into UK cinemas, *Alone* features some flashy, fairly innovative camerawork and editing from Phil Claydon as we experience through the eyes of "Alex" (the killer is never seen) a series of brutal murders of young girls: One pushed down a flight of stairs, another force-fed to death, a strangling. Is Alex male or female? His/her parents died 13 years back, and he/she now lives in a sterile environment, wearing surgical gloves to eat, drink and kill.

Miriam Margolyes puts in a star turn as a chain-smoking caseworker, two warring detectives (John Shrapnel and Isabel Brook) are superfluous to plot requirements and in the final scenes, intended victim Laurel Holloman is pursued down hospital corridors strangely devoid of both patients and doctors. As psychodramas go, it's atmospheric in parts, shoddy and incomplete in others, with touches of *Halloween* here and there. But that sudden ending ruins all the preceding hard work and will leave those watching feeling short-changed.

Black Cadillac
Painting Entertainment 2003; es;
Director: John Murkowski *****

Two brothers and their buddy go for a drinking/let's chat up the women session at a roadhouse bar deep in the Wisconsin woodlands. On leaving after a fight, they're pursued relentlessly by a mysterious black Cadillac manned by an anonymous psychotic driver.

Shot at night (apart from the final few minutes), *Black Cadillac* is a nifty, suspenseful *Duel*-type thriller benefiting from Randy Quaid's burly presence, a sheriff who the guys (Shane Johnson, Josh Hammond and Jason Dohring) pick up by his broken-down patrol car. As the chase proceeds through dark, snow-laden Wisconsin woods and across

ice-bound lakes, has the sinister Quaid got something to do with the boys' plight? He's shot dead midway through, but is he in fact dead? It seems that one of those psycho rednecks thoroughly objected to Dohring trying to lose his virginity with his flighty wife and Quaid is in cahoots with him—these young interlopers who have invaded their hick territory need to be taught a harsh lesson! Robert Clunis is the loony driver who eventually crashes the Cadillac into a frozen lake after unsuccessfully trying to murder the trio. A tautly directed edge-of-the-seat thriller, thankfully lacking the usual banal teen dialogue and delivering the goods in breathtaking style.

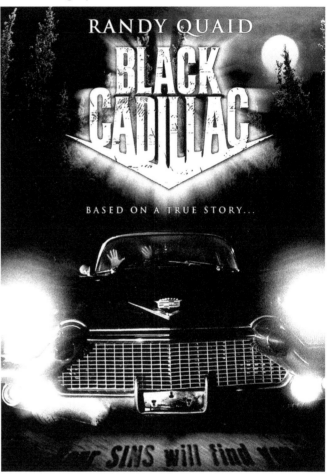

Blood Car
Fake Wood Wallpaper Films 2007; 76 minutes;
Director: Alex Orr ****

A geeky children's teacher, experimenting with a new fuel, discovers that his car can run on human blood.

21st-century schlock brimming with bad taste, graphic sex, crude humor, blood and guts while underneath it all, we have a biting satire on man's obsession with the automobile. With gasoline prices at $32 a liter, cars have become more or less obsolete, creating "car graveyards" where youngsters hang out to engage in sexual activity. Mike Brune's vehicle runs moderately well on a wheat grass liquid (obtained from besotted Anna Chlumsky), but

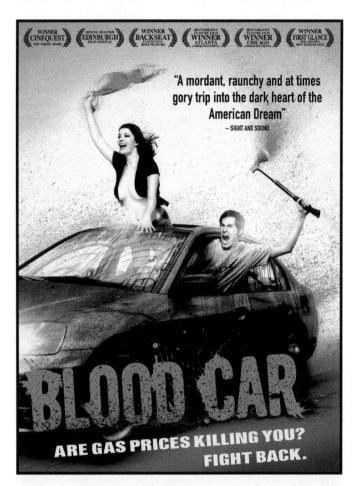

"A mordant, raunchy and at times gory trip into the dark heart of the American Dream"
— SIGHT AND SOUND

BLOOD CAR

ARE GAS PRICES KILLING YOU? FIGHT BACK.

Shot in 18 days on a $200,000 budget, Mason's spare thriller is superb moviemaking by anyone's standards; think *Wolf Creek* with supernatural undertones and you'll get some idea of what this multi-layered little gem is all about. Superficially, the story is simple: Ian Duncan and pregnant Tess Panzer have to slog it down an endless highway to the desolate town of Blood River in the middle of the desert when their car suffers a blow-out. A stranger arrives in the shape of Andrew Howard who quickly begins to rub Duncan up the wrong way, paying far too much attention to his wife. One's first thought is "Aha! Serial killer or religious nut." But no, you'd be on the wrong track. Howard slyly states that everyone has a dark secret, including Duncan, and must ultimately atone for their wrongdoings. What develops is a psychological battle of wills between all three as slowly, pieces of a very disturbing jigsaw puzzle fall into place, revealing that this couple's life isn't so perfect after all and that Duncan does indeed harbor a dreadful secret involving Panzer's young son from a previous marriage. Yes, it's payback time and the increasingly vile Duncan, exhibiting a darker side to his personality, has met his nemesis, as has Panzer in her own small way. Mason fleshes out his characters so that you can totally identify with each one while the panoramic desert landscapes are beautifully observed. In the sphere of independent psychological horror cinema, sun-blasted *Blood River* outshines most of its competitors by a mile and grabs from beginning to end.

when he accidentally cuts himself and blood drips into the mix, the engine roars into life and he realizes he has hit upon a novel form of fuel. Constructing a metal, saw-toothed fan in the trunk, the skinny vegan-turned-babe magnet cruises the streets, shoving unsuspecting victims into the fan where their blood powers the vehicle as efficiently as gas, and more cheaply! All the while, he's being shadowed by government agents, anxious to acquire the secret formula behind this revolutionary fuel. Jumping from no-holds-barred sex (Katie Rowlett—what a fox!) to scenes of a distasteful nature (Brune shooting animals with a BB gun; a baby tossed nonchalantly into the trunk; everyone connected with Brune killed at the end, including schoolchildren) to the question of whether vegans can take to meat-eating, Orr's low-budget 18-rated eco-horror show is a gas from start to finish, backed by an intriguing soundtrack that effectively utilizes classical music. Roger Corman might have come up with something as quirky as this in the early '60s, but nowhere near as explicit.

Blood River

Leonidas Films/Epic 2009; 104 minutes;
Director: Adam Mason ****

A couple driving across Nevada have to walk to a ghost town when their vehicle breaks down; there, they are confronted by a drifter who claims to have been sent to Earth as an avenging angel of death.

"INTENSE, VIOLENT & THOROUGHLY THRILLING" Quietearth.us

FROM THE DIRECTOR OF **BROKEN** & **THE DEVIL'S CHAIR**

BLOOD RIVER

DVD VIDEO

IF YOU CROSS HIS PATH... IT'S ALREADY TOO LATE

UNDER TEN MILLION? ANYTHING'S POSSIBLE!

B.T.K.

North American Ent. 2008; 90 minutes;
Director: Michael Feifer ***

Mild-mannered city compliance officer Dennis Rader, married with two children, minister of the local church and scout leader, turned out to be one of America's most sadistic serial killers, embarking on a murder spree in the Wichita area from 1974 to 1991.

Director Feifer and actor Kane Hodder reunited after 2007's *Ed Gein: The Butcher of Plainfield* to come up with a nightmarish study of mental psychosis, misogyny and twisted sexual deviance: Bind, torture, kill was Rader's tenet, the man breaking into houses, tying up, shooting, suffocating or strangling his victims, sometimes photographing the bodies with himself lying beside them and, like many such psychopaths who like to broadcast their acts, teasing the police with cryptic notes. Rader was eventually convicted in 2005 and given a 174-year sentence. Hodder plays him as the nerdy guy next door who wouldn't harm a fly, his inner turmoil and ruthlessness bubbling just beneath the surface, and the vicious murders depicted are quite hard to stomach. Perhaps the movie does stray from the true facts on occasions, but in the recent spate of features based on these real-life monsters, *B.T.K.* is better than most.

The Cellar Door aka Broken 2: The Cellar Door

Six Sense Productions/Tricoast 2007; 85 minutes;
Director: Matt Zettell ***

A mentally unstable man kidnaps a girl and imprisons her in a huge crate in his cellar.

Nothing new here—Terence Stamp and Samantha Eggar did all this in William Wyler's classic 1965 thriller *The Collector*. Forty years later, hulking James DuMont and Michelle Tomlinson go through the same scenario, albeit with more gore and nudity to titillate the modern-day audience. DuMont, with the mental age of a 10-year-old, also bludgeons a girl to death for calling him a jerk and captures another, stabbing her repeatedly. In the final frenetic 15 minutes, Tomlinson breaks free and manages to turn the tables on the nutter by incarcerating him in his own crate. Zettell orchestrates a tingling sense of frisson between the two as Tomlinson attempts to bond with her tormentor to save her skin, and as screen psychos go, DuMont is just as good as a thousand others of his ilk. A satisfactory effort for all slasher lovers.

Ed Gein: The Butcher of Plainfield

North American Ent. 2007; 90 minutes;
Director: Michael Feifer **

Wisconsin, 1957: A farmer who keeps himself to himself murders, mutilates and skins the corpses of his victims, eventually gaining notoriety as one of America's most infamous serial killers.

Playing hard and fast with the facts, *Ed Gein* is bolstered by the burly presence of Kane Hodder as the psycho—take him out of the equation, and you are left with a mundane sequence of events where the soundtrack at times drowns out all dialogue and the police are shown to be a bunch of blundering fools. Michael *The Hills Have Eyes* Berryman puts in a guest appearance as Gein's only friend but ends up dead very quickly following an argument over digging up dead bodies; the murders are fairly low-key in depiction and the killer's charnel house of a barn is only hinted at in shadowy glimpses. When you consider the raft of horror movies based on Gein's depraved exploits—*Psycho*, *The Silence of the Lambs*, *The Texas Chainsaw Massacre*, among others—you might have expected a more full-blooded version than what we have here. Shawn Hoffman (a young deputy) and Timothy Oman (the sheriff) play the two main incompetent law officers who, give them their due, didn't possess the modern-day technology to track Gein down—but they're still useless! This is Hodder's show and it's his performance alone that engages the interest, a star turn in a rather disappointing true-life serial killer flick.

Ed Gein: In the Light of the Moon aka Ed Gein

Overseas Filmgroup/Tartan 2000; 89 minutes;
Director: Chuck Parello ***

A sober reconstruction of Ed Gein's rise to infamy as one of America's most reviled serial killers.

Steve Railsback stars as the farmer who, in the mid-1950s, inadvertently started the craze for a whole slew of

horror films, from *Psycho* onwards. Focusing mainly on the murders of storekeeper Carol Mansell and flirty bar owner Sally Champlin and photographed in warm pastel colors to convey an authentic '50s period atmosphere, this version of Gein's appalling "achievements" tones down the horrors (it was 15-rated in Britain) and seems content to concentrate on the schizo's strained relationship with his bullying parents and brother, the catalyst for his deranged acts. Carrie Snodgress plays Gein's mother, a religious fanatic goading her son from beyond the grave to commit one foul deed after another. A few scenes are included to remind us exactly what Gein got up to in his spare time—a headless body strung upside down; Gein dancing in the moonlight, dressed in an outfit made from human skin; the madman cooking meat carved from a victim—and Railsback is all-too believable in the role. It's rather plodding at times, but with actual newsreel footage opening and closing the film, this is a more accurate record of events than many other interpretations of the Ed Gein case history.

Elsewhere
Lost Toys Productions 2009; 106 minutes;
Director: Nathan Hope ***
A teenage slut hooked on chatrooms and internet dating mysteriously disappears after arranging a meeting with "Mister X."

The dangers associated with internet dating are brought home to roost in a compelling little feature. Quiet Anna Kendrick and flighty Tania Raymonde are bored waitresses, both looking for their very own Mr. Right. Spending $300 a month on text messages, Raymonde tells Kendrick that she has bagged herself an internet boyfriend and plans to meet him one night. The teenage tramp then vanishes, but not before texting her friend with a disturbing image of her on a bus, ending in a high-pitched scream. Kendrick, plagued by dreams of Raymonde and another girl who went missing five years back, takes on the role of amateur detective as she and computer buff Chuck Carter attempt to establish the sinister reasons behind Raymonde's sudden disappearance; for starters, is Hendrick's other pal, mousy Olivia Dawn

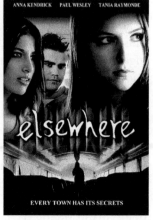

York, hiding knowledge concerning Raymonde's plight? Part drama, part psycho thriller, *Elsewhere* scores because of its understated approach, the abductor (John Gries) dispatched by Kendrick in a maize field without revealing the whereabouts of the bodies of the girls he has murdered over many years. Raymonde is bewitching as the vulnerable tart with a heart of gold and Kendrick eschews cuteness for streetwise savvy, while Hope's direction is assured. A modern-day warning on getting too wrapped up in technology to the detriment of one's well-being.

The Fear Chamber
Night Light Films 2009; 91 minutes;
Director: Kevin Carraway **
A cop with a troubled past has a heart transplant following a tussle with a serial killer and starts to have horrific visions of the maniac's future victims.

Indie regular Rhett Giles is on good form as the police officer on the trail of psycho Richard Tyson, a lunatic who abducts young women, sells their internal organs to dealers and disposes of the corpses in acid. When psychic Miranda Kwok meets Giles in a bar and tells him he has got to pursue the case because he also is gifted with psychic powers, he goes all out to nail the killer, even

though boss Steven Williams has pulled him off the case. *The Fear Chamber* follows in the footsteps of countless others and is let down by a soggy script with too many loose ends: What were the circumstances behind the death of Giles' wife at the hands of a criminal—is that why he has a drinking problem? What went on between Tyson and his mother? Why did Tyson dig up and behead a corpse. What is the significance of that partly constructed grotesque female mannequin Giles stumbles across in the killer's den. The supernatural denouement—Kwok is a ghost; Giles received *her* heart in his transplant operation—is enough to raise the eyebrows an inch or two, but by then the movie has run out of steam. A pity—this could have worked if all involved had tightened up the script and plot development to make the scenario more cohesive.

Gacy
DEJ Prods./Peninsula Films 2003; 88 minutes;
Director: Clive Saunders ***
A semi-factual account of the John Wayne Gacy case, a notorious sex killer who tortured and murdered 33 young

men during the late 1970s, storing their dismembered corpses in the crawl space beneath his house.

Flatly directed but held together by the riveting performance of bulky Mark Holton in the lead role, *Gacy* is better than your average true-life serial killer thriller, even though it doesn't really stick to the facts (but then, none of them do). Humiliated by his bullying father, Gacy grew up to be a sadistic murderer, although he was married with two daughters. Cutting up the bodies of his victims, he shoved the remains under his floorboards, leading to complaints by the local residents about the stench emanating

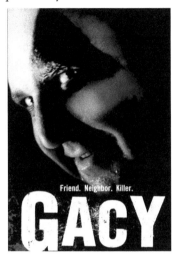

from his home; eventually arrested, Gacy was executed in 1994. If you are familiar with the case, then the movie has very little dramatic impact because you'll know what's coming but to its credit, *Gacy* tones down the sadism and gore (it was rated "15" in England) and concentrates on the killer's twisted persona—really, this is a one-man show, with Holton excelling in the part.

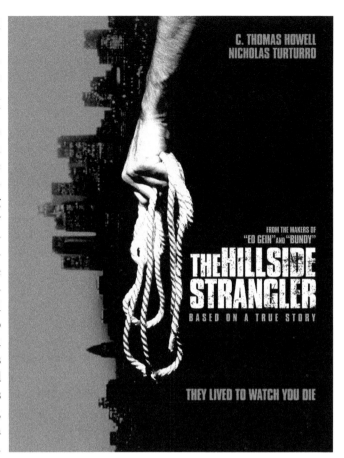

The Hillside Strangler
Tartan Films 2004; 97 minutes; Director: Chuck Parello ****

In revenge for their prostitution racket being busted by a rival gang, two men cruise the streets of Los Angeles, picking up hookers and strangling them.

Based on the celebrated Hillside Murders case of the late 1970s, Parello's cut-price docudrama doesn't make for pleasant viewing: The language is explicitly foul, the actions of the two slimeballs even more so, the murders clinical rather than sensationalistic, adding to rather than detracting from the director's crudely effective semi-realistic technique. C. Thomas Howell plays Kenneth Bianchi, an out-and-out loser, forever trying to force his way into landing a job with the LAPD; Nicholas Turturro is his cousin, Angelo Buono, a woman-hating mechanic living for cheap thrills. After a string of murders, the sadists are eventually caught when Howell's long-suffering girlfriend (Allison Lange), sick of his constant lying, discovers evidence connecting him to one of the dead prostitutes; she then shops him to the police. It's unsavory and tasteless in the extreme but pieced together proficiently by Parello; Howell (one of indie's better actors) portrays Bianchi as a weasel-faced dreamer, flitting from one dead-end job to another, while Turturro reverts to Joe Pesci mode when his temper flares up. Many female viewers will want to give this a miss and the coldness of the subject matter might not appeal to some males either. But there's no denying the fact that, out of the numerous cinematic adaptations of real-life murder cases that have made the headlines over the past 40 years, *The Hillside Strangler* is preferable to others of its type.

Lonely Joe aka Haunted Traxxs
Emmemax Films/NuFilms 2009; 95 minutes; Director: Michael Coonce **

A New York reporter arrives in the town of Solvay to investigate the death of her brother 10 years previously at the hands of a local mass murderer.

The main fault with this bloodless outing is one of bafflement: Director Coonce attempts to intermingle a supernatural detective drama with a serial killer thriller, topped off by tagging on a *Sixth Sense*-style finale, perhaps hoping that something of value will be achieved from the mix. Unfortunately, the end result is a plodding exercise, low on thrills, in which resolute reporter Erica Leerhsen takes up an inordinate amount of footage interviewing Solvay's residents, being hounded by suspicious officer Peter Speach and, in one ridiculously interminable sequence, traipsing

endlessly along roads with ex-boyfriend Matthew S. Harrison, only for the guy to vanish into thin air. Is he a ghost? Is *she* a ghost? Why are people scared of the rail tracks bordering the killer's old farm? What made the loony (David Fine) cut up victims with a scythe and bury 30 bodies in his field. Why are townsfolk still disappearing from time to time? What is the meaning behind Leerhsen's repeated visions and violent dreams. That closing resolution points to mysterious occurrences dating back to the American Civil War, the area long known for entities and hauntings. There's simply too much going on in what is after all a standard horror setup and the finale is hurriedly pieced together, making little sense. A pity, because *Lonely Joe* had all the makings of a serial killer movie with more wit and intelligence than others.

The Lost
Silver Web Productions 2006; 119 minutes;
Director: Chris Sivertson ****

A narcissistic youth, unable to form proper relationships with women, shoots them for kicks.

American Psycho meets *Psycho* meets … well, think of any number of psychopath movies and they'll feature in *The Lost* somewhere. In fact, one scene in Sivertson's compelling, if disturbing, journey into a particular individual's deranged world is a frame-by-frame copy from Hitchcock's

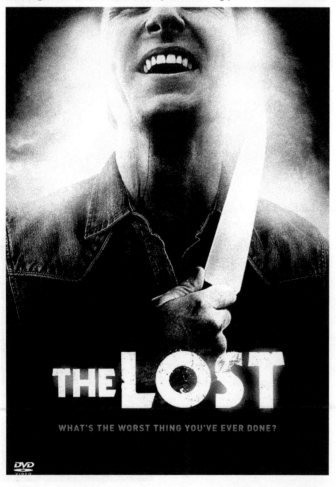

masterpiece: Police officer Michael Bowen questions killer Marc Senter in the lobby of his mother's hotel, bringing to mind Martin Balsam's quizzing of Anthony Perkins at the Bates Motel; oh well, if you're going to plagiarize, you might as well plagiarize from the best. Senter turns in a turbo-charged performance as the preening, ingratiating teen who stuffs crushed beer cans into his boots to increase his height; charming, repellent, irritating and unbalanced in equal measures. In a densely plotted screenplay, Bowen knows for certain that the kid shot dead two girl campers four years ago and is determined to prove it; 60-year-old cop Ed Lauter is shacked up with teenager Megan Henning who has to reject Senter's persistent overtures (she works at the motel); Robin Sydney is a raven-haired beauty with hang-ups of her own, also the object of the youth's perverted lust; and Shay Astar plays Senter's long-suffering girlfriend who decides to sleep with Alex Frost, his equally long-suffering buddy, as an act of pure spite. The climax, in which Senter, completely insane, takes Astar, Henning and Sydney hostage, driving them to a house where a couple are in the throes of moving, is deeply unpleasant but fits in with what has come before—Senter stabs the pregnant woman in the back, performs a crude Cesarean section and is then beaten to a pulp by Bowen who bursts in on the bloody scene. And catch that buzzing mosquito sound each time Senter goes off the rails, a cunning little motif if ever there was one. If *The Lost* is supposed to be a modernistic parable on an aimless portion of today's young society, then it achieves what it sets out to do, at the expense of alienating many viewers. As an added treat, porn princess Misty Mundae appears full-frontal naked within the first five minutes, a lighter touch in what turns out to be a very dark picture.

Midnight Movie
Bigfoot Ent./Peace Arch 2008; 82 minutes;
Director: Jack Messitt ***

An insane killer who both starred in and directed an obscure 1970s horror flick (*The Dark Beneath*) escapes from an asylum; when the movie is screened at a local cinema, his evil persona transfers from film to reality and the murders commence once again.

A film within a film— it's a novel slant on the old slasher theme, that's for certain. An assorted group assembles in the local flea-pit for a rare midnight showing of *The Dark Beneath*, including two detectives who

UNDER TEN MILLION? ANYTHING'S POSSIBLE!

reckon that the killer, missing for five years, will be lured there to appease his perverted ego. As the black-and-white picture unfolds (three girls and a guy are stranded when their vehicle breaks down; they find a farmhouse run by an elderly woman; her son is a depraved butcher), the events on the screen revert to events in the cinema; the masked butcher (Lee Main), who homes in on people's sense of fear, materializes, savagely putting to death the cops, the teens and a Harley-loving couple, the slayings then appearing in the film itself. It's a clever device to produce something fresh and, by and large, it works. Even the climax—everyone's souls trapped on celluloid and only little Justin Baric leaping from the screen, thereby saving himself—is a winner. Messitt directs a low-budget quickie that is fairly absorbing, and that's something of a recommendation when you consider how saturated the world of horror cinema has become with this class of fodder.

Mum & Dad
Film London Microwave/BBC Films 2008; 84 minutes;
Director: Steven Sheil ****
A family living near London's Heathrow Airport kidnaps immigrant workers, subjecting their victims to prolonged sexual abuse before murdering them.

Steven Sheil's stark essay into depravity and degradation, filmed on a shoestring budget with a cast of relative unknowns, evokes memories of the notorious Fred and Rose West case which shocked England in the 1990s. Intensely shot, using everyday noises (a dripping tap; doors creaking) as aural wallpaper instead of music, the director's telling of perverted Perry Benson and wife Dido Miles' lust for sexual gratification through domination, pain and torture is not mainstream cinema by a long chalk. A Polish airport cleaner (Olga Fedori) is bamboozled into returning to Ainsley Howard's home after a late shift and finds herself a virtual prisoner in a scabrous house from hell, presided over by owl-faced Benson and predatory Miles. Sheil hints at, rather than shows, the dirty side of murder (body parts in bags; victims' belongings sorted and burnt; rotted teeth on the kitchen floor) but doesn't question the degenerate couple's motives; they're simply stark raving mad, period. A couple of scenes are not for the easily offended: The Christmas party, a mockery of what Christmas stands for; and the unedifying sight of Benson pleasuring himself with a slab of raw meat taken from a corpse. But this sober picture grips from its slow-burning commencement to the uncompromising ending: It's a refreshing alternative (if you can class this material as refreshing) to the usual blood and guts serial killer flick; *Mum & Dad* is the kind of work the British excel in, as Sheil so ably demonstrates.

Parasomnia
American World Pictures/Rising Storm Prods. 2008; 103 minutes;
Director: William Malone ***
A young girl suffering from narcolepsy, a disease whereby a person spends most of their time asleep, has her dreams invaded by the evil thought processes of a serial killer who was once a hypnotist.

At 103 minutes, William Malone (he directed 1999's *House on Haunted Hill*) overstretches this fantasy/horror vehicle by at least 20 minutes; there's simply too much going on here, a clash of differing styles that in some instances doesn't come off. The premise is promising: Cherilyn Wilson is virtually bedridden in a clinic, sleeping her life  away; Dylan Purcell, visiting his druggie pal, spots her and instantly falls in love, spiriting the girl out of the ward to his apartment. However, mass murderer Patrick Kilpatrick, tethered to the wall in an adjacent room, wants the girl to himself; he continually enters her dream state and turns it into a dark netherworld populated by misshapen ghouls, mirroring his own perversions. He can also order her to kill and very soon, Purcell and Wilson are on the run after a string of brutal slayings, both from the police and the psycho who has broken free of his bonds. Kilpatrick manages to produce a passable Hannibal Lecter impersonation (many of the scenes featuring him in his cell are straight from *The Silence of the Lambs*) while winsome Wilson's dreamscape looks like something Guillermo del Toro left on the cutting room floor during the making of *Pan's Labyrinth*. Add to that a bizarre final sequence featuring mechanical puppets (plus two abducted musicians) playing a piece from Prokofiev's *Romeo and Juliet* as Kilpatrick dresses Wilson up as an angel, and a final shot of the pair suspended in a tank of liquid at a Sleep Study Center (Wilson asleep, Purcell in a coma, both regressed to children in their joint dreams) and what you are presented with is a perplexing brew that covers a wide horror spectrum with spasmodic success.

Passed the Door of Darkness
Night Light Films 2008; 100 minutes;
Director: Traxler Mervis *****

New on homicide, a young detective teams up with a disgruntled old pro carrying too much emotional baggage and is soon up to his neck in a series of grisly slayings, performed by a serial killer dubbed The Shadow of God.

An engrossing, low-budget shocker with Freudian undertones that poses the old question—who is the murderer and what are his/her motives? Mark Colson plays a world-weary detective at constant loggerheads with young partner Matthew Prater, both on the graveyard shift. A city

is plagued by a number of brutal massacres whereby innocent people have inadvertently set off booby-traps, killing those closest to them, the maniac leaving cryptic notes at the crime scene. Colson regards Prater as a wet-behind-the-ears rookie but gradually warms to him as the hunt for the killer takes off. Prater then forms a tentative relationship with Colson's angst-ridden daughter (Kathryn Avery Hansen) and an already dark thriller (shot in the style of *Se7en*) gets even darker when it transpires that screwed-up Colson

has brain cancer. He's also nursing a deep-seated psychosis regarding the death of his wife, stabbed during a robbery. Eventually, a man is arrested, but is he the culprit? Has Colson been committing these vile acts? Why does he want Prater to shoot him and make it look like suicide. Why does young Prater suffer from disturbing visions, mostly involving his father who died in the Gulf War. Why have the victims all had their faces rendered unrecognizable. There's a great deal going on here and the various intricate plot threads are tied up beautifully in the final few minutes. The murders are truly horrific in detail, Colson and Prater form a prickly double act and Mervis directs with a real sense of purpose. Bear in mind that this is an indie psycho thriller, not big-budget, and viewed as such, *Passed the Door of Darkness* is astonishingly well-constructed. Top marks all round for this grimly effective outing.

Red Mist aka Freakdog
Geronimo Pictures/Revolver 2008; 85 minutes;
Director: Paddy Breathnach **

A stammering, backward janitor is teased, ridiculed and put into a coma by his so-called student friends; when one of the interns tries to resuscitate him in hospital by administering an experimental drug, he undergoes an out-of-body experience, possessing members of staff and murdering his tormentors, then returning to his own recumbent form.

Filmed on a higher budget than most indie movies, this Northern Ireland horror film, like Breathnach's previous effort, *Shrooms* (2007), features a predominately young American cast on the run from Andrew Lee Potts' malicious entity which can body-jump into other people, commit murder, and then body-jump back. Again, this bunch of unbearable teens leaves no room for sympathy as they're sliced up (one is forced to drink acid), and that goes for Arielle Kebbel, the only female to feel sorry for Potts in the first place. Token Brit actor Stephen Dillane plays a doctor who decides to use his untested drugs on Potts after realizing Kebbel has been doing it, with dire results, and Kebbel herself ends up in a psychiatric ward after her mates have all been butchered—and is *she* now possessed? The intriguing opening minutes, outlining the reason for Pott's disturbed persona (as a child, he saw his prostitute mother beaten to death) isn't extended into the remainder of what turns out to be an unenterprising slasher opus that really has little in the way of surprises up its sleeve.

UNDER TEN MILLION? ANYTHING'S POSSIBLE!

Red Riding Hood
KOA Films 2003; 92 minutes;
Director: Giacomo Cimini ***

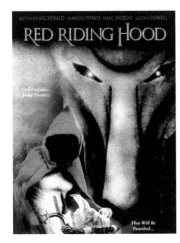

A warped, moralistic young girl and her six-foot masked, bicycle-riding puppy called George brutally murder those people who have committed misdemeanors.

It sounds absurd, yet this wacky Italian feature based on the *Little Red Riding Hood* tale succeeds most of the time. Kathleen Archebald plays a grandmother, visiting Rome to take Susanna Satta back to New York. Satta's politician father was shot by an anarchist and her mother ran off with a young lover, so the girl is screwed-up, big time. Butchering a shoplifter in a subway, Satta and her strange accomplice (George wears a cape and white mask) subsequently track down her dentist and his lover, slaughtering them with a nail gun. The bothersome Archebald then has both kneecaps drilled out to prevent her from returning to America, and even tutor Rob David (who Satta fancies) is knifed to death. Six months later, back in New York, the killing spree continues in a twist ending that involves her resurrected father. This offbeat, gory horror outing is held together by Satta's cunning vixen of a girl, all sweetness and light one minute, radiating pure evil the next. George represents the giant rabbit character in *Donnie Darko* (what *is* behind that grinning mask?) and Archebald is fine as the unfortunate girl's grandmother. The one jarring note is an inappropriate, cheesy soundtrack that ruins the mood, epitomized at the conclusion when Satta and her father, for some odd reason, break into a rendition of "Que Sera Sera." Minus that awful score, this could have been a minor classic.

Resurrecting the Street Walker
2nd Floor Productions 2009; 80 minutes;
Director: Ozgur Uyanik ****

A wannabe filmmaker discovers a serial killer flick in a Soho storage basement that was never completed; ignoring advice, he decides to resurrect the picture and reshoot the ending, but this has unforeseen consequences.

Very cleverly pieced together, Uyanik's picture-within-a-picture is an artful combination of mock documentary and nightmarish sadism as, through interviews, we follow the exploits of James Powell; he works as a runner for Portland Films but cherishes ambitions to become a director. Filmed by his pal Tom Shaw in video diary format, Powell decides to complete a lurid black-and-white

shocker called *The Street Walker*, shelved in the 1980s for falling foul of England's strict censorship laws regarding video nasties. He's convinced that a girl was accidentally killed during the production, so has he got a snuff movie on his hands? Why did the original director commit suicide. Is the film jinxed? Intercut with Powell's quest for stardom are scenes from the film itself which are disturbing to say the least, and the ending perplexes; Powell, his finances withdrawn, goes off the rails, murders Lorna Beckett, the bitchy PA who gave him the run-around at Portland Films (her body is never found) and disappears. Individualistic and original, *Resurrecting the Street Walker* bucks the trend of most other serial killer features and for this must be admired for its sheer bravado.

Seed
Pitchblack Pictures/Boll Kino 2006; 90 minutes;
Director: Uwe Boll ****

A convicted mass murderer, surviving two bouts of the electric chair, is buried alive but claws himself free from his grave, hell-bent on killing those responsible for his premature interment.

Shock Horror! Uwe Boll produces an acceptable feature AND Michael Paré turns in a dependable performance. From the man who brought us the pitiful *House of the Dead* (2003) comes a serial killer thriller in the sick tradition of *Saw*, *Hostel* and all those hardcore slasher flicks of recent years. Insane killer Will Sanderson (the Max Seed of

Scully up with a job there; the eager-to-please youngster gets concerned over the comings and goings of Robert Mammone—in unit 830, the guy is found sobbing and holding a gun, but just *what* is he hiding in that red barrel? Scully's investigations trigger off a catastrophic series of events involving wrongful murder, abduction and imprisonment; it transpires that the unhinged Garvey has been killing wrongdoers, disposing of the bodies in sulfuric acid. Afraid that Scully might call the cops to investigate, and with sexy girlfriend Saskia Burmeister caught sneaking around the facility, Garvey has decided to kill the pair to cover his tracks. An involving Australian psychodrama featuring believable performances, taut direction and a low-key but effective soundtrack; yes, it does tail off slightly in the final 15 minutes, but it's still a neat low-budget shocker that delivers a fair degree of suspense and originality.

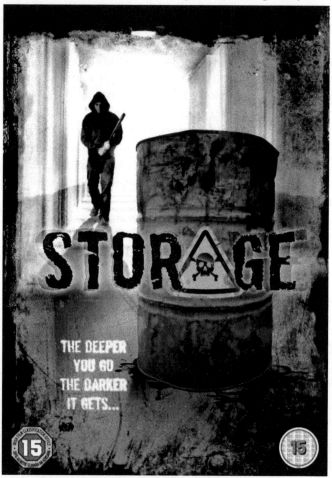

the title) is given two doses of the electric chair but survives (the equipment is faulty); warder Ralf Moeller, to save face, buries Sanderson to make it appear that he actually died and is out of harm's way. But the lunatic lives on, hunting down the Sufferton Prison staff and homing in on detective Paré's family, determined to make everyone suffer as he did. Commencing with grainy images of animals dying and decomposing, thus setting the overall tone of death and decay, *Seed* makes for grimly horrific viewing; unfortunately, it's saddled with a cop-out ending that solves nothing, and too much overactive camerawork. The hulking Sanderson, hooded and silent throughout, acts as though he's a refugee from *The Texas Chainsaw Massacre* while Paré convinces as the cop for whom there is no escape. Boll acquits himself well with *Seed* after a string of low-budget clunkers. This is a cracker of a serial killer flick.

Storage
Rich Vein Productions 2009; 95 minutes;
Director: Michael Craft ****

Following the death of his father at the hands of a mugger, a 17-year-old youth goes to live with his uncle, unaware that the man is a homicidal psychopath.

Matthew Scully's uncle, Damien Garvey, is manager of the City Storage facility, whereby clients place their goods into storage for a determined period. Garvey fixes

Ted Bundy aka Bundy
Tartan /First Look Media 2002; 99 minutes;
Director: Matthew Bright ****

The life and crimes of Ted Bundy whose murderous exploits in the 1970s coined the phrase "serial killer."

College student Bundy (played with calculated relish by Michael Reilly Burke) was proved to be the killer of 19 young women, although, according to police files, the charismatic monster could have slaughtered at least 35.

UNDER TEN MILLION? ANYTHING'S POSSIBLE!

A straightforward, no-frills account of his heinous, sex-based crimes which the director details more explicitly as the movie progresses. Because it's factual, the film is that much more disturbing in content and you wonder just how a smarmy, good-looking charmer (but ultimately, a sexually repressed misanthrope nursing a shedload of insecurities) like Bundy could get away with so many

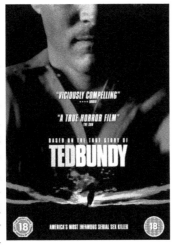

murders, even escaping from police custody twice. The drawn-out execution scene is not for the faint-hearted, and neither are the numerous murders themselves; Boti Bliss is exceptional as the killer's long-suffering girlfriend, unaware of her boyfriend's dreadful deeds, and director Bright paces the movie just right. "Mostly, I just wanna be normal," states Burke at one point. Normal Bundy certainly wasn't, as this excellent docu-horror drama ably shows.

Thr3e
Fox Faith Movies/Namesake 2006; 101 minutes;
Director: Robby Henson *

A murderer known as The Riddle Killer targets a young man with a disturbing past of his own.

Released theatrically but bombing at the box-office, *Thr3e* is an unoriginal low-budget psychological drama trying its damned hardest to be an edgy big-budget psychological drama, but falling far short of the mark. Why so? The potential is there: Unknown killer giving his victims so many minutes to solve a riddle before their car/bus/fridge blows up, and them with it; angst-ridden theology student Marc Blucas hiding a terrible childhood secret; Laura Jordan, raised in the same foster home as Blucas, refusing to consummate their friendship; people wired up with explosives; a bitter cop (Justine Waddell) whose brother

was murdered by the killer; and a storyline that revolves around Christian beliefs in good and evil and multiple personality disorders. It's difficult to put a finger on but where the film falters is in the execution: Characters you can't identify with, disjointed direction, clichéd script and a scenario played out in dozens of other, much better, movies. Then there's the acting: Blucas

is more or less believable but Jordan looks facially paralyzed most of the time, Waddell goes through the female cop motions without too much savoir faire while Priscilla Barnes, playing the scatty woman who once looked after Blucas, would be highly suitable as a pantomime dame but is totally unconvincing in this setup. Fair enough, the conclusion—Jordan and the killer (Bill Moseley) are figments of Blucas' fevered imagination; the guy is a schizo, the result of childhood abuse—comes as a bit of an eye-opener, leading to a schmaltzy final few minutes; Blucas is a patient in a mental hospital, recovering fast judging by the looks he keeps giving Waddell, both seated on a bench. An offshoot of 20th Century Fox, Fox Faith Movies' apparent intention was to produce Christian-themed thrillers with (hopefully) audience appeal but judging by this half-hearted effort, perhaps they shouldn't have bothered.

Tony
AbbottVision/Chump 2009; 76 minutes;
Director: Gerard Johnson ****

One week in the life of a lonely sex killer who wanders through London's grimy backstreets looking for possible friends.

Lacking emotional depth of any kind, Gerard Johnson's matter-of-fact portrayal of the meaningless existence of loner Peter Ferdinando (based on the notorious Dennis Nielsen murders that took place between 1978 and 1983 in Muswell Hill) is all the more disturbing *because* of its no-frills approach. Meeting by chance people as marginalized as he is and full of sexual self-loathing, he strangles his male victims, either sleeping with selected corpses or dismembering the bodies and disposing of the remains in the River Thames. Ferdinando cannot relate to the female sex (his visit to a prostitute is a disaster), is unemployable and is repelled by human contact, but we are not allowed any inklings into what makes this man tick and in this respect, the movie could have benefited from more length. But the dingy environs co-existing with London's West End and Soho

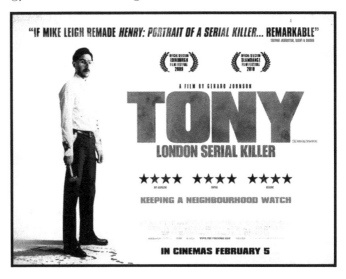

districts (underlined by a spare score) perfectly match Ferdinando's pale, matchstick figure as it forlornly tramps the cheerless streets and sink estates, a lost soul with nowhere to go. Slight in plot and as cold a ice, this is a stunning debut from Johnson that lingers long in the mind after the final fade-out showing Ferdinando aimlessly disappearing into the busy city thoroughfares.

2:13
Anthem Pictures 2009; 96 minutes;
Director: Charles Adelman **

A killer is at large in Los Angeles, torturing his victims, placing a mask on their faces and leaving quotes from Shakespeare at the crime scene.

Like an extended episode from Britain's *Wire in the Blood* or *Cracker*, *2:13* strives for originality but ends up confused and implausible: For instance, how can killer Mark Pellengrino, as a young adult, meet police profiler Mark Thompson as a 10-year-old and then, when detained by Thompson who has obviously grown-up, look *younger* than the cop does? With deep-rooted mental problems of his own, crumpled-looking Thompson is on the trail of a psycho who tortures his victims before ripping off a limb and placing a mask on the corpse. Female officer Teri Polo has an on/off relationship with Thompson, shrink Kevin Pollak is trying to fathom out what occurred when the cop was a 10-year-old (his mother was left horribly scarred in a car accident and had to wear a mask created by Pellengrino, hence the mask motif) and it isn't too hard to guess that Pellengrino is the murderer from the first moment you see him. Stacks of flashbacks, quick-cuts of the victims' violated bodies and Polo mumbling her lines adds up to a derivative serial killer flick where you wish, just for once, that the killer would quote lines (as they all do) from anyone else other than England's most famous playwright.

The Ungodly aka The Perfect Witness
Dream7 Ent./Zip Films 2007; 100 minutes;
Director: Thomas C. Dunn **
A young filmmaker shoots a serial killer stabbing a woman to death and decides to contact him with a view to making a documentary of his exploits.

There are echoes of *Henry: Portrait of a Serial Killer* in Dunn's unsatisfactory maniac-on-the-loose thriller, unsatisfactory because after 40 minutes or so, the movie loses its

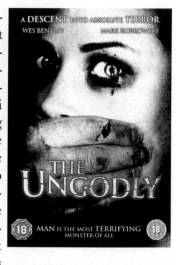

rhythm and becomes inconsistent in plot development and narrative drive. Filmmaker Wes Bentley, looking for his big break, contacts killer Mark Borkowski with the idea of producing a movie showing a real-life murderer at work and the motives that spur him on to remove the eyes of his victims. What starts out to be a conventional psychodrama changes course when it transpires that Borkowski's supposedly dead mother (yes, it's *always* the mother!) isn't dead but incarcerated in a psychiatric ward. When the killer learns of this, he abducts Bentley's mother and so begins a tit for tat with the two protagonists on the trail of each other's mothers, Bentley suddenly lumbered with a stack of personal problems (drug addition, alcohol abuse) not previously hinted at. Hitchcock was a genius at delving into the troubled psyche of a killer; lesser mortals like Dunn can't carry it off and *The Ungodly* meanders all over the place until the end when Bentley smothers Borkowski's mother to death and batters the killer into oblivion, thus becoming unhinged himself. Disturbingly graphic in places, this joint Spanish/American outing isn't that far off from being a very good picture—judicious editing would have worked wonders in tightening up the various plot threads and reducing the running time by 10 minutes. Another "it could have been so much better" movie.

Wolf Creek
AFFC/403 Prods./Emu Creek Pictures 2005; 99 minutes;
Director: Greg McLean *****
Three backpackers drive through the outback to view the meteorite crater at Wolfe Creek in Western Australia and encounter a psychopathic tourist-hating loner

who slaughters all those who stray onto his hunting grounds.

Loosely based on the infamous backpacker murders committed by Ivan Milat in the 1990s, writer/director Greg McLean's mesmerizing shocker (his film debut), produced on a $1,000,000 budget over 35 days, has now taken on the mantle of a cult movie, and that's down to John Jarratt

UNDER TEN MILLION? ANYTHING'S POSSIBLE!

Jarratt), the graphic torture of Morassi, Magrath helping her to escape, Magrath's capture, her spinal chord severed, Morassi's brutal slaying on the highway and Phillips, hands nailed to a wall in a mine adit, breaking free and making it back to civilization. A lot of it isn't pleasant to watch, particularly for women, but McLean's expert pacing and editing ensures that this is one harrowing Aussie thrill-ride that is nigh on unmissable.

Wolf Creek 2
Screen Australia/Emu Creek Pictures 2013; 106 minutes; Director: Greg McLean ****

A lone British tourist finds himself the plaything of pig shooter Mick Taylor, a murderous sadist inhabiting Australia's remote outback regions.

Greg McLean focused much more on John Jarratt's (Taylor) grisly exploits and twisted persona than in *Wolf Creek*, kicking off in classic style with a terrific opening 11 minutes: Two bored cops on traffic duty in the outback decide to pull Jarratt over for speeding (he isn't) and, minutes later, regret doing so, a terrific (but bloody) curtain raiser to all the gore-drenched fun that follows. Butcher Jarratt terrorizes two young German backpackers (Philippe Klaus and Shannon Ashlyn); Klaus is carved into chunks of meat like a pig (Jarratt grabs the boy's severed penis: "Jesus, part bloody donkey! Who's a lucky girl, then!"), Ashlyn escap-

as pig hunter Mick Taylor: Taylor's a sadistic butcher of the first order, mixing rough Aussie charm with unspeakable acts of atrocity, foul language and an insane chuckle that are right at home in his charnel house of a camp, situated inside a remote derelict mine stuffed with decomposing bodies. Jarratt, like a lot of pros, lived the part on set and off, creating one of modern-day horror cinema's most beguiling, most comically horrible deranged mass murderers, but that's not all McLean's blood-drenched thriller has going for it. Australian Film Institute award winner Will Gibson's diamond-hard photography, capturing the desolate Australian outback in all its scenic glory, is absolutely superb, painted in deep bold colors like glossy pages direct from *National Geographic Magazine*, while composer François Tétaz's funereal music underlines both the vastness of the territory Nathan Phillips, Cassandra Magrath and Kestie Morassi are driving through and their fateful encounter with Jarratt at Wolfe Creek crater. McLean divides his narrative into three segments: Phillips and the two girls flirting, partying, then heading out to the impact crater (the second largest of its type on Earth); on the 39th minute, their car having broken down, meeting Jarratt as he drives up in the dark ("What the bloody hell are you lot doing out here? Scared the shit outta me!"); and, commencing at 49 minutes after the trio have drunk drugged water ("Rainwater from the top end," chortles

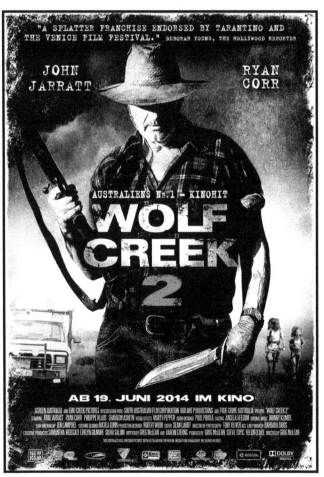

John Jarratt and Ryan Corr in *Wolf Creek 2*

ing, finding refuge in Ryan Corr's 4WD and then shot dead by the madman. Now it's Corr's turn to be the mouse that the cat is after, chased down the highway by chuckling Jarratt ("Welcome to Australia, cocksucker!"), crashing, going on the run through parched, arid bush, reaching a farmhouse, the two elderly residents gunned down when Corr's pursuer arrives ("You in there, hero?"), Corr slugged unconscious and waking up in Jarratt's corpse-filled lair ("Definitely a Pommy. Weak as piss!"). After several verses of "Tie Me Kangaroo Down, Sport," Corr, plied on rum, resolves to get on the xenophobe's better side (if he has one), especially when Jarratt announces he's going to play a game. He'll ask Corr 10 questions on Aussie history. If the "Pommy bastard" gets all 10 correct, he's free to go; for each one wrong, he loses a finger—by buzz saw. Minus two digits, Corr whacks the killer with a hammer, turns himself loose, traverses Jarratt's abattoir-like labyrinth of tunnels, becomes cornered, is headbutted ("Foreign vermin!") and regains consciousness on a town sidewalk, a note stuck to his torn, battered body stating "LOSER." Based on true events, *Wolf Creek 2* is an undiluted stomach-churner filmed in gleaming color by Australian Film Institute award winner Toby Oliver in South Australia, not around Wolfe Creek as in the first movie. Maybe the material is formulaic at times, but Jarratt's energetic, tremendously effective role playing of the comically horrible Aussie monster towers above plot deficiencies; if the film was in any other genre, the man would win an Oscar for his mesmerizing performance, one that holds the attention for every single minute. In Jarratt's profanity-littered vernacular, you are certainly *not* welcome in Australia!

X Moor aka The Beast of X Moor
Precision Pictures/The Fyzz Facility Film Two 2014;
79 minutes; Director: Luke Hyams ****

Two American film students team up with an animal tracker to hunt down the Beast of Exmoor, reputed to be a large black cat that has been slaughtering sheep in the area for the past 40 years.

In writer/director Luke Hyams' taut little debut feature, Mark Bonnar and Melia Kreiling, spurred on by a £25,000 reward to provide evidence of the beast's existence, drive out to the bleak moors and meet rough-and-ready tracker Nick Blood, busy amusing himself with a drugged-up prostitute at a derelict, trash-filled farmhouse. Parking their VW Campervan on the moors, the trio enters dense woodlands, Bonnar having serious doubts over Blood's credentials ("I'm beginning to get the scent of bullshit."). CCTV surveillance cameras are positioned on trees before they realize that the stench emanating from the spot they've chosen to film the creature comes from the decomposing corpses of six women, all prostitutes; the place is a serial killer's dumping ground, Blood revealing that his true motive in taking the job on was to trap the person responsible and get the kudos for doing so ("We're so fucking dead," complains Bonnar). Night falls, noises are heard, one of the bodies is in fact alive (Olivia Popica: "Him bad man. He kill us." "We'll kill him."), Kreiling shouts at Blood, "This isn't the cat of the Baskervilles!" and all three are soon on the run from the masked, boiler-suited psycho (James Lecky) who has returned with his half-blind daughter (Jemma O'Brien) to gloat over his victims, among other perversions. Thankfully, the dim photography in the movie's first half lightens up in the second, thus enabling us to figure out who's doing what to whom. Blood is knifed to death, Popica is brutally slain and Kreiling plunges a deer's antler into the killer's back, only it's not the killer; it's Bonnar, dressed in his clothing to provide a decoy. The maniac then drives his Land Rover at Kreiling and O'Brien who sidestep, the vehicle plummeting over a quarry, putting paid to the loony driver. Hand in bloody hand, Kreiling and traumatized girl wander back to civilization; the final shot is of one of the wrecked CCTV cameras showing the face of a big black cat; the beast exists after all! Filmed on moorland near Belfast in Northern Ireland (NOT Devon's Exmoor National Park), *X Moor* plays to its serial killer strengths well enough, the desolate, exposed locale (the aerial views are striking), plus Kreiling's sparky performance, adding greatly to the suspense. Note: Not only has Exmoor a mythical beast roaming the countryside, first reported in the 1970s, but also Bodmin Moor to the south in Cornwall; neither animal, be it real or an elaborate hoax, has ever been identified.

UNDER TEN MILLION? ANYTHING'S POSSIBLE!

Monsters/Creatures/ Dinosaurs

Abominable

Red Circle Productions 2006; 94 minutes;
Director: Ryan Schifrin **

Bigfoot goes on a rampage near the mountain resort of Flatwoods.

An attempt to emulate the Yeti cycle of films of the 1950s, *Abominable* features, yes, a man in a shaggy suit (no CGI effects here), a jokey script that misfires most of the time, forced acting from the leads and a guest appearance from grizzled Lance Henriksen. The busy but dated score comes from none other than Lalo Schifrin and seems to belong to another movie altogether. Wheelchair-bound Matt McCoy and physiotherapist Christien Tinsley head for a mountain cabin for a spot of relaxation, their peace disturbed by the arrival of five young girls staying in an adjacent lodge. When McCoy, peering through binoculars, sees red eyes in the bushes and one of the girls goes missing, he tries to convince everyone that Sasquatch is alive and well and on the prowl. With McCoy doing a James Stewart turn from *Rear Window* and one lass, Haley Joel, coming to his assistance, the scene is set for a risible climax in which hero and heroine abseil down the side of the cabin to escape Bigfoot who hauls Joel up on her rope *King Kong*-style (he even sniffs her) before being rammed against a tree with an axe embedded in its back. Resembling an '80s movie in parts, this odd concoction only works in patches, and to be honest is no better or worse than Jerry Warren's infamous *Man Beast*, made 51 years earlier on a tenth of this movie's budget.

Arachnoquake

Active Entertainment 2012; 86 minutes;
Director: Griff Furst **

In the Louisiana Bayou, earthquakes caused by fracking create fissures that unleash fire-breathing spiders on the population of New Orleans.

Eight Legged Freaks revisited, a comic book-fashioned creature-feature that really should have played it straight. After all, Nu Image's *Spiders* (2000) put the lid on infantile antics, coming up with an indie classic; here, the pink, blind spiders hop and scuttle like clockwork toys, emerging from out of their victims' skins in blisters and bursting into flame when hit with a baseball bat. The scenario plays in two parts: Tour guide Bug Hall and his group on the run in the swamps, and bus driver Edward Furlong's attempts to get his posse of short-skirted co-eds to safety. "Jumbo spiders. Some as big as dwarves," states one startled

onlooker as the albino beasties increase in size, leading to a climactic confrontation (set to loud metal music) with the queen arachnid, a huge red specimen that crawls into New Orleans (excellent CGI here), spins a web between two skyscrapers and is blown to bits by Hall who dons a protective suit, sliding down the monster's gullet to ignite the gas inside its stomach—somehow, he miraculously survives the explosion. Cast-wise, it's left to Tracey Gold to overcome the trite script and present us with a biologist who's determined to defeat the creatures at their own game; Olivia Hardt, Hall's blonde sister, does nothing but preen and pose, while indie regular Furlong looks ill, as though he's just crawled out of bed after a heavy night on the town. If more on the serious side, *Arachnoquake* could have been a winner; as it is, the lighthearted approach kills it.

Banshee!!!

American World Pictures/Synthetic Cinema Intl. 2008;
86 minutes; Director: Colin Theys **

A group of teens hiking through the Connecticut woodlands encounter a ferocious winged creature spoken about in Irish legends.

The best part of *Banshee!!!* is the opening 10 minutes, set in 1970—three dudes driving down a dark country road see in the headlights a dazed young blonde dressed

in a white robe. The woman clambers into the back, slaughters two of them and the other dies when the car plunges off the road into a flooded quarry. Flash forward three decades; the vehicle is retrieved from the swamp and in the trunk is a black cocoon from which the monster of the title hatches, causing havoc among the local rednecks and those flirting teenagers. The thing can switch into human form at the blink of a CGI eye and force people to hallucinate; confusion ensues as the cast wonder who is, and who isn't, who they say they are. Eventually, David McCarthy, in a frankly ridiculous scene, drives the creature away by banging out a rock tune on his guitar (apparently, it detests high-pitched sound), although judging by video footage at the end, the shape-changing banshee is still at large. Ashley Bates plays the obligatory pouting blonde bitch, Kevin Shea the hick who discovered the cocoon in the first place. Colin Theys' flashy quick-cut direction muddies the waters while the flamboyant monster is only seen in its entirety towards the closing minutes, creating a mixed bag that doesn't really gel as much as it should.

The Bay
Alliance Films/Automatik/Haunted Movies 2012; 84 minutes;
Director: Barry Levinson ***

On July 4, 2009, the inhabitants of Claridge in Maryland's Chesapeake Bay are virtually wiped out by flesh-eating crustaceans of the species Cymothoa exigua, mutated from contaminated water.

A found footage, documentary-style ecological horror movie in which amateur reporter Kether Donahue Skypes tells her story (in 2011) of events leading up to Claridge's population becoming covered in boils, blisters and lesions, black Isopods chomping their way through their victim's bodies to grisly effect; radioactive waste, fertilizers and chicken effluent leaking into the sea means that Chesapeake Bay's waters are "40% lifeless," a "toxic soup" unfit for humans. Flicking between Donahue in 2011, Donahue in July 2009 and video footage shot by an oceanic research couple in May/June 2009, carrying out investigations as to why thousands of fish were dying from parasitic infections, the narrative at times is a confusing mess, as messy as the vomiting, chewed-up patients crowding the town's overworked Atlantic Hospital, only settling down towards the latter stages when Will Rogers, Kristen Connolly and their baby enter Claridge at night, the sidewalks littered with grotesque corpses. Frank Deal plays the ingratiating mayor trying to cover up the disaster in the name of tourism and profit, the whole matter swept under the carpet by the government after massive doses of chlorine dumped into the Chesapeake channel kill off the Isopods; an unseasonable rise in sea temperatures is the explanation given for the town's missing population. A sick, stomach-churning message to us all regarding the real dangers of polluting our rivers and oceans, *The Bay* will make you think twice about drinking a glass of water, making you question just what that innocent-looking liquid contains.

Black Sheep
Singlet Films//New Zealand Film Com. 2006; 87 minutes;
Director: Jonathan King ****

Recovering from a childhood phobia to sheep caused by his brother's stupid prank, a man returns to his father's farm which is in imminent danger of being overrun by genetically mutated sheep.

Nathan Meister and environmental activist Danielle Mason manage to keep their heads above water as hordes of flatulent mutated sheep with a taste for body parts descend on Meister's farm; Peter Finney, his brother, transforms into a were-sheep, as does pal Tammy Davis and activist Oliver Driver when they're bitten. Finney's presentation to a group of businessmen, to promote a new genetically bred specimen called the Oldfield, ends up in a welter of severed limbs, spilled guts, savaged faces and gallons of blood after Meister and Mason have crawled through a pit of stinking offal to escape a ravenous ewe. Davis and Driver return to normal after administered an antidote;

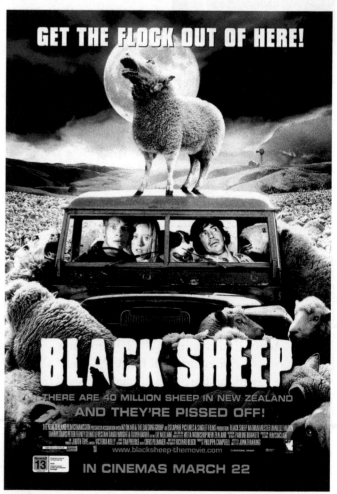

Finney, part sheep, part man, is blown to bits alongside his grotesque flock when his brother tosses a lighter into their methane-filled ranks. Following the end of the carnage, Mason unwittingly tucks into a plate of fried sheep's testicles and the final shot is of Meister's dog opening its jaws and bleating, not barking. Writer/director Jonathan King's gore-laden black comedy-cum-parody of a sort has terrific effects, especially when Finney morphs into a giant sheep monster, and some hilarious lines of dialogue: Driver to Finney: "I know all about your Frankensheep"; Davis: "What about the sheep?" Finney: "Fuck the sheep." Davis: "No time for that now, Bro. Go. Go, go"; Driver to a rampaging sheep: "The little baaaaaastard"; Meister, bitten, to Mason who suggests he calms down by pretending to be a tree: "I'm not a tree. I'm a fucking sheep!" If you concentrate between laughing your head off, there are plenty of genre in-jokes to savor, but the whole gruesome exercise might put some people off eating roast lamb for a very long time! A quite unique horror/creature-feature from New Zealand, though sensitive animal lovers may well turn away in disgust.

Black Water
ProdigyMovies/AFC 2007; 90 minutes;
Directors: Andrew Traucki and David Nerlich *****

On a fishing trip down a river estuary in Northern Australia, three people become trapped in mangrove swamps, at the mercy of a 20-foot crocodile.

Co-director Andrew Traucki cranked up the shark-filled tension in *The Reef*; here, alongside David Nerlich, he performs a similar heart-pounding job with a giant estuarine crocodile (called "Salties" by Australians) that targets Andy Rodoreda, newly pregnant wife Diana Glenn and Glenn's younger sister, Maeve Dermody, after their fishing boat has capsized, guide Ben Oxenbould reduced to a headless, armless chunk of croc bait. Can the three make it to safety, either by using the boat or by clambering over trees to the banks of the river to enable them to be spotted ("No one knows we're here. We're miles from anywhere," says Rodoreda). That's the premise and the $700,000 movie delivers: Little music, the silence only broken by ominous splashing sounds, thoughtful, slow-moving interludes followed by moments of absolute fright as the monster reptile (a real crocodile, *not* a model!) floats implacably into view, rears its head and grabs Rodoreda between its massive jaws when he rights the boat; his wife has her leg badly mauled after wading through the swamp, Dermody, in the boat which is rammed by the croc, finding safety on a mudbank, Oxenbould's mutilated torso waiting to be feasted upon. Retrieving his gun, she goads the croc into attacking her by using the guide's dismembered limb to churn the water; looming into view, the beast closes its jaws over her arm and she fires a shot, blowing its brains out. Back

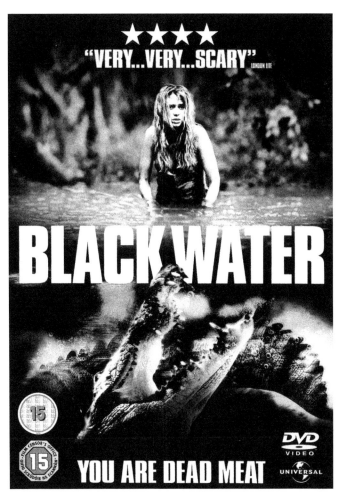

at their tree refuge, Glenn has died due to blood loss from her gaping wound and shock; the last we see of Dermody is the girl rowing out into the river, her sister's body beside her. Filmed around Darwin in Australia's remote Northern Territories, *Black Water* (like Greg McLean's *Rogue*, released the same year) will have viewers in a sweat on the edge of their seats and banishing from their minds all thoughts of embarking on a fishing expedition in an Aussie backwater lagoon!

Blood Glacier aka The Station
Allegro Film/FilmVergnuegen 2013; 98 minutes;
Director: Marvin Kren ****

Scientists at an Alpine research station 3,500 meters up in the mountains discover a glacier steeped in blood, the liquid containing alien organisms that mutate local animal life into hybrid freaks of nature.

An Austrian creature-feature that to its credit discards CGI effects in favor of good old-fashioned giant models, the claustrophobic tone very much based on John Carpenter's *The Thing*. Splendidly filmed in Italy's grand South Tyrol area (photography: Moritz Schultheiß), Gerhard Leibmann is one bad-tempered member of a squabbling team who finds the red glacier and a cave harboring a rabid fox/beetle-like creature that bites his dog Tinni. Back at base, something grotesque ransacks the food supply and a huge woodlouse is killed, its blood revealing single-celled organisms that are not of this Earth. Meanwhile, Minister Brigitte Kren and her colleagues, trekking over the mountains on a visit to the station, are set upon by a flying feathered predator and flesh-eating insects. When they reach the station, a girl has a nasty squirming bug cut out of her leg, Michael Fuith crashes through the door, now a human mutation, flies pouring out of his disfigured body, and the base comes under attack from a malformed ibex, Kren finishing the thing off by drilling into its skull. A helicopter arrives to rescue the survivors; on board, Leibmann and his ex, Edita Malovic, cuddle the new addition to their family, a mutant human/puppy infant that Tinni hatched before he was put down. What it will grow into is beyond comprehension! The perils of global warming seems to be the message here ("The gates of Hell are open. We melted them open!"), wrapped up in an eco-horror setting without (thank goodness) a single angst-ridden, self-obsessed teen in sight. And the final shot of another glacier tainted red, a squawking monstrosity flying at the camera lens, rams home that message. *Blood Glacier* is credible, meaty monster thrills, suitable for perhaps an older audience brought up on the mutated creature movies that populated horror/sci-fi cinema in the 1950s.

Bone Eater
Cinetel Films/Eagle Pictures 2007; 90 minutes;
Director: Jim Wynorski (as Bob Robertson) ***

On a building site, construction workers uncover old Indian artifacts and bones, disturbing a legendary 15-foot-tall skeletal creature, the Torag, that turns humans to dust.

Shot around California's scenic Alabama Hills and Vasquez Rocks area, *Bone Eater* is a glossy, highly enjoyable Cinetel Films creature-feature that boasts an original-looking monster, part CGI, part stop-motion animation, almost resembling one of Ray Harryhausen's fabled creations. Green eyes blazing from a skull head and exhaling deadly, bone-disintegrating breath, earth tremors announcing its appearance, the creature

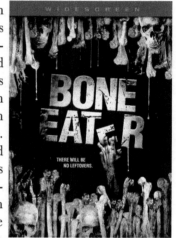

brings death and destruction to Sheriff Bruce Boxleitner's Sweet Water desert community, all because bull-headed businessman James Storm is determined to proceed with his leisure complex, Indian curse or no Indian curse. Yes, it's corporate greed versus the Katonah Indians and their superstitious beliefs: Michael Horse (Storm Cloud) wishes to undo the evil and get rid of the thing, Adoni Maropis (Black Hawk) wants it to continue on its rampage against the troublesome developers and delectable Jennifer Lee Wiggins (Kaya) acts as go-between, flitting from her reservation to Boxleitner's office. Clara Bryant plays Boxleitner's teen daughter, feeling her father's wrath when she dates the town's bad guy, Jesse Janzen. But, in the end, Janzen comes good: That sacred bone war axe resting on the back seat of his car is the one and only weapon that can defeat the Torag so, in a confrontation on the highway prior to a solar eclipse, the skeletal menace, after eliminating most of the cast including sleazeball Storm, mounts its skeletal steed and goes head-to-head with Boxleitner who hurls the axe into its chest, whereupon it falls apart, bone by bone, disappearing under the tarmac in a cloud of dust. An energetic, decently acted monster romp filmed in attractive locales more suited to the Western genre than outlandish beings of legend, but all the better for it.

Creature aka The Creature of the Sunny Side Up Trailer Park
Digi-Flicks/Plastercity 2006; 105 minutes; Director:
Christopher Coppola *

Two arch-rival brothers (one black, one white) are summoned to the desert town of Whiterocks Valley to collect their inheritance, a property built near excavations that have unearthed a legendary monster.

The credits sequence depicts hooded Ku Klux Klan figures carrying torches, blood sacrifices and a half-seen, hideous scaly monster, lulling you into thinking that what's coming up could be rather mouth-watering. It isn't. Beefcake brothers Andre Ware and Steve Hedden arrive at desolate Whiterocks

Valley and meet promiscuous trailer-trash doll Lynda Carter, clingy kid Andre Marcus and veteran comedian Frank Gorshin (one of the town leaders), the siblings fighting and arguing over who-owns-what. Forty long minutes into the movie, the creature appears, biting off the head of a cinema projectionist. Next comes a visit from the ghost of the brothers' mother, letting them in on the secret: When she was prospecting for gold, she uncovered a golden shell which unleashed a monster called Bloodhead—the creature is secretly worshipped by the locals. A climactic fight with the thing leads to its death (youngster Marcus was the monster in human disguise all along) and the cloaked worshippers are sprayed with its acid blood, thus leaving the brothers to reclaim their legacy without further hindrance. Unfortunately (and this *is* 2004!), the lumbering creature is a man in a red lobster suit, resembling one of those cardboard creations that used to populate the Amicus fantasy adventures of the 1970s, such as *At the Earth's Core*, and if the aim was to produce a horror-comedy, then in that respect, *Creature* fails on all counts, as it does in every other area. You have to be a real glutton for punishment to weather this limp clunker.

Curse of the Talisman
Telescene Film Group/UPN 2001; 92 minutes;
Director: Colin Budds **

A student, his girlfriend and a priest battle a living gargoyle from the Dark Ages, an "instrument of punishment," that intends to awaken dozens of others and destroy the world.

In Yorkshire, England, 1100 AD (where the movie begins), a village is set ablaze, a terrified lad on the run falling victim to a horned flying beast with talons. Flash forward to the USA of today (filming actually took place in Australia): A crate of artifacts from a Yorkshire consignment destined for the Elmsford Museum is stolen, given to the owner of a bookshop to fence; he passes a grotesque statue of a gargoyle plus a box of trinkets to student Jesse Spencer for safekeeping. Spencer finds an ornate book in the

box, together with a silver talisman whose red eyes glow ominously as the statue shakes and crumbles, releasing a beaked horned devil that flies here and there, creating mayhem. The creature eventually homes in on a rack full of similar statues housed in the museum that harbors more winged demons; by bonding with its brethren, the statues will liberate their hosts, the combined force reducing the town to ashes. Lukewarm creature fare for the younger set—Spencer and girlfriend Sara Gleeson dash around in

an effort to avoid the thing's claws, particularly at a Halloween party, while Father Rod Mulliner studies the ancient text in the hope of finding an answer that will bring about the flock of demons' demise. Water combined with the power of prayer is the answer, sprinklers reducing the gargoyles, who have all hatched, to dust, Spencer impaling gargoyle number one on the end of a sword and getting a kiss from Gleeson in just reward.

Deadly Descent: The Abominable Snowman
UFO International Productions 2013; 85 minutes;
Director: Marko Mäkilaakso **

When a man goes missing in the mountains in search of a mysterious creature that killed his father, his ex-army friends join in the hunt and encounter the Yeti.

Filmed in Bulgaria's mountain region, *Deadly Descent's* main failing is its Abominable Snowman, or all two of them. Like big fat cuddly toys with fangs, these furry monsters are shot in blurred, fuzzy motion, even in daylight; they're neither scary nor particularly ferocious, more "let me take you home and give you a bowl of food" bundles

of fun, almost cute. Therefore, Lauren O'Neil, Nicholas Boulton, Elizabeth Croft, Sean Teal, Chuck Campbell and Sam Cassidy's woes on that snow-laden glacier amount to very little, even when the things are battering down the doors as the team becomes trapped in a ski lodge. You need a monster with bite to raise the fright factor, not the innocuous specimens on display here; the gore count is also exceedingly low. Ex-alcoholic Adrian Paul (his macho charms wasted on this occasion—he should have been the hero) rescues the survivors in his chopper (even though he's suffering a hangover), following scenes of creature mayhem, a couple of avalanches and too much snowboarding/skiing across the frozen wastes. *Not* one of the better of the indie movies featuring the legendary beast inhabiting the snowy heights.

Deadly Stingers aka Mega Scorpions
Shadow Entertainment 2003; 73 minutes;
Director: J.R. Bookwalter **

Six-foot scorpions go on a rampage, spewing green acid over their victims.

Fans of a certain age (50-plus) will fondly remember Warner Bros.' 1957 *The Black Scorpion*, an archetypical, full-blooded '50s monster movie featuring tremendous stop-motion effects by Willis O'Brien and Pete Peterson. Well, *Deadly Stingers* has CGI scorpions, albeit a lot smaller than those featured in O'Brien's seminal flick and although it's a $150,000 indie picture, a short-lived collaboration between Full Moon's Charles Band and 20th Century Fox, the budget of *The Black Scorpion* wasn't that huge either. The message here is that over a gulf of 46 years separating the two movies, the old methods of bringing these creatures to the silver screen are the best; Bookwalter's monsters resemble cartoons and are just as harmless. The plot

consists of Nicolas Read (bad-boy), Marcella Laasch (she runs a halfway house for ex-cons), Sarah Megan White (her daughter), Jay Richardson (interfering mayor) and Sewell Whitney (forensics expert) warding off very large scorpions mutated by the illegal dumping of toxic waste. It's Whitney who finally deduces that by giving the monsters a dose of their own medicine, a vial of venom tipped over the head, they expire. Unaccountably given an "18" rating in Britain, *Deadly Stingers* is to *The Black Scorpion* what *Eight Legged Freaks* was to *Tarantula*, another classic '50s monster outing.

Deadly Swarm
Cinetel Films 2003; 93 minutes;
Director: Paul Andresen **

A strain of wasp bred by Indians is smuggled over the Mexican border in a crate; when the lorry crashes, the insects escape, descending on a town preparing for local festivities.

Here we go again—the military (led by burly J. Patrick McCormack) eager to abduct the one person immune to the wasps' stings so that they can create a biological weapon from their DNA; that one person happening to be hysterical heroine Kaarina Aufranc; entomologist Shane Brolly saving the day by unleashing a horde of bats on the buzzing pests; a scatty UFO nut convinced the wasps are aliens; and let's not forget that dastardly town mayor

French poster for *Deadly Swarm*

(Roger Nevares) who sure ain't gonna stop the festival from taking place, wasps or no wasps, threatening to relieve the sheriff of his duties if he so much as mentions the word "cancellation." We've been down this route so many times before that it's a case of comparing *Deadly Swarm* to others of its kind, namely *Killer Bees* and *Swarmed*. Andresen's overlong addition to a distinctly underwhelming genre of horror cinema kicks off in fairly intriguing *Indiana Jones*-style and finishes on the same note—what happens in between amounts to nothing more than a string of clichés poorly acted by a wooden cast. No getting away from it, *Deadly Swarm* is deadly dull.

Devil in the Woods aka The Barrens
Genre Co./Empire Film and Ent. 2012; 94 minutes;
Director: Darren Lynn Bousman ***

A family on a bonding trip set up camp in New Jersey's Pinewoods National Park and encounters the Jersey Devil, a creature of legend said to have been the product of union between a witch and Satan in the 1750s.

First off, why is it that today's teenage girls have such a downer on their new stepmother? Jealousy? Fear of rejection? Allie MacDonald, constantly glued to her cellphone, harbors such feeling towards Stephen Moyer's attractive new wife, Mia Kirshner, so what better than a family outing to the woods to mend all those broken fences. Once there, however, Moyer slowly but surely goes bonkers. Yes, he was bitten by his dog, but also claims to have seen the Jersey Devil when hiking through the woods with his father many years ago ("It's no myth. It's real and it's after me."). Soon, MacDonald and Kirshner *are* bonding, a case of having to as unshaven, unhygienic Moyer foams at the mouth (has he got rabies?), drags young son Peter DaCunha into a pond and has repeated visions of a monstrous winged, cloven-hoofed creature with fangs lurking among the trees. We are never quite sure whether pill-pop-

ever put together since the halcyon days of Bert I. Gordon, while fending off the advances of the sexiest bunch of prehistoric women since Raquel Welch decided to don a bikini in Hammer's 1966 classic. Never mind the jerry-built plot—the men are looked upon as gods but have to defeat the "Great One" in order to marry the girls—simply relax and relish the following: Sharp, occasionally crude, dialogue ("You're right, John. This *is* Club Med!"); babe-chasing Richard Gabai's smiley-face tattoo being mistaken for a sign from the gods as prophesied in the sacred scrolls; a nude hot-tub sequence; a green plastic-looking Brontosaurus; the "Great One" itself, the fattest dinosaur ever to waddle onto a film set; an animated (well, sort of) Triceratops; Queen Toni Naples coming on to tough-guy Hagen; a lascivious trio of "let's all bare our ample breasts" chicks (Antonia Dorian, Griffin Drew, Michelle Bauer); and a host of naked sex romps. And look closely—a lot of those writhing, dancing damsels have nothing on underneath their loincloths! The final shot of a giggling baby dinosaur sums it all up; even this reviewer (and generally speaking, I avoid comedy piss-takes in *any* genre of film) had to smile. *Dinosaur Island* is to all those *Lost World* potboilers like *Airplane!* was to all those disaster features of the 1970s/1980s. It's a hoot!

ping Moyer is hallucinating or plagued with mental problems, especially when he brutally attacks Kirshner after she's tied him to a tree; what's bugging the man is what audiences will be asking themselves. However, *something* must be at large, hence all those ripped-open bodies spilling entrails. The toothed devil is only really put on display in the final reel, leaping from the treetops onto Moyer and his terrified family plus two Park Rangers, the screen fading to black, leaving us to guess the outcome. Part psychological horror, part creature-feature, *Devil in the Woods* builds up a smattering of tension within its enclosed rural setting, let down somewhat by an inconclusive denouement.

Dinosaur Island
New Horizons 1994; 85 minutes;
Directors: Fred Olen Ray and Jim Wynorski ****
Six lusty marines end up on an uncharted Pacific Island after their plane crashes, discovering a lost world inhabited by prehistoric monsters and frisky, busty cave-girls.

An outlandish slice of hokum cooked up in 12 days on a $190,000 budget, a kind of spoof on *One Million Years B.C.*? Or grade Z drivel. Let's all lighten up and enjoy the antics of Captain Ross Hagen and his sex-obsessed platoon as they combat the ropiest collection of dinosaurs

The Dinosaur Project
Kent Films/Moonlighting Films 2012; 83 minutes;
Director: Sid Bennett *****

Lost footage from the British Cryptozoological Society's expedition to discover dinosaurs roaming the Congo River basin, found in a rucksack, shows the startling facts behind the expedition's mysterious disappearance.

Compiled from found footage, Bennett's involving dinosaur adventure, steeped in *Lost World* atmosphere, strikes all the right notes for movies of this type: Marvelous, primordial-looking South African locations; good performances; a literate script; and an array of believable CGI monsters. Tough explorer Richard Dillane, stowaway son Matt Kane, right-hand man Peter Brooke, journalist Natasha Loring, Abena Ayivor from the Congolese Environmental Agency and camera crew set off to find Mokele Mbembe, "Africa's answer to the Loch Ness monster." Crashing their helicopter in thick jungle when the blades are hit by flying reptiles, their camp, an abandoned village, is attacked by unknown winged creatures. Loring is killed, forcing the team to commandeer two native boats; they then have one prehistoric encounter after another. Kane befriends a group of small carnivores, attaching a mini-cam to one, allowing us unique views from the dino's perspective, Ayivor wishes to turn tail and run, afraid of a

gateway to something evil ("We weren't supposed to come here. No one has ever come back.") while Brooke seethes with jealousy, wanting to take credit over his boss for the venture, even to the extent of murdering Kane. No happy ending here, but in many ways an uplifting one: After avoiding a plague of giant bat monsters and near-escapes in caves, Brooke is eaten alive by the big parent of one of Kane's new buddies, Ayivor and camera crew perish when their boat is capsized in a gorge by a Pliosaur, Dillane falls over a cliff and Kane, alone, throws his rucksack full of video hard drives into the river, wandering down to a fantastic Lost World valley, side-by-side with his reptilian friend Crypto, the very place that the mythical gateway leads to. One of the better indie dinosaur lost/found footage offerings which, at 83 minutes, doesn't outstay its welcome, a highly enjoyable exercise in prehistoric *Jurassic Park*-type thrills.

Dracano aka Dragon Apocalypse
Odyssey Media/Pulser Prods. 2013; 91minutes;
Director: Kevin O'Neill **

Volcanic eruptions in the Whatcom County's Mount Baker area spew forth rock cocoons containing embryonic dragons that hatch and go on a rampage.

An over-abundance of Oedipal emoting from daughter Mia Faith towards father Corin Nemec and nowhere near enough dragon action sums up *Dracano*, an uninspired giant flying reptile flick that is far too talkative for its own good. Why is it that these young females refuse to accept the fact that Dad (after Mom has died) has acquired another partner, in this case Victoria Pratt? Every time Pratt gets near to Faith, the teen's eyes roll up in shock horror and she shudders. Get over it, girl! As for Nemec, he's booted off his university KRONOS project (a method of preventing catastrophic volcanic activity) when dozens of dragons from erupting Mount Baker wipe out a few citizens; somehow, he's blamed for the massacre. Wannabe news reporter Dominika Juillet discovers that Mount St. Helens was blasted from the air (!) to seal thousands of embryos lying in magma chambers, Nemec, Faith, Pratt and General Troy Evans try to figure out a way of entombing 20,000 rock eggs, there's a colossal mother waiting to burst forth and, once in a while, a flock of the things appears to remind us that we are watching a monster movie, not a personal drama between daughter and Dad's new girlfriend.

A bomb forces the mother dragon from her lair, she's hit by missiles before the president has a chance to nuke Oregon and Faith, hidden inside a cocoon, is instrumental in sealing the lava tubes using the KRONOS device, the offspring at last lying dormant (until the next eruption, that is). Four months later, Juillet is now a fully-fledged reporter, about to be consumed by a huge dragon, thus ending her short career in front of the TV cameras.

Dying God
Metaluna/Buenos Aires Rojo Shocking 2008; 85 minutes;
Director: Fabrice Lambot ***

Prostitutes on their beat in a South American city are being horribly raped to death by something that, according to doctors, isn't human.

The perpetrator happens to be a humanoid monster born in the surrounding jungles, a deity of sorts, a native shaman his protector. Sporting an enormous phallus, it roams the city streets at night, raping hookers. If they prove to be infertile, he kills them; if fertile, they're taken to an abandoned warehouse to be properly impregnated. Hot on the thing's trail is seedy cop James Horan, a chain-smoking, cocaine-snorting, boozing, womanizing maverick, not averse to knocking his girlfriend about either (porn princess Misty Mundae plays her. Check this tasty babe out in *An Erotic Werewolf in London* [Seduction Films 2006]). As the body count mounts up, Horan forms a truce with the city's leading pimps, headed by wheelchair-bound Lance Henriksen: Let's all hunt the killer down, otherwise the girls won't want to do business. This leads to a confrontation in the warehouse with the beast, a green, skeletal-type being that Horan slices open with a buzz-saw. However, a pregnant woman is last seen running away, carrying the monster's fetus. At the extreme end of the splatter cinema spectrum, the Argentine-produced *Dying God* is both sleazy and repellent, a gritty, 18-rated take on the 1960s continental horror output, with explicit dialogue and scenes to match that will offend many.

Fire Serpent
Cinetel Films/Reel One Ent. 2007; 89 minutes;
Director: John Terlesky ***

A globule of incandescence containing a living alien entity travels from the sun and lands on Earth, absorbing fuel from power stations and causing catastrophic fires wherever it goes.

Did William Shatner really supply the idea for the fiery serpent of the title, as stated in the credits? If indeed the *Star Trek* legend did, then let's all applaud the man for coming up with something more unusual and intelli-

gent than the norm; in fact, *Fire Serpent* is quite talky for a cheapo creature-feature, the script literate, the acting above par. In 1966, a young firefighter investigating a forest blaze sees his fiancée die after she spots a glowing ball of fire embedded in the ground which releases a monster lurking within the flames. Forty-one years later, the embittered man (Randolph Mantooth) teams up with fireman Nicholas Brendon and agent Sandrine Holt to figure out just what kind of being they are dealing with after a fire officer is killed in identical circumstances. An added complication comes in the shape of Robert Beltran, playing a religious fanatic who captures the radiant orb in a canister, wanting to cleanse the Earth in an inferno as punishment for mankind's sins. The blazing payoff takes place in an oil refinery, the serpent dispersed in a gigantic explosion, although in the closing seconds, a second ball of fire heads towards Earth, obviously containing another alien, so the battle isn't quite over. First-rate special effects and careful pacing contribute to a compelling creature/sci-fi thriller that maintains the interest.

Flu Birds aka Flu Bird Horror
Nu Image/Castel Film Romania 2008; 89 minutes;
Director: Leigh Scott ***

Seven delinquent teenagers sent to a remote island by their counselor are attacked by vicious bird-like creatures that carry a deadly virus.

The birds of the title don't resemble birds at all, more like scaly clawed Pteranodons. And when they bite, the victim turns into a suppurating mess whose touch can be lethal. It's science versus the military again as the army moves in to destroy the animals *and* the infected teens (led by the nasty Jonathon Trent), the scientists, headed by

Clare Carey, wishing to study the creatures and the effect they have on humans. Several gory deaths later, the things are incinerated in a gas-filled passage under an abandoned fort. Leigh Scott ups the pace to capitalize on the general unease felt by 2008's Bird Flu pandemic and the monsters are suitably ferocious in act and appearance, while the argumentative youngsters are pure teen lunch for the reptilian birds. Nu Image's features are always a cut above the average, and *Flu Birds* is no different to the rest.

Glass Trap
Itasca Pictures 2005; 90 minutes;
Director: Fred Olen Ray (Ed Raymond) *

Radioactive giant ants, brought into a skyscraper on infected nursery pot plants, run amok.

We're not talking *Them!* here, not by a longshot—these ants, around seven feet in length, stalk the corridors of the Waldman Building while a stock bunch of indie character actors go through the motions: C. Thomas Howell as the ex-con janitor; Siri Baruc the hysterical secretary; Stella Stevens her chain-smoking, workaholic boss, editor of *Hooray* celebrity magazine; cigar-chomping grunt Martin Cove; a guy who plans to illegally  copy computer information and his precocious daughter; an ex-FBI agent; and a photographer with two tarty glamour models. Put them all together and you have a bottom-of-the-barrel variation on *Eight Legged Freaks* that is a pretty feeble creature-feature, the silly antics of the cartoon-like cast at odds with the doom-laden score. And just how many times can Baruc shriek "Oh my God!" before you fervently wish that one of those big ants would do us all a favor and crush her in its mandibles. After three barrels of DDT have finished off the critters and their eggs, Howell the reluctant hero gets a peck on the cheek from Baruc plus the promise of a dinner date and, not before time, the picture mercifully comes to a close. A monster movie to forget.

Goblin
Cinetel Films/Reel One 2010; 92 minutes;
Director: Jeffery Scott Lando ***

Halloween night, 1831: Near the town of Hollow Glen, a malformed infant is tossed into a bonfire to ensure a good harvest but his mother, a witch, curses the town and conjures up a fearsome being that will bring death to future generations of children in the area.

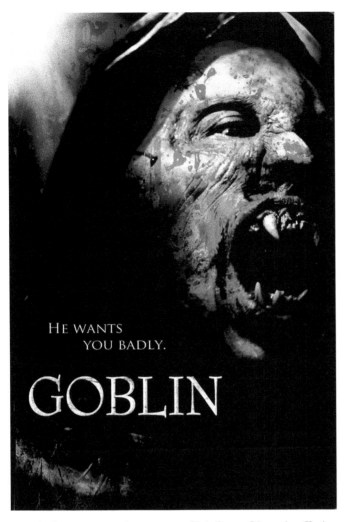

HE WANTS
YOU BADLY.

GOBLIN

A decent-enough monster flick from Cinetel, offering no real surprises in plot and execution but far more professionally produced than a lot of other similar B fodder. Take note—the seven-foot skeletal, bat-eared, fanged goblin of the title bears little resemblance to that pictured on the DVD cover, even though it is cloaked. Dad Gil Bellows, wife Camille Sullivan, headstrong daughter Tracy Spiridakos and tarty friend Erin Boyes drive to Hollow Glen and stay in a cabin a stone's throw away from where the creature appeared out of the flames all those years ago. As Sullivan is nursing an infant, she gets more than her fair share of nervous glances from the townsfolk and, this being Halloween, very soon the cloaked goblin emerges from the ashes, swooping through the air, stalking the woods and ripping up those who cross its path. Two dudes (Reilly Dolman and Brett Dier) meet up with the flighty teens but are simply lambs for the slaughter, although Spiridakos, Dolman, Bellows and the baby make it to the final reel after most of the leading players have been made mincemeat of by the malevolent CGI beastie; a sacred dagger plunged into its chest defeats the monster. Familiar territory, perhaps, but the cast, sparkling photography and creepy atmosphere all contribute to a lively offering from these Canadian indie moviemakers.

Growth
New Artists Alliance/KGM Films 2010; 90 minutes;
Director: Gabriel Cowan *

In 1988 on Kuttyhunk Island, scientists create an intelligent parasitic organism that enhances, and even manipulates, human DNA when introduced into a person's body; 20 years later, the squirming, slithering customers have wiped out most of the island's inhabitants and some survivors now possess super-strength.

Remember Tobe Hooper's *Lifeforce* (1985)? I quote this as a classic example of a movie containing a great opening sequence, only to rapidly fall flat on its face. Which is what *Growth* does. The credits sequence, filmed in pseudo-documentary fashion, points to greater things to come, showing the disastrous side-effects of the so-called Growth program. Unfortunately, they fail to materialize. Mircea Monroe travels to the island to collect a $2,000,000 inheritance on a property left to her by her mother. With her is boyfriend Brian Krause, Christopher Shand and Nora Kirkpatrick. Soon, all four become acquainted with the worm-like maggoty menaces as they slide in and out of orifices, consuming their hosts from the inside. Shand becomes infected, changing into a ravaged superman, Kirkpatrick is slaughtered by a hooded figure in a PVC coat and even heroine Monroe succumbs at the end, throwing herself into the sea so as not to contaminate the mainland; salt water is the element that disposes of the parasites. Underdeveloped in characterization, plot and drama, *Growth* meanders all over the place without achieving anything worthwhile, its one saving grace the CGI creatures themselves. Like a stale recipe, it seems to run out of ideas very early on, as if everyone involved had simply given up on the project. A lackluster outing that should have been heaps better than the finished product—even the surprise final few minutes can't save it.

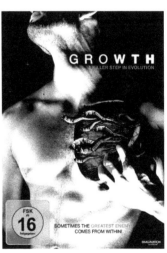

The Hollow
Lighthouse Pictures/Sonar Entertainment 2015;
85 minutes; Director: Sheldon Wilson **

On an island near Vancouver, a woody, fiery monster wreaks havoc on Halloween night in revenge for six girls burned at the stake in 1915, falsely accused of witchcraft.

Turn the volume down, or wear ear plugs, as teens Stephanie Hunt, Sarah Dugdale and Alisha Newton scream their way through a good-to-look-at but formulaic "something is in the woods" outing featuring a novel crea-

ture constructed of branches and twigs, an inner fire burning like a furnace. Following the death of their parents (in a fire, naturally!), the three siblings take a ferry to the island, discover that their aunt, Deborah Kara Unger, has been slain by the thing and a few local townsfolk are holed up in a diner, waiting for these Halloween horrors to end. The last third of the movie takes place inside the bowels of the island's underground power plant, Newton's voice rising to uncomfortable decibel levels ("Time to die, you bastard!") as the glowing monstrosity scuttles over ceilings, conduit pipes and walls, breathing flames. Eventually, it dissolves in sunlight, Newton and Dugdale hobbling off towards the rising sun, the curse lifted. An unusual looking creature running amok in a movie ruined by mass hysterics from the young cast.

Hydra aka Hydra The Lost Island
Cinetel Films 2009; 94 minutes;
Director: Andrew Prendergast ****

A modern-day big game hunter plans to deposit four of his enemies (all rich, but crooked, businessmen) on a deserted island and then hunt them down as human prey: Unknown to him, a monstrous, mythical multi-headed serpent lives there and has been disturbed from its lair by a group of archaeologists.

A briskly paced monster movie from Cinetel featuring a tremendous CGI creature of mythology, emerging from the Chamber of Zeus after archaeologist Polly Shannon and her pals have wandered in. Once captives George Stults, Texas Battle, Dawn Olivieri and James Wicek are dumped on the island by captain Michael Shamus Wiles, they find themselves doggedly chased by both hunters and the legendary monster. We get bodies ripped apart, limbs separated from torsos and blood a-plenty, the Hydra able to regenerate its torn-off heads at will. Near the end, William Gregory Lee retrieves a magic sword from a lava pit and supposedly kills the beast, lopping off its heads; however, the hydra revives, managing to storm the boat and gobble up the baddies before finally being slain for good. There's not many flaws here in an enjoyable indie creature-feature romp containing decent effects and credible performances; and the monster looks the business.

Hyenas
American World Pictures/Entertainment Dome 2011;
92 minutes; Director: Eric Weston **

After his wife is killed by shapeshifting creatures, a man teams up with a hunter to exterminate the monsters in their hideout, an abandoned copper mine.

Narrated by hunter Meshach Taylor, *Hyenas* is marred by a semi-comical undertone which goes against the grain,

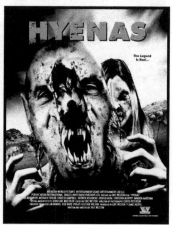

poor CGI transformation scenes and an uninteresting subplot concerning two rival gangs led by Joshua Alba and Derrick Kosinski. Curvy Christa Campbell is leader of a pack of humans that shapeshift into hyena-type monsters, her position under threat from foxy Amanda Aardsma whom aggrieved widower Costas Mandylor picks up; conveniently forgetting his recently slaughtered wife and unaware that the woman is one of the creatures, he impregnates her. A farcical showdown in a disused mine has Alba and Kosinski squaring up to each other to see who's top dog, Taylor and Mandylor wiring the tun-

nels up with dynamite and Campbell and Aardsma fighting to the death to determine who will lead the clan. And that almighty explosion *doesn't* finish them off—the last few minutes shows two of the creatures (in sexy babe guise) in New York, pouncing on an unsuspecting male victim. Some amusing lines ("So, you wanna play?" "No, I wanna eat!") and ferocious make-up raises this oddly mixed up, routine horror movie to two-star status.

Hypothermia
Dark Sky Films/Monsterpants 2010; 73 minutes;
Director: James Felix McKenney **

Two families fishing on a frozen lake fall prey to an amphibious humanoid creature inhabiting the icy waters.

A partly effective little thriller set in unusual surroundings (New York's Great Sacandaga Lake), but what a crying shame about that monster, sporadically putting in an appearance during the final 20 minutes. *Hypothermia*'s "gill-man" is right up there with the rubber-suited alien in *Reptilicant* (2006) and the reptile man in *Creature Unknown* (2004) as one of indie's worst humanoid monstrosities, a man in a black plastic costume with webbed feet (diving flippers?) wearing a goggle-eyed mask sporting fangs. It's pretty awful, a real letdown, nullifying all that has come before it, which, in all honesty, isn't much: Michael Rooker, wife Blanche Baker, son Ben Forster and girlfriend Amy Chang meet Don Wood and son Greg Finley on the lake for a spot of fishing, only to be picked off by the monster which emerges through holes in the ice, just the two women surviving its attacks. Plenty of red distorted shots from the thing's perspective, a few gory images, the notion that those wounded will morph into clones of the creature (it's never followed up) and a sense of bleak isolation jog matters along, but as soon as the aquatic terror (or non-terror) comes into view, caught in the glare of a spotlight, even diehard indie buffs will feel betrayed, gasp "Oh no!" and probably switch off. This is 2010, for heaven's sake, not 1955. A poor excuse for a creature-feature.

Jurassic Attack aka Rise of the Dinosaurs
Titan Global Ent./Little Dragon Prods. 2013; 83 minutes;
Director: Anthony Fankhauser ***

An elite team of commandos rescues a biochemist from a jungle rebel base; on the flight back, their helicopter is hit by a missile and they crash inside a crater populated by dinosaurs.

Predator (1987) has a lot to answer for. Ever since Arnie and his grunts dropped in on jungle rebels to bring back people of importance, only to encounter something they never expected, filmmakers large and small have jumped onto this particular cinematic bandwagon with varying degrees of success. So *Jurassic Attack* is packed with clichés: Grizzled Gary Stretch and company combating T-Rex's and 'raptors by the score, plus the odd Triceratops; Natasha Berg's biochemist resembling a catwalk model, and talking like one; Israel Sáez de Miguel's rebel chief glowering like mad; Alicia Ziegler sighing and rolling her eyes every time Stretch disagrees with her useless tactics; Corin "Get the job done or die trying" Nemec's colonel at base, threatening cold-eyed boss Vernon Wells with extinction if he proceeds to "glass" the area where the team is located because of possible fallout from a chemical warhead; and Michael Worth's Professor Roxton (Roxton as in *The Lost World*), a cross between Jeff Goldblum's twitchy doctor in *Jurassic Park* and Henry Brandon's half-crazed survivor in 1957's *The Land Unknown*. The effects are not to be sneered at—20-odd years ago, these would have been deemed state of the art; now, they're quirky but serviceable. Filmed in picturesque Belize, *Jurassic Attack* is colorful, fast-paced dino-fun containing a neat beginning, explaining how dithery Worth ended up in his beloved prehistoric paradise, a paradise he refuses to leave; there are many more similar movies worse than this one out there on the market.

Jurassic City
International Production Bridge/Little Dragon Prods.
2015; 88 minutes; Director: Sean Cain ***

Three Velociraptors taken to the Elkwood Detention Facility for study break loose and terrorize the freed inmates.

Made by the same team behind *Jurassic Attack*, *Jurassic City*'s action mostly takes place within the confines of a detention center at night where four girls, two lesbians, a couple of old cons, a killer rapist, the head warden and assorted guards are menaced by three monsters that have broken out of the back of an armored truck. In the final five minutes, as a smoking Los Angeles is overrun by dinosaurs of every shape, size and variety, fish-eyed agent Vernon Wells informs chief black ops grunt Jack Forcinito, "I set them free. A test run. All my pets are on the loose." Forcinito finishes off the deluded madman with a well-aimed rocket grenade and goes out into the night,

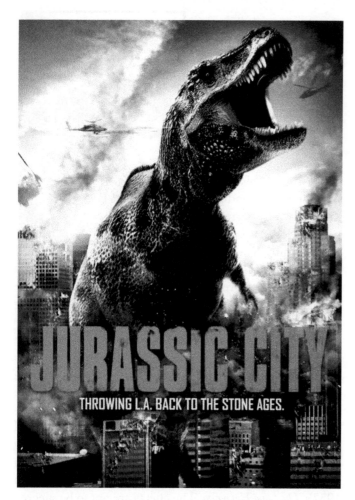

radioactive crater out of which pour hundreds of dinosaurs that terrorize the nearby community.

Rib Hillis playing a sleepy-eyed ex-rodeo star drifting into town, determined to win back lost love Casey Fitzgerald from hick sheriff John Freeman; his father, Eric Roberts, a drunk loser behind bars; college grad Sara Malakul Lane trying hard to boss around a bunch of beefy miners that could eat her for breakfast; Vernon Wells perfecting his corrupt boss act; Heather Foote a blonde, gun-toting babe; and Kelcey Watson armed to the teeth. Add a town full of chicks attired in hot pants and cowboy boots, questionable acting from all concerned (including veteran Roberts), moments of gore and lively CGI effects (the T-Rex stomping down the main street is terrific, as are the acid-spewing Velociraptors) and you have a daft but enjoyable monster romp from the hands of producer Anthony Fankhauser, the man behind many of these *Jurassic Park*-type rip-offs. Hillis lassos a 'raptor, rides rodeo-style on a bucking Triceratops and finally lures the beasts back into their prehistoric domain with a whiff of methane gas. But, as he smooches with Fitzgerald at the end, a massive winged creature flies out of the crater, staring down at the pair—it ain't all over yet!

armed to the teeth. Come daybreak, the two survivors from the detention center carnage, Dana Melanie and Kayla Carlyle, survey a city in ruins, helicopters flying overhead engaging with giant Pteranodons. If you can get past the early sequence of partying-on gals squawking in teen-speak, then what we have on offer is a taut dinosaurs-on-the-prowl thriller featuring an engaging performance from burly Kevin Gage as the psycho, a real charmer in spite of his terrible crimes (as a nine-year-old, he bludgeoned his mother to death). It's a futile exercise comparing the monsters in *Jurassic City* to those in *Jurassic Park* as many do—here, in this low-budget setup, they're perfectly adequate, biting off heads, munching on bodies, chewing on severed limbs and creating bloody mayhem. Remember, we're in indie land, not Universal-International land. A pretty decent entrant in a number of movies made over the past few years featuring the word "Jurassic" in their title; Mario Salvucci's opening score isn't too bad either.

Jurassic Hunters aka Cowboys vs. Dinosaurs
Epic Pictures/Oracle Film Group 2015; 89 minutes;
Director: Ari Novak ***

At the Lando iridium mine in Montana, workers take a short cut, setting off explosives at surface, exposing a vast

UNDER TEN MILLION? ANYTHING'S POSSIBLE!

KillerSaurus

88 Films/Creativ Studio 2015; 75 minutes;
Director: Steve Lawson *

A scientist creates, by "bio-printing," a Tyrannosaurus Rex in a research facility which his backers want to use in times of war, as a "soldier of the future."

Ten minutes of pseudo-scientific chat in a spartan lab, followed by three minutes of credits (two minutes too long) does not bode well for things to come. And it's no good screaming "Get a move on!" because British-made *KillerSaurus*, possibly the worst (and cheapest) dinosaur picture ever made, steadfastly refuses to do so, crawling through the remaining 56 minutes like a snail nursing a colossal hangover (the film ends on the 69th minute, the rest of the time given over to outtakes and bloopers). "For everyone fed up with CGI creatures" states the blurb. Well, this is one case where CGI, even in its poorest form, was urgently needed. After 44 paralyzing minutes, we get a shot of the beast's head and jaws enveloped in clouds of gas, and in the final moments, it's shunted out from its chamber, only for the movie to end abruptly. Helen Crevel is the scientist resembling Professor Steve Dolton's dead daughter, Kenton Hall plays her snoopy journalist boyfriend, Julian Boote is the corporate creep wanting to deploy T-Rex ("A fighting carnivore.") on the battlefield while Sergeant Adam Collins gets blasted by twin laser beams, stumbling around sporting a T-Rex head and T-Rex claw (*The Alligator People* this film isn't!). "What have you got in there? King Kong?" asks Hall at one point. If only! A slower-than-slow-moving, talkative, embarrassingly awful monster-not-on-the-loose flick backed by a funereal soundtrack that promotes Asylum's often derided dinosaur outings to the level of *Citizen Kane*.

Lavalantula

Cinetel Films 2015; 81 minutes; Director: Mike Mendez ***

Volcanic eruptions in Los Angeles' Santa Monica Mountains cause fissures to open in the streets, spewing forth giant, lava-breathing spiders.

Nice spiders—shame about the acting and script. Cinetel's monsters are always a cut above the opposition and these scaly arachnids look just dandy, especially the mighty queen at the end. But why, in this *Eight Legged Freaks* meets the Disaster movie offering, did the scriptwriters insist on going down the semi-comical route? Steve *Police Academy* Guttenberg plays ex-'90s action movie star The Red Rocket, attempting to round up kickboxing wife Nia Peeples and teen son Noah Hunt with the blundering assistance of clownish sidekick Patrick Renna, Ralph Garman attired in pirate costume and forever-acting-the-fool Michael Winslow, all the time dodging those fire-breathing horrors erupting in droves from the cracked sidewalks. There's loads of action and telling shots of devastation, together with a splendid middle section when the creatures emerge from the LA's La Brea Tar Pits, going on a rampage in the George C. Page museum; however, these exciting scenes are canceled out by the sight of Guttenberg dressed in his Red Rocket outfit like a third-rate superhero, zooming from one building to the next as he takes on the big queen, tossing explosives down her gullet. Bombs dropped into the underground network of lava tubes defeat the spiders, Guttenberg crashing into a swimming pool, Hunt exclaiming (as kids do in today's films) "Dad, you're so cool." "I smell a sequel coming on," states Winslow, but hopefully minus his continual mugging and irritating habit of breaking into silly voices (the inferior *2 Lava 2 Lantula!* arrived in 2016). *Lavalantula*'s genuinely funny moment? In the 33rd minute, Guttenberg bumps into Ian *Sharknado* Ziering running down the street who informs him, "I'd love to help you, but I got shark problems right now!" It's monster fun but would have worked better if a certain amount of gravitas was allowed to creep in on occasions.

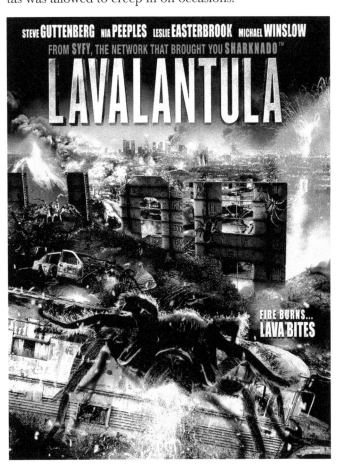

Lightning Strikes
Paradox Pictures/WST Productions 2009; 90 minutes;
Director: Gary Jones **

Destructive bolts of blue lightning contain an entity

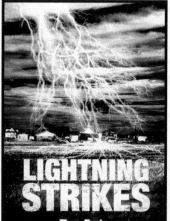

created by electrical force that feeds off human beings.

One minute a disaster movie—the next, a *kind* of monster movie. The normally reliable Kevin Sorbo wanders through this screwy vehicle with a look of bemusement as the town of Roscoe, gearing itself up for the annual Pumpkin Festival, is bombarded by bolts of lightning in which a weird entity (resembling a gray, skeletal alien) perches on rooftops, electrocuting the populace. A team of weather chasers appears in town, grizzled David Schofield is determined to trap the thing in a lightning conductor because it killed his son, survivor Annabel Wright flashes her eyelashes at Sorbo and mincing mayor Todd Jensen refuses to evacuate the town, placing (as these mayors *always* do) profit before safety. Filmed in Bulgaria, the movie kicks off encouragingly (streaks of electrical energy pursuing a car down a lonely road) but then degenerates into a hysterical mishmash. The idea of an electrical monster is intriguing (check Nu Image's *The Black Hole*, 2006), but it's not fully realized in this flatly directed picture.

Mandrake
Cinetel Films/RHI Ent. 2010; 85 minutes;
Director: Tripp Reed **

An expedition is sent to the jungles of South America by a rich industrialist to retrieve a sacred dagger hidden inside the 500-year-old tomb of a conquistador; when the dagger is removed from the skeleton, a deadly walking tree comes to life, bent on revenge.

Way back in 1957, the Milner Brothers let loose *From Hell It Came* on an unsuspecting '50s audience, a glorious piece of grade Z schlock featuring a man in a rubber tree suit. Over 50 years later, *Mandrake* has a CGI walking tree made up of jungle vines and creepers, a big red eye peeking out between the tendrils. But is it any better than the Allied Artists' classic? "No"

has to be the answer. An unsympathetic cast made up principally of Max Martini (grizzled anti-hero), Betsy Russell (acting-by-numbers token blonde), Jon Mack (female boss, barking out orders with a permanent pained expression) and Benito Martinez (rich financier, devious and wooden) combat the living tree when a jeweled dagger is plucked from the bones of a conquistador, unleashing the monster of the title and a horde of bloodthirsty savages to boot. Filmed in the Louisiana swamps, *Mandrake*, after a promising, fairly atmospheric start, rapidly becomes repetitive and predictable, the only pleasure on offer seeing the various cast members being ripped apart by the woody menace as it prowls the forest. Martini saves the day, stabbing Martinez with the dagger, the monster frozen into a statue, its power gone. Filmed with Cinetel's customary sheen, this is okay fodder for those who have never witnessed any similar production prior to 2000; for much older fans, Todd Andrews, Tina Carver, Gregg Palmer and the unforgettable Linda Watkins, together with Paul Blaisdell's immortal creation from the 1950s, win hands down in the "walking monster tree" stakes.

Maneater
Canal Street Films 2009; 92 minutes;
Director: Michael Emanuel *

A number of savage deaths and disappearances are attributed by local townsfolk to be the work of a wendigo, a mythical Indian shapeshifting creature.

Do you like rom-coms? If so, *Maneater* will be right up your street. On the other hand, if you relish good old-fashioned creature thrills, it won't be. Far too much time is wasted on police profiler Dean Cain's daughter (Lacy Phillips) giggling and going all gooey eyed over weedy new kid on the block Stephen Lunsford; face up to it girl, the guy ain't no Brad Pitt! Added to that the frequent domestic spats between Cain and Phillips and plenty of lulls in the action,

plus dim photography, and you will find it extremely difficult to stifle a yawn every five minutes or so. Yes, believe it or not, there *is* a monster—the creature of Indian legend can shapeshift from human form into that of a hag-like fiend with glowing eyes and is driven to kill by people's lust and infidelity. If you dare stare into its baleful eyes, you too will become a wendigo, and the twist in this rather plodding tale is that Cain himself is one of them (*and* his grizzled Indian deputy with the gloved hands), as we see him changing in the final seconds. A couple of explicitly

UNDER TEN MILLION? ANYTHING'S POSSIBLE!

nude sex scenes might stop the eyelids from drooping, but overall, *Maneater* could have been a lot, lot better if the domestic/teen hang-ups had been tossed overboard in favor of full-on creature mayhem.

Metal Shifters aka Iron Invader
Cinetel Films/Reel One Ent. 2011; 87 minutes;
Director: Paul Ziller ***

A green alien bacteria attaches itself to a Russian satellite—the machine crashes to Earth and the bacteria latches onto an 18-foot-tall metal sculpture called the Golem, imbuing it with life and causing it to go on a rampage.

A lively monster yarn featuring a creation of the kind countless English kids used to construct out of Meccano sets in the 1950s—it resembles a sizeable variant of the T-800 cyborg from the *Terminator* movies. Scrapyard owner Donnelly Rhodes buys the satellite wreckage from brothers Kavan Smith and Colby Johannson for 800 bucks, unaware that a creeping bacteria feeding off metal is plastered all over the fragments. When the green goo comes into contact with Rhodes' robotic sculpture, the contraption takes on a life of its own, stomping off towards the town of Redeemer; when it closes its claws on humans, the bacteria strips the blood of iron, the victims expiring. Smith bumps into old college flame Nicole de Boer (handy for him, she's about to divorce) and the redneck bar crawlers accidentally discover a substance dear to their hearts that can render

the Golem harmless—alcohol, or neat whiskey! "Have a drink, you alien sonofabitch!" yells Rhodes as he pours liquor over a crawling chunk of metal; yes, Cinetel's take on *The Blob* is slightly daft in places, but enjoyable with it.

Mongolian Death Worm
Cinetel Films/RHI Ent. 2010; 90 minutes;
Director: Steven R. Monroe ***

A company drilling for oil in Central Mongolia uncovers the tomb of Genghis Khan, guarded by a giant species of mythical worm.

Fast-paced nonsense combining sub-*Indiana Jones* thrills and creature-feature mayhem: Sean Patrick Flanery plays the devil-may-care adventurer who discovers that the LBK drilling company has located, by chance, Genghis Khan's burial chamber, complete with millions of dollars worth of treasure. Unfortunately, giant worms resembling huge multicolored slugs have≠≠ been disturbed and begin to emerge from their burrows, gobbling up the interlopers intent on raiding their master's tomb. Tomboy medic Victoria Pratt supplies the female interest, first of all loathing Flanery and then falling for his rugged charms. Although the plant is blasted to bits and pieces at the end (and the creatures with it), Flanery and Pratt are showered in gold coins, their reward for defeating both the worms and crooked oil chief Drew Waters. Romania stands in for the Mongolian Desert (and not very convincingly), the acting is above average and the 10-foot-long CGI worms look splendid, making this 90 minutes of undemanding monster fodder that doesn't bore for a single second.

Monsterwolf
Bullet Films 2010; 90 minutes;
Director: Todor Chapkanov **

A company drilling for oil accidentally unearths an Indian relic, unleashing the spirit of a medicine man that manifests itself in the form of a giant, flesh-eating wolf.

The environmentalists versus the oil company scenario rears its head again, Leonor Varela a bright young lawyer hired to ward off (legally) those who want the hallowed site left alone, boss Robert Picardo doing his best to ride roughshod over the townsfolk's objections. Meanwhile, a ragged-looking CGI wolf embarks on a rampage, chomping up the local residents. The cast, led by Jason London, go through the motions as everyone tries to slay the brute, there's a short cartoon sequence showing how the wolf legend got started which is completely out of place and the dim photography disguises the fact that this is one big wolf that is not particularly fearsome. And could you honestly insert a sacred bone into a rifle and shoot the creature dead with it? A smattering of gore and blood juice up some scenes but in all honesty, *Monsterwolf* is PG-rated lukewarm horror fodder even by these standards.

Mothman
Upload Films 2010; 89 minutes;
Director: Sheldon Wilson ***

When a youth is accidentally drowned during a prank, the teens responsible cover up the deed; 10 years later, a supernatural monster exacts justice for the unlawful death.

Jewel Staite is the reporter returning to Point Pleasant, West Virginia, the scene of the tragedy—her editor wants her to write an article on the local Mothman legend. Staite meets up with all her old pals who were in on the crime and

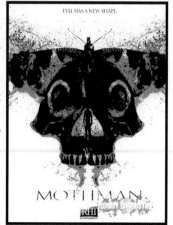

triggers off a series of grisly events when the evil Mothman makes its presence felt; the creature can only crawl out of reflective surfaces such as mirrors and when it does, those who stare into its eyes die horribly. According to blind Jerry Leggio, the Mothman is the phantom of an Indian who was tortured, sliced up and buried in a glass-lined coffin; it seeks out those who have not reported a death. He ran over a kid years back, hid the body and blinded himself so that he couldn't attract the Mothman by sight. Comparisons will be made to 2002's pretentious *The Mothman Prophecies* but at least this movie has a monster, not the half-seen entity that featured (or didn't feature) in the Richard Gere flick; it's black, has large red eyes, wings and a mouth full of fangs. As a nod to the 2002 picture, there's a brief bridge-collapsing scene and just when you thought the thing had been vanquished (Staite stabs it with a sacred bone dagger), Staite herself, eyes glowing like red coals and surrounded by dozens of moths, appears to be the new Mothman, or should that read Mothwoman. A lively horror tale with convincing creature effects that, to be honest, knocks spots off Gere's glossier, though muddled, thriller.

Ogre
Cinetel Films/Insight Film Studios 2008; 90 minutes;
Director: Steven R. Monroe ****

1859: In the town of Ellensford, Pennsylvania, townsfolk are dying from a pestilence, forcing the community's elder to enter into a devilish pact to get rid of the epidemic, but at a cost; a huge being is created that demands one blood sacrifice every year.

Cinetel Films' fantasy products have more gloss than most other indie offerings and *Ogre* doesn't buck the trend. Monroe directed the marvelous *Wyvern* (also, like *Ogre*, filmed in Canada) so he's at home here in the snow-laden forests as four teens become lost in the dense woods (à la *Blair Witch Project*) and one of them opens the trap door to an old plague pit, unleashing what can only be described as a cross between an X-rated Shrek for adults and the Incredible Hulk. Yes, 150 years on, Ellensford still stands, populated by about 50 residents all blessed (or cursed) with eternal life because of John Schneider's unholy pact. Crafty Schneider is also choosing for himself who should die each year, saving himself until last. When Ryan Kennedy and Katharine Isabelle are captured, Kennedy is offered up for sacrifice, the villagers, tired of living forever, stage a revolt and the giant ogre embarks on a killing spree. Chelan Simmons eventually defeats the thing and by doing so, she and her companions, released from their curse, vanish in balls of golden light. Remember, *Ogre* is low-budget monster thrills, so don't expect million-dollar graphics as the 12-foot-high troll stomps around, breaking into houses, biting off heads, stamping on heads and tearing off limbs; it's adequately done and works well in this particular context. Combined with a half-decent script, crisp photography and moderately good acting (apart from Isabelle, the whining teen),

UNDER TEN MILLION? ANYTHING'S POSSIBLE!

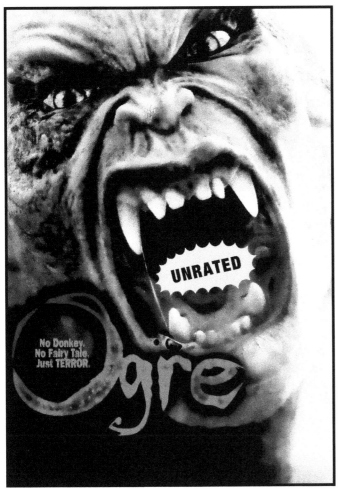

monster movie on your hands here which cannot be taken seriously, although it must be admitted that the Everglades scenery is photographed in crisp colors to add some degree of atmosphere. Doug Swander plays an animal control officer up against Simon Page's scatty scientist (an odd performance from the British actor); in between the gory deaths, the harmonica-playing lothario indulges in sexual antics with ex-wife/town sheriff Kathleen LaGue. Escaped convicts, student interns, canoeists, local rednecks, dogs—all are gobbled up or savaged by the giant Asian swamp eel before Swander wrestles with the creature and it swallows a grenade; the two lovers are drenched in blood as the eel explodes, although this doesn't prevent them from entering into some serious canoodling. But hang on—as they walk off camera, a group of baby eels slithers into view, so we are back to square one. Fair entertainment if you're sprawled on the sofa with your mates and a few beers, the brain disengaged; for fans of more meaningful indie monster fodder, *Razortooth* is utter poppycock.

Reptisaurus

Retromedia Ent. 2009; 81 minutes;
Director: Christopher Douglas-Olen Ray ****
(chiefly for the monster)

Scientists create a "mutated biological weapon" from an unknown species of reptile and a bat, the end product a

this is a fast-moving picture with a touch of M. Night Shyamalan's *The Village* about it (but more entertaining); it won't disappoint lovers of cut-price monster fodder.

Razortooth

Push/Gravedigger Films 2007; 92 minutes;
Director: Patricia Harrington **

A genetically engineered 20-foot diabetic eel goes on a rampage in the Florida Everglades.

Those pesky swamps have thrown up colossal crocs and

'gators, mutated fish, mega snakes and walking trees, so why not an enormous carnivorous eel. The drawback is, this monster has the face of a piranha stitched onto it and is the CGI equivalent of the tatty puppet featured in 1962's dire classic, *Reptilicus*; this means that, together with a semi-comical script and a cast of rednecks uttering every cliché in the creature-feature book, you have one very predictable

giant flying self-reproducing monster that wreaks havoc on an island military base.

An obscure US/Bulgarian creature-feature (DVDs emanate from Thailand) that showcases one of indie's most engaging monsters, a 20-foot flying dinosaur resembling a gigantic harpy from Greek Mythology (or even 1982's *Q The Winged Serpent*); pinning its victims to the ground under massive claws, Reptisaurus pecks their heads off before discarding body parts like so much chewed-up trash. That's the good point. The bad is the acting, woeful even on this low-budget level, the raspberry award going to blonde crybaby Annmarie Lynn Gracey whose incessant whining ("I don't wanna be eaten!") is mercifully silenced when she *is* eaten! First seen knocking a jet fighter out of the sky, the creature then dispatches two marines on an island. Three months later, five youths are washed up on the beach when their boat sinks; bumping into two more marines (Bernard Fredericks and Eric Fischer), all seven make it to a wrecked research facility where they find Doctor Yahaira Love who relates how she and Doctor Frank Forbes created the thing as a military biological weapon before he hightailed back to the States. General Gil Gerard orders the island to be nuked but Fredericks saves the day, blowing the monster to bloody chunks; he's then flown off along with three others. But in the monster's cave, there's a clutch of eggs, and one is about to hatch. So ignore the idiotic behavior of the five that appear on the island, the dumb script ("I'm gonna blast Godzilla's ass!") and the dire performances; just concentrate on Ray's energetic direction, a quirky soundtrack and fabulous Reptisaurus, straight out of a Japanese monster flick of the 1960s and looking all the better for it.

Riddles of the Sphinx
Insight Film Studios/Sci-Fi Channel 2008; 89 minutes;
Director: George Mendeluk **

To prevent the world being decimated by the Plague of Isis, an archaeologist and his two helpers must unravel riddles inscribed in various languages on cipher stones in order to defeat a giant living sphinx that has escaped from a lost Egyptian tomb.

Take Indiana Jones clone Lochlyn Munro, team him with Angelina Jolie/Lara Croft look-alike Dina Meyer, have 15-year-old know-it-all daughter Emily Tennant along for the ride, toss in a dose of Noah Wyle's *The Librarian* series and produce a monster that changes into Arnold Vosloo's Imhotep from 1999's *The Mummy* and what have you got? A recipe for disaster, saved to a certain extent by that eye-catching creature. Cold-looking British Columbia stands in for Egypt (a dense wood on the banks of the Nile?), Iraq (a quarry instead of a desert) and Greece (moss-covered stone columns and gray skies at the Temple of Zeus?) as Munro dashes from one country to another in a plane, pursued by the flying sphinx, deciphering four cryptic

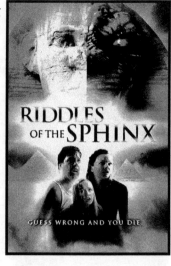

messages set in matching pairs of golden ammonites, all relating to the four elements and the fabled Hall of Knowledge (or Ark of Destiny; take your pick) where his dead father's spirit resides. None of it makes much sense, simply a series of mad stunts pinched from *Raiders of the Lost Ark* and the two Jolie *Tomb Raider* movies; too well-fed Munro simply doesn't cut it as a second-rate Harrison Ford (get that huge hat!) while Meyer mumbles her lines through clenched teeth—you cannot understand a word she is saying. "We only have a couple of hours before Armageddon," shrieks Tennant as a handful of people are discovered dead, a result of the imminent plague; on cue, Munro plunges a golden sword into his own midriff, his sacrifice killing the sphinx. Reunited with Dad in the ethereal Hall of Knowledge ("I'm okay. I've stopped the plague."), he's given a choice; spend all eternity delving into that vast room of archives and the secrets of the universe, or love. Munro chooses good old-fashioned love, returning in one piece to Tennant and Meyer and immediately engaging in lip action with the leather-clad, gun-toting babe. "At last, Dad's getting some action," grins Tennant, but the only decent action to be had from this million-dollar clunker is from the mighty CGI sphinx, a colorful creation that wouldn't have looked out of place in one of Ray Harryhausen's mythological pictures and about the only reason to tune in.

Scourge
PHD Productions 2008; 92 minutes;
Director: Jonas Quastel **

Following the burning-down of Harborford church, an ancient parasitic creature is released from an underground chamber, requiring new bodies to inhabit every six hours and leaving its previous hosts dead.

Give *Scourge* its due, at least it's played straight with no teen shenanigans, but we are in clichéd creature-feature territory here: Bad boy from the wrong side of the tracks (Nic Rhind) rekindling a romance with nice young lady Robyn Ledoux;

UNDER TEN MILLION? ANYTHING'S POSSIBLE!

Russell Ferrier, the sheriff and Ledoux's uncle, firmly against the romance *and* convinced that Rhind is behind the spate of bloody deaths overtaking the town; a couple of sloppy interludes whereby Ledoux stares dreamily into space, thinking (or lusting) about her ex-beau; and a plot taken direct from *The Hidden*, *Shivers* and many others—even indie outfit Artist View Entertainment gave it a go with 2005's *Disturbance* (aka *Choker*). As the death toll mounts, Ledoux discovers in an old book on demonology that the only method of exterminating the squirming, tentacled creature that enters the human body via the stomach is by electrocution; it also hates alcohol. This leads to her and Rhind setting a honey trap for the thing's latest host, an overweight photographer. Lured to a hotel room with a promise of sex, he's electrocuted and the creature emerges from his mouth; a modern-day demonic practitioner working with the FBI incinerates it, but, surprise, surprise, a vestige of the parasite appears to be alive and well at the end. The creature effects are adequate, the two young leads proficient enough, but we've seen all this before which gives *Scourge* a slightly unoriginal, predictable air that doesn't work in its favor.

Slugs
Dister Group Productions 1988; 92 minutes;
Director: Juan Piquer Simon **

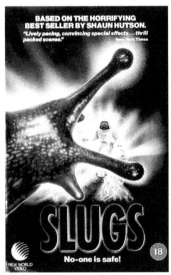

Thousands of meat-eating black slugs begin feasting on a town's inhabitants.

Slugs has one major flaw—if this particular gastropod is one of the slowest-moving creatures on Earth, how come humans are unable to escape from its slimy clutches? Well, they don't in this joint American/Spanish creature-feature; people get munched to bloody shreds as the things emerge from sewers contaminated with toxic waste, and it's up to Michael Garfield, sanitation supervisor Philip MacHale and kooky scientist Santiago Alvarez to fathom out a way to exterminate them. It's a proven fact that the 1980s has gone down in celluloid history as one of the worst decades for films per se, and looking at *Slugs*, you can see why. The movie has a horribly dated Hispanic look about it: Drab color, tacky décor and art direction, the cast all sporting big hair and flared trousers. This, together with a stilted script, makes *Slugs* quite an unattractive picture to experience, let alone enjoy. Alvarez blows up the sewers (and half the town with it) in the end with his own cocktail

of chemicals, although the final frame hints that he hasn't finished off *all* of the slithering terrors. *Slugs* wasn't granted a wide release in the United Kingdom and viewed today, it's not hard to understand why.

Snow Beast
Silver Peak Productions 2011; 88 minutes;
Director: Brian Brough *

An expert in animal behavioral patterns takes his teenage daughter deep into the Canadian mountains where

they team up with a couple of conservationists and encounter the Yeti.

And this rubber-faced, white-haired Yeti is of the tatty variety, looking like a 1980s reject from Britain's *Dr. Who* television series. John Schneider, sulky daughter Danielle Chuchran, Paul D. Hunt and Kari Hawker-Diaz are the foursome combating a monster that makes the Abominable Snowmen in Jerry Warren's infamous *Man Beast* (1955) look positively artistic in design. Slicing up snowboarders, the stomping menace goes after the occupants of Hunt's remote cabin (Yeti perspective shots are in distorted amber), killing Hawker-Diaz, dragging Schneider off to its polystyrene cave and slaying Hunt. In the end, the thing is wiped out in an avalanche, but is it? Two hikers trek through the snow, the man dragged into a drift by something with big claws. At least the stop-start action shakes Chuchran out of her eye-rolling "why doesn't anyone understand me?" mode, enough for her to realize that Schneider isn't the ogre she makes him out to be. The scenery is attractive, but that's about it, a lame, tame creature-feature lumbered with an unconvincing protagonist that's more suitable for the under-10s than adults.

Surviving Evil
Fries Film Group/Focus Films 2009; 90 minutes;
Director: Terence Daw ***

A wildlife-documentary film crew camps on a remote island in the Philippines for a shoot, unaware that shape-changing carnivorous creatures known by local legend as Aswang inhabits the surrounding jungles.

A joint South African/UK creature-feature featuring a solid cast of well-rounded characters: Billy Zane (the outdoor survival guy), Colin Moss (cameraman), Louise Barnes (director), Christina Cole (assistant), Natalie Mendoza (zoologist) and Joel Torre (expert on tribes). The opening hour concentrates on the interaction between the crew—Cole is pregnant after a quick fling with Zane, Moss lusts after Mendoza, Barnes, Moss' ex, is seething with jealousy and Torre has a hidden agenda; he knows the exact spot where the Japanese deposited a hoard of gold bullion during the war and wants to lay his hands on it. With all this going on and those lush tropical locations to savor, you might be forgiven for asking "When are the monsters going to appear?" Well, they do, nearly 65-odd minutes into the movie, winged, devil-faced humanoids that change form (dogs, natives) and feed on human flesh. Unfortunately for Cole, the things also have an unnatural inclination towards the blood of pregnant women, so she is in real danger of the fetus being torn from her body. Nobody makes it out alive, not even the personable Zane—Cole *does*, in a dinghy, but is washed ashore on another island where *all* the women are in various stages of pregnancy, so what chance does she have there. Professionally pieced together and favored with a succinct script, *Surviving Evil* does go off the boil a shade near the end; however, the strong performances, savage creatures and colorful cinematography more than make up for any lapses in the narrative.

Swarmed
Reel One Ent./S.V. Scary Films 2005; 88 minutes;
Director: Paul Ziller ****

A genetically enhanced pesticide has an alarming effect on yellow jacket wasps, mutating the insects into super-aggressive miniature killing machines armed with lethal stings.

Hooray—Paul Ziller has pulled off the nigh on impossible by producing a "killer flying insect" movie that works! The blueprint for all such pictures (and there have been an awful lot of disposable ones) is this: Scientists create a substance that has an adverse effect on bees (or in this instance, wasps); the local town (Dundas) has a festival coming up (here, it's the National Burger Cook-Off); the unscrupulous mayor refuses to call off the festivities because of profits (income vs. fatalities); the swarm embarks on a stinging spree, feasting on raw burgers, wreaking havoc and putting paid to both slimeball mayor and equally dishonest chief of police; the swarm is eventually destroyed (in this case, by fire *and* tire sealant gas!); and

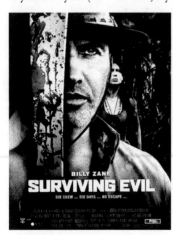

male scientist cuddles up to female entomologist in the final seconds. The CGI effects in *Swarmed* are splendid: Distorted sepia wasp viewpoint shots and close-ups of the yellow/black buzzing terrors as they zero in on their victims. Oh, the cast: Michael Shanks (hunky scientist); Carol Alt (attractive entomologist); Christopher Bondy (slimy mayor); Richard Chevolleau

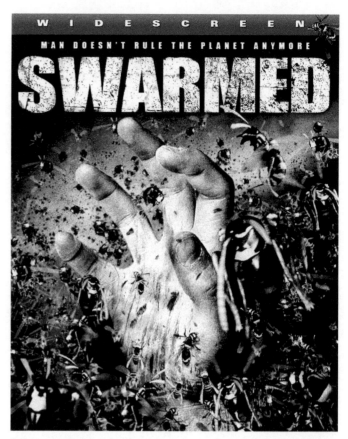

(who runs Bugbusters); and, among others, Tim Thomerson, sleazy head of Washburn Sauces—all turn in efficient performances while managing to keep a straight face. The climax is a direct steal from Regent's *Killer Bees* (2002) but hey, you have to get your source references from *somewhere*, don't you? And naturally, the queen survives, busy laying eggs in a vacuum pump. Apart from one or two daft moments (can you honestly kill a single wasp with a shotgun?), *Swarmed*, as far as the numerous "deadly swarms" genre goes, is very near the top of the pile, if not THE top!

Ticks aka Infested
Overseas Filmgroup/First Look 1993; 85 minutes;
Director: Tony Randel ***

On a camping trip near Los Angeles, a group of problem teenagers on an Inner City Wilderness Project pitch their tents next to an illegal marijuana farm and is menaced by hordes of mutant ticks.

The big ticks are the result of hick farmer Clint Howard treating his marijuana plants to herbal steroids, the juice of which has leaked out of a barrel, infecting tick larvae—soon, the creepy-crawly terrors

PIONEER MOTION PICTURES
presents

TREES

"Good ol' fashioned sappy fun!"
-Denis Sheehan, ASKEW REVIEWS

"TREES will leave you in splinters!"
-Stephen Seward, BURIED.COM

ITS BITE IS WORSE THAN ITS BARK!

emerge from their gelatinous pods and scuttle about, attacking Rosalind Allen, Ami Dolenz, Seth Green and friends, causing skin to blister and other gross-out effects (a body split in half as a monstrous tick emerges from within). The rubbery, clawed creatures, hand-sized and man-sized, were created at a time when CGI didn't rule the roost and are all the better for it; one of the things manages to make its way back to LA on the underneath of the teens' bus after the remainder have presumably perished in a forest fire. *Ticks* is rollicking, gruesome horror fun of the old-fashioned variety, aimed at a younger audience, with its tongue planted firmly in its cheek.

Trees
Pioneer Motion Pictures/Mazzarella Bros. Prods. 2000; 88 minutes; Director: Michael Pleckaitis * or *****

The town of Hazelville comes under attack from a man-eating tree known by locals as the Great White Pine.

A goofy frame-by-frame, word-by-word pastiche of Steven Spielberg's *Jaws* made on a $20,000 micro-budget without a solitary CGI effect in sight; they don't come much weirder than this oddity. So, as millions of cinemagoers are fully acquainted with the plot of the giant shark classic, there's no need to relate the plot of *Trees*. Simply substitute *Jaws'* familiar sequences for those in this movie, the shark now a tree! Roy Scheider becomes Kevin McCauley, Richard Dreyfuss is now Philip M. Gardiner, Robert Shaw changes into Peter Randazzo, and so on, and so forth. All the notable scenes are in place: The disemboweling of the shark (tree), the obnoxious, money-grabbing mayor protesting about the beach (campsite) being closed, the grizzled seafarer Quint (now Squint) scratching his nails down the board, the singsong on the boat (truck), even the reverse-zoom shot that Spielberg copied from Hitchcock. And catch that priceless dialogue—"You gotta tree in there with pine needles THAT big!"; "We're gonna need a bigger axe."; "Smile, you sonofasapling!" Tom Destefano's ominous score is a rarity in independent filmmaking, a fairly memorable soundtrack that complements the silliness (even if it does ape John Williams' music) while the tatty monster is nothing more than a large pine being towed from behind by the production team. And you thought Allied Artists' *From Hell It Came* (1957) was bad! Seriously, if you're in the right frame of mind, *Trees* is a five-star indie hoot, almost deserving a cult reputation. If not, then you might consider it to be complete and utter rubbish, deserving one-star status.

Vampire Bats
VZS Films 2005; 93 minutes; Director: Eric Bross **

Vampire bats that have fed off deer contaminated with toxic waste turn nasty and attack the residents of Mercier, Louisiana.

It's slightly more agreeable than the similar *Bats* (1999), but not much. Husband and wife teachers Dylan Neal and Lucy Lawless, new to the town of Mercier, investigate a number of killings whereby the bodies are covered in bite marks and contain traces of waste chemicals. Ritualistic murders are ruled out as a possible cause when a huge colony of bats descends on two parties; a posh do on a riverboat, and an underground teen bash in the college's steam room. Timothy Bottoms plays a slippery mayor who is actually on the side of good this time, exposing Ranger Liam Waite's shady dealings with a chemical company who have been pouring poisonous sludge into the swamps, affecting the food chain. The winged terrors are finally conquered by luring them into the steam room via amplified signals and giving them a deadly steam bath. "We've seen it all before" springs to mind when sitting through this distinctly average thriller: Acting, direction and photography are all adequately presented, but there's nothing here to stir the blood, and older viewers

will undoubtedly want to give the teen party sequences and all that they entail a big miss.

Warbirds aka Mega-Raptor vs. Humans
New Symphony Pictures/Clockwork Planet 2008; 85 minutes;
Director: Kevin Gendreau **

In the spring of 1945, Americans and Japanese stranded on a Pacific island battle a species of ferocious winged dinosaur.

Jamie Elle Mann, her team of glammed-up W.A.C.s and soldiers led by sour-faced brass hat Brian Krause crash-land on an island populated by the remnants of Tohoru Masamune's patrol; three months earlier, the Japs blasted

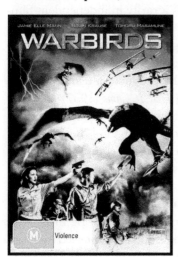

into a cave system, discovering hundreds of huge eggs and their angry prehistoric owners. The B-29 bomber that Mann commands houses an atomic bomb, to be dropped on Japan; only grumpy Krause knows about the mission, hence the reason for his abrupt manner and stony countenance. The ladies, the grunts and the Japs forget their differences and fight off the flying monsters in a series of land

and aerial battles using Japanese Zero jets. Only Mann, her co-pilot and the pilot of the escort Zero make it off the island alive, Krause sacrificing himself by letting loose the big nuclear warhead from the bomb bay and jumping out after it; there's an almighty explosion, destroying the pursuing dinos, but Mann manages to steer the B-29 clear of the blast. The dialogue is straight from 2008, not 1945, the girls' lipstick stays a bright red throughout, their '40s hairdos remain unruffled, their tunics are unsoiled after 80-odd minutes of mayhem and pain-in-the-ass Krause defines the very meaning of the word "wooden." It's those flying 'raptors that make the whole dullish exercise reasonably viewable.

Yeti aka Curse of the Snow Demon
American World Pictures 2008; 87 minutes;
Director: Paul Ziller ***

A plane carrying an American football team to Tokyo crash-lands in the Himalayas; not only are the survivors up against cold and hunger, but a ferocious strain of the Abominable Snowman.

Kicking off with a pretty alarming plane crash filched from 1992's *Alive*, Ziller's take on *The Snow Creature*, *Half Human* and other '50s B Yeti pictures is perky horror fodder for the indiscriminating punter. Blond hunk Marc

Menard plays the jock trying to hold everything together as one of the white-haired monsters (there are two of them) emerges from its cave, salivating at the sight of all those dead passengers laying there in the snow, a ready-made feast just waiting to be snacked upon. Two of the survivors trek through the wastes to retrieve a radio and have a confrontation with the beast in its lair, Menard has to make the difficult decision for the survivors to eat meat from the corpses to combat starvation and a chopper off-loads two rescuers, inept rescuers as it turns out—both are torn to pieces by the Yeti. The movie is chock-a-block with incongruities: First the creature has blood all over its face, then it doesn't, then it does; the survivors search for matches among the dead, anxious to build a fire, even though the area is littered with burning wreckage; the Yeti leaps over considerable distances as though it's on a pogo stick; the Canadian Rockies stand in for the Himalayas; and when Menard ends up in a five-minute kiss with Carly Pope after one of the monsters has plummeted down a cliff, bear in mind that the two of them haven't cleaned their teeth for several days *and* have partaken of human flesh. Ugh! The "just when you thought it was all over" climax works, as does the semi-surprise/shock closing seconds. Notwithstanding its faults, *Yeti* is decent monster hokum that keeps up a speedy pace throughout.

Sci-Fi

Apex aka **A.P.E.X.**
Green Comms./Republic 1994; 98 minutes;
Director: Phillip J. Roth ****

In the year 2073, a scientist is accidentally hurled back 100 years in time; when he returns, he finds himself in an alternative world to that which he left, the population affected by a virus carried by himself.

For a low-budget effort, *Apex* is surprisingly imaginative sci-fi; the movie has pace, decent effects, a script that makes sense and believable performances, especially from Richard Keats, the unfortunate scientist who finds himself back in a very different world to the one he left; nobody recognizes him (and that includes wife Lisa Ann Russell) and Earth is a wasteland patrolled by robots originally designed to sterilize and eliminate paradoxes in time—now they hunt humans in packs. To put matters right in his own dimension, Keats has to locate the facility he disappeared from, create a new time window and travel through it. Commando leader Mitchell Cox refuses to believe Keats' tales of time travel, even when people are sucked into thin air right in front of him as the time paradox grows stronger. It all ends on a high note, Keats reunited with his now

pregnant wife, the parallel world he left behind destroyed along with its infections. Slightly *Terminator 2* in drift, *Apex* contains enough action and set pieces to satisfy most sci-fi addicts, doesn't drag its heels and looks good to boot.

Apollo 18
Dimension Films/Bekmambetov Projects Ltd 2011;
86 minutes; Director: Gonzalo López-Gallego ****

Classified footage reveals the true reason why NASA canceled its Apollo space program; *Apollo 18* landed near Earth's satellite's South Polar region in December 1974 and was never heard of again.

Made for $5,000,000 and raking in $25,000,000 on its limited worldwide release, Canada/US-produced *Apollo 18* is composed entirely of scratchy color/black-and-white 16mm film footage, lacks any form of music and will force all those who were handed free samples of moon rock by the Nixon administration to give much closer inspection to their collections. In Gonzalo López-Gallego's cleverly constructed thriller, those rocks contain spidery crustaceans that have nourished themselves on the sole crew member of a Russian lunar module (on a top secret mission), the craft and shriveled corpse of the astronaut discovered by Lloyd Owen and Warren Christie; Owen soon has one of the things crawling inside his face helmet (and his body) and staggers back to the *Liberty* module with Christie, only to find communications with NASA and Commander Ryan Robbins, orbiting in *Freedom*, down. There are several striking (a very authentic-looking) shots of the astronauts on the moon's surface near a vast impact crater and the creatures are just that *tiny* bit believable, bearing in mind the moon is composed of lifeless rock (or supposed to be!). Needless to say, the three men have to perish in the name of science, protocol and American self-esteem, NASA's Department of Defense left with no alternative ("We made a decision. We can't bring you home. We can't take the risk. We'll let your families know you all died as heroes. This decision is final."). Owen, covered in the mini-monsters, is now a gibbering human wreck, so Christie leaves him behind, blasting off to dock with Robbins, NASA warning that they will terminate the mission in 60 seconds. Rocks in the *Liberty*'s cabin explode into hundreds of creatures, Christie panics and his module, out of control, crashes into the *Freedom*; end of mission *without* NASA's cold-hearted intervention. A riveting faux space documentary opus that conjures up a genuine sense of claustrophobic terror set in a desolate, totally isolated, environment. Note: Online sources state the *Apollo 18* landing took place in December 1973; on the seventh minute, Owen clearly states that touchdown is on December 25th, 1974.

The Blackout
Starway Pictures 2009; 80 minutes;
Director: Robert David Sanders ****

Christmas Eve: Los Angeles is rocked by a series of tremors, releasing from deep underground ferocious humanoids that start to prey on humans. Earthquakes, power surges, unseasonably high temperatures, electrical malfunctions, erratic mobile phone reception—what phenomenon is causing this?

That's the intriguing premise and for 40-odd minutes Sanders keeps us guessing by placing his relatively small cast within the confines of the Ravenwood apartment block, trapped while all around them their cozy close-knit world collapses. Joseph Dunn and Barbara Streifel Sanders' two kids disappear in the basement and a group of partygoers invades their apartment when one of their friends is slaughtered by a shadowy figure lurking in the darkness; meanwhile, deep down in that basement, crustaceans resembling prehistoric arthropods slither across the floor, sulfurous gas circulates and huge shafts of rock burst out of the foundations. *The Blackout* is a sci-fi horror film without a proper resolution, but before you criticize the abrupt ending, think on: *Cloverfield* and *The Mist* are just two examples of recent, big-budget horror movies that didn't end conclusively and both had excellent reviews in the press. *The Blackout* contains that carefully edited, compelling opening 40 minutes, atmospheric sets, artful direction, lucid dialogue (not a single "Oh my God!" is uttered) and deadly, green-eyed, scaly humanoids sporting tails tipped with pincers. The fatalistic closer has Sanders, daughter Abigail Droeger and radio ham Anthony Tedesco on the rooftops, staring out over a Los Angeles in complete ruins, colossal volcanic vents spewing fiery liquid over the streets. Ignore those negative comments posted on the internet—*The Blackout* is short, tension-filled and very sweet.

The Cold Equations
USA Pictures/Alliance 1996; 92 minutes;
Director: Peter Geiger ***

An astronaut is commissioned to deliver a quantity of viral vaccine to LC10, a distant mining planet, but a female stowaway upsets the ship's equilibrium and he is ordered to jettison her into space to enable him to land safely.

This low-key sci-fi flick is principally based around a moral dilemma—should Bill Campbell disobey orders and save his argumentative, unwanted passenger (Poppy Montgomery), or should he get rid of her in order to deliver the vaccine (which, it transpires, is not all that important). As the two form a close attachment, various parts of the vessel are disposed of through the escape hatch to lighten the load but it all turns out to be in vain and, in the end,

UNDER TEN MILLION? ANYTHING'S POSSIBLE!

Montgomery sacrifices herself for the good of all; Campbell is subsequently given 15 years hard labor for his pains. Nice interaction between the two leads and a well-worn subplot concerning corporate skulduggery versus the downtrodden minority is ruined by dismal cinematography—most scenes are so dark, it's hard to see what's going on. The special effects are negligible

but *The Cold Equations* is all about human drama in a confined setting and as such is slightly more thoughtful in its approach than most cheapo space operas.

Cold Fusion

UFO 2011; 90 minutes; Director: Ivan Mitov *

A terrorist force in the Ukraine has created EMP (Electro-Magnetic-Pulse) weapons using alien technology gleaned from the wreckage of a flying saucer, shot down over the Soviet Union in 1979 and taken to a secret research facility, their aim to start a world war by way of a doomsday device.

And it's up to kick-boxing secret agents-cum-babes Sarah Brown and Michelle Lee to infiltrate the hidden military base and destroy the weapons before the Middle East's major cities are blown to smithereens by Kitodar Todorov and his gang, triggering a Holy War. Like two episodes of 1960s *Star Trek* stitched together, this sci-fi/disaster/cloak-and-dagger mystery adventure includes a lengthy, fairly erotic lesbian dance rehearsal whereby Lee tries it on with Brown, successfully as a matter of fact! It's

all rather dull, indie tough guy regular Adrian Paul's talents wasted playing the girls' commanding officer, the sets unimaginative, the action scenes laughable, the narrative bland to the point of boredom. Even the sight of the repaired alien UFO trying to take off from its hangar near the end is poor compensation for a paucity of ideas. Filmed in bleak-looking Bulgaria, *Cold Fusion* is one for diehards to catch once before resigning it to the attic of their memory.

Digital Man
Green Comms./Sci-Fi Pictures 1995; 95 minutes; Director: Phillip J. Roth ***

A prototype cyborg, the D1, is sent to wipe out terrorists who have downloaded launch codes to 250 nuclear missiles: Mission accomplished, the army then orders an assault team to destroy the machine because it could use the information for its own advantage.

Easier said than done—the armor-plated D1 model (a cross between RoboCop and Terminator) possesses awesome destructive powers, seemingly too much for Ken Olandt and his squad to handle when they track the killing machine down to the town of Badwater, deep in the Nevada Desert. Unknown to Olandt, three of his colleagues are androids, and he's also completely unaware that General Ed Lauter is double-crossing all and sundry, wanting the disc containing the launch codes for himself. After all, they're worth $2 billion in reward money. A fast-paced shoot-up filmed with more flair than usual in harsh desert surroundings: Matthias Hues is splendidly deadpan as the D1, local white trailer-trash Susan Tyrrell, Don Swayze and Chase Masterson overact to the point of parody and the action sequences hit the right buttons; the baddies get their just deserts after an explosive climax in an underground nuclear silo. Played out to a pseudo-Ennio Morricone soundtrack, *Digital Man* is super-duper fun for video game fanatics, and even older hands might find it watchable.

Escape from Mars

Credo Entertainment 1999; 100 minutes;
Director: Neill Fearnley ***

In 2015, three men and two women blast off to Mars in the *Sagan* spacecraft and find themselves stranded on the Red Planet in survival mode when a meteor storm disables their means of returning to Earth.

It's highly improbable that Ridley Scott caught this straight-to-TV movie before embarking on his $108,000,000 production of *The Martian* (2015), but there are vague similarities in plot and characterization; Touchstone's *Mission to Mars* and Warner Bros.' *Red Planet*, both released in 2000, figure in there somewhere as well. Commanders Christine Elise and Peter Outerbridge, scientist Allison Hossack, space architect Michael Shanks and Russian biochemist Kavan Smith all turn in understated, believable performances as they try to come to terms with being stuck on Mars; mission control, headed by kindly Julie Khaner and corporate sleazeball Ron Lea, boss of IMV, do their utmost to come up with a solution to bring the astronauts back in between arguing over the mission's merits at the expense of human life. Exploring a network of caves that harbor minerals, primitive chemical protozoans and frozen water, Smith's spacesuit is punctured during a storm when their buggy overturns. Outerbridge, distraught at his recent divorce, sacrifices himself, giving

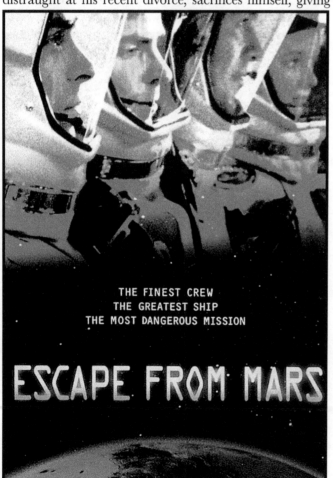

THE FINEST CREW
THE GREATEST SHIP
THE MOST DANGEROUS MISSION

ESCAPE FROM MARS

the Russian his own oxygen and expiring. With one less drain on their depleting air supply and fuel, the crew make repairs to their ship (resembling a space shuttle) and are eventually able to take off from Mars. Yes, the effects are cheap-looking but strangely effective, towering rocky cliffs set in an orange glow standing in for the Martian surface, while the space scenes are not much better than those depicted in the original *Star Trek* 1960s television series, though adequate enough in this setup—it's the acting that counts here, giving this entertaining little space opera an unassuming air of expertise made on low finances.

Fallout

Royal Oaks Entertainment 1999; 90 minutes;
Director: Rodney McDonald ***

An experimental space shuttle is sent to engage with terrorists who have taken command of a joint Russian/American space station.

Russia is on the point of invading neighboring Tadjikistan. Soviet astronaut Frank Zagarino and his confederates have seized control of the *Gateway* space station and inform NASA that if Russia doesn't withdraw its troops from the conflict in 12 hours, they will blitz major American cities with nuclear missiles. Enter Daniel Baldwin who, although concerned about the shuttle's capabilities in

space, flies the X33 prototype to the *Gateway* with a team of commandos in the hope of stopping Zagarino from nuking the Earth. Solid and old-fashioned, rather like the Cold War/space co-features that proliferated throughout the 1960s, *Fallout* has a reasonably cohesive script, basic but serviceable model work and workmanlike performances. It's not exactly pumped-up entertainment, but you could do a lot worse than give it a go. One question: Why do filmmakers insist on kitting out their female boffins with over-large black spectacles. Does it make them look more intelligent than they really are?

Fugitive Mind

Royal Oaks Entertainment 1999; 94 minutes;
Director: Fred Olen Ray **

Discharged from a US Special Forces unit, a homeless sniper is snatched by agents, given a new identity via a mind implant and programed to assassinate a local senator.

A poor man's *Manchurian Candidate* whose cast includes David Hedison (the senator), Barry Newman (head of

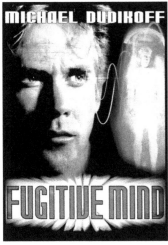

GENCOM) and Ian Ogilvy (the doctor dealing in mind implants). They're probably the best things in a dull thriller that treads old ground, hampered by a stilted lead performance from Michael Dudikoff as the subject of Ogilvy's experiments in brainwashing, mind manipulation and cloning. Dudikoff constantly suffers from flashbacks to his previous life, involving girlfriend Heather Langenkamp (also captured), and disturbing visions of a future which sees him bumping off Hedison. After numerous escapes from GENCOM's goons, Dudikoff is recaptured and reprogramed ("Are You Ready?" is the signal for him to act), but the company's plans to eliminate the senator go belly-up. The ex-marine accidentally shoots corrupt politician Chick Vennera, the stooge who was double-crossing Hedison behind his back. Newman is then ordered to restore Dudikoff to normal—his old self again, the guy waltzes off with Langenkamp in the final few minutes. Full of guilt at his unethical actions, Newman does the decent thing and shoots himself. A mundane direct-to-video effort that passes the time pleasantly enough, similar to one of those Cold War feature films that were *de rigueur* in cinemas during the 1960s.

The Last Days on Mars
BFI/Irish Film Board/Qwerty Films/Fantastic Films
2013; 89 minutes; Director: Ruari Robinson ***

In the 2040s, a crew member from Mars base Tantalus, part of the *Aurora 2* mission, falls into a pit that opens at his feet and emerges a flesh-eating zombie, infecting his comrades.

Britain's BFI and the Irish Film Board splashed out an unprecedented £7,000,000 on their ambitious space opera which could so easily have been titled *Zombies on Mars*, because that's precisely what the movie is all about. Despite impressive Martian landscapes (filmed in Jordan) at the start (almost as good, in parts, as many scenes that would appear in Ridley Scott's *The Martian*) and realistic space hardware, plus a tense buildup, the second half of the film consists of Liev Schreiber, Romola Garai and Johnny Harris on the run from six other crew members who have turned into black-faced ghouls able to survive in the thin Martian atmosphere without helmets. At the end of a six-month stint on the planet, and due to be relieved in 19 hours time by the orbiting *Aurora*, Goran Kostic is the reckless astronaut responsible for wrecking the homeward bound trip, insisting on exploring fungus-like growths

found on rock faces at a nearby site with Yusra Warsama and tumbling into a gaping crater. Schreiber visits the spot in Rover 1 and is lowered down the crevasse which is covered in the growths that have the ability to transform humans into aggressive zombies lacking all traces of their former personalities; but Kostic and Warsama have disappeared, their footprints wandering off into the night. The pair returns like savage animals, attacking the base domes; after repeated assaults, Schreiber scrambling from one base to the other via a lengthy, claustrophobic connecting tunnel (images from *Alien* and *It! The Terror from Beyond Space* spring to mind here), it's a case of "nobody makes it out alive." Garai, suffering from a deep wound that is immune to antibiotics, staggers out into the desert wastes, morphing into a zombie, Schreiber bashing her head in with a rock to put her out of her misery. The *Aurora* landing craft's crew is slaughtered by the Martian walking dead; on board the lander, Harris, after blasting off for the mother ship, begins to mutate; he's killed by Schreiber, the body jettisoned into space. But Schreiber *could* be infected; taking no chances, he contacts mission control, informs them of the situation and elects to plummet back onto the Martian surface, the craft burning up on re-entry, thus saving himself from becoming cursed with zombieism. Kicking off as an

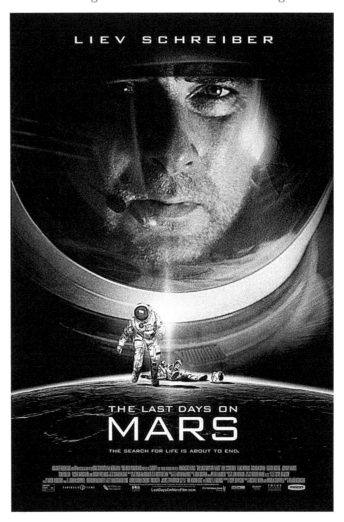

A feature, then escalating into indie-zombie shenanigans, it's easy to see why *The Last Days on Mars*, distributed by Universal on a limited release basis, was unsuccessful. The feature comes across as yet one more zombie outing, albeit in a novel setting, all show and very little substance; what was required was not only a named star but a much stronger storyline to carry the action than the one on display here, to match those eye-catching visuals, one case where a Martian monster of some kind was urgently needed to attract more interest from a wider audience.

Living Hell aka Organizm
Dark Lot Entertainment/MWM 2008; 92 minutes;
Director: Richard Jefferies ***

A rapidly growing mutated biological organism escapes from an underground bunker and only one man, immune to its disease, can stop it.

Living Hell has, for a low-budget sci-fi actioner, a quite brilliant opening 15 minutes: A military installation is being shut down and Johnathon Schaech, whose parents worked there in 1958, has to get an urgent message to the authorities—on any account, do *not* disturb the contents of vault 12, sub-level 3. But when he delivers the message to the base in person, the military do just that, releasing a deadly creature resembling pulsating tree roots that spreads like wildfire and threatens the nearby community.

Because Schaech's father created the thing as a biological weapon, his genes are immune; after discovering his blood can cause it to shrivel and die, Schaech heads back to the base with Erica Leerhsen to drip blood into the organism's nucleus which happens to be in the chest cavity of his father's preserved corpse. Nicely paced and containing decent creature effects, *Living Hell* delivers the thrills with a certain amount of aplomb, even if you have to wonder how on earth Schaech doesn't lapse into unconsciousness after continually slicing his hands and wrists with broken glass to either smear blood over Leerhsen to keep the creature at bay or spill the red stuff over its tendrils.

Nautilus
Royal Oaks Entertainment 2000; 97 minutes;
Director: Rodney McDonald ***

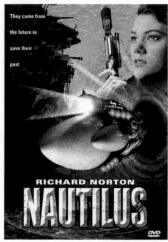

In the year 2099, Earth has become a polluted wasteland, so submarine *Nautilus* travels back in time to 1999 in order to prevent a possible catastrophic boring operation damaging mankind's future.

The operation is taking place on the *Prometheus* rig, drilling into the Earth's crust to tap its molten energy. Captain of the *Nautilus* Christopher Kriesa reckons that the detonations used to break into the magma will cause worldwide cataclysms that will ultimately lead to the kind of future he has arrived from. When the time traveling submarine appears at the rig site, Kriesa warns everybody that he will destroy the structure if operations don't cease forthwith. Head of operations Victor Eschbach thinks he's a fraud. In the meantime, a gang of terrorists has infiltrated the rig, keeping security boss Richard Norton on his toes. *Nautilus* is *20,000 Leagues Under the Sea* in a different guise and of its type is reasonably entertaining hokum. Kriesa's attractive daughter (Miranda Wolfe) ferries two scientists plus Eschbach and Norton to the *Nautilus* via a mini-sub, where the captain shows them recordings of the planet's grim future to prove that his warning is the truth. The sting in the tail here is that the *Prometheus* project is ultimately doomed; Kriesa realizes that his submarine is the catalyst for things to come and, Jules Verne style, blows it to pieces, and him with it. A cut-price Victorian-looking *Nautilus*, bags of incident and a robust performance from Kriesa, playing the Captain Nemo figure, all filmed at a quick pace, will ensure that your attention won't lag over the movie's 97-minute running time.

UNDER TEN MILLION? ANYTHING'S POSSIBLE!

The Sender

PM Entertainment 1998; 98 minutes;
Director: Richard Pepin *

A young girl whose grandfather disappeared over the Bermuda Triangle in 1965 while engaged in a skirmish with a UFO has inherited the "sender gene," a unique alien characteristic that enables its hosts to transport objects to other worlds by force of will alone.

Naturally, the bad old Area 51 government agents, headed by stone-faced Steven Williams, want to get their grubby hands on the girl (Erica Everage) and her other-worldly powers, no matter who gets hurt in the process. If ever there was an Oscar awarded for the title of "Daftest independent science fiction production of the 1990s," *The Sender* would win it, no contest. Badass Michael Madsen plays Everage's father with all the conviction of a person caught sleep-walking; the man looks bored to death. Robert Mitchum perfected this style of acting to a tee in his illustrious career but possessed Hollywood star charisma by the bucketload. Madsen doesn't. Then you have chief grunt R. Lee Ermey—in Kubrick's *Full Metal Jacket*, the pint-sized drill instructor was up against a squad of raw recruits; here, he's up against a gorgeous-looking female alien dressed in silver lamé who sunbathes nude to restore her energy. She's also Everage's "angel," curing the girl of cancer; no wonder Ermey wears a look of frozen bewilderment throughout. Director Pepin throws in a high-speed car chase every few minutes to keep us all on our toes, followed by multiple vehicle pile-ups (including helicopters), everything interspersed with shoot-outs galore (a highlight, or lowlight, of PM's rota of 1990s sci-fi thrillers) as the bad guys try to get their hands on Madsen, his daughter and alien goddess Shelli Lether; all three zoom around Los Angeles in a clapped-out UFO which can mask itself in invisibility, Lether tossing green balls of light at her enemies. Robert Vaughn puts in a guest appearance as Madsen's old buddy; his wife (Dyan Cannon) double-crosses him and gets a bullet for her deception. The baddies are eventually vanquished and Lether (who has monitored Madsen's family for years) is beamed up into a giant *Close Encounters*-type craft in tears after a trio of stick-thin aliens have waved goodbye to Madsen and daughter. Madsen's father then steps down from the ship, reunited with his son (even though they're now the same age); Everage, looking at the pair, fittingly speaks the one line that mirrors the viewer's desperation at sitting through all

of this twaddle: "Can we go now?" "Yes please!" I hear someone shout at the back. Mindless beyond belief, *The Sender* is a hodgepodge of styles and ideas that comes apart at the seams very early on, hindered by bad acting, far-fetched conceptions and soul-destroying, repetitive action sequences. Send this one to another galaxy forthwith!

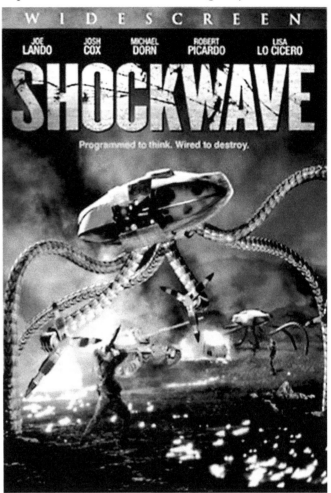

Shockwave aka A.I. Assault

Cinetel Films 2006; 94 minutes;
Director: Jim Wynorski ***

A military plane carrying several experimental robots crash-lands on a deserted Pacific island and a team of commandos is sent to destroy the machines before they run out of control.

Predator meets *The War of the Worlds* as Joe Lando and his grunts troop through the undergrowth in pursuit of the combat robots which resemble the Martian fighting machines from H.G. Wells' classic novel—oval bodies perched on four flexible tentacle-like legs, two flexi-arms at the front which open up, firing laser beams. Meanwhile, the authorities, worried about a possible humans versus aliens war, want to nuke the island regardless of the success of the commandos' mission. *Shockwave* is a lively sci-fi actioner featuring commendable (considering the budget) CGI effects: Okay, you have the hysterical dumb blonde

(Hudson Leick) and the inept female scientist (Lisa LoCicero) charging around aimlessly as the spidery mechanical terrors wreak havoc, and even a short appearance from *Star Trek*'s George Takei, but all in all, this is fast-moving cheapo hokum. After impregnating a man's brain with electrodes to utilise his intelligence, two of the robots are destroyed while cannibalizing a helicopter; the third is crushed under a falling girder that has been struck by lightning. Jim Wynorski and Cinetel Films specialize in this kind of low-budget monster fodder and this is one of their better efforts.

Star Runners aka Termination Shock
Celestial Production/Sci-fi Channel 2009; 80 minutes;
Director: Mat King ***

Two rogue space traders are ordered by the government to transport a top secret crate to Rigel 4; attacked by terrorists, their ship crash-lands on an uncharted world populated by giant bugs.

Star Wars collides with *Starship Troopers* and *The Fifth Element* (plus quite a number of others) in an enjoyable Bulgarian space opera that has rough diamonds Connor Trinneer, James Kyson and assorted passengers on the run from giant crab/spider-type bugs that, it transpires, originated from Earth centuries back and mutated due

to solar flare activity. The crate contains an amnesic girl (Toni Trucks), the sole survivor of the total annihilation of a human colony on Centauri 3; the people were wiped out because they were developing telekinetic powers which the authorities wanted to suppress, seeing it as a threat to civilization. Trucks, her memory restored, has the psychic ability to force out high energy beams from her lithe body, very handy when combating the rampaging spiky monsters, a terrorist group led by Atanas Srebrev and bigwig Michael Culkin's military cruiser—both are after Trucks because of her unusual powers. Their battle cruiser disabled by Trinneer in a neat "avoid those missiles" space maneuver, Culkin plus sidekicks Hristo Mitzkov and lethal female assassin Aja Evans end up marooned on the barren planet, surrounded by hundreds of bugs; Trinneer and Trucks take off for new adventures, planning to expose the real truth behind the destruction on Centauri 3. The effects and hardware are fairly impressive, particularly the opening sequences taking place in a congested asteroid belt and meteor storm, Trinneer does a cheeky take on Harrison "Han Solo" Ford and the monsters (especially the big mother) look the business, as all outer space creatures indeed should. Cheap-looking round the edges, maybe, but *Star Runners* is 80 minutes of diverting, unpretentious space fodder with its tongue set firmly in its cheek.

Stranded aka Black Horizon
Phoenician Entertainment 2001; 92 minutes;
Director: Fred Olen Ray *

Space station *Avna*, fed incorrect re-entry details from saboteurs on Earth, drifts out of orbit towards destruction and a shuttle is sent into space to rescue the crew.

It's very hard to muster up any enthusiasm for this below-par space frolic. First the cast: Michael Dudikoff, playing the space shuttle commander, is about as animated as a wooden plank; Yvette Nipar, the shuttle's captain, is pretty but dumb; Ice-T tries to act the hard-man Federal agent but fails; and Hannes Jaenicke is apparently an aeronautics expert of some kind, sent to repair the *Avna* after it has been bombarded by meteorites. Trouble is, the guy hates heights, suffers from space-sickness and has no special skills—so why on earth include him on such an important mission. The technical effects in Paramount's *Conquest of Space* (1955) were more authentic than those exhibited here, and as for that space walk— you can see the wires! The

tiresome storyline involves espionage, rescuing a couple trapped in the space station's elevator and Ice-T up to his neck in baddies. It goes without saying that Dudikoff and a few others make it to Earth in two capsules after the shuttle has been nicked by Chick Vennera following the break-up of the *Avna* station. You could probably sit through this feeble tosh in 1961, but not in 2001. Out of this world it isn't.

Stryker
HCI Intl. Pictures 1983; 86 minutes;
Director: Cirio H. Santiago **

In a post-apocalyptic world, water is a much-fought over commodity; who controls the water rights controls the planet.

Cheapo *Mad Max* shenanigans filmed mostly inside a vast quarry somewhere in the Philippines with blond hunk Steve Sandor taking on the Mel Gibson role; he's up against baddie Mike Lane and his mob who are anxious to control a freshwater spring found in a hilltop cave. Near the cave is the Colony, a bevy of Amazon-type females equipped with crossbows who guard the precious water. Also thrown into the cobbled-together mix is a tribe of midgets clad

in sackcloth who help out Sandor and his gang from time to time. Vehicle chases across the arid desert landscapes, shoot-outs, rescue missions and a showdown in the cave—all play their part in a sci-fi flick that is extremely rough around the edges, backed by a bizarre avant-garde piano/drum score that seems to belong to a different time and place altogether; the grimy photography doesn't help matters, either. But at least it moves at a blistering pace and in that respect, *Stryker* is reasonably presented futuristic nonsense for the kids. One question: If Earth is critically short of water, how can they afford to run all those vehicles—cars, motorcycles, buggies, trikes, tanks—in a hot climate?

T-Force aka Dark Force: Aliens in Black
PM Entertainment 1994; 95 minutes;
Director: Richard Pepin ***

A scientist is ordered to disable a squad of android soldiers when they inadvertently cause the death of a number of hostages during an anti-terrorist operation—on learning about this, the cybernauts go into "self-preservation" mode and rebel against their creators.

The first 25 minutes of *T-Force* treads *Die Hard* territory: Terrorists who have infiltrated an embassy are eliminated by the cybernauts in one almighty shoot-up, typical

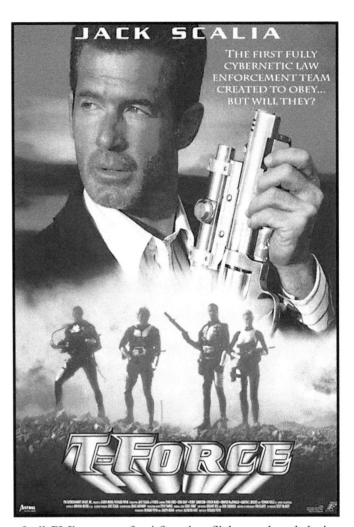

of all PM's quota of sci-fi action flicks produced during the 1990s. Robot-hating Jack Scalia is only too pleased when the mayor's office orders their termination; however, Evan Lurie (leader of the droids) finds out what's going on, wipes out the doctor and his team responsible for their creation and, together with two others, embarks on a murder rampage. Scalia teams up with goodie cybernaut Bobby Johnston to put an end to their reign of terror, meaning a succession of gun battles and explosions before Lurie and his unstoppable colleagues are, one by one, blown to bits. Among all the flames and bullets, Scalia develops a soft spot for Johnston, almost looking upon him as human, and the plot dips its toes into the hoary old "do robots have a useful role to play in society?" theme before jettisoning it in favor of more shoot-outs in a disused steel mill. *T-Force* has slightly more depth than most of Pepin's other efforts but still resembles an extended video game aimed at arcade fanatics.

Terminal Error
Porchlight Entertainment 2002; 90 minutes;
Director: John Murlowski **

Sacked by the boss of computer firm AutoCam, a disgruntled ex-employee creates a super-virus in revenge that runs out of control and targets nuclear power stations.

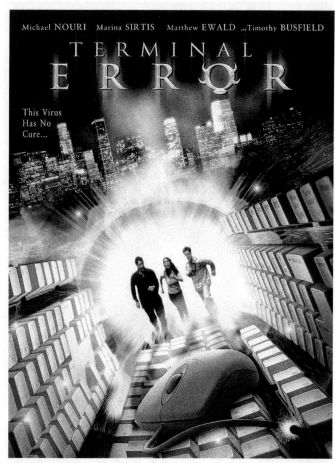

For computer buffs only—most non-techno fans will quickly tire of repeated scenes showing the cast staring into monitors while an intelligent virus sounding like HAL from *2001* taunts them with his superior knowledge. Following a venomous email sent by the virus, a power station in the Ukraine is the first to explode. In Del Vista, California, Michael Nouri's company AutoCam is next on the virus' hate list, each destruction preceded by an irritating musical jingle. Soon, Nouri's precocious son (Matthew Ewald), ex-wife (Marina Sirtis) and wheelchair-bound boffin David Wells (a Stephen Hawking clone) are at their wits' end, trying to figure out how to disable the virus before it decimates the city in an atomic blast. Timothy Busfield plays the guilty computer nerd (and why are these people always portrayed as overweight, unshaven and geeky?) who gets his comeuppance in a plane collision and Nouri's family are reunited after the virus has been vanquished by Ewald's handheld Gameboy. A fairly uninteresting excursion into the world of rogue computers that patently fails to grip.

Termination Point
Cinetel Films/Eagle Pictures 2007; 89 minutes;
Director: Jason Bourque **

An airliner gets caught up in a time vortex and a scientist on board has to repair a damaged teleporter before the plane, the Earth and the universe are all annihilated.

An intriguing premise, perhaps, but unfortunately not given its due in this leaden time travel opus which sinks under the weight of poor performances and stock situations. Grieving security officer Jason Priestley attends the site of a plane crash because his wife and daughter had been on board. However, scientist Lou Diamond Phillips was also a passenger and has a device that can revert time by a day. In other words, all the events that occur over 80 minutes when the plane is sucked into a wormhole in space are reversed once Phillips has managed to activate his handheld machine: Wife Stefanie von Pfetten (shot by a terrorist on the plane) is okay, the plane *doesn't* crash and, most important of all, the massive swirling vortex that is demolishing cities with bolts of lightning and growing larger all the time, threatening to end life on Earth, is dissipated. A crooked agent crops up, after both Phillips' secret and Priestley, so there are a few shoot-ups en route to the happy ending. An uninspired offering from Canadian indie filmmakers Cinetel, one of their lesser efforts by a long way.

Time Under Fire aka Beneath the Bermuda Triangle
Concorde-New Horizons/Royal Oaks Entertainment
1997; 92 minutes; Director: Scott P. Levy **

A submarine commander returns to the year 2077 via a time vortex in the Bermuda Triangle in order to overthrow a corrupt regime.

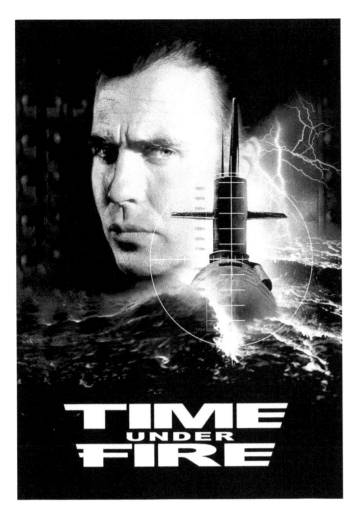

oxygen system; only three of the crew of five can survive on the depleted oxygen, but who will make it to Venus before the air runs out?

Based on Arthur C. Clarke's 1949 short story, *Breaking Strain*, *Trapped in Space* was farmed out to Paramount Television by its producers and has "TV movie" written all over it: Cheap-looking color; static direction; and *Star Trek*-type effects. But there's a fair degree of suspense to be had in the way the disparate crew members react to the catastrophe: Self-centered womanizer Jack Wagner; tough family man Jack Coleman; earnest cadet Sigrid Thornton; loose cannon Craig Wasson; and twitchy Kay Lenz, left in charge when Captain Kevin Colson jumps ship in a lifeboat to save his own skin; all argue and bicker as to who should stay, and who should be the sacrificial lambs by drinking a euthanasia mix. But fate takes a hand in reducing their numbers: Thornton is the first to go in a bloody manner, her body imploding in

A dreary nautical time travel opus featuring a stilted Jeff Fahey in duel roles, the commander and the commander's long-haired son. Six years after disappearing with the loss of 100 men, Fahey returns from his time travels and convinces the authorities to mount an expedition into the future to terminate despot Bryan Cranston's reign. Flashing backwards and forwards between the first trip into the future and the second, the action (and plot) is confusing to say the least, with an over-abundance of shoot-ups, and if the future is as bleak as depicted here, God save us all (apparently, it's the result of an American-Iraqi nuclear war). There are human clones who foam at the mouth with what appears to be green paint splashed over them, and the end segment has you wondering who is a replica of their former selves, and who isn't. You also get the old time travel standby: If Cranston is eliminated in the present, how will it affect the future? A rather dull sci-fi adventure redeemed somewhat by the convoluted twists and turns in the final 10 minutes.

Trapped in Space

Village Roadshow Pictures/Wilshire Court Prods. 1995; 87 minutes; Director: Arthur Allan Seidelman ****

Five months into its six-month mission, cargo vessel *Venture*'s hull is pierced by a small asteroid, damaging the

its spacesuit as she attempts to repair the damage to the hull, the suit snagged on metal and puncturing. Next is Wasson who's gone berserk, his throat cut by Lenz after he's killed her pet dog; grief-stricken, she then commits suicide. With now only enough oxygen left for one astronaut, Wagner and Coleman draw lots; in a trick ending, Coleman, who drew the short straw, is saved along with Wagner, replacing the unknown passenger in frozen suspension and revived when a rescue team boards the *Venture*. Colson is unmasked as a cowardly deserter, and the curtain closes on the ship cruising down to the surface of Venus. A neat little sci-fi thriller that would have been a worthy addition to the Allan Sandler and Robert Emenegger productions discussed elsewhere, of which it closely resembles.

UKM: Ultimate Killing Machine
235 Films/Archetype Films 2006; 90 minutes;
Director: David Mitchell **

Recruitment is down, so the army takes on dropouts and, by experimentation, changes them into super-soldiers. Unfortunately, their first experiment has turned out horribly haywire—decorated Gulf War hero Simon Northwood, pumped full of drugs and other chemicals, his stem cells mutated as a result, is now an indestructible madman, prowling the corridors and reducing people to mincemeat.

When four misfits turn up (Mac Fye, Steve Arbuckle, Victoria Nestorowicz, Erin McKinnon) as the next batch of so-called killing machines, Northwood runs riot and the Millhaven Research Institute becomes a slaughterhouse. One day, Michael Madsen is going to make a decent movie but *UKM* isn't it. The actor goes through his tried and tested grunting, dead-eyed routine as the center's commanding officer, while the younger members of the cast argue, brawl and swear their way through the dimly lit

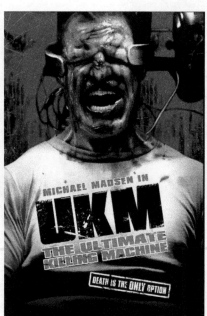

complex, on the run from both Madsen and Northwood. Two make it out, the institute blown up by Fye after the zombie-like soldier has killed Madsen and the scientists responsible for his condition. Mundane and tiresome, *UKM* plays like an 18-rated video game, lacking cinematic finesse in most areas. Madsen won't be winning any awards for this one.

French poster for *Velocity Trap*

Velocity Trap
UFO 1999; 86 minutes; Director: Phillip J. Roth **

A federal space vessel carrying $40 billion is hijacked by space pirates.

Ken Olandt stars as the pirate leader, tough-guy Olivier Gruner the opposition Olandt and his team run into. A run-of-the-mill outer space actioner from UFO which gets off to a slow start, dealing with Gruner's frame-up over the death of a leading figure on a mining planet. Once we're in outer space, and the pirates are on board the ship, the action livens up, with plenty of gunplay and two delectable babes in the form of Jorja Fox (the baddie) and Alicia Coppola (the goodie). Another spanner in Olandt's plans (apart from Gruner) is an asteroid looming large on the horizon. The ship is on a collision course with it, meaning all that money will count for nothing if they smash into the rock. Naturally, Gruner wins the day, winding up in hibernation sleep next to Coppola, with that stack of cash at their disposal. The special effects are excellent (including a brief attack on Gruner by a sanitation robot), compensating for a less-than-sparkling storyline and stodgy script. All right in parts, but not particularly riveting.

SHARKS

Avalanche Sharks aka Snow Sharks

Odyssey Media/Pulser Prods. 2014; 82 minutes;
Director: Scott Wheeler *

Tourists at a ski resort in the Mammoth Mountains are attacked by sharks appearing under the snow, as prophesied in ancient Indian legends.

Something has to be seriously amiss in an 82-minute horror shark movie when all you get is five minutes of shark action and even then, the only things you'll eventually see are blue fins cruising above the snow and close-ups of reptilian shark skin; the gore count is also too low. A corrupt businessman, a local hick shouting doom and gloom, a skirt-chasing nerd, an inept sheriff, a few teenage idiots, dumb chicks in bikinis and an abundance of shots of the attractive mountain scenery will lead to restless bums on seats as military hero Alexander Mendeluk, sheriff Richard Gleason and blonde Kate Nauta sit around, talk, gossip and argue while one or two skiers are picked off by the predators, all because a few Indian totem poles have been knocked askew. "There's nowhere to hide," somebody yells at one stage, reflecting the feeling of those viewers brave enough to sit through this lamer than lame effort, summed up in its weak ending: Mendeluk tosses a bomb, destroying two sharks, the totems are straightened by a female skier (an

Indian?), the creatures vanish but, when the totems topple sideways again, the sharks reappear. What a shame that the avalanche that crashed down the mountain side didn't bury the whole production team in reel two.

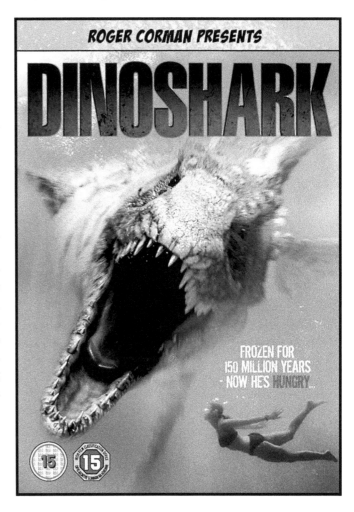

Dinoshark

Concorde/New Horizons 2010; 92 minutes;
Director: Kevin O'Neill **

One hundred and fifty million years after it was imprisoned in an Arctic glacier, a gigantic prehistoric shark revives, makes its way to Puerto Vallarta in Mexico and begins a feeding frenzy.

If producer Roger Corman (he also has a cameo role) had been in the director's seat, would he have injected a bit more zing into this pretty-to-look-at but oddly lifeless monster shark flick. Lanky Eric Balfour (hunk) and fulsome Iva Hasperger (superwoman scientist) are attractive but wooden, the highlights are over in the blink of an eye and the curtain closer (shot in slow motion), whereby Balfour leaps off a jet ski and hurls a grenade at the looming, armor-plated predator, Hasperger yelling, "Welcome to the endangered species list, you bastard," is faintly ridiculous. Throw in a sub-*Jaws* theme and splashes of gore, together with the monster attacking boats and chomping up members of an aquatic polo team, bikini babes, surfers and parasailers, and you are left with soggy fare that could have done with a hefty dose of Corman's renowned suspense and tension—after all, this was the man who thrived on low-budget fodder, bringing us a string of minor '50s classics such as *Attack of the Crab Monsters*, *The Wasp Woman* and *Not of this Earth*, not forgetting his Edgar Allan Poe films. Surely some of his undoubted expertise could have rubbed off on O'Neill's shoulders and made *Dinoshark* a higher-rated movie than it turned out to be.

Ghost Shark
Active Entertainment 2013; 87 minutes;
Director: Griff Furst ***

The coastal resort of Small Point is menaced by the ghost of a Great White Shark whose evil entity is somehow connected to a cave with mystical properties.

In the redneck community of Small Point, a giant blue-glowing shark gobbles up fisherfolk, beach bimbos and jocks, alcoholic lighthouse keeper Richard Moll knowing its secret but not letting on. Years back, he murdered his wife and blamed it on the Great White whose body lies in the mystic cavern. According to superstitious legend, those suffering a violent death in the cave are resurrected to seek retribution; Moll now has one angry, finned son-of-a-bitch on his hands! It sounds preposterous, but director Griff Furst drives the action along as teens Mackenzie Rosman, Sloane Coe and Dave Davies form an unlikely

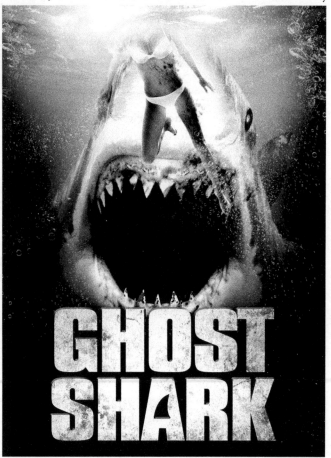

alliance with Moll in order to rid the seas, and even the local pools and water supplies, of the translucent monster (this thing's a ghost, able to materialize anywhere!). An inordinate number of victims are cut in two (Mayor Lucky Johnson is dismembered) in a higher-than-high gore level scenario that finishes with Moll eaten by the phantom predator after facing the spirit of his wife, the cave plus shark blown sky-high in a fountain of blue light. An enjoyable supernatural shark romp leaving the viewer with two burning questions: Where are the parents of all those kids who troop in and out of their houses as if they own them? And why has Furst introduced so many grossly overweight young males into the proceedings? Was he trying to put some form of cryptic social message across?

Jurassic Shark
TopCat Films/Dudez Prods. 2012; 90 (75) minutes;
Director: Brett Kelly *

Drillers break into a subterranean ice cavern situated above an oil bearing zone, unleashing a giant prehistoric shark that goes on a rampage in a freshwater lake.

"Ladies and Gentleman, the Oscar for Worst Independent Giant Shark Movie goes to … *Jurassic Shark*." Awful sums up Brett Kelly's cheapo Canadian shark offering, both in acting, direction, script, continuity and special effects. There can be no excuses for this genre travesty, even if we are in low-budget land. To kick things off, we have an opening eight minutes where two bimbos in bikinis preen on a beach, every sentence highlighted with "totally awesome/cool," "spaz" and "what the fuck." After they've been thankfully eaten, it's the turn of vocally challenged Angela Parent and her bunch of numbskull thieves who have just stolen a painting worth $62,000,000. Rowing across to an island on the lake, the Megalodon capsizes their boat, the painting sinks and, once ashore, Parent squawks incessantly. Then Emanuelle Carriere, Christine Emes and Celine Filion arrive, their boat having been head-butted by the predator, their male companion chomped to bits. Forced to tag along with Parent's mob, they troop over to the other side of the island to a research center where Vin Diesel look-alike Duncan Milloy tosses the girls into the water with instructions to fish that

painting out, shark or no shark, even though they're on the opposite side to where the painting sank! Note the lack of sound as explosives hit the lake (a dull crack) and *no* sound when Emes empties a gun into the shark's plastic head. Mercifully, Parent's strangulated vowels are silenced when she's swallowed whole, Emes and Carriere the sole survivors after blowing the thing's head off. But unfortunately, it's not over yet. "Even big ugly things can have offspring," says one fisherman to his pal, perched on a rock, only for the pair to disappear in a flash as another flying (yes, flying) monster shark devours them. Giant shark movies *can* work—Asylum's *Mega Shark* efforts are worth catching, while Nu Image's 2004 *Shark Attack 3: Megalodon* is a classic of its type. This isn't the case here—Kelly's creation, when it deigns to appear, that is, resembles something out of a 1930s Walt Disney cartoon (but that's an insult to Disney), increasing and decreasing in size from one frame to the next; the effects in Fred Olen Ray's *Super Shark* seem state of the art by comparison. A 21st-century Edward D. Wood, Jnr. film by any other name that should carry the following health warning: Do *not* purchase this movie at *any* price!

Malibu Shark Attack
Insight Film Studios/Limelight Intl. 2009; 87 minutes; Director: David Lister *

A tsunami caused by an earthquake floods the Californian coastline and hundreds of Goblin sharks home in on the stranded survivors, including a group of lifeguards trapped in a wooden shack and construction workers marooned on a building site.

One of the more inept indie sharks-on-the-prowl offerings: The computer-generated tsunami looks totally unrealistic (pieces of rubbish and an overturned traffic sign the only visible indications of the disaster), the spike-backed sharks, sporting horny protuberances, even more so. The first 20 minutes might just as well be titled *Having Fun on the Beach* because that's all it is; bikini babes and hunky guys arguing over who's dating who, water skiing, paragliding etc, etc. Peta Wilson, Renee Bowen and the rest are easy on the eye but can't act, there's the usual carnage (severed arms and legs, bloodstained water) but not all that much and the script is clichéd beyond belief. Added to that you have a bunch of immature jocks (led by Remi Broadway) fighting over the women's charms and ridicu-  lous scenes of the CGI predators being sliced up underwater by chainsaws, the entire cast fighting them off in the confines of the half-submerged building site. Five eventually survive from both groups as a chopper picks them up. You'll get far more enjoyment, and professionalism, out of Nu Image's trio of *Shark Attack* movies, or Asylum's *Sharknado* series, than can be received in this tawdry effort.

Megalodon aka Sharkzilla
100% Entertainment/Corbitt Digital Films 2002; 90 minutes; Directors: Pat Corbitt and Gary J. Tunnicliffe ****

Off the coast of Greenland, deep sea oil rig *Colossus* breaks into a vast cavern 5,000 feet down on the seabed, releasing shoals of prehistoric fish and a gigantic shark that proceeds to lay siege to the rig and its workforce.

One of the earliest of the Giant Shark series of movies, *Megalodon* has to be commended for its slow, careful build-up, eye-catching set design, intelligent script and believable acting. True, you don't get to see the mighty predator until the 55th minute, but what comes before holds the interest. Reporter Leighanne Littrell and cameraman/boyfriend Fred Belford are given permission to shoot a documentary on *Colossus*, mainly to highlight environmental issues, but oil boss Robin Sachs is having none of it. He argues that what his small team is doing benefits modern-day society and the rig won't pollute the sea. To prove his point, the reporters descend to the seabed in a reinforced elevator to get a close-up view of operations. The effects come into their own here, with imaginative shots of the giant rig and mini-subs at work on the ocean floor. But when tremors are felt and a suction pipe becomes blocked by a ferocious prehistoric fish, the Dinichthys, Sachs realizes all is not well ("This is a juvenile. An adult would be eight foot long. You don't want to find Mum and Dad!"). On the 35th minute, Jennifer Sommerfield steers her mini-sub into a vast cavern that has opened under the drilling head, spewing forth those ancient fish; gliding through darkness lit by masses of exotic phosphorescent creatures, she's enchanted by this fairy tale world in the ocean depths, despite it harboring hidden menaces, a terrific sequence. Megalodon then makes its long-overdue appearance, grabbing a sub in its jaws, ramming the rig and disabling the elevator's guide runners, the occupants having to float to surface and taken off an ice floe by helicopter which crashes onto the rig's platform, killing Belford. Sommerfield loses her life when her sub is seized, boyfriend Al Sapienza navigating his sub into the maw of the monster and setting off depth charges, blowing the thing in half. Three months later off the French coast, Littrell is relaxing on deck, unaware that a 60-foot-long Megalodon has just swam underneath her boat. For purists, Dinichthys and Megalodon existed in different geological ages, but that makes little difference to a hybrid of *The Abyss* and the Giant Shark genre made with a tad more care and attention to plot detail and characterization than is normal in these films.

Raging Sharks
Nu Image/Tosca Pictures 2005; 92 minutes;
Director: Danny Lerner ***

Two alien vessels collide in space and a cylinder breaks free, plummeting to Earth, crashing into a ship and coming to rest in the Bermuda Triangle—five years later, above the very same spot, deep sea complex *Oshona* is carrying out survey work on the wreck, pestered by swarms of aggressive sharks.

Another Nu Image killer-shark fest to add to their *Shark Attack* trilogy and *Shark in Venice* (which Lerner also directed), but this time containing a sub-aliens plot chucked in to spice up the mix. And what a mix. Corin Nemec and pouting Vanessa Angel play husband and wife researchers on board the *Oshona*; mysterious orange crystals scattered over the sea bed (and embedded in the cylinder) are driving sharks crazy; Todd Jensen turns up as a vicious government agent; and a battered-looking Corbin Bernsen is the captain of a sub sent to rescue the *Oshona*'s team when the lab starts to disintegrate. Those crystals, when mixed with deuterium, produce a cold fusion, an unlimited form of energy, and the government wants first in on the action, regardless of who gets hurt. You get a splendid *Star Wars*-type

opening sequence, umpteen gory shark attacks, (including the massacre of dozens of surfers on a Bermudan beach), Jensen running berserk on the *Oshona* and an *Abyss*-type climax as the aliens arrive and retrieve their cylinder. Oh, and Angel's pumped-up scarlet pout is a sight to behold. The continuity is all over the place, as is the overwrought acting and stilted dialogue, but you have to hand it to Nu Image—this addition to their very own *Shark* franchise is a scream from start to finish.

The Reef
Lightning Ent./ProdigyMovies/Screen NSW 2010; 94 minutes; Director: Andrew Traucki *****

When their hired yacht *Boomerang* hits rocks and capsizes on the Great Barrier Reef, four friends attempt a 12-mile swim to an islet, pursued by a Great White Shark.

The Reef, one more in a long line of must-see features from Down Under, is based on an actual event that took place in 1983: Andrew Traucki's lean, mean feature, utilizing frightening footage of a real shark (not a model in sight), wracks up the tension as Damian Walshe-Howling, ex-girlfriend Zoe Naylor and sweethearts Gyton Grantley and Adrienne Pickering, using a surfboard cut in half for floats, head toward Turtle Island, chased by a huge shark. Boat owner Kieran Darcy-Smith elects to stay on the

UNDER TEN MILLION? ANYTHING'S POSSIBLE!

ripped hull of his upturned vessel; he's never seen again. It's the primal fear of what lies beneath those fathomless blue depths that the director skillfully plays upon, filming the action in POV/water level mode; a minimalistic score heightens the stark reality of the situation. Sheer panic sets in as first a large turtle shell floats by, its occupant chewed to grisly pieces. Then Walshe-Howling, the only one wearing a face mask, spots the prowling shark on the hunt for prey. Grantley is the first to go as the predator charges in for the kill, expiring from shock and loss of blood, his leg bitten off; ("I can't swim. Fucking leg's gone."); next is hysterical Pickering, vanishing under the waves in pools of blood, the islet (not the one they were aiming for) in sight. Naylor cuts her foot on sharp rocks when they reach the shallows; the makeshift bandage comes off, the shark homing in on the blood trail and gobbling up Walshe-Howling just as Naylor tries to haul him onto the barren islet; she's rescued the following day. Similar to 2003's *Open Water*, in which two scuba divers are left stranded in shark-infested waters after their tour boat departs without them, *The Reef* will put many off swimming in deep Australian seas for life, such is the sense of overwhelming alarm, the terror of becoming shark bait and the buildup of suspense manufactured

Japanese poster for *The Reef*

in Traucki's pared-to-the-bone, but superior, shark thriller, one of the best of the "sharks at loose in Aussie waters" movies available on the market.

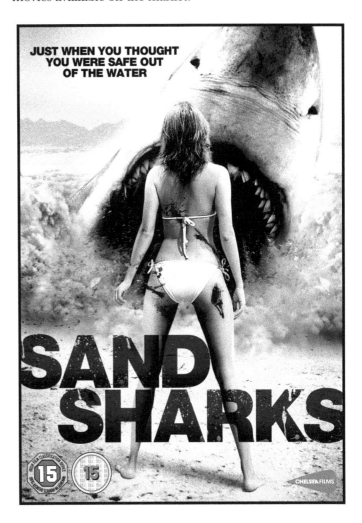

Sand Sharks
American World Pictures/Little Dragon Prods. 2012; 86 minutes; Director: Mark Atkins **

A promoter who plans "the world's biggest beach party" has his major event ruined by jaw-chomping prehistoric sharks that can travel under the sand.

Filmed on California's South Catalina Island and including among its retinue a number of names from Asylum (Mark Atkins, Scott Wheeler, Anthony Fankhauser), *Sand Sharks* is a semi-comic parody of Spielberg's *Jaws*, right down to the "we need a bigger beach" line and Robert Pike Daniel's Quint-like grizzled sea dog. "The beaches stay open. Mayor's orders," barks self-deluded promoter Corin Nemec and we all know exactly what's coming next: Nemec, in the name of profit, chooses to ignore warnings that scaly sharks swim beneath the sands, ready to finish off those partying-on teens and every other cast member, including the main man himself. Sheriff Eric Scott Woods and Brooke Hogan (from *2-Headed Shark Attack*), a blonde, busty scientist with attitude, decide to lure the creatures into a pit by playing Wagner's "The Ride of the Valkyries," melt the sand and imprison them in a glass tomb. It works, but not before Nemec, the mayor, cop Vanessa Evigan, DJ Delpaneaux Willis and lawyer Gina Holden ("Beach parties are to die for," she yells as she's seized between two rows of teeth) have vanished into the maws of the sand-dwelling predators. The effects are variable, Nemec overacts like crazy and the whole tiresome exercise could have been better handled by Asylum who at least would have shown more of the sharks, plus extra helpings of gore; this is *not* as humorous as its makers would have us believe.

Sharktopus
Concorde/New Horizons 2010; 89 minutes;
Director: Declan O'Brien *

A shark/octopus hybrid bred as a military weapon discards its electronic tag and embarks on a killing spree along the Mexican coast.

None other than Roger Corman produced this supremely silly monster caper boasting picturesque sunny scenery and little else. Tired-looking Eric Roberts stars as the creator of S-11 (or Sharktopus) and when the abomination runs riot, chomping up beach lovers, surfers and bungee jumpers, Roberts, daughter Sara Malakul Lane and Iraq veteran Kerem Bursin set out to kill it using an explosive dart. A surfeit of honed bikini babes coupled with dreadful acting, a trite script, several scenes padded out to bolster the running time and a truly ludicrous, plastic-looking monstrosity that wouldn't frighten a five-year-old—Corman (who has a minor part, not much more than a walk-on) could get away with hogwash like this during the 1950s (and did, quite frequently!), but not in 2010. It doesn't even fall into the "it's so bad it's good" category.

Super Shark
Synthetic Filmwerx/Boomgates 2011; 87 minutes;
Director: Fred Olen Ray ***

An oil rig pumps a chemical weathering agent into bedrock off the coast of California in an attempt to locate oil but causes an earthquake, unleashing a gigantic prehistoric shark into the ocean.

In the plethora of giant shark movies to have been foisted onto the public by the independent film outfits since the 1990s, *Super Shark* is no better or worse than many others of its kind. Sarah Lieving puts in a measured performance as the marine biologist attempting to uncover John Schneider's shady methods of drilling, charging his company, Treymar Oil, with contaminating the ocean, while skipper Tim Abell backs her cause. As for the shark, this one can walk ("They say it came out of the water and walked on its fins!"), home in on radio waves and even leap out of the sea to grab aircraft. Feeding on a bevy of hot beach babes, the mighty Megalodon head-butts a submarine, capsizes boats, battles a walking tank and is finally dispatched in a cave by Lieving after she throws explosives down its gullet. Full marks to the producers for having giggly, puerile Shane Van Dyke, Carolyn Martin and Rya Meyers gobbled up in the first 20 minutes, but black marks for including Jimmie Walker as flamboyant DJ Dynamite Stevens, an irritant of the first order. Filmed in glossy widescreen, *Super Shark* maintains the interest due to decent acting, lively direction, plenty of attractive young girls and a corny looking CGI monster that looks perfectly at home within the movie's cheapo framework.

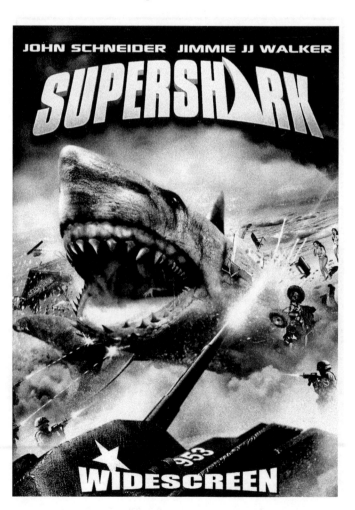

Albino Farm

Labor 13 Films 2009; 89 minutes; Director: Joe Anderson ***

Four teenagers driving through the Ozark Mountains on a cultural history project stop at the town of Shiloh and decide to investigate a condemned farmhouse, despite warnings from the locals to steer clear of the place.

Bigheaded Nick Richey, flighty girlfriend Alicia Lagano and more sensible couple Sunkrish Bala and Tammin Sursok shouldn't have been so dismissive about Shiloh's legend concerning a farm where souls cursed with eternal damnation take out their vengeance on the local redneck population by having them produce deformed children. After all, the signs are there for all the world to see that something is not quite right: A scabrous midget scraping up road kill; a blank-eyed hick quoting a passage from the Book of Leviticus relating to lost spirits; a waitress with a deformed left hand; a dumb boy carrying a chalk board for communication; the elderly church warden suckling a grotesque infant; and three youths who state that they will take them to the farm if Lagano flashes her twin assets at them (which she does, much to our delight as well as their's). But no—Richey and Lagano decide to ignore the alarm bells and check the old farmhouse out but are left stranded when the three hicks drive off in the dark; at least this shuts up the garrulous Richey. We are then plunged into "let's get the hell away from here" territory as Richey, Lagano and their two friends (escorted to the place by the dumb boy) are terrorized by a gang of pug-ugly hillbillies all brandishing meat hooks, the deviants inhabiting a system of caves and feeding on raw flesh. Surviving the ensuing carnage after Bala has destroyed the caves by igniting gas cylinders, bloodied Sursok runs off and staggers into a packed marquee, much of the congregation suffering from physical defects, presided over by an albino Bible-thumper, having no choice but to join in and repent her sins. Briskly shot and oozing menacing rustic atmosphere, *Albino Farm* is a well-presented addition to the *Wrong Turn/Timber Falls* category of redneck horror and won't disappoint fans of the genre.

Altitude

Darclight Films/Foundation Features 2010; 86 minutes; Director: Kaare Andrews **

Five teenagers embark on a trip in a twin engine light aircraft, fly into a huge storm and become entwined in supernatural events relating to the pilot and her boyfriend.

Years ago, Jessica Lowndes' mother piloted a plane that was in collision with another; her mother died in the crash, as did Landon Liboiron's parents, but he survived. Now he's Lowndes' boyfriend, terrified of flying, and she's unaware of the connection between the two of them. Her twin engine craft takes off, Julianna Guill, boyfriend Jake Weary (a tiresome jock) and Ryan Donowho aboard. Heading straight into a massive storm, turbulence loosens a bolt which jams the elevator controls, Weary thinks he may have seen and heard something strange outside and Liboiron realizes that the weird events they are experiencing are somehow mirrored within the pages of the comic book he's reading ("A fantasy world come to life."). A *Twilight Zone/Final Destination*-type teen outing containing the usual barrage of bad language, stupid behavior and one-upmanship antics between the guys, *Altitude* also fea-

tures for good measure a tentacled monster of the kind last seen in 1958's *The Trollenberg Terror* (*The Crawling Eye*), but what the thing is doing thousands of feet up in the clouds is anyone's guess, and that goes for the mystical ending; Lowndes and Liboiron are reunited as children in a golden light, their parents looking on, their three buddies all dead. But were this bunch all dead in the first place? That is the question, a conundrum you may not want to fathom out after sitting through all the noisy shenanigans, wondering how on earth that aircraft can stay on course when Lowndes spends most of her time out of her seat, arguing and shouting.

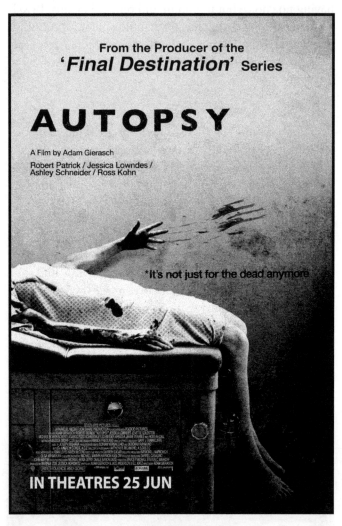

Autopsy
FlipZide/A-Mark Ent. 2008; 84 minutes;
Director: Adam Gierasch *******

Following a car accident, five teenagers are driven to the Mercury Hospital for treatment of a kind that they could only imagine in their worst nightmares.

Head of the hospital is Robert Patrick. His wife (now a withered old crone) has a life-threatening condition. Patrick (assisted by nurse Jenette Goldstein and two psychotic orderlies) abducts unsuspecting body donors to keep her alive; those donors whose organs are incompatible are butchered and left to rot or, in some cases, fall apart at the seams. Once you get past that ear-shattering opening sequence showing drug-sniffing, boozing, shrieking, posing, partying-on teens rocking their socks off (guaranteed to make even the most battle-hardened horror fan call it a day), persevere with this blood-drenched shocker. Gierasch commendably steers clear of the usual teen horror histrionics and directs in leisurely pace, his camera prowling through the dimly lit white-tiled corridors, delivering the grisly jolts with flair: A stomach lifted from an abdomen; Ashley Schneider jumped on by a naked patient, intestines spilling out over her; a ward full of hacked-off body parts; a welter of stabbings; and a primitive drill entering Jessica Lowndes' skull. To cap it all, the entire contents of Ross Kohn's insides are suspended above his body like a grotesque chandelier, connected via pipes and a monitor to Patrick's wife. Ignore the absurdities—how does Lowndes manage to run around and evade capture after the doc has bored into her skull with a hand drill, and who exactly are all those ill-looking patients wandering the corridors—and wonder if Gierasch got his inspiration from Dario Argento; *Autopsy* strongly resembles one of that director's more bloodier works (and even *Saw*) and is, for a teen horror movie, far better than usual. It might put you off eating meat for quite a while, though.

Boo
Kismet/Graveyard Filmworks 2005; 94 minutes;
Director: Anthony C. Ferrante ******

Halloween: A group of teenagers decides to spend the night in a reputedly haunted hospital, knowing that one of their friends has already cased the joint and set traps.

The director strives for all-out atmosphere in a retread of 1999's *House on Haunted Hill* but is let down by an illogical narrative. Trish Coren, Jilon Ghai and friends break into the abandoned Santa Mira Hospital to test their courage, unaware that cop Dig Wayne is observing their illegal antics. Michael Samluk is also investigating the building as his sister disappeared there; it's not long before Samluk and the teens meet up and begin to be possessed by M. Steven Felty's corrupt spirit. There are numerous ghostly apparitions, a levitating, maggot-infested killer clown, Coren's blotchy faced dead mother materializing in a ward, the usual banging noises, warnings about the third floor, a spooky child and the possessed teens exploding when shot, but it's all put together in such a

haphazard fashion that you lose interest in both plot and characters long before the end. The final scene is of the hospital restored to its former glory but in keeping with the rest of the movie, why isn't made at all clear.

Buried Alive
Horror Two/Dark Lot Entertainment 2007; 94 minutes;
Director: Robert Kurtzman **

Six teenagers seek out a family fortune in gold that is guarded by an evil spirit.

A teen horror movie with little bite, even with the inclusion of Tobin *Saw* Bell in the cast. Terence Jay's great-grandfather discovered gold out in the desert, his first Indian wife disappeared (rumored to be buried alive) and his second wife (also an Indian) gave birth to four children, three of whom burned to death in a house fire. Therefore, it stands to reason, states Bell, the family caretaker, that the place is cursed, even though he himself has been digging for gold nuggets in the sub-cellar. Once Jay, his tetchy cousin Leah Rachel, dude Steve Sandvoss, geek Germaine De Leon and two dumb sorority chicks (Lindsey Scott and Erin Reese) are ensconced in the refurbished house, a visitation in the form of a wizened-looking hag announces its presence, slicing in half with a chopper first De Leon, and then Sandvoss. Rachel is protected by a talisman originally worn by her relative's second wife but still winds up being

buried alive in a crate with Jay after the other teens, and Bell, have been butchered. One or two moments of tension and female nudity ensure that you won't fall asleep entirely, but the climax patently lacks a killer punch, a flat ending to a rather flat production.

Candy Stripers
Wind Chill Films 2006; 89 minutes;
Director: Kate Robbins ***

Following an automobile accident, a blind girl infected with an alien organism is admitted to the hospital; with her final dying kiss, she transmits the entity to a nurse.

A fun-filled spoof on '50s sci-fi classics such as *Invasion of the Body Snatchers*, *Candy Stripers* doesn't take itself too seriously, even though it was 18-rated on its British DVD release. Jock Brian Lloyd, girlfriend Nicole Rayburn, pal William Edwards, Jr. and his sister, Tori White, are among a group of teens rushed to the hospital after a violent fracas at a baseball game. Unknown to them, and the hospital's staff, nurse Deanna Brooks has been taken over by an alien host, her deadly kiss producing a slimy green proboscis that infects all the other nurses, leaving them with a craving for sugary confectionery, hard liquor and hot sex. Halfway through the action, White hits upon the solution to defeat the things—inject them with insulin via an air gun. Effects are minimal, allowing one a glimpse of alien claws and victims cocooned in sticky webs, spewing blood,

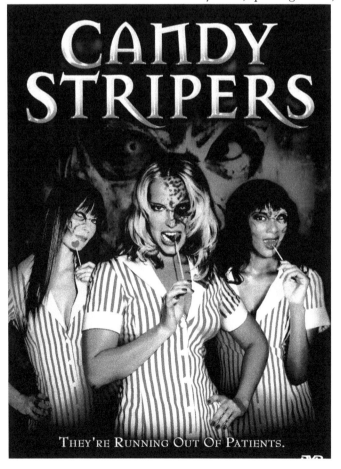

and just when you thought it was all over (White blows the hospital to pieces, surviving with Lloyd), a girl dragged from the rubble whispers "Kiss me Mummy"—and we all know what that kiss will lead to! A teen horror mickey-take that more or less hits the target.

Cemetery Gates
Kismet Ent./Graveyard Filmworks 2006; 92 minutes;
Director: Roy Knyrim **

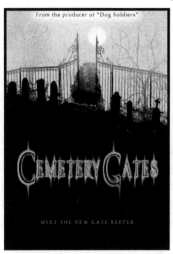

Animal activists liberate a genetically enhanced Tasmanian devil from a secret laboratory; the creature breaks loose from its crate and embarks on an orgy of bloody mayhem.

It's difficult to tell whether or not this creature-feature was played for laughs as the mutated monster, resembling a huge shaggy dog with deformed features, rips people apart, limbs hurled into the air, blood and guts cascading from gashes; in addition, you have some truly vile teens whose idea of fun is to play a CD containing noises of flatulence, and Kristin Novak is simply one blonde, dumb bimbo too many. Peter Stickles and his mates are shooting a zombie flick in the Southern Cross Cemetery which just happens to be the spot where the monster was dumped by its liberators. Soon, ravaged bodies are flying through the air as the slavering hairy terror begins a killing spree. Stickles' father, Reggie Bannister, who created the beast, turns up with assistant Aime Wolf and the climax takes place in tunnels under the cemetery where the monster is finally defeated, but not before giving birth to two grotesque offspring. If played straight, this might have worked better, but the semi-comical approach (and those brain-dead teens) renders the movie tiresome and derivative, with only a few moments of genuine suspense in among the buckets of gore.

The Craving
Biscuits and Gravy Prods. 2008; 98 minutes;
Director: Sean Dillon ***

Five teenagers cruising through the desert are waylaid by a man who wants to use them as bait for a flesh-eating creature that inhabits the arid countryside.

Shot direct to video on a rock-bottom budget, *The Craving* is a surprisingly effective thriller that limits the usual boring teen excesses and concentrates on edgy tension. Grayson Berry, Jesse C. Boyd, Anselm Clinard, Wallis Herst and Lesley Paterson find themselves stranded when,

in the middle of nowhere, a man punctures their van's tires with a shotgun blast and promptly disappears inside his dilapidated house. A Golem-faced monster lives in the area, emerging at night to feed on raw flesh, be it dog or human. The thing gives off an alluring aroma and those who come into contact with it (but aren't slaughtered) develop weird orange eyes. Dillon includes two raunchy sex scenes before night falls and the creature (which is only partly glimpsed) gallops on all fours towards its prey, grunting and hooting. Ranger Jason Kehler arrives on his motorcycle but doesn't assist the surviving teens; rather, he's on the monster's side, judging by his orange orbs. Herst appears to be the one that gets away, her slanting eyes glowing with an unearthly orange light as she salivates over a tethered dog in the nearby town. Correct—there is no clarification as to the origins of this strange creature, why it is there, where it is from and why people are tainted by some aspect of its touch, but perhaps that isn't necessary (although the dude with the shotgun is seen carving a small wooden idol). For low-cost creature thrills set in isolated desolation, Dillon's feature is a pretty cool effort all round.

Deadgirl
Hollymade Films 2008; 101 minutes;
Directors: Marcel Sarmiento and Gadi Harel ****

Two students break into an abandoned mental hospital and discover a strange girl trussed up on a bed in a secret room; they then decide to use her as an object for their sexual desires.

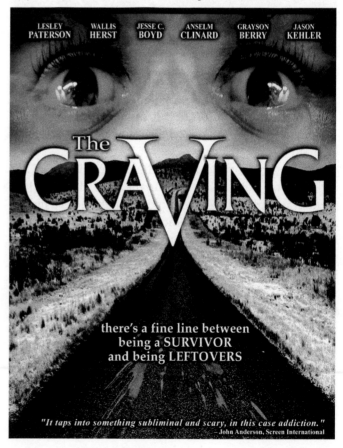

UNDER TEN MILLION? ANYTHING'S POSSIBLE!

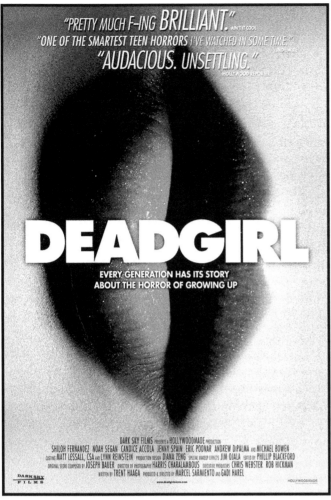

Segan and Podner's increasingly warped behavior, loosens her bonds; like a wild animal, she attacks her tormenters, spares Fernandez and disappears into the woods, a raving, screeching harpy. Accola, infected by her bites, is last seen manacled to the bed, replacing Spain; Fernandez, at school, his mates all dead, looks forward to visiting her when he feels the urge! Minimal background music, telling performances, forceful direction—*Deadgirl* is compelling indie horror, opening up ungodly areas in some people's psyche that they would rather not acknowledge.

Dearly Devoted aka Devil in the Flesh
Le Monde/Prostar Ent. 1998; 99 minutes;
Director: Steve Cohen ***

A young student develops a serious crush on her teacher—when she is rebuffed, her psychotic persona manifests itself in a string of murders.

The Crush and *Fatal Attraction* revisited: Rose McGowan plays the femme fatale who lusts after tutor Alex McArthur; trouble is, the guy has a sexy blonde girlfriend and isn't interested in McGowan's flirtatious come-ons, or skimpy clothes. Having already dispatched her bullying parents by burning the family house down, McArthur's refusal to yield to McGowan's charms is the last straw,

Is the girl simply a metaphor for man's darkest sexual fantasies, fantasies that verge on necrophilia? Why can't she be killed. Why, when she bites chunks out of people, do they die a horrible, painful death. Why is a ferocious dog guarding her. These questions are never answered but probably aren't meant to be. Although acted by teenagers, *Deadgirl* is not your average teen horror flick, rather an exercise in sexual deviance, fragile relationships and the less-palatable side of male testosterone gone berserk. Nice Shiloh Fernandez and nasty Noah Segan stumble across Jenny Spain in a disused institution, bound to a bed, gagged and naked. Succumbing to lust, they rape the girl but Fernandez has qualms about the deed, even more so when hippie pal Eric Podnar is invited by Segan to sample the delights to be had. But who is she, and how can she be impervious to beatings, being shot and sexually abused each and every way? As Spain's condition deteriorates (green pus oozes out of bullet wounds; she smells like rotten meat), the movie plummets into morbidity and sordidness—Fernandez's one-time girlfriend (Candice Accola) who rejects his offers to rekindle the friendship, her obnoxious beau (Andrew DiPalma) and his jock pal all get caught up in the act, DiPalma paying the ultimate price for engaging in oral sex, and Spain escapes after Accola, tied up and earmarked to be the next unwilling playmate of

pushing the disturbed student over the edge; her domineering, religious fanatic of a grandmother (Peg Shirley) is murdered, followed by her social worker and the leering, sex-obsessed school jock. It all ends in a frenetic, slasher-type payoff, McGowan arrested after almost killing the object of her desires and his girl. This by-now much-copied material benefits from McGowan's edgy star turn as the screwy student (although, at 24, she looks too old to be playing a teenager), taut direction from Steve Cohen and a sensible script. Give this low-budget effort its due, in some instances it even outclasses *The Crush* in tension and thrills and between the two is probably the better bet.

Decoys
Sci-Fi Prods./Téléfilm Canada 2004; 95 minutes;
Director: Matthew Hastings **

A trio of blonde babes attending the Ice Queen contest at a sorority shindig are aliens in disguise who turn their victims into blocks of solid ice after copulation.

It sounds promising, but this Canadian teen horror outing unfortunately camps things up to the point of annoyance, especially as dudes Corey Sevier and Elias Toufexis (anxious to lose their virginity) are your typical teen students—imbecilic, dumb and infantile. The shrieking, whooping, eye-rolling female fraternity are just as guilty, leaving older viewers to wait for the effects to kick in; Stefanie von Pfetten and Kim Poirier climb on top of their chosen mates, tentacles sprout from between their breasts, one passes down the throat of the victim who is frozen to death from within. When subjected to heat, the girls revert to type, shedding their human camouflage, resembling H.R. Giger's creature

in *Species*. After Sevier defeats the deadly duo plus Carrie Colak with a homemade flamethrower, Matthew Hastings adds a twist (which you *know* will happen) by having Meghan Ory turn into an alien as she makes love to boyfriend Sevier. The transformation sequences work (saving the movie from one-star status), but the rest of *Decoys* doesn't. Standard teen horror for the under-20s.

Detention
NHP/American World Pictures 2008; 90 minutes;
Director: James D.R. Hickox **

In 1976, a youth is locked inside Reseda High School's incinerator and fried to a crisp. Thirty years later, his spirit takes vengeance on the offspring of the perpetrators.

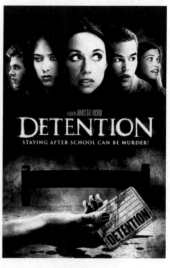

The "F" word included in every sentence, along with "shit"; every female cast member referred to as a "bitch"; "Are you serious?" repeated over and over again; and frequent eye-rolling, giggling and general stupid behavior. One day, a half-decent teen horror movie might come along that will appeal to those over the age of 25, where the actors don't all display the traits of a bunch of retarded infants. Until that day arrives, we have *Detention*, a standard "let's get the hell outta here" slasher flick in which seven teens are locked in the school after class and finished off by the smoking, burning phantom of Gregory Mikurak (who also possesses nerd Michael Mitchell), assisted by his evil mother, Alexa Jones. David Carradine makes a brief appearance as the college head, but even his presence can't save the film from becoming just one more derivative "teens in peril" offering, enlivened with random flashes of bloody mayhem—Preston Jones and his girl are the only two to make it out alive. It's all been seen before, and with lines like, "This is like a fucked-up Scooby-Doo show" and "The building's pissed at us," older hands will do well to give *Detention* a miss; watching it could seriously affect your sanity!

Fear Island
Waterfront Pictures 2009; 95 minutes;
Director: Michael Storey **

Five teenagers plus a stowaway take a boat ride to an uninhabited island and find themselves at the mercy of a cold-blooded killer.

In the opening minutes, Haylie Duff is arrested by police as six bodies (including the boat's pilot) have been found dead on the island. Whisked away to a hospital ward, Duff relates the events of what happened on the island to a doctor and skeptical detective, so we flash backwards and forwards from island to ward as one by one, Duff's companions are slain by an unknown assailant. Although competently made, there is nothing of note to distinguish this Canadian teen horror mystery from countless others. The murders are neither graphic nor suspenseful, the acting so-so and the twist ending predictable: Tousle-haired Romeo Kyle Schmid and his brother accidentally killed a girl at a party and buried her on the island; her sister (the stowaway) has coming looking for revenge. However, the stowaway (Lucy Hale) *isn't* the demented sister—Duff is, and having fooled both doctor and cop all along, she walks out of the hospital, driving off to a new life. A very ordinary teen horror movie that patently fails to generate any kind of excitement whatsoever.

The Final

After Dark Films/Agora Ent. 2010; 93 minutes;
Director: Joey Stewart ****

"The good news is, we don't plan to kill you. The bad news is, you will wish we had."

So states Marc Donato to chained-up jerk Justin Arnold, pouting wannabe Whitney Hoy and the rest of their thoroughly loathsome cohorts who have made Donato's life, and the lives of his pals (especially shy Lindsay Seidel), an absolute misery at college. Lured to a spacious house where a fancy dress party is in full swing and drugged, Donato's tormentors wake up to find themselves shackled to one another, five masked figures waiting in the wings to make them suffer, by torture, for their crass behavior. A serious teen horror movie with real depth for a change, the theme of catharsis tellingly put over without the usual amateur dramatics, the ending (all five commit suicide after seriously damaging a number of captives) downbeat yet leaving the viewer as cleansed as the perpetrators of these vile (but justifiable) acts. And the repercussions live on—one girl facially scarred, hiding behind a hood, another on pills, Arnold paralyzed from the neck down. Distressing, maybe, but in all fairness, they richly deserved all that they had coming to them.

Forget Me Not aka Haunted Souls

Vindicated Pictures 2009; 103 minutes;
Director: Tyler Oliver ****

A group of teenage friends is punished by the evil phantom of a girl they tormented as a youngster in the town's graveyard.

As hard as it may seem, try and get past *Forget Me Not*'s opening 12 minutes, portraying teenage students at their most hideous: Drinking, flirting, necking, having sex, shouting and acting like a bunch of brain-dead idiots. When this disagreeable bunch decides to play ghost games at night in the local graveyard, Tyler Oliver's movie rapidly changes tack for the better, gets serious and starts to pack a punch: Carly Schroeder spots a mysterious female (Brittany Renee Finamore) perched on a gravestone. "Do you remember me?" the girl asks before suddenly falling backwards over a cliff and disappearing. In flashback, we learn how Schroeder befriended orphan Finamore when they were youngsters but, being shy, Finamore was picked on by the members of Schroeder's gang, ending up in a coma when she stumbled and hit her head on a slab outside a convent. Now her hate-filled entity wreaks havoc, killing Schroeder's buddies one by one, the twist being that once they're dead, no one can remember they ever existed. Finamore's ghoulish doppelgänger, there one minute, gone the next, is effectively macabre, moving in jerky motions when working her way through the teens who themselves are turned into ghouls in a series of bloody, spine-chilling encounters. The final payoff sees Finamore, a smile on her face, recovering from her six-year coma after Schroeder, her one-time friend, has foolishly turned off her life support system; Schroeder herself is now in a coma, a case of role reversal taken to nightmarish extremes. Quite harrowing in parts, this is one teen horror picture that delivers the goods in spades, once you have persevered through that initial spell of infantile stupidity.

Horror 101

Valmax/Taurus Prods. 2001; 89 minutes;
Director: James Dudelson **

A psychology teacher asks her students to enact one of their member's projects after class, and they find themselves at the mercy of a serial killer.

The '70s revisited in this toothless, uneventful picture where the only thing worth looking at is how well Bo Derek (starring as the teacher) had aged over the years. Six students decide to play the parts in bullyboy Justin Urich's paper on the psychology of fear but start to disappear within the confines of the college as the night wears on. Virtually

blood-free, Dudelson has his cast walking into one room, then another, and then another, with no sense of tension, the bland photography as lifeless as the "action" itself. Derek turns out to be the mother of fruitcake Josh Holland, the pair responsible for the murders of 16 people; their little experiment ends up with all seven students locked in a deep freezer, carted off on a lorry to be used as dog meat. There's the germ of a good idea here but it's not fully realized; the one thing going for it is that the teens eschew the standard eye-rolling, shrieking tantrums that dominate so many other movies of this caliber.

Horror 102: Endgame

Valmax/Taurus Prods. 2004; 85 minutes;
Director: Ana Clavell **

Students renting rooms in what was once the Bellepark Mental Hospital are preyed upon by the disturbed spirits of former inmates.

The story has it that in 1989, the hospital was closed following the disappearance, in one night, of 32 patients. Now two of the students (Melissa Frederick and Anna Lerbom) play games with the others, a case of who survives to the last, only in this movie, these two students are egged on by the asylum's original mad doctor, Michael Moon, posing as a caretaker. When the asylum goes into self-curfew mode, doors and windows locked from 10:00 p.m. until six in the morning, the teens (who are there to attend a field trip run by Christopher Hawkins) are slaughtered. Frederick turns out to be the winner in this muddled feature after stabbing rival Lerbom to death, her reward a file of research papers handed to her by Moon. Not really a follow-up to *Horror 101* (and heaven forbid the two would ever go the rounds as a double bill as depicted on the DVD cover), Clavell's mundane teen horror show will have you checking your watch to see how much longer it goes on for long before the final reel.

House of Fears

Lonesome Highway/Black Orchid 2007; 86 minutes;
Director: Ryan Little **

Six teenagers break into the House of Fears, a themed haunted house attraction, where a statuette unearthed in Africa has the power to make each teen confront their own phobias.

A hit-and-miss affair— Corri English, Sandra McCoy, Michael J. Pagan, Corey Sevier, Alice Greczyn and Eliot Benjamin decide to continue their party in a make-believe spooky house, but their deep-rooted fears (suffocation, electricity, scarecrows, clowns) manifest themselves via a malignant stone statue. The initial 30 minutes is reasonable enough, with the youngsters wandering from one dark creepy room to the next, but when Benjamin goes missing and is found slashed to death, it's the old "we gotta get the hell outta here" procedure; mummies come alive, there's a killer clown on the loose and a murderous scarecrow stalks English. Pagan emerges tops in the acting department (he also had a hand in producing the picture) but it's all rather unexciting, like a watered-down *The Funhouse* (1981), and falls flat at the end.

Husk
After Dark Films 2011; 83 minutes;
Director: Brett Simmons ***

Five teens driving through extensive farmland veer off the road when crows hit the windscreen; finding shelter in a deserted farmhouse, they're menaced by malevolent scarecrows inhabited by the spirits of the house's former owners.

Concocted in 18 days, *Husk* delivers a few tension-filled jolts in a claustrophobic manner, the action set amid a dense cornfield where decades ago, a jealous farm boy, tormented by his bullying father, shot dead his brother and strung him up on a pole dressed as a scarecrow (seen in a series of visions by Devon Kaye). Now the murdered boy's spirit seeks fresh victims, slicing their flesh and turning them into blank-eyed zombies that stitch together grotesque hoods before joining others in the cornfield. It's predictable, nicely atmospheric fodder, the derelict farm building almost a work of decaying Gothic art design in itself, but the sudden ending in which a family is seen investigating the group's wrecked vehicle, obviously the next batch to fall foul of the killer scarecrow, followed by a sudden fade-out, is unsatisfactory, although widespread in today's horror cinema. For a refreshing change, the young cast (Kaye, Wes Chatham, C. J. Thomason, Tammin Sursok, Ben Easter) put in believable performances without resorting to screaming teen histrionics; that, plus a few spells of gore (nails through fingers) add up to a neat little shocker that would have benefited from a more satisfactory all-rounded conclusion.

Mine Games
Vitamin A Films/Yellow Brick Films 2012; 92 minutes;
Director: Richard Gray ***

Seven teenagers lost in woods stumble across a house situated near abandoned mine workings that harbor a terrible secret.

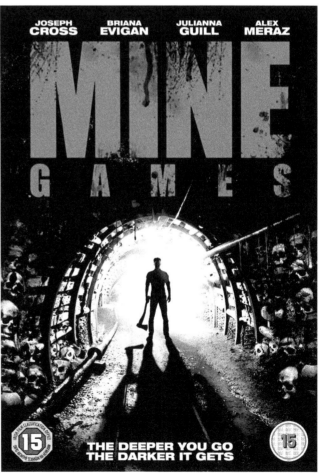

The Twilight Zone meets the "Cabin in the Woods" genre in Richard Gray's muddily photographed, tortuous but still intriguing semi-supernatural/horror thriller where, halfway through, we know all seven teens are dead, trapped in a vicious loop of events; it's how they got dead that is the puzzle for us to figure out. Joseph Cross, who by accident (or is it?) crashes his van at the start of the trip, appears to be the culprit, a schizophrenic not taking his medication and terrorizing the other six. Rebecca Da Costa plays a psychic who can see all this coming in a series of visions, beer-swilling Rafi Gavron is the first to see his own bloodied corpse deep underground ("We just saw our bodies—dead!"), Ethan Peck is determined to "break the cycle" and the rest—Julianna Guill, Briana Evigan and Alex Meraz—haven't a clue what's going on (and neither will some members of the audience). There are numerous chilly touches: A note discovered in the house that reads, "Wait here. Back soon," is the selfsame note written near the end, the gloomy mine workings are the stuff of nightmares (something dwells down there connected to mythology, but what we are not privileged to know) and the pieces of the jigsaw more or less fit into place, even the shock ending connected to that billboard headline seen after the credits: Unidentified girl found dead in forest. Backed by an eerie soundtrack, *Mine Games* is a lot more cerebral than most teen horror outings, offering food for thought, not a bad thing within this kind of low-budget framework.

Murder Loves Killers Too
Radar Dog Productions 2009; 80 minutes;
Director: Drew Barnhardt ****

Five teenagers drive to a mountain lodge for a weekend break and are picked off wholesale by a perverted killer.

Two reasons for giving this cheapo teen slasher flick a pat on the back—hyperactive Kat Szumski meets her end within 10 minutes, sparing us the sight of any more of her silly, whooping girly antics; and Barnhardt racks up the nail-biting tension in the movie's lengthy middle section as Christine Haeberman, the only youngster left alive, plays cat and mouse with psycho Allen Andrews. Why the unappealing Andrews gets pleasure from plunging knives into people's stomachs and ripping out their innards isn't made clear, although the final 15 minutes hints at sexual repression: Back home, his wife is conducting an affair, and does this dull oaf lust after his daughter? After all, he dressed Haeberman to resemble her, instructing the tied-up girl to "Call me Dad." The shock ending, whereby Haeberman emerges intact from the trunk of Andrews' car (after we thought she had been strangled), yanks out the killer's tongue and suffocates him with it, wife and daughter looking on, glad to be rid of the nuisance, satisfies from a retribution angle and for lovers of nubile female flesh, there is

a writhing sex romp on a pool table. Despite the eccentric title, this is a briskly directed, pleasing little feature with a lot more suspense than usual and (apart from Szumski) reasonably acted. Viewers would love to know the symbolic significance (if there is one) of the lingering close-up of that dead bee in the sink, though.

Poison Ivy: The New Seduction
Cinetel Films/MG Ent. 1997; 93 minutes;
Director: Kurt Voss ***

A student with psychopathic tendencies inveigles her way into the household of her childhood friend, intent on using her sexual allure to cause maximum disruption.

First, Drew Barrymore in 1992's *Poison Ivy*; then Alyssa Milano in 1996's *Poison Ivy 2*; now Jaime Pressly in this direct-to-DVD third instalment which, if you can tear your eyes away from her well-honed butt, is okay fodder in the tradition of the *Single White Female* school of filmmaking and a vast improvement on the 1995 flick. The convoluted who's-related-to-who plot needs to be worked out from the start: When she was a small girl, Pressly's mother was having sex with friend Megan Edwards' father, played by ex-singer of glam-rock band Silverhead, Michael Des Barres. Des Barres' neurotic wife eventually killed herself,

UNDER TEN MILLION? ANYTHING'S POSSIBLE!

as did Pressly's mother. So years later, the teenage temptress turns up at Edwards' house, intent on revenge for her mother's death. Seducing her pal's boyfriend (nice-but-dim Greg Vaughan), she then moves onto Des Barres' himself who takes one look at that naked, curvy body and gives in to lust, in this case bondage. Then matters turn nasty: The housekeeper is murdered, as is Vaughan, and so finally is Des Barres, locked in a gas-filled car—or is he? That's the tease—Pressly is pushed down the stairs by Edwards and may, or may not, be dead; Des Barres may, or may not, be dead; and Edwards may, or may not, have flipped over into madness herself. Notwithstanding the raunchy sex scenes, the main reason to watch this melodramatic semi-psycho thriller is the scheming Pressly; her blonde elfin features combined with a very fit, slinky figure are enough to have any male viewer's eyes on stalks, regardless of plot issues and that ambiguous climax. This girl is hot!

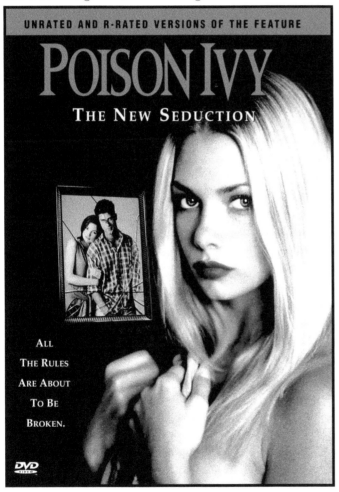

Poison Ivy 2: Lily
Cinetel Films/MG Ent. 1996; 101 minutes;
Director: Anne Goursaud *

A young art student finds the diary of a former psycho housemate and transforms herself into a sexually liberated woman with manipulative designs on two men.

You have to wait a very long time for anything to happen in this vapid low-budget follow-up to 1992's *Poison Ivy*

and when it does happen, it's not worth the wait. Alyssa Milano discovers Drew Barrymore's diary (from the first in the series), dons some of her clothing left in a box, slaps on the make-up and lustfully pursues sculptor Johnathon Schaech. As if he wasn't enough to satisfy her needs, she plays fast and loose with randy married tutor Xander Berkeley, leading to a showdown between the trio in which Berkeley, mad with desire, falls to his death from a roof. Following his demise, Milano is back in submissive cutie mode, snuggling up to Schaech. A thriller without thrills, with far too many soft-focus sexual antics, *Poison Ivy 2* is an overlong, uninteresting flop; and Milano, apparently, hated appearing in it.

Pray for Morning
Blu Nile Films 2006; 91 minutes;
Director: Cartney Wearn ****

Eight teens decide to spend the night in the abandoned Royal Crescent Hotel, aware that in 1984, the bodies of five teenagers were discovered there, horribly butchered.

If you can weather the childish antics on display in the teen party at the beginning, stick with this haunted house opus which is a little too ambitious in scope for a teenage horror movie at times. Jonathon Trent, Jessica Stroup, Dennis Flanagan, Ashlee Turner and friends break into the vast hotel and start to see the spirits of former residents. One by one, the kids are torn asunder by an invisible force. Udo Kier (always good for the odd shudder) is the catalyst for the hauntings. In 1921, he was a magician-cum-serial killer at loose in the hotel. Caught and executed by the proprietor, his corpse,

minus the hands, was bricked-up behind a fireplace. Now he's returned for fresh blood. Flashing backwards and forwards from the 1920s to the present day, the storyline is confusing at times, and the photography muddy. Nevertheless, *Pray for Morning* has a degree of uncanny atmosphere and smartly avoids the usual pitfalls evident in many other flicks of this type.

Primal

AV Pictures 2010; 80 minutes; Director: Josh Reed **

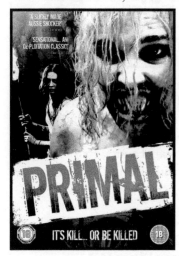

Six students go in search of 12,000-year-old aboriginal cave paintings in the outback and fall victim to an ancient supernatural virus.

An Australian teen horror movie that is no different in its portrayal of insufferable, uncouth youngsters than the American teen horror flicks. When will filmmakers ever learn—if your leading characters are foul-mouthed, hormonal dunderheads, both dudes and babes, any punter over the age of 25 is going to wish them all dead from reel one; it is *impossible* to empathize with such people, so you end up rooting for the killer/monster, which surely isn't the idea—or is it? So *Primal*, after an intriguing start, spirals into teen lunacy once giggling bimbo Krew Boylan goes skinny-dipping in a lake near the paintings, emerges covered in leeches, becomes infected with some form of virus and changes into a fanged, flesh-hungry wild animal. But why? This is never explained, even though the cave art itself is supposed to give clues. And just what is that giant slug up to, attempting to penetrate Zoe Tuckwell-Smith as she lies spread-eagled on the cave floor, held by tentacles. Tuckwell-Smith turns out to be the only survivor of whatever it is turning her mates into mutants, smashing a rock onto Boylan's head before the final fade-out. Too much bad language, a half-jokey script, buckets of gore and an incomprehensible plot—only the vivid color photography and those initial 20 minutes saves *Primal* from becoming a one-star teen disaster.

The Pumpkin Karver

Mannatee Films 2006; 90 minutes;
Director: Robert Mann **

Halloween: A teenager stabs his sister's uncouth boyfriend to death in the mistaken belief that the guy, wearing a disfigured pumpkin mask, was going to murder her. A year later, attending a party, the youngster is certain that

his victim has returned from the grave, still sporting the selfsame mask and bent on revenge for his untimely demise.

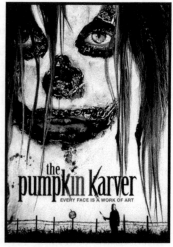

This humdrum movie gets two stars for the grotesque pumpkin make-up—take that out of the equation, and what you have is an extremely irritating teen shocker. Will today's filmmakers ever learn that populating their productions with the kind of one-dimensional characters you wouldn't want to be seen dead with is so off-putting. The drawn-out party scenes in *The Pumpkin Karver* give a whole new meaning to the word "idiocy" and you'll be rooting for the killer (David J. Wright) to finish these kids off pronto; trouble is, he only dispatches a couple of girls and you are left to wonder whether Michael Zara, the lad who originally knifed Wright, is the masked psycho himself—or is it the town's old pumpkin carver, Terrence Evans. The title character, firing off bolts of electricity from both hands, maintains the interest; when he's not up to bloody mischief and you are faced with those mugging, clowning teens, you might wish to leave the room and make yourself a stiff drink.

Satan's School for Girls

ABC/Spelling 2000; 87 minutes;
Director: Christopher Leitch ****

A student adopts an alias and goes undercover at a college to determine why her sister apparently committed suicide under mysterious circumstances.

A rarity—a teen horror flick that is more sensible than others, with a young cast, for once, cutting down on the amateur dramatics and acting sensibly. Shannen Doherty (who possesses mild psychic powers) is investigating the reason why a card bearing the inscription "The Five" was left on her sister's grave. Kate Jackson, dean of Fallbridge College for Women, is behind it all, leader of a pack of females who have sold their souls to the Devil for the right to achieve fame and fortune beyond their wildest dreams. The girls, who can shapeshift into dogs and ravens, conduct satanic rites within a pentagram beside an ancient cursed oak tree and murder all those who attempt to delve too deeply into their evil practices. Unknown to Doherty, boyfriend Daniel Cosgrove and blonde roommate Julie Benz are also members of the cult. Although PG-rated in Britain, Leitch's witches' brew serves up a frothy helping of none-too-gory shocks to please a younger audience; Doherty is personable in her role, the plot has a few twists

UNDER TEN MILLION? ANYTHING'S POSSIBLE!

killer in *Silent Scream* but you don't care a jot about any of them. Obsessed with sex, drinking and who's dating who, this idiotic bunch deserves everything that's coming to them, and boy do they get it: A face pushed into a fire; strangulation; dismemberment; decapitation; asphyxiation; drowning; and an axe murder. The trick ending reveals that it's all been a horrible dream—Professor of Psychology Peter Carrey has exploited their minds during a semester, but as his devious methods of thought control are top secret, he will have to do away with the lot of them when he takes them to his retreat, meaning a *Dead of Night* twist conclusion as the events begin to repeat themselves. The snow-laden location work and one or two grisly moments boost the degree of suspense somewhat; however, that young cast let down the proceedings badly, but that's to be expected in the modern-day teen horror genre.

Solstice
Endgame Ent./Key Creatives Prod. 2008; 91 minutes;
Director: Daniel Myrick ****

Five college graduates meet for a Summer Solstice party at a rambling old house at Nowell Lake in the Louisiana Everglades, one of them nursing a dark secret that manifests itself in the form of a vengeful wraith.

A solid, well-rounded teen horror flick from *The Blair Witch Project*'s co-director, cutting down on annoying girl/

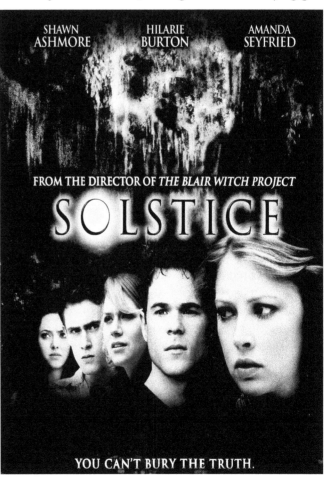

and turns and the climax is satisfying without being stupidly over-the-top. A made-for-TV occult thriller that might not raise the hackles (hence that UK PG rating) but entertains regardless.

Silent Scream aka The Retreat
Charity Island Pictures/Freetown Ent. 2005; 90 minutes;
Directors: Matt Cantu and Lance Kawas **

A large group of "let's party on" students, enjoying a weekend break at their professor's cottage in remote woodland, are slaughtered by a hooded maniac.

"God, this sucks on so many levels," sobs one female after most of her friends have been slain by a figure wearing an anorak. Never a truer word spoken! When will scriptwriters present us with a modern-day screenplay, even on *this* level, that *isn't* liberally laced with expletives? Yes, 14 hateable teenage students are horribly murdered by a serial

guy antics by presenting an intriguing plot boosted by moments of shock; the opening credits are eerily presented in a green tint to set the right haunting mood. Elisabeth Harnois, mourning the death by suicide of her twin Sophie (Harnois plays both parts), isn't in the party mood but volunteers to attend her parents' house for a Solstice shindig where she was present when her troubled sister took an overdose. Shawn Ashmore, her sister's boyfriend, is drawn towards her, but so is good-looking garage attendant Tyler Hoechlin, an avid believer in the supernatural. Once at the house, Harnois is subjected to a barrage of frightening visions: Black mud oozes from taps, her hands appear bloody and torn, a sinister shape with glowing eyes is seen behind her and a teddy bear keyring keeps popping up. Is her sister trying to tell her about something evil from beyond the grave, as Hoechlin suggests ("The dead speak on the 21st June.")? Why does the group's car stall on that bridge? And is gun-toting hick R. Lee Ermey as harmful as he appears to be? Myrick cleverly focuses our doubts and mistrust on loudmouthed jock Matt O'Leary and Ermey, fooling us into believing that Ashmore is caring and innocent of any misconduct. He isn't. In flashback, the truth unfolds: Ashmore and Sophie, on a previous trip to the house, became distracted in their car, running into young Jenna Hildebrand, Ermey's now-missing granddaughter, on the bridge. Her body (and bike) was unceremoniously buried in the swamps surrounding a ruined mansion by the thoughtless couple, the deed hushed-up; guilt over the girl's death was the main reason behind Sophie killing herself. Now the twin's spirit is pointing the finger, leading to Harnois, Hilarie Burton and Amanda Seyfried unearthing Hildebrand's decaying remains; the key fitted her bike's padlock. The emerging ghoul chases Ashmore through the woods; terrified, he runs out onto the road, is hit by a police car and badly injured; he's arrested and carted off in an ambulance. Her twin finally at rest, Harnois and Hoechlin place flowers on Hildebrand's grave, walking off together and making plans for the future.

Somebody Help Me
Codeblack Ent./Basement Films 2007; 100 minutes;
Director: Christopher B. Stokes ***

Ten youngsters decide to spend the weekend in a woodland cabin; on arrival, six are immediately captured, imprisoned and mutilated by an insane plastic surgeon.

Take one cabin situated in remote woods; a bunch of sex-obsessed, partying-on teens; a maniac on the loose responsible for murders dating back years; a nosy neighbor who *could* be the killer (but usually isn't); blundering police officers; and a twist ending. What do you have? The recipe for a standard teen/slasher horror movie which is either brilliant, middling or lacking in style. *Somebody Help Me* falls into the middle category—two black couples (Marques

Houston, Brooklyn Sudano, Omarion Grandberry, Alexis Fields) drive to the cabin, having invited three more couples to join them. Unfortunately, a deranged plastic surgeon (Sonny King) lives nearby; after accidentally killing his wife, he escaped from an asylum years back and proceeded to murder nine other people. Somehow abducting the three visiting couples and holding them captive in cages, the masked loony performs one grisly operation after another (although his motives aren't made clear): An ear removed, a girl scalped, a guy blinded, another subjected to primitive dentistry. The original two couples manage to survive, Houston aided in his endeavors to free the hostages by a mysterious girl (Brittany Oaks) who is there one minute, and gone the next. Naturally, King proves to be indestructible—just when you thought he was dead, up he pops in the very last frame. The operation sequences are definitely *not* for those prone to queasiness, Stokes' direction is assured and the script avoids most of the usual clichés associated with this particular sphere of horror. Milking the "lonely cabin in the woods" scenario for all it's worth, this is not bad at all.

Spiker
Laurel Lane Pictures/Moodude 2007; 90 minutes;
Director: Frank Zagarino *

A depraved killer whose specialty is plunging railroad spikes into people's backs breaks loose from captivity and terrorizes six teenagers staying at an old house.

Teen horror? Ghost story? Serial killer flick? *Spiker* attempts a shot at all three and falls flat on its face in the process. Giselle Rodriguez-Forte and her five pals visit a house left to her by her long-dead aunt; hot on their heels comes an albino killer (played by the director) who has an association with the house—years ago, he was going to marry Rodriguez-Forte's aunt but she ditched him for another man on the eve of their wedding and later died giving birth. Now her ghost, kitted out in a wedding dress, flits around the dingy rooms as one dim, goofy teen after

UNDER TEN MILLION? ANYTHING'S POSSIBLE!

another is murdered by Zagarino while her ex-beau David Fralick, the killer's sworn enemy, sits alone upstairs, awaiting his fate. The opening few minutes of *Spiker* does show some promise, but that promise evaporates very quickly—there are several sequences in the movie (notably the séance segment) where the young cast, judging by their bemused expressions, seem to have forgotten their lines, or whatever it is they are supposed to be doing—were they improvising, or making things up as they went along? Low on thrills, atmosphere and cinematic ability, Zagarino's tawdry effort is 90 minutes of sheer horror purgatory.

Tamara
Armada Pictures 2005; 98 minutes;
Director: Jeremy Haft **

In love/lust with her English tutor and tormented by mindless classmates, a plain, timid student who delves into witchcraft and magic spells is accidentally killed by her tormentors but returns from the grave, a vamped-up predator thirsting for revenge.

Tamara received the cold shoulder from Britain's cinema chains, an unremarkable, regurgitated *Carrie/I Know What You Did Last Summer* teen horror romp that appears oddly unfinished in some areas, like a rough cut. Jenna Dewan-Tatum is the shrinking violet harboring an almighty crush on teacher Matthew Marsden. When six students, led by brain-dead jocks Bryan Clark and Gil Hacohen, set up a fake tryst between lovelorn Dewan-Tatum and Marsden in a motel room, camcorder at the ready, it all goes horribly wrong; Dewan-Tatum, during a struggle, hits her head on a table and dies. The guilty six bury her in a woodland grave but she returns to school the next day, wearing a red killer dress and make-up, with attitude to match, intent on bedding Marsden and destroying the others. By stroking their faces, the girl can make her persecutors do as she wishes, turning each against the other with murderous results. An unsatisfactory closer has Marsden and Dewan-Tatum leaping from a roof to their deaths, while Melissa Marie Elias, one of the surviving six, has turned into a witch herself. Dewan-Tatum acts everyone else off the screen as the unholy temptress, making *Tamara* marginally watchable, but the heavy intrusive score drones on and on, destroying the atmospheric set pieces, and the gore quota is pretty low for a film of this type. Mundane fare for the teen horror set.

Teen Monster aka Big Monster on Campus; Boltneck
Regent Entertainment 2000; 92 minutes;
Director: Mitch Marcus ***

College student Frank Stein places a serial killer's brain into a high school geek who dies through a freak accident; once revived, the geek is now a womanizing smart-ass.

A rough-and-ready satire on the old Universal-International *Frankenstein* flicks (you can spot the source referenc-

es a mile off) that unfortunately doesn't sustain the momentum built up during the first 30 minutes or so. Picked-upon Matthew Lawrence puts to work his theories on "electronic reanimation" when nerd Ryan Reynolds falls backwards into an empty pool, sustaining fatal head injuries. Revived with the brain of a murderer implanted in his head, Reynolds changes into an obnoxious nuisance and Lawrence has to eventually put another brain in his cranium to calm him down; he emerges from the operation a babe magnet for young female Goths! Elfin Christine Lakin is a delight as the object of Lawrence's desires while Justin Walker and Christian Payne's exuberant "numbskull jocks" double-act provides comic relief of a sort. What a pity about that saggy middle section—it really spoils what could have been a fabulous little horror comedy.

Warriors of Terra aka Biohazard: Death Plant
Archetype Films 2006; 91 minutes;
Director: Robert Wilson **

A group of teenage animal activists break into a large complex, become trapped in a deep underground laboratory and fall victim to a mutated female with a lust for flesh.

What is the normally reliable Edward Furlong doing starring in a dour Canadian "experiment gone wrong" thriller? At least he tries to give a credible performance as a security officer helping a bunch of teens enter a building where unethical experiments on animals are supposedly taking place. When the youngsters take the one and only elevator to a lower level, followed by a bevy of grunts, they all meet up with pale-faced, lank-haired, scantily dressed Trina Brink and wish they hadn't. Brink, once suffering from cancer, had her DNA messed around with by Andrew Gillies, in search of a cure—the cancer was expelled from her body, but in doing so she changed into a killer who injects her prey with toxins before feeding on them. There's lots of prowling around in dingy industrial corridors, Ellen Furey and Andrea Lui spend all of their time snarling "Bitch!" at one another and Brink is distinctly unscary as the biologically enhanced female creature. Not even immersion in a decontamination tank finishes her off—she emerges at the end after pouncing on the hapless Furlong. Wilson strives to raise the tension but in this setup, you need a decent protagonist to engage and excite the senses. Unfortunately, *Warriors of Terra* doesn't have one.

Torture/Slasher/Gore

Are You Scared?
Mainline Releasing/Albatross 2006; 79 minutes;
Director: Andy Hurst **

A scarred madman kidnaps six youngsters, incarcerates them in an abandoned warehouse and forces them to undergo a series of fiendish tests for a fake reality show.

Saw 10 would be more of an apt title for this mediocre slice of torture/horror in which Alethea Kutscher's insane father (Brent Fidler) is after retribution of sorts: She burnt the family house down and escaped with her mother to be free of him but, like Vincent Price in *House of Wax*, he lived on, horribly scarred and deranged. One bloody torture sequence follows another in quick succession, the cops take their time in getting to the warehouse and Kutscher plus mother survive the day—or do they? Cue for mandatory shock ending as Fidler, thought to be dead, reappears in Kutscher's new apartment. If you've managed to catch the complete *Saw* franchise, *Are You Scared?* will offer nothing new in the way of gory jolts. It's competently put together but really is a pale imitation of the real thing, in this case 2005's *Saw 2*. Primetime Pictures' *Cruel World* (2005) explored this selfsame territory to far greater effect.

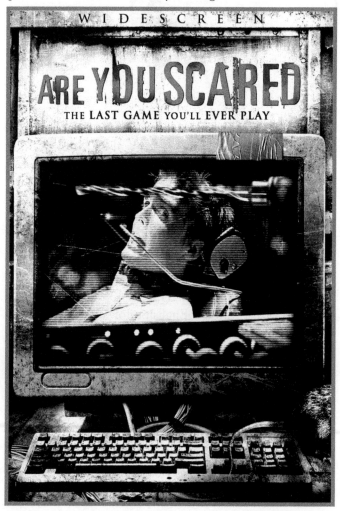

UNDER TEN MILLION? ANYTHING'S POSSIBLE!

disturbingly graphic (one girl is stuck on a meat hook and trundled into a furnace for instant cremation), the direction hard-hitting but in the end, one becomes desensitized to all the carnage, leaving you with the impression that *Bereavement* is just one more in a never-ending stream of gore/slasher flicks that show no signs of abating.

Broken
Brand Mason/Renegade 2006; 110 minutes;
Directors: Adam Mason and Simon Boyes ***

A woman awakes to find herself held prisoner in woodland by a loner exhibiting psychopathic tendencies.

Spread over a 41-day period, *Broken* is torture-porn fare with little plot, no motive behind the loner's antisocial behavior but well performed by Eric Colvin and Nadja Brand as abductor and captive. And that's the problem—*why* does Colvin insert a razor blade into women's stomachs, sew up the wound and then force them to retrieve the blade by yanking out the stitches, making sure their intestines don't spill out either. These two scenes alone might have your gorge rising, as will the sight of Colvin stamping on Brand's leg and breaking it after an escape attempt, or the loner cutting out the tongue of another victim, *or* Brand blinded by a face-full of buckshot at the end when she discovers her daughter in a shack. And that's after she's bludgeoned her captor to death with an iron bar. The cat and mouse situation between the two raises

Bereavement
Darclight/Crimson Films 2010; 103 minutes;
Director: Stevan Mena ***

Six-year-old Martin, who suffers from a congenital resistance to pain, is abducted by a psychopath who forces the boy to witness the horrific slaughter of women in an abandoned meat packing factory.

In modern day slasher movies, no one makes it out alive. Heroine Alexandra Daddario, her uncle, Michael Biehn, and his family, troubled boyfriend Nolan Gerard Funk—all slaughtered by crazy Brett Rickaby who, in the final frame, is chopped to pieces with an axe by his creation, Spencer List, now a stark raving mad 11-year-old. A prequel to 2003's *Malevolence* which told what happened to the kid after the events depicted in this picture, director Stevan Mena lays on the blood and guts with a trowel, mostly in the gloomy confines of the dilapidated Sutter Meat and Poultry premises, Rickaby driving around in a battered truck in search of victims to satisfy his perverted desires. But what are those desires? It's never made clear, an area where the movie fails to deliver in not nailing to the wall Rickaby's motives, if any. The lunatic talks to someone wearing a longhorn cow mask who may or may not be sharing the factory with him (is it all in his mind?), cuts the boy before slicing open his trussed up lambs to the slaughter and spouts gibberish about repentance. Why he does what he does remains a mystery. The murders are

the tension (try not to ponder on Brand's toilet arrangements over those 41 days—she's permanently shackled to a tree) but the lack of any psychological reasoning behind Colvin's bizarre actions lets the film down (why does he require a family of women to attend to his every need if he's so self-sufficient?); however, at least it's different and, for once, played by adults and not teens.

Crushed aka She's Crushed
Hold It Now Films 2009; 90 minutes;
Director: Patrick Johnson *****

A mentally disturbed young woman stalks her neighbor, brutally torturing and killing those women (and men) who stand in her way.

Fatal Attraction with balls. You won't find gratuitous savagery like this in mainstream horror cinema, unless it's on the underground circuit. Natalie Dickinson chews the scenery, playing a maladjusted woman (no, hold that—she's a complete basket case!) who attaches herself like a limpet to pleasant-but-drippy Henrik Norlén. After a one-night stand, he wants nothing more to do with her; after all, the guy's engaged to nice blonde girlfriend Caitlin Wehrle. But Norlén can't shake the woman off—despite spurning her advances, she won't let up. Tipped over the edge of sanity (her mother resides in a psychiatric ward), Dickinson's twisted world escalates into sexual violence. She kidnaps and murders a babysitter, a stranger and his girlfriend, Norlén's female boss

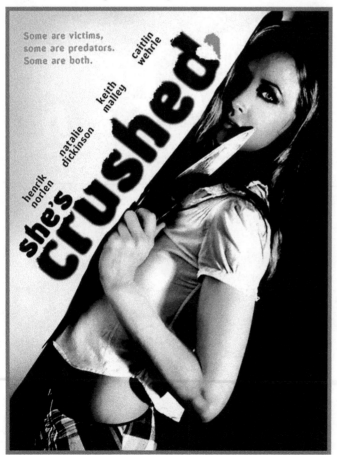

and his moronic, sex-obsessed work buddy (Keith Malley) before abducting both Norlén and Wehrle, subjecting them to sadistic torture. Dickinson is still on the loose in the final reel, having slaughtered Wehrle and given the object of her desires a full-frontal lobotomy with an electric drill. *Crushed* contains bucketloads of gore and many scenes might make you turn away in nauseous revulsion, especially the make-shift dentistry part. Notwithstanding the blatant bloodletting, this is vivid, finely executed in-your-face psycho horror produced on a shoestring budget, and Marilyn Manson look-alike Dickinson really gets under the skin of her character; she's terrifyingly realistic as the totally deranged, self-harming femme fatale.

The Death Factory Bloodletting
Ominous Productions 2008; 94 minutes;
Director: Sean Tretta ***

A bunch of degenerates lured to an abandoned factory to view an actual murder are in fact targeted for death themselves by an insane killer.

Sean Tretta was on much more surer, and saner, ground with the excellent *Death of a Ghosthunter* (2007)—here, he plunges us into a cesspit of torture-porn, S&M, depravity and vileness. Claudia Vargas joins a group that includes a child molester, a prostitute, an anarchist, a collector of snuff movies and a leather-clad lesbian and her slave. Vargas is there to find out who the pervert was that abducted and killed her daughter—Noah Todd, looking like Charles Manson, is running the show, acting (so he believes) on God's wishes by sending out flesh-eating Michelle Mousel, with her metal claws and pointed teeth, to rid Phoenix of this human trash. Played out to a death metal soundtrack, the director bombards the senses with scenes straight out of a slaughterhouse, with many a nod in the direction of *Saw*, and finishes with a couple of twists up his sleeve. It won't be to everyone's taste but in the grindhouse context in which it was conceived, Tretta's brash, gore-laden flick won't disappoint fans of this kind of stuff.

Frontier(s)
EuropaCorp/Cartel Prods. 2007; 108 minutes;
Director: Xavier Gens ***

Following civil unrest riots in Paris, four young thieves on the run drive out to an isolated guest house run by cannibalistic Nazis.

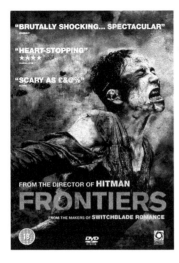

Pregnant Karina Testa, her ex-boyfriend Aurélien Wiik and their two buddies, after a gun battle with the cops, have far more to cope with when they find themselves prey to fanatical Nazi Jean-Pierre Jorris and his band of deviants who butcher passing travelers, keeping their salt-preserved corpses in nearby mine workings. Torture, degradation, strong sex, shoot-outs, three mutant children, their deformed mother, Chems Dahmani fried in a steam room, Samuel Le Bihan sliced to ribbons on a circular saw, foul language, rants about a new Master Race—Xavier Gens goes for the throat but in doing so appears to be trying just a bit too hard to shock his audience into submission. Some dazzling camerawork in the opening scenes, where the movie promises much, degenerates into *Texas Chainsaw Massacre/Saw/Hostel* savagery to a point where one becomes immune to it all. The one moment of frightening tension is when Dahmani and David Saracino almost get stuck while worming their way through a tortuous underground passage; the rest is simply one scene of carnage and brutality after another. But it is robustly put together with expertise.

Garden of Love
aka **The Haunting of Rebecca Verlaine**
Benfeghoul & Goldberg Films/Imas 2003; 86 minutes;
Director: Olaf Ittenbach *****

A girl's entire family is brutally slaughtered by two assailants wearing clown masks—years later, suffering from amnesia, the young woman is tormented by powerful visions of that terrible night and enlists the aid of the police to help trace the killers.

German splatter meister Ittenbach serves horror fans a dish of dripping raw meat in this superior gore-fest—the opening credits sequence alone is enough to turn most viewer's stomachs. But if you've managed to sit through the likes of *House of Blood*, you'll know what to expect from the man, appreciating that Ittenbach infuses his carnage-laden features with more depth than most, elevating them to the "must-see" category for aficionados of his works. Natacza Boon, living with psychology lecturer Daryl Jackson, has repeated visions of the night her family was butchered. Moreover, her dead father frequently visits her, stating that all is not over—both himself and the family's tortured souls need revenge and closure. But creepy chief cop James Matthews is covering up for something,

and so are Boon's adoptive parents (her uncle and aunt). The conclusion is wrapped up in typical Ittenbach horrendous style: The adoptive parents, insanely envious of the family's wealth, hired Matthews *and* Jackson to do away with them in a serial killer-type manner so that they could lay their hands on the money. Revelation done and dusted, the four guilty parties are ripped to shreds by the avenging spirits. But there's a sting in the tail that involves Matthews' daughter, so all, apparently, is *not* done and dusted. An edge of parody (mainly in Matthews' overstated performance as the unbalanced cop) runs through *Garden of Love* but in top-notch fare such as this, you can ignore it. In this particular area of horror cinema, Ittenbach has come up trumps again and reigns supreme.

Harpoon: Reykjavik Whale Watching Massacre
Icelandic Film Company 2009; 90 minutes;
Director: Július Kemp ***

Ten disparate tourists charter the *Poseidon* to take them on a whale watching trip, only to end up fighting for their lives on another ship, home to a family of crazed butchers.

Two sex-starved German women and one sex-starved Icelandic lady of questionable age, a gay negro, an alcoholic Frenchman, a Japanese family and two young girls are dumped on board a rusting, rat-infested hulk in a remote bay near Reykjavik after the *Poseidon*'s captain has acciden-

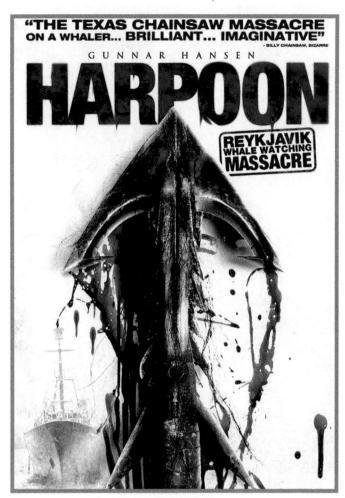

"THE TEXAS CHAINSAW MASSACRE ON A WHALER... BRILLIANT... IMAGINATIVE"
- BILLY CHAINSAW, BIZARRE

GUNNAR HANSEN

HARPOON

REYKJAVIK WHALE WATCHING MASSACRE

tally been run through with a harpoon. From thereon in, this Icelandic gore-fest doesn't let up, with enough blood and guts to appease all those who wallow in this kind of thing—a hammer buried in the skull, decapitations, death by harpoon, a flare shot into an eye, a cut throat and the crazy mother (Gúdrun Gisladóttir) burned alive are just some of the treats on offer. Sassy Japanese chick Nae Tazawa is the sole survivor, her homeward plane flying over Miranda Hennessy, floating in the cold desolate waters in her lifejacket, miles from anywhere. Add to this a ridiculous guy pretending to be disabled to sell his model whales, nudity, an unpleasant rape, vomiting and opening scenes of whales carved-up in the flensing sheds, followed by a heavy metal group, and you have a dumb-scripted slasher movie shot in pristine widescreen that leaves a nasty taste in the mouth, however well it's been pieced together.

High Lane aka Vertige
Gaumont/Studio Mad 2009; 90 minutes;
Director: Abel Ferry ****

Five rock climbers become cut off in a remote region of Croatia's Risnjak Massif and encounter, to their cost, a deranged hermit living in an isolated forest shack.

The Descent in reverse—it's not what you meet up with down there, but what you meet up with *up* there. The first half of Ferry's adventure/horror is nerve-racking cinema as expedition leader Nicolas Giraud, girlfriend Maud Wyler, vertigo-prone Johan Libéreau, girlfriend Fanny Valette and Valette's jealous ex, Raphael Lenglet, ignore a "Way Closed" sign in a ravine and begin to ascend a terrifying rock face above a deep gorge. The first 50 minutes will leave you with sweaty palms and a palpitating heart as the five negotiate a series of vertical rock faces high above a river, hindered in their progress by Libéreau's constant hyperventilating and his endless rows with Lenglet over Valette. When a rickety bridge gives way (a truly hair-raising scene), thus preventing their return by the more conventional route, they are forced to climb even higher and find themselves in a forest, home to a maniac (Justin Blanckaert) who traps and chops up any persons unfortunate enough to find themselves on his patch. From this point, *High Lane* morphs into a *Wrong Turn* slasher-type flick; Giraud is the first to meet his end, followed by Wyler. The other three become imprisoned, the cowardly Libéreau escapes with the crossbow-armed madman in hot pursuit and a bloody showdown results in survivor Valette zooming over a zip-line cable to her possible doom. Filmed in the French Alps, it's a real shame that *High Lane* doesn't sustain the giddy (in more ways than one) heights that it attained in that first exhilarating, tension-filled half, and in the opening shot, you just know that when a

camera lingers on a photo of a group of friends going off into the wilds, those friends aren't going to make it back alive. The film's one major weakness is Blanckaert's loony, a lank-haired Klaus Kinski look-alike that fails to convince. Nevertheless, for the mountain climbing sequences alone and the magnificent scenery, this French thriller is a real nailbiter of a picture.

The Horseman
Kastle Films 2008; 96 minutes;
Director: Steven Kastrissios ****

Grief-stricken after his daughter dies from a drug overdose, a man vows bloody retribution on all those he feels responsible for her death.

Uncompromisingly brutal, vicious and downright nasty—Kastrissios' cut-price Aussie revenge thriller makes for tough viewing and is certainly *not* suitable for shrinking violets. Peter Marshall is magnetic as the ordinary father caught up in a sordid world of drugs and pornog-

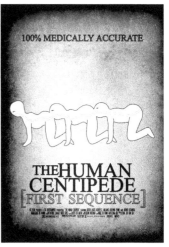

In the first of Tom Six's trio of stomach-churning, taboo-breaking, politically incorrect affronts to human dignity, a mad surgeon stitches two girls and a man together, anus to mouth, creating a "Siamese Triplet," the film ending with two of the three dead, only the unfortunate middle section female alive. Dieter Laser plays the surgeon, Ashlynn Yennie, Ashley C. Williams and Akihirio Kitamura his three tortured victims. The second (shot in black-and-white) has underground car park guard Laurence R. Harvey, a sick psychopathic loner fantasizing over the first movie, abducting 13 people (including a pregnant woman who escapes and gives birth), dragging them to a warehouse and joining them anus to mouth using a staple gun. But is it all a figment of his warped imagination? As he stares at the picture for the umpteenth time, we hear a baby cry … The third instalment again features Laser as the 100% certifiable warden of a prison ("A vile, sadistic asshole."), Harvey his mouse-like accountant. Governor Eric Roberts wants to sack the insane pair, so Laser, by using straps and stitches, produces a 500-man centipede (or caterpillar), Roberts approving of his method of keeping pris-

raphy; discovering that his daughter "starred" in several blue movies and then overdosed alone in a dingy flat, he ruthlessly tracks down the men behind the trade in porno (headed by Jack Henry) and in a series of savage vignettes murders them one by one. Teenage hitchhiker Caroline Marohasy provides a welcome antidote to Marshall's turbulent existence, bringing moments of tenderness to the heartless world he has been forced to enter, the guy carrying out a platonic father-daughter relationship with her, even though the girl is a complete stranger. The ending is suitably bleak but you wouldn't expect it to be anything else in this scenario. Exceptional direction, knockout performances and stark photography make *The Horseman* one hell of an Aussie horror drama; one man's descent into frenzied madness has very rarely been better portrayed than in this little gem.

The Human Centipede (First Sequence)
Six Entertainment 2009; 92 minutes;
Director: Tom Six ***
The Human Centipede II (Full Sequence)
Six Entertainment 2011; 91 minutes;
Director: Tom Six ***
The Human Centipede III (Final Sequence)
Six Entertainment 2015; 102 minutes;
Director: Tom Six **

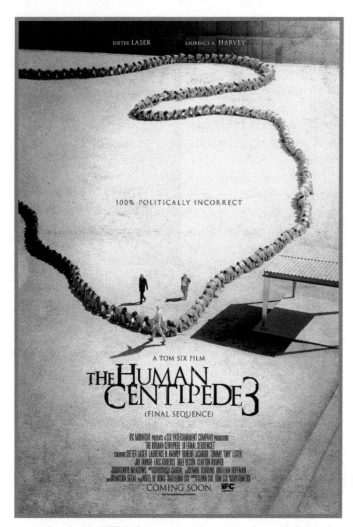

ons them in caskets and then butchers them, filming his deeds on tape.

The first is a classic helping of gore, centering on a girl (Bobbi Sue Luther) wanted by the police (for prostitution?) who wakes up in a locked casket, not knowing how she got there. Managing to escape from the funeral parlor, she's picked up by Kevin Gage and taken to his house for safe-keeping—and then the carnage begins. From the opening frenzied, mortuary-style images behind the flashy credits, backed by Deadbox's pounding industrial music, you'll know what to expect: Gage's girlfriend, Lena Headey, is graphically slaughtered by the relentless psycho, wielding a huge serrated knife, known as Chromeskull (played by Nick Principe) who sports a video-cam on his shoulder; Luther and Gage flee, meeting Sean Whalen and spending the remainder of the action wallowing in blood, gore, behead-ings, viscera, dismemberment, throat hacking and every-thing else you can conjure up to guarantee your last meal not staying put in your stomach. The pace doesn't falter, Hall going for unsubtle maximum shocks, even a whiff of humor here and there (timid Whalen has to cope with his mother's stitched-up corpse, used as bait by Chromeskull). The killing machine dispatches cops, a garage attendant, Gage and Whalen (his head explodes after glue is pumped

oners in check ("This is exactly what America needs!"); the director himself makes a guest appearance. Tom Six's ode to excess gets grosser by the minute if you're brave enough to watch all three in one sitting (as this author did): Mouth to anus operations in close-up; laxatives given to expedite the flow of excreta; anal rape; the rape of a coma victim; digging a hole in a patient's back to allow intercourse of a different kind; a stoma bag ripped from a patient; knee ligaments cut; dismemberment; a jar of dried clitorises; castration; fried testicles for lunch; masturbation; oral sex; senseless shootings; bludgeon by crowbar; ass wiping; vom-iting; force-feeding via funnel and tube; and a barrage of obscenities to top it all off. But one vital question will re-main on many viewers' lips after wallowing in nearly five hours of gore, blood, filth and degradation—why?

Laid to Rest
Dry County Films 2009; 90 minutes;
Director: Robert Hall *****
Chromeskull: Laid to Rest 2
Dry County Films 2011; 93 minutes;
Director: Robert Hall ***
In writer/director Robert Hall's two homages to the modern-day torture-porn/slasher genre, a maniacal killer wearing a chromium mask kidnaps young women, impris-

as Dekker, is the hero, rescuing Michaels after a platter consisting of dismemberment, axe in head, decapitation, a head plunged into boiling metal plating solution, a face ripped in half, throats hacked to shreds, nudity, a female cop pushed face downwards onto a five-bladed sword, a girl slashed across the mouth and other bloody visual delights has been served up. Chromeskull lives to carry out his grisly work, at large on the streets before the closing credits—can we expect to see a third instalment? (*Laid to Rest: Exhumed* is in conception as of 2019.)

The Loved Ones
Darclight/Film Victoria 2009; 84 minutes;
Director: Sean Byrne ****

A psychotic teenager, spurned by her student idol, takes him hostage on the night of the college dance, determined to be the queen of her own perverted ball.

Carrie meets *Misery* in yet another in-your-face Aussie shocker that delivers its torture/gore a-plenty. Unfortunate tousle-haired Xavier Samuel is the object of demented Robin McLeavy's desires, abducted, tied up in her home, both feet anchored to the floor with knives and a picture carved on his chest with a fork; McLeavy and her bug-eyed, incestuous father (John Brompton) also drill a hole

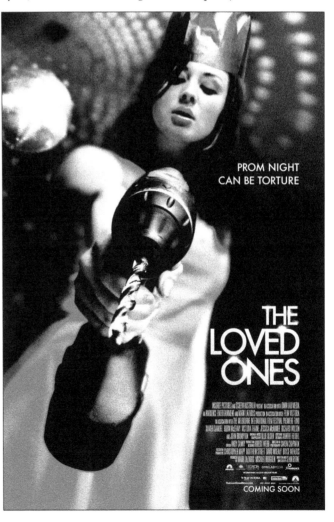

into his ear) before Luther, spotting the loony using adhesive to fix the mask to his face, mixes a superglue; he uses it and rips his face to shreds trying to remove the mask. Luther then reduces his features to pulp with a baseball bat, driving off to Atlanta with survivor Thomas Dekker as the cops arrive on the crime scene. Hall's movie is 100% in-your-face extreme splatter, not for those of a delicate nature; who's bothered by a dumb script when wholesale butchery such as this is presented in such a ferociously expert manner.

As with a lot of sequels, *Chromeskull: Laid to Rest 2* doesn't quite reach the heights attained in the first movie. Commencing where we left off in number one, Chromeskull is somehow patched up and gives orders via video-messages to his assistant, corrupt FBI agent Brian Austin Green, working with stern-faced Danielle Harris; the masked maniac has now been created into something akin to the Frankenstein monster. The bulk of the film takes place in a vast workshop where Green, also wearing a chrome mask, imprisons teenager Mimi Michaels; protracted scenes of violence are dimly lit and drag a bit, simply carnage for carnage's sake, with very little in the way of plot development, even in fare that doesn't really require a strong storyline. Police officer Owain Yeoman, aided by Thom-

through Samuel's forehead to fry his brains. As if this wasn't enough, in a cellar underneath the floorboards, the girl's past victims live like cannibalistic ghouls, feeding off human flesh. Perhaps *The Loved Ones* overdoes it on the sadistic front, lapsing into feverish parody at times (Brompton overacts like crazy), and the tone lurches from angst (Samuel guilt-ridden over the death of his father in a car accident), to comedy (Richard Wilson trying to handle oversexed Goth Jessica McNamee—hilarious!) to out-and-out depravity (McLeavy forcing Samuel to urinate in a cup on threat of his penis being nailed to the chair). The bleak, bloody ending, with Samuel's girlfriend (foxy Victoria Thaine) coming to the rescue, has a touch of Tarantino about it, but that's no bad thing. Once again, the Australians prove that their horror fare has oodles of bite, more so than a lot of similar fodder, and produced on far less cash to boot, and McLeavy is absolutely riveting in the role of the maniacal, thoroughly disturbed, teenager with no friends.

Madison County
Dunn-Rite Prods./Southern Fried Films 2011; 81 minutes;
Director: Eric England ***

A college student heads off to Madison County with friends to interview the author of a book detailing the exploits of a notorious serial killer, only to find that the psycho still haunts the area.

Slasher maestro Robert Hall (*Laid to Rest* and its sequel) had a hand in the make-up and effects in Eric England's neat little slasher movie containing watered-down shades of *Wolf Creek*, shot over 18 days in Arkansas on a budget of $70,000. The other *Laid to Rest* connection is Nick Principe; he played Chromeskull in Hall's two movies and is the pig-masked maniac here, appearing on the 45th minute (if you discount the brief opening sequence). Until then, student pals Colley Bailey and Matt Mercer, girlfriends Joanna Sotomura and Natalie Scheetz, and Sotomura's protective brother, Ace Marrero, take a languidly paced drive through attractive sunlit wooded scenery, the mood darkening when they stop at Adrienne Harrell's diner to ask directions to author Dayton Knoll's house; the local rednecks don't like what they see, staring the kids out. Knoll's house appears deserted and Marrero takes a stroll in the woods, chancing upon two topless girls bathing, but they're the bait; he's stabbed in the back by a man wearing a pig's mask. The oinking, snorting maniac then stalks the other four and it's no good turning to those ugly looking town hicks for help, or even Harrell—she's Pigface's old Mum, hacking Sotomura to death in the final seconds as wounded Bailey and Knoll hightail it in a truck, Mercer and Scheetz both slaughtered (an axe and the jagged end of a broken baseball bat). Written with conviction by director England who commendably tones down on the usual crass girly/guy antics, *Madison County*, even from a scenic angle, is an agreeable slasher opus to take in, not too grisly, splatter suitable for the younger set, if you like—and Pigface/Pighead is an arresting addition to indie cinema's catalogue of loony masked killers.

Martyrs
CinéCinéma 2008; 99 minutes;
Director: Pascal Laugier ****

Abused, tortured and held captive as a child, a young girl and her friend take out a terrible revenge on the family responsible but in doing so uncover a secret involving a covert organization attempting to discover what lies beyond death.

Sickeningly violent, shockingly brutal, repulsively gore-laden to the point of overkill, with a profound ending*Martyrs* is all of these and more, another cutting edge addition to French New Wave splatter-horror guaranteed to nauseate more sensitive viewers. The film plays as two halves—first we have the wholesale slaughter of Mylene Jampanoi's adoptive family, aided by an unwilling Morjana Alaoui, and very bloody it is as well. But when Jampanoi cuts her own throat and a crazed, mutilated being enters the frame, we have a very different, and very complex, proposition to contend with; Alaoui is captured by a mysterious group (all dressed in black) and chained up in a cell. Catherine Bégin is Mademoiselle, austere leader of a

sect who are obsessed with the hereafter. By imprisonment in isolation, deprivations and beatings in a sterile environment, young women are systematically de-humanized, the unfortunate souls taking on the sins of the world. Subsequently skinned alive, it is believed by Bégin and her cronies that these "martyrs," through their pain and suffering, will experience a near-death experience and then relate what they have seen to the organization. The payoff here is that whatever Alaoui (after her appalling treatment, she resembles an alien suspended in a tank of fluid) tells Bégin, it is potent enough for the woman to blow her brains out and therein lies the rub—*is* there an afterlife or isn't there, and if the answer is "yes, there is," what exactly does it consist of? The prolonged de-humanization of Alaoui—force-fed, beaten, head shaved, the skin stripped surgically from her battered body—does go on far too long for comfort, but the actress turns in a remarkable performance given what she has to go through. Cruel, heartless and cold, *Martyrs* is a formidable horror brew, even though many will question its right to be called entertaining.

May
2 Loop Films 2002; 93 minutes;
Director: Lucky McKee *****

When she was a young girl, May was ridiculed at school because of a patch covering her lazy left eye; later, she also had an inward-turning right eye. Now a shy adult nursing deep-rooted mental scars, she exacts bloody retribution on those she feels affection for but who reject her innermost desires.

Winsome Angela Bettis turns in a poignant, beautifully observed portrayal of a deeply disturbed young woman whose mantra of "If you can't find a friend, make one" reaches untold levels of carnage. Continually talking to the stary-eyed doll in a glass case her mother made for her, she attempts physical contact and companionship but is rebuffed every faltering step of the way. Mechanic Jere-

my Sisto, he with the manly hands, rejects her; lesbian workmate Anna Faris, she with the pretty face, spurns her; punk James Duval, he with the rugged torso, thinks she's a freak; and bimbo Nichole Hiltz, she with the lovely legs, ridicules her. Even the blind kids at a school smash her beloved doll and tear it to rags. So what else can a poor girl do than to go crazy, kill all four and stitch the parts of their bodies she so admires together to create a bloody, life-sized doll. The only ingredient missing is an eye. Bettis stabs her right eye with scissors (this will have you jumping out of your seat in revulsion), extracts it and places it on the doll whose hand caresses her sleeping form. The splatter commences on the 63rd minute after a carefully orchestrated buildup, modern music used as an aural backdrop to emphasize the fact that *May* is a contemporary psycho shocker, and one of some note. Surely destined to become a cult classic, Lucky McKee's excursion into loneliness and ultimate madness is a riveting piece of horror cinema, quite moving in a grotesque fashion; the director virtually topped it with 2011's *The Woman*, also reviewed in this chapter.

ANDREW DIVOFF   ERIN BROWN

ROBERT KURTZMAN'S

THE RAGE

A MEGA-DOSE
OF PURE TERROR

"THIS YEAR'S
ULTIMATE PARTY MOVIE"
– FANGORIA

"A NEW SPLATTER
CLASSIC"
– DREAD CENTRAL

"ONE HELL OF A
GORY GOOD TIME"
– HORROR HOUND MAGAZINE

FEATURING MUSIC FROM MUSHROOMHEAD

The Rage
Precinct 13 Ent./Whacked In The Head LLC 2007;
85 minutes; Director: Robert Kurtzman ****

A mad scientist creates a rage mutagen; once introduced into the human system, he hopes that the resultant plague will decimate mankind.

There's nothing remotely subtle about Kurtzman's over-the-top splatter-fest. In a lunatic, overpowering mix that takes in facially deformed mutants munching on human flesh; ravenous zombie vultures; sex-crazed mutated midgets; a distasteful scene showing a man bludgeoning his nephew to a pulp; various implements (axe, knife, screwdriver, steel rods) plunged into craniums and other (unmentionable) orifices; two-foot, bloodsucking leeches; decapitations; bare boobs and full-on sex; and enough of the red stuff to stock several blood banks, the director's frenzied method of serving up this mammoth helping of juicy gore might leave viewers feeling a bit green around the gills. Andrew Divoff plays a modern-day Frankenstein, aggrieved that his breakthrough cure for cancer was filched by his employers for profit while he was thrown into an asylum. Now free, he plans to wipe out America in revenge by creating a deadly contagion. Porn actress Misty Mundae (billed as Erin Brown) and Ryan Hooks defeat the doctor and his pug-ugly minions (plus that horny dwarf

sporting a blonde wig) after a bloodbath finale but, hang on, those CGI vultures are still on the loose, hovering over the pair as they drive away from Divoff's burning laboratory. Shot in gaudy color at breakneck speed, *The Rage* unashamedly wallows in excess from start to finish and, of its type, almost deserves classic status.

Scarce
Bloodlife Films 2008; 93 minutes;
Directors: Jesse T. Cook and John Geddes ****

Stranded in a blizzard after their car skids off the road, three buddies are unaware that a nearby house which they see as a welcome refuge from their predicament is the residence of a cannibalistic redneck.

What a shame about *Scarce*'s depressing opening sequence: A parade of beer-swilling, dope-smoking, partying-on snowboarders all hoping to get laid, plus a lesbian romp, death metal blasting away in the background. Don't give up, though, however much you're tempted; what follows is a trip to redneck hell for three of these dudes (the joint directors and Thomas Webb), a hell from where nobody escapes. In Pennsylvania, Cook's vehicle veers off the icy road and he breaks a leg, leaving Geddes and Webb to venture into the woods where they chance upon loner Steve Warren in his ramshackle house. Hospitable at first, the pair soon discover that lanky Warren (looking like a cadaverous John Carradine) has hidden depths—him and his two equally sadistic pals (Gary Fisher and Chris Warrilow) practice cannibalism; Cook, shackled in chains, is being primed

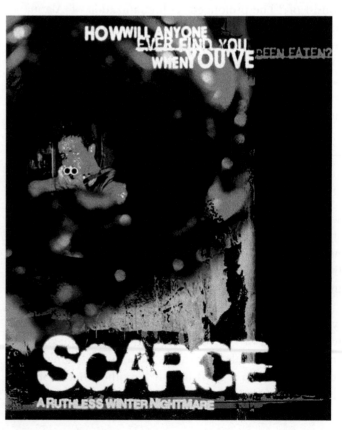

HOW WILL ANYONE
EVER FIND YOU
WHEN YOU'VE BEEN EATEN?

SCARCE
A RUTHLESS WINTER NIGHTMARE

for the evening's feast, with his friends earmarked as a future supply of human meat. There's an unsuccessful escape attempt that ends up in Fisher's own house of horrors and enough blood-dripping viscera on show to satisfy those with the appetite for it. *Scarce* is a gore-fest supreme, containing a standout performance from the spooky Warren, a man who ate his own wife but couldn't stop there. Uncompromisingly wallowing in degradation, nausea and filth, it's not the kind of movie your grandparents (or even parents) would ever approve of, but you might! A word of warning—watching this will put you off tomato soup for life!

Skeleton Crew aka Snuff Massacre
Northern Discipline/Timeless Films 2009; 90 minutes;
Directors: Tero Molin and Tommi Lepola **

The director of a crew shooting a horror movie based on events that took place in an abandoned asylum 30 years ago becomes obsessed with a stash of old snuff films found in a hidden room and decides to turn his production into a snuff masterpiece.

For the initial 25 minutes, you are caught up in Rita Suomalainen's attempts to escape from a vast derelict mental hospital where she and her boyfriend have taken refuge for the night following a car accident. On the run from a crazy nurse, she discovers her bloodied boyfriend on a bed in the basement, one arm and a leg hacked off, the guy in agony. She goes to put him out of his suffering with a cleaver and Steve Porter yells "Cut!" That's right—what we have been watching is Porter's bumbling attempts to make a decent slasher flick, a lively, atmospheric beginning that unfortunately goes off the rails once Porter stumbles across a pile of snuff features made by the hospital's former doctor. After watching every single one, he then takes on the mad doctor's mantle, butchering the crew and filming his deeds to come up with the ultimate snuff movie. This Finnish-produced *Hostel/Saw* clone could, and should, have been a winner—the shots of Porter glued to scenes of stomach-churning atrocity on scratchy celluloid, surrounded by the pale, blank-eyed specters of those put to death, chill the marrow, but once Porter switches into hammy maniac mode and starts to polish off his colleagues, *Skeleton Crew* travels down the modern-day carve-'em-up route, ditching suspense and terror in favor of all-out gore. A lesbian romp chucked in to titillate does nothing to redeem a feature that begins so well, and ends so dismally.

Switchblade Romance
aka Haute Tension; High Tension
EuropaCorp/Alexandre Film 2003; 91 minutes;
Director: Alexandre Aja *****

A desperate student attempts to rescue her friend from the hands of a psychopath after her entire family has been slaughtered in their farmhouse.

Relentless vicarious thrills highlight Alexandre Aja's French slasher flick which wasn't widely screened in the United Kingdom because of its graphic violence. Her mother, father and baby brother brutally slain by a hulking killer (Phillipe Nahon), Maiwenn Le Besco is chained, gagged and bundled into the back of his van; Cécile De France gets in with her and manages to break out at a gas station. The attendant is murdered with an axe and Nahon quickly drives off without De France, the girl commandeering a yellow Ford, in hot pursuit. The director piles on the tension, suspense and gore in every frame with finesse, right up to the unexpected shock twist—De France is the killer; what we have experienced are the workings of a tortured, sexually twisted mind, Nahon her barbarous doppelgänger, and, in hindsight, you can pinpoint the exact moment (and the film's major clue) when the tomboyish student changed from being a bossy friend to a possessive, murderous psycho—that masturbation scene 15 minutes in. Spoiled somewhat by too-obvious dubbing on its UK DVD release, this is a superior example of foreign-made slasher horror that far outstrips many bigger-budgeted efforts from the States and elsewhere.

Terror Trap
American World Pictures 2010; 86 minutes;
Director: Dan Garcia *

Drivers on an isolated stretch of road are apprehended by a sheriff and taken to a seedy motel where they are indecently assaulted and butchered, watched by paying customers on monitors.

A blatant rip-off of 2007's *Vacancy*, Garcia's trashy "almost a snuff movie" will repel many viewers with its scenes of full-frontal bloody torture, but is this really what people want to see curled up on the sofa with Coke and popcorn?

Kicking off with a certain amount of tension, first a young woman and then quarrelsome couple David James Elliott and Heather Marie Marsden are waylaid by sinister cop Jeff Fahey who takes them to a filthy hostel called the Motel Royal Vista. There, for the sum of a few thousand dollars, a group of deviant rednecks sits in front of a monitor as the girl is sexually molested and murdered while the couple attempt to escape from their predicament. Allied to this, hulking Michael Madsen (one of the actor's worst performances) arranges for a van load of Ukrainian prostitutes to be taken to the motel to undergo similar treatment. The two storylines oddly fail to gel, Madsen seemingly in a different production altogether, and the movie plummets into sick depravity after that fairly diverting first 15 minutes. The ending is a complete shambles, leaving nothing resolved, leading one to believe that by then, everyone concerned had said "enough is enough" and thrown in the towel. Violent torture-porn fodder for sadists only.

Timber Falls
Ascendant/A-Mark Ent. 2007; 100 minutes;
Director: Tony Giglio ***

A pair of religious fanatics seize young couples and force them to procreate in order to produce a child, compensating for the woman's string of miscarriages.

Given a pasting by UK critics and disappearing without trace from the circuits, Tony Giglio's combination of *Deliverance*, *Hostel* and *Wrong Turn* will appeal to hardcore/ torture horror freaks only—those of a saner disposition will turn way in disgust. Couple Josh Randall and Brianna Brown are innocently hiking through picturesque Lake Kimbrabow National Park. When Brown is abducted after skinny-dipping in a lake, Randall goes in search, steps into an animal trap, is taken to Beth Broderick's cabin for repairs and then finds himself trapped. Broderick and Ranger hubby Nick Searcy are religious nutters, several of Broderick's aborted fetuses kept in bell jars. What they require is a child of their own. The captured couple are given a mock marriage ceremony and then ordered to have sex, pronto; if they don't comply, each will be punished or, in this case, tortured. *Timber Falls* is slickly produced for a low-budget feature and Giglio piles on the hard-to-stomach shocks with gusto, but in all honesty, is seeing a woman's finger chopped off, a branding iron plunged into Randall's chest, a graphic whipping, various implements stabbing into writhing bodies and a disfigured maniac (Sascha Rosemann) sexually assaulting Brown *really* entertaining? Even the opening credits sequence showing a woman nailed to a bed and painfully yanking out both hands from the metal spikes will have many squirming in revulsion. Savagery in horror movies is now *de rigueur*, but *Timber Falls* does overstep the decency mark on occasions.

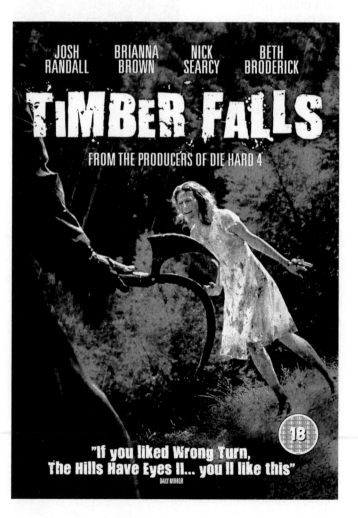

UNDER TEN MILLION? ANYTHING'S POSSIBLE!

The Wizard of Gore
Sick-A-Scope Motion Pictures 2007; 94 minutes;
Director: Jeremy Kasten **

A journalist becomes obsessed by master magician Montag the Magnificent and his unending succession of gory illusions.

A remake of the Herschell Gordon Lewis splatter groundbreaker of 1968 (released in 1970) and a pretty messy one at that. Kip Pardue visits the local carnival with his girl (Bijou Phillips) and is mesmerized by Crispin Glover's stage act; the magician plucks females from the audience, practically dismembers them in an orgy of blood, guts and entrails and then—hey presto—they're back to normal. But days later, these women are found dead with exactly the same injuries inflicted to them on stage. Pardue decides to investigate what's behind it all and in doing so descends into a world of drug-induced paranoia. Director Kasten goes flat out for Gothic decadence and *film noir*, shooting from all manner of odd angles; sadly, the murky photography hinders and confuses, while Glover's demented "crazy magician" turn goes far beyond the realms of overacting. A mind-controlling drug is behind the gruesome illusions but you need to be concentrating hard to get to the bottom of why Pardue takes on the mantle of the magician in the end. An unfathomable muddle at times, *The Wizard of Gore* is a splatter-fest gone awry; a straightforward approach would have been more appropriate here.

Wrestlemaniac
Blue Cactus Pictures 2006; 75 minutes;
Director: Jesse Baget ***

Three men and three women, driving through Mexico with the intention of making a porn movie, stop off at the ghost town of La Sangre de Dios where lurks a murderous wrestler whose specialty is ripping the skin from his victims' faces.

Suffer the first 30 minutes of Baget's splatter-fest and gore-freaks will be in for a real treat. That initial half introduces us to a cast of pretty unappealing, all-swearing characters: Stud Adam Huss, pothead Zack Bennett, overweight cameraman Jeremy Radin and three leggy tarts: Leyla Milani, Margaret Scarborough and Catherine Wreford. After a portion of simulated sex on a bar bench, filmed with drooling relish by Radin, Wreford feels sick, wanders off and is attacked. Next is Bennett and then the remaining four are fighting for survival; crazed masked wrester El Mascarado (Rey Misterio, Sr.) is on the prowl, looking for more skin to tear off more faces. The sicko has been constructed by scientists from the body parts of several expert wrestlers and now possesses invincible strength, and the only way to kill him is to somehow pull the mask off *his* face. It's standard shocker fare, containing a fair number of stomach-churning set pieces, but presented with more panache than usual by Baget who ensures that nobody gets out alive. But then, they never do in these modern-day horror outings.

VAMPIRES

Bled aka Bloody Days
FatKid Films/Indie Ent. 2009; 95 minutes;
Director: Christopher Hutson **

An artist specializing in erotic paintings is given a drug by a master vampire that transports her to a dark netherworld populated by bloodsuckers.

Bled is a one-woman show—Sarah Farooqui as the dark-haired painter-turned-vampire puts in a compelling

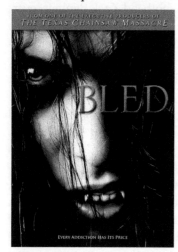

performance, compensating for deficiencies found in abundance elsewhere: poor acting, murky photography and an intrusive orchestral score that refuses to let up. Suave Jonathan Oldham introduces Farooqui to the drug, produced by boiling sap from a mystical twig. Inhaling the smoke, the woman finds herself in a misty forest, stalked by a demon and a young man who bears an uncanny resemblance to her on/off boyfriend, Chris Ivan Cevic. Soon, friends Alex Petrovitch and Michelle Morrow are partaking of the smoke with Farooqui but Cevic refuses to join them, particularly when he sees an alarming change come over the participants. The result of Farooqui's frequent journeys into this Brothers Grimm fairy tale world is that she transforms into a vampire herself, killing Morrow and eventually winding up dead in that dark forest, Cevic (who takes the drug once) forcing a tree branch into her heart. There's a lot of mention of eternal life and the blood of the young, but how all this fits in with the muddled scenario is anyone's guess. *Bled* tries very hard to be an opulent tale of the undead and if made on a bigger budget might well have succeeded. As it stands, the terrifying sight of the voluptuous Farooqui changing into a gray-faced, addled snarling vampire is the only thing that, alone, is worth the price of the DVD.

Embrace of the Vampire
Cinetel Films/Reel One Ent. 2013; 91 minutes;
Director: Carl Bessai **

A young girl attends college on a trust scholarship, aware that her blood disorder could be the result of an ancient vampiric curse.

Filmed in the wooded mountains of Vancouver, *Embrace of the Vampire*, a loose remake of Anne Goursaud's 1995 movie of the same title, fails to grip, meandering in-

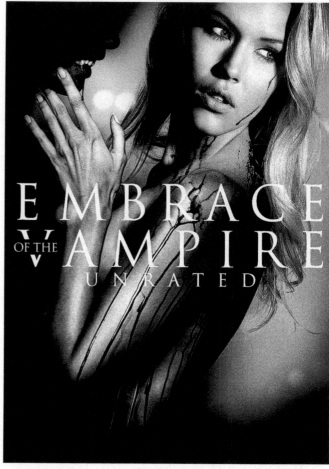

stead of nailing the action. Opening in 1735, rival vampires squabbling over a terrified girl whose vein has been opened, we next see withdrawn Sharon Hinnendael meeting roommate Kaniehtiio Horn and her tarty, obnoxious pal C.C. Sheffield. The shy co-ed, who wears her dead mother's ancient necklace (it leaves a burn mark on her chest), suffers from horrific visions (cups full of maggots; teeth falling out), becoming the butt of much wicked female taunting, including a lesbian pass in the shower. Craftily, we are led to believe that Doctor Robert Moloney *could* be a vampire, with his piercing blue eyes and aversion to bright light, but this is a red herring calculated to throw the unwary off the scent; handsome fencing coach/professor Victor Webster is the undead one, lusting after Hinnendael, a virgin. If he takes her, he will return to a state of normality and she, in turn, will become a fully-fledged bloodsucker. Mystic Keegan Connor Tracy tries to warn the girl of her dreadful family inheritance, that she'll be damned for eternity if she has sex ("It's my destiny to help you."), boyfriend Ryan Kennedy is slaughtered right on the point of penetration, half-naked Sheffield is bitten to death and Moloney murdered. Webster, in a showdown with Hinnendael at his lodge, has a silver cross plunged into his heart after he nips her neck; she quickly draws the curtains and sunlight floods the room, reducing the vampire to ashes. Relieved, Hinnendael rests against a wall, convinced she's now free from the curse of vampirism—or is she? *Embrace of the Vampire* looks good, particularly the forested Vancouver backdrops, but lacks punch and, dare I say it, bite; 56 years on, Herbert L. Strock's 1957 *Blood of Dracula* (*Blood is My Heritage*) still remains the best co-ed vampire picture ever made in terms of X-rated undead teenage shocks.

Fist of the Vampire
KillerWolf Films 2007; 93 minutes;
Director: Len Kabasinski *

Thirty years after witnessing the death of his entire family by vampires, a detective resolves to infiltrate their sect by way of illegal fights and eliminate them.

For those brought up on a diet of Bela Lugosi, Universal-International, Christopher Lee and Hammer Films, turn away right now. Kabasinski's muddily shot outing, mixing aspects of both *Blade* and *Fight Club*, seems to be aimed at martial arts-loving, beer-swilling, bike-riding metal freaks who aren't too particular about their horror fare roots. Brian Anthony carries the show as the cop out to get vampires Leon South and Brian Heffron, who are burdened with their own problems; loose cannon vam-

piress Darian Crane can't stop eating her female victims (after sexually abusing them), leaving a trail of corpses in her wake, thus drawing unwanted attention to the sect. One tedious fight follows another, the bloodsuckers going up in flames when exposed to sunlight. Even vampire fans will find this hard to swallow—for real indie undead thrills, try Richard Brandes' *Out for Blood* (2004) instead.

The Hamiltons
San Francisco Ind. Cinema 2006; 86 minutes;
Directors: Mitchell Altieri and Phil Flores ***

Left to cope on their own after the death of their parents, three brothers and a sister kidnap young girls, torture them and drain their blood—but for what purpose?

The purpose is made clear in the final 10 minutes. Up to then, you are convinced that sociopaths Joseph McKelheer, Samuel Child, and lesbian sister MacKenzie Firgens are simply deranged serial killers, only baby brother Cory Knauf sensitive to the girls' plight; two of them are shackled in the basement, awaiting death or even worse. And who, or what, lurks in that gated box in the basement, feeding on raw meat? Shot on and off in camcorder mode to

highlight the terror the victims are being put through, *The Hamiltons* is more or less successful in depicting a young, parentless family disintegrating into some form of nightmarish hell, containing a subtle performance from teenager Knauf who eventually discovers the horrifying truth behind the killings; the family are infected by a "disease" (vampirism?), meaning continual supplies of fresh human blood in order for them to survive, and what's more, the thing in the basement is an even younger sibling, locked up because of his animalistic tendencies. If classed as a modern-day vampire shocker, at least the movie is a departure from the norm, with a high gore quota (the murder of a girl in a bath is not for the squeamish) and a denouement that will come as quite a surprise.

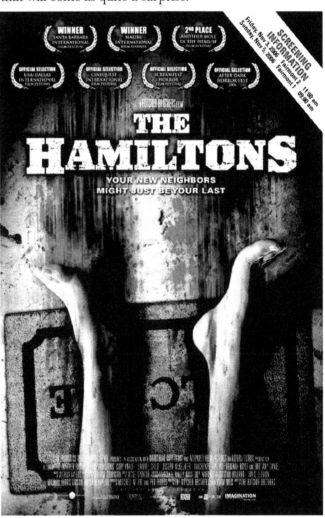

I've Been Watching You aka The Brotherhood
Rapid Heart Pictures 2001; 85 minutes;
Director: David DeCoteau *

A sinister fraternity named "Doma Tau Omega" who have discovered the secret of eternal youth wants to recruit a young freshman into their ranks as "new blood."

From the director of the abominable *Ancient Evil: Scream of the Mummy* (1999) comes another abomination, a tepid, talkative vampire farrago that simply appears to

be an excuse for a group of super-honed hunks to strip down to their Calvin Klein pants and drool over each other. Homoeroticism may exist in the cinema, but not in this cheapskate form. Sam Page and roommate Josh Hammond home in on college babe Elizabeth Bruderman, oblivious to the fact that frat leader Bradley Stryker and his three acolytes are homing in on *them*, in particular pretty-boy Page. These beefed-up dudes are 100 years old, have sold their souls to the dark forces, and need Page's soul to prolong their youthful existence. DeCoteau directs with the pace of a snail with migraine, some shots dragging on for over eight minutes; close-ups of heaving male buttocks and lascivious looks from Stryker and his blood-brothers as Page is drugged and forced to grovel over Bruderman in her underwear. An axe through the chest puts paid to Stryker, the other three perishing in clouds of smoke. For lovers of soft-porn gay movies only. For genuine horror buffs—forget it!

Kiss of the Vampire aka Immortally Yours
HMPC/Artist View Entertainment 2009; 100 minutes;
Director: Joe Tornatore *

A sect of modern-day vampires preys on the inhabitants of a small town but their leader falls in love and wishes to become mortal.

Beware any vampire movie that carries a PG rating (in England) on its DVD release. And this flaccid *Kiss of the Vampire* is light years away from Hammer's colorful 1963 classic of the same name. What we are presented with here is pretty-boy vampire Daniel Goddard falling for winsome Katherine Hawkes (she co-wrote the script) at the opera and wanting to lose his vampirish ways with a little help from her doctor father. Meanwhile, an Illuminati headed by Eric Etebari is trying to make a deal with the bloodsuckers because *they* want the secret of eternal life, and chief-vampire-in-waiting Gary Daniels is out with his pack when the moon is full, pouncing on teenagers in a feeding frenzy. After a century of pictures dealing with the

undead, one would have thought that today's moviemakers could have come up with a fresh perspective on the old legend, but they patently failed to do so here. Bland and lifeless in all departments, Joe Tornatore's offering is flat and indigestible: Long-haired Matthias Hues plays the obligatory vampire slayer, carrying a crossbow and arrows; Goddard has a midget assistant; tough-guy Daniels is hopelessly out of his depth as a snarling bloodsucker; that "heads in space" sequence towards the end, when members of the Illuminati grow fangs above the Earth, has to be seen to be believed; and the dialogue verges on the atrocious ("I'm madly in love with Alex." "What's wrong with that?" "He's a vampire."). The sect all go up in smoke in the finale, when exposed to brilliant light, and the two lovers are last seen getting cozy, bathed in the rays of the sun, just to get the message across that Goddard is now a normal human being. Watered-down horror fare—lovers of the *Twilight* saga might enjoy it, lovers of adult, meaty vampire fodder most certainly won't.

Midnight Son
Free Lunch Productions 2011; 88 minutes;
Director: Scott Leberecht *****

A malnourished young man suffering from a childhood skin disorder cannot venture out during the day and finds that the only way to stop his continual craving for food is by drinking copious amounts of blood.

Forget the teenage vampire antics of the *Twilight* Franchise—this is how a doomed romance based on the vampire myth *should* be done, Scott Leberecht's expert eye cloaking his production in a kind of sordid, blood-soaked depravity, a depravity that eventually takes over the lives of lovers Zak Kilberg and Maya Parish. Owing a lot to George A. Romero's 1977 *Martin* in style and mood, *Midnight Son* relates how Kilberg, a pale, ill-looking night security guard-cum-artist, discovers by chance that blood, human or animal, satisfies his stomach cramps, even though the result is a pair of yellow eyes, brought on in moments of sexual lust. Striking up an awkward relationship with coke-snorting Parish, the youth turns to unethical hospital orderly Joe D. Jonz for sachets of discarded blood from the accident and emergency department, his life spiraling out of control as he contaminates first Jonz, then Parish, with his curse. Fired for beating up an employee who refused to

UNDER TEN MILLION? ANYTHING'S POSSIBLE!

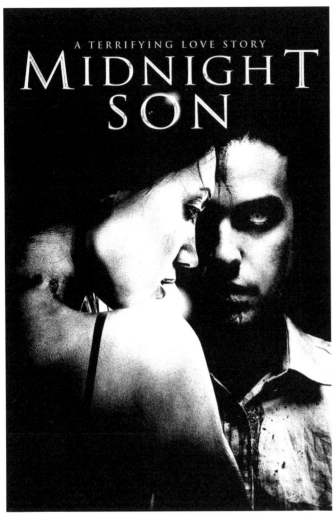

A TERRIFYING LOVE STORY

MIDNIGHT SON

Candlelit soft-porn toothless vampire frolics for the dirty raincoat brigade. Eighty minutes running time equates to 70 minutes of unbridled sex, 10 minutes of watered-down vampire action; 400-year-old vampiress Julie Strain and sidekick Michelle Bauer, their silicone-enhanced breasts popping out of the screen in mock 3-D, lure dumb waitress Raelyn Saalman to the Blonde Heaven agency on the promise of fame and fortune, hick boyfriend Alton Butler in hot pursuit. Umpteen sexual antics (and corny music video shoots) later, Butler has been vampirized, so has horror cinema's most ineffectual vampire hunter (Jason Clow) and the whole tacky enterprise comes to a close. Not released until 2001 (and why the title *Morgana?*), David DeCoteau's modernistic take on the undead (factor 200 sunblock allows vampires to operate in daylight?) needs a stake through its celluloid heart to put viewers out of their misery.

Night Junkies
Scanner-Rhodes 2007; 90 minutes;
Director: Lawrence Pearce **
A young prostitute is ordered by her boss to walk the streets and snare a killer who has murdered 13 women, all hookers.

sign the "in" book, Kilberg confesses to cop Larry Cedar that he may have killed a woman, but is disbelieved. Following a violent row, Jonz, who has been draining blood from corpses, is chained to a wall and left to fry in the sun, Parish reduced to inhabiting Kilberg's boarded-up basement flat, unable to face sunlight. The final shot is downbeat and moving, Leberecht drawing his camera slowly back, framing the bloodstained couple (Cedar has just been slashed to death) lolling against each other, yellow eyes rimmed with dark circles, like two strung-out drug addicts on Planet Heroin—there's nothing remotely glamorous or romantic about this pair of vampire lovers! Grimy and compelling, containing low-key but riveting performances from the two leads, *Midnight Son*, if granted a bigger budget, could have been a minor winner at the box-office, catering for the more discerning horror fan who knows a good thing when he sees it.

Morgana aka Blonde Heaven
Torchlight Ent./Cult Video 1995; 80 minutes;
Director: David DeCoteau *
A coven of vampires, under the guise of an escort agency, recruits women off the Los Angeles' streets to become new members.

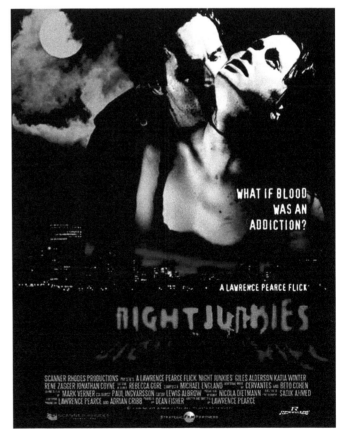

Pearce's contemporary reading on the vampire legend is allied to drug addiction; both vampire and junkie need a regular fix to survive. Shot solely after dark in seedy London locations, *Night Junkies* is simply too gloomy and glum to maintain much interest. Katia Winter plays the unwilling decoy, Giles Anderson the vampire she falls for and who enrolls her into his world. However, Anderson is not the only killer on the block. Headstrong vampire René Zagger has a hatred of prostitutes, loves Winter and wants to vampirize her to death. There are no fangs in this vampire thriller, even though necks are bitten and chewed on. The dialogue is suitably foul, with an unpleasant misogynistic tone underlying the scenario; the message seems to infer that women of a certain type are there to be abused, beaten and disposed of. In the end you care little for the characters, even though Winter dies and Anderson heads for Edinburgh for a possible cure. Not for vampire purists, that's for sure.

Shower of Blood

Film Fusion 2004; 90 minutes;
Director: Tiffany Kilbourne *

Three hot chicks and two sexed-up dudes drive to a mansion owned by Uncle Marty who turns out to be a 300-year-old vampire.

Belches, farts, puking; a ridiculous music score; dumber than dumb acting; an abundance of female nudity; and vampires looking like throwbacks to the 1970s period of horror filmmaking. Was *Shower of Blood* meant to be taken as a joke, a parody of the much-revered B movie? Surely, this camcorder disaster can't have been produced as a serious piece of work. Granted, babes Lia Montelongo, Melissa Mountifield and Robin Brown are guaranteed to have any male with certain problems ditching those Viagra tablets, spending most of their screen time partly or totally undressed, but working against this bevy of busty beauties is Dave Larsen, acting (to use the term loosely) like a

robot running on flat batteries; pal Peter Renaud is no better, and neither is Martin Shannon as the playboy vampire, trying to out-ham the likes of Vincent Price but failing miserably. Devoid of any real atmosphere and thrills, the clumsy climax sees Shannon choking on a crucifix and crumbling into a skeleton (to the tune of "Roll out the Barrel"), although niece Montelongo has inherited the family vampir-

ic curse, turning her fangs and lust on Mountifield in the closing credits. Yes, even the 911 operator the girls telephone is a half-clad tarty vampire! *Perhaps* a great wheeze for a lads' night out—otherwise, Tiffany Kilbourne's crass movie is unbelievably dire in every respect.

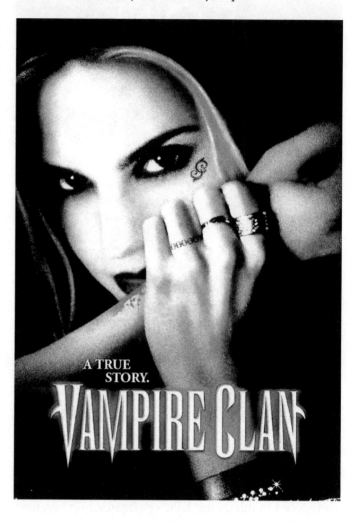

Vampire Clan

Langley Productions 2002; 87 minutes;
Director: John Webb ***

Based on a true series of incidents that took place in Eustis, Texas in 1996: A brutal murder leads to the arrest of five teenagers; each relates to the police their story of the circumstances leading up to the slaying.

Warning: This is *not* a movie about vampires in the true sense of the word. It's about charismatic (but psychotic) 17-year-old Drew Fuller, a young dude obsessed with vampirism, who gathers around him one guy (Timothy Lee DePriest), three Goth chicks (Marina Black, Kelly Kruger, Alexandra Breckenridge) and initiates them into his twisted creed—drink each other's blood (from the wrists), break into houses, steal cars and commit bloody murder with a crowbar. The horrific killing of Kruger's parents leads to their downfall, the girl realizing she is on the road to some kind of hell and wanting out from the

UNDER TEN MILLION? ANYTHING'S POSSIBLE!

self-styled "Clan." Gloomily put together by John Webb, flashing backwards and forwards between the police interrogation rooms and the disturbing chain of events, the film doesn't make for comfortable viewing. However, in its own low-key way, *Vampire Clan* is a relevant study of teenage antisocial behavior taken to extreme lengths that can sometimes spiral alarmingly into much darker depths than thought possible, even by those indulging in such foul practices.

Vampires vs. Zombies
aka Carmilla, the Lesbian Vampire
Creepy Six Films 2004; 81 minutes;
Director: Vincent D'Amato *

A father, his daughter and her lesbian vampire lover converge on a derelict convent overrun by zombies to put an end to the vampire's reign.

Cheap and dreadful sums up Vincent D'Amato's vampire/zombie clunker (distributed by Asylum), the kind of horror movie college film students could knock up in a week on peanuts as part of their thesis. Badly acted and scripted, blonde Maritama Carlson plays seductive vampire Carmilla, giving oral sex with added bite to willing Bonny Giroux while C.S. Munro and General Peter Ruginis fight off the odd rampaging green-faced zombie. None of it makes much sense, one uncoordinated scene of bloodletting and decapitation followed by another, with a couple of red herrings chucked in—is Giroux a patient in a mental hospital, imagining all this, or is it for real? Dialogue such as "All right, you zombie fuck" as one of the undead is run over will make purists yearn for better times (and better pictures), and what, if any, is the meaning behind that tub full of green goo, and the vampiress in white who yells "Baaaath!"at Giroux? Stakes through chests, close-ups of viscera spilling out of torsos, Munro creating carnage with a power saw, Giroux shouting, "What is this? A fucking zombie convention?" and the living dead munching on body parts add up to an amateurish mishmash that, for aficionados of both genres, makes depressing fare. To see how it *should* be done, tune in to Jesús Franco's *Vampyros Lesbos* (1971) which itself was cheaply produced but made with an expert eye for lesbian vampire thrills of the salacious variety.

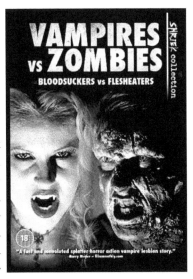

Werewolves

Animals
American World Pictures/T & C Pictures 2008; 93 minutes;
Director: Douglas Aarniokoski (Arnold Cassius) **

A man down on his luck is befriended by a young woman and becomes embroiled in a world of savagery linked to man's primitive animal instincts.

There's a lot of raunchy, explicit sex in *Animals*—sex on a table; sex on the bonnet of a car in the pouring rain and sex in a bed. Nicki Aycox is the vixen; she's one of a select breed of humans who have the ability to transform themselves into slavering werewolf-type beings during moments of passion, and she's latched herself onto Marc Blucas, seeing him as a possible mate. But jealous shapeshifter Naveen Andrews, her erstwhile partner, appears on the scene, leading to a ferocious showdown between the threesome plus Eva Amurri, a shy bar girl who has the hots for Blucas big time. *Animals* is vaguely unsatisfying—the opening 15 minutes, with characters drifting in and out of the scenario, will faze many fans, the photography is too dark and the transformation sequences, filmed in a shimmering blue light, are clumsily handled for a modern-day horror film. The movie plays more like a soft-porn number and in that respect it delivers in spades; where it doesn't deliver is serving up the necessary man-into-beast thrills to keep fans happy.

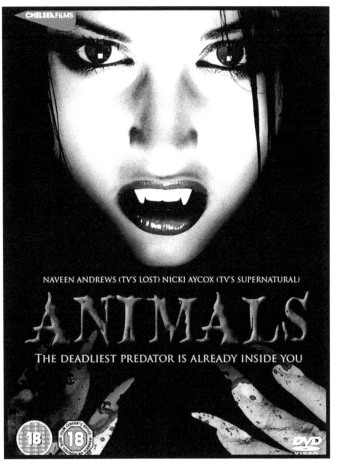

into werewolves but are exterminated, along with their unholy brethren, by lone survivor McKidd; he severs gas pipes, blowing the cottage and its unwelcome visitors to bits. "Werewolves Ate My Platoon" states the headline at the end under the news that Germany lost to England 5-1 in a soccer match that Pertwee's squad desperately wanted to see, rather than slogging through the Scottish forests (filming took place in Luxembourg) and being set upon by creatures that had no right to exist in the year 2001. Neil Marshall used the movie (not a success on its limited release) as a springboard for the superior *The Descent* (2005), one of the best British horror pictures made since 2000: *Dog Soldiers* is pure man versus savage hairy beasts fodder, nothing more, nothing less, but shot in a ferocious, down-to-earth manner; the pithy, oath-strewn dialogue is highly amusing while the non-CGI werewolves (animatronics and dancers in lycanthrope costume were employed because of their balletic skills) are up there with the very best that horror cinema has to offer within the werewolf arena.

Dog Soldiers

Kismet Ent./The Noel Gay Motion Picture Company 2002; 105 minutes; Director: Neil Marshall ****

An eight-man army patrol on exercise in the Scottish Highlands comes under siege from a pack of werewolves, taking refuge in a cottage occupied by a mysterious female.

No surprise that the woman (Emma Cleasby) turns out to be a lycanthrope herself ("They're as real as you and me."), as is belligerent special forces commander Liam Cunningham who knew about the beasts all along, hoping to capture one for the military to use in their weapons division. Cleasby, fancying Kevin McKidd and viewing him as a possible mate, has kept her primitive urges under control—for the time being. His insides hanging out following an attack, Sergeant Sean

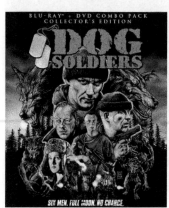

Pertwee and his five men, after encountering bloody body parts in the forest and wounded Cunningham, barricade themselves inside the cottage, the wolf men snarling, smashing, grabbing and ripping their way through the building and cast. Cleasby, Cunningham and, lastly, Pertwee (both men infected by their injuries), transform

Ginger Snaps
Copperheart Ent./Water Pictures 2000; 108 minutes; Director: John Fawcett *****
Ginger Snaps 2: Unleashed
Copperheart Ent./49 Films 2004; 90 minutes; Director: Brett Sullivan ***
Ginger Snaps Back: The Beginning
Copperheart Ent./49 Films 2004; 94 minutes; Director: Grant Harvey ***

UNDER TEN MILLION? ANYTHING'S POSSIBLE!

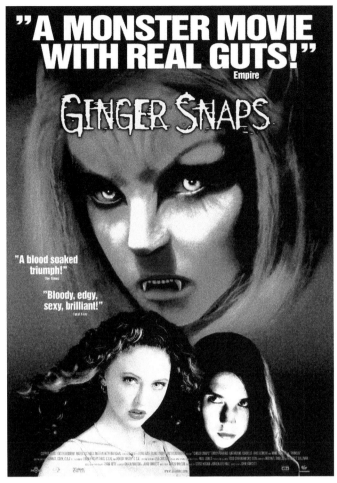

"A MONSTER MOVIE WITH REAL GUTS!"
Empire

GINGER SNAPS

"A blood soaked triumph!"
The Times

"Bloody, edgy, sexy, brilliant!"
Total Film

body (pointed ears and teeth, unwanted body hair, an enhanced sense of smell), the morose Perkins, with the aid of young Tatiana Maslany, a girl sporting strange homicidal tendencies, escapes from the hospital and goes to the youngster's house, followed by odious sex-pest orderly Eric Johnson. Isabelle puts in a guest appearance as Perkins' ghostly lycanthropic conscience and the movie ends in complete mayhem with all involved under siege from a huge werewolf; the beast is slain on a bed of spikes and the weird Maslany locks Perkins in the cellar, content to sit in her bedroom and write a book about the whole episode. Tension-filled and gruesome, *Ginger Snaps 2* doesn't quite live up to the standards set by its predecessor but nevertheless holds its own as a darned good werewolf thriller.

The third instalment is something of an oddity, taking the werewolf action right back to 1815 and re-examining the sisters' death-obsessed relationship in an entirely different setting. In the snowy Canadian forests, wendigos (ancient mythical monsters) have been on the prowl, killing Indians and traders. Following a boating accident in which their parents drowned, Perkins and Isabelle arrive at the Northern Legion Trading Company and immediately come under suspicion, particularly as Isabelle has been bitten by a nameless animal in the woods and is growing sharp teeth, a silver streak highlighting her ginger mane. Fort Commander Tom McCamus has a malformed,

Three low-budget Canadian-produced werewolf flicks that bombed at the UK box-office (the two sequels never made it onto the circuits) but stand up as excellent examples of the genre.

Ginger Snaps (*I Was a Canadian Teenage Werewolf* would be an apt '50s title!) is a stunning interpretation of the werewolf myth in modern guise: Two suicide-obsessed Goth sisters (Emily Perkins and Katharine Isabelle) are attacked by a ferocious animal that has been slaughtering the dogs of Bailey Downs. Following the assault, Isabelle slowly undergoes a change, from bullied 15-year-old to aggressive teenage slut, and thereafter into a fully-fledged werewolf. An infusion concocted from Monkshood leaves, drummed up by caring drug dealer Kris Lemche, slows down the transformation but soon, Isabelle is a savage monster on the prowl, even biting her own sister and contaminating her. Taking in sibling rivalry, puberty problems, sexuality, peer pressure and undying love ("Together, Forever"), the film, a witty and bloody (there's an awful lot of skin-slicing on show) mix of *Carrie* and *An American Werewolf in London*, skillfully avoids all of the pitfalls evident in so many other teen horror movies and emerges an outright winner.

The second interlude sees Perkins incarcerated in a care facility, injecting herself with the Monkshood infusion to avoid becoming a werewolf but finding its effects wearing off pretty quickly. As signs of lycanthropy take over her

EMILY PERKINS TATIANA MASLANY ERIC JOHNSON KATHARINE ISABEL

GINGER SNAPS
UNLEASHED 2

driver Sean Pertwee wanders out to investigate and is attacked by something monstrous with glowing yellow eyes and sharp talons; soon, the carriages and their terrified occupants are under siege from howling, prowling werewolves. Horror cinema's favorite hairy monster is alive and kicking in Paul Hyett's blood-soaked £1,000,000 tribute to the werewolf genre, the creatures more ape-like in appearance than of old: Young guard Ed Speleers attempts to "man up" as teen Rosie Day is dragged through a window, later found hanging in the branches of a tree, one of the beasts feasting on her entrails; Shauna *The Descent* Macdonald meets a similar demise; Duncan Preston's infected wife grows fangs ("She's one of them!") and rips open her husband's throat; fat complainer Calvin A. Dean is torn to shreds in a toilet; and obnoxious bad guy Elliot Cowan runs for his life, locking the train doors and leaving the others to their fate. Only Speleers and waitress Holly Weston make it into the woods, but Speleers, in an ambush, sacrifices himself to enable Weston to escape to Eastborough where she's last seen staggering down the platform, bloody and disheveled. In a final act of retribution, Cowan, wandering through the forest, finds that he's surrounded by werewolves—and Speleers, now transformed, fangs bared, eyes blazing, goes in for

half-werewolf son locked away, there's a maniac preacher at loose wanting to burn wrong-doers and slavering werewolves are queuing up outside, licking their fangs at the thought of all that food inside the barricades. This is basically a retread of *Ginger Snaps*—if you can push John Fawcett's beguiling entrant into the trilogy to one side, *Ginger Snaps Back*, while losing a little of the original's freshness, makes for rewarding period horror with more bite than most, and both young actresses are on top form, as they were in the other two movies in the series; the picture ends with the two clasping each other's bloody hands, "Together, Forever," their private creed, on both girls' lips.

Howl
Starchild Pictures/AV Pictures 2015; 89 minutes;
Director: Paul Hyett ****

On the overnight train from London's Waterloo Station to Eastborough, a dispirited guard recently denied promotion has to contend with not only a bunch of disgruntled passengers but a pack of rampaging werewolves.

When the train grinds to a halt in a mist-laden forest lit by the full moon, due to having run over the body of a butchered deer, thus fracturing a fuel line,

UNDER TEN MILLION? ANYTHING'S POSSIBLE!

the kill! Some amusing lines ("We're just a train full of bear bait." "No, it was more like a man.") plus atmospheric filming in Wexham's Black Park Country Park contribute to a splendidly gory, nerve-jangling British wolf man outing, the best of its type since Neil Marshall's *Dog Soldiers*; werewolf buffs won't be disappointed for one minute.

War Wolves
Curb Entertainment 2009; 104 minutes;
Director: Michael Worth *

A soldier and his unit return from the Middle East; each has been infected by a werewolf virus and find themselves hunted by a special forces unit.

Veteran John Saxon leads the military group that are out to exterminate the werewolves in a $500,000 tiresome, overlong horror thriller that unsuccessfully combines war action, bar-room brawls, fistfights, martial arts, talks of Gulf War syndrome (the possible cause for lycanthropy?) and cheap-looking werewolf make-up, among the worst committed to celluloid (or tape in this instance). Sometimes, it's a big mistake to update the werewolf legend into such a modern setting (as with vampires) and to try and present the film as a *Matrix*-style shoot-'em-up, which is the case here, although, give the film its due, Michael Worth, hitting the drugs/alcohol trail to suppress his body changes and deadly urges, takes on the alias of Lawrence Talbot, a direct reference to Universal's *The*

Wolf Man, dating from 1941. You care even less about the characters than the unremarkable effects (Natasha Alam, delighted with her newfound evil power, tries it on with Michael Worth) and the film drags throughout. It's good to see old pro Saxon back in action again, and Adrienne Barbeau puts in a decent performance as the one person believing in werewolves, aliens and Bigfoot, but they're the only things remotely watchable in this substandard, unlikeable werewolf flick; *War Wolves* fails miserably on all counts.

Autumn
Renegade Pictures 2009; 110 minutes;
Director: Steven Rumbelow ****

Mankind is virtually wiped out by a deadly virus; a band of survivors takes refuge in a school and then has to deal with the reactivated corpses.

A post-apocalyptic zombie thriller that works. And why, in a genre saturated with all manner of cinematic variations on the walking dead, does it work? Because director Rumbelow slows things down, infuses the film's look with some striking cinematography and a degree of intelligence, concentrates on the human aspect and doesn't have his zombies lurching all over the place like demented, ravaged puppets. Basically, you have a cast of three (Dexter Fletcher, Dickon Tolson and Lana Kamenov) realizing that the dead who are at first blindly stumbling around are slowly regaining their faculties; therefore the need to find an isolated house is paramount to their survival chances. One hour 30 minutes into the action, David Carradine makes an appearance as a scatty survivor who refuses to leave the tied-up zombie that used to be his mother behind when Tolson requests that he joins his group. The pessi-

mistic ending has Fletcher and Kamenov in a car, gazing out to sea and wondering what the future has in store. No, it's not *28 Days Later*, *I Am Legend* and a host of others; in a class of horror cinema open to self-parody (think *Shaun of the Dead*), at least *Autumn* possesses a degree of intelligence about it and cuts down on the sometimes unintentionally hilarious zombie histrionics than can ruin many a horror flick. Uneven sound balance in a few scenes doesn't detract from what is a compelling, low-budget zombie flick that is a lot more palatable than most.

Days of Darkness
Motor Pictures/Swag Ent. 2007; 89 minutes;
Director: Jake Kennedy **

Remnants of a comet enter Earth's atmosphere, creating a dust cloud that turns humans into zombies.

Following a hike through the mountains, Travis Brorsen and Roshelle Baier are attacked by flesh-hungry zombies as they get in their car; following Chris Ivan Cevic, they end up at a compound run by trigger-happy Tom Elpin, home to, among others, an ex-porn actress, her screwed-up daughter, her zombie son (chained to the wall in a basement cell) and the obligatory religious nut played with zeal by John Lee Ames. Zombie movies come and go, and *Days of Darkness* treads familiar territory, *until* halfway through, that is; the film then switches rather awkwardly to *Alien*/*Invasion of the Body Snatchers* mode as it transpires that the cloud has brought with it parasites that enter the body (male and female) and incubate, producing humanoid creatures that control minds via a

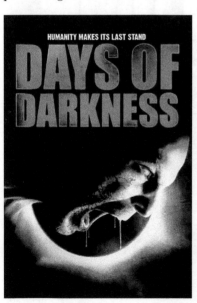

vein into the back of the head. So we now have a humans versus zombies *and* aliens scenario that becomes increasingly frenetic as each cast member is finished off in a welter of blood; only the two lovers seen at the outset are left intact at the end, having discovered that the alien hosts are allergic to, of all things, alcohol. Fundamentally, there's nothing all that wrong with the movie, but there's not much to get the juices flowing either, and the final shot of an intoxicated Brorsen and Baier shooting their way out of the compound appears rushed and unresolved. Average fare for all lovers of zombie flicks.

Dead and Deader
Mindfire Entertainment 2006; 89 minutes;
Director: Patrick Dinhut **

A green beret returns from Cambodia, part human, part zombie; his infected squad are brought back in body bags, but return from the dead as flesh-eaters, contaminating all those that they bite.

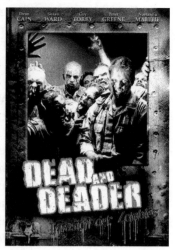

Comedy zombie flicks? Hmmm—*Fido* (Anagram Pictures 2006) wasn't too foolish, but *Dead and Deader* is stretching things a bit, even if blessed with a fairly witty script. After all, is a woman (in this case, foxy Susan Ward) enticing the creatures with raw meat on a stick, saying, "Come here, zombie" really *that* hilarious? Dean Cain and his squad become infected by stings from an abnormal species of scorpion in Cambodia. Back in California, Cain (exhibiting no pulse or heartbeat) rips a scorpion out of his arm; although he still craves fresh meat, he's not 100% zombie. The marine is on the side of the goodies, wanting to exterminate the zombie hordes. Teamed up with Eddie Murphy clone Guy Torry and babe Ward, much of the movie consists of the trio on the run from the military (who still think Cain is a danger), battling the zombies and meeting up with withered-looking Peter Greene, a doctor suffering from cancer. He's after a cure and reckons it lies in Cain's blood somewhere. Gory effects abound as bodies are decapitated in ceiling fans, limbs gnawed on, fingers minced in a grinder, faces blasted with guns and throats torn open, but it all sits uncomfortably with the comedic element and refuses to gel. Cain is wooden, Torry you might find amusing if you're a fan of Eddie Murphy and Ward looks great when stripping down to her black underwear. But it's still not an ideal mix to blend camp farce with out-and-out horror, and it doesn't work here.

Dead Meat
Horrorthon Pictures/Three Way Prods. 2004; 80 minutes;
Director: Conor McMahon **

Ireland is swept by a zombie epidemic caused by feeding cows contaminated meat.

There is a school of thought among some members of the horror fraternity that once you have sat through one zombie movie, you have seen the lot. To a certain extent, that's true—as soon as the explanation as to how and why the local populace has been reduced to a mass of shambling flesh-eaters is done and dusted, it's a case of a select band of survivors battling against the odds, besieged by the walking dead masses. *Dead Meat* is no different to hundreds of others of its ilk: Couple David Ryan and Marian Araujo motor down a country lane in Leitrim, run over a guy, stick his body on the back seat, he comes alive, bites Ryan, infects him and the zombie ball starts to roll. In the space of a day,

Araujo turns from a self-obsessed, designer-clad diva to seasoned zombie killer: She meets David Muyllaert and another couple and after a series of bloody clashes, Araujo ends up in the back of a military truck with dozens of normal people. Irish horror films have a tendency to appear cold, gray and grubby (due to the country's damp climate) and *Dead Meat* is no exception; there are plenty of gory exterminations shot in close-up, the pace is quick and the zombies are ghoulish. Dark photography (occasionally, you are looking at a black screen for what seems like minutes) is a hindrance but, after all, what can any director do to improve the genre apart from simply paying homage to what has gone before. Zombie fans will lap it up—non-aficionados will find it ever so slightly old hat.

Mutants
Spotlight Pictures/K2 Pictures 2008; 83 minutes;
Director: Amir Valinia *

The ruthless boss of the Just Rite Sugar Company employs an unethical scientist to doctor sugar cane, making it so addictive that consumers crave for the product, thus boosting profits. Unfortunately, the subjects of his experiments are turned into drooling zombies.

You'll need copious amounts of caffeine (and sugar!) to stay awake through this woeful feature, even with heavyweights Michael Ironside and Tony Senzamici in the cast. The Just Rite Sugar Company drags down-and-outs off the

streets, turns them into sugar-crazy zombies and locks them away in a warehouse for further experimentation. Cue for Sharon Landry to search for her missing brother and uncover the company's awful secret, leading to one protracted shoot-out after another. Landry, Senzamici and cohorts blow the factory up at the end, but not before hospital wards are packed to the rafters with patients infected by a hungering for the sweet white stuff (and we're not talking cocaine here). Tedious in the extreme, a very poor zombie flick that goes nowhere fast.

The Plague
Armada Pictures 2006; 88 minutes;
Director: Hal Masonberg **

Overnight, all of the world's nine-year-old children fall into a deep coma. Ten years later, they suddenly awake, now transformed into flesh-eating zombies.

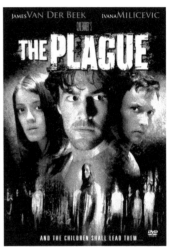

Village of the Damned merges with the zombie genre in a movie that has a striking initial 20-odd minutes as you are left to conjecture on just what *is* afflicting the children (now young adults, albeit ghoulish-looking ones), but then goes quickly off the boil once they wake up and start assailing the grown-ups. You are then firmly in *Day of the Dead* territory. James Van Der Beek and ex-wife Ivana Milicevic lead the adults attempting to escape the confines of the town to safety, thwarted at every stage by the zombies who disable all the vehicles. There is one tremendously blood-freezing moment in the film—a nurse presiding over a ward full of comatose 19-year-olds turns to see scores of dead, dark-rimmed eyes staring at her as the awakening begins. Heaps of grisly slayings to slake the thirst of zombie lovers abound but *The Plague*, unfortunately, cannot sustain its splendid first part and peters out on a peculiarly flat note.

Rise of the Dead
Develement/Crook Brothers 2007; 72 minutes;
Director: William Wedig **

A young woman fears her life is cursed when people around her that she knows change into zombie-like killers.

Actually, it's her infant son who was cursed; given to foster parents, a pair of religious zealots, who placed a curse on him because, in their eyes, his mother was a harlot, the child was then adopted and accidentally (or was it?) shot himself after watching his adoptive parents attack each other. Now his disturbed spirit seeks revenge by possessing those close to his mother, Erin Wilk, resulting in people morphing into flesh-eating zombies every few minutes, including, at the end, boyfriend Stephen Seidel; by mating with him, Wilk becomes pregnant again and lifts the zombie spell. Shot on a paltry budget, this sub-ghost-cum-zombie flick has moments of promise, including a couple of savage murders, but it's Wilk who virtually carries the movie on her own back and saves it from being a ridiculous (check that plot!) bore.

Shadow: Dead Riot
Fever Dreams Prods. 2006; 81 minutes;
Director: Derek Wan ***

A voodoo-practicing killer is resurrected from the dead and, with his zombie minions, wreaks havoc in a women's prison.

Comic strip zombie action featuring Tony *Candyman* Todd as a mass murderer of pregnant women, storming Nina Hodoruk's prison in search of the one unborn baby that got away, in this case black kick-boxing babe Carla Greene. Twenty years earlier, scores of prisoners, along with Todd, were shot by prison guards and buried in a pit; now they're back, the rotting horrors feasting on naked nubile flesh as Todd bares his ground-down teeth and pursues Greene who, injected with Todd's blood by mad doctor Michael Quinlan, is now superhuman. Oh yes, there's a particularly nasty, flesh-eating baby that Cat Miller gives birth to, straight out of *It's Alive*. Supremely silly and over-the-top, *Shadow: Dead Riot* is surprisingly well-directed by Wan with enough lively zombie incident and bloody gore on show to appease all addicts of the genre.

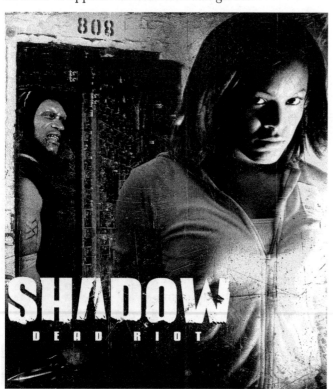

Toxin
IndustryWorks Pictures 2014; 73 minutes;
Director: Tom Raycove **

An embittered soldier seeks revenge on his corrupt military boss who allowed his men to become zombies on Archer Island following experiments in biological warfare, using a powdery substance known as NRX.

Pizza-faced drooling zombies run amok on an island while Lieutenant Douglas Chapman tries to prevent a bunch of disparate tourists from joining their ranks. Filmed around Vancouver, Tom Raycove's cheapskate zombie outing (you only get to see a couple of living dead) has two things going for it: Chapman's uncanny likeness to a young Clint Eastwood and spoiled brat Katherine Gauthier's hilarious denunciation of her brand-new husband, Graeme McComb. "You're a fucking loser!" she screeches at the poor sap when their charter flight crashes on Archer Island, weakling McComb at a loss what to do. "You've got a small dick. I only married you for your money, and I was fucking your best friend Nick behind your back!" Having manly vest-wearing hunks Chapman and Giles Panton in her vicinity doesn't help McComb's case; anyway, he winds up a zombie, as does Gauthier. Chapman, meantime, sets his jaw and squints his eyes à la Eastwood mode and sets about raking up evidence of what occurred on the island to make him so angry. At the end, Colonel Philip Granger, the villain of the piece, lands in a chopper, taking Chapman and tasty Kyra Zagorsky off (the others are all dead); Chapman could be an antidote to the disease and his DNA is wanted by the government. Approaching the city, zombified Panton, on the roof of the helicopter, pulls Granger out to his death; crashing on the city outskirts, Chapman and Zagorsky, weapons in hands, march towards more chaos and mayhem. Short and ordinary sums up *Toxin*, neither particularly good nor particularly bad, and Chapman is no Clint Eastwood, even though he shares the actor's same granite-set jawline.

Undead or Alive
Dark Lot Entertainment/MWM 2007; 89 minutes;
Director: Glasgow Phillips **

In the Old West, two cowboys team up with Geronimo's niece, helping her to wipe out the cavalry unit who killed her uncle, the trio pursued by a posse of zombies.

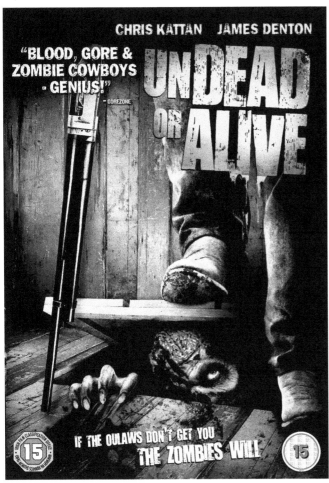

In 1913, the Carlton Mine in Addytown, Pennsylvania was closed after a number of immigrant children were buried alive in a preventable pit explosion. The owner was brought to trial but acquitted for the deaths; however, those long-dead children aren't happy, stalking the gloomy woods as zombies at night and feasting on raw meat, unable to rest until they have had their revenge. Mum Lori Heuring, daughters Scout Taylor-Compton and Chloë Grace Moretz, plus hick Ben Cross and Martin McDougall, the last in the Carlton line, spend much of the film running through the darkened trees as the pasty-faced kids, all armed with pickaxes, hack their bloody way through Taylor-Compton's three teenage pals, various animals and lastly McDougall himself, chopped to pieces in a barn. Moretz, who has befriended one of the little zombie girls (Helia Grekova), says goodbye to her undead playmate as Heuring drives away at the end, leaving her house unoccupied—except for one zombified child who slams the door in our faces. Some amusing lines (McDougall's friend, leveling his rifle: "I can't shoot a kid." McDougall: "They're already dead.") plus eerie location work (the production was shot in Bulgaria) make up for the almost pitch-black nighttime photography where a miner's lamp is required to see what's taking place. For lovers of the zombie genre, *Wicked Little Things* has pace, atmosphere and solid acting, and, because of its forest setting, is slightly different from most fare of its type.

Out of all the constituents that make up the horror genre, none have been more lampooned than the zombie movie. *Undead or Alive* is one more in a long line of zombie comedies that either bring a smile to the face or grate on the nerves. This one grates and you'll need a few beers inside of you to gain any satisfaction from it. James Denton and Chris Kattan play the wisecracking cowpokes, Navi Rawat the sexy, raven-haired Indian (speaking with a swank New York accent) and Matt Besser the addled-faced sheriff in pursuit. It's standard zombie fare played out like *Dumb and Dumber* and backed by an intrusive rock 'n' roll soundtrack; the trio reach a fort, fight off zombie troopers and battle with Besser and his lurching, flesh-eating mob. Kattan and Denton become zombiefied, blow up the garrison and its undead hosts, decapitate Besser and revert back to normal again. For non-aficionados, Phillips' self-claimed "zombiedy" is a pain to sit through; the younger set might find it amusing in parts.

Wicked Little Things aka Zombies
Millenium Films 2006; 94 minutes;
Director: J.S. Cardone ***
Following the death of her husband, a woman and her two daughters travel to their new home on the outskirts of a remote forest populated by flesh-eating children who perished in a mining accident in 1913.

To be continued...

Barry: "Well, after that little lot, what do you reckon of the indie scene so far? Has that sense of reluctance I sensed when we first talked about this project been swept away?"

Gary: "Yes, I suppose it has. Agreed, much of this stuff is marvelous and I can spot plenty of historic influences in many of the films, particularly from the '70s and '80s."

B: "Ah, yes, the gorier, splatter features. But no doubt you will have noticed that a lot of, say, the Asylum fodder is nothing more than '50s and '60s genre tropes presented in a glossy format but perhaps lacking the actors and technicians we were so familiar with back then, although, having said that, some names do stick in the mind after a while. I mean, *Bigfoot* could easily have been made in the 1970s or 1980s, not with CGI, granted, but with a man in a Bigfoot suit. And *Alien Siege* is *Earth vs. the Flying Saucers* revisited in another guise."

G: "Yep, you're right on the button there."

B: "Right, on with part three then, the dessert to the main course. I've chosen a further 85 movies that I've

caught between mid-2017 and June 2019, the period covered being 2010 through to 2019 with the exception of *Creep*, *Half Light* and *Lake Placid 2*; only a couple of disasters this time round! In this varied selection, you'll find ghosts, giant monsters, huge crocs, haunted houses, vampires, werewolves, body modification, dinosaurs, evil entities, witches, psychological horror, rampant robots, Bigfoot, poltergeists, underground horror, aliens, sci-fi, a smattering of Irish horror other worlds and a few foreign delights; in addition, I've thrown in a couple of new-age Frankenstein flicks. There's something for everyone, none of it mainstream, all made for less than that ceiling of $10,000,000. I've tried to steer clear of the better-known productions which hover around the $10,000,000 figure like *Hereditary*, *Trollhunter*, the two *Haunting in Connecticut* movies, *The Secret of Marrowbone*, *The Girl With All the Gifts*, the four *Insidious* outings, the two *Sinister* flicks because these had a limited theatrical release in some parts of the world and made a bit of money. I had to draw the line somewhere. Much of what follows is straight-to-DVD/TV material, or screened at FrightFests, and not generally known to the general public or older film buffs, which was the case with the Asylum/Full Moon/Sandler and Emenegger section in part one and the movies listed in part two."

G: "Right, I'm with you."

B: "So, the ways of presenting things as they were done in the golden age are clear for all to see, proving that in all honesty, nothing *that* monumental has altered over the past 60 years except for computerized effects and a tad more sophistication. *The Pyramid*, for starters, is nothing more than a variant on United Artists' *Pharaoh's Curse* made in 1956; an Egyptian setting with a monster, plain and simple. Fifty-eight years separates the two, yet in essence, it's an almost identical scenario. *The Innkeepers* has that slow buildup favoured by Boomers, *American Mary*, *The Void* and *The Woman* hark back to the 1980s, *The Ritual* is a modern-day monster movie, *Cold Skin* is a modern-day gill-man movie and, hey, *Frankenstein* is in there, still going strong after a century! Remember that old '70s classic *The Legend of Boggy Creek*? Well, what about *Willow Creek* and *Exists* which I've featured. And *Redwood* is a vampire tale straight from the 1960s. Take *Hereditary* which, as I've said, I haven't included. It's packed to the rafters with genre tropes, from *Rosemary's Baby* through to *The Shining* and *The Exorcist*, a touch of the haunted house scenario, witchcraft, possession, you name it, the whole shebang has been done before countless times. What I'm saying is that there's *nothing new* in *Hereditary*, although the younger set may not realize it. No, what *is* new is the way that director Ari Aster has pla-

Some children are more special than others.

H E R E D I T A R Y

Every family tree hides a secret.

IN CINEMAS 21 JUNE

A24

sometimes springs to mind, although I'm sure that's not always the case. *Dead Mine*, *The Ritual* and *It Follows* are three classic examples of decent movies containing inconclusive, open-ended or abrupt finales, leading to one yelling at the screen "What? Is that it?" It can be bloody annoying for us Boomers; after all, even the cheapest '50s second-feature, yes, *even* Ed Wood's efforts, had a beginning, a middle and a proper end. It's as though everyone, notably the scriptwriter, has run out of ideas and the director's shouted out of frustration "It's a wrap." Take note, all you modern horror filmmakers; it simply ain't good enough! But that's the modern-day method of doing things for you and it doesn't detract from the fact that there's some terrific viewing to be had among this low-budget-cum-indie fodder which I really want to share with you, and others, if you've got the time, that is. And, Gary, after doing a bit of online research, there's definitely a fan base out there for this kind of material; I've come across several "Top 20/50/100" lists that contain an awful lot of new-ish indie/low-budget material, compiled by buffs of *all* ages who are searching, and coming across, something that bit more different than your normal blockbusting popcorn epic."

G: Okay, okay! Message received and fully understood! I've got plenty of time! Let's get the show on the road!"

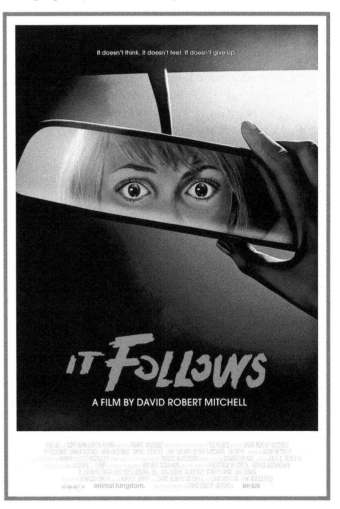

giarized the horror catalogue and presented his opus in such a way that the film appeals to that newer audience while satisfying the taste buds of the older punters. A clear case of the new colliding with the old if ever there was one. And what about *Clown*?"

G: "Whoa! Slow down! What about it?"

B: "When the monster dies in the end, he reverts back to normal. Now how many times did *that* happen in past movies? Want a list?"

G: "I'm sure you could quote examples off the top of your head, but that's all right, I haven't seen *Clown* but I get what you're saying."

B: "The one major worrying difference I find, though, with not only this indie/low-budget stuff but a great many post-2000 blockbusters as well is that, apart from too much dark photography and inaudible snatches of dialogue, plus repeated inclusions of people vomiting—must we *really* have to see all *that*?—plus an over-reliance on the cellphone as a plot device, we are now in the age of the unresolved ending."

G: "Care to elaborate?"

B: "No proper wrap-up or explanation, no matter how good the film is. It's left for the viewer to decide on what happens after the closing credits. The word "cop-out"

Alien Code
The Men Productions 2017; 97 minutes;
Director: Michael G. Cooney ***

A down-on-his-luck cryptographer is assigned by a government agency named ARIST to decode a message in a machine retrieved from a space satellite that is not of human origin.

At the start, Kyle Gallner walks into his house and sees his own body lying on the carpet, an envelope containing the message "WATCH ME" clutched in the hand, inside the envelope a computer stick. Gallner plugs it into his laptop, is confronted by himself and the story unfolds. Gripped? Well, in this low-budget sci-fi puzzler, you may have difficulty in remaining gripped throughout a tortuous narrative concerning aliens, who have the ability to control time, existing in a multi-dimensional universe and attempting to inhabit our one-dimensional world. Those hired to break the alien binary code develop life-threatening brain tumors, so Gallner, after figuring out what the message means, is on borrowed time—and so is previous cryptographer Azura Skye, suffering from dizzy spells and other ailments. Doctor Richard Schiff, a third code-breaker, informs the couple that another satellite appeared 50 years ago: "They want to tether themselves to our dimension. They exist on a different plane. We're primitive; they're advanced. The new machine will allow them access to our world." Schiff also has a "pet alien" in his backyard that "hasn't moved for 30 years." (unfortunately, we don't get to see it). As time bends and distorts in a series of slow-motion loops, Gallner, shadowed by two white-faced beings, one giant specimen outside his bedroom, plus government agents, sets out, with Skye's assistance, to sabotage the machine, which may be "the most powerful weapon the world has ever known," in ARIST's mountain facility, ending up in a sparse room facing a black-faced otherworldly inquisitor. "We can't understand you living in linear time," the being states, Gallner creased up in pain because he's in *their* environment: "I can't exist here. It's making me sick." ARIST executive Mary McCormack is killed ("They're on to me. I've been trying to stop it.") and the conclusion has Gallner writing that note on the envelope and falling to the floor, hinting to his other-self that, "It's already happened. The message has been decoded. Forget the message. Warn her (Skye). Just live." Gallner is last seen standing on a ridge overlooking Los Angeles—but in what dimension? Top marks go to Gallner's full-on performance in holding the entire shaky scenario in check; a larger budget would have helped cement all the seams together, thus producing a more coherent, at least *understandable*, thinking man's sci-fi opus that, in its present form, contains a multitude of concepts that are not fully realized.

American Mary
Industryworks/Evolution Pictures 2012; 103 minutes;
Directors: Jen and Sylvia Soska *****

Abused and raped at an office party, a promising young medical student quits college and turns cold-blooded surgical killer, entering the illegal world of body modification and exacting a terrible revenge on those who wronged her.

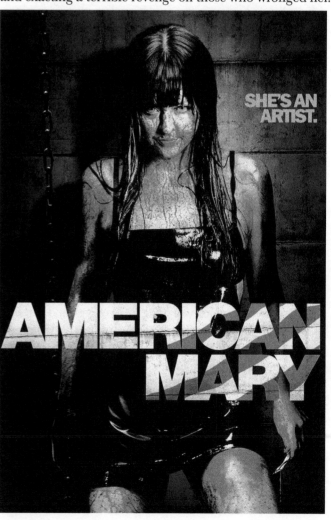

Distributed by Universal-International at various FrightFests, Canadian-produced *American Mary* comes across like a contemporary freak show presented tastefully (Shubert's haunting "Ave Maria" is played over the credits), despite the let-me-not-look-at-this surgical procedures on graphic display, including nipple removal, vagina tuck, penis enhancement, tongue splitting and amputation, all in the name of some form of perverted self-esteem. Yes, we live in a look-at-me society where personal image is paramount in many people's lives, but to this extent? Katharine Isabelle (from *Ginger Snaps*) is utterly brilliant as young Mary Mason: Invited to a drinks party by Doctors David Lovgren and Clay St. Thomas, she's drugged, half throttled and raped by Lovgren who videos the act, a big mistake on his part; he should have given more thought to his number one student's skill with a scalpel. Very soon, Lovgren finds himself strapped to a bench, the subject of a 14-hour procedure that transforms him from man to gibbering, limbless idiot. Into this heady brew we have Tristan Risk as a model made to look like Betty Boop, Paula Lindberg wanting to appear like an asexual dummy and the Soska twins themselves, needing to be joined by surgery, not by mind. Isabelle operates from a room behind Antonio Cupo's seedy sex club; the guy has the hots for her, fantasizing about her body (and Isabelle has one hell of a body!) but she's not interested, a cold, clinical surgical/killing machine in it for the money. You know it won't end happily-ever-after and it doesn't: Cupo's offer of a two-week break in Los Angeles is snubbed, enchanting Risk is beaten to death by a client and cold-eyed Isabelle, tailed by a police officer, is fatally stabbed by Lindberg's twisted boyfriend. She tries to stitch her gaping wound, but fails, the camera panning away from her bloodied, beautiful corpse as the police investigate the scene. "Appearances are everything," wrote one critic. Maybe, but the Soska twins' riveting exploration of the murky world of body modification proves that it doesn't always lead to happiness. An original and unforgettable journey into one person's decaying soul.

As Above, So Below

Brothers Dowdle Prods./Legendary Entertainment 2014; 93 minutes; Director: John Erick Dowdle ****

A young female professor in alchemy gathers a group together to hunt for the legendary philosopher's stone in the Paris catacombs, knowing that the artifact can turn base metal into gold and grant eternal life.

Universal-International took up the distribution rights to John Erick Dowdle's $5,000,000 shaky camcorder journey into Paris' vast ossuary which contains the bones of over six million people, permission granted by the French authorities to use the site. Bossy Perdita Weeks coerces five volunteers to accompany her into the labyrinth of galleries lying beneath the Paris streets; she has calculat-

ed that the chamber that houses not only the stone but tons of treasure is situated hundreds of feet below the tomb of Nicholas Flamel whose tombstone contains vital clues written in Aramaic. The first 50 minutes is frightening stuff if you're prone to claustrophobia, especially the scene where cameraman Edwin Hodge (in reality, he was scared of enclosed spaces) gets trapped in a tight passage filled with bones and freezes in panic (the fear on his face is truly palpable). Thereafter, it all gets a bit frenetic, like a chaotic ride on a ghost train, the team meeting Cosme Castro who apparently vanished in the catacombs years back, descending deeper and deeper through a series of shafts, discovering the preserved body of an old knight and the hallowed chamber and then, to their misfortune, unwisely squirming into a gallery that has "Abandon All Hope All Ye Who Enter Here" inscribed over the portal; yes, they've ventured into a gateway to hell and are now prone to ghoulish visitations from the dead, plus disturbing events from their lives. By carrying on *downwards* (hence the movie's cryptic title), survivors Weeks, Ben Feldman and Ali Marhyar emerge through a manhole cover into the Paris streets outside Notre Dame Cathedral, dazed and confused. The unique setting's the thing here, those endless tortuous winding galleries exerting a baleful influence over the viewer to the extent that the hysterical cast comes second best to their gloomy, forbidding surroundings. As "underground horror" movies go, *As Above, So Below* is a winner for fans of this particular subgenre.

Attack of the Werewolves
aka **Game of Werewolves**; **Lobos de Arga**
Telespan 2000/Vaca Films 2012; 98 minutes;
Director: Juan Martinez Moreno *****

An unsuccessful writer returns to his ancestral home in the Spanish village of Arga after a spell of 15 years, unaware that his family is cursed with lycanthropy.

In 1901, the Marchioness Mariño of Arga kidnapped a Gypsy knife-thrower, seduced him and destroyed the camp, but not before the man's wife had placed a curse; if the Marchioness gave birth, the child would become a werewolf on his 10th birthday. One hundred years later, a descendent (Gorka Otxoa) of the Mariño family plus his dog Vito visits the abandoned mansion in Arga, bumping into friends Carlos Areces, literary agent Secun de la Rosa and Manuel Manquiña. However, Manquiña, a priest, has a hidden agenda, to allow the wolf man inhabiting an underground cellar (existing on a diet of visiting pilgrims for a century) to kill Otxoa, thus ridding Arga of its unholy curse ("Your sacrifice will save the village."). Director Juan Martinez Moreno was responsible for the blacker-than-black script crammed full of dark humor, steering his werewolf opus just clear of

outright parody; the laughs (mostly based on sex) are expertly entwined with tremendous wolf man make-up effects and fine rustic photography from Carlos Ferro, producing a horror semi-comedy of considerable note. Rescuing a disheveled lad (Marcus Ruiz) from the wolf man's lair, the boy ("He's over 100 years old. Why hasn't he grown up?") is fed two of protesting Otxoa's severed fingers to see if he's the real thing; nothing happens during the full moon, Manquiña and the villagers reverting to werewolves ("It's the curse for not breaking the curse.") and going on a rampage. Following a series of near-fatal scrapes on the road and at the mansion ("They may be villagers but they've got a bit of brain!"), Otxoa, Areces, de la Rosa, cop Luis Zahera and Otxoa's grandmother, Mabel Rivera, seek refuge in the church barn; in a battle with the lycanthropes, de la Rosa loses his right arm, Rivera is throttled and the creatures are dynamited. In the graveyard, the chief werewolf has a metal spike plunged into its heart; Ruiz, the Marchioness' son, ages into an old man and expires. But all is not over: The epilogue has Otxoa morphing into one of indie horror's most fantastic-looking wolf men, minus two digits, roaring and homing in on his two chained-up, scared-as-hell buddies in revenge for losing those fingers! A terrific Spanish werewolf offering whose final lines of dialogue sum up the whole madcap exercise:

De la Rosa: "When he bites us, he'll remember the taste and that we cut off two of his fingers. What the fuck do we do now?"

Areces: "Let him bite us. We'll become werewolves and that's that. We'll form a little pack."

De la Rosa: "What? How can I be a werewolf with just one arm?"

Areces: "We'll be creatures of the night, roam the Spanish countryside, terrorize the locals, we'll breed, attack flocks of sheep … it's not such a bad life."

De la Rosa: "You're crazy!"

The Autopsy of Jane Doe
42/IM Global 2016; 86 minutes;
Director: André Øvredal *****

The flawless body of an unidentified young woman discovered in the basement of a house littered with mutilated corpses is taken to a morgue where it begins to exert a diabolical force.

André *Trollhunter* Øvredal's debut horror feature grabs the attention throughout; just who, or what, is that beautiful corpse laid out on the slab in father and son coroners Brian Cox and Emile Hirsch's morgue, waiting to be opened up? And why are the police suggesting that the victims in that house were trying to escape—and from what? When they begin to perform the autopsy, lights flicker and cabbalistic objects, symbols and script are discovered inside her body, *and* imprinted on her inner flesh; she also has strange scarring on her internal organs. As the terror

UNDER TEN MILLION? ANYTHING'S POSSIBLE!

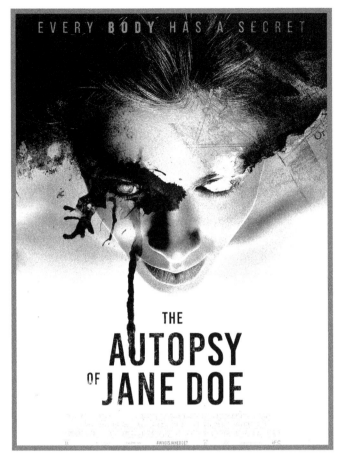

firecrackers, carting around a dangerous crossbow, thrown out of school ("He has significant behavior problems," is the school's classic understatement), shouting to Davis with her friend Daniel Henshall in earshot, "I hate you. You won't let me have a birthday party and (turning to Henshall) *she* won't let me have a dad," and finishing off with, "Do you wanna die?" this is one kid that's far more monstrous than the black, clawed apparition lurking in his bedroom closet. Hell, he even jumps on his mother when she's pleasuring herself in bed. Kudos to the six-year-old actor in pulling it off, but did writer/director Jennifer Kent *have* to make him quite so obnoxious? His ghastly antics detract from a standard "something spooky in the house" movie which focuses on Davis and Wiseman's attempts to escape the malicious clutches of the comic book, gravelly voiced boogeyman that finally winds up living in the basement of Davis' house,

fed on a bowl of grubs and earthworms, Mum and son cuddling up contented (or as contented as they'll ever be) at the end. Davis goes through the wringer (and looks it), Wiseman calms down a bit in the final 30 minutes (thank goodness) and Mister Babadook at least appears different from your normal, run-of-the-mill creepy monster; in some scenes, he's quite scary. But for many viewers, that annoying kid and his tantrums completely sabotage what could have been something far more relevant (tapping into a child's inherent fear of the dark) than it turned out to be.

mounts, it appears that what Cox and Hirsch have on their hands is a 17th-century witch, an innocent girl involved in the Salem witch trials of 1693; she's remained indestructible throughout the centuries, carted from one locale to the other and destroying all those who cross her path in revenge. Even setting her ablaze has no effect. The director ladles on the grisly shocks in the last 20 minutes, horrible-looking corpses coming alive, both coroners perishing under the being's baleful influences. When the cops arrive on the scene, Jane Doe (commendably played by Olwen Catherine Kelly, whose expertise in yoga won her the part) is as untouched and perfect as ever and, in the ambulance escorting her to Virginia's Commonwealth University, her big toe twitches; the lass ain't finished yet! A genuinely chilling thriller filmed in England; Cox and Hirsch are excellent, while Kelly's pale unblinking features and sheer *stillness* will haunt your dreams for a long time after.

The Babadook
Causeway Films/Screen Australia 2014; 94 minutes;
Director: Jennifer Kent ***

A widow and her temperamental five-year-old son come under attack from the Babadook, a demonic entity straight out of the pages of an old book.

Essie Davis is the mother looking more careworn and frazzled by the minute, and coping with clinging son Noah Wiseman, who could blame her. Screaming, shouting, crying, kicking, breaking his cousin's nose at a party, letting off

Bedevilled
Filma Pictures/Tori Pictures 2010; 115 minutes;
Director: Jang Cheol-soo *****

A stressed-out bank official in Seoul goes on vacation to Moo-do Island where her childhood friend suffers relentless physical and mental abuse from her odious husband and his family.

It's no wonder that in the 72nd-minute, Kim Boknam (Seo Young-hee) picks up a scythe and slices two woman to death. She was Hae-won's (Ji Sung-won) teenage friend, now living a cruel, brutalized existence: Continuously raped, beaten, kicked and stamped on by her husband Man-jong (Park Jeong-hak), forced to endure him having graphic sex with a prostitute, knowing that the human ape is molesting their 10-year-old daughter (he's not the father), treated like a slave by the elder women and having to bury her daughter in the yard when, during a fight, the girl hits her head on a rock and dies. Hae-won,

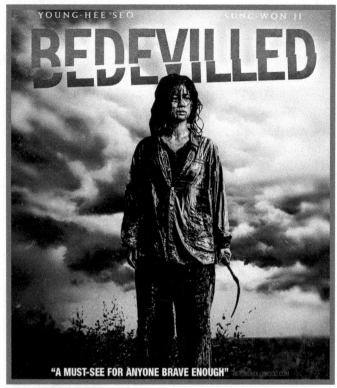

YOUNG·HEE SEO   SUNG·WON JI

BEDEVILLED

"A MUST-SEE FOR ANYONE BRAVE ENOUGH" BEYONDHOLLYWOOD.COM

on the island for some peace and quiet, remains indifferent to the carnage as Bok-nam snaps and, totally deranged, pressurizes her loathsome aunt into falling off a cliff; she then decapitates Man-jong's brother and hacks her detested husband to pieces, blood spattering over the camera lens. Managing to catch the boat to Seoul and dressed in Hae-won's clothes, Bok-nam follows Hae-won to a police station to kill her for not coming to her aid, bludgeoning a police officer with a sledgehammer before Hae-won pushes a flute into her throat, putting the poor girl out of her misery. It then transpires in the poignant conclusion that Bok-nam had repeatedly written to Hae-won, pleading for help, but the letters had remained unopened due to the banker's angst-ridden lifestyle. Beside herself with grief, Hae-won self-cleanses in cold water and reposes on the floor in her apartment, the outline of her figure matching that of the island's contours. Until recent times, isolated male-dominated communities such as the one depicted in this superior South Korean shocker actually existed but were subsequently outlawed by the government. *Bedevilled* makes for uneasy viewing in portraying a harsh way of life far removed from 21st-century ideals, but Seo Young-hee's magnificent playing of the exploited, unloved Kim Bok-nam elevates Jang Cheol-soo's picturesque, gore-drenched revenge thriller into must-see status.

Black Mountain Side
A Farewell to Kings Production 2014; 99 minutes;
Director: Nick Szostakiwskyj ****

An archaeological team stationed in a remote Canadian outpost falls prey to an ominous presence somehow associated with an ancient structure thought to date back to 20,000 BC.

John Carpenter's *The Thing* encounters H.P. Lovecraft-style cosmic terror in a Canadian horror show that may disappoint on first viewing but will reward if you grant it another throw of the dice. It's slow-moving and bereft of a score; and don't expect a full-blooded monster to materialize because it won't. What it does have is an abundance of icy ambience, an unsettling mood of fear, dread and uncertainty and pristine photography courtesy of Cameron Tremblay. Michael Dickson plays an archaeology professor puzzled by a partly buried massive stone artifact of unknown date and origin inscribed with inexplicable animal symbols and deformed humans lacking appendages ("Is it a temple?" he wonders). With only five hours of sunlight each day and temperatures dropping to minus 50c at night, the team starts to feel jittery in the solitude of their surroundings. Steve Bradley and Timothy Lyle hear a strange deep voice giving them unholy orders ("Follow my voice. Open your eyes."), three workers disappear from camp ("They're spooked and superstitious."), communications with the outside world are cut off and Bradley, vomiting blood, has a seizure, forcing Doc Andrew Moxham to sever his right arm as *something* was crawling inside it. When Lyle blows his brains out (after hacking off his hand), Moxham analyzes his and Bradley's blood; the cells aren't human, more like a cephalopod's ("Wells is turning

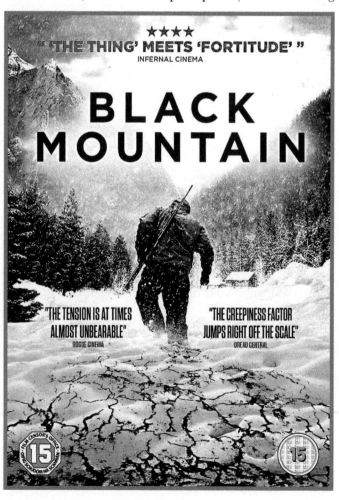

★★★★
"'THE THING' MEETS 'FORTITUDE'"
INFERNAL CINEMA

BLACK MOUNTAIN

"THE TENSION IS AT TIMES ALMOST UNBEARABLE"
ROGUE CINEMA

"THE CREEPINESS FACTOR JUMPS RIGHT OFF THE SCALE"
DREAD CENTRAL

    UNDER TEN MILLION? ANYTHING'S POSSIBLE!

into an octopus?"). Could bacteria in the vicinity of the dig, frozen for thousands of years, be causing this mutation? Bryce McLaughlin then sees a creature resembling a giant shaggy deer standing on its hind legs and we are in *Thing* territory, Mark Anthony Williams, out of his mind, on a shooting spree, Shane Twerdun attempting to blow the mysterious being to bits and Dickson running after the thing into the snow-laden forest at night. As dawn breaks, Dickson emerges into a clearing and steps into a concealed bear trap, no doubt perishing in that freezing wilderness. Legends of the Deer God, from Mesoamerican folklore, plus (naturally) aliens interweave in a low-budget production that commendably relies on atmosphere, and not welters of gory effects, to get its chilling message across, that Man is not alone in the universe and never has been.

The Canal
The Orchard/Park Films/Treasure Ent. 2014; 92 minutes;
Director: Ivan Kavanagh ***

A depressed film archivist is convinced that his house is haunted by the spectral presence of a murderer who could be responsible for the disappearance of his wife.

A tangled web is spun in this Irish supernatural yarn as Rupert Evans' unfaithful wife (Hannah Hoekstra) goes missing; is Evans responsible, as the police think, or is it her boyfriend Carl Shaaban? Evans discovers old film footage of a multiple murder that took place at his residence in 1902; is the event linked to Hoekstra's disappearance? Ivan Kavanagh piles on one disturbing image after another: The hulking killer from 1902 appearing in Evans' bedroom; a graffiti-marked public subway/toilet harboring a baleful presence; Hoekstra's blue-tinged body (she's discovered drowned in the canal) giving birth to a baby in a foul sewer; and Evans strangling his doting assistant, Antonia Campbell-Hughes. It's all in Evans' mind, of course; he murdered his wife by pushing her into the canal, his troubled psyche prey to all kinds of demons. At the end, he's drowned in the canal's turbid waters, winding up as a ghost in his own house and instructing his five-year-old son to join him ("I'm here with your mother. Stay here with us."). The kid does, jumping out of his grandmother's car to his death, his spirit last seen in the house by an estate agent. Confusingly shot and edited, the one chilly moment is when Hoekstra's phantom, caught on cine-film, lurches towards camera and slithers into Ev-

ans' room; otherwise, despite the leading man putting in a good, angst-ridden performance, *The Canal* could have worked better if presented in a slightly calmer style. Occasionally, less is more.

Clown
Cross Creek Pictures/Vertebra Films 2014; 100 minutes;
Director: John Watts ****

To star as the main attraction at his son's birthday party, a father dons an old clown's outfit found in a house refurbishment, but the cursed suit changes him into a Nordic, child-eating demon.

Killer clowns don't come much creepier than in John Watts' thriller; Eli *Hostel* Roth produced, so expect plenty of blood and gore. Andy Powers is the unfortunate man unable to shed his Dummo clown costume, his hair merging with the wig, the bulbous nose ripped off (his dog eats it and turns rabid), leaving a festering sore; even a hand saw can't remove the suit which is gradually adhering to his skin. Rapidly deteriorating like Jeff Goldblum in *The Fly* ("It's not a costume. It's the skin and hair of a demon!") and staggering around the woods in Frankenstein's monster fashion, stomach rumbling from an ever-increasing hunger, Powers learns that Peter Stormare, the previous

owner of the house where the costume was discovered, was similarly jinxed with the outfit. He managed to rid himself of it when his physician brother smuggled, out of a cancer ward, five dying children which Stormare devoured, thus freeing him of the curse. Either Powers similarly eats five kids or has to be beheaded in order to destroy the Clöyne, the Nordic demon he is morphing into. After a well-developed buildup, the final third of the movie goes down the splatter route, Powers unable to kill himself (by bullet and buzz saws), gobbling up four children, spitting out their bones and homing in on his son (Christian Distefano); if he's consumed, Powers will be released, returning to normal. Now completely transformed into a hideous demonic being ("Bring a child to me," he growls to pregnant wife Laura Allen), Powers murders his father-in-law (Chuck Shamata) and attempts to grab his unborn child from Allen's belly before she decapitates him with a hammer, yanking his head clean from his body. As Powers expires, he reverts to his natural self, the Clöyne skin melting away; the costume is packed up by the morticians to be analyzed and used for police evidence. *Clown*'s framework and look appears to be paying homage to the horror movies of the 1980s, John Watts directing with vigor, while Powers is on top form playing the tragic evil clown; if the youngsters are watching, his ragged, murderous creation will put them off the gentler, funnier circus variety for a very long time.

Cold Skin
Babieka Films 2017; 108 minutes;
Director: Xavier Gens ****

In September 1914, a meteorologist begins a year-long tenure on a remote island that suffers from nightly invasions of subhuman fish-men.

A Spanish/French production filmed in the Canary Islands that some have compared to Guillermo del Toro's $20,000,000 *The Shape of Water* in that both deal with the relationship between man and subhuman beast. Here, that relationship is given a more hard-edged treatment, David Oakes' uncouth companion on the island, Ray Stevenson, bullying and even having sex with blue-skinned Aneris (Aura Garrido), a female of the species that he treats like a dog. Stevenson, occupying the fortified lighthouse, wants to exterminate the creatures; Oakes comes to realize that they have a degree of intelligence and rebels at even shooting them as they clamber over the black rocks en masse in order to get their claws into their vile persecutor. Stevenson, it turns out, is the island's missing signal technician; rejected by his wife and muttering "Love, love, love," he has taken out his hatred of mankind on the fish people ("Here, I'm master of my own destiny. They're the enemy.") but in the end, knowing he has done wrong by creating carnage among their ranks with explosives, he walks out into their arms and is ripped to pieces. Oakes is spared;

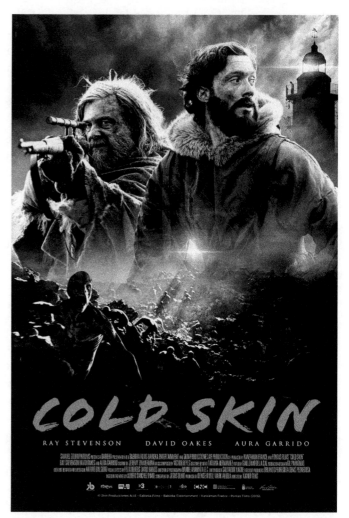

a new vessel arrives, the captain encountering the lone man, now bearded, eyes glazed over, uncomprehending. As the ship steams away, Aneris dives into the clear waters, she and her people free of Stevenson's brutal predations. Sparkling cinematography from Daniel Aranyó and rugged volcanic-like location work, plus a spot-on turn from Garrido playing the tormented Aneris possessing almost human feelings, contribute to a modern-day gill-man feature that a lot of buffs reckon trumps del Toro's feature in more than one department.

Confined aka The Abandoned
C Plus Pictures/Darclight 2015; 86 minutes;
Director: Eytan Rockaway ****

A student on anti-psychotic pills takes a night security job in a vast building and decides to investigate what lies behind the locked door to Room 441, with unforeseen consequences.

Filmed in Manhattan's huge Prince George Ballroom, we journey into the warped mind of Louisa Krause, the single mother of Clara, as she investigates poorly lit tunnels, dark corridors and an old dormitory behind the steel door to 441, her movements monitored by night guard Jason Patric. The only other occupant of the residence is

Mark Margolis, a down-and-out who has begged shelter for the night. Eytan Rockaway utilizes the edifice's capacious dimensions to great effect, an atmosphere of Gothic doom hanging in the air, helped by Max Aruj's creepy score—and pay attention to Ido Fluk's script because all the clues are there as to Krause's mental state. She discovers that the cobwebby dormitory, named Wellville, used to be the home to deformed, mentally handicapped children, abused and neglected by their doctors who were found guilty of malpractice, the kids drinking contaminated water to calm them down. When wheelchair-bound Patric answers Krause's cries of terror, he's dragged under the pool and Krause encounters a facially deformed girl who tells her, "It's not your fault." The payoff is that what we have sat through is all in Krause's disturbed mind: She was a patient in Wellville and has been in a coma for years; *she* is the deformed girl, Patric her father, Margolis a patient at the hospital. As for her daughter Clara—she happens to be a doll. Krause dies in the closing minutes, but we see her unblemished self run out of the building into sunlight, smiling and laughing, free of her mental burden at last. A telling production all round, one of a number of low-budget movies made in this period to explore the mind of a troubled person by creating a framework in which to delve into that person's tortured psyche.

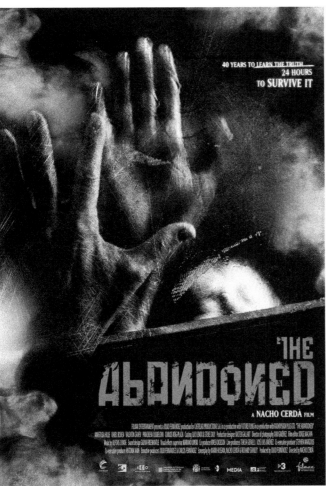

Creep
UK Film Council/Dan Films 2004; 85 minutes;
Director: Christopher Smith ***

Finding herself locked in a tube station for the night, a socialite goes on the run from a deformed human with a taste for butchery and raw flesh.

Christopher Smith never takes his foot off the gas pedal as Franka *The Bourne Identity* Potente dozes off on Charing Cross Underground station, awakes and falls prey to a deranged monster who, it appears, was a survivor from a group of malformed children inhabiting an underground clinic (their shriveled bodies are in bell jars); unable to speak, only mimicking sounds and shrieking hideously, this loathsome mutated specimen carves up anyone accidentally wandering into his dark, labyrinthine domain. Not only Potente but obnoxious admirer Jeremy Sheffield, homeless couple Kelly Scott and Paul Rattray and sewer worker Vas Blackwood encounter the sicker-than-sick abomination (well-played by Sean Harris), Scott's death by saw particularly harrowing. Potente, bloody and battered, eventually makes it out alive with Rattray's cute little dog after virtually severing Harris' throat with a length of chain attached to a rail track. Filmed mainly within the confines of London's long-disused Aldwych Underground tube train network, *Creep*, a British/German production, is a grisly shocker that isn't for those who find endless gloomy tunnels claustrophobic; it's also extremely violent in parts. Okay, Potente's full-on feminist character (she's in London to meet George Clooney!) isn't really one you would necessarily root for, but Smith's helter-skelter pace and the novel tube tunnel settings more than make up for her less-than-ladylike demeanor and, it has to be said, a few gaping plot holes.

A Dark Song
Irish Film Board/Samson Films/Tall Man Films 2016;
100 minutes; Director: Liam Gavin ****

Grieving the loss of her son in a ritualistic murder, a woman rents an old house in Wales and hires an occultist with the aim of contacting her boy and taking out her vengeance on his killers.

Filmed in Ireland, Liam Gavin's supernatural drama is as bleak as the surrounding moorlands, boosted by an eerie drums/clanging score from Ray Harman. Distraught Catherine Walker, against the advice of her worried sister ("You have two fucking healthy children. I have a hole.")

is prepared to literally put herself through hell in order to contact her dead son, seven at the time of his death. The occultist she enlists, Steve Oram, is a mentally damaged, uncouth, foul-mouthed bully who, for £80,000, demands that Walker purges her mind and body, memorizes certain pagan rituals, fasts, freezes in icy water and, dressed like a tart, performs a strip in front of him as he masturbates; and the perimeter of the house is sealed with salt, a barrier against possible harmful influences. Hopefully, all these extreme (and very grueling) measures will invoke the forces that will enable her to converse with her boy. But in having lied to Oram over her motive (she doesn't let on that revenge is on her agenda), the forces they eventually conjure up (it all starts on the hour) are of the dark variety: The lights go out, noises are heard, hideous, malformed demons stalk the dusty corridors, the voice she hears not of her son but a mimicking fiend ("Mummy. Open the door." "No. I know you're not him."). Oram, accidentally knifed in the guts by Walker during a row, gets sick and expires from an infection; she's grabbed by the ghouls and tortured, screaming, "I'm so sorry," before escaping their clutches and entering a room bathed in dazzling light, confronting a massive, beatific angel clad in armor, a truly goosebumpy, unnatural yet oddly calming scene. "I want the power to forgive," she tells the golden-eyed being, cry-

ing, and she is allowed peace and serenity at last, pushing Oram's body out into the lake and driving off to a new life. Slow-moving, maybe, but dripping in "what's going to happen" atmosphere, *A Dark Song* sticks in the mind, nervy Walker and disagreeable Oram's tour de force a potent mix if you can stomach the occasional bouts of unpleasantness.

Dead Mine
Infinite Frameworks Studios 2012; 87 minutes;
Director: Steven Sheil ***

On the Indonesian island of Unauna, a team of soldiers and treasure hunters searching for the legendary Yamashita hoard of gold discover an abandoned mine where, during WWII, the Japanese created mutants from experiments in biological warfare.

An Indonesian horror movie filmed in the area around Batam that kicks off in fine fettle. On a Jap-held island during the war, a soldier wanders into a mine entrance, stumbles on the floor and is hauled under the ground to his doom. Over 60 years later, rich kid Les Loveday, girlfriend Carmen Soo, Japanese scientist Miki Munzo and a team of marines led by Sam Hazeldine and Ario Bayu are on the island, trying to locate (the marines are led to believe) the lost treasure of Yamashita (which has never, to date, been found). Under attack from rebels, they retreat into an old mine, the entrance is sealed by a bomb blast and after traversing one gloomy passage after another, Loveday's true agenda comes to light: The place was once utilized by the Japanese as a biological research facility for chemical warfare, Australian prisoners of war used as guinea pigs, giving rise to sub-human creatures wearing leather muzzles that inhabit a large cavern, feeding on human flesh. One normal survivor from 1942 is astounded to discover, via Soo's tablet, that the war ended decades ago; he's been stuck in the bunker for 70 years, unaware of the fact. What Loveday is after is an experimental serum that can both prolong life and create "human weapons; indestructible soldiers," Soo injecting him with a syringe-full of the liquid as the entire cast go on the run from an army of reactivated armored Samurai warriors, wielding deadly swords; the Imperial Guard has come to life! Loveday morphs into something not quite human, bashing his girlfriend's brains all over a rock wall, while Hazeldine and Munzo swim through a tunnel, emerging in a lake. Munzo staggers ashore, the

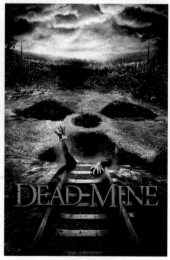

UNDER TEN MILLION? ANYTHING'S POSSIBLE!

Samurai appear, one big feller stands over her, raises his sword, and … end of film! Yes, it's that modern-day curse of the abrupt ending in all its annoying glory. Did the writers simply run out of ideas for a cohesive conclusion, or was there to be a sequel? A pity, as the mine passages, shafts and narrow tunnels are effectively forbidding and Hazeldine shines playing the rough-and-ready ex-army guy trying to hold everything together as all and sundry are skewered to death by the Samurai.

Don't Blink
EchoWolf Prods./WindowLight Pictures 2014; 92 minutes; Director: Travis Oates ***

Ten people arrive at the Mountainbrook Cabin Retreat to find the place completely deserted; then they start to disappear, one quickly followed by the other.

What strange phenomena is causing the cast (let's give them a mention; they all play their part: Zack Ward,

Mena Suvari, Fiona Gubelmann, Brian Austin Green, Joanne Kelly, David de Latour, Leif Gantvoort, Samantha Jacober, Curtiss Frisle, Emelie O'Hara) to vanish into thin air at, literally, the blink of an eye. "Don't blink" and "Help me" are scrawled on a mirror and cupboard door, food has been left uneaten on the dining room table, a bath is full of water, a tap is running, a baby's feeding bottle lies in a crib, cars in the parking area have no fuel and, needless to say, there's no phone connection. The nearby lake is frozen solid, even though it's summer and warm elsewhere, and there are no signs of any birds or animals. It also proves impossible to drive away from the lodge's perimeters. There's a fair degree of suspense built up by Travis Oates as you are left on tenterhooks, wondering what's behind it all as first one, then another, of the ten bickering characters fades from sight. Unfortunately, you are never destined to find out. Kelly, the last girl standing, goes outside to meet the police and fire services who have turned up en masse; she sits in a patrol car, looks up and they've all disappeared, just like her companions; end of movie. You might argue that *Don't Blink* fails to capitalize on its tantalizing potential as a mystery/supernatural thriller but, give the film its due, it manages to hold the interest and leaves it to the viewer to decide exactly what was behind all those startling "here one minute, gone the next" incidents.

Dream Home
852 Films 2010; 96 minutes; Director: Ho-Cheung Pang ****

In Hong Kong, a young bank teller will go to any lengths to obtain the flat of her dreams—even multiple murder of the horrific kind.

A pregnant woman trussed up like a chicken, then suffocated by a plastic bag placed over her head, the air vacuumed out; strangulation by nylon cable; entrails spilling from a barely alive man's ripped-open torso; a wooden slat rammed into a girl's mouth; a penis sliced off; a spike shoved through the back of a victim's head, emerging through the eye; graphic sex; drug taking; and vomiting, stabbings, a head battering and brains blown out. And all because Josie Ho has been turned down for a bank loan, even though it's her job to sell them to clients, has not reaped any benefits from her dead bullying father's insurance policy, is unable to get her married lover to part with any money and has had her lowly offer rejected by the elderly owners of the property she so desires. So what better way than to ferociously butcher 11 occupants in that apartment block, forcing a horrified Mr and Mrs Tang, now anxious to move because of the adverse publicity, to drastically drop their asking price, thus enabling her to purchase the flat with that all-important Victoria Bay view

for peanuts. Blood-spattered carnage on a nihilistic scale highlights Pang's gut-wrenching psycho-slasher, shot in glossy color amid striking Hong Kong locations and incorporating within its framework a series of short flashbacks that gradually reveal the motives behind Ho's abominable killing spree. Apparently based on a real-life police case, *Dream Home* is well-made, the cinematography superb, and beautifully acted by Ho, an angelic she-devil in upwardly professional mobile guise, whatever you may think of the film's dubious, sickening content. And yes, that flat is hers in the end, just as the Hong Kong stock market crashes, probably leaving the murderess penniless—but she had to pay for her crimes somehow! To be viewed on an empty stomach!

The Dyatlov Pass Incident aka Devil's Pass
Midnight Sun Pictures/Aldamisa Ent/A.R. Films 2013; 100 minutes; Director: Renny Harlin *****

Five students decide to make a documentary about nine climbers who were found dead in Russia's Northern Ural Mountains in 1959, the whole incident shrouded in mystery and speculation, and are never seen or heard of again.

Fact: In 1959, the bodies of nine climbers were discovered in the Ural Mountains (some state that 11 went up), their deaths put down to government secrecy, avalanches, hypothermia, the Yeti and, naturally, UFOs. Fiction: Five American filmmakers set off to put the record straight and vanish (the news of their disappearance is broadcast on TV), their recording equipment later located. Filmed in Russia, Renny Harlin's found footage thriller intrigues from the off, more polished than most and that's down to his expertise behind the camera. Harlin (to the eternal gratitude of sci-fi conspiracy buffs) goes down the extra-terrestrial route for an explanation of the truth behind the puzzle. Once in the mountains, Holly Goss, Matt Stokoe, Luke Albright, Ryan Hawley and Gemma Atkinson (they should have taken heed of that "Stay Away" sign held up

by a survivor of the original tragedy) see bare footprints in the snow, a severed tongue in a weather tower and hear odd noises. Hawley and Atkinson have a romp, hear shots and an avalanche sweeps all the tents away; Atkinson lies dead, Hawley has a busted leg and Albright is wounded with a bullet. Leaving Hawley, the three enter a forbidding door located earlier in a snow drift, and this is where their troubles *really* begin. Harlin ups the ice-cold tension as the students explore an intricate military facility, but built for what purpose? Perhaps those old Indian legends were right, that the area is a place where two worlds collide. Ghastly distorted humanoid figures clamber over the walls and ceilings, there's reference to the infamous 1943 Philadelphia Experiments on board USS *Eldridge*, blackened bones litter cell floors and Albright perishes horribly. The payoff works, a disturbing stunner: Goss and Stokoe stumble across a strange tunnel that, they surmise, could be a wormhole and possible way out by teleportation ("It has no controls or buttons."). They chance it, walking into swirling, dazzling light, a big mistake! Their frozen figures are hauled back inside the complex by the military who fire warning shots at a party of inquisitive tourists. Both bodies are stripped and hung in a cell on chains; they're still alive, but distinctly *not* human in appearance. And to ram home the point, the camera closes on the female's neck as it stares at her partner, displaying Goss' wing tattoo. The Dyatlov Pass mystery still remains to this day just that, an unsolved mystery; whether Harlin's film offers a logical exposition or a fanciful one, we shall probably never know. But it's a well-crafted exercise in sci-fi terror all the same, one of the very best among the profusion of found footage outings available today.

The Endless
Snowfort Pictures/Pfaff Pfaff Prods. 2017; 111 minutes; Directors: Justin Benson and Aaron Moorhead ****

Two brothers receive a video cassette containing a cryptic message in the mail from a UFO death cult they once belonged to as youngsters and decide to revisit the place to see if anything's changed.

Justin Benson and Aaron Moorhead, the team behind the magnificent *Spring* (2014), directed, produced, wrote, edited and even photographed this mind-bending sci-fi puzzler with a difference that both intrigues and infuriates in equal doses. The Ascension cult, run from remote Camp Arcadia, is presided over by Tate Ellington and his cohorts, all wearing silly grins (are the males castrated?), as though they're on happy pills; and none has aged over 10 years. Benson and Moorhead are given a guarded welcome by this "Stepford" community, especially sex-starved gals Callie Hernandez and Kira Powell, before realizing that everyone around them is being controlled by an alien presence, living out their lives in a time loop. No one can

UNDER TEN MILLION? ANYTHING'S POSSIBLE!

in the dawn sky, birds now flying naturally. "You figure it out," says Benson, which might well sum up the thinking of a lot of buffs watching the film. A sense of other-worldly dread hovers in the air, H.P. Lovecraft one of the duo's influences, in a thought-provoking movie that will appeal to those wishing to get to grips with a complex alien mystery where a great deal is tossed into the mix; others may well be scratching their heads in confusion after 30 minutes and simply give up; if so, they would be missing out on something distinctly left field in the sci-fi genre.

The Enfield Haunting
Eleven Films/Sky TV 2015; 136 minutes;
Director: Kristoffer Nyholm *****

In August 1977, a family living in Enfield, North London, is plagued by poltergeist activity which appears to center around the 11-year-old daughter.

One of England's most celebrated cases of urban haunting caught the nation's attention between August 1977 and mid-1979 when the Hodgson family's younger daughter, Janet, became the focus of intense media coverage; the girl levitated, was hurled against walls, could speak in various dialects, saw moving lights and was subjected to flying furniture, thrown objects and unusual marks on her body. In the television adaptation of Guy Lyon Playfair's book *This House is Haunted*, Timothy Spall played Maurice

escape beyond those carved poles emitting a force field; if they do, they're compelled to return. Seems the god-like alien entity is observing its human "prey," communicating by the usage of old media (film, reel-to-reel tapes), but why is never made clear; and the group's mantra is that meeting death at the hands of whatever it is and came from is preferable to leading a menial existence elsewhere. Glancing over the fact that the brothers managed to get out of the area when they were young adults, *The Endless* contains some unsettling imagery: Birds forever wheeling in a circular formation; members playing tug-of-war on a rope that ascends towards the night sky; three moons glowing in the heavens; clouds of dust stirred up by a large unseen object; a weird rock formation in the desert; a vast unearthly shape gliding under the brother's boat on a lake; and other unexplained phenomena. Disappointingly, the second half tends to lapse into a certain amount of disorder, Benson and Moorhead going their separate ways while various people witness their own violent deaths over and over again. Finally, the brothers reunite, zooming off in a vehicle lacking fuel after the community has been beamed up and returned, the semi-visible alien destroying Camp Arcadia in fury. Crashing headlong into an approaching car, they emerge unscathed, one moon showing

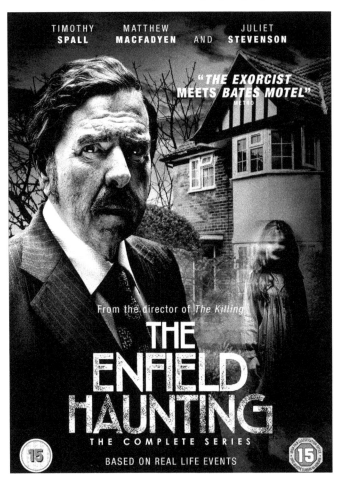

Grosse, a paranormal investigator from the Society for Psychical Research, called upon by Rosie Cavaliero (Mum Hodgson) to conduct a study into the violent disturbances after newspapers had taken up the story. Spall forms a close bond with lively Eleanor Worthington-Cox (Janet) as his own daughter Janet died in a motorcycle crash a year earlier; both Spall and wife Juliet Stevenson, grieving over their loss, blame each other for the accident, and Spall is after forgiveness from the spirit world. *The Enfield Haunting* is a far cry from 2016's frenetic, and vastly more expensive, *The Conjuring 2* which dealt with this particular incident; it's given a typically British low-key treatment as Spall, joined by skeptical (at first: "They're in it for the money.") Matthew MacFadyen (Playfair), engage a medium (chillingly portrayed by Amanda Lawrence) to pinpoint who, or what, is possessing Worthington-Cox ("You should not communicate with it. This is a house of death."); the pair are then thrown off the case but later reinstated after the Society's president realizes the whole thing isn't some gigantic hoax (many still believe it was). The shocks are few and far between, but the feeling of malevolence and dread from a presence in the house is palpable and Worthington-Cox is brilliant in the role of the profanity-spouting child coming to depend on Spall's kindly, caring persona (she was awarded a BAFTA in 2016 for Best Supporting Actress). Hospitalized, newspaper headlines screaming that the "Poltergeist girls" were faking it, Worthington-Cox is released when Cavaliero states to the disbelieving authorities that the whole business was a charade, a bit of fun ("It was nice having men around the place. She's made things up and wasted people's time."). At the house, in Spall's words to his anxious wife, "It's back. She needs me," a disastrous séance with the ashes of a man called Joe Watson who died there in 1961 and apparently is causing all the trouble (they're eventually scattered over a football pitch) ends with Spall and MacFadyen bringing in Lawrence once more in a last attempt to lay the poltergeist to rest. The moving climax sees Spall communicating with his daughter via Worthington-Cox and given closure; the house is now at peace (and has been ever since), Spall and Stevenson are reconciled and MacFadyen goes off to write his best seller. To the sound of David Bowie's "Young Americans," the camera closes on Worthington-Cox at her bedroom window, the faintest of enigmatic smiles flickering over her pretty face; was she fooling the experts all along? Perhaps we shall never know. A minor television supernatural classic, carefully rendered and performed with 100% conviction by the entire cast; the mighty Spall dominates the proceedings with a lovely, understated star turn, as his legion of admirers would expect from one of the UK's most highly respected actors. He, alone, makes *The Enfield Haunting* essential viewing.

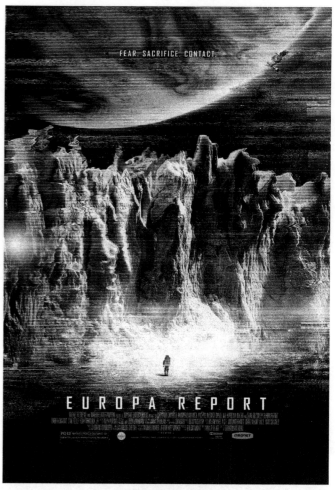

FEAR. SACRIFICE. CONTACT.

EUROPA REPORT

Europa Report
Wayfare Ent./Misher Films 2013; 90 minutes;
Director: Sebastián Cordero ****

Found footage discovered by NASA reveals that the crew of the *Europa One* mission encountered alien life on Jupiter's icy moon.

Narrated by mission commander Embeth Davidtz, Sebastián Cordero's faux documentary space thriller, although produced on modest funds, is one of only a handful of films that shows you what an alien life form *could* actually look like, it's that authentic. Split screen and multiple images chart the 19-month voyage of the spacecraft and its six crew; it finally enters Jupiter's orbit, landing on Europa 100 meters off the target zone. The movie looks good in a pristine, sub-*2001* fashion (there's even a snatch of classical music at one stage), the frozen, pockmarked surface of Europa, Jupiter's bulk filling the dark heavens, instilling a cold, eerie, other-worldly atmosphere that has the crew in a state of high nerves; Earth seems so, so far away. Drilling through the ice, a vast underground sea is located but a solar storm damages their vessel. Sharlto Copley, repairing a panel with Michael Nyqvist, gets covered in hydrazine and floats into space to his death through fear of contaminating the ship. Next to perish is Karolina Wydra, falling beneath the surface on a reconnaissance trip down

UNDER TEN MILLION? ANYTHING'S POSSIBLE!

a valley after observing glowing blue lights moving in the water. Captain Anamaria Marinca decides to blast off; the ship has an engine problem, crashing back onto the moon and killing Daniel Wu. Christian Camargo and Nyqvist venture out to inspect the damage, both spotting those mysterious lights before tumbling under the crust of ice. In the closing moments, the vessel begins to sink beneath the brittle surface; Marinca, terrified, looks down to see a massive bioluminescent octopoid creature emitting a blue radiance emerging from the turbulent waters into the ship, its tentacles unfolding and reaching out for her. "That last final image," intones Davidtz to camera. "Startling. Terrifying," and the film closes on that haunting image, that utterly alien creature that inhabits a world 370,000,000 miles from us. Note: In 2023, NASA plans to send the *Europa Clipper* on a flight to explore Jupiter's ice-covered moon and investigate possible life in that fathomless sea. Is *this* what the cameras and sensors will pick up?

Exists
Haxan Films/Court Five 2014; 80 minutes;
Director: Eduardo Sánchez *******

Five youngsters embark on a vacation at their uncle's cabin in remote Texas woodlands; the partying comes to an abrupt end when Bigfoot decides to eliminate them in revenge for the accidental death of its infant.

Eduardo Sánchez's finest hour outside of *The Blair Witch Project*? Many would agree—this is a Bigfoot movie with teeth, the director, by cunning usage of camcorder and "normal" footage, conjuring up a scenario drenched in genuine terror, especially in the seven-minute sequence whereby Chris Osborn, Roger Edwards, Dora Madison Burge and Denise Williamson endure a pulverizing assault in Jeff Schwan's cabin; a similar scene in an abandoned camper is just as hair-raising. En route to their holiday retreat, Osborn's brother, Samuel Davis, hits an unseen object in the road, blood and hair found on the bumper; then a fallen tree blocks their path. Yes, we have to suffer some minor irritants (Osborn filming Edwards and Williamson about to have sex; Osborn in the woods, observing a large figure, whispering, "We can be friends, man."), but when cries and screams are heard and something prowls around outside the cabin at night, grunting and testing the doors, things get serious. Blood-curdling howls echo through the trees and, in the morning, their car has been wrecked, a branch wedged through the windscreen. "No one knows we're here," admits a terrified Davis, cycling off to obtain a phone signal so that he can contact his uncle for help. Followed by a hairy creature, Davis is knocked off his cycle, his right leg smashed, and dragged away. Sánchez piles on the ordeal (for the group *and* us) with that extended attack on the cabin, a terrifying seven minutes of pure savagery; Williamson, mauled by a huge claw, dies, the place trashed,

Davis' buckled bike found on the porch come morning. The remaining three run like hell down overgrown tracks, unwisely take what they think is a shortcut, see an old camper and haul Davis out of a tunnel (Bigfoot's lair), taking cover in the camper where they come under a second all-out blitz. Burge and Davis expire, Edwards (he sets off a firework to alert Schwan) is bashed to oblivion and Osborn, feigning death, is towed by one leg to a spot where the bodies of his friends lie side-by-side, covered in flies; nearby is the corpse of the Sasquatch's infant. "It was an accident. We didn't mean to kill your baby," sobs Osborn as Schwan shows up, armed; he's quickly cut down, the beast chasing Osborn to a bridge where the two eye each other warily. Osborn lays down his rifle ("This is Brian Talbot. This is my last video."), staring at the wounded, bloodied creature in front of him and fearing the worst. But perhaps the monster has had enough slaying for the time being; slowly, it ambles away, leaving Osborn sobbing in relief. Shot in Texas' Big Thicket National Park, *Exists* goes for the throat, unlike some Bigfoot outings which tend to pussyfoot around ("They're only violent if provoked," claims the pre-action blurb). Here, we are presented with a creature of such unbridled hate and animal ferocity that it's enough to put anyone thinking of tracking down the legendary half man/half beast off for life; an intense 80-minute thrill-ride of some note.

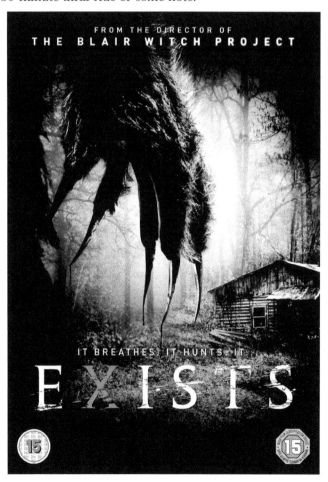

Extraterrestrial aka The Visitors

Abduction Films/Vicarious Ent./Manis Films 2014; 101 minutes; Directors: Colin Minihan and Stuart Ortiz (The Vicious Brothers) ***

Five friends drive off to spend a weekend at a cabin in the woods and have to defend themselves against aliens.

The 1980s collides with *The X-Files* and even *Close Encounters of the Third Kind* in The Vicious Brothers' brash $3,000,000 "alien abduction" feature which veers from puerile juvenile behavior and mediocrity one minute to a genuine sense of imaginative alarm the next; it doesn't seem to be able to make up its mind whether to be serious sci-fi/space fodder or simply dumb popcorn entertainment. Brittany Allen, boyfriend Freddie Stroma, moronic Jesse Moss and two babes, Melanie Papalia and Anja Savcic, set off for Allen's parents' cabin which is up for sale. Nearby resides grizzled UFO hunter/Vietnam vet/cannabis dealer Michael Ironside who's been monitoring covert military activity in the area ("The US government has a treaty with the aliens since Roswell. They turn a blind eye to them abducting humans."). The idiotic antics come courtesy of Moss, a stereotypical jerk of the first order; even a splendid flying disc crashing into the woods doesn't prevent motor-mouth from shutting up, spouting lines of "Dude. That's a dead fucking alien" when one of the bony creatures is shot in its stomach, falling into a swimming pool. The visual effects are excellent when you consider the budget: A vast mother ship beaming up victims in a white shaft of light, red light bathing the cabin as the beings prowl around and the H.R. Giger-type interior of the ship during the final 15 minutes, humans encased in sticky membranous tissue ready to be medically experimented on or released ("Some have been up there for years, others returned," states a traumatized woman). Feisty Allen refuses Stroma's marriage proposal, Savcic disappears in that beam of light, Papalia overdoses because, "I don't want to go up there," skeptical law officer Gil Bellows finally accepts that the aliens took his wife 10 years back, despite Deputy Sean Rogerson's crass comment of, "You can't be serious. This

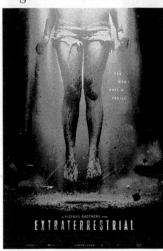

is horseshit," and Ironside comes off second-best in a tussle with a large alien specimen. As for Moss, he's hauled into the mother ship, leaving his handcuffed left arm in a tree, and given a well-deserved anal probe. The climax is downbeat and moving, Allen and Stroma, reunited on board the ship, beamed back down to Earth where they're shot by the military and incinerated in a pit; there must be no witnesses to what has occurred in Echo Lake over the years. A fun, rather clichéd, alien invasion ride that at times appears curiously dated in its heavy mix 'n' match approach (loud rock music blasting out in some scenes); a bit more finesse in some quarters would have elevated the movie to a more praiseworthy level.

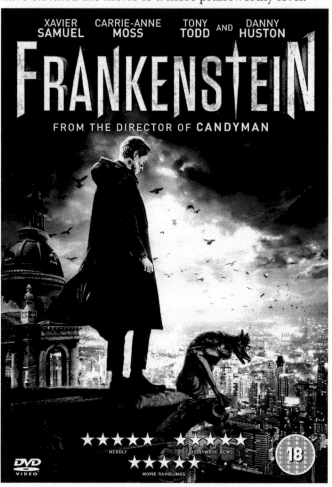

Frankenstein

Bad Badger/Eclectic Pictures 2015; 89 minutes; Director: Bernard Rose ****

Husband and wife research scientists create a human being that breaks out of the lab and roams the streets of Los Angeles looking for a friend.

Bernard Rose leans heavily on James Whale's *Bride of Frankenstein* in this gory updating of the old legend, Xavier Samuel giving a fine performance as the youth called Adam who gradually mutates into something resembling Jeff Goldblum in *The Fly*. Aware that he's about to be euthanized on the orders of Danny Huston (as Victor—who else?) and Carrie-Ann Moss ("Put him down? Murder? He's never been born."), Samuel breaks free, kills two scientists (one is a Dr. Pretorius) and prowls the streets, eating insects and roadkill, befriending a dog and throwing a little girl off a jetty into the water (1931's *Frankenstein* anyone?), his looks becoming more festering by the hour. Surviving a savage beating by cops (and a bullet in the head), he links up with blind busker Tony Todd, mirroring the Karloff interlude with the lonely blind hermit (plus large chunks of the dialogue. Todd: "I can't see. You need a friend, Monster." Samuel: "Friend!"). After the leprous-looking creation has smothered a prostitute to death, he accidentally kills Todd, takes to the streets and shoots dead the officer who shot him. Making his way to the lab, his birthplace, he destroys his new body ("That's how we made you!") in a fit of rage. In a frenetic climax, Huston slashes Moss' throat with a brain saw by mistake and Samuel carries "Mum" to the woods, setting fire to her corpse, going up in flames himself, screaming "I am Adam!" A surprisingly refreshing take on a story that's been filmed over 100 times, the producers honoring the old classics by presenting them in a new guise; and Aussie actor Samuel in the lead part is, as stated, superb.

The Frankenstein Theory
Rocket/Inner Station 2013; 87 minutes;
Director: Andrew Weiner ***

A brilliant young college professor and film crew travel to the Arctic Circle to put to the test his startling theory that his descendant, Professor Venkenheim, created the Frankenstein monster, not Mary Shelley, and that the creature still stalks the wastes, responsible for hundreds of unexplained deaths over the past 190 years.

Don't expect to see too much of the Frankenstein monster in Andrew Weiner's camcorder footage slant on the old tale. It appears in longshot on the 75th minute and crashes through a log yurt door at the end, tramping away into the distance with Heather Stephens' body slung over its shoulder, Kris Lemche's decapitated head clasped in its hand. Beautifully filmed in Canada's Arctic Circle region (photography: Luke Geissbühler), Weiner's minor low-budget gem is all about the paranoia and panic brought on by the sense of "where is it" felt by the six-man expedition as it treks through the limitless snowy tundra towards Potter's Gulch, led by local guide Timothy V. Murphy who scoffs at Lemche's "bullshit" theories. Snatches of Mozart's somber "Requiem in D Minor" adds to the air of icy loneliness, Lemche and company halting at a gloomy log cabin, the possible location for a sighting. Murphy is later found dead, his snowmobile wrecked, then others disappear and alarming growling noises heard, finally leaving just terrified Stephens and a distinctly nervous Lemche to face the awful truth: The bestial creature is alive and

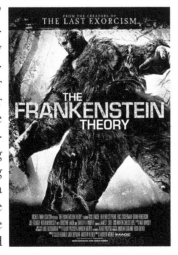

not the least bit interested in making friends with anybody, least of all the bloodstock of his creator ("We must appeal to its humanity."). *The Frankenstein Theory* is a mood piece, pure and simple, a cut-price but nonetheless interesting addition to the long list of movies based on Mary Shelley's novel. It may indeed be cheap, but those mesmerizing landscapes and atmosphere of dread more than make up for the lack of a full-blooded monster.

Half Light
VIP3 Medienfonds/Lakeshore Ent. 2006; 110 minutes;
Director: Craig Rosenberg ****

Following the death by drowning of her five-year-old son in a London canal, a thriller writer rents a small cottage by the sea in Scotland and befriends a lonely lighthouse keeper with a troubled past.

Demi Moore stars as the successful author attempting to exorcise her demons by getting away from it all, becoming romantically involved with lighthouse keeper Hans Matheson whom locals say committed suicide seven years ago after killing his wife and her lover in the lighthouse. She sees the spirit of her dead son, fridge magnets are arranged to spell out a warning and the local psychic tells Moore her life is in danger. Moore's best friend and business acquaintance, Kate Isitt, arrives at the cottage;

unknown to Moore, she's having an affair with her husband, Henry Ian Cusick who, jealous of Moore's success compared to his own feeble attempts at writing a novel, has decided to bump her off and lay his hands on her fortune. When Isitt is apparently murdered by Matheson in the lighthouse, Moore doubts her sanity but it's a put-up job concocted by Cusick, Isitt and a man called Patrick who strongly resembles Matheson (the actor played both roles). By driving Moore over the edge, they hope that her murder will appear like suicide; she's drugged, bound in chains and dumped in the sea. But Moore manages to free herself and, at the lighthouse, watches as, during a struggle, Isitt falls and bangs her head, dying; Patrick, the bogus lighthouse keeper, possessed by the spirit of the real one, kills Cusick, mirroring the tragic events of seven years back, and jumps to his death from the tower, just as Matheson had done. Moore then leaves the cottage, hoping that Matheson's restless spirit can finally rest in peace. Shot mainly on Llanddwyn Island, Anglesey in North Wales, *Half Light* is an involving supernatural thriller whose picturesque coastal location plays just as important a role as Moore's guilt-ridden author.

The Hallow aka The Woods
Irish Film Board/Occupant Ent./Fantastic Films 2015; 97 minutes; Director: Corin Hardy ***

A conservationist/botanist is sent to an isolated area of Ireland to survey a forest for possible tree felling, not knowing that he is trespassing on ground inhabited by legions of demonic creatures.

Irish filmmakers love to set their darkly shot productions in dense woodlands, so *The Hallow* doesn't buck the trend; shooting took place at scenic Letterfrack in County Galway. Joseph Mawle is the man frowned upon by the locals, especially farmer Michael McElhatton, as he places a cross on trees earmarked for destruction ("He's trespassing. It's dangerous."). The forest harbors something deadly; when Mawle places blood from a savaged deer under the microscope, he observes unusual parasitic organisms preying on

blood cells with the ability to cause mutation. McElhatton attempts one more time to force Mawle, his wife (Bojana Novakovic) and their baby son out of their rented mill house by laying the facts on the line: The villagers are superstitious, the forest belongs to the Hallow with its banshees and baby-stealers and he lost his daughter to whatever lurks in the woods; if you decide to stay and vio-

late their haven, he concludes, replace the iron grills over the windows and barricade the doors. He leaves the couple with an ancient book on Irish folklore but Mawle chooses to ignore the farmer's warnings and soon regrets it: Black sticky gunge seeps out of cracks in the walls and floors, Mawle's left eye is penetrated by a gooey proboscis, his dog is badly mauled, the house is ransacked and, at night, the woods are alive with crawling, taloned humanoids bent on causing mayhem; only light can scare them off. The first 45 minutes builds the tension strongly but thereafter, we enter formulaic "can we escape from the creepy monsters" fight-for-survival territory, a case of whether Novakovic can prevent the ghouls from stealing her infant while her husband quickly morphs into one of the things that are causing them so much grief, presenting a further danger to his wife. Oozing masses of black vine-like fungus sprouts everywhere, the climactic showdown taking place in a forest glade: McElhatton's missing daughter, now a grotesque changeling, like a fairy tale zombie, appears from a cave, holding a baby; it's exchanged for Novakovic's child which, in fact, was an infant from the Hallow. As dawn breaks, the creatures scuttle from sight, the swapped baby gruesomely explodes in the sun's rays and Mawle, transformed into a horned monstrosity, dies, knowing that his son is safe. Back at the house, Novakovic clutches her baby to her chest, mourning the loss of her husband. And keep watching when the closing credits roll up: A logging company is felling trees en masse; a lorry loaded with black fungus-covered logs thunders by and as it passes, a denizen from the Hallow roars in anger at camera. A fast-moving Irish indie creature-feature that doesn't hang about to begin with, Martin Van Broekhuizen's glossy photography just right; but the frenetic pacing runs out of steam during the final 20 minutes which drag and spoil what could have been a real little gem of a horror outing.

Haunt
Revolver Picture Company/Covert Media 2014; 86 minutes; Director: Mac Carter ****

A family moves into a house that, unknown to them, suffers from the Morello curse due to the previous family all dying in mysterious circumstances except for their deranged mother.

In the opening minutes, Sebastian Barr, head of the Morello family, attempts to contact his dead siblings via a boxed transmitter; he's dragged backwards by a ghoulish figure and falls to his death down the stairs. And those ghoulish figures feature prominently in Mac Carter's (his sole director's credit) spine-tingling supernatural tragedy as Harrison Gilbertson, the new inhabitants' elder son, befriends Liana Liberato, living with her abusive father in a nearby trailer and somehow drawn to the house. Forming a relationship, the pair sets out to discover the secret of that spooky residence and use the old radio transmitter to dial into the

UNDER TEN MILLION? ANYTHING'S POSSIBLE!

So, you want to hear a ghost story?

It's Groundhog Day of a sort as Abigail Breslin (a charming performance) gets out of bed, sees her baby brother (Peter DaCunha) playing with his computer games, talks to Mum and Dad (Peter Outerbridge and Michelle Nolden) about her 16th birthday, due the next day, practices on the clarinet to Prokofiev's "Peter and the Wolf," deals with the laundry and watches a television show; the next day, the same, and the day after. Then things gradually change: Outerbridge turns into a bad-tempered grouch and starts smoking, taking out his anger on the family car, DaCunha talks to an invisible pal called Edgar, Breslin hears noises in the rooms, uses an Ouija board to figure out who's there and discovers an old mine tunnel littered with human bones beneath the laundry room. She then finds herself in the house, modernized which it will be in the future, occupied by another family. And why is it that Breslin and *her* family cannot escape that thick fog surrounding the place? A complex French/Canadian supernatural offering that moves through an intriguing, twisty-turny plotline to its payoff. Since 1953, numerous young girls who have lived in the house have gone missing, murdered by a psychopath (Stephen McHattie) whose entity is out to get the new family and can possess the fathers, hence Outerbridge's unnatural behavior; and Edgar, DaCunha's friend, is young

netherworld ("I wanted to see if there was a heaven, not a hell," Liberato tells Gilbertson later), conjuring up a series of disturbing events: odd voices, banging doors, rattling floorboards, a hideous-looking wraith and spectral shapes hovering in the background. Jackie Weaver (Mrs. Morello) is the cause: The mentally unstable pediatrician not only murdered her own children but killed the woman who was having an affair with her husband, burying her body under the floorboards; the baby she gave birth to is none other than Liberato who, possessed by her mother's vengeful spirit at the end, slaughters Gilbertson with a hammer. The new family departs, Liberato is taken into custody and the house has one more entity to prowl its empty rooms—Gilbertson. Nicely acted by Gilbertson and Liberato, with Weaver putting in a downright nasty performance as the venomous doctor, *Haunt* is a disturbing haunted house thriller that admirably delivers the goods on minimal funds.

Haunter
Copperheart Ent./Wild Bunch 2013; 97 minutes;
Director: Vincenzo Natali ★★★★

A 15-year-old girl wakes up to the same routine every day, becoming convinced that her family met with a dreadful fate linked to a serial killer whose presence still inhabits the building.

McHattie. The phantom of Samantha Weinstein, one of McHattie's victims, informs Breslin what took place; Breslin subsequently attempts to warn Eleanor Zichy, the new family's teenage daughter, that her life is in danger. A satisfactory climax sees the wraiths of the dead girls materializing in the mist and tearing McHattie to shreds, consigning him and his murderous soul into the basement incinerator. Breslin reaches her birthday at last and is presented with a new bike, cycling out into a blinding white light; the family is finally free of McHattie's malevolent curse.

A Haunting at Silver Falls
Outside Pictures/Enderby Ent. 2013; 96 minutes;
Director: Brett Donowho ***

An orphaned teenager sent to live with her aunt and uncle is followed by the ghosts of twin girls who were reputedly murdered by their father, an unproven serial killer.

A terrified, screaming girl is seen being murdered in woods at the start, her body dragged away, leaving a dismembered ringed hand. Twenty years later, Alix Elizabeth Gitter finds the ring, puts it on but can't take it off; at night, the ring's bedraggled, pale emaciated owner tries to reclaim it by wrenching Gitter's finger, after which the teen has the phantom (Nikita Ramsey) as unwelcome, but not altogether unfriendly, company ("I'm being followed by a dead girl."), Ramsey trying to communicate to her something of importance. Silver Falls has a history of deaths and suicides; is there a killer in the town's midst, or is James C. Burns (Ramsey's father), due to be executed, the culprit? Brett Donowho and his trio of scriptwriters (Cam Cannon, Rachel Long and Brian Pittman) lead the viewer down a maze of blind alleyways to keep us on our toes: Steve Bacic (uncle) and Tara Westwood (aunt) reckon Gitter is in need of psychiatric help, sending her to prying doctor Erick Avari whose geeky son (James Cavlo) Gitter is unaccountably dating; Burns gives Gitter an identical ring to the one she is wearing, claiming he didn't murder his girls; Ramsey is joined by her equally ragged twin, Jade Ramsey (real-life twins); there are hints that Bacic murdered Gitter's alleged crazy mother, making her death appear like a drowning accident; and it's made obvious that Westwood and Bacic are up to no good, falsely accusing Gitter of stealing and lying. Bacic and Westwood turn out to be the unhinged psychopaths, locking Gitter in the basement so that pervert Bacic can indulge in "playtime"

before killing her. Cavlo of all people comes to the rescue, belting the demented uncle with a spade, Gitter whacking Westwood unconscious. Dumped in a pit covered by a trapdoor, the two homicidal maniacs wake to discover that both are wearing the accursed rings; the trapdoor rises and the ghoulish dead twins leap in to feast on their revenge. Screened on the American Lifetime Channel, *A Haunting at Silver Falls* is the type of supernatural thriller shown on British television at three o'clock in the afternoon; despite its "15" rating, the feature is fairly tame but, considering the low budget, surprisingly well pieced together in all departments, an inoffensive ghost story for the family to enjoy over a cup of tea and packet of biscuits.

The Haunting of Borley Rectory
Greenway Ent./High Fliers Films 2019; 92 minutes;
Director: Steven M. Smith ***

Wounded in the Battle of Monte Cassino, Italy, in 1944, an American lieutenant is seconded to a cottage near Borley in Essex, England, where he is subjected to disturbances caused by a ghostly nun.

For non-English readers, a note on Borley Rectory, still reputed to be the country's most haunted building: Constructed in 1862, the Gothic-styled Rectory first gave rise to supernatural incidents as early as 1863; over the years, numerous families occupying the house reported a raft of uncanny noises, poltergeist activity, unusual phenomena and sightings, the most famous being the figure of a nun that walked in the Rectory grounds. In 1929, celebrated paranormal detective Harry Price paid the first of many visits to Borley, even renting the place for a year in 1937 (he wrote two books on the case). On February 27, 1939, the Rectory was gutted by a fire, thought to have been started deliberately, and was demolished in July 1944; Price died in 1948, and alleged manifestations in the vicinity of the site still persist to this day. Steven M. Smith's £50,000 take on the Borley legend fabricated a storyline whereby recovering American serviceman Zach Clifford (as Robert Vincent O'Neill), tasked with decoding German transmissions, was troubled by the glowing-eyed nun wielding a bloody axe from the nearby Rectory ruins; Rad Brown (Harry Price) is called in for an opinion, thinking that Clifford's suffering from shellshock, and the Yank eventually marries Sonera Angel (Marianne Foyster) in 1945; Foyster *did* marry a man called O'Neil, but he was a local laborer. Where does this leave us re-

UNDER TEN MILLION? ANYTHING'S POSSIBLE!

garding the film *as such*, and *not* a concise history of the Borley hauntings? Shot around rural Borley, this modest, idiosyncratic production is blessed with bright cinematography (Peter Panoa), spotlighting England's peacefully green, wooded countryside bathed in sunlight, and the 1940s period feel is pretty accurate, even if the facts aren't. Acting is low-key (like the production itself), the nun effects tingle the spine ever so slightly while Smith's directorial style verges on the clumsy at times, leading you to believe that Clifford himself *may* be a spook. It's similar to the kind of British television two-part drama you might catch on a Sunday night—but it fares much better than North Bank's *A Haunting at the Rectory* (2015), another hazy version of strange occurrences at the Rectory. An unpretentious little English ghost picture that isn't as awful as some online reviews suggest; for a comprehensive study of the complex events surrounding the psychic manifestations at Borley Rectory and all those involved, Peter Underwood and Paul Tabori's *The Ghosts of Borley* (Underwood Press reprint, 2017) comes highly recommended.

The Hole in the Ground
Savage Prods./Bankside Films/Irish Film Board 2019; 90 minutes; Director: Lee Cronin ****

A mother is convinced that the disturbing change in her young son's behavior is attributed to a vast sinkhole that has opened up in a nearby forest.

Seána Kerslake and James Quinn Markey move to a house on the edge of a forest to start a new life, but an odd encounter with elderly neighbor Kati Outinen (she claims her son *wasn't* her son but an imposter) plus a huge mysterious sinkhole in the forest forces her to question her decision to go there. Markey vanishes into the forest, returns, and changes from docile seven-year-old to mini-monster, eating spiders and food that he previously disliked and throwing his mother across the kitchen, staring at her malevolently. Outinen shouts at her, "He's not your son" and is then found dead, her head pushed into the earth. Ker-

slake captures on camera an image of Markey's face that is *not* human, and after the boy tries to kill her in the manner that Outinen met her grisly death, she locks her bogus son in the cellar where he screams like a wild animal. Venturing into the cavernous depths of the sinkhole, Kerslake encounters slimy subhumans before dragging her real son out; back home, she sets fire to the house and the thing in the cellar. Months later, everything is back to normal—or is it? Kerslake is seen photographing Markey at play, closing up on the image of his face; she has also positioned a mirror to catch his reflection; it's obvious that's she's still not sure. Stephen McKeon's loud spooky score contributes greatly to a moody horror film containing one of indie cinema's most malevolent kids in Markey's chilling performance; this, plus Kerslake's psychologically fraught mother and that ominous sinkhole in the dense forest, makes this a recent Irish gem worth catching.

I Origins
WellWork Studios/Bersin Pictures 2014; 106 minutes; Director: Mike Cahill ***

A graduate's hypothesis on evolutionary science related to the human eye is questioned after meeting a girl at a Halloween party.

Distributed by Fox Searchlight Pictures and a flop on its limited release, Mike Cahill's $1,000,000 second feature (his first was *Another Earth*, 2011) was an overly ambitious little movie which proved too slow-moving for mainstream audiences, cerebral content taking precedence over action; its heart was in the right place, even if the execution wasn't. Twenty-six-year-old PhD student Michael Pitt, researching into the eye and the organ's place in the natural order of things, meets Astrid Bergès-Frisbey at a party, photographing her vivid pupils; they have sex, start a relationship and almost get married before she dies in an horrific lift accident. Lab assistant Brit Marling has succeeded in transplanting a man-made eye into the blind worm *Eisenia fetida*, thus going some way in proving Pitt's theories on scientific

evolution. Seven years later, Marling and Pitt, now married, have a baby, Tobias; on a routine eye scan, his details are identified with those of a man who died just prior to the baby's conception, shaking Pitt's stubborn refusal in accepting creationism. Checking an iris database, Bergès-Frisbey's eyes are studied, the pattern matching those scanned of a person in Delhi, India only three months previously. Pitt travels to India and meets community leader Archie Panjabi, tracking down an orphaned girl living rough on the streets, the match of Bergès-Frisbey's pupils. In a series of tests, the girl (Kashish) identifies certain images only Bergès-Frisbey could have known about, *and* she becomes terrified when they go to enter a lift. Pitt is now forced into believing that man's very existence, the afterlife and even reincarnation, has a religious aspect; Kashish cuddles Pitt and stares into his face in recognition, the pair walking out of his hotel into blazing sunlight. In a post-credits sequence, Pitt scans the pupils of famous deceased persons to determine whether any of them has a counterpart. Cahill's script is littered with pseudo-religious teasers (cremation; recurring numbers; no proof of God; Bergès-Frisbey talking in riddles) as is the narrative (what is the point of William "I serve the Lord" Mapother appearing in the hotel where Pitt is staying?); and would Pitt seriously be allowed to take a 10-year-old girl up to his room without questions being asked? "How do you feel," asks Marling to Pitt on Skype after he's semi-convinced of a divine intervention. "I feel foolish," is his lame response. Part whimsical romance, part sci-fi mystery, *I Origins* suffers from that malaise in modern-day cinema, the unresolved ending, a half-baked "science versus religion put to the test" essay that disappoints despite sharp, colorful cinematography and Pitt's winning, occasionally bemused, performance.

I Remember You
Zik Zak Filmworks 2017; 105 minutes;
Director: Óskar Thór Axelsson ****

A doctor whose eight-year-old son went missing three years ago starts to unravel the story of an abused, missing child dating back over 60 years.

Cinematographer Jakob Ingimundarson's pristine shots of a desolate Iceland landscape shadowed under heavy skies adds punch to this atmospheric Icelandic chiller that requires a great deal of concentration before the picture's startling denouement (filming took place at the deserted town of Hesteyri in remote Westfjord). There are two plotlines running on parallel lines which ultimately converge, director Axelsson switching from one to the other in the blink of an eye. First we have doctor/psychiatrist Freyr (Jóhannes Hauker Jóhannesson); his diabetic son Benni disappeared without trace three years ago and the doctor is convinced he died in mysterious circumstances. Freyr and policewoman Dagny (Sara Dögg Ásgeirsdóttir) are investigating the suicide of an elderly woman found hanging in an old desecrated church. Numerous crosses are carved on her back and on searching through newspaper archives, it appears that in 1956, the woman was at a school where eight of its pupils bullied and tormented a boy named Bernódus who was abused by his father,

crosses etched into *his* back; the lad vanished decades ago. In a faded photograph, six of the eight have their faces scratched out; all died from various accidents, leaving two still alive ("A 70-year-old serial killer?" says Freyr). In the second storyline, Garðar (Thor Kristjansson), wife Katrin (Anna Gunndis Guðmundsdóttir) and Lif (Águsta Eva Eriendsdóttir) travel to a small abandoned town and take up residence in a derelict house, the aim being to turn it into a bed and breakfast. Katrin sees Bernódus' ghost by a creek, sprains her ankle and, in the house's cellar, stumbles across the desiccated corpse of the boy she saw (Bernódus reached the town because his mother was buried there and perished in the cellar, her photo clutched in his hand). Terrified out of their wits, the trio moves into a nearby doctor's empty house where it transpires that, in the previous summer, Garðar had a fling with Lif—and she's now pregnant. The final revelation is that Garðar and Lif died years earlier when Bernódus' wraith lured the pair into a disused whaling station which collapsed on them. Freyr and Dagny discover Katrin's body in the cellar alongside Bernódus' remains while Freyr's son Benni is found in an adjacent green septic tank; CCTV footage shows that he crawled inside the tank playing hide and seek with a pal while Garðar, Katrin and Lif were at a petrol station having a meal. As Freyr and Dagny leave the isolated site with

UNDER TEN MILLION? ANYTHING'S POSSIBLE!

Benni's body, the spirits of Katrin and Bernódus watch from a window, holding hands. A compelling supernatural mystery that demands an immediate second viewing in order to fully understand its labyrinthine framework and all of its implications which, in the end, *do* make sense.

I Spit on Your Grave
Cinetel Films/Anchor Bay 2010; 108 minutes;
Director: Steven R. Monroe *****
I Spit on Your Grave 2
Cinetel Films/Anchor Bay 2013; 106 minutes;
Director: Steven R. Monroe *****
I Spit on Your Grave 3: Vengeance is Mine
Cinetel Films/Anchor Bay 2015; 92 minutes;
Director: J.D. Braunstein ****

Writer/director Meir Zarchi's $600,000 1978 notorious cult classic *I Spit on Your Grave*, dealing with female degradation and rape (original title: *Day of the Woman*), was controversial fare for its time, banned in several countries and heavily cut in others. Cinetel Films' trio of remakes were released in less-stricter cinematic climates but still remain strong meat—and all are surprisingly well made, given the X-rated content. The $2,000,000 2010 version of the rape-revenge 1978 feature (Zarchi co-wrote and was executive producer) had budding author Sarah Butler

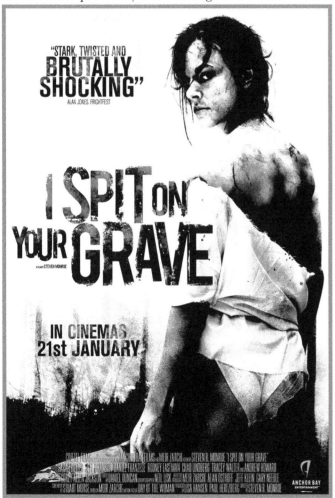

(as Jennifer Hills) terrorized by five retards in an isolated rented cabin in the Louisiana swamps; Jeff Branson, Daniel Franzese, Rodney Eastman, simpleton Chad Lindberg and perverted sheriff Andrew Howard. Abused, humiliated ("A big city cock-teasing whore," Branson shouts into her face) and gang-raped, Butler, naked, traumatized and covered in filth, throws herself off a bridge into a river before Howard has a chance to shoot her. The girl returns and how; retribution is very sweet, although not for those easily offended: Lindberg is throttled unconscious, to be used later; Franzese is tied to a tree, his eyes pecked out by crows; Eastman dies in agony, his face plunged into a tub of caustic lye solution; Branson has his teeth yanked out with pliers ("It's date night. Show me your teeth!"), his penis severed for good measure; and the vile Howard receives a shotgun blast up his anus ("I thought you were an ass man."), the trigger unknowingly set off by Lindberg. The first 50 minutes focuses on Butler's harrowing violation, the second 50 minutes her sickening revenge, a film of two bloody halves competently put together by Steven R. Monroe, the director of many of Cinetel's finer fantasy/sci-fi efforts. Neil Lisk's glossy cinematography combined with Corey Allen Jackson's spot-on score results in a marginally superior remake of Zarchi's original torture-porn groundbreaker, Butler rock steady in her role despite having had reservations in taking on the sordid material.

Monroe was back in the driving seat for *I Spit on Your Grave 2* (Zarchi was again executive producer), Jemma Dallender the aspiring New York model (Katie Carter) who wants to add more glamorous photos to her portfolio and by doing so gets bundled off to Sofia, Bulgaria, the victim of a sex trafficking gang. Before Dallender disappears, she's raped by Yavor Baharov and pumped full of drugs; in Sofia, she wakes in chains  on a filthy mattress in a basement where she's stripped and assaulted before managing to escape through a window. Unfortunately, Mary Stockley, a seemingly benevolent Samaritan, takes her back to her house, the one she fled from; Stockley happens to be the mother of this bunch of sadists and the trafficking ringleader. Drugged, tortured with an electric prod, raped by loathsome pair Aleksander Aleksiev and Peter Silverleaf, savagely beaten by Joe Absolom (strange to see the British actor of family television series *Doc Martin* appearing in something so far removed from family entertainment) and left buried alive in a box, Dal-

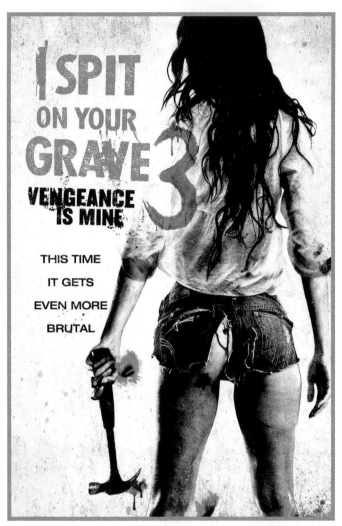

roe, the result not quite as full-on violent as the previous two but still containing more than enough moments of gory carnage to appease aficionados. Sarah Butler reprised her role as Jennifer Hills, now attending group and solo therapy sessions under the assumed name of Angela to rid herself of her inner demons; she has constant nightmares harking back to her previous ordeals and imagines killing anyone who crosses her path. When her friend at group therapy, Jennifer Landon, is raped and murdered by her boyfriend who's released on a technicality, Butler embarks on a bloody trail of vengeance, not only against the perpetrator, Andrew Dits, but other lowlifes involved with group members: Christopher Hoffman (he's continually raping Megan Raich, his stepdaughter) and Adam Dunnells (he raped Doug McKeon's daughter, was let off, and the girl committed suicide). Dits is bludgeoned to death with a crowbar after Butler slits open his penis, Hoffman has a lubricated metal pipe rammed deep into his anus, expiring in unendurable pain ("Forgive me, Father, 'cos I don't give a shit," Butler laughs after committing the deed) and Dunnells is slashed with a knife before Detective Gabriel Hogan shoots him dead; the cop has been on Butler's tail, convinced she's behind the slayings. "You want justice? You take it for yourself. I'm not finished yet," Butler tells therapist Harley Jane Kozak, going on to bite off the tip of sex pest Walter Perez's pecker and stabbing at his throat before arrested by Hogan. In the twist reveal, it transpires that Butler has been undergoing personal therapy sessions for two years due to lack of evidence on the murders she committed; leaving Kozak's office, she repeatedly knifes two inmates and then Kozak, walking down the corridor, smiling. Sane or insane? It's for the audience to decide. Braunstein directs with purpose while Richard J. Vialet's inky photography bathes the movie in *noir* overtones, completing a trio of glossy slasher epics that, if they weren't so darned well made, might not have been worth a dime. That they *can* be appreciated on repeated viewings is all down to the skill and proficiency displayed by Cinetel Films' roster of technicians; three revenge-rape features, nightmarishly innovative in their own unique fashion, that rise above the congested pack and can be enjoyed (if that's the right word) as pieces of expertly crafted horror cinema. (Note: In 2019, Meir Zarchi released *I Spit on Your Grave: Déjà Vu*, a direct sequel to his 1978 opus; original star Camille Keaton was back as a 70-year-old Jennifer Hills, the movie running at a lengthy 148 minutes. It doesn't form part of the Cinetel triumvirate and is not reviewed in this volume.)

lender forces herself out of her shallow grave, prowls the dark, dank sewage tunnels, finds refuge in a church ("Little mouse" is what Father Valentine Pelka calls her) and stalks her attackers, each meeting a well-deserved but hard-to-stomach demise: Baharov is tethered to a wall, sliced open and muck smeared into his wounds, dying of infection; Aleksiev is drowned in a toilet bowl brimming with excrement; Silverleaf is electrocuted, his genitals and mouth scorched by the prod; Stockley finds herself in the same grave that Dallender got free from; and Absolom has his testicles ripped from his body, the psycho shot by cop Michael Dixon who has been on Dallender's trail. Her vengeance satiated, the broken, bruised girl warily approaches the American Embassy to face an uncertain future. Yes, it's grim, grimy and nasty but produced with lashings of unholy style; Monroe's direction never flinches from the awful events taking place, Damian Bromley's photography accentuating the cold grays of the Eastern European locations. For fans of this kind of hardcore stuff, the film's a top-scorer—and note Dallender's prophetic words to her friend near the outset as she sets a trap for a rat: "I know how to catch me some vermin." She certainly did!

The last of the trio, *I Spit on Your Grave 3: Vengeance is Mine*, had J.D. Braunstein taking over the reins from Mon-

In the Dark Half
Cinema Six/BBC Films/Regent Capital 2012; 85 minutes; Director: Alastair Siddons ****
A confused 15-year-old girl feels alone in her isolated world, retreating to a bunker in the woods where she finds solace among the spirits of dead animals.

UNDER TEN MILLION? ANYTHING'S POSSIBLE!

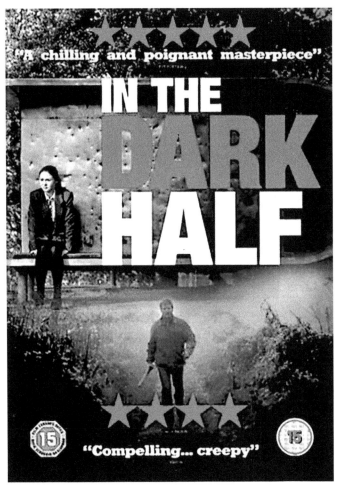

Not all is what it seems in Alastair Siddons' £300,000 UK supernatural/psychological drama filmed around the bleak outskirts of Bristol. Jessica Barden plays the angst-ridden teen, arguing incessantly with her bad-tempered mother (Lyndsey Marshal) and befriending her neighbor, poacher Tony Curran, drawn to him sexually, even though she steals his "kills" and lays the dead rabbits to rest in the bunker. Tragedy strikes when Curran's young son dies suddenly from heart seizure while Barden is babysitting. She blames herself, Curran blames *himself* and the girl's imagination becomes distorted by the events that are unfolding around her, seeing the spirits of animals that Curran has shot. Ultimately, *In the Dark Half* is all about grief, repression, guilt and redemption: In a *Sixth Sense*-type payoff, Barden's mother, who we have seen throughout the film, is a ghost; depressed, she hanged herself on the stairs and it is Barden's *father* (Simon Armstrong) whom the girl has been conversing with. As for Curran, he elects to commit suicide in the bunker, cuddling the ashes of his beloved son ("I can't live without him."). Finally coming to terms with the loss of Marshal, Barden resumes a normal relationship with Armstrong, now free of her inner demons. A beautifully observed study in one person's troubled psyche produced on a micro-budget, both Barden and Curran in highly believable form.

Inanimate aka Harbinger Down

Studio ADI/Dark Dunes Prods. 2015; 82 minutes; Director: Alec Gillis ***

The crew of the crabbing trawler *Harbinger*, operating in the Bering Sea, fishes out of the ocean a huge block of ice containing the remains of a soviet spaceship that crashed in the area in 1982; aboard are two dead astronauts and something far more deadly.

Writer/director Alec Gillis' first feature should have been a welcome addition to the cycle of *The Thing*-type of movie; the special effects ace worked on 2011's *The Thing* as well as a heap more high-profile pictures. Here, though, Gillis' inexperience behind the camera showed up in a profusion of clumsy, casually handled scenes combined with uneven acting; Matt Winston's university professor is a boorish, loudmouth bully ("It's salvage and we own it," he cries, not realizing what lies in the wreckage) while student Camille Balsamo, on the ship to study pods of Beluga Whales, whispers instead of projecting her vocals. The block of ice that Captain Lance Henriksen (excellent as usual) hauls out of the icy depths houses a Russian experimental moon lander (a "hunk of junk."), designed to take tiny animals known as Tardigrades into space as they can withstand intense radiation. It goes without saying that the reactivated creatures have infiltrated the body of one of the astronauts, mutating into a tentacled monstrosity, absorbing humans ("It can change shape, take on different forms. It can reprogram its host's DNA.") and erupting into a worm-like writhing mass ("Some things should stay frozen."). As we wonder just who's human, and who isn't, liquid nitrogen turns out to be the answer to stopping the ever-evolving monster in its tracks, Henriksen wryly announcing "We'll need a bigger bucket" when he first lays eyes on the slimy shapeshifter. Russian agent Milla Bjorn becomes part female, part monster, and Henriksen, covered in alien muck, is infected as the crew all succumb to the horror below decks. Balsamo survives the mayhem, the *Harbinger* colliding with a berg and showering the thing in ice as she lies on a floe, a rescue helicopter approaching. Studio ADI created the creature effects in traditional 1980s fashion, discarding CGI, and they work, but unfortunately the moderate budget tells: The film is too short, characters underdeveloped, the pacing hurried and not measured; with bigger finances, it could have been something a whole lot juicier, and meatier, for monster fans to get their teeth into.

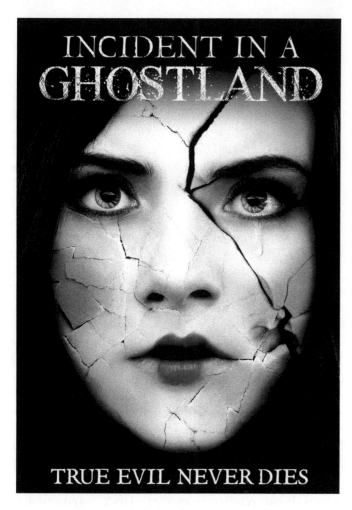

INCIDENT IN A GHOSTLAND

TRUE EVIL NEVER DIES

Incident in a Ghostland aka **Ghostland**
5656 Films/Inferno Pictures 2018; 91 minutes;
Director: Pascal Laugier ****

A successful author returns to her family home where, 16 years earlier, she, her mother and her sister were subjected to a barbaric assault by a woman and her retarded, doll-fixated companion.

Pascal Laugier brought us the gore-soaked *Martyrs* in 2008; in this French/Canadian shocker, he treads similar territory in a psychological horror jump-scare fest that might have the more easily offended turning away in disgust. Emilia Jones (as Beth; she's obsessed with H.P. Lovecraft), Mum Mylène Farmer and argumentative sister Taylor Hickson (Vera; she and Beth dislike each other intensely) are savagely attacked in their isolated house by a couple driving a candy truck. Jones escapes the harrowing ordeal; years later (her new book *Incident in a Ghostland*, based on what she suffered, is a best seller), she receives a frantic call from her sister: "You have to come back. Don't leave me alone, Beth." Beth (now Crystal Reed) arrives at the house which is stuffed to the rafters with antique dolls, meets her mother and finds that Vera (now Anastasia Phillips) inhabits a padded room in the basement, traumatized by what happened all those years ago. But history repeats itself, the nightmare returning as that woman (Kevin Pow-

er) and her hulking, bald grunting pal (Rob Archer) come back to carry on where they left off. The last third of the picture is pitched at near-hysterical levels, Archer torturing (with a blowtorch) and sexually molesting dolls, then brutalizing Reed after Power makes her up to look like a doll, Phillips screaming her bruised, battered head off and Farmer trying to ward off the maniacs. Then Phillips spells out the truth to Reed: "Mum was murdered on that night." She was, her throat cut; what Reed has been witnessing is her spirit, attempting to thwart the killers and reunite the two warring sisters. A cop finally puts paid to Power and Archer with a hail of bullets, the two sisters, bloody but alive, bonding at long last on their way to hospital. Disturbing, unflinching and violent, Laugier's in-your-face splatter feast will appeal to those who appreciate the more extreme form of horror flick on their menus; it certainly isn't for the faint-hearted.

The Innkeepers
Dark Sky Films/Glass Eye Pix 2011; 101 minutes;
Director: Ti West *****

During the final days of the Yankee Pedlar Inn, two employees dabbling in the paranormal awaken the angry manifestation of a woman who hanged herself on her wedding day.

A GHOST STORY FOR THE MINIMUM WAGE

The Innkeepers

The shock-a-minute, jump-scare brigade hated this slow-burner, divided into four chapters; for others, writer/director Ti West's supernatural, Hitchcockian-type thriller hit all the right notes, a quirky, at times downright chilling, exercise in haunted goings-on, shot in the actual Yankee Pedlar Inn in Torrington, Connecticut (built in 1891; closed 2015; and reputedly haunted). Goofy asthmatic Sara Paxton (an engaging performance) and Pat Healy (sporting a Tintin haircut) attempt to record on tape the ghost of Madeline O'Malley; the woman hanged herself after being jilted by her fiancé on their wedding day. Guest Kelly McGillis is a psychic, aware that something's wrong with the place, and George Riddle arrives, booking himself into the same room he spent his honeymoon in. Assisted by Jeff Grace's nicely-judged score (light one minute, doom-filled the next), West opts for the slow buildup (a tinkling piano; an indistinct voice on tape) before going for the jugular. Paxton's first sight of O'Malley's hollow-eyed wraith in her darkened room will have your flesh crawling while the scene in the cluttered basement, Paxton whispering to Healy, "She's right behind you," is spine-tingling cinema. And no happy conclusion, either. Riddle slashes his wrists in the bath, his phantom turning up in the basement and pursuing the terrified Paxton, the girl dying as the ghoulish O'Malley in her soiled bridal dress homes in on her; McGillis (she sensed this would all happen) and Healy leave after the police have removed Paxton and Riddle's bodies. In the final 70 seconds, West's camera slowly moves along the corridor, turns into Paxton's room and freezes for a full 25 seconds, the temperature dropping (is *this* what a haunted room would be like? It feels so *wrong*.). What is in there? Then the door slams shut. Look *very* closely at the drapes pulled back from the net curtains on the right; you'll spot Paxton's vague apparition *in* them (above and below the tie cord), her head turning as the door suddenly closes with a bang, another clammy (and rather sad) moment in a perceptive, well-directed ghost story full of psychological nuances that grows on you after two to three viewings.

It Comes at Night
A24 Pictures/Animal Kingdom Prods. 2017; 92 minutes; Director: Trey Edward Shults ****

In a virus-ravaged post-apocalyptic world, a family cautiously welcomes another family into their home with disastrous consequences.

What comes at night? Is it nightmares associated with the disease that has decimated mankind, or the disease itself, airborne and a constant threat to survival? Most post-apocalyptic movies, by their very nature, are dark, somber downbeat affairs; *It Comes at Night* is no exception to the rule and after it finishes, a strong drink followed by a dose of happy pills will be urgently required to lift you out of the depressive rut. Notwithstanding the film's grimmer-

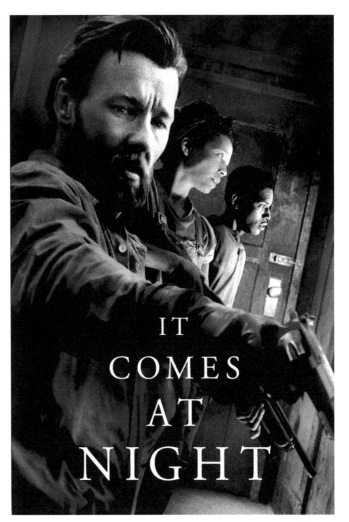

than-grim aspect, writer/director Trey Edward Shults' feature (distributed by Universal) is an attention-grabber admirably acted by a small cast. Joel Edgerton, Carmen Ejogo and 17-year-old son Kelvin Harrison, Jr., holed up in their woodland house, allow into their ranks Christopher Abbott, Riley Keough and toddler Griffin Robert Faulkner, satisfied that they are disease-free. In the woods, trigger-happy Edgerton, suffering from acute paranoia (he's already shot Ejogo's father in the opening minutes and incinerated his corpse) callously guns down two men without checking to see whether they're infected or not; Harrison's dog contracts the virus and the poor boy has to lay in bed hearing both couples indulging in noisy sex games (he dreams of Keough astride his body, drooling liquid into his mouth). Then young Faulkner gets sick and the final act develops into a frantic "who's got the virus, and who hasn't" scenario. Following heated arguments, the two families are separated, each to their own room ("We can't take any risks," growls Edgerton), leading to Edgerton blindly killing the mother, father and boy when they decide to leave. Indoors, Harrison, coughing up blood and covered in sores, dies, leaving Edgerton and Ejogo alone at the kitchen table, facing a very bleak future indeed. A gritty slab of intimate drama based on mistrust and the genuine fear of an uncertain future, *It Comes at Night* serves its particular subgenre well, even though it's far from being uplifting fare, a spirit-crusher if ever there was one.

It Follows

Northern Lights Films/Animal Kingdom/Two Flints
2014; 100 minutes; Director: David Robert Mitchell *****

A 19-year-old girl is relentlessly pursued by a murderous entity, a "paranormal STD," that is passed from one person to another through casual sexual activity.

Budgeted at $2,000,000, David Robert Mitchell's dread-filled essay into the perils of casual sex (he based it on childhood nightmares) is one of most cleverly constructed flicks of its type in recent years, packed with the kind of telling detail that many directors in this genre miss. Maika Monroe plays the not-so-innocent teen spending an hour of passion with Jake Weary in a disused parking lot. Afterwards, he chloroforms her, she comes to, strapped in a wheelchair, he points out a ragged-looking girl slowly approaching through the gloom and delivers a disturbing message: "This thing is going to follow you. Someone gave it to me but I passed it on to you. It could look like someone you know. Or it could be as a stranger in a crowd. But whatever else, it will get close to you. It

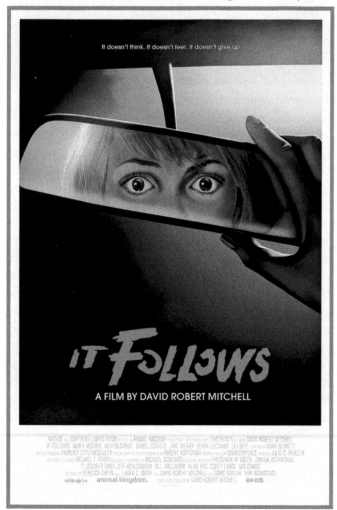

can look like anyone. But there's only one of it." Later, when Monroe tracks him down at his home, he tells her, "Just sleep with someone else." From that point onwards, she's doggedly pursued by the entity that takes on a variety of forms: A haggard old crone, a naked man, a diseased, urinating, hollow-eyed female ghoul and, in a scene designed to make your skin crawl, a seven-foot-seven ghostly pale youth (played by Mike Lanier, one of the world's tallest twins). Director David Robert Mitchell begs you to look behind the actors to see what's occurring in the background, even though it may be only momentary—in one sequence, shot in a school, Mitchell's camera performs a 360-degree scan, a figure seen plainly moving close and closer to Monroe who, with her sister Lili Sepe and pals Olivia Luccardi, Keir Gilchrist and promiscuous Daniel Zovatto, goes to stay at a beachside residence, only to be attacked by the thing in front of her friends. Monroe has sex with Zovatto in hospital, the targeted youth raped and killed by the haggard, obscene specter of his own mother. After trying to trap the unholy being in an abandoned swimming pool, Monroe finally allows besotted Gilchrist to seduce her, the pair holding hands and walking down a darkened sidewalk as the screen fades to black, the nightmare continuing—someone is following them in the distance, *not* the happy ending many might be expecting. Two interesting facts: There's not an adult in sight (where are all these kids' parents?) and Mitchell purposely juggles with the time frame to create an air of uncertainty and hopelessness: Old/modern automobiles, *Charade* (1964) playing at a 1960s-type cinema and a pink compact mirror device that doubles as an e-reader/light. An erie chiller containing obvious warnings about STDs and loose morals, *It Follows* deserves to be seen several times in order to winkle out all those visual nuances and subtle hints of "something lurking" that are artfully peppered throughout the compelling narrative; and the young cast turn in totally believable performances to match the overall feeling of impending doom.

Jurassic Galaxy aka Jurassic Planet

Dual Visions 2018; 77 minutes;
Director: James and Jon Kondelik ****

Luxury space liner *Galileo* splits in two and crashes on a barren planet populated with dinosaurs and a crazed survivor from a previous flight.

Garish photography from Joel Hodge; an imaginative Christopher Cano score; striking panoramic views of an alien skyline containing two moons and a planet; an engaging AI drone called PAL; and above-average CGI dinosaurs: *Jurassic Galaxy* is the '50s revisited in color; Boomers will quickly recognize shades of Universal's 1957 monster-fest *The Land Unknown* thrown into the scenario. Security tough guy Eric Paul Erickson leads a ragbag bunch of

UNDER TEN MILLION? ANYTHING'S POSSIBLE!

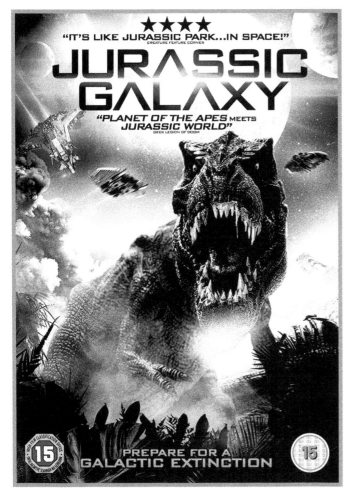

colored concept; all credit to the producers for this all-important point, one that indie fans will appreciate.

The Jurassic Games
High Octane Pictures 2018; 86 minutes;
Director: Ryan Bellgardt ★★★★

Once a year, America's 10 most dangerous criminals compete in a television virtual reality game, transporting them back to the dangers of the Jurassic Age, the winner granted his freedom.

With a worldwide audience of over 300,000,000, host Ryan Merriman and director Perrey Reeves have a major success on their hands ("The Greatest Game Show on Earth."), 10 criminals strapped to benches, VR headsets fitted to each, all 10 finding themselves battling dinosaurs and each other, knowing the sole survivor will be freed; the rest will be executed. Fans of *Jurassic Park* and *Jurassic World* may well scoff, but it's a cinematic fact that only a few short years ago, dinosaur CGI effects such as are on display here were considered the business; in this $10,000,000 prehistoric romp, they're perfectly serviceable and look okay: Several T-Rexes; a triceratops; the obligatory Velociraptors; a briefly glimpsed giant spider; two Brontosauri; Pterodactyls; a flesh-eating plant; man-eating bugs; a saber-toothed tiger (in the Jurassic era? I don't think so!); and

survivors across rocky, sun-bleached, volcano-erupting terrain to gain access to a shuttle in *Galileo*'s tail-end wreckage which will enable them to blast off from a planet stuck in the Jurassic era, PAL, a whizzing metallic globe, scouting out the route ("Did we time travel or something?" queries Jonathan Nation). Erickson argues with bearded "lifer" Nation (a dead ringer for a latter-day Oliver Reed), rookie flight commander Madison West sobs that she's landed them in this mess, the AI is disabled (a pity; it was rather cute) and Frankie Ray, a mentally unstable lost soul who has spent years on the planet, takes a shine to pregnant Tamara Stayer ("You stay here with me, my queen. We rule this world, my love."). Plenty of gory attacks by Velociraptors, Pterodactyls wheeling in the air and a Tyrannosaurus on the prowl mean there's no shortage of dino-action, Stayer the one who blasts off in the shuttle after Ray has been gobbled up by a T-Rex protecting its infant from a pack of 'raptors; Nation, badly injured, acts as sacrificial lamb to six flesh-eaters while Erickson (suffering from cancer, the planet's fierce radiation not helping) and West go out in a blaze of glory, encircled by dozens of rampaging dinosaurs. If you don't expect anything like the caliber of *Jurassic World*, the Kondelik Brothers' sci-fi dinosaur feature is an okay prehistoric jaunt that presents the viewer with another world that at least looks alien in its brightly

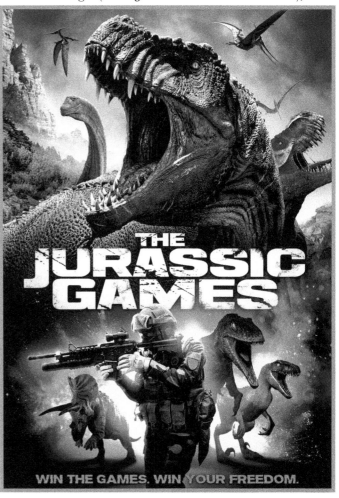

an eye-catching volcanic diorama shot in a red tint. A covert group calling themselves the Cavemen are attempting to infiltrate the studios to halt the show, which they view as barbaric, while Adam Hampton, falsely accused of slitting his wife's throat, and the other nine contestants have to negotiate four stages before reaching the safety zone. The frenetic pace sags when the squabbling criminals, reduced to eight mainly through in-fighting, worm themselves through a maze, pursued by a pack of 'raptors; matters then pick up, the grand finale taking place between Hampton, multiple killer of men Katie Burgess (she murdered Tucker's wife because she hates him) and three T-Rex's. In the main studio, the Cavemen burst in, shooting Reeves and effects man Lucan Ross; Merriman, wearing his silly monster mask, is strapped down and sent back to the not-so-safe safety zone where he's swallowed by a T-Rex. Then the cops take over, gunning down program editor Erika Daly and her Cavemen cohorts. Hampton is announced the winner, reunited with his adoring kids, and the "All-New Jurassic Games" features a Tyrannosaurus Rex built like a robotic war machine; that will sort out the criminals! Resembling a higher-class Asylum production, *The Jurassic Games* is great, goofy fun, gory one moment (get that scene when Luke "Cannibal" Wyckoff is reduced to a skeleton by thousands of big black beetles), tongue-in-cheek the next; just don't take it all so seriously!

The Keeping Hours
Blumhouse Productions 2017; 91 minutes;
Director: Karen Moncrieff ***

A divorced father returns to the old family home where the ghost of his five-year-old son conveys by subtle means that he wants to be reunited with his mother, in this life and the next.

Completed in 2016, copyrighted in 2017 and issued on DVD in 2018 by distributors Universal-International, *The Keeping Hours* is a rather twee ghost tale, more rom-com in execution than out-and-out haunted thrills, but not without a few heart-jumping elements. Lawyer Lee Pace is the man delighted to be in contact with his boy Sander Thomas (he died in a car crash, unbuckling his seat belt as the vehicle went into a skid), even though touching him produces an electric shock. Pace's ex-wife, Carrie Coon, skeptical at first, sees Thomas' spirit for herself and moves in with Pace; soon, the couple are forgetting their differences (each blames the other for their son's death), smooching and having sex at the expense of Coon's marriage to Cliff Chamberlain. Psychic medium Ana Ortiz warns the lawyer that "You can't keep him here. Let him go. This world is for the living" but to no effect, Pace and Coon playing with their beloved son, oblivious to the fact that he's an apparition. But Thomas has returned for a reason. Coon, on antidepressants, is diagnosed with terminal blood cancer and the boy wants to reunite with his mom in the afterlife which he does at the end, the pair disappearing in a brilliant white light, leaving a sorrowful Pace on the beach to mourn his losses. However, with attractive divorcée Amy Smart and her lively son (Julian LaTourelle) as neighbors, it won't be too long before good-looking Pace is playing happy families again. A supernatural offering for the ladies; men might find it just a tad *too* sugary for their tastes.

Kill Command
Vertigo Films 2016; 99 minutes;
Director: Steven Gomez ****

An elite team of marines sent to an island used for military training find themselves under threat from assorted robots which have developed a subversive intelligence.

Despite the foreign-looking location scenes at the beginning, UK production *Kill Command* (budget: £1,000,000)

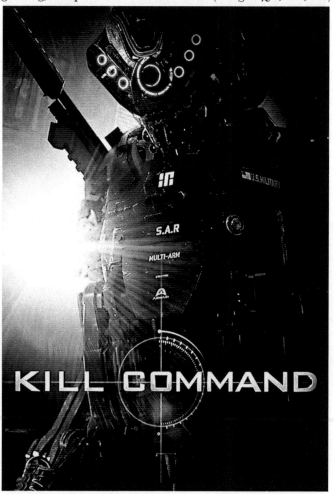

was filmed in the woodlands at Coldharbour near Dorking, in England's county of Surrey. And although shot on low finances, the effects and hardware on display are impressive, robotic S.A.R.'s (Study, Analyze, Reprogram) resembling big metallic spider crabs, the buzzing surveillance drones like mechanical flowers, opening up to scan the humans. Vanessa Kirby leads the seven-man squad; she's a cyborg, chipped when she was 11, her gleaming blue eyes able to read information others cannot see. She also designed the prototypes to these killing machines but is unable to figure out what has turned them against the marines when they begin to attack in force; and who, or what, is blocking the global communications network? Head grunt Thure Lindhardt doesn't trust her an inch but recognizes Kirby's unusual capabilities, especially when the big daddy of the droids, 15-foot-tall S.A.R.-003, turns vicious, dissembling its victims in pincer-like claws; Kirby, who can disable one of the things with her mind alone, is urgently required! A climactic showdown in the concrete facility near the drop zone (shot at the Hayes' disused vinyl factory near London) sees the metal monsters destroyed; Kirby finishes off the S.A.R.-003 unit using an EMP device, the robot transferring its data to the woman before collapsing. When the three survivors board the tiltrotor to take them off the island, the camera zooms up on Kirby, disclosing the S.A.R.-003's seven staring blue eyes embedded in her circuitry; she now contains the deadly, anti-human mission protocol, the robots being groomed by the Harbinger Corporation as soldier replacements of the not-to-distant future. *Terminator/Transformer* fans might well enjoy this modest man versus robots sci-fi thriller that, to its credit, remains serious throughout, not once resorting to a barrage of foul language and army stereotypes.

Lake Placid 2
UFO/Sci-Fi Pictures 2007; 88 minutes;
Director: David Flores ***
Lake Placid 3
Stage 6 Films/UFO 2010; 93 minutes;
Director: Griff Furst **
Lake Placid: The Final Chapter
UFO 2012; 90 minutes; Director: Don Michael Paul **
Lake Placid vs. Anaconda
SyFy/UFO 2015; 92 minutes;
Directors: A.B. Stone and Griff Furst ****
Lake Placid: Legacy
Out of Africa Ent. 2018; 93 minutes;
Director: Darrell Roodt *

Following in the claw prints of Fox's successful *Lake Placid* in 1999, budgeted at $35,000,000, came five sequels of varying quality, each produced for around $2,500,000 and farmed out to television. The first of the bunch featured Sheriff John Schneider, son Chad Collins, Fishery

and Wildlife Officer Sarah Lafleur, big game hunter Sam McMurray and assorted guys/babes fighting for their lives against three, then another four, giant crocs in a lake near Aroostook; the creatures have been nurtured by dotty old Cloris Leachman who treats them like her "babies." Shot in Bulgaria (as were the next three) and backed by Nathan Furst's burbling musical tonalities, the movie moves languidly through its paces, most of the cast eaten by the predators before Schneider finishes them off with a grenade launcher, leaving him and Lafleur time to smooch, Collins likewise with Alicia Ziegler. Eighty-one-year-old Leachman's acerbic "lady with attitude," plus the big CGI crocs and a fairly high gore count, makes the whole thing entertainingly watchable in an undemanding kinda way.

Game Warden/zoologist Colin Ferguson had his hands full in *Lake Placid 3*, what with son Jordan Grehs feeding meat stolen from the local supermarket to several hungry crocodiles, huntress Yancy Butler, jaw firmly set, out to bag herself a trophy, wife Kirsty Mitchell pulling her hair out in a perpetual state of panic and various brain-dead teens providing tasty morsels for the huge killer reptiles. Much trooping around woods on the edge of Black Lake culminates in the scaly predators attacking Ferguson's house, then the supermarket; he dispatches the chief monster croc with petrol fuel ignited by a handy lighter

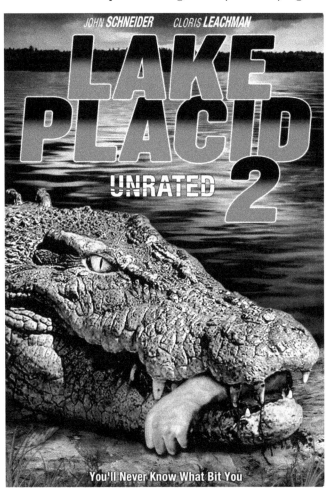

DON'T FORGET YOU'RE LUNCH!

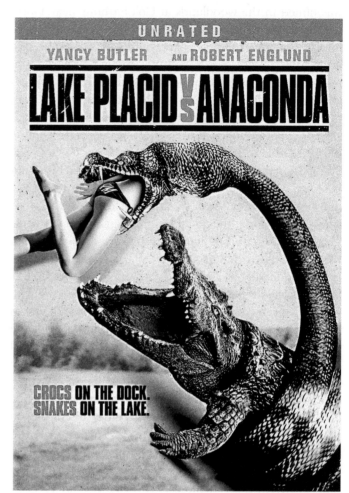

UNRATED

YANCY BUTLER AND ROBERT ENGLUND

LAKE PLACID vs ANACONDA

CROCS ON THE DOCK.
SNAKES ON THE LAKE.

and is last seen lecturing to a group of students on the lakeshore: "The marine river crocodile is extinct," he states authoritatively. Judging by those enormous jaws that rise up out of the waters behind him, it isn't! The grisly effects aren't bad but the film has a definite "seen it all before" air that will cause you to fidget in your seat. On the positive side, the half-naked gals look babelicious.

Feisty cougar Yancy Butler was back, bloodied but unbowed, in *Lake Placid: The Final Chapter*, along with leering poacher Robert *Freddie* Englund and David Reed's tongue-in-cheek script (Butler: "I know how to blow these bastards to high hell if things go all apeshit!"; Englund to an approaching croc: "Come to daddy, you fuckin' bitch!"); Martin Chichov's cinematography also sparkled. An electrified fence now encircles Black Lake, turned into a crocodile sanctuary, but that doesn't prevent a coach-load of partying, jet-skiing teens from gate-crashing the place where they become fair game for those ravenous predators. Several blood-spattered interludes are ruined by the inclusion of a schmaltzy love subplot featuring Sheriff Elisabeth Röhm making gooey eyes at Lieutenant Paul Nicholls, and her daughter Poppy Lee Friar simpering over Nicholl's Anthony Perkins-look-alike son, Benedict Smith. Don Michael Paul spends far too much time closing up on the foursome's drippy faces (especially Friar) at the expense of exciting "severed body parts" monster action; this is supposed to be a horror movie, not a romcom! The end result is a bit of a damp squib—and, as expected, adjacent Clear Lake is *not* "100% croc free," judging by the fate of a jogger in the woods

Time to beef things up a little: *Lake Placid vs. Anaconda* featured giant crocodiles and enormous snakes clashing in two resort lakes, the species genetically engineered to produce a croc/anaconda hybrid. It's all here: A beach chockablock with bikini-clad sorority chicks (or "bitches" as their leader screams incessantly); put-upon Yancy Butler (now promoted to town sheriff) and her bungling deputy (Oliver Walker); a square-jawed, wooden hero (Corin Nemec); a "profits before lives" mayor (Nigel Baber); Wexel Hall Pharmaceutical's devious backer, Annabel Wright; mercenary Steve Billington; and eye-patched, hook-handed, peg-legged Robert Englund (how he survived from the chomping he received in the previous film is anyone's guess). Mix them all together and you had a lively though clichéd exercise in cheapo monster frolics taking place around Clear Lake and Black Lake in Maine. Nemec played the fisheries and wildlife officer coming to the aid of beleaguered Butler as the huge crocs gobble up the gals, the snakes crushing cars and those stuck inside them, Baber ranting that "my ass is on the line" if the mess isn't cleared up before the tourists arrive. "Go deep, beach bitches! Get in the water!" yells Laura Dale to her soon-to-be croc bait as they hesitate over wading into Clear Lake's monster-infected waters; in the meantime, Billington, Englund and Wright plus an army of grunts are on the hunt; the hybrids' secretions, when mixed with the rare Blood Orchid (see the previous entrants in the *Anaconda* franchise for an explanation!), produces a serum that can prolong human life. Following a crocs versus snakes battle (one snake is hurled into a helicopter), Billington, rifle focused on one of the big reptiles, is swallowed whole, detonating a grenade in its stomach; his severed head is spewed out of its guts. Wright

UNDER TEN MILLION? ANYTHING'S POSSIBLE!

is arrested, Englund somehow survives minus his eye-patch and the final shot is of a batch of eggs hatching, a baby "crocanaconda" emerging. The fifth *Lake Placid* outing is amusing, gory fun of the dumb variety, with passable blood-spattered creature CGI effects; the "babes on the beach" sequence is worth the price of the DVD alone!

If you thought it was all over, it wasn't; three years later came *Lake Placid: Legacy* in which a group of eco-warriors investigate an abandoned facility on an out-of-bounds lake (filmed in South Africa), only to be hunted by a 40-foot crocodile. Vivid cinematography by Trevor Calverly and taut direction from Darrell Roodt, yes—but where's the croc? Most of the drawn-out action is spent in the gloomy facility, Tim Rozon and company on the run from a shadowy reptilian form; only during the final five minutes do we fully get to see the beast which is pinned down by an excavator and blasted into "the world's biggest barbecue" by babes Sai Bennett and Katherine Barrell, the two survivors. And as the girls swim across the lake to safety, an enormous fanged head rears up behind them (cue for yet another sequel?). Glossily shot mayhem that fails to deliver in the "monster crocodile" stakes and becomes one very tedious exercise to sit through; for a *Lake Placid* movie (after all, they're meant to be fun romps, aren't they?), it takes itself far too seriously.

Landmine Goes Click aka Dead Mountain
Sarke Studio/Scatena & Rosner Films 2015; 105 minutes;
Director: Levan Bakhia ***

On a hike in Eastern Europe's Georgian hills, one of a trio of friends steps on a landmine and is taunted by a local pervert.

Only the landmine is a fake, although Sterling Knight doesn't know it; he's been lured onto the device by pal Dean Geyer who's incensed by the fact that Knight has been having a fling with his intended bride,

Spencer Locke; Knight can't move an inch, afraid that if he does, he'll blow himself to bits. As Geyer leaves Knight and Locke ("You're a whore!") to sort out the problem, along comes a second problem in the shape of uncouth beekeeper Giorgi Tsaava, who torments the couple by playing cruel games, ordering Locke to strip and fetch her panties to him like a dog before brutally raping her. Managing to grab Tsaava's shotgun, Knight lets off a round, the recoil sending him tumbling to the ground; the dummy mine doesn't explode, and Locke accidentally receives the bullet, killing her. End of Act one. Act two is the revenge, Knight, now a crazed psycho, inveigling himself into Tsaava's home where the tables are reversed; it's now *his* turn to play the same games that Tsaava carried out, running over his dog, shooting him in the kneecap, tying up his wife and engaging in Russian roulette with the man's terrified daughter in a prolonged one-take sequence, the gun's single shot killing the girl, probably against Knight's better judgment; he slumps to the floor in anguish and remorse, horrified at what he has done. An unpleasant, overlong revenge tale filmed in Georgia, embellished with a sadistic undercurrent that makes for unsettling, somewhat depressing viewing; a stiff shot of whiskey will be required after the camera closes in on Knight's crumpled, boyish features.

Lights Out
Atomic Monster/RatPac-Dune Ent. 2016; 81 minutes;
Director: David F. Sandberg ***

A malicious entity that was once the companion of a girl in a mental institution still follows her around years later, killing all those who dare to interfere in their warped relationship.

The skinny, croaking entity named Diana inhabits the dark, disappearing when the lights are on. Without doubt, she's an unnerving creation, killing Maria Bello's husband in the first few minutes, tormenting her son (Gabriel Bateman) and getting her blackened talons into Bello's daughter, Teresa Palmer, who decides to rid her mentally unstable mother of the thing's influence with the help of boyfriend Alexander DiPersia. Warner Brothers took up the option to distribute David F. Sandberg's debut feature (budget: $5,000,000) and the film made money on its sporadic release, coming across in some areas like a cut-price version of Andy Muschietti's *Mama* (Universal, 2013). It thrills and tantalizes for the first half of its short running time, but once the origins of the entity are made clear to the audience (Diana as a child suffered from a severe skin disorder, befriended young Bello in the Mulberry Hill Psychiatric Hospital and died as a result of experimental treatment), we go down the jump-scare route, Palmer and DiPersia attempting to defeat the murderous phantom in Bello's home where none of the lights work. In the final minutes, the LAPD arrives and Bello, realizing that she's the key to the thing's existence, blows her brains out, Diana vanishing in clouds of glowing cinders; Palmer, DiPersia and Batemen hug each other outside. A case of "what might have been" if the movie was a few minutes longer (it runs at 79 minutes plus end credits) and didn't pander to the thrill-a-minute punters during its final half.

The Lodgers
Irish Film Board/Epic Pics./Tailored Films 2017; 92 minutes; Director: Brian O'Malley ***

Approaching their 18th birthday, twin siblings remain isolated in a huge decaying mansion, a sinister presence preventing them from ever leaving the ancestral home.

Filming was undertaken at one of Ireland's most haunted buildings, Loftus Hall in County Wexford, Richard Kendrick's sumptuous cinematography imbuing the musty neglected rooms with the right degree of chilly foreboding. Taking place just after World War I in the 1920s, pretty Charlotte Vega and morose brother Bill Milner are the young couple living under a centuries-old family stain. The near-derelict house, bordering a lake, has its own set of rules which must be obeyed: Vega and Milner have to be in bed by midnight; no one else is allowed over the threshold; and if one attempts to escape, the other's life will be in jeopardy. Venturing into the village on a shopping trip, Vega meets ex-soldier Eugene Simon (part of his right leg is false) and trouble rears its ugly head. Simon awakens in Vega hidden sexual desires, Milner in a jealous sulk as he's fondled his sister and been rebuffed ("I'll die if you leave me."). Solicitor David Bradley visits the house

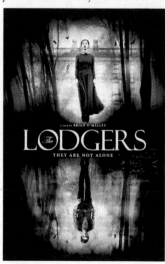

to inform Vega that the estate is heavily in debt and they should sell up ("*They* would never allow it," she says mysteriously), Vega sees her dead parents (they committed suicide) drifting over the lake's surface and at midnight, black water wells up out of a trapdoor set in the hall floor, the unseen entities angry that Vega spent too long outdoors, phantom figures hovering in the shadows. The payoff is that Vega

and Milner's parents, and their parents, and their parents before them, conceived through incest; Vega has to remain pure for Milner to impregnate her, thus carrying on the perverse family tradition. Bradley is stabbed to death by Milner after foolishly entering the mansion, his body dumped through the trapdoor opening, Simon perishes in the lake in an attempt to rescue the girl from the clutches of her long-dead, naked look-alike ancestors, Milner expires from falling on his own knife and Vega departs the cursed edifice, a crow (her mother collected birds in cages) flying after her as she walks down a leafy lane to the outside world and possible freedom. The movie looks gorgeous in a darkly saturated wash and the oppressive Gothic flavor is spot-on, but it could have been just that *little* bit creepier, the climax having an "I've witnessed this a dozen times before" cliched air about it; however, *The Lodgers* (15-rated in the UK) is a lot more atmospheric and meatier than the lukewarm 12A-rated *The Woman in Black* (2012) which some critics have compared it to (the definitive version of Susan Hill's classic ghost story remains the Channel 4 1989 telefilm, scripted by Nigel Kneale of *Quatermass* fame.)

The Monster
Atlas Independent/Unbroken Pictures 2016; 91 minutes; Director: Bryan Bertino ****

A young girl and her alcoholic, chain-smoking mother are left stranded on a rain-lashed road at night when one of their tires bursts, both at the mercy of a bloodthirsty creature inhabiting the woods.

Do monsters exist? Well, in abused Ella Ballentine's tortured world, they come in two forms—her alcoholic, uncaring mother and the multi-fanged creature lurking in the woods. So, a pair of monsters for the price of one, Zoe Kazan and the ferocious black nightmare (first glimpsed in the 33rd minute) that munches on breakdown driver Aaron Douglas before finishing off two members of an ambulance team that arrives and then focusing its deadly intentions on Kazan. Mum sacrifices her worthless life to save Ballentine who sets fire to the beast with lighter fuel and emerges into a clearing at dawn: "I'm not afraid anymore," she says, relieved, both demons in her life vanquished. Filmed over one dark night (and the visuals are *very* dark indeed), writer/director Bryan Bertino's joint US/Canadian effort is interspersed with short flashbacks highlighting Ballentine and Kazan's toxic relationship, no doubt to enhance their blossoming bonding sessions while trying to combat whatever it is that's stalking them. The bulk of storyline can therefore be interpreted as a psychological study in a poisoned mother/daughter union, both as flawed as one another, rather than a straightforward monster movie and in this respect, many fans will feel let down, the snarling, bestial protagonist only really coming into its own during the final 10 minutes. Unfortunately, the dialogue during these climactic moments suffers, Kazan switching from scream queen to a sobbing wreck full of remorse for what's she's put her daughter through ("I hope you grow up to be a better person than I was."); you have to tweak the volume control to understand their whispered verbal exchanges. But Bertino expertly maintains the suspense at fever pitch and both women act their socks off in an emotionally storm-wracked, tightly edited exercise depicting two females each coming face-to-face with two different kinds of monsters in their troubled lives.

Monsters
Vertigo Films 2010; 93 minutes;
Director: Gareth Edwards ***

Six years after a NASA space probe crashed in Central America, bringing with it alien life forms, a photographer is ordered to escort his boss' daughter through the Mexican infected zone to the safety of the American border.

Filmed on a micro budget of $500,000, Edwards' enterprising alien creature-feature, coming across like an upmarket Asylum production, is to some extent a genre misnomer, disappointing many older purists because of its blatant lack of monster excitement; a green-tinted night vision scene of a towering squid-like alien fired on by the military at the start, an attack on a convoy of trucks in the middle and two of the creatures engaged in a courtship ritual at the end, and that's  it as far as any monster action goes. *Monsters* runs along the lines of a road movie with *Cloverfield* leanings, a burgeoning love affair between photographer Scoot McNairy and vulnerable Whitney Able played out against a backdrop of alien chaos, a chaos imaginatively conjured up by the director—a wasteland of ruined buildings, wrecked aircraft and shipping, a massive electrified fence, quarantine centers and a colossal wall separating the American border with the infected area. Edwards soaks this disturbing scenario with a genuine sense of paranoia, and the two leads turn in commendable performances; however, it has to be said that the proceedings are let down by an abrupt ending and too much constraint on the "what's out there" front. Given a limited, unsuccessful UK release, *Monsters* works well as human drama facing unknown odds, but as an alien monster movie, it simply doesn't cut the mustard. The follow-up, *Monsters: Dark Continent* (2014), was set in the Middle East, a war movie masquerading as a monster movie, an unsuccessful, foul-mouthed mix that didn't go down well with critics and fans; it bombed on its original theatrical release.

Nails
Fantastic Films/Irish Film Board/House of Nether Horror 2017; 84 minutes; Director: Dennis Bartok ***

Hospitalized following a hit-and-run accident, a seriously injured woman is terrorized by the evil phantom of a former worker who hanged himself after killing five young patients.

Shauna Macdonald, rigged up to a life support machine in the Hopewell Rehabilitation Hospital and able to converse only through her laptop, is the unfortunate damsel in distress, at the mercy of Nails (Richard Foster-King), an abused, neglected soul who was a patient in 1972 and, after recovery, given an attendant's job. In 1984, the maniac murdered five girls, took clippings from their nails and committed suicide in a supplies cupboard, the doors of which face Macdonald's bed. Husband Steve Wall reckons his wife is paranoid, refusing to believe her when she tells him of the nightly visitations from the lanky, white-eyed creep who doesn't appear on CCTV footage (do they ever!); daughter Leah McNamara half-believes her, orderly Ross Noble thinks he has seen the entity hovering over Macdonald's bed while both haughty hospital director Charlotte Bradley and sinister Doctor Robert O'Mahoney know all about Nails' wicked exploits but prefer to keep the unsavory episode under wraps. There's a modicum of suspenseful shocks/jolts during the first 45 minutes, Nails determined to get his bony claws into Macdonald because, being a child patient there herself 30 years ago (she had meningitis), she escaped his taloned clutches ("I miss you," is scratched on her stomach), but the final half plummets into the standard "who will escape the loony" routine, lights flickering, doors slamming shut, Noble, Bradley and O'Mahoney all put to death by the rampaging ghoul; Wall is slain by his daughter's new athletic coach Muireann D'Arcy who's possessed by the demon. To prevent McNamara from becoming a victim, Macdonald sacrifices herself, facing Nails who batters her to oblivion. The final scene is of Foster-King in human form, cutting Macdonald's nails as she lies in bed, captured on CCTV footage. Macdonald is excellent in her traumatized female role, one that, since *The Descent*, she has specialized in, her bloodied, stitched face reminiscent of something out of a '60s continental horror movie, while British comedian Noble turns in the film's second-best performance. Old Nails himself will give the kids nightmares but for seasoned buffs, the picture's scenario, although produced in a glossy sheen, is slightly predictable and stale; this has been done so many times before and offers nothing fresh to get one's teeth into.

Nothing Left to Fear
Slasher Films 2013; 100 minutes;
Director: Anthony Leonardi III *****

A new pastor and his family arrive in Stull, Kansas from the big city, unaware that the town is a gateway to hell and their youngest daughter is to be sacrificed to a nameless satanic entity that emerges once a year from the pit on Festival Day.

James Tupper, Anne Heche, Rebekah Brandes, Jennifer Stone and young Carter Cabassa are welcomed into the community by outgoing pastor Clancy Brown who sports mysterious scars over both arms. And why do all the residents bear a scar on their right wrist? Brandes smells a rat, even though reserved hunk Ethan Peck takes an instant shine to her; she's spotted him slitting a sheep's throat, the blood dripping into a bucket, feels her family is being watched and reckons the citizens are acting weird, almost shunning her in the street. Also, what was the significance of that carved tooth found in a cake that had been left on their kitchen table? Hick communities nursing dark secrets are no strangers to the horror genre and here, Anthony Leonardi III has fashioned a tension-filled shocker that doesn't warrant all those negative online reviews. Yes, the buildup is slow but there's nothing wrong with that, the audience on tenterhooks, left wondering what the hell (being the operative word) is going on, especially when devious Brown tells Peck that there are to be "no mistakes. The choice has been made." On Festival Day, Stone is drugged, taken to an arcane hall and tied to a pillar; in front of watchers, Brown draws blood from his arm (hence those scars), the droplets drip into an oily pool and out of that pool emerges an entity of black tendrils, possessing Stone's body and changing her into a ragged, black-eyed

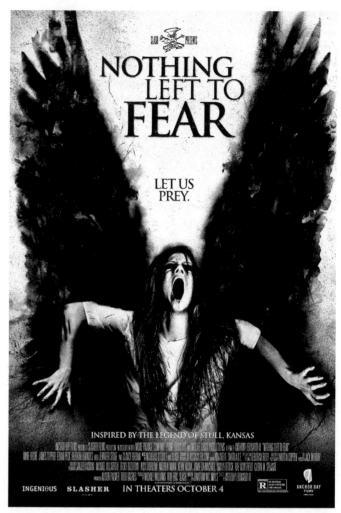

ghoul that prowls the empty streets, sucking the life out of its victims—and that includes Heche, Cabassa and Tupper. To close the portal to the hellish pit, Peck frogmarches Brandes into the hall and slices her wrist open, her blood forcing the thing, now resembling a monstrosity that's crawled from the pages of an H.P. Lovecraft story, back to where it came from. The final frame shows Brandes cutting a sheep's throat, a scar on *her* wrist, as another new family arrives on the scene, more lambs to the slaughter. A literate script, good acting, forceful direction and the terrifying sight of Stone the monster, grunting and lurching down darkened streets with black creeping tendrils spreading from her tread (great make-up and effects), everyone's houses marked with a red cross to ward off evil, make for a satisfying excursion into small-town devilry that packs a hefty punch and, for a change, doesn't have the obligatory happy ending; low-budget horror at its best.

The Ones Below
BBC Films/Tigerlily Films 2015; 87 minutes;
Director: David Farr ****

A couple expecting the birth of their first child experience disturbing behavior from their new ground floor neighbors who are also awaiting the birth of *their* first baby.

Shades of *Rosemary's Baby* as Clémence Poésy and Stephen Campbell Moore become increasingly perturbed by David Morrissey and heavily pregnant Laura Birn's queer manners. Birn is too friendly, verging on the unhealthy, by far, while Morrissey remains aloof and non-talkative. David Farr leads us down a semi-supernatural route to begin with: The lower flat belonged to a dead man (a real red herring, this), Morrissey and Birn both appear scared of Moore's pet cat (are they witches?), Poésy, who has a history of mental instability, visits the grave of her baby brother (and her mother won't go near her) and there are repeated shots of Morrissey's garden, as orderly as the couple is in stacking their shoes in a neat line outside their door. Matters turn nasty when Birn, tripping over the cat, falls down the stairs and loses her baby. Moore and Poésy are maliciously blamed and when Poésy gives birth to Billy, she's convinced that the almost demonic Morrissey and Birn are trying to steal her infant, by fair means or foul. Farr ratchets up the tension, Poésy failing to prove to stubborn Moore that the pair is up to no good, especially when, horrified, she spots Birn breastfeeding Billy in the garden. And they're *not* up to any good: Poésy is drugged through drinking spiked milk, found sprawled on the floor by Birn who suffocates her in the bath, and the baby is presumed

drowned in a pond. In fact, it was the cat wrapped in a bundle we saw Birn (dressed in Poésy's clothes) throw into the water; her and Morrissey are last seen in Germany, playing happy families with Billy, renamed Peter in honor of Birn's dead infant. Produced on a tiny budget and filmed in London, Farr's psychological essay is a minor nerve-shredder of considerable merit; it didn't make a dime on its limited release, but this isn't mass audience material, it's more suited to the discerning psycho-horror buff who will find much to appreciate in its spare framework.

The Other Side of the Door
42/Fire Axe Pictures 2016; 96 minutes;
Director: Johannes Roberts ***

Desperate to contact her young son who died in a car accident, a woman enters an ancient Hindu temple to undergo a sacred ritual, hoping to communicate with him on the other side of the temple door.

Sarah Wayne Callies unwisely ignores the advice of her housekeeper (Suchitra Pillai): "Scatter the ashes on the steps. Go inside, wait for nightfall and then you can speak to your boy. But DON'T open the door." She does just that, unleashing not only the angry spirit of her son (Logan Creran) but chanting shamans covered in gray ash and the Myrtu, a crawling, gurgling abomination that is the Gatekeeper to the Underworld. Shot in Mumbai, India (the UK/US/India production was distributed by 20th Century Fox), the movie starts well, intriguing and tension-filled, especially the atmospheric temple sequence; and the chilling incidents that occur in Callies' home are unsettling to the nerves: Vegetation withering and dying, something ghostly in Creran's bedroom moving a book and chair, daughter Sofia Rosinsky talking to her dead brother, piano keys played by invisible fingers and a hostile entity, husband Jeremy Sisto oblivious to it all. But the picture's second half undergoes a downturn, dropping away into formulaic ghost/horror territory, suffering badly from too much dim-to-dark photography; in several scenes, you simply cannot see what's taking place. Pillai, after advising Callies to burn all of Creran's toys and photographs ("You don't know what you have done. His soul will putrefy. She has come to claim him. Destroy all his belongings and he may return."), is drowned in a pond, Rosinsky becomes possessed by Creran's decomposing wraith, Callies stabs Sisto during an argument and is herself possessed by Creran, pleading with a shaman to "take me instead." She's knifed through the heart, dying, the ghoulish Myrtu taking her to the afterlife. Callies then finds herself on the temple steps amid her own ashes, Sisto calling for her from within the building; despite her screams for him not to, he opens the door, and the nightmare starts again …

Prospect
Depth of Field/Gunpowder and Sky 2018; 97 minutes;
Directors: Christopher Caldwell and Zeek Earl ****

On a distant mineral-rich moon named Bakhroma Green, a young girl has to fend for herself in an inhospitable environment when her father dies during a skirmish with rival gem hunters.

Although commencing with an eye-catching shot of a vast freighter orbiting a green moon, don't expect space battles or alien monsters in *Prospect*. Writers/directors Christopher Caldwell and Zeek Earl plump for the human, intimate touch and other-world atmospherics, the dense forest that Sophie Thatcher and Jay Duplass negotiate humid and toxic, poisonous dust motes drifting in the breeze, necessitating the use of face helmets (filming was undertaken in Washington State's unique Hoh Rainforest). Valuable gemstones are located in plant bladders which

have to be harvested, but dangerous rivals are on the hunt for the stones as well, all and sundry seeking the legendary Queen's Layer, worth billions. In a tense encounter with two mercenaries, Duplass and one of the men are killed, forcing Thatcher to form an uneasy alliance with Pedro Pascal, both having to deal with the moon's hostile inhabitants, the dregs left over from a former booming mining community, and their own disabled spacecraft. How to reach the freighter from Central is the burning question and, en route through this forbidding land, Thatcher has to amputate Pascal's right arm due to an infected wound inflicted by herself. Striking panoramic views of the mother planet looming over the hazy landscape plus the constant exertion of breathing through filters adds to the air of alien unfamiliarity; the hardware is battered-looking, rusty, dirty and authentic. The film ends with Thatcher and Pascal blasting off for the giant Central freighter after stealing a vessel from a bunch of ruthless mercenaries, Thatcher beaming and relaxing—she has triumphed over so many adversaries and is on her way home at last. Budgeted at $3,900,000, *Prospect* is minimalistic in approach, simple in design, non-hi-tech and highly imaginative, proving that you can produce a fairly memorable little space opera without the need for fights and explosions every few minutes; the futuristic score is also a bonus.

Pyewacket
JoBro Productions 2017; 90 minutes;
Director: Adam MacDonald *****

Tired of her mother's temperamental behavior, a teenager conjures up an evil entity to kill her but finds it is too late to reverse the spell when Mum becomes much nicer.

It's a case of not what you see but what you *don't* see in Adam MacDonald's artful psychological shocker, performed with minimal music and effects but still managing to raise the goosebumps, a mood piece that hits all the right notes. Nicole Muñoz is the angst-ridden teen, dragged off to live in the woods by Laurie Holden, a grief-stricken widow who can't control her temper and depression. Sick of being separated from her college friends, Muñoz consults a book on the occult and sneaks into the woods one night, performing an unholy ritual to get rid of Mom. But Mom unexpectedly changes into a better person to live with, leaving her daughter faced with a dilemma; how to attempt a reversal of the ancient spell to put things right. Too late. Banging noises are heard around the house at night, a shadowy figure creeps through the rooms after dark and pal Chloe Rose, on a sleepover, is terrified out of her wits after waking and staring into the face of something not human, choosing to spend the night in Holden's car. The horrifying climax has Muñoz dousing Holden in gasoline and burning her to cinders in the belief that her

Buckley, Christa Nicola and Amir K have followed the trail left by NASA rover Shorty, leading them into a labyrinth of square-cut galleries, deep shafts, eerie rooms and booby traps left by the ancients, plus cat-like creatures that tear humans to pieces. Hinshaw, suffering from an infection, nearly makes it out alive after the others have perished (Amir K by a falling slab; Nicola on a bed of spikes; Buckley and O'Hare by Anubis) but is grabbed in the dying seconds by that jackal-headed terror and dragged to her doom. English actor Buckley (of British TV's *The Inbetweeners* fame) shines as the grumbling camera operator and the gloomy settings possess a creepy aura redolent of old musty tombs. Yes, fans, it's the '50s revisited of a kind, complete with a '50s-type monster; surely that can't be a bad thing, can it?

mother is the baleful entity; she isn't, and the girl, paying the price for meddling in matters best left alone, is held on a murder charge. The message is clear—do *not* dabble in the supernatural, it will only bring heartache and grief, as this superior little slow-burner ably proves.

The Pyramid
Aja/Levasseur/Sahara Prods. 2014; 89 minutes;
Director: Grégory Levasseur ****

Five archaeologists venture inside a 5,000-year-old three-sided pyramid that lies buried beneath the sands, unaware that the edifice was designed to keep something evil from getting out.

20th Century Fox took up the distribution rights to Grégory Levasseur's $6,000,000 found footage movie, hoping for a financial killing; it backfired on them, a limited release schedule leading to scathing reviews and poor box-office receipts. A B movie by any other name, *The Pyramid* is not as atrocious as online reviews suggest, containing a terrific monster in the form of the jackal-headed Anubis who prowls this dark, dusty domain, weighing its victims' hearts to determine the fate of a dead person's soul. Until the thing makes its savage entrance, squawky-voiced Ashley Hinshsaw, her father, Denis O'Hare, cameraman James

Radius
EMA Films/Peripatetic Pics. 2017; 93 minutes;
Directors: Caroline Labrèche and Steeve Léonard ****

A man staggers from the wreckage of his car after a crash to find that anyone that gets within a certain distance of him, both human and animal, drops down dead.

An intriguing Canadian indie flick from writing/directing team Caroline Labrèche and Steeve Léonard that contains elements of horror, the supernatural and even

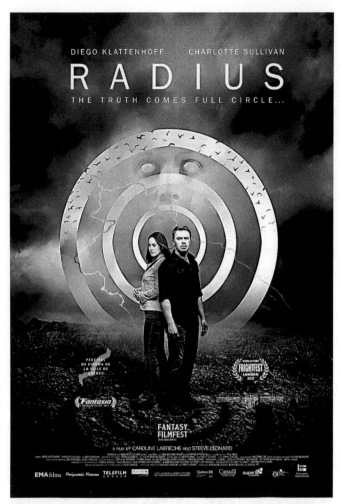

sci-fi in its tantalizing mix. When Diego Klattenhoff walks away from a car crash near the town of Woodmore, panic sets in as people begin dying in his immediate vicinity; a woman in a car he flags down and customers/staff in a diner. Even birds drop out of the skies. Suffering from loss of memory, Klattenhoff experiences sudden flashbacks: He's in a boat on a lake, meets a girl on the Smithburg-Oakdale Bridge and the same girl is with him in his car on the night of the crash. Breaking into a house, that mysterious female (Charlotte Sullivan) turns up, as confused as he is, amnesic and plagued with similar flashbacks, thinking that she's met him before; in addition, she's immune to his lethal power and, by staying at his side, can prevent people from expiring. The radio transmits news of Klattenhoff's "murder spree," and on visiting the site of the accident, they're confronted by a vast blackened, charred circular area. As if this isn't enough to get your head in a spin, Sullivan's husband (Brett Donahue) enters the fray, worried on two counts: What is his wife doing with this wanted stranger, and what happened to her in her quest to locate her twin sister, missing for a year? "I cause people to die," states Klattenhoff, Donahue forced into believing it when the cops arrive in force, the entire bunch wiped out after Klattenhoff and Sullivan become separated. With news bulletins broadcast from NASA of a "cosmic event" in the county, the couple drives north to Klattenhoff's retreat in the woods, their memories slowly returning. At the shack, Klattenhoff goes for a row on a nearby lake, leaving Sullivan to light a fire. She unearths a diary in the grate, discovering to her horror that her companion is a serial killer; the pages are packed full of graphic details relating to the brutal slayings of several women, including her sister, their bodies dumped in the lake—and she was next on the list. A climactic flashback shows that Klattenhoff targeted Sullivan when he picked her up on the bridge. Out on the road, he attacked her with a metal spike, causing the vehicle to swerve and crash. The two clambered from the upturned car, stood facing one another and were hit by a gigantic ball of lightning, a cosmic anomaly that changed the physical characteristics of both. Sullivan confronts Klattenhoff over the killings as three men arrive at the cabin, bent on mischief. They're felled by Klattenhoff, but not before one puts a bullet in Sullivan's stomach. Driving her to hospital, Klattenhoff deposits her with the medics and shoots himself in the head before he can do any further damage. A fast-paced and highly involving mystery filmed near Manitoba that will appeal to fans of the unusual; the two leads play well off each other, while Simon Villeneuve's photography bathes the cold landscape in a somber wash to match the fatalistic tone.

Redwood

Stern Pictures 2017; 80 minutes;
Director: Tom Paton ****

A couple sets out to hike through the isolated Redwood National Park and encounters a sect of vampires.

Musician Mike Beckingham and twitchy girlfriend Tatjana Nardone are the bickering pair ignoring Ranger Muzz Khan's warning to "Stay out of the gray zone, it's dangerous" and "Special kind of Ranger" Nicholas Brendan's hints of "creepy local tales" relating to the woods; they take a shortcut off the designated path to reach a waterfall and mountain top, trespassing on land populated by bloodsuckers. Good use is made of the dense, ominous woodlands and the shrieking noises heard during the night as the couple cower in their tent are unsettling; shadowy figures flit around outside, adding to the tension and making you forget, for a while, hyperactive Nardone's constant eye-rolling and mugging to the camera. The twist in this tale is that Beckingham is suffering from leukemia; he's heard that by sacrificing Nardone in front of an arcane statue standing inside an ancient mausoleum, he will cure himself ("You're going to save me, Beth."). Following a few near-death confrontations with the zombie-like vampires, he commits the life-saving deed by cutting Nardone's jugular beside the statue, her blood spattering over the ground. Immediately feeling much better (a hand wound miraculously disappears) and driving off from the cursed wood-

lands, he hesitates about going back, then continues on his way, leaving his girlfriend to become one of the scuttling undead—and a final shot of the unfortunate Nardone, pointed fangs and black eyes glaring at the audience, confirms it. A neat little vampire outing that could have been a few minutes longer to pack in more in the way of shocks; however, it possesses a suitable disturbing aura, particularly in the night scenes, the whole package expertly pieced together by director Tom Paton.

The Remaining
Affirm Films/Cinematic/Triumph Films 2014; 88 minutes;
Director: Casey La Scala ***

During a couple's wedding ceremony, the Earth is hit by an apocalyptic event as foretold in the Bible.

Affirm Films was set up by an evangelical Christian organization in 2007 to promote Christianity within their product. Therefore, *The Remaining* is part horror/part religious statement, an uneasy mix containing references to God, faith and personal belief that are littered throughout Casey La Scala and Chris Dowling's turgid script. Unfortunately, the opening camcorder credits sequence, presenting (yet again) a bunch of youngsters whose infantile behavior might prevent older viewers from proceeding further, means that you have little or no empathy with those surviving the thunderbolts, a plane crash, tremors,

exploding buildings, hailstorms, citizens dropping dead like flies (instant death syndrome), the sound of celestial trumpets and half-seen entities (the Fallen) that pluck their victims off the streets: Johnny Pacar, Alexa PenaVega, Shaun Sipos, Bryan Dechart and Italia Ricci are the five almost convinced that what they're experiencing could be the Biblical End of the World as told in the Rapture—an end of time event; pert blonde Liz E. Morgan later joins the group. In church, John Pyper-Ferguson explains that all over the world, people are being "Raptured" by God if they're believers, their souls transported to Christ in Heaven; if they're unbelievers, they appear to be cursed ("This is our wakeup call. I can now show you the way."). PenaVega expires from a ghastly infection caused by a demon's claws, summing up the film's drummed-home tenor: "I forgive you for everything (Dechart, her new husband, was having a fling just prior to their marriage). I never really believed. It's so bright. It's beautiful." In desperation, Dechart runs outside, a giant feeler piercing his body which is whisked upwards. Ricci, skin ripped open and dying, has left a message on tape, stating "I feel real faith. These demons are here to remove the word of God. We must believe or live selfishly and ignore God. I choose God." At a makeshift military camp, Sipos is hastily baptized but plucked into oblivion as countless thousands of winged creatures descend from the dark skies, attacking everyone, Pacar and Morgan watching in terror, the evil versus the good. *The*

Remaining's religious themes seem at odds with the horror/monster elements, the constant ramming home of "what will happen if we decide *not* to believe" coming across as a tad sanctimonious at times; the best part of the feature is the series of cataclysmic disasters depicted in the first part, a superb montage of destruction very well executed by the filmmakers.

The Ritual
Imaginarium Productions 2017; 94 minutes;
Director: David Bruckner ****

Four English friends trek through dense woodlands on the Norwegian/Swedish border, stalked by a giant mythical beast that picks them off, one by one.

Rafe Spall, Arsher Ali, Robert James-Collier and Sam Troughton are the argumentative, foul-mouthed foursome who become lost in the endless dark Scandinavian forests (actually filmed in Romania) where ritualistic signs and gutted animals are all around them in the trees. They are forced to spend a stormy night in a derelict, *very* spooky,

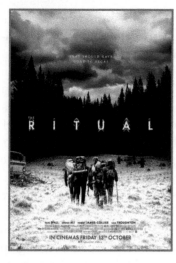

building, one upstairs room containing a headless wooden statue with antlers for hands. Director David Bruckner piles on the suspense and terror as Spall realizes that *something* out there is hunting them down; trails are leading nowhere, darkness is closing in and they've lost their bearings. Ali and James-Collier are horribly slaughtered by the unseen assailant, Spall and Troughton making it to a village straight out of the medieval age where the uncommunicative locals worship the Jötunn, a creature of Norse legend that grants them immortality in return for the occasional blood sacrifice. Troughton is tied to a stake and given up to the monster which then pursues Spall to the edge of the forest, demanding obedience; Spall, refusing to be cowed, wounds it with an axe and runs into a meadow, back to civilization, leaving the thing standing among the dense undergrowth, roaring in frustration and rage, unable to leave its domain. A creature-feature with a difference, *The Ritual*, like *Redwood*, utilizes its claustrophobic woodland setting to great effect and the monster is at least different to the norm; the film is also well-acted by the small cast and possesses bags of dread-filled atmosphere.

Road Train aka Road Kill
Screen Australia/Prodigy Movies 2010; 87 minutes;
Director: Dean Francis ***

In the vastness of the Australian outback, two men and two women encounter a juggernaut truck that doesn't run on petrol, only blood and human remains.

Aussie filmmakers have utilized the country's awe-inspiring outback wilderness in many a horror production, Greg McLean's two *Wolf Creek* movies being prime examples of Down Under bloodbaths expertly conceived for maximum, palm-moistening shocks. *Road Train* doesn't match up to the high voltage terror factor exhibited in those films, even though it begins well. Bob Morley, Sophie Lowe, Xavier Samuel and Georgina Haig are driving down the highway when a monster truck (the

Road Train of the title) which they have overtaken rams them off the road. Their vehicle a wreck, Morley nursing a busted arm, they spot the stationary truck with its two huge containers and cautiously approach it. It's empty—no driver, and no driver's mate. Dean Francis wracks up the suspense *Duel*-style, leaving you wondering what's in those containers and who that crazy guy is (the driver?) running towards them, firing a gun. Samuel takes to the wheel, they drive off, doze in the sun and wake with a start, to find that the lorry has veered down an unpaved side track into an abandoned mine, poised dangerously on the lip of a quarry. From this point, we're in blood and guts territory: The truck operates on human remains, not fuel, Morley its master, intent on shoving his three companions into the innards inside the first container (annoyingly, we are left to guess what's in the rear trailer). Too much psychobabble from Morley drags the pace, a simple case of who will get out alive. And what is the significance behind umpteen shots of Cerberus, the mythical three-headed canine, an emblem of which adorns the truck's bonnet. After the juggernaut hurtles down the road, smashing into a car towing a caravan, Lowe pumps four bullets into Morley who has fed Haig and Samuel to the machine and ends up the deranged sole survivor, running towards a couple who have unwisely commandeered the bloodthirsty vehicle, her warning cry ignored. *Road Train* is effective in parts, particularly the initial 20 minutes, but the "machine lives off humans" angle was done so much better in 2007's *Blood Car*.

The Sand aka Blood Sand
Scatena & Rosner Films/Allegra Pictures 2015; 84 minutes;
Director: Isaac Gabaeff ****

Following an all-night graduation party on a beach, eight teens wake up to discover something nasty and life-threatening lurking beneath the sands.

Put the remote on fast forward for the first six minutes of camera mugging, binging, boozing and infantile partying-on antics, then try to relax (it's a very noisy movie) as Brooke Butler, Mitchell Musso (in a lifeguard shack), Cynthia Murell, Dean Geyer, Meagan Holder, Hector David, Jr., (in a car) Nikki Leigh (asleep on the beach, topless) and Cleo Berry (stuck up to his waist in a blue trash bin) discover to their cost that hair-like tendrils rise up from the sand to snare and devour their prey. Could they be connected to that enormous gelatinous blob that was found on the beach during the party? Leigh is the first to be gobbled up, followed by David, turned into mincemeat before vanishing bloodily from sight ("This shit is crazy! We're all gonna fucking die!"). Geyer makes it to a bench by stepping over surfboards but is impregnated in the torso by the glistening threads, Murell gets her hand trapped in the car's trunk and big fat black guy Berry, a man's genitals drawn on his perspiring cheek, shouts in frustration, delivering some

UNDER TEN MILLION? ANYTHING'S POSSIBLE!

apparently was) heading towards a packed seaside resort for another feeding extravaganza. Decent acting, that hilarious script, a better-than-average score (Vincent Gillioz) and commendable CGI effects; yes, *The Sand* cuts it as a modern-day creature-feature, once you get past that initial brain-shredding six minutes.

The Shrine
Brookstreet Pictures 2010; 85 minutes;
Director: Jon Knautz *****

A photographer and two journalists travel to a village in Poland in search of a missing reporter and stumble across an ancient, evil force, held in check by a ritualistic cult.

Cindy Simpson, Meghan Heffern and Aaron Ashmore are told to stay away by the villagers, but that strange shifting fog hovering over the treetops is too enticing for the trio to ignore. In the woods, the two girls enter the mist, Simpson coming face-to-face with one of budget horror cinema's scariest stone statues, a 12-foot-high winged gargoyle holding a heart in its clawed hand that begins to drip blood. Emerging from the fog, the women and Ashmore enter a mysterious underground sacrificial chamber shown to them by a small girl, discovering bodies with mutilated

priceless snatches of dialogue courtesy of Alex Greenfield and Ben Powell: "Fuck you, I'm dying," he yells, and when dumber-than-dumb beach patrolman Jamie Kennedy arrives on the scene, he too gets some choice bits of speech: "You look like a fucking art exhibit," he says to the hapless Berry, seeing him wedged in the bin. "This is fucking worse than the lady with a horseshoe crab up her ass." Kennedy loses his right arm, then disappears screaming under the sand, Berry roars, "We are fucked, man!" Musso is the next to succumb to the thing, whatever it is, dragged under in pools of blood, Berry delivers the funniest line in the picture ("I don't wanna die with this dick on my face!"), Butler jumps into the car and gives Holder a hard slap for stealing boyfriend Geyer ("That's for screwing my boyfriend, bitch!"), Murell almost makes it to Kennedy's vehicle but unfortunately slips to her doom, Berry gets sucked to oblivion by a mass of writhing tentacles and at night, huge blue luminescent tentacles menace Butler and Holder in the patrol car, Butler setting light to the monster with two cans of gasoline ("Burn, you motherfucker!"). Come morning, Geyer has expired from his festering wounds, babes Butler and Holder limping off ("It's gone."), the area of infestation clear for all to see. But it ain't all over yet—the final shot is of that colossal jellyfish (for that is what it

faces in coffins. Breaking out of the locked door, they're pursued by hooded priests, captured and taken back to the shrine. Heffern is roughly seized, scrutinized and tied to a slab, a spiked mask placed over her face which is brutally hammered down into her eyes. In a state of shock, Ashmore and Simpson run for it, taking refuge in a farmhouse, pursued by the priest-like figures—and here the film cleverly springs a genuine surprise. Those murderous hooded guardians aren't the bad guys; Simpson is, morphing into an *Evil Dead/Exorcist*-type demon from hell in the grisly, frenetic climax, meeting the same fate as Heffern after the priests have managed to pin her down, the girl's penance for foolishly entering that infernal mist and encountering that unholy statue; the evil contained within the area mustn't be allowed to spread. Ashmore, dazed and confused, departs, asking, "What is up there, in the trees?" "This is curse," he is told. "Left here on our land long ago. It cannot be undone." And this enthralling little Canadian horror movie closes on that devilish gargoyle staring balefully at the viewer, sending out its ungodly message: "If you venture too close to me, you'll pay."

The Siren aka The Rusalka
Signature/Blackshear 2019; 80 minutes;
Director: Perry Blackshear ***

A mute brought up by the church goes to stay in a house by a large lake that has given rise to the Slavic legend of the Rusalka, a spurned female entity who drowns anyone getting too close to her.

Virtually a three-man job: Perry Blackshear produced/wrote/directed/edited and photographed, his repertory pals Evan Dumouchal and MacLeod Andrews chipping in along the line. A dark fairy tale presented in semi-professional, almost student, fashion, shot over 17 days in Vermont, Dumouchal plays the young man encountering water-bound Margaret Ying Drake, the girl never emerging fully from the lake. In a nearby property, Andrews spies on the pair through binoculars; he's on the vengeance trail because Drake, who met his husband, drowned him. The picture is moody, arty, ham-fisted in parts, strikingly effective in others: Drake takes a fancy to her new non-speaking admirer, suppressing her animalistic instincts (growling sounds; eyes turning black) and even imagining what life (specifically sex) would be like with him outside of the lake, opening up to the guy about her murderous addiction ("All the drownings. They were all me. I can't stop."). Granted, not a great deal happens, the pace deliberately slow: Dumouchal, whose throat was crushed in a swimming accident, allows Drake to ease him into the water to test his fear, Drake, consumed by desire, snuggles up close to him on the jetty, one foot left in the lake, and Andrews meets his watery demise after attempting to bludgeon her to death with a sledgehammer. Dumouchal, crestfallen because Drake hasn't returned (she's hidden in her lakeside "nest"), departs at the end, leaving the lass alone in her lake domain. An atmospheric score (traditional Eastern European folk songs sung by the Kitka Women's Ensemble) complements the somber, tragic ambience; yes, *The Siren* was obviously made on shoestring finances but Blackshear's fatalistic romance must be applauded for its offbeat approach instead of relying on blood and thunder to get the message across.

Spring
XYZ Films/Rustic Films 2014; 109 minutes;
Directors: Justin Benson and Aaron Moorhead *****

Escaping his train-wreck of a life, a bar worker travels to Italy where he meets a mysterious girl harboring an ancient, terrible secret.

A Romeo and Juliet love story with a difference: Lou Taylor Pucci encounters medical student Nadia Hilker at the resort of Polignana a Mare in Bari, unaware that she's a 2,000-year-old mutant, requiring pregnancy every 20 years to provide her body with the embryonic cells needed to sustain a human image and live forever. There's lot to take in here, and for those seeking something individual on their menu, *Spring* delivers the rewards. The first 18 minutes focuses on Pucci's foul, miserable existence, complete with excessive swearing to ram home the point; in finally discovering Hilker *as she is* in the movie's lengthy stomach-churning transformation scene (tentacles, claws, a slithering reptilian tail, fangs), he prefers to stick with her, even though it might lead to his ultimate death ("You dumped me and became a monster."). The directors subtly highlight Hilker's savage, primordial other-self: Paintings and frescos showing her to be alive centuries ago (her eyes are contrasting colors), plants withering at her touch, bugs and insects appearing in her wake, dead animals in the streets, parts of her body breaking out in suppurating sores, the girl shedding her old skin, eating raw flesh, snarling at Pucci when he goes to kiss her and zoom shots of the resort's enclosed, rather forbidding rocky bay, everything punctuated by Jimmy Lavalle's menacing score. The make-up of Hilker in her various transformation stages is also suitably repulsive; repeated injections return her to human form. In the end, love conquers all: After showing Pucci the ash-covered bodies of her parents and brother in the ruins of Pompeii, the couple rests on a wall, cuddling up; Pucci, hearing grotesque sounds, becomes aware that

UNDER TEN MILLION? ANYTHING'S POSSIBLE!

Ring and Vernon Wells) are dragged out and the Yowie is not really fully seen. The best part is the opener: In 1825, a Chinaman is panning for gold, finding a large nugget. Along comes a robber who relieves him of his prize; then Andy Bramble (Thunderclap) relieves him of *his* prize. Suddenly there's a scream, a growling and the Chinaman, followed by the first robber, are savaged to death by something large and hairy. Fast-forward 180 years: Shawn Brack and Ring are hunting for Bramble's treasure; it's located in a cave, Ring double-crossing his partner and trying to kill him in the river. Park Ranger Melanie Serafin comes to Brack's rescue and Wells makes a brief appearance playing a detective searching for clues as to why nine people have vanished without trace in the area. Wells is decapitated by the beast that terrorizes the other three before Brack, having drowned two-timing Ring, blows the Yowie to kingdom come with a stick of dynamite. Amusingly shot in "Yowiescope," the movie closes with the logo "For Ray Harryhausen" and contains obvious references to *Creature from the Black Lagoon* in its claustrophobic setting, plus other Bigfoot features (a bottle of Boggy Creek wine, anyone?). But it's very amateurish-looking a lot of the time and the monster, although sounding great, doesn't *look* great. The novel fact that it's an Aussie Bigfoot outing, plus the attractive scenery, makes it worth seeking out for fans of the Bigfoot legend.

Hilker is changing into something terrifying while in the background, a volcano starts to erupt. Scared at what he might see, he looks down to find that Hilker is normal. By falling in love, she has become mortal and thereby prone to a mortal's lifespan which, after 2,000 years, she welcomes at last. Pucci and German actress Hilker strike sparks of each other, Pucci's moments with farmer Francesco Carnelutti are a joy and the novel locations lend the production a haunting air of a timeless horror that has survived the ages; *Spring*, for discerning horror buffs, is superb, memorable fare.

Throwback

Sapphire Pictures/Monster Pictures 2014; 93 minutes;
Director: Travis Bain ***

In the North Eastern Australian outback, two adventurers seeking the lost treasure of 19th-century outlaw Thunderclap Newman encounter the Yowie, Australia's answer to Bigfoot.

Writer/director/photographer Travis Bain spent three years on-and-off filming his pet project in Cairns National Forest, Queensland, on limited funds. *Throwback*, for the most part, looks gorgeous, complemented by Richard Band and Amotz Plessner's rich score. However, there's a noticeable unevenness in continuity and color matching, some scenes (especially the interchange between Anthony

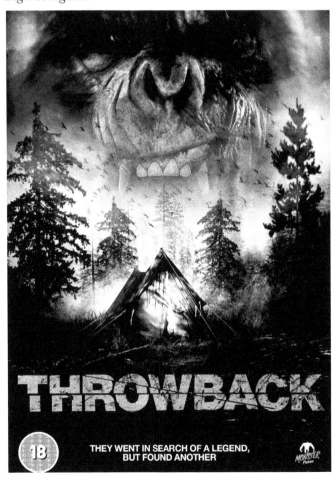

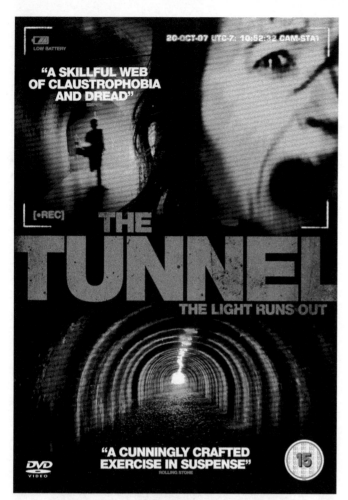

"A SKILLFUL WEB OF CLAUSTROPHOBIA AND DREAD"

[•REC]

THE TUNNEL

THE LIGHT RUNS OUT

"A CUNNINGLY CRAFTED EXERCISE IN SUSPENSE"
ROLLING STONE

15

and scattered utensils, there are no signs of any homeless persons said to occupy the passages. Soundman Luke Arnold hears weird grunting noises through his headphones and suddenly disappears from a room containing a huge bell, a snooping security guard is snatched from behind and an indistinct "something" with glowing eyes is spotted emerging from that black lake, breaking the neck of someone *minus* his eyes. Everything gets a bit frenetic in the final 15 minutes, Deliá giving in to hysteria, Davis determined to locate an exit route and Andy Rodoreda attacked by whatever's down there; and what is the significance behind that closet containing a mass of eyeballs? Rodoreda dies from internal injuries, Deliá resigns, Davis carries on in his position, the police close their case files and Arnold is never found (in an alternative ending, Arnold *is* found, winding up in a hospital ward suffering from loss of memory and scars around both eyes). Expertly put together in widescreen to heighten the visceral effect, *The Tunnel* gives little explanation as to what lies beneath; the aim is to convey claustrophobic terror felt in deep, confined spaces and in this respect, it scores highly. For lovers of horror movies set below ground (count the author among them), Ledesma's Aussie offering is one hell of a nightmarish, subterranean thrill-ride.

The Tunnel
Distracted Media/DISHS 2011; 90 minutes;
Director: Carlo Ledesma *****

A documentary team ventures into Sydney's abandoned subway train tunnels to find out why the government vetoed plans to recycle water flooding the galleries and encounters the frightening reason behind the scheme being dropped.

The Tunnel is partly based on fact: Around 2002, plans were discussed by the New South Wales government regarding various methods of utilizing reserves of water from St. James Station's network of broken-down railway tunnels in drought conditions but were later scrapped. Carlo Ledesma was granted permission to shoot his found footage documentary in those selfsame creepy, oppressively silent man-made galleries, manufacturing an exercise in paranoia and dread, a paralyzing fear of what was lurking down there in that labyrinth of gloomy vaulted chambers and interconnecting rooms that projects itself to the watcher. Filmed in green night vision mode and normal vision, journalist Bel Deliá and cameraman Steve Davis are interviewed throughout, so you know out of the four who fails to make it. The crew breaks open a locked gate, entering the forbidding abandoned tunnels with the aid of an inaccurate map, descending a shaft and locating the vast underground lake. Disturbingly, apart from a few clothes

Under the Shadow
Wigwam Films 2016; 84 minutes;
Director: Babak Anvari ****

During the Iraq-Iran war in the 1980s, a mother and daughter are haunted by a malignant Djinn that has arrived in their apartment block via a military missile.

In Tehran, leftist medical student Narges Rashidi, turned down for further studies at university because of her political beliefs, takes out her frustrations on daughter Avin Manshadi and husband Bobby Naderi. Manshadi begins suffering from nightmares, her beloved doll Kimia goes missing, Naderi, a doctor, is seconded to the war zone, sirens go off at regular intervals, a missile crashes through the building's roof and we then enter supernatural territory. Rashidi is told of the legend of the Djinns that "ride on the wind," Manshadi claims there's a presence in the apartment and develops a fever, and the occupants of the block gradually depart due to the ongoing fighting, leaving Rashidi and Manshadi alone to combat the evil entity that has latched onto them. A ceiling crack repairs itself and harrowing apparitions appear, the creepiest being a huge floating chãdor (open cloak) that attempts to suck them to oblivion; finally, they manage to escape, leaving Kimia's head on the apartment stairs, along with one of Rashidi's textbooks, implying that the Djinn, or whatever it may be, has items with which to hound them even further. A UK/Jordan/Qatar/Iran collaboration filmed in Amman, Jordan, *Under the Shadow* possesses a definite uniqueness due

UNDER TEN MILLION? ANYTHING'S POSSIBLE!

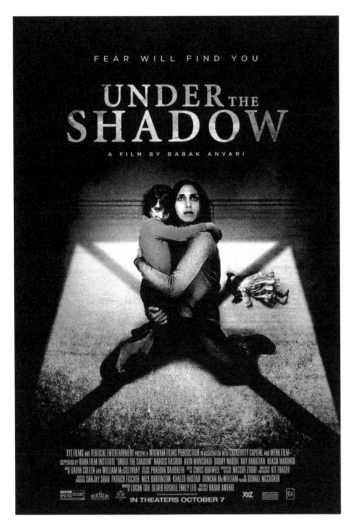

to its unusual (for a horror film) setting and Middle Eastern cultural nuances; it's also shot in relatively bright light, so you can experience all that is taking place instead of squinting into dark corners. What Western audiences are presented with is a familiar plotline but in *unfamiliar* circumstances and in this respect, writer/director Babak Anvari's debut feature works splendidly, real-life trauma combined with chilling scares to produce something a little bit left field in this over-populated genre. The ending may be slightly abrupt, but then, aren't most of them these days …

The Unfolding
Robin Films Limited 2016; 90 minutes;
Director: Eugene McGing ★★★

A couple of amateur paranormal investigators set up their equipment in a rambling 14th-century house on Dartmoor, the threat of a possible nuclear war transmitted over the airwaves.

Fans of camcorder footage movies (there are many!) will lap up Eugene McGing's debut feature, initially filmed on mist-shrouded Hound Tor, Dartmoor in Devon before moving to the next location, a large haunted house (shot in Maidenhead, Berkshire). Lisa Kerr and Lachlan Nieboer play the pair unraveling a centuries-old murder mystery

over an eight-day period with the help of friend Nick Julian, Professor Robert Daws and medium Kitty McGeever. Apparently, three spirits occupy the building: That of a girl abused by her uncle from the age of nine to 18, when she died in childbirth; the wicked uncle himself (he practiced black magic); and the cries of all the dead babies to which she gave birth. Filmed mainly in monochrome with a dash of color, the obligatory conveyor belt of whisperings, screams, moving furniture, temperature drops, bangs, crashes, utensils stuck in walls, billowing drapes, slamming doors, ghostly visions, frozen pipes and marred film footage is trotted out, broadcasts of an imminent nuclear catastrophe heard on the radio. Following three séances, McGeever frees the spirit of the girl by giving a Christian incantation but pays with her life when she tries to do the same for the murderous uncle: "I will never leave this place!" his presence roars. Julian gets shut in a room and as Nieboer, hysterical Kerr and Daws drive off after a prolonged bout of supernatural mayhem, the sound of a siren shatters the dawn stillness, a series of terrific explosions lighting up the sky, followed by a blinding white light; as forecast, H-bombs have been dropped. Perhaps a writer of Nigel *Quatermass* Kneale's experience and inventiveness could have made more of the combination of the supernatural and science fiction in the shape of a World War III; here, it counts for very little, a tenuous link at most, apart from hints that "It's safer in here than outside" and that the warnings of a nuclear disaster leads to an increase in paranormal activity, the spirit world just as afraid as we are. Nevertheless, McGing knocks up a few camcorder shocks to

keep buffs happy, the house (reputedly haunted and since demolished) looks eerie, Leslie Rothwell provides a creepy score and the cast give it their all. But, on higher funds, you get the impression that something more could have been made out of this particular (and unusual) melding of two classic genre tropes.

The Void
XYZ Films/JoBro Prods. 2016; 90 minutes;
Directors: Jeremy Gillespie and Steven Kostanski ★★★

At the Marsh County Memorial Hospital, the chief medical surgeon has opened a portal to another world and has the power to change humans into grotesque mutants.

H.P. Lovecraft meets *Hellraiser* and even *The Thing* in a darkly shot horror film smacking of the 1980s; not a CGI

effect in sight, only an array of tentacled, gooey monstrosities conjured up by mad doctor/cult leader Kenneth Welsh in his insane quest to conquer life after death; his experiments have resulted in a basement full of inhuman body parts and mutants. As white-cloaked Ku Klux Klan figures hover outside the hospital keeping guard, inside, battered cop Aaron Poole tries to cope with father and son Daniel Fathers and Mik Byskov wanting to kill whatever's causing people to change into deformed creatures, heavily pregnant Grace Munro about to give birth (to what?), estranged wife Kathleen Munroe suddenly pregnant, giving birth to a multi-tentacled being (put there by Welsh in honor of his dead daughter) and rookie nurse Ellen Wong screaming her head off, totally unable to handle the escalating situation. It's a frenetic concoction, the muddy plotline adding to the confusion, climaxing in a basement morgue where Welsh, transformed into a skinless, skeletal being, informs Poole that he can be reunited with his wife if he jumps through a triangular portal in the wall into the void, the gateway to another world. Grace Munro hatches another aberration with the face of a skull that devours Fathers before being set on fire by Poole who tumbles into the void with his wife. In a striking final scene, the two stand together hand-in-hand in an utterly alien landscape, staring up at a vast black pyramid that fills the sky; Byskov and Wong are the only two to make it out of the cursed hospital in one piece. If you like slimy monster flicks that don't make a great deal of sense, *The Void* will be right up your street; for others, the disjointed action, relentless swearing and dim photography might grate on the nerves after the first 40-odd minutes.

We Are Still Here
Snowfort Pictures/Dark Sky Films 2015; 84 minutes;
Director: Ted Geoghegan ***

Mourning the recent death of their son in a car crash, a couple sets up home in their rural New England residence, unaware of the house's terrible reputation.

Snowy, wintry backdrops add to the bleak atmosphere in a fairly effective but derivative thriller in which Andrew Sensenig and Barbara Crampton's new home demands a sacrifice every 30 years. Built in 1859, the Dagmar family ran the place as a funeral parlor but were caught selling bodies to local universities, burying empty boxes instead. They were allegedly run out of Aylesbury, old man Dagmar drinking himself to death; in reality, the townsfolk burned the family to death and the "darkness that lies under the house" will bring natural disasters to the district if its thirst for sacrifices is not appeased (newspaper cuttings shown during the closing credits tell of these catastrophes; wilting crops, sick livestock, polluted rivers). Cue for Crampton to hear her dead son banging around in the house, for an electrician to be badly scorched by a charred ghoul in the cellar, for town bigwig Monte Markham to make plans for ensuring Crampton and Sensenig don't make it out alive and for friends Jacob Lewis and Lisa Marie to arrive and contact the troubled spirits; Lewis ends up possessed, shoving a poker in his eye. The movie climaxes in a showdown, roasted ghouls versus townsfolk, the blackened spooks winning by a mile, Markham's head squashed to a bloody pulp by Dagmar's white-eyed phantom; it closes with Sensenig peering into the cellar and whispering "Hey, Bobby." Yes, his son's spirit *is* there, one reason for him and his wife electing to stay on in the house. Very gory in parts (hence the British "18" rating), *We Are Still Here* is standard post-2000 horror fodder, put across with style but with a slight air of "We've seen this kind of stuff before."

UNDER TEN MILLION? ANYTHING'S POSSIBLE!

down the highway without breaking into a cold sweat. *We Go On* is a tidy little ghost yarn that contains decent performances from all concerned, especially Annette O'Toole playing Freeman's skeptical, overprotective mother.

White Settlers aka The Blood Lands
Not a Number/Warwick Films 2014; 80 minutes;
Director: Simeon Halligan ***

A couple escapes the hustle and bustle of living in London by purchasing an isolated Scottish farmhouse, the local residents taking brutal steps to ensure their stay is shorter than they envisaged.

"The Thriller That Fueled The Scottish Independence Debate" states the DVD blurb; well, the Scots and English have never really seen eye-to-eye, old enmities dating back to the time of William Wallace versus King Edward I in the 13th century. Perhaps Lee Williams and Pollyanna McIntosh should have disregarded that "Scotland Welcomes You" road sign as they set up home in Castle Farm, built on the site of a "ferocious battle between Scots and English," the estate agent has previously informed them, adding, "Scotland's a very friendly country." Well, maybe to the locals it is, but not to this couple. McIntosh sees a young boy standing in the doorway and, during a long night, their first in the house, she and her husband come under attack from a group of violent men wearing pig masks and wielding axes who invade the property

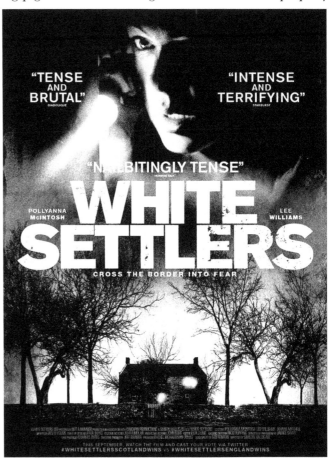

We Go On
Filmed Imagination/Untethered Films 2016; 90 minutes;
Directors: Jesse Holland and Andy Mitton ****

Following a near-fatal car crash, a man suffering from all kinds of phobias offers $30,000 to anyone who can provide proof that there is life after death.

Video editor Clark Freeman plays the troubled soul who encounters down-and-out airport runway worker Jay Dunn after rejecting three unsuitable candidates; Dunn shows him his own raddled corpse in a deserted, rubbish-strewn building as positive proof of the hereafter and from then on, Freeman can't shake off Dunn's ever-present zombie-like phantom ("I'm haunted. It's my ghost now. He's scared to be alone."). Freeman begins seeing and hearing dead people all around him and eventually meets Dunn's twitchy girlfriend (Laura Heisler) who admits that she detested Dunn so much that she purposelessly overdosed the rat on drugs to be rid of him ("He wore me down. I had a boy from another man."); reluctantly, she shoots Freeman so that he can join his unwelcome pal in the afterlife and leave her alone. But Freeman, after going into cardiac arrest from the wound, survives ("I died and came back alone."), finally free of Dunn's unwelcome ghoulish presence and now able to drive a car at speed

("We'll make the bastards pay," one shouts). Williams is badly beaten, abducted and tied up in a workshop; McIntosh escapes and frees him, the two going on the run in the woods and getting their own back by flooring two of their assailants but ultimately defeated: Williams is trapped in an animal snare and the boy leads McIntosh, limping from a cut ankle, to a bridge, but not to safety; a land rover pulls up and she's gagged, a hood roughly shoved over her head. The next day, husband and wife, bloodied and bruised but alive, wake up in a park in the middle of Manchester, 150 miles from the Scottish borders, while at their farmhouse, a Scots celebratory party is in full swing, the kid wearing a pig's mask. Sexy McIntosh (so good in Lucky McKee's *The Woman*) carries the film (she gets to strip during the opening minutes), a telling "damsel in distress" performance of some note, and the tension-filled pace never lets up. However, the movie will do absolutely nothing to repair historical Scottish/English antagonism which still rumbles on to this very day, judging by the UK political scene as of 2019; is this why the shoot took place in Derbyshire's Peak District, not Scotland?

Willow Creek

Jerkschool Productions 2013; 80 minutes;
Director: Bobcat Goldthwait *****

A couple go on the road to Bluff Creek and Willow Creek to hopefully capture on film the celebrated Bigfoot, spotted in the area over a period of 50 years.

In 1967, Roger Patterson and Robert Gimlin shot their now famous, endlessly discussed footage of a Sasquatch at Bluff Creek in Northern California. In Bobcat Goldthwait's found footage Bigfoot feature, filmmaker Bryce Johnson and girlfriend Alexie Gilmore drive to Willow Creek, taking in all the sights relating to the elusive creature and interviewing various locals, some of whom have had close encounters with the beast (not actors; the public was asked to take part in the production). A slow but nevertheless interesting opening 30 minutes whets the appetite, presented in bright sunshine and attractive wooded scenery around Willow Creek itself. "There's nothing down there. Turn that camera off. Turn round, go back and fuck off," is the blunt message from a burly Park Ranger barring their path to Bluff Creek, but Johnson finds an alternative track, drives through the dense forest, parks up and sets off on foot with skeptical Gilmore. Then their troubles begin. Setting up camp, Johnson goes for a swim in a nearby creek; on their return, one of his socks is high up on a tree branch and the tent has been flattened. "I wanna go home," mutters Gilmore, starting to feel uneasy, and at night in their tent, they are subjected to a barrage of frightening noises: Whoops, cries ("That ain't no human."), howls, twigs snapping, wood knocked together, growls, snorts and something outside, scratching the tent

fabric. At this point, the movie has a 20-minute, one-take shot of the pair in their sleeping bags, the stationary camera focusing on every scared, cautious movement; the couple was told to improvise and the mounting claustrophobic terror they feel is palpable. Thrill-a-minute buffs won't enjoy it; in the context of this movie, the scene works, and full marks to the two young actors in pulling it off. Dawn arrives, preparations are made to leave and all hell breaks loose. Becoming lost in a maze of tracks, they wander in circles ("We don't know where we are!" yells Gilmore hysterically), reach Bluff Creek, see huge footprints in the mud and hear a roaring sound. Running for their lives (it's now dark), they stumble across a filthy, near-naked woman (her missing poster was seen in Willow Creek) and are attacked, the fallen camera capturing their screams (and a cacophony of howls) as they're dragged through the undergrowth to their deaths. The closing image is of broken grass stems, which the film opened with. *Willow Creek* doesn't show the big feller of folklore as such but remains one of the better of the independent productions to tackle this enduring legend; two engaging central performances plus authentic location work add up to a nerve-wracking 80 minutes that you wish had been another reel longer, it's that good.

UNDER TEN MILLION? ANYTHING'S POSSIBLE!

The Witch in the Window
One Bad House Films 2018; 77 minutes;
Director: Andy Mitton *****

A father and his 12-year-old son take up residence in a newly purchased home haunted by the malicious spirit of a former owner who preys on people's insecurities.

Three cheers for writer/director Andy Mitton for coming up with a carefully composed modern-day ghost story bereft of a single puerile teenage student; Mitton also wrote the atmospheric music and uses it sparingly to good effect. Dad Alex Draper and son Charlie Tacker (highly believable interplay from the pair) set about bonding with each other and repairing the place, unaware that a woman (Carol Stanzione) is watching them through the windows and doorways (observe the background shots closely). The moment when they both cautiously approach the chair she was found dead in, seeing the still arm of someone seated looking out over the garden, is as creepy as it gets, as is the scene where Tacker, sent back to New York to his mother (Arija Bareikis), returns to the house; sitting side-by-side, Draper calls his estranged wife and, astonished, speaks to Tacker *on the phone*, his "son" next to him frozen in an icy silence before morphing into the malevolent hag, several minutes of sheer fright. Stanzione wants to be "free" of the property and to carry out her wish, Draper sacrifices himself to enable Tacker and Bareikis to live there in peace; he dies of a heart attack, sitting in that ominous chair (why didn't they burn the thing in the first place?). Mother and son now reside in the house ("It doesn't feel bad in here."), Stanzione prowls the New York streets and Tacker can feel his father's shade in the walls, just as he first felt Stanzione's (Draper left a note to Tacker: "It's a good house again if you want it. I haven't left. I never will."). Justin Kane's sharp photography adds to the unsettling tone of a supernatural chiller that delivers on all bases; the jump-scare crowd will scoff, others will find the experience a refreshing and rewarding change.

Without Name
Irish Film Board/Lovely Productions 2016; 93 minutes;
Director: Lorcan Finnegan ****

A land surveyor hired by a private contractor to assess isolated woodlands for a possible housing development comes under the malevolent influence of the surrounding trees that begin to exert a non-rational presence of their own.

Nature fights back! Lorcan Finnegan's debut feature, made for £300,000 in Ireland, is a mini-psychological *tour de force* involving troubled surveyor Alan McKenna; his marriage on the rocks, McKenna is having an affair with assistant Niamh Algar which isn't running smoothly.

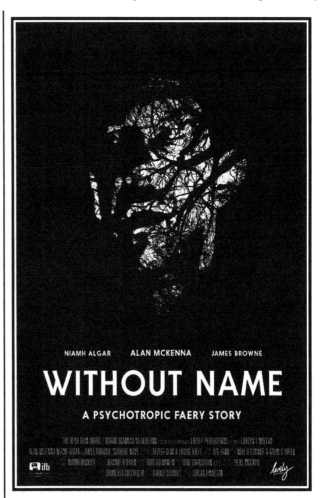

Renting an old cottage once owned by Brendan Conroy, a recluse who had written a journal, *The Knowledge of Trees*, concerning the area and its natural habitat and managed to catch on photograph the aura that surrounds plants, McKenna, setting up his equipment, begins seeing a vague nude figure lurking among the copses as a mist closes in; later, when he drinks an infusion made from magic mushrooms, his damaged psyche goes into overdrive. Is what we are experiencing, the effects of the potent brew or visions from McKenna's paranoia? Finnegan artfully puts the point forward that nature represents a far more powerful force than Man and shouldn't be tampered with. The huge quarry at the start is a stab at the total destruction of plant/wildlife; McKenna spots a leaf emerging from concrete, nature exerting itself; there's a 35-second surreal shot of trees in the forest, alternately glowing and darkening in the changing light; as McKenna sleeps, a gusty wind and creaking noises prelude the shadows of branches drawing ever closer to his pillow, like spindly, clutching hands; peg holes in the moss constitute some form of plant murder; and is that naked figure Conroy (he's in hospital in a state of catatonic shock) or McKenna, who also appears to wind up in hospital. Reality and dreams merge together under the shadow of those lofty watching trees, a trip of sorts fueled by the mushrooms, McKenna's mind or both. Finnegan employs a great deal of visual style in a haunting, slow-moving but memorable essay into the age-old agencies that the natural world still possesses; Gavin O'Brien and Neil O'Connor's menacing score underlies those visuals to perfection.

The Woman
Moderncine 2011; 101 minutes;
Director: Lucky McKee *****

A lawyer kidnaps a feral woman to satisfy his own perverted appetites, keeping her prisoner in his outdoor cellar and attempting to civilize her, with unforeseen results.

Lucky McKee's powerfully disturbing psychological thriller begins with a four-minute montage showing wild woman Pollyanna McIntosh at work and play in her natural element, the backwoods. Smarmy lawyer Sean Bridgers out hunting, captures the woman and chains her to the cellar walls, thus precipitating a catastrophic series of events leading to the gruesome slaughter of his wife and son, and of himself. Is McKee's gut-wrenching picture an indictment on some aspects of modern-day society, on abusive relationships and on downtrodden feminism—after all, every female in the picture is a victim of sorts. Bridgers is an out-and-out control freak, a 100% asshole whose word is set in concrete, knocking wife Angela Bettis to the floor if she speaks out of turn, barking orders to son Zach Rand and nursing unnatural desires towards teen daughter Lauren Ashley Carter, younger offspring Shyla Molhusen taking it all in her stride, munching on cookies. Within this

dysfunctional family setup, malicious Rand is exhibiting his father's sadistic traits, at school and at home, torturing McIntosh with pliers after Bridgers has raped her, while teacher Carlee Baker shows concern over morose Carter, clearly pregnant but by whom? *The Woman* doesn't make for comfortable viewing: McIntosh is scrubbed clean, then hosed down and dressed to cover her nudity, Bridgers coercing his reluctant family into his illegal, disturbing activities, even though the question on horrified Bettis' lips is "Why?" The last 15 minutes packs one almighty punch: Bettis is beaten unconscious for daring to question Bridgers who then drags Baker off (she's turned up to query Carter's pregnancy) to a dog pen where McIntosh's savage offspring, kept in a cage, rips the girl to shreds. It's Carter who frees McIntosh; the vengeful woman disposes of Bettis by tearing her face to raw meat and finishes off Rand and Bridgers, pulling his heart out and giving it to her daughter to eat. The final lingering shot is of McIntosh, her daughter and little Molhusen (she licks McIntosh's bloody finger and grins) walking away to the woods, Carter watching them depart. Backed by an effective indie rock soundtrack, *The Woman* is a brilliantly directed shocker that has a lot to say and mull over after its shattering conclusion, a horror film with depth and meaning, with standout performances throughout. It's something you won't forget for a long, long time.

Barry: "Well, have you formed a different, if not more favorable, opinion of the indie/low-budget scene after sitting through that assortment? Has your mind been opened up to the possibility that there is life in the indie/low-budget market after all? Has, in fact, your appetite been whetted for *more*?"

Gary: "It most definitely has. I really had no idea that movies like *Confined*, *The Shrine*, *The Ritual*, *The Innkeepers*, *Pyewacket*, *The Pyramid*, *Spring*, *Jurassic Galaxy*, *Incident in a Ghostland*, *Cold Skin*, *The Woman*, *Under the Shadow* and even a real cheapo like *Willow Creek* could be so damned good. I even enjoyed the *I Spit on Your Grave* trilogy, although Sue wouldn't watch for obvious reasons! [Sue here: they would have been much more impactful if they had been directed by women—because what woman hasn't wanted to take a butcher knife to evil men?] And great to see that those two new *Frankenstein* movies you included proves without doubt that the old legend is still alive and kicking after all these years. And, yes, I now have to agree with you, they are, in the main, the B movies for a new generation. This is a terrific bunch of material you've made possible for me to indulge in once in a while, Barry. Most of it I wasn't aware existed."

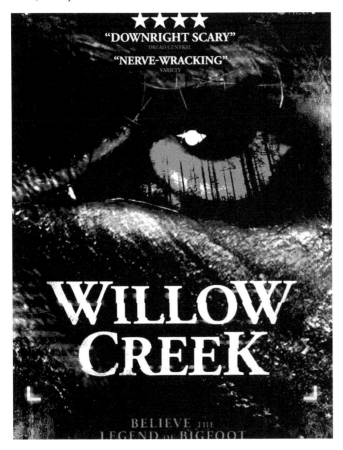

B: "Only happy to oblige. But "new and indie" and "post-2000" shouldn't be a barrier to the older among us watching and enjoying them, should it?"

G: "No, and in future, I'll keep an eye open for them for myself, unless you care to inform me on a regular basis what's available on the market in this low-budget horror arena. As always, I value your judgement on this matter!"

B: "Consider it done. I seem to have converted you, well, at least a little bit; now go forth and preach to the unconverted!"

G: "Will do!"

B: "But before you do, I've chosen one more title for you to sink your teeth into, a feature that perhaps in its own way epitomizes the whole indie/low-budget deal; yes, before you say it, it's got to be an Asylum movie and it is, a recent addition to their "we can try and do it just as well as you can, but on less money" stable. An apt choice for finishing off the book, I reckon."

G: "Good stuff. I'll grab a couple of beers, or any other liquid refreshment you may care to imbibe, and then you can put the film on."

B: "Beers will be fine!"

On 1 June 2019, Asylum/SyFy released Mark Atkins' *Monster Island* on American television, budgeted at $500,000; on May 31, 2019, Warner Bros.' 132-minute, $170,000,000 *Godzilla: King of the Monsters* hit US cinemas. Asylum's 89-minute kaiju mockbuster undoubtedly cashed in on the enduring and seemingly unstoppable popularity of the whole Godzilla/Kaiju phenomenon, and while cries of "rip-off" echo throughout the land, *Monster Island* has to be viewed within the context of an Asylum production, not a multi-million dollar Warner Bros. production. Both have their faults and that includes Michael Dougherty's hyped-up blockbuster. Too much uninteresting human drama at the expense of the Big G who only really makes his mighty presence felt in the movie's final 25 minutes, inaudible dialogue and murky, fuzzy nighttime photography (Lawrence Sher) which doesn't do justice to Godzilla, Rodan, Mothra and Ghidorah. In contrast, writer/director Atkins' photography in *Monster Island* is as bright as a button *and* shot in daylight, so one up for Asylum on that score. But let's look at the film in more detail.

Benthic's deep-sea mining machine, prospecting for minerals over volcanic rifts and irregular-sized nuggets in the Kermadec Trench, is wrecked by something monstrous. Boss Adrian Bouchet, assistants Donna Cormack Thompson and Chris Fisher, plus marine environmental observer Natalie Robbie, board Jonathan Pienaar's boat and head for the site to investigate. Plumbing the ocean depths in their submersible, they encounter a gigantic six-limbed marine kaiju, a cross between a starfish and an octopus, which rises from the sea floor, setting off a tsunami and posing a threat to mankind; the thing is armor-plated and has magma for blood, feeding on volcanos for energy ("Born of fire from the sea!"). Enter Eric Roberts as General Horne (who, naturally, has a Japanese sidekick, Toshi Toda), sporting the longest hair of any naval commander seen on the silver screen; Roberts won't take advice from anybody, his flotilla of cruisers homing in on the enemy. Bombs have no effect, a submarine is wiped out, a ship smashed, the dialogue becomes muffled during a few sequences on the submersible and Robbie flies by helicopter to meet her former mentor Margot Wood, an expert in Kaiju mythology ("I have the knowledge of the ancients."). Only a kaiju-killer can destroy the beast (which is called a Tengo, or destroyer) she says, and this particular giant has to be enticed from its volcanic lair on Monster Island by the blood of another kaiju. After 50 minutes, the action hots up. Hundreds of winged monsters hatch from eggs ejected into the air from the Tengo's body, the creatures spitting out streams of magma. Fisher is incinerated, leaving Bouchet, Robbie, Thompson and Wood to make their way to New Zealand's Taupo volcanic region (filming took place around Capetown, South Africa and the Stadsaal Caves) where they waken Asylum's answer to Godzilla, a colossal kaiju that emerges out of a volcanic mountain, defeating the army of flying menaces by breathing jets of blue fire and engaging in battle with the Tengo ("A quarter-million ton nuisance.") that has now sprouted wings; a huge explosion results in both titans perishing and the formation of a massive armored egg that the foursome promise to protect.

Asylum knockers may well have had a field day with

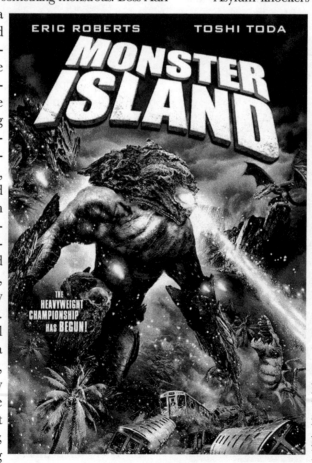

Monster Island, but the picture remains one of the company's worthier latter-day efforts, albeit a minor addition to the kaiju cycle. The monsters, when they're given screen time, are pretty impressive, the girls keep the hysterics down (which Vera Farmiga failed to do in *Godzilla: King of the Monsters*), you can clearly see what's going on, the sunny South African scenery is attractive and the plot is cohesive to a point; just try and ignore Roberts' overactive performance and the fact that Bouchet and company travel across the Pacific in a helicopter at what appears to be the speed of light. *Monster Island's* framework just about sums up the entire indie/low-budget movie scene to a tee; entertaining, unpretentious and wearing its cheapo credentials proudly on its sleeve, a "big finger" to all those sniping critics who persist in putting this kind of fare down. All power to Asylum's elbow! Rating? Four stars—and why not?

Barry: "Gary—I thought I'd finished, having completed 300 pages and reviewed 581 movies, but I've still got a load more to watch and write-up on!"

Gary: "Okay. Choose another 20 and make it snappy!"

B: "How about 21?"

G: "Twenty-one and that's it. Finito!"

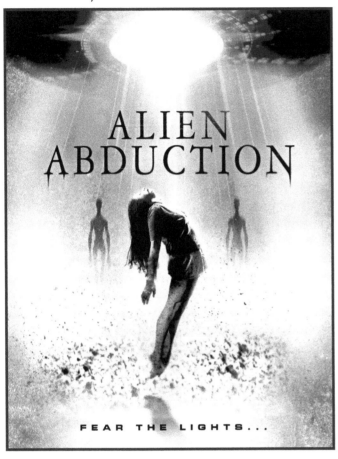

Alien Abduction
Big Picture Prods./Exclusive Media Group 2014;
85 minutes; Director: Matty Beckerman ****

"October 2011. Project Blue Book case no. 4499. Twenty-seven people missing." Young Riley Polanski's camcorder footage, recovered in a field, provides compelling evidence of UFO activity related to numerous sightings of the mysterious Brown Mountain Lights in North Carolina, recorded as far back as 1913. Polanski's family embarks on a trip to the wooded mountainous region and, one by one, are abducted by distinctly unfriendly aliens, beamed up in agony to what one supposes to be their spacecraft; exactly one year later, 155 missing people are returned, Dad Peter Holden found on a bridge by the police, filthy and incoherent. At times fairly alarming, Matty Beckerman piles on the tension with gusto (creepy alien figures; flashing lights; the vessel's noisy, forbidding interior), his camera (or Polanski's) on overdrive, a full-throttle found footage opus that makes us hope that these malefic beings from another world aren't actually out there. God help us if they are!

Bigfoot: The Lost Coast Tapes
New Breed Ent./Freeway Studios 2012; 90 minutes;
Director: Corey Grant ****

Paranormal reality TV show boss and Bigfoot skeptic Drew Rausch heads an argumentative team that drives to Northwest California in order to blow holes in Bigfoot hunter Frank Ashmore's claim that he possesses the body of a juvenile Sasquatch, hidden in a sea cave. What they stumble across is something totally unexpected, another ferocious species (alien?) inhabiting the wooded area that is hunting and killing both Bigfoot and inquisitive humans straying onto its chosen territory. 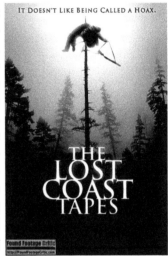 Everyone ends up slaughtered in a suspenseful *Troll Hunter*-type found footage chiller containing a brief but neat twist payoff (is that shaggy leg and hoof of *this* world?), the clue lying in the DVD cover blurb: "Bigfoot is hiding—but not from us!" A Bigfoot movie with a difference.

The Cured
BAC Films/Tilted Pictures/Irish Film Board 2017;
95 minutes; Director: David Freyne ****

Mirroring the Protestant/Catholic uprisings in Northern Ireland, David Freyne's post-apocalyptic thriller focused on the "Cured," those 75% of the population that survived the Maze virus and are attempting to integrate into a deeply suspicious society; the remaining 25% are still disease-ridden, locked in military facilities and due for elimination. Sam Keeley is allowed to live with Ellen Page, even though he killed her husband (his brother), while nasty-piece-of-work Tom Vaughn-Lawlor stirs up trouble with the authorities, leading to another zombie outbreak. The bleak conclusion has Keeley and his infected nephew seeking a center where, hopefully, a cure will be found. The scenario catapults into standard "zombies loose in the streets" action which somehow lessens the impact built up in the first hour, but, like 2016's similar *The Girl with All the Gifts*, it's still a thoughtful slant on the zombie genre, as gray-looking as its subject matter.

Estranged
Face Films/Room 101/Vicarious Ent. 2015; 101 minutes;
Director: Adam Levins ***

Hospitalized following a scooter accident in Brazil, Amy Mason, suffering from amnesia, returns to her home in England with boyfriend Simon Quatermain but doesn't find welcoming arms. Dad James Cosmo, Mum Eileen Nichols and brother and sister James Lance and Nora-Jane Noone treat the pair with open hostility and soon, wheelchair-bound Mason finds herself held prisoner in the cellar, Quatermain carried off and murdered. Kindly Butler Craig Conway passes her a newspaper cutting; her mother shot herself when Mason was eight years old, so who, in fact, *is* this family, and what do they want with her? Filmed at the Gothic-styled Lambton Estate in County Durham, *Estranged* features a dysfunctional brood bordering on the sociopathic, so after several plot reveals, it's a treat to see that Mason, almost out of her mind and pregnant with Cosmo's child, shoots the perverted lot. A nervy psychological thriller featuring beefy British movie stalwart Cosmo as a bad guy for a change.

Evidence
RynoRyder Prods. Inc. 2012; 78 minutes;
Director: Howie Askins ***

Produced on a $12,000 budget, Howie Askins' *very* shaky found footage cheapie has two guys (Ryan McCoy and Brett Rosenburg) and two gals (Ashley Bracken and Abigail Richie) documenting their camping trip, ignoring the "NO TRESPASS" signs, spotting a strange animal lurking in a ravine and straying onto a government restricted area where scuttling, shaggy, simian-like monsters and crazy bloodstained zombies roam, the result (or so it appears) of some form of covert scientific experiment gone terribly wrong. Sit through the frenzied lengthy end credits to see if all those flashing images make sense of what you've witnessed; odds are that they won't! However, faults apart, it's still worth a look.

Evidence
Bold Films/FilmEngine 2013; 94 minutes;
Director: Olatunde Osunsanmi ***

Evidence commences with a camera panning over a frozen picture of a crime scene, a massacre at a gas station in Kidwell, Nevada. Cellphones are collected, cops Radha Mitchell, Stephen Moyer and their team view what they can salvage from sim cards and we are in found footage domain, Moyer searching for clues to establish who was behind the mass killing. Starting off innocently enough, aspiring filmmakers Torrey DeVitto and Caitlin Stasey boarding a bus to Las Vegas, the narrative quickly plunges into a confusing jumble of images: The bus overturns on a dirt track, passengers making it to Kidwell where they're confronted by a maniac in a protective suit and mask, wielding a welder's torch. Moyer sifts through the forensic evidence, watching in horror as all and sundry are incinerated by the lunatic:

Various suspects enter the frame before the surprise reveal; DeVitto and Stasey were the killers ("We're gonna make a movie one day," they state at the start), video footage showing exactly how they accomplished the deed. "That's it. Thanks for watching!" the deranged duo grin at the camera, Moyer and Mitchell staring in disbelief. That shock ending compensates for a messy middle section where it's difficult to determine who's doing what to whom, although, on a second scrutiny, the signs are there for all to see (as Moyer discovers in the final minutes.)

Feral
Alternate Ending Films 2017; 90 minutes;
Director: Mark H. Young ****

Six student campers (two straight couples and a pair of lesbians) fall foul of a rabid flesh-eater in the forest. The grunting, gurgling freak is Ranger Lew Temple's son, infected by the feral virus; the thing either rips its prey to shreds or infects them, turning its victims into what he has become. Mistrust among the group and gory attacks from those that

UNDER TEN MILLION? ANYTHING'S POSSIBLE!

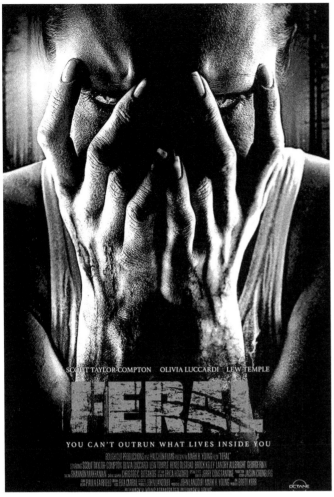

falling, temperatures dropping, frostbite lurking, panic setting in and savage wolves prowling below. Ironically, after discussing the worst possible way to die, Ashmore and Zegars meet grisly ends, Bell (who was terrified throughout the all-too-realistic shoot—and it shows!) hitting the ground when the chair throws a bolt, struggling through the snowy woods and reaching a road where she's picked up and taken to hospital. You'll need to wipe your clammy palms dry after sitting on the edge of your seat through this nervy, chilly (in more ways than one) exercise in human survival.

Honeymoon
Fewlas Entertainment 2014; 87 minutes;
Director: Leigh Janiak ****

Harry Treadaway and Rose Leslie honeymoon in the family cottage beside a wooded lake. One night, bright lights beam through the windows and Leslie wanders off, returning subtly changed, not remembering her past life or likes/dislikes, refusing sex with increasingly puzzled Treadaway and tugging at something hideously slimy between her legs—and neighbor Hanna Brown is behaving in exactly the same odd manner. An alien possession spine-tingler made for $1,000,000 that scores highly, mainly due to Leslie's icy turn as the young newlywed changing from fun-loving lass to a cold, unfeeling being that is not of this Earth. The climax has Leslie and Brown, both looking unhuman, walking towards an intense radiance and their new masters, having both killed their husbands. Heather

have contracted the disease leads to Scout Taylor-Compton the sole survivor; she leaves partner Olivia Luccardi to shoot herself, thus preventing her changing into one of the ravenous undead, walking off alone. Grotesque creature make-up and tense cabin situations add up to an above-average zombie/virus shocker effortlessly performed by the small cast and directed with force by Mark H. Young.

Frozen
A Bigger Boat/ArieScope Pictures 2010; 93 minutes;
Director: Adam Green ****

In Adam Green's sweaty, claustrophobic and plain un-

comfortable thriller, filmed in Utah, three skiers (Emma Bell, Shawn Ashmore and Kevin Zegars) find themselves suspended 50-feet above ground in a chairlift after the Holliston ski resort closes down for a week. Following an initial 20 minutes of dude-speak, the movie settles down into a question of how the hell the trio will manage to escape their frozen, perilous predicament, what with snow

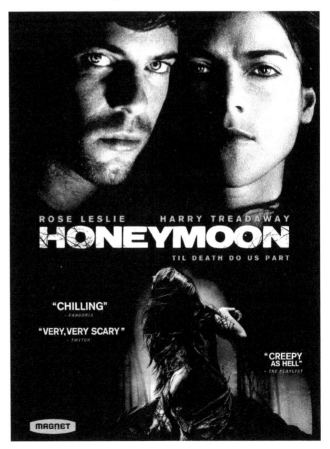

McIntosh's discordant violin-based score contributes to the mounting sense of unease in writer/director Leigh Janiak's persuasive debut feature.

House of Dust
aka The Haunting of Redding Hospital
Budderfly Prods./Goodnight Films 2013; 90 minutes;
Director: A.D. Calvo **

Four students explore an abandoned psychiatric hospital, breathe in toxic dust from the crematorium and become possessed by the mad, restless spirits of the former inmates, including a homicidal doctor. Inbar Lavi playing the heroine isn't all  that bad, but the rest of the bunch are woeful, as are the limp shocks and odd grisly "drilling into eyes" scene. Decent cinematography and a cute ending that has a dust cloud from the asylum settling on a bunch of kids at play, changing one of them into something unholy, cannot disguise the fact that A.D. Calvo's flop was reissued on disc in 2019 as *The Haunting of Redding Hospital*, shorn of 14 minutes, to grab more dollars from an unsuspecting public. Could have been much, much better.

The Nursery
Three Tortured Minds 2018; 87 minutes;
Directors: Christopher A. Micklos and Jay Sapiro **

Babysitter Madeline Conway and friends Carly Rae James Sauer, Emmaline Friederichs and moronic Claudio Parrone, Jr. are terrorized by the malignant ghost of a nanny who drowned the family's seven-year-old daughter and then hanged herself; she's now after their three-month-old baby. The golden spirit of the dead daughter comes to the rescue, dragging the ugly crone off into a world of purity and whiteness. Containing cheap-looking shocks, unevenly acted and erratically presented in garish colors, *The Nursery* is a mediocre rehash of indie's oft-used "evil nanny" 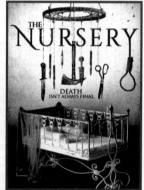 plot device; Boomers will be amused at the site of Parrone (his mind off sex for a change) watching Bela Lugosi's *The Devil Bat* on TV and pronouncing PRC's old 1940 potboiler as "awful." Well, it's not quite as awful as this one!

Piranha Sharks aka Jurassic Piranha
Bitter End Media Group/Imaginarium Prods. 2016;
79 minutes; Director: Leigh Scott *

Amy Blackman's company produces a genetically mutated cross between a Great White Shark and a pira-

nha, the highly profitable little predators reproducing like crazy, bursting out of aquariums, infiltrating New York's water supply and eating people from the inside out. A rare misfire from Leigh Scott whose jokey screenplay (along with writers Barney and Mark Burman) focuses on a group of tiresome, disparate jerks (including two lap dancers) who all eventually meet after several disconnected vignettes and succeed in wiping out the tiny menaces before the military has a chance to drop an atomic bomb on Manhattan (poison in the water system does the trick). It's neither comedy nor horror, the gore count is disappointingly low and the CGI effects are poorly conceived; an indie "Shark" effort to forget.

Quarries
Diamond Cutter Films/Indiesyndicate Prods. 2016;
83 minutes; Director: Nils Taylor *****

Six troubled women are led on a wilderness expedition by Sara Mornell, only to find themselves facing an endurance test, hunted by scarred hillbilly James Devoti and his four feral cohorts. *The Descent* meets *Deliverance* sums up Nils Taylor's taut, lean exercise in female survival against

UNDER TEN MILLION? ANYTHING'S POSSIBLE!

the odds, Nicole Marie Johnson holding center stage as the feisty heroine escaping her abusive boyfriend but having to confront far more dangerous foes; she comes out on top, along with Carrie Finklea and Nicole DuPort, Devoti and his loathsome sadistic pals all slaughtered in a manner that befits them. Authentic wooded locations and solid acting add up to a pulsating "girls on the run from sick psychos" horror drama that successfully attempts to avoid most genre clichés and in doing so packs quite a punch, as does Isaias Garcia's vibrant score.

Ravenswood Asylum
Becker Ent./Ignite Pictures 2017; 88 minutes;
Director: Jon Cohen **

Filmed at the Gledswood Homestead, Catherine Fields in NSW, four American youths are conducted on a ghost tour around a notorious derelict asylum where, in the 1950s, lunatics were subjected to Electroconvulsive Shock Therapy (EST) by an insane doctor. Needless to say, the doctor's evil spirit awakes, first entering the body of Shane Savage, then Isabel Dickson, to exact revenge on his original patient Sara, the girl responsible for his downfall 65 years ago; Sara now inhabits Madeline Marie Dona's luscious body. After a promising spooky 30 minutes, it all falls apart, mainly due to poor performances from everyone except Dona and uneven direction, Sara's entity, having escaped the asylum's confines, surviving on in yet another fresh female at the end; *not* the best Aussie horror film you'll come across.

Rosewood Lane
Hollywood Media Bridge Productions 2011; 97 minutes;
Director: Victor Salva ***

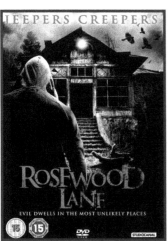

Victor *Jeepers Creepers* Salva came up with a *Halloween*-type thriller where radio agony aunt Rose McGowan, haunted by her own childhood demons, is stalked by a psychopathic paperboy (Daniel Ross Owens), a genuine creep who just won't leave her alone. Trouble is, she's not taken seriously by the police or on/off boyfriend Sonny Marinelli. Was the black-eyed pest responsible for her father's death? Why does he continually chant nursery rhymes? Why do dogs hate the sight of him? "He's a trick of the light," warns her elderly neighbor. "Something dark. Don't attract his attention." The suspense-laden narrative presents a constant guessing game, spoiled by the unresolved payoff. Owens is hit by McGowan's car, his torn body suspended from a tree; at his funeral, cop Ray Wise sees *two more* Owens, one in bandages. Were they triplets, or was the guy some form of supernatural, indestructible being? Annoyingly, we are not allowed to find out.

Rust Creek
Lunacy Pictures 2018; 108 minutes;
Director: Jen McGowan ****

Lunacy Pictures' mandate is to support female filmmakers on their projects; is this why every male in *Rust Creek* (apart from Deputy Jeremy Glazer) is a lowlife rat? Putting that aside, Jen McGowan's thriller, mixing a psycho sheriff with murderous hicks, drug-making and a girl in dire peril (Hermione Corfield) is engrossing stuff containing one twist after another, right up to the final reel. Corfield, on her way to a job interview, takes a wrong turn off the highway, drives deep into the Kentucky woods and is brutally assaulted and wounded by brothers Micah Hauptman and

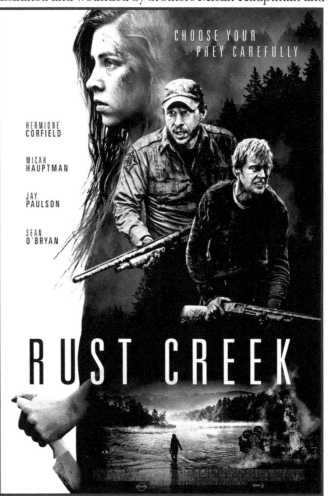

Daniel R. Hill, whose cousin, Jay Paulson, cooks up meths in his trailer. Paulson takes in Corfield, the brothers plus corrupt cop Sean O'Bryan (in on the drug deal) determined to kill her after they've had their fun. One tense situation after another culminates in Hauptman, Hill and Paulson all dead, O'Bryan (having gunned down his honest deputy) dispatched by Corfield in a river as the State troopers arrive. Corfield stands out as the student at the mercy of a bunch of deviants you wouldn't care to meet on a dark night; O'Bryan also shines as the lawman without a conscience.

Skinwalker Ranch aka Skinwalkers
Deep Studios 2013; 86 minutes;
Directors: Devin McGinn and Steve Borg *****

In 2010, an eight-year-old boy vanished in a ball of light in front of his father on a ranch in Utah. In August 2011, a team from Modern Defense Enterprises arrives to investigate the barrage of UFO sightings, reports of flashing lights, strange animals, extraterrestrial beings, poltergeist activity and cattle mutilations that date back to the 1960s (these happen to be based on real events). Presented documentary fashion, *Skinwalker Ranch* is a superior, hair-raising offering of its type, straying into *Paranormal Activity* territory at times as the missing boy (Nash Lucas) is caught on camera rushing through rooms and disappearing in a shed; farmer John Gries' truck is found mangled; a savage wolf-like

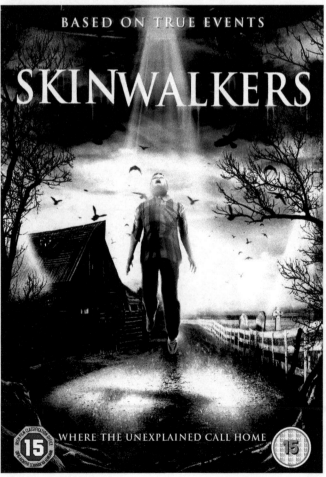

creature prowls the fields, impervious to bullets; Matthew Rocheleau is picked up by an invisible force and hurled to the ground; wise old Indian Michael Horse warns the crew to "get the fuck out of here," and grainy video footage from a secret MDE visit made in the 1970s shows that a strange girl was discovered on the ranch—but she wasn't human! In a frenzied climax, Steve Borg and his team are subjected to balls of light, the sound of overhead engines and a malicious alien up to no good; at 3.03 am on August 19, a massive ship hovers above the ranch, Lucas, caught in a shaft of brilliance, staring upwards. A terrific, goose pimply, well-constructed UFO thriller; the fact that the entire site is now deemed private property, fenced and "off limits" to the general public speaks volumes.

Tank 432 aka Belly of the Bulldog
Belstone Pictures 2015; 88 minutes;
Director: Nick Gillespie **

In Nick Gillespie's £150,000 drama, a bunch of British mercenaries on the run hole up in an abandoned tank with two female hostages, not realizing that they are victims of a toxic substance experiment, resulting in hallucinations, visions of masked monsters and bouts of sickness; it's all linked to a deadly orange powder called Kratos. Rupert Evans and the bodies of his squad are eventually incinerated by men  in white suits and gas masks, one girl captive escaping. Claustrophobic tension is maintained within the vehicle's cramped confines but the anti-climax is inconclusive and repeated shots of Evans vomiting, plus Steve Garry emptying his bowels in close-up and a depressing storyline will repel most viewers.

Tape 407 aka Area 407
Cloud Nine Pics./Suzanne DeLaurentiis Prods. 2012; 90 minutes; Directors: Dale Fabrigar and Everette Wallin ***

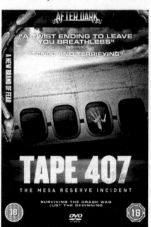 On New Year's Day, Flight 37A from New York to Los Angeles crashes in a government top secret zone, the survivors picked off by genetically engineered dinosaurs. Made over five days on an $80,000 budget and mostly ad libbed, this frenzied found footage cheapo delivers a few gruesome shocks and explosive incidents, a juvenile T-Rex caught on camera in the dying seconds after an

UNDER TEN MILLION? ANYTHING'S POSSIBLE!

inspector completes a final sweep of the area, shooting the last two passengers dead. A word of warning: Teenager Abigail Schrader's nonstop, high-pitched quack-quack delivery during the first 15 minutes will have you gritting your teeth; her shrieking tones more or less cease (thank goodness) after the plane crash. A proposed follow-up in 2013/2014 was never completed.

Terrordactyl aka Jurassic Wars
3rd Films 2016; 95 minutes;
Directors: Don Bitters III and Geoff Reisner ****

Meteorite showers hit Los Angeles, bringing with them eggs that hatch into Pterodactyls that go on a rampage of destruction. Only yard care business partners Jason Tobias and Christopher John Jennings, together with grizzled ex-marine Jack E. Curenton and gals Candice Nunes and Bianca Haase, can save the city from destruction. A goofy sci-fi/horror semi-comedy featuring grand CGI effects that unequivocally gives a nod in the direction of all things 1950s, Japanese kaiju movies, *Q The Winged Serpent* and even *King Kong*. Don Bitters III's witty script brims with droll lines (Tobias to Jennings on spotting an egg: "Dude. They're worth a fortune!"; Nunes to Tobias and Jennings: "How about you guys stow your drama, drop your dicks,

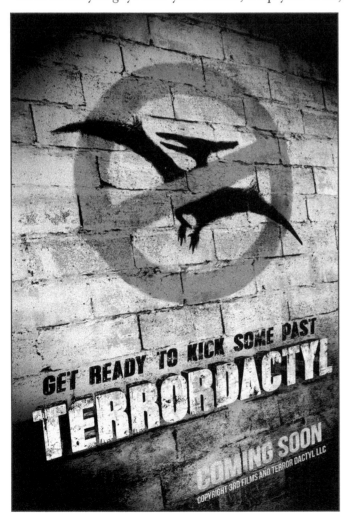

pick up your guns and kill some reptiles!"), there's great monster action in the streets and in the closing seconds, more meteorites are on the way, one containing a gigantic specimen. Earth is far from safe yet!

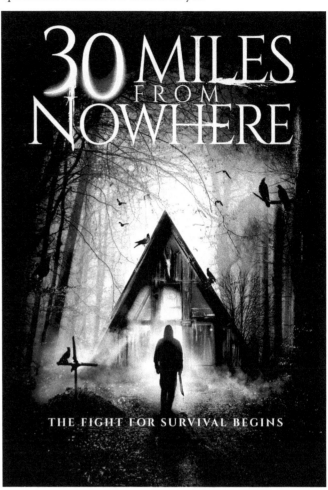

30 Miles from Nowhere
Film Camp Productions 2018; 84 minutes;
Director: Caitlin Koller **

Carrie Preston invites five of her old college friends to her summer home in Wisconsin to attend the funeral of her husband, shot dead by a student—or was he? Caitlin Koller's debut feature plays games with us as the group of horny, soulless 30-somethings, nursing enough sexual hang-ups and grudges to fill several casebooks, get increasingly suspicious over Preston's disturbing behavior. Everything is hurriedly explained in the final unsatisfactory minute as William Smillie is arrested for Preston's murder: The deranged woman was conducting a study in the effects of fear on the human brain, her husband not dead at all ("My film. My work."), the house rigged with cameras that filmed their every move. A modicum of suspense and a feeling of "what the hell is going on" is evident, but you care not one iota for any of the characters involved and, as you have no one to root for, therein lies the film's one major flaw.

"I have a question for Barry. Why aren't any of *my* indie films included in his book?"

Fair comment on an email received from publisher Gary Svehla's wife, Susan, who has indeed directed three of her own quirky (she won't mind me saying that!) mystery/horror/science fiction productions on limited funds, featuring a cast of unknowns and amateurs, each movie an affectionate homage to the given genre they represent. After all, if Asylum, Full Moon and others can do it, why not Midnight Marquee?

In 2007, *Terror in the Pharaoh's Tomb* was the second MidMar opus to hit the DVD stands, coming shortly after 2006's *Terror in the Tropics*, produced by Gary and written/co-edited/directed by Sue. The story unfolds as follows: Undisciplined, skirt-chasing photographer Ace Zucco (reprised from *Terror in the Tropics*), accompanied by feisty reporter/sidekick Fay Kendall and stone-faced detective Mike Flannigan, are sent on a mission by Daily Dispatch chief Mac to locate Rick Banning, the fiancé of Mac's niece Kate, who's gone missing on an archaeological dig in Egypt while searching for the fabled Lost City of Lemuria. The zig-zag quest takes our intrepid heroes and a

Professional Wrestler Nikolai Volkoff, Gary Svehla, Bill Littman and Nikita Breznikov behind the scenes on *Terror in the Pharaoh's Tomb*.

disparate bunch of individuals associated with the lost city to London, then on to Scotland, and finally to Egypt where the group encounter mad Queen Amanetor who rules the city, all trespassers to her domain slain by a 3,000-year-old mummy—the lady requires a fresh body every century to rejuvenate herself and Banning's new wife, "The Beautiful Nadjia" (he's apparently forgotten all about Kate), is the chosen unwilling victim. After many confrontations amid the lost city ruins, the over-sexed queen bitch loses her magic pendant and, her evil powers gone up in smoke, is reduced to a near-skeletal state; the mummy is vanquished by unraveling its bandages, Rick kisses Nadjia and Indiana Jones-lookalike John drops his whip, taking full advantage of the fact that Rick is married by smooching furiously with Kate.

Standard *Mummy* fare, then, but judicious use of striking digital backdrops against which the actors play out their roles, combined with archive shots of New York and other places, plus artful insertion of vintage footage from features starring Bela Lugosi (he gets the lion's share), Lon Chaney, Jr., Lionel Atwill, Peter Lorre, George Zucco, Leo Gorcey and even Barbara Stanwyck (you'll have to see the film to figure out why *she's* in it!) and a bombastic, stitched-together soundtrack courtesy of Bill Littman, give *Terror in the Pharaoh's Tomb* the look and feel of a 1930s/early1940s Poverty Row serial, almost (but not quite) on the level of a Sandler/Emenegger production; the whole rather endearing shebang was shot in a Baltimore warehouse during a heatwave in 2006 using bluescreen for the technical effects. The tatty-looking mummy (Karl Hopf) vaguely resembles that which appeared in United Artists' *Pharaoh's Curse* (1957) and, without doubt, acting honors go to Leanna Chamish as vampish Queen Amanetor;

Above: A local Baltimore Dance Studio provided glam and choreography in *TIPT*.
Below: Suzanne Herr applies makeup to Leanna Chamish as the evil queen and Karl Hopf as the mummy in *TIPT*.

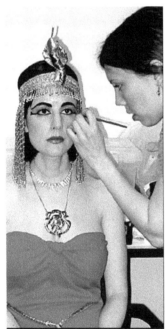

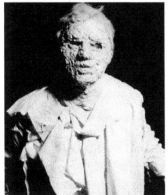

and polished in scope, *and* shot in color to boot, the space opera *Stellar Quasar and the Scrolls of Dadelia* (great title!). Taking its cue from any number of '50s influential sci-fi/fantasy movies you care to mention, golden cinematic treasures which we all sat through in darkened auditoriums during that heady period of fantasy filmmaking (*World Without End*, *Cat-Women of the Moon*, *This Island Earth*, *Missile to the Moon*, *Forbidden Planet* among others), plus, of course, 1960s *Star Trek*, *Star Wars* and even *Alien* (George Stover as the pasty-faced Ike the Android), *Stellar Quasar*'s plot was basically a simple one: Captain Stellar Quasar (Nichole Chimere) and the ragbag crew of the *Aticus Lem* are on a hazardous mission to locate the Scrolls of Dadelia which hold the key to peace in the trouble-torn universe. Pursued by a Repo ship, mad cult leader Zoltan (Shawn Anthony: "No one escapes Zoltan the Magnificent!"), a bunch of religious fanatics and a Corporation fighting vessel, they head for the forbidding Uncharted Quadrant, picking up, en route, a passenger stranded on an uninhabited jungle-covered planet and finally reaching the forested world of Imperium Prime where the Keepers of the Scrolls, Sayang and Amanay (Veronica Carlson and Caroline Munro, attired in fetching yellow and blue gossamer dresses), preside over a number of ornate caskets. Following a fracas between all interested parties, the bad guys, back on board their respective ships, open the cas-

she chews the scenery with undisguised (and hammy!) relish, managing to be both wildly over-the-top and seductively orgasmic all in one go. Film students and horror aficionados of a certain age (over 60?) will derive great fun working out which of the old classics *Pharaoh's Tomb* is deriving its source material from as well as spotting the amount of name dropping on display (Rick Banning? Wasn't Peter Cushing *John* Banning in Hammer's *The Mummy*?). *Terror in the Pharaoh's Tomb* is nothing more or less than 87 minutes of sheer black-and-white cheapo enjoyment, made by horror film fans *for* horror film fans—serious po-faced critics should stay well clear! (The movies which were plundered for their footage are *The Sphinx* [1933], *The Return of Chandu* [1934], *A Scream in the Night* aka *Murder in Morocco* [1935], *Bowery Blitzkreig* [1941], *Lady of Burlesque* [1943], *Midnight Manhunt* [1946], *The Chase* [1946] and *Scared to Death* [1946]).

The Svehla's third and final project (Sue has no plans for another of her mini "epics") was far more ambitious

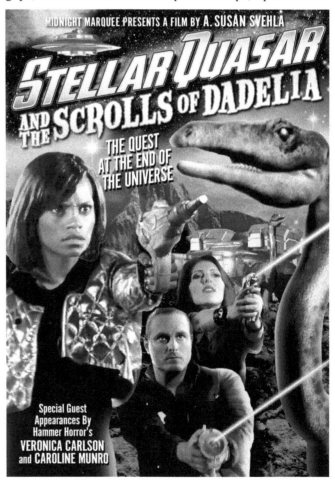

The *Aticus Lem* from *Stellar Quasar*

kets which have been beamed up and are vaporized, leaving the galaxy in a much more peaceful state.

Filming commenced in 2011 on a minimal budget (IMDb quotes $10,000) and wasn't wrapped up until 2016, suffering one setback after another. In an interview Sue gave to Full Moon's *Delirium* magazine in 2021, she expressed her dissatisfaction with some of the scenes on display as well as other elements in the finished product. In fact, the variety of intergalactic vessels on show resemble the real-deal [Sue made the models and Mitch Klein computer animated them], as good as if not better than many that appeared in American and British television sci-fi programs during the 1960s, especially the impressive space wheel *Herculon 3* [Pond 5] which, throughout the narrative, broadcasts UNN News—it's these rapid-fire news bulletins that contain most of the in-jokes and genre references but they whizz past so quickly you really have to watch the movie at least twice, or have your finger poised on the pause button; blink, and you'll miss images of John Agar and Ingrid Pitt. The overall color rendition is dazzling verging on the psychedelic (courtesy Sue's editing), the various planets, complete with dinosaurs, exotic lizard-like creatures, unicorns *and* that old 1950s standby, a giant spider, are imaginatively realized, the vast galaxy systems that the *Aticus Lem* has to navigate are authentic to a degree and whoever thought of the idea of utilizing the Incan ruins at Machu Picchu on an alien planet deserves a

Hammer film stars Veronica Carlson and Caroline Munro from *Stellar Quasar*

round of applause for sheer audacity! And it's a nice touch to include the Svehla's beloved pooch, Buddy, cast as a crew member with an R2-D2-type robot as a companion! OK, a few of the opening scenes are a tad baffling, with so many weird and wonderful characters coming and going, not to mention the numerous star systems and assorted hardware (a space station; a UFO; fighter ships), but once the storyline settles into focus, sit back and indulge in 83 minutes of pure sci-fi/fantasy escapism c/o an out-and-out enthusiast that, through trial and tribulation and her own tireless efforts, managed to get her pet project on screen. You've got to be a real sourpuss not to like and appreciate it! Both productions reviewed here merit a 5-star rating—it would be downright churlish to award anything less!

From Sue Svehla: I think Barry might have been a little too kind. We had to do these so fast and so cheap that I couldn't make them nearly as well as I wanted. I drafted fiends, err. friends to act and crew all the films (and our FANEX film conventions as well). So most of our budget went toward food. I was really happy with *TIPT*. We had villains, heroes, feisty heroines horses, donkeys, dancing girls... But I had always wanted to do a science fiction film, because that is my true love.

We were having drinks at our convention Classic FilmFest with Roger and Julie Corman. She encouraged me to make my sci-fi movie. So I threw in every sci-fi reference that I loved—, and have more in jokes in there that I can even remember.

At Midnight Marquee's Classic FilmFest (2000) Gary Svehla, Julie Corman, Susan Svehla and Roger Corman

-WARNING: don't watch these films unless you are a true fan of old horror films and old sci-fi books and movies.

Midnight Marquee DVD Titles

Films:
Terror in the Tropics (Alpha, 2006)
Terror in the Pharoah's Tomb (Alpha, 2007)
Stellar Quasar and the Scrolls of Dadelia
(Alpha, 2016)

Documentaries:
Samuel Z. Arkoff (Alpha, 2007)
Fanex Files: Hammer Films (Alpha, 2008)
American Filmmaker: Robert Wise (Alpha, 2013)
Christopher Lee: A Legacy of Horror (Alpha, 2013)

Monster Madness:
The Golden Age of the Horror Film
(Alchemy Films, 2014)
Monster Madness:
Mutants, Space Invaders and Drive-Ins
(Alchemy, Films 2014)
Monster Madness:
The Gothic Revival of Horror (Alchemy Films, 2015)
Monster Madness:
The Counter Culture to Blockbusters
(Alchemy Films, 2015)

About the Author

Atkinson, a Renaissance man, originally from Brighton, UK, studied at Cornwall College and lives in St. Columb, Cornwall. Barry enjoys writing, watching and writing about movies, of course, (especially 1950s horror), reading, walking, exploring Cornwall's old mines, music (rock to classical), geology, fossils and his and wife Janet's cats.

Visit
www.midmar.com
for a complete listing
of our books
or visit Midnight Marquee
on Amazon.com:Midnight Marquee